W9-BEF-096

LABOR-MANAGEMENT RELATIONS

McGraw-Hill Series in Management

CONSULTING EDITORS

Fred Luthans
Keith Davis

Also available from McGraw-Hill

Schaum's Outline Series in Accounting, Business, & Economics

Most Outlines include basic theory, definitions, hundreds of example problems solved in step-by-step detail, and supplementary problems with answers.

Related titles on the current list include:

Advanced Business Law
Bookkeeping & Accounting
Business Law
Business Mathematics
Business Statistics
Calculus for Business, Economics, & the Social Sciences
Contemporary Mathematics of Finance
Cost Accounting I
Financial Accounting
Intermediate Accounting I
Intermediate Accounting II
International Economics
Introduction to Mathematical Economics
Investments
Macroeconomic Theory
Managerial Accounting
Managerial Economics
Managerial Finance
Mathematical Methods for Business & Economics
Mathematics of Finance
Microeconomic Theory
Money and Banking
Operations Management
Personal Finance
Principles of Accounting I
Principles of Accounting II
Principles of Economics
Statistics & Econometrics

Available at most college bookstores, or for a complete list of titles and prices, write to: Schaum Division
McGraw-Hill, Inc.
Princeton Road, S–1
Hightstown, NJ 08520

LABOR-MANAGEMENT RELATIONS

FIFTH EDITION

Daniel Quinn Mills

Graduate School of Business Administration
Harvard University

McGRAW-HILL, INC.

New York   St. Louis   San Francisco   Auckland   Bogotá
Caracas   Lisbon   London   Madrid   Mexico City   Milan   Montreal
New Delhi   San Juan   Singapore   Sydney   Tokyo   Toronto

This book was set in New Aster by The Clarinda Company.
The editors were Lynn Richardson, Dan Alpert, and Bernadette Boylan;
the production supervisor was Denise L. Puryear.
The cover was designed by Andrew Cantor.
R. R. Donnelley & Sons Company was printer and binder.

LABOR-MANAGEMENT RELATIONS

 This book is printed on recycled, acid-free paper containing 10% postconsumer waste.

2 3 4 5 6 7 8 9 0   DOH   DOH   9 0 9 8 7 6 5 4

ISBN 0-07-042512-4

Library of Congress Cataloging-in-Publicaton Data

Mills, Daniel Quinn.
    Labor-management relations / Daniel Quinn Mills. — 5th ed.
       p.   cm. — (McGraw-Hill series in management)
    Includes bibliographical references and index.
    ISBN 0-07-042512-4 (alk. paper)
    1. Industrial relations—United States.   2. Industrial relations.
I. Title.   II. Series.
HD8072.5.M54   1994
331'.0973—dc20   93-21687

ABOUT THE AUTHOR

DANIEL QUINN MILLS holds the Albert J. Weatherhead, Jr., Chair as a Professor of Business Administration at the Harvard University Graduate School of Business Administration. He has taught for many years and is the author of numerous books and articles.

Professor Mills is widely and often quoted in the national media, including *The New York Times, Wall Street Journal, Chicago Tribune, Los Angeles Times,* and *Business Week.* He has appeared on the Today Show on NBC.

CONTENTS

PREFACE

Important developments in American society are occurring in the 1990s. Although union membership has been declining in recent decades, the material included in a course on labor-management relations is of continuing interest and importance both for its own sake and for the light it sheds on our society as a whole.

The workplace is a focal arena in a time of rapid social, demographic, and economic change. This text on labor-management relations presents the opportunity to address these matters in an exciting, up-to-date, and relevant way.

Much new material has been included in this fifth edition. Several of the most important additions are described below.

1. The American work force is increasingly diversified and the concerns of minorities (by age, race, gender, ethnic background, and education) are very important. Material on diversity has been expanded into a full chapter entitled "Human Diversity in the Workplace" and given prominence at the front of the book. The great opportunities created by diversity are stressed.

2. The American workplace is undergoing significant changes. New work systems are giving much greater freedom to employees, who often now work in teams and without close supervision. Other innovations include enhanced employee involvement and the empowerment of rank-and-file workers. Unions, which in the past have been slow to accept these changes because they impose greater responsibilities on employees, are now sometimes highly supportive. The success of such an effort at the Saturn Corporation is described.

3. Competition from firms abroad is challenging American companies and unions to develop better quality, productivity, and relationships. Automation, quality consciousness, downsizing, and the new way of working are all responses. The competitive challenge and its results are described in the chapter on the new workplace.

4. Unions are beginning to change. They've begun to recruit nontraditional employees and to accept "associate" members.

5. The chapter on benefits has been updated for changes in medical care plans, for early retirement initiatives, for child care, and for the extensions in the frequency and use of employee stock option plans.

6. The chapter on wage theory has been made more accessible to noneconomists by a less formal presentation and the inclusion of more behaviorial science contributions.

7. Since the fourth edition of this book there have been several major interpretations of the laws that have affected labor relations. Discussions of these court decisions are included.

8. New data show that about one-third of U.S. employers now hire permanent replacements for strikers. As a result, unions have lost many major strikes in recent years. The unions have been pressing for a federal law to limit the use of replacements by companies. The pros and cons of such legislation are described.

9. The role of unions in the economy and society has been much explored by researchers recently. Unions are said to have two faces: economic monopolists and mechanisms to give workers a say in society. The text explores the different aspects of unionism.

A great strength of this book in its first four editions has been its thorough grounding in research findings about the topics it addresses. The new edition maintains this characteristic.

The overall structure of the text has evolved over the previous editions in response to suggestions by instructors who use the book. I am deeply grateful to those who reviewed drafts of this new edition and have assisted me with their many insightful suggestions. In particular, I much appreciate assistance from Thomas P. Gilroy, University of Iowa; David A. Gray, University of Texas, Arlington; Denise T. Hoyer, Eastern Michigan University; David Jacobs, American University; Ronald Miller, Oregon State University; William L. Moore, California State University, Hayward; Herman A. Theeke, Central Michigan University; and Elizabeth C. Wesman, Syracuse University.

Daniel Quinn Mills

LABOR-MANAGEMENT RELATIONS

CONTEMPORARY LABOR-MANAGEMENT RELATIONS

Work is a central concern in the lives of most people—it is the method by which they support themselves and their families, and it is where they spend much of their lives. As a result, most of us care very much about the features of our work environment. Many aspects of work are established by employers; others by technology; and still others are governed by laws administered by various government agencies. Important features of work depend on labor-management relations, which is why the subject of this text is important to many people. What occurs in labor-management relations hinges on individual and group psychology, economic factors, sociological trends, and power relationships.

The first section of this book discusses the elements of labor-management relations, what its study is about, and why it is an important topic in today's world.

CHAPTER 1

THE INDUSTRIAL RELATIONS SYSTEM

MODERN ECONOMIC SOCIETY

The economic and social status of most people in modern economic society depends, to a large degree, on their occupations. Most adults in our country hold jobs. We spend a considerable amount of time at our place of work. Through work, we develop many of our personal associations, attitudes, and other aspects of our lives. Work is crucial to most people's economic security. Jobs provide the mechanism by which each of us contributes to the economic wellbeing of the society as a whole. In return, jobs provide us with an income. The amount of the income a job provides helps to determine an individual's, and a family's, standard of living, especially in terms of the goods and services consumed. Income also provides people with opportunities, such as the opportunity to travel, to engage in hobbies or in recreational activities, or to develop talents, such as those in music, art, or dancing. The income and benefits associated with many jobs also provide protection against weakness, injury, and even, to a degree, loss of the job itself.

As we all know, some jobs are better than others. Good jobs provide higher pay, better benefits, and better working conditions than poorer jobs. And since we spend so much time on the job, the personal relationships at the workplace are important to all of us. But what causes some jobs to be better than others? Who sets the standards that apply to various jobs, and by what process is it done?

Ours is a society of employees and managers. In the past, many more people worked for themselves or for members of their families, but this is no longer the case in industrialized countries. Instead, most people work

3

for organizations that vary in size from small to very large.[1] Some private business organizations now have several hundred thousand employees, and some levels of government, like the federal government, have several million employees. Most organizations are smaller, of course, but they also have policies and procedures, and each individual is only a small part of their functioning.

PLAN OF THE BOOK

It is through an interaction of employers and workers that the conditions of employment are determined. This book is about that interaction. It is divided into eight major sections which describe aspects of the relationship of management and labor, and it includes exercises from which the reader can develop some personal experience in handling labor relations problems.

The book is organized as follows:

Part A examines the American industrial relations system.

Part B relates the history of employee-management relations in America and describes American labor unions.

Part C describes the current setting of labor-management relations including the increasing human diversity of the American work force and the changing workplace. It also contrasts union and nonunion firms.

Part D examines the legal setting the government has established for labor relations in the United States.

Part E describes how labor and management interact in the private and public sectors of the economy and compares American employee relations practices with those of some key trading partners.

Part F describes the collective bargaining process.

Part G considers some of the most important subjects that arise in collective bargaining.

Part H assesses the consequences of the American system of labor relations and glances ahead into the future.

Throughout the text runs the theme of the inequality of power that is inherent in the relation of employer to employee and the various limitations that are imposed, whether by law, union influence, or management self-discipline, on the ways in which power is exercised.

WHAT IS AN INDUSTRIAL RELATIONS SYSTEM?

Labor-management relations are part of what may be described as an industrial relations system. The concept of such a system is a very broad

---

[1]John T. Dunlop, "Introduction," in John T. Dunlop and Walter Galenson, eds., *Labor in the Twentieth Century* (New York: Academic Press, 1978), pp. 1–10.

one, so that one may speak of the industrial relations system of a nation; and within a nation one may speak of the industrial relations system of a particular industry. An industrial relations system is characterized by having certain active institutions, a context in which they operate, and a certain output. It is important to think of industrial relations as being a system because the concept of a system focuses attention on interrelationships among the system's parts. In fact, the industrial relations system of each country constitutes a method of dealing with certain fundamental problems of labor relations that exist in all countries, but that assume different forms as a result of the peculiar form in which they occur.[2]

How is the term "industrial relations systems" to be defined? First, the system is industrial in nature because we do not include in it the relationships that exist in the agricultural sector, which explicitly involves the growing of crops and husbandry of animals. In most countries these activities still consume most of the labor force. Also, traditional agriculture has its own special systems of organization, which in many countries depend primarily on land ownership and tenancy. The organization and the conduct of agriculture are important topics, but ones that are generally excluded in discussion of industrial relations systems. (However, in the United States the number of persons engaged in agriculture has declined to such a low proportion of the total labor force—only 3 or 4 percent—that some parts of agriculture are now being reorganized on the basis of models taken from the industrial sector.) The distribution, processing, and retailing of agricultural commodities are, of course, industrial activities that are included in our definition of an industrial relations system.

Further, the term "industrial" is meant to include the labor-management relations that exist in service industries and in public service. In this sense, the term "industrial" is not meant to be limited to industry (i.e., manufacturing), but hearkens back to an older meaning of industry which refers to the way a person earns a living. Hence, "industrial" in industrial relations systems refers to the workplace—whatever and wherever it is.

"Industrial relations" may be defined as the processes by which human beings and their organizations interact at the workplace and, more broadly, in society as a whole to establish the terms and conditions of employment. The process of relations between persons and organizations is stressed, not just the resulting standards. Finally, a "system" is spoken of in order to emphasize the interrelations among persons, organizations, and standards in the industrial environment.

Each nation may be said to have some characteristic fashion of dealing with the social, economic, and legal problems that arise among its citizens. If each of these areas is conceived to involve a system, then the

[2]John T. Dunlop, *Industrial Relations Systems* (New York: Holt, 1957).

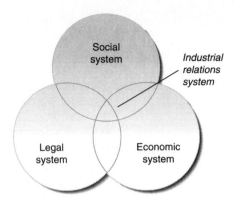

FIGURE 1-1 Identification of an industrial relations system.

industrial relations system may be described as an area in which they overlap. Thus, the industrial relations system is seen to involve important aspects of the social, economic, and legal systems of a country as they relate to the industrial workplace and the relationships among employees and managers. Figure 1-1 provides a diagrammatic identification of an industrial relations system. The diagram shows that the industrial relations system is derived from the intersection of the other, more basic systems.[3] It also shows that the other systems overlap two by two outside the industrial relations system. Thus, in the United States, the economic and legal systems overlap a great deal in areas other than industrial relations, such as commercial law. Similarly, the social and economic systems overlap broadly outside industrial relations, including, for example, income maintenance programs like Social Security and welfare assistance. Thus, we see that the industrial relations system is deeply embedded in our country's basic framework and is not a thing apart. In fact, many persons who make their livelihood in industrial relations have been broadly trained as tradespeople, lawyers, or business people and come therefore from the legal or economic system, bringing their attitudes and practices into the industrial relations system. To further illustrate the point, in the United States, the federal courts that ordinarily handle labor relations cases are not specialized courts, but instead handle the full range of legal activity that comes before the federal judiciary. (The National Labor Relations Board is not a court, but rather an administrative tribunal. It is much like a specialized court.) Thus, industrial relations matters are not separated from the broad range of legal activities in the United States, but are in fact deeply intermingled with them.[4]

[3]Dunlop described the economic and industrial relations systems as part of an encompassing social system. The formulation used here is, therefore, not Dunlop's, but a modification.

[4]Nicholas Bain, "Approaches to Industrial Relations Theory: An Appraisal and a Theory," *Labor and Society*, 3:2, April 1978, pp. 199–216.

The industrial relations systems of various industrialized nations that John Dunlop described in the 1950s are undergoing change. "Technological change and internationalization [of business] have reduced the viability of both Keynesian economics [by which government intervenes to keep the economy stable] and the mass production system, once integrally related to the industrial relations systems."[5]

Although union membership has undergone a dramatic decline as a portion of the labor force in many countries, this is not true in all. In general, the more the government, unions, and corporations cooperate to determine economic and social policy, the stronger the unions have remained. Where wages are determined in a centralized manner, unions have remained stronger; and where there is centralized national bargaining, unions have remained stronger. In effect, the success or decline of unions is said to be related to the overall political structure of different societies. This observation relates a key aspect of a nation's industrial relations system to its broader political system. [6]

Twenty years ago it was reasonably accurate to speak of the industrial relations system of each nation and to compare and contrast them. In recent years, however, there has been much change, so that in important instances today there are greater differences within a nation than between nations. In the United States, for example, the union and nonunion sectors of the economy are sometimes very different, while the union sector in America is very much like the union sector in some other countries. This increasing complexity of labor-management relations does not invalidate the concept of an industrial relations system—which stresses that law, society, and labor-management practices each play a role—but does suggest that the concept should be used with care. It is still possible to compare the industrial relations systems of different nations, but the degree of difference identified is likely today to be less dramatic than in the past. This is less the result of an increasing convergence, or likeness, of the systems, than it is of increasing diversity within each nation.[7]

HOW DOES OUR INDUSTRIAL RELATIONS SYSTEM OPERATE?

An industrial relations system involves certain institutions, which we may term "actors" in the system. In the United States the major actors are,

[5]Ray Marshall, "The Future Role of Government in Industrial Relations," *Industrial Relations*, 31:1, Winter 1992, p. 31. Ray Marshall was secretary of labor during the Carter administration, 1977–1981.

[6]David G. Blanchflower and Richard B. Freeman, "Unionism in the United States and Other Advanced OECD Countries," *Industrial Relations*, 31:1, Winter 1992, p. 72.

[7]Richard M. Locke argues that the more important variations among industrial relations systems often lie within a nation rather than between nations. That is, he suggests that nations do not have only one system but several. R. M. Locke, "The Demise of the National Union in Italy: Lessons for Comparative Industrial Relations Theory," *Industrial and Labor Relations Review*, 45:2, January 1992, p. 229.

broadly defined, three: management and management organizations, employees and their organizations, and the government in its role as a regulator and judge. These actors together determine the output of the system, which we may describe as a set of arrangements, understandings, or rules about terms and conditions of employment. Described in this way, the system seems simple enough—but unfortunately, there are many complications. For example, there is not one government in the United States but many governments, with different levels of government (e.g., federal, state, and municipal) and many branches of government (executive, legislative, and judicial). It is a basic characterization of government in America that these different levels and branches are kept more separate than is ordinarily the case abroad. We refer to this separation as the "balance of powers," or "separation of powers," doctrine. Because of this separation, the many agencies of government are each, to a degree, separate actors in our industrial relations system. (In addition, governments are major employers in the United States, so that they also belong in the category of management and management organizations as well as in the category of regulators.)

Figure 1-2 is a diagrammatic representation of an industrial relations system in the United States. This representation is also accurate for the

FIGURE 1-2   A diagram of the industrial relations systems in the United States.

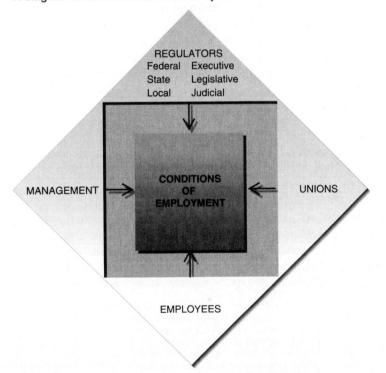

systems in most Western European countries.[8] In other countries, certain other institutions, such as the church, a particular political party, or a national movement, may serve as independent actors in the system also. The actors in the system interact with one another to develop the basic output of the system, including a set of rules or understandings about working conditions and standards of employment. Employees must be compensated, trained, assigned work, and transferred in ways that are mutually understood and accepted by both managers and employees. The most formal method of establishing how actions are to be taken involves the creation of specific arrangements. Arrangements may be as formal as rules, but informal understandings and working relationships between managers and employees are also of great significance. We will have much to say about various types of arrangements in the next section of this chapter.

When arrangements have been established, they have an impact on both management and labor, who with government participated in their establishment. Sometimes the impact, or feedback, is what was expected and intended. When this is the case, the actors in the industrial relations system may turn their attention to other problems. However, sometimes the arrangements that have been created have unexpected consequences. Management or labor may be surprised and upset at the unintended consequences of a rule. In this case, the actor that is aggrieved is likely to seek further changes in the rule, or may go to the regulatory agencies to attempt to get the rule changed. Thus, feedback plays an important role in the operation of the industrial relations system.

For the most part our industrial relations system operates peacefully to determine the standards and conditions of work for more than one hundred million American workers. Most union-management contracts are resolved without work stoppages. Most nonunion employers modify terms and conditions of work without substantial objection by their employees. Cooperation among management, employees, and unions is much more often the case than conflict.

However, conflict may occur among the actors in the industrial relations system. Strikes, which are often the product of disputes between management and labor, occur frequently in the United States. Conflict causes considerable public attention, but it is not the primary product of the industrial relations system. To adopt the view that conflict is the primary output of the system, that is, the most significant thing to be studied and explained, risks the absurd conclusion that when there is little conflict, there is little or nothing to be studied. However, we will see that rules about how conflict is to be managed and controlled are an important element of the output of the system.

[8]Hugh Armstrong Clegg, *Trade Unionism under Collective Bargaining* (Oxford: Basil Blackwell, 1976).

In the next two chapters we will carefully examine the union movement in America, but it is useful to introduce it briefly here.

Unions exist for a number of reasons. To a degree they reflect our history. In the past employees were generally treated much more badly by employers than today, and unions arose to liberate employees. In this regard, unions today may be said to embody the collective memory of working people—the memory of a struggle against exploitation.

But unions also have current purposes. They are a device by which employees band together to persuade or compel employers to provide better pay and working conditions. Also, they provide employees with a common voice in dealing with employers, expressing employees' concerns and needs. They provide a supplementary mechanism by which employees participate in the social and political life of their communities and the nation. Finally, unions serve as a means for members to improve themselves through study, education, and leadership.

An industrial relations system may also be said to operate within a set of constraints involving both the technology available to the economic system and the ideology of the society as a whole. Technology is very important, for it helps to determine the types of jobs available and the amount of output that can be produced and in turn can support living standards. Improving technology is both a blessing and a curse to the industrial relations system. It creates the capacity to provide higher living standards, but it also generates disputes among labor and management about work assignments, pay levels, and similar matters associated with new processes and equipment.

The ideological direction of a society is also an important constraint on an industrial relations system. In the United States people generally accept privately owned business as a legitimate part of our economic system, and the attempts of management to make a reasonable profit for private stockholders are accepted (although people may argue about what is "reasonable"). In contrast, in many other countries the legitimacy of private ownership of business is far less acceptable. Where government, unions, and managers do not accept each other's legitimacy, very great difficulties can develop for the industrial relations system. Stability in industrial relations requires a degree of correspondence among the actors' views of industrial society, although the specific nature of the views (e.g., favorable or unfavorable to private business or favorable or unfavorable to unions) is less significant.[9]

---

[9]A critical review of the concept of an industrial relations system can be found in S. J. Wood et al., "The Industrial Relations System Concept as a Basis for Theory in Industrial Relations," *British Journal of Industrial Relations*, 13, 1975, pp. 291–309. See also A. J. Geare, "The Field of Study of Industrial Relations," *Journal of Industrial Relations*, 19:3, September 1977, pp. 274–283. See also William K. Roche, "Systems Analysis and Industrial Relations," *Economic and Industrial Democracy*, 7:1, February 1986, pp. 3–28.

UNDERSTANDINGS ABOUT WHAT?

There is much to be said about the understandings or arrangements that are the product of the industrial relations system. First, they may concern many types of matters, including compensation, discrimination, hiring, and workers' rights. Second, they may be either substantive or procedural. This is a very important distinction, to which we will return often in later chapters.

Substantive arrangements establish a matter exactly, as, for example, the amount of compensation, the length of the workday, and the size of the overtime premium (e.g., time and a half).

Procedural rules establish how things are to be done, as, for example, what steps a company must take to set a new rule or to discharge an employee. Procedural rules generally describe how substantive rules are to be made or implemented. We usually think mostly about substantive rules, but procedural rules are equally, or often more, important. When management and labor cannot agree on what the substantive rule will be (e.g., how much a particular employee should be paid), often they can agree on how the rule will be decided (e.g., by reference to an impartial arbitrator, who will issue a decision as to what amount the employee will be paid).

The arrangements produced by an industrial relations system may be in several different forms. In many instances they are in the form of the personnel policies, practices, and procedures of various companies. In many other instances they are found in the collective bargaining agreements between companies and labor unions. In some instances they are in written form; in other instances they are in the form of tacit understandings and/or unwritten practices.

Some union-management agreements are very brief and treat only a few matters. Other agreements are quite lengthy and involve many provisions. Many agreements are more than 200 pages long. Tables of contents include such headings as:[10]

- Local working conditions
- Contracting out (i.e., subcontracting)
- Recognition and union membership
- Rates of pay
- Job classifications and incentives
- Hours of work and overtime
- Holidays
- Vacations
- Seniority
- Adjustment of complaints and grievances
- Discharge of employees

[10]Each heading involves a topic that will be treated later in this book.

- Management functions
- Safety and health

Understandings are also drawn from the decisions of arbitrators and courts and from statutes (i.e., laws) passed by legislatures and applying to companies, employees, and unions. Since governments, management, and labor are all deeply interested in the rules of the workplace, it is no surprise that government tries by regulation to affect the rules that management and labor establish, and, conversely, that management and labor try through political activity and lobbying to affect the laws that governments pass concerning the rules of the workplace.

There is very great diversity in the arrangements that exist within the American industrial relations systems. Few collective bargaining agreements have the same provisions. Agreements within the same industry often show substantial similarity, but those from another industry are likely to be very different. For example, seniority provisions are of great importance in agreements involving railways and in many manufacturing agreements (especially in the steel industry, for example), but collective bargaining agreements in the construction industry are virtually silent about seniority. In most instances, seniority does not even exist in the construction industry. For another example, agreements in manufacturing are virtually silent about supervisors and managers, since these persons are not represented by the unions. But in many industries supervisory personnel are unionized, and the agreements include provisions about supervisory jobs (e.g., supermarket agreements commonly cover department managers, construction and utility agreements cover forepersons, and maritime agreements cover ships' officers).

Examples of differences in arrangements may be multiplied many times over. For brevity's sake, only two additional instances are described here:

- Grievance procedures in collective bargaining agreements ordinarily end in binding arbitration by a neutral party, but in some industries (including trucking and electrical construction) the final resolution is made by a joint labor-management committee without the participation of a neutral person (see Chapter 10).
- Incentive pay is common in some industries (e.g., steel, textiles, apparel) but almost altogether absent in others (supermarkets, automobile manufacturing, construction). In industries that use incentives, the incentive pull (i.e., the amount of earnings beyond base pay accounted for by incentives) may be as much as 70 to 80 percent in steel, but only 10 to 15 percent in textiles and apparel.

American labor law has many provisions that differ by industry or class of worker. For example, the garment manufacturing industry is exempt from the general prohibition against secondary boycotts. A secondary boycott is a strike (or other action) directed by a union against employer A in order to bring pressure on employer B, with whom the union has a dispute. The construction industry is exempt from the general prohibition against "prehire" agreements. A prehire agreement involves an employer's recognition of a union as the representative of workers the employer has not yet hired. Railway and airline employees are covered by laws that are different from the laws operative in other private companies. Public employees are covered by still other laws.

What accounts for this diversity? Which differences are appropriate? Which are not? Should there be greater diversity or less? Questions like these are at the heart of the analysis of an industrial relations system and its output. The function of analysis is to discover not only similarity but also difference, and to assist in the explanation and understanding of both.[11]

WHAT ARE THE MOST DISTINGUISHING CHARACTERISTICS OF OUR INDUSTRIAL RELATIONS SYSTEM?

Certain characteristics distinguish the American industrial system from those abroad. The characteristics of our system will become apparent in later chapters, but it is useful to summarize them at the outset to give the reader a sense of the most distinguishing aspects of our system.

1. *The principle of exclusive and sole representation holds that for a given group of workers there shall be one and only one union with the right to represent the workers.* This principle has its origins in the doctrine of exclusive jurisdiction, which developed in the nineteenth and early twentieth centuries in the American Federation of Labor. The doctrine holds that in any given job territory (such as an occupation or an industry) there shall be one and only one legitimate union. (See Chapter 2.) It is now embodied in a somewhat modified form in American law.

In practice today this principle means that there is only one union that represents an employee at his or her workplace. Unlike some European countries in which many unions purport to represent the same workers, we have in America sole unionism, but also our own form of pluralism. We have many unions, each trying to be the sole representative of workers.

In 1935 an altered form of this doctrine was included in the National Labor Relations Act. The act conveys on a union certified by the National Labor Relations Board (NLRB) to represent a group of workers the right and duty to be the exclusive representative of those workers. The employer may not deal with another union, nor may another union interfere with the bargaining relationship (except at certain specified intervals and in cer-

---

[11]Peter B. Doeringer, "Industrial Relations Research in International Perspective," International Industrial Relations Association Congress, September 1976 (mimeographed); and Kenneth F. Walker, "Toward a Useful General and Comparative Theory of Industrial Relations," International Industrial Relations Association World Congress, September 1976 (mimeographed).

tain conditions), and the union cannot decline to represent any member of the unit of workers certified by the board.

This principle of exclusive representation is different in significant ways from the doctrine of exclusive jurisdiction from which it emerged. Exclusive representation is founded on the will of the majority of workers in an employee unit as expressed in a secret-ballot election conducted by an agency of the government. The exclusive jurisdiction of a trade union in the old practices of the American Federation of Labor rested solely on decisions of the AFL itself. Furthermore, the AFL based its jurisdictional lines largely on the craft in which a worker was employed, while the principle of exclusive representation is largely independent of the occupation of employees.

Despite these differences, the principle of exclusive representation had its origins in the practices of the AFL and has been widely accepted by the American trade union movement. Exclusive representation today stands in marked contrast to the multiple unionism (based on religious or ideological orientation) that is common in much of Western Europe. The principle of exclusive jurisdiction, accepted and enforced both by the courts and by the trade union federation (the AFL-CIO), has given American labor relations a stability that is unusual (though not unknown) abroad.

2. *With respect to the rights of the individual employee at his or her workplace, the American system places much more responsibility on the union and much less on the law than in almost any other nation.* Whether it's a matter of paid vacations or holidays or pensions Americans look to the workplace—to employers and/or unions—rather than to government to determine to what employees are entitled. This is quite different from the practice in many other countries.

3. *There are few limitations placed by American law on the authority of employers to hire or fire employees or to lay them off for lack of work.* Every other economically developed nation has extensive legal protection for employees against discharge or layoff. In fact, employment security is a major concern of law in most nations, and people from abroad often cannot believe that the government here leaves such matters in the hands of management and labor.

4. *Bargaining between employers and unions is very much decentralized in the United States.* Collective bargaining agreements tend to be comprehensive, and bargaining tends to involve only one tier of relationships, for example, between a company and a union, or between a plant and a union.

In most of Europe, negotiations tend to be more centralized and to involve multiple tiers. For example, industrywide negotiations between a union or group of unions and an employer association are common in Europe but unusual in the United States. And in Europe it is common for the industrywide negotiations to dispose of certain matters, while others are left to company-level or plant-level negotiations (though in some countries, different tiers bargain over the same issues as well).

In some countries the government, together with national union and employer federations, takes a role in determining the outcome of collective bargaining. The United States has no counterpart to this except in unusual periods of national crisis, especially wartime.

5. *There is a direct line of authority or responsibility from a national union to a local union in a particular workplace.* Thus, the unions function fully at the national level and at the plant level. This is in very great contrast to the situation in Europe, where the national union federations may be very weakly organized at the individual workplace. In Germany, for example, the industrywide collective bargaining agreements are negotiated by labor unions, but the plant-level agreements are negotiated by works councils, which are separate from the unions. The United States has no institution that is a counterpart to a works council.

6. *An employer has a much greater opportunity to remain nonunionized in the United States than in Europe or Japan.* American law confers the right to oppose unionism on both employees and employers. Many American employers do oppose the unionization of their employees and actively campaign against unions that are trying to organize at their facilities. Furthermore, an employer able to remain nonunion is not covered by laws that extend the practices and terms of collective bargaining agreements to nonunion companies, in contrast to what is commonly the case abroad.

7. *Unions are relatively numerous in the United States.* There are some 110 national unions in the United States, in contrast to 17 in Germany. American unions cooperate in some instances but compete vigorously with each other for membership and political influence.

8. *The ideological orientation of most American unions is more moderate than that of the trade union movement in Europe and Japan.* American unions for the most part accept capitalism as an economic system and have little confidence in or commitment to a socialist alternative. In Germany and Britain, the trade unions are predominantly socialist in orientation, while in France and Italy the strongest elements of the labor movement are communist.

9. *Institutions for the resolution of labor-management conflict are highly developed in the United States.* Grievances are handled by binding arbitration by neutrals (see Chapter 20) and disputes over contract terms by mediation and by procedures for negotiation prescribed by law (see Chapter 11). As a result, there is probably less conflict and social disruption in labor-management relations than would otherwise be expected in so large and diverse a democracy. The commitment of the unions to centrist political ideologies also contributes to overall political and social stability in the country.

10. *In stressing that there is an industrial relations system, we emphasize that the various parts of the labor relations process in America have a systematic relationship to each other.* But this should not be taken to imply

that the system is static. Change is occurring slowly in our industrial relations system.[12]

In recent years a series of important developments have occurred. The role of collective bargaining has diminished as the proportion of the labor force in unions has declined. In collective bargaining there has been a shift in emphasis away from labor-management conflict toward a broader role for cooperation as management and labor try to preserve profits and jobs against nonunion and foreign competition.

At the workplace various tasks are divided among the workers. One type of division is according to workers' skill levels. Another relates to supervisory responsibilities and accounts for one of the most general classifications of the members of an organization: the supervisors and the nonsupervisory personnel. It is symptomatic of the changes going on in our society that we do not have a precise pair of terms representing this distinction. We might say managers and employers, but managers are also employees. We might say managers and workers, but most employees today are not workers in the sense of blue-collar production workers. Instead, most employees are salespeople, clerks, or professional or paraprofessional people. For example, nurses, and even doctors, are generally employees of some hospital or clinic, often in a nonmanagerial capacity, and it seems inaccurate to refer to them simply as workers. So when we wish to be precise, we should say that there are supervisors and nonsupervisory personnel. When we are talking less precisely, we may follow a common convention in describing supervisors as management and nonsupervisory personnel as labor. Hence, we speak of labor-management relations. As the terms imply, management has essentially a supervisory or leadership role at the workplace and labor has essentially a performance role. Management and labor may be said to constitute the human side of an organization.

Management and labor are not all there is to producing a product or to providing services, however. The economic system also requires other inputs, including energy, materials, machinery, physical facilities (such as a building), technological know-how, and working capital (or cash). These inputs are used in various degrees by different types of organizations, but all, including government agencies, require some of each. Economic society involves the combination of these inputs in various proportions and different ways to produce goods and services, which our population consumes. Management and labor are the human factors that organize and combine these inputs in order to produce goods and services.

---

[12]D. Quinn Mills and Janice McCormick, *Industrial Relations in Transition* (New York: John Wiley & Sons, 1985), especially chap. 1. See also Thomas A. Kochan, Robert B. McKersie, and Harry C. Katz, "U.S. Industrial Relations in Transition: A Summary Report," Proceedings, The Industrial Relations Research Association Annual Meeting in December 1984, published in 1985.

Management and labor together determine most of the conditions at the workplace. In some manner or another, wages and salaries are established, benefits are provided, hours of work are set, job assignments are made, and disagreements and disputes are handled. Often in the past, and in some instances today, a single individual owned a business establishment personally and would hire and fire people, setting the conditions of work and inviting employees to "take it or leave it." But that day is largely past. Today managers represent a large and often diffuse group of stockholders who own the company, and policies are set on the owners' behalf. In many instances workers are organized collectively into unions, which bargain with management over the terms and conditions of their employment.

Table 1-1 presents some general examples of elements of the bargaining power of business management and unions. Both strengths and vulnerabilities are listed, since either side's power in bargaining has both its positive and negative elements.

TABLE 1-1   SOME GENERAL EXAMPLES OF THE ELEMENTS OF BARGAINING POWER

Management or business	Unions
Strengths	
Ownership of jobs	Support of employees
Ownership of facilities	Support of other unions
Control over business plans, decisions, and financial resources	Financial resources
Control over management organizational structure	Some management structure
Shared interests with business community	Legal protection through laws, regulations, and contracts
Communication resources	Communication resources
Vulnerabilities	
Survival requires economic viability, which depends on:	Union leaders depend on the support of majority of members
Availability, capability, and attitude of workers	Leaders can deliver to employees only what employer will concede
Age, efficiency, and cost of plant and equipment	Activities are subject to legal restrictions in use of strike and picketing
Cost of production	Financial survival depends on maintaining employment and membership
Method of receiving raw materials and distributing product	
Customer satisfaction	
Stockholder control	
Uncontrollable market forces	
Wide-ranging laws and regulations	

Source: E. Robert Livernash, "Note on the Analytical Framework of the Labor Policy Association Seminar on the Dynamics of Power in Employee Relations," Washington, D.C., Labor Policy Association, 1979 (mimeographed).

LABOR-MANAGEMENT RELATIONS AND YOU

Should you know something about labor-management relations? How do the activities of management and labor affect people? Does it help a person to understand these matters? In what way?

There are many reasons why you should make an effort to know something about labor-management relations. Among the most important is the fact that decisions about the workplace affect:

The quality of your life The type of environment that exists at the workplace helps to determine the satisfaction you and those you care about have in life and the attitude you hold toward others. America is changing rapidly: our population is more diverse, our workplaces are more varied. Labor and management will play a key role in determining how our nation adapts itself to these changes.

Economic wellbeing The economic health of the working people and their families—even that of whole communities—depends on decisions about the workplace.

Social status In our society the position of people in the social hierarchy is affected by their occupations. Whether or not this is appropriate, it nevertheless affects all our lives. Decisions by management and labor about jobs therefore affect not only our economic lives but our social lives as well.

Political activity Management and labor, especially where workers are members of unions, play a very significant role in our political life and affect decisions of government at all levels. In one very dramatic recent example that does not involve our own country directly but another country about which many Americans care a good bit, the Solidarity Union in Poland not only overthrew the communist government and instituted democratic reforms, but it provided leadership and support to the new government.[13]

In general, in the United States management and labor constitute a kind of private government of the workplace that to some degree affects all our lives, even the lives of those who have no direct dealings with either management or labor. Furthermore, because business organizations and labor unions are large aggregations of people and involve the livelihoods of many individuals, they are able to influence other people and organizations, including government, in substantial ways. They are, therefore, a major factor affecting the economic, social, and political institutions of our country. The citizen who wishes to understand and influence our society and, thereby, his or her own life, needs to know a good deal about management and labor.

---

[13]Robert A. Senser, "How Poland's Solidarity Won . . . ," *Monthly Labor Review*, 115:9, September 1989, pp. 34–38.

Finally, knowledge about labor-management relations, like knowledge about any important topic, prevents one from appearing a fool. For example, in the late 1960s a wave of strikes swept Louisville, Kentucky, leading a *Wall Street Journal* reporter to describe Louisville as the strike capital of the world. He speculated that the excess of industrial unrest was caused by southern labor encountering northern management in the border-state city. But this was all foolishness.

Louisville had nothing to do with the rash of strikes; the city was simply a victim of decisions made elsewhere for reasons that had nothing to do with it. The major strikes in Louisville were all a result of nationwide work stoppages between national unions and national companies, of which their Louisville plants were only a minor part. Local people had essentially no part in the decisions that led to the strikes. So all the speculation that appeared in the newspaper about the poor labor climate in Louisville and how it led to strikes was merely the result of ignorance.

LABOR-MANAGEMENT RELATIONS AND THE MANAGER

It is a somewhat bewildering fact that while people generally recognize the importance of studying labor-management relations, many managers do not. Instead, managers often assert that they are too busy with other business problems to think about labor relations. But this is shortsighted, for a major part of any manager's job involves interaction with other people, and the firm's employees as a group are sometimes the largest single cost factor in its operations.

When managers fail to study labor relations, they often make costly errors. Because of poor preparation, they then find the area intimidating. For example, this is how a seminar for managers about labor relations at a major business conference in 1992 was promoted in the conference program:

> Labor relations. It's a challenge that can strike fear in the hearts of the most courageous business managers. A challenge that has begun to embrace every aspect of your operation and influence many of your major business decisions.
>
> Effective labor relations begins with a full understanding of law . . . and how to motivate, prevent, and deal with issues that arise in the employment context. From employee benefits to affirmative action, from age discrimination to employment at will, from corporate mergers to corporate downsizing, employment and labor . . . will play an integral role in determining the future of your business.

Below is a list and brief description of five major reasons why managers need to study and understand labor-management relations.

To Enhance Profitability

A major factor in whether a company is profitable or not is its labor relations. Not all companies manage labor relations the same way, of course, but when these relations are well managed the company may have a considerable profit advantage. Strikes, low productivity, rapid turnover of key personnel, and similar characteristics of a company with poor labor relations are profit destroyers. Newspapers, commercial magazines, and the trade press are full of articles entitled, for example, "Labor Is Key to Profits for Corporation" or "Strike Causes Losses at Corporation."

Many managers presume that they know how to handle labor relations well, as if somehow they were born with an instinct to manage well. But, in fact, people learn to manage labor relations in the same way they learn to do other things: by experience, thought, and study.

Managements in government and in private, not-for-profit organizations—such as hospitals, museums, and orchestras—must meet budgets and keep from losing money. They, too, must be concerned with labor relations and minimizing any unfavorable impact on their organization. For example, a headline can also read "New Labor Agreement with Police Causes Increase in Tax Rate."

To Aid in the Climb[14]

Many managers are ambitious. They want to get to the top of their organization, or at least to obtain as responsible and financially rewarding a position as they are able. In various companies there are certain managerial jobs that lead to the top more quickly and directly than others. In some companies it is a financial background that sets a "comer" apart; in others it is sales or marketing or production. But in many companies, the personnel, or labor relations, specialist also has a good chance.

In part this is because American companies are beginning to realize the great importance of people in a business organization. Japanese and European competitors have for years given greater attention to the morale and performance of people than have many American firms. But human performance is at the heart of successful competition in the world economy.

Another factor is that training and experience in labor-management relations involves learning how to accommodate conflicting interests between different groups of people. Problems of accommodation are increasingly important to business and other organizations, especially so at the top of the organization. People who can analyze and understand such problems are rare and valuable, and even more so are those with the capacity to solve them.

---

[14]"Personnel—Fast Track to the Top," *Dunn's Review*, 105:4, April 1975, pp. 74ff.

To Help Avoid Disputes

Among the more obvious advantages that some knowledge of labor relations confers on an executive is an enhanced ability to cope with labor relations problems in his or her own organization. These problems do occur in all organizations from time to time, regardless of whether employees are represented by a union. A manager who is acquainted with labor relations should be better prepared to understand the context of such a problem and better able to develop a method to resolve it.

To Master Poorly Structured Problems

For many managers, labor relations problems are a source of frustration because they seem so difficult to define and to handle objectively. Indeed, as compared with most other management problems (whether of finance, production, sales, or research and development), labor relations problems are poorly structured. They do not lend themselves readily to unambiguous definition and to optimal solutions. Instead, labor relations problems require solutions in the form of accommodations. Often the specific action taken to resolve a problem is less important than the fact that whatever action is taken must be one on which all those involved can agree. In many instances, managers are not able to find optimal solutions, and the best they can hope for is that they and the company will survive the problem.

Managers often refer to such problems as "people" problems, to distinguish them from more technical difficulties. People problems require a form of "muddling through" and compromise, or bargaining, that executives may find distasteful. But people problems are important. And, although labor relations problems are often poorly structured, they can nevertheless be handled well or ineptly. Study of such problems allows a manager to handle them well. A manager may, by study and experience, develop the capacity to resolve people problems.

Managers so often handle people problems badly that it is useful to examine why this is so. To a surprisingly large degree, managers' problems in labor relations arise not out of the objectives that managers have, but rather out of how managers try to get things done. To put it bluntly, it is not what managers do that causes so much trouble, but how they do it.

Many managers will devote considerable time and effort to discovering a potential solution to a production problem, for example. Often the solution that the manager has worked out requires that other people in the organization carry it out. Yet these same hard-working managers often try to put their solution into effect without giving any consideration to how the solution should be implemented. When problems arise with other people in carrying out the proposed solution, the managers often invent reasons for the difficulty that absolve them of any responsibility. They describe the people problems as nontechnical, political, or psychological and insist that they, as managers, cannot be expected to deal with such issues. They lack, they say, the conniving, manipulative nature that the resolution of human problems requires. They are, they believe, above such concerns. And, to excuse a failure to implement the technical solution, they blame the shortsightedness, stubbornness, or ill will of others, as if these conditions were complete and acceptable excuses for a manager's failure.

Good managers recognize, however, that human problems are as important a constraint to the solution of a difficult situation as are technical problems. They recognize that a problem is not solved simply when an idea is developed, but only when the idea is successfully implemented. They know that leadership and supervision of employees are critical elements of the manager's role and that to approach people problems in a way that conforms to known principles greatly increases the chances of success. The successful handling of people problems is necessary to get the job done.

Labor relations problems are not the only poorly structured problems a manager may confront. Difficulties with customers, suppliers, government officials, and community groups may be akin to labor relations problems. The knowledge and techniques derived from studying labor relations are likely to be helpful when applied to other areas, just as statistical and quantitative techniques may have a general applicability to the problems that confront a manager.

To Develop Professional Management

Management is in many ways assuming the characteristics of a profession. A body of knowledge about management is developing. Graduate schools now award thousands of master's degrees each year in business administration or management. Managers' behavior is increasingly judged by the standards of good behavior established by managers as a whole.

In the area of labor relations the increasingly professional character of management is especially important. This is so because in the past managers often felt free to pursue any tactics in order to repress concerted activity among their employees. Violence, intimidation, bribery, and similar undertakings were once common. They still occur, unfortunately, but on a far smaller scale than in the past.

Managers used to excuse such tactics on the grounds of expediency—it was necessary to keep the union out, or to break a strike, and, ultimately, to make a profit. Today expediency is no longer a very effective justification. Most of the community of managers and teachers of management does not accept such tactics as right and appropriate methods, regardless of their success or of the provocation.

In the area of labor relations there are certain principles emerging as standards of the profession of management that are valued for their own sake. They are not a blueprint for managerial action, but rather broad standards of conduct. Among the more important are:

- Giving personal financial considerations is not an appropriate method of resolving disputes.
- Employing violence, using intimidation, and especially accepting the assistance of organized crime in settling disputes are not appropriate.

Unfortunately, there are still a significant number of situations in the United States in which these methods are in common use both by employers and by labor union officials. On the other hand, there are also many situations in which arrangements can be made on a handshake basis and in which a person's word is his or her bond.

Personal dealings are at the heart of labor relations matters, and the increasingly professional standards applied to labor relations behavior are an important constructive factor in American life.

WHY STUDY UNIONS?

Most American employees are not represented by labor unions or employee associations. Yet in this book about labor-management relations we devote what may seem a disproportionate amount of attention to unions and to union-management relations. After all, if unions represent only about 17 percent of all employees, shouldn't they receive only about 17 percent of the attention in this book? In fact, they receive considerably more than that amount of attention. Why is this so?

There are three reasons for making a careful and complete study of unions and union-management relations.

Unions Are Pattern Setters

Through collective bargaining, unions are pattern setters in establishing wage levels, fringe benefits, and working conditions. Many nonunion companies, even many of the largest and most profitable ones, simply adopt the standards established by their unionized competitors. Thus, in order to understand the operations of the nonunionized sector of American industry, the student must take a long and careful look at the unionized sector.

Unions Are an Important Political and Economic Force

Unions provide a mechanism through which millions of American employees take action in the general economic and political spheres of their communities and the nation. Unions constitute a separate and significant force in a way that has no counterpart in the nonunionized sector. Thus, in order to understand the environment in which all Americans operate, unions deserve careful study.

Unions Have Intrinsic Interest and Importance

Unions are large and important human institutions that deserve study for their own intrinsic interest. A well-educated citizen must know something about the institutions of our society, including, for example, business corporations, churches, private foundations, governmental organizations, and the communications media. Unions are institutions also. Furthermore, as we will see below, the activities of unions have an intrinsic interest to anyone who wants to know how human organizations operate and what they do. Again, there are no counterpart organizations of similar interest among nonunionized employees.

Unions Preserve Elements of the History of Our Nation

Unions grew up in adversity, emerging out of difficult struggles with management and government (see Chapter 2). They preserve in their organization, rituals, and modes of thought the times that shaped them. Some unions developed in the nineteenth century when there were still pioneers and industrialization was just beginning. These are the craft unions, and in a sense they are the custodians of the lessons of the building of the nation and what it meant for working people—both good and bad. Other unions developed in the 1930s and continue the legacy of the great depression and the so-called labor wars. These are the industrial unions. Finally, other unions—those in government and services—date primarily from the 1960s and 1970s and remember most of all the times of rapid economic growth. Studying unions is therefore a way in which we can get in touch with our past.

Do Numbers Matter?

Critics of the current leadership of the American labor movement charge that it has failed to expand the role of unions. The proportion of employees who are members of labor organizations has been declining rapidly, and it forms a distinct minority of all employees. To many observers, the failure of the American labor movement to gain a greater proportion of all employees implies (indeed, is evidence of) its stagnation. Only dramatic new initiatives in the policies and orientation of the unions will correct this, critics maintain. Only with the new policies and growing numbers will the labor movement be able to play the progressive role in American society that it should play.[15]

While numbers are important, they are not critical, the current leadership seems to reply. Unions that represent only a minority of all employees

---

[15]Solomon Barkin, "Diversity in Industrial Relations Patterns," *Labor Law Journal*, 27:1, November 1976, pp. 678–685.

still make gains that are often extended to workers who do not belong to unions. These extensions occur either by governmental action or by the action of nonunion employers.

Unions, their leaders argue, set standards for many more employees than they actually represent. There is, therefore, no reason to pay undue attention to the size of union membership. In fact, a small, cohesive group can often achieve more than a large but unwieldy organization. A management representative has given some support for this view:

> It is a common assumption that growth in the influence of organized labor is proportioned to growth in union membership. [Yet] we have seen labor's influence in both collective bargaining activities and in the political arena grow steadily in the past, and I know of no basis to predict a decline in union influence in the future. The facts of union membership . . . are seemingly at variance with this growth of influence.[16]

MODELS OF LABOR-MANAGEMENT RELATIONS

A "model" is a mental construct with which people organize their thoughts about a topic. When people consider labor-management relations, they usually think about a single company dealing with a single local union. This is, of course, a model. It may be represented diagrammatically as in Figure 1-3 by showing the management of company A dealing with union local No. 100, which represents company A's employees. The line between the company and the union has arrows pointing both ways and indicates that each side influences the other. Also, the absence of any other organizations or lines indicates that the relationship between company A and local No. 100 is all there really is to know about the system of labor-management relations indicated here. Figure 1-3 represents a model, in that it identifies the parties involved, indicates their relationship to each other, and excludes other organizations and relationships as insignificant (i.e., extraneous).

Unfortunately, most labor-management relations are not so simple. Instead, both company A and local No. 100 may be found to be at the center of a web of relationships to other organizations, of which their relationship to each other is only a single instance. In Figure 1-4 we examine the web of relationships involving company A. We see that company A has responsibilities to its stockholders and customers as well as to local No. 100. It also has relationships with other companies through an association to which it belongs; it has obligations imposed by governmental regulatory bodies; it has commitments to the communities in which it operates; and it has responsibilities to other unions with which it deals.

---

[16]Joseph W. Shuster, "Manpower and Labor Relations," paper delivered at the American Mining Congress Convention, 1975 (mimeographed).

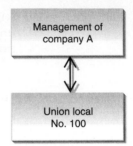

FIGURE 1-3   A simple model of labor-management relations.

This is a more accurate model of the relationship of company A to local No. 100 because it shows that the company must also deal with many of these other groups on issues that affect local No. 100. For example, in considering whether to give in to wage demands by local No. 100 or to take a strike, company A must consider the impact of its choice on its customers, its stockholders, the communities in which it operates, its nonunionized employees, and the other unions with which it deals. Often the strong preferences of one or more of these groups will determine company A's decision.

The local union is also involved in a web of relationships. Figure 1-5 shows that local No. 100 must consider in its own activities the views of its national union, other unions, the community in which it is located, its political friends (whom it should not embarrass by its activities), other companies with which it has contacts (if any), and the management of company A itself.

Figures 1-4 and 1-5 together constitute an alternative model to Figure 1-3. The alternative is much more complex and shows that there are many more factors involved in the relationship between company A and local

FIGURE 1-4   Company A and its relationships.

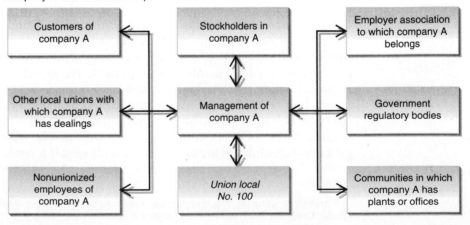

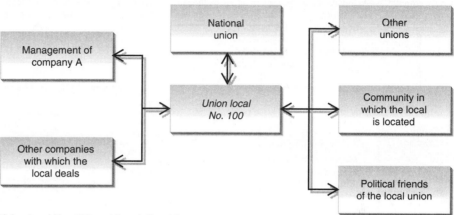

FIGURE 1-5   Union local No. 100 and its relationships.

No. 100 than just the two organizations alone. As such, the more complicated model is generally a more accurate reflection of reality.

The model in Figure 1-3 may be referred to as a "one-to-one" model. The few situations in which it applies in reality are not difficult ones to analyze. Most often, however, labor relations are of the type diagrammed in Figures 1-4 and 1-5 and are not simple at all.

In the remainder of this book we shall often describe labor relations using the model of Figure 1-3 for convenience and simplicity. But the reader should remember that this is an oversimplification, and in many instances we shall try to reflect reality better by using a model of the type given in Figures 1-4 and 1-5.

The reader will recall that John Dunlop's model of the industrial relations system focused on the development of arrangements for the workplace as the ultimate outcome. There are other outcomes of significance, however, including the political activity of unions, the decisions by companies about where to locate facilities, and decisions by managers and unions about lockouts and strikes.

A model (see Figure 1-6) offered by Sethi and Dimmock illustrates these additional outcomes, as well as the rules determined to apply at the workplace, and also shows the influences. It stresses, to a greater degree than Dunlop, the ethos (i.e., the values, philosophy, and ideology) of the participants in the system. In part because of the importance of ethos and choices in the model, its authors refer to it as a "transactional model."

In essence, the transactional model implies that management and union are influenced in their actions by other factors than economics. This implication is consistent with much of the psychological and behavioral research now being conducted on labor relations.

The model begins with environmental variables that include not only ecological factors but also economic, legal, political, social, and technolog-

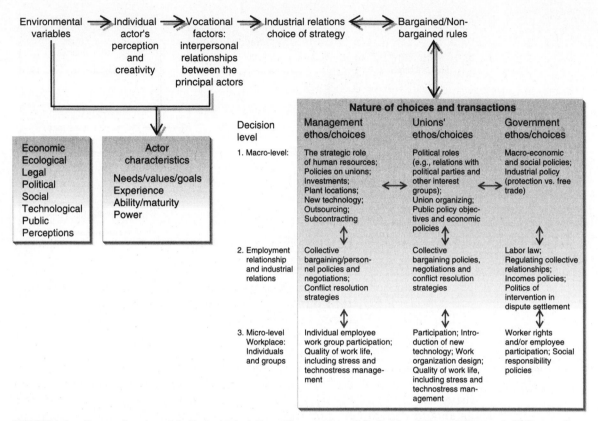

FIGURE 1-6 Transactional model of industrial relations. (Source: Amarjit S. Sethi and Stuart J. Dimmock, "A Transactional Model of Industrial Relations," *Labour and Society*, 12:2, May 1987, p. 180. The figure is adapted from Thomas Kochan, Robert McKersie, and Peter Cappelli, "Strategic Choices and Theory," *Industrial Relations*, 23, Winter 1984, p. 23.)

ical factors as well. These factors affect the actors in the industrial relations system via their own needs, values, goals, power, and other factors.

What individual actors decide to do is also affected by their personal relationships with other people. For example, a potential controversy between an employee and a manager may be avoided if the two people like one another; or a conflict between a union and a company may be avoided if the union leader and the company's top executive trust each other.

All the factors mentioned so far determine the strategy that each actor will choose for dealing with other actors. The union, employer, and government each then determine how to proceed to achieve its goals. Unions and companies try to achieve objectives through bargaining with one another. They are also concerned to see that conflict does not get out of hand. The government passes legislation and acts in the courts to enforce its laws.

At the level of the workplace, the individual is affected by the processes occurring between the organized entities of management, labor, and government and to a degree participates in them. The union member, for example, votes on the union's leadership and ordinarily is asked to vote to approve or disapprove a contract that the union negotiates with management. Furthermore, an individual employee may participate via discussions with his or her supervisor or through a work team. Finally, the individual has rights conveyed on her or him by government legislation and regulation.

CHAPTER SUMMARY

Modern economic society is made up largely of organizations such as business firms or government agencies and the people who work for them (i.e., who are their employees). The processes by which the wages, benefits, and other conditions of work are determined may be termed an industrial relations system.

The industrial relations system is composed of numerous organizations of management and employees, and different levels and branches of government. It is deeply embedded in our country's basic social, economic, and legal systems. The processes of the industrial relations system mold the terms and conditions of employment and the rules about how conflict is to be expressed and controlled. There is a great diversity between industries and between classes of workers in the types of rules that apply.

The American industrial relations system has a number of characteristics that tend to distinguish it from those of other countries: (1) There is usually exclusive representation by one union of any given group of workers; (2) bargaining between employers and unions is very much decentralized, although there are direct lines of authority and responsibility between a national union and a local union in a particular workplace; and (3) it is easier for an employer to be nonunionized in the United States than it is abroad. Also, there are a greater number of unions in America than in most other countries, and the industrial relations system here has a more moderate ideological orientation than elsewhere.

It is important for people in general to know about labor-management relations because these relations are a significant factor affecting the economic, social, and political institutions of our society. For employees labor-management relations affect the wages and conditions of their jobs. For managers such knowledge and understanding are indispensable. Employees are often the largest cost factor in whether a company is profitable or not. Skill in labor-management relations includes the valuable ability of accommodating the interests and needs of different groups of people.

QUESTIONS FOR THOUGHT AND DISCUSSION

1 What are some of your already-established attitudes about labor, unions, business managers, and government regulation of labor relations? How have these ideas been formed—through personal experiences? Family attitudes? The mass media? Formal education?

2 In what way does American practice in industrial relations make up a system?

3 What outcomes produced by an industrial relations system are most important, in your opinion?

4 What is the most appropriate role for government in the industrial relations system?

6 Why is there such a great diversity in the United States in the arrangements and conditions of work, both between industries and between types of workers? What are some of the differences you are aware of at present?

7 What factors limit management's power in the workplace?

SELECTED READING

Dunlop, John T., *Industrial Relations Systems* (New York: Holt, 1957).

Dunlop, John T., and Derek L. Bok, *Labor and the American Community* (New York: Simon and Schuster, 1970).

Heckscher, Charles C., *The New Unionism: Employee Involvement in the Changing Corporation* (New York: Basic Books, 1988).

Kochan, Thomas A., and Harry C. Katz, *Collective Bargaining and Industrial Relations*, 2d ed. (Homewood, Ill.: Richard D. Irwin, 1988).

Kochan, Thomas A., Harry C. Katz, and Robert B. McKersie, *The Transformation of American Industrial Relations* (New York: Basic Books, 1986).

Mills, D. Quinn, "Reforming the U.S. System of Collective Bargaining," *Monthly Labor Review*, 106:3, March 1983, pp. 18–22.

Somers, G. G., ed., *Essay in Industrial Relations Theory* (Ames, Iowa: Iowa State University Press, 1969).

B

THE HISTORICAL AND INSTITUTIONAL CONTEXT

Management has been hostile to unions during most of American history. For a variety of reasons, this has not been equally true in many other industrialized nations. Abroad national governments often intervened on behalf of labor, but until the 1930s such intervention was rare in the United States. Instead federal and state governments more frequently supported employers than unions in periods of conflict. Wherever possible, most American employers have opposed the growth of unions, often with the assistance of the law and the courts. In this hostile environment isolated local unions of workers at the plant, office, or construction site would not long survive. In order to provide mutual assistance and protection unions have banded together to form large national organizations.

National union organizations have gone beyond assisting the activities of local unions. They also conduct lobbying and other political activities at the state and federal levels. Through the activities of national unions, employees have extended their countervailing power against management beyond the work site and into the broader stream of American social and economic life.

CHAPTER 2

HISTORY AND PHILOSOPHY OF AMERICAN UNIONS

THEMES IN AMERICAN LABOR HISTORY

Unions are not a recent development in American history. Organizations of craftspeople and workers originated at about the time of the American Revolution, which established the independent United States. Nor are strikes a new development, for, as we will see, associations of skilled tradespeople in American cities conducted strikes as early as the late eighteenth century. However, American trade unionism has not had a simple and straightforward line of development.[1] Rather, the progress of American trade unionism has been accompanied by as much failure as success, by as many false starts as enduring accomplishments, by serious blunders that took generations to rectify, and by sudden and largely unforeseeable achievements.

In this chapter we review briefly the history of American unionism. It is convenient to approach the history in a generally chronological order. However, there are certain themes that run throughout the story that the reader should bear in mind.

1. *The impact of the business cycle on labor unions* Early trade unionism arose in periods of business expansion and collapsed during depressions. It was not until the late 1800s that some few unions were able to survive depression and not until the mid-twentieth century that labor organiza-

---

[1] Three general sources for material on the American union movement are Richard B. Morris, *Encyclopedia of American History* (New York: Harper, various editions); Maurice F. Neufield, *A Representative Bibliography of American Labor History* (Ithaca, N.Y.: Cornell University, 1964); and Daniel J. Leab, ed., *The Labor History Reader* (Urbana: University of Illinois Press, 1985).

tions as a whole seemed able to endure the strains of recession. In part, this development is the result of a moderation in the severity of downturns caused by modern governmental economic policy. The development is also a result of the increased size, diversification, and financial and administrative strength of unions as organizations. In the early days of unionism each economic crisis caused the institutional or organizational framework of unionism to collapse. This no longer occurs.

2. *The impact of the growth and development of the American economy on unionism* The rapid industrial expansion of the United States in the last quarter of the nineteenth century and the first quarter of the twentieth century provided both the opportunity for expansion of unions and the threat of a very difficult environment in which to act. Emergent big business was politically and economically powerful. With some few exceptions, American trade unions first gained a foothold in the mass-production industries, then lost it. Violent struggles, costing many lives, characterized the period of union collapse and resurgence many years later. But the union organization of the mass-production industries in the 1930s brought to labor relations a period of relative peace, which has continued to this day.

3. *The ebb and flow of radical and Marxist influence in American trade unionism* Reformist, politically active trade unionism first appeared in the 1830s and later in the nineteenth century became a militant and radical force. Efforts to organize American labor into a Marxist or socialist mold, like so much of European trade unionism, occurred with great regularity. Examples include the socialists' and anarchists' efforts of the late nineteenth century, the formation of the International Workers of the World (IWW) in the early twentieth century, and the emergence of the communist-dominated unions in the 1930s. Again and again leftist groups have attempted to capture the American trade union movement and to divert it to a radical political orientation. The 1990s, however, were a period of very little influence for radical leadership within the trade union movement.

4. *The progress of government regulation of trade unionism* Unions have never been free of legal restraint, and much of the history of American trade unions involves their efforts to free themselves of limitations on their activities imposed by courts or legislative bodies. For most of the history of American trade unionism the federal government exerted only a small influence on labor relations between private-sector employers and workers, although federal officials did intervene in important instances in major disputes. The labor turmoil of the 1930s reached such proportions, however, that the federal government intervened by statute to establish a legal framework for unionism and collective bargaining. In consequence, the activities of American unions and employers have become increasingly subject to legal oversight and are now the subject of public regulation to a degree previously unknown in the United States.

5. *The development of the mainstream of the American labor movement*
Throughout the turmoil accompanying labor-management conflict in
America and the rapidly changing forms of its political manifestations,
there has continued the somewhat unspectacular growth of the national
trade unions, which first emerged with a central body, the American Federation of Labor (AFL). Founded in 1886, the AFL has weathered repeated depressions and has fought off challenges from both the radicals, who criticize it as too moderate, and those business people who have fought all labor
unions. In competition with other forms of unionism, including geographic
councils, single big unions, and, finally, industrial unions, the national trade
union structure of the AFL survived and emerged as the most common form
of American unionism. But the AFL has been much affected by the movements that have challenged it. In particular industrial unionism has also
survived and in the merger of the AFL and its industrial union counterpoint,
the Congress of Industrial Organizations (CIO), in 1955 American unionism
combined the strengths of craft and industrialism unionism into one.

BEGINNINGS OF LABOR UNIONISM, 1794–1886

The First Unions

It is often thought that labor unions are essentially a response by workers
to unbearably oppressive employment conditions. Certainly some unions
have developed from such a background. But most American labor union
activity has been among skilled or semiskilled workers and is the outgrowth of their attempts to regulate in their own interest the trades at
which they make a living. Our earliest trade unions appear from today's
perspective much like medieval guilds. The distinction between employer
and employee was not so sharp then. There were few corporations and few
large employers. Craftspeople worked for themselves, or in small shops,
and were often in conflict with their customers or with the merchants to
whom they sold their products. In order to raise their earnings directly, or
to shut out competitors, working people formed organizations, ostensibly
for the purpose of regulating a trade by imposing standards of training,
quality, and price on those practicing it. In some instances, these organizations came into conflict with the employers, merchants, or potential competitors and conducted work stoppages. For example, the Federal Society
of Journeymen Cordwainers (shoemakers) of Philadelphia was formed in
1794 and conducted a strike in 1799. New York City printers struck in
1794, cabinetmakers in 1796, and Pittsburgh shoemakers in 1809. The issues in dispute ordinarily involved hours of work, earnings, the regulation
of apprenticeship, and demands that only members of the particular jour-
neyman society should be hired by employers (a so-called closed shop) or
patronized by merchants. Some theorists of labor history are of the view

that these earliest elements of trade union concern have endured in the American labor movement, and they characterize the movement as "scarcity-conscious" unionism.[2]

Not surprisingly, the associations were often prosecuted as illegal conspiracies under the common law, especially when strikes occurred. The decision of state courts often went against the associations until 1842, when Chief Justice Lemuel Shaw of Massachusetts ruled in *Commonwealth v. Hunt* that trade unions were lawful and strikes for a closed shop were legal. Although not binding outside of Massachusetts, Justice Shaw's decision was accorded substantial weight as a precedent by judges in other states and marked an important liberalization of judicial tolerance for union activities.

The first unions did not arise for the purpose of collective bargaining with employers, either in the United States or in England, from whose unions American workers drew much of their leadership. "The object of trade unionism used to be to uphold the price of labor against the encroachments of the employers," wrote one historian of the British labor movement. "'Collective bargaining' is an afterthought, forced on capital and labor alike because of the straining after industrial peace and the apparent necessity for securing it for lengthened periods."[3]

Printing and textile manufacturing were two of the first economic activities to be practiced on a large scale. Businesses hired labor for work in plants, and disputes developed over earnings and conditions in the plants. In 1824, for example, the first recorded strike by women workers occurred among weavers at a Pawtucket, Rhode Island, factory. Labor organization advanced to such a degree that by 1836, some 13 cities had central trade association councils. Political participation by workers was accelerated by the removal of property qualifications for voting in various states in the period from 1818 to 1843, and so-called labor parties became active in Philadelphia, New York, and Boston. In 1834 President Andrew Jackson intervened with federal troops to put down a strike by Irish laborers trying to obtain a closed shop on construction of the Chesapeake and Ohio Canal in Maryland; this was the first such use of federal troops against workers but not, as we will see, the last.[4]

The National Trades Union

Early trade union activity culminated in the formation of the National Trades Union in 1834 by delegates from central trades councils of various

[2]Selig Perlman, *A History of Trade Unionism in the United States* (New York: Macmillan, 1929); and Perlman, *A Theory of the Labor Movement* (New York: Macmillan, 1928).

[3]Fred Knee, "The Revolt of Labor," *Social Democrat*, November 1910; reprinted in K. Coates and A. Topham, eds., *Industrial Democracy in Great Britain*, vol. 1 (Nottingham: Spokesman Books, 1975), pp. 44–47.

[4]Arthur M. Schlesinger, Jr., *The Age of Jackson* (Boston: Little, Brown, 1945).

cities meeting in New York. A New York City congressman from the Tammany Hall political organization, Ely Moore, became the chief officer of the organization. In a remarkable demonstration of political effectiveness, Moore and the NTU prevailed on President Andrew Jackson to establish the 10-hour day in the Philadelphia Navy Yard and on President Martin van Buren to extend the 10-hour day to all workers on federal public works. At this time most manufacturing workers were on an 11- or 12-hour day. This cooperation between labor officials and a national Democratic administration has caused some historians to see great parallels between the 1830s and President Franklin D. Roosevelt's administration a century later. Attempts to form national associations in various trades were also begun at this time, but the panic of 1837 (an early depression) brought the collapse of most of the local associations and eventually of the NTU itself.

National Unions Emerge in Various Trades

The 1850s and 1860s saw the emergence of a group of national trade unions. The National Typographical Union was formed in 1852, the Hat Finishers in 1854, the Stone Cutters in 1855, the United Cigarmakers in 1856, and the Iron Molders (i.e., steel and iron workers) in 1859. The panic of 1857 shattered the weaker organizations, but some survived. The National Typographical Union still exists today, while the cigarmakers and stone cutters have been absorbed into other organizations (the cigarmakers, for example, numbering 2500, merged with the Retail, Wholesale, and Department Store Union in 1974). Attempts at trade union organization continued during the Civil War, and in 1865, for example, delegates from several Midwestern cities formed the Bricklayers National Union. The railway brotherhoods also originated in this period, including the Locomotive Engineers (1863), the Conductors (1868), and the Firemen (1873). By 1866 enough trade associations existed to form the National Labor Union, with the immediate objective of an 8-hour working day. The failure of the 8-hour campaign led to a concentration on political reform, and in 1872 the National Labor Union became the National Labor Reform Party with a nominee for President of the United States. The nominee was unsuccessful, and the movement collapsed. However, in 1868, largely as a result of National Labor Union influence, Congress established the 8-hour day for government laborers and mechanics.

In the early 1870s there were about 30 national unions, and total union membership was perhaps 300,000. In the depression of the 1870s, starting about 1873, the number of unions and membership fell by 80 percent or so. The depression generated radical labor activity, including riots in New York City, the formation of the Molly Maguires, a radical organization of Irish coal miners (10 members were hanged for murder in 1875), and, finally, the general railway strike of 1877 against wage cuts. The strike was broken by federal troops and state militia in battles at Pittsburgh and in West Virginia, with 35 people killed.

Knights of Labor

Out of the turmoil of the 1870s emerged the most substantial labor organization yet seen in the United States, but in a form that appears very strange to those familiar with the modern American labor movement. Called the Knights of Labor, this organization was a sort of fraternal organization of working people. It began among tailors in Philadelphia in 1869 as a secret fraternal order and grew to national prominence under the leadership of Terence V. Powderly in the period from 1879 to 1886. The Knights grew to a membership of more than 700,000 in the mid-1880s, organized in some 6000 local assemblies, and the organization exerted considerable political influence. In the eastern states, assemblies were primarily of industrial workers; in the western states, of farmers. Assemblies could be organized on a trade or industrial basis, and the Knights were so significant that many local trade unions affiliated as assemblies. The Knights stressed the unity of all labor—farm and industrial alike, and advocated the succor of the unskilled by the skilled. In the depression of the mid-1880s the assemblies of industrial workers and trade unionists turned to strikes to protect their earnings and jobs. A series of strikes against various railway companies was successful, even against the opposition of financial magnate Jay Gould. Gould is said to have boasted at the time that "I could hire one half of the working class to kill the other half."[5]

However, the Knights' success did not continue. A strike against the Southwest Railroad System failed, and a general strike for the 8-hour day in Chicago collapsed. On May 4, 1886, in Chicago, a bomb was thrown at police breaking up an anarcho-communist rally at Haymarket Square. The bomb exploded, killing 6 police officers outright and causing wounds of which another later died, and injuring 70 others. In the riot 4 workers were killed and 50 injured. A trial of alleged conspirators resulted in the execution of several radical leaders, although the actual bomb thrower was never identified.[6] In a general wave of public reaction against strikes and labor agitators, the Knights began to lose membership. As membership among workers declined, the farmers' assemblies seized control of the Knights. Thereafter, the Knights rapidly declined as a workers' movement and in 1893 disappeared into the agrarian movement entirely.

[5]Sidney Lens, *The Labor Wars* (New York: Doubleday, 1974), p. 7.
[6]Leon Stein and Philip Taft, eds., *The Accused, the Accusers, the Famous Speeches of the Eight Chicago Anarchists in Court, 1887* (New York: Arno, 1969).

TRADE UNIONS, 1886–1905

Formation of the AFL

The American Federation of Labor was formed in the aftermath of the 1886 debacle. Meeting in December 1886 in Columbus, Ohio, some 25 groups representing perhaps 150,000 members established another central trade union federation. Like the Knights of Labor, the AFL was committed to advancing the interests of working people. But to a large degree the AFL was created in reaction to the approach that had failed for the Knights of Labor. Predominantly, the delegates who formed the AFL represented workers who were organized on a trade basis. Unlike the Knights of Labor, the AFL did not include farmers, skilled workers predominated, and there were no locals or lodges of mixed occupational membership. Many of the groups involved had been cooperating previously through the Federation of Organized Trades and Labor Unions (founded in 1881), which was now abolished. The AFL selected Samuel Gompers, a leader of the Cigarmakers Union, as president.[7]

Gompers was to be president of the AFL for 37 of the next 38 years (until his death in December 1924, at 74 years of age). He was an Englishman by birth, apprenticed in London as a cigarmaker, and came to the United States in 1863. He is probably the single most important individual in American trade union history, for he kept the AFL together despite internal divisions and external opposition. He maintained a commitment to principles that we now perceive to be fundamental to American unionism, including organization by trade (rather than the establishment of one union of skilled and unskilled alike) the primacy of the national union (rather than of the federation of all workers), and unionism directed at gaining from employers improvements in pay and working conditions, socalled business unionism (rather than social reform through political action). He was particularly influential in opposing socialist ideology (though originally a socialist himself) and in insisting that the AFL remain unaffiliated with any political party.[8]

Problems in the 1890s

The AFL experienced very difficult times in the depression of the 1890s, but thereafter made rapid gains. At this time it was the only effective national organization of workers in the United States. As such, it began to encounter substantial opposition from the business executives who controlled the rapidly expanding manufacturing sector of the economy. In

---

[7]Lee M. White, "The Founding Convention," *AFL-CIO Federationist*, 88:11, November 1981, pp. 1–5.

[8]Irwin Yellowitz, "Samuel Gompers," *Monthly Labor Review*, 112:7, July 1989, pp. 27–33.

1895 the National Association of Manufacturers was formed, and it engaged the AFL in a struggle that the AFL itself was never able to resolve successfully (though the CIO did so in the 1930s).

Nonetheless, the AFL prospered and by 1904 claimed almost 2 million members.[9] Membership was concentrated among railway and building trades workers and in the coal industry. Organization in manufacturing was much more spotty and in fact was being weakened. In 1892, for example, a strike against Carnegie Steel Corporation at Homestead, Pennsylvania, was broken by private police (of the Pinkerton detective agency) and state militia. Another steel strike, in 1901, was beaten by the newly established United States Steel Corporation so effectively that steelworkers remained largely nonunionized until 1937 (although an unsuccessful attempt was made in 1919 to organize the industry).

The Pullman Strike

In 1894 a strike against the Pullman Company (a railway car manufacturer), in opposition to a wage cut, began among nonunionized workers at a company-owned town outside Chicago. Eugene V. Debs was a leader of the Brotherhood of Railway Firemen and organizer (in 1893) of a multi-trade, industrial-type union, the American Railway Union (not affiliated with the AFL). Debs felt obliged to assist the strikers. A nationwide rail strike was called and was particularly effective in the Midwest. Alleging violence, the railways sought federal assistance in keeping the trains running. The attorney general of the United States was a former railway corporation legal counsel. He supplied 3400 men as federal deputies to help the railways maintain operation. When violence ensued, President Grover Cleveland sent federal troops to Illinois to break the strike, over the protest of the governor of Illinois. A federal court injunction (i.e., a court order to cease and desist certain activities) was issued against the strike, and Debs was jailed for contempt of court. The strike was broken.[10] Debs's American Railway Union collapsed, and he left trade unionism to become the longtime head of the Socialist party in America (five times a candidate for President of the United States).[11] The AFL, however, was relieved that it had resisted overtures to join the strike. Once again the AFL had confirmed its view that general social crusades or assistance to oppressed workers when they lacked the capacity to defend themselves was a dangerous sort of idealism that would likely result in the destruction of the AFL itself (as the Pullman strike had resulted in the destruction of the American Railway Union). The

[9]Leo Wolman, *Ebb and Flow in Trade Unionism* (New York: National Bureau of Economic Research, 1936).

[10]Leon Stein and Philip Taft, eds., *The Pullman Strike* (New York: Arno, 1969).

[11]Irving Stone, *Adversary in the House: The Life of Eugene V. Debs* (New York: Doubleday, 1947).

AFL continued its moderate course, emphasizing collective bargaining by its affiliates and the achievement of gains by political activity.

RADICAL UNIONISM IN THE UNITED STATES, 1905–1920

Did violence and repression by employers spawn radical unionism? Or did radical unionism require such a response? Perhaps this issue is debatable, but certainly the two went hand in hand. By the early twentieth century employers in many industries had crushed labor union activity, and the federal government and, in some instances, state governments had become their willing accomplices. In 1902, for example, federal courts began to apply the Sherman Antitrust Act (passed in 1890) to the activities of trade unions, further increasing the extent of federal resistance to unions (see the so-called *Danbury Hatters* case[12]). Injunctions obtained from federal courts under the Sherman Act soon became an especially powerful tool for employers in resisting union organization.

A radical response to the success of employers in repressing unions, and to the supposed moderation of the AFL, was already developing by 1900. In mines of the far West radicals had formed the Western Federation of Miners, and in 1895 a federation to rival the AFL had been formed, the American Labor Union. Finally, in 1905 in Chicago, these two groups established the Industrial Workers of the World (IWW), or "Wobblies," as they came to be called. The IWW stood for abolition of capitalism, the end of the wage system, and industrial unionism. In the West the IWW organized unskilled and migratory workers in lumber, agriculture, and shipping; but they also made some headway in organizing large-scale industrial strikes, as in the Lawrence, Massachusetts, textile mills in 1912. The IWW lived a short and violent existence. Its leaders preached revolution, but in action it was possibly as sinned against as sinning. For example, in 1906 government authorities from Idaho virtually kidnapped Bill Haywood, the IWW's leading organizer in Denver. He was tried for murder, but the state failed to get a conviction. Haywood was released. Meanwhile, however, the IWW had dissolved into internal bickering.

The struggle for the allegiance of workers was waged between the AFL and the socialists (who were deeply involved in the IWW) continually in the years around the turn of the century. The AFL repeatedly rejected the revolutionary rhetoric of the socialists. In 1903, speaking at the Federation convention, AFL President Gompers replied to his socialist critics:

> I want to tell you Socialists that I have studied your philosophy, read your works upon economics. . . . I have heard your orators and watched the work of your movement the world over. I have kept close watch upon you, and know what you have up your sleeve. And I want to say that I am entirely at variance with

[12]*Loewe v. Lawler*, 208 U.S. 274 (1908).

your philosophy. . . . Economically, you are unsound; socially, you are wrong; and industrially you are an impossibility.

But the AFL was not always able to extricate itself from the situations created by the agitation of leftists, and sometimes this inability led to disastrous results.

During World War I the AFL supported the war effort and joined in government-sponsored committees to keep production going. The IWW, however, opposed the war effort. The AFL, in consequence, grew and prospered during the war, while the IWW suffered increasing prosecution. In 1919, following the Bolshevik revolution in Russia, a communist party was established in the United States. In the ensuing public scare, the federal government's Department of Justice conducted nationwide mass arrests of political and labor agitators, and hundreds were deported from the country. On a single day, January 2, 1920, federal agents carried out raids in 33 cities and arrested 2700 persons for radical political or union activity. The IWW was destroyed as a significant force in the process. (In the 1990s the IWW still exists as an organization representing some one thousand workers nationally and committed to its traditions and to the objectives of its founders. Its one official has recently moved the IWW's headquarters from Chicago to San Francisco.)

The AFL attempted to distinguish itself from the radicals. With some governmental support, it attempted to retain the gains in membership and collective bargaining that had been achieved during the war. But in 1919 the communist labor organizer William Z. Foster provoked the AFL into urging a strike in the nation's steel industry. The strikers sought union recognition, collective bargaining, a shorter workday, and wage increases. Thousands of workers supported the strike, which continued for 3 months before collapsing. Organization of the steel industry was still 2 decades away, and both the AFL and its steel industry affiliate, the Amalgamated Association of Iron, Steel and Mine Workers, were badly damaged by the struggle.[13]

All through these decades of often violent clashes between labor and management—the historical crucible, as it were, in which the American labor movement was formed—unionism was largely, though not exclusively, the province of men. But women were moving into the commercial labor force in large numbers. Already female clerical workers, who would become so numerous as the twentieth century progressed, were emerging in the big cities. But unionism failed to enroll them, both because of employer opposition and because of the disinterest of many male unionists.[14]

[13]See David Montgomery, *Workers' Control in America* (Cambridge: Cambridge University Press, 1979), and David Brody, *Labor in Crisis: The Steel Strike of 1919*, 2d ed. (Urbana: University of Illinois Press, 1987).

[14]Lisa Pine, *The Souls of the Skyscraper: Female Clerical Workers in Chicago, 1870–1930* (Philadelphia: Temple University Press, 1990).

SETBACKS IN THE ROARING TWENTIES, 1920–1932

A sharp recession in 1921 and 1922 and strong opposition from employers weakened the unions in the 1920s. In the aftermath of the recession economic conditions improved steadily, but most large companies were unwilling to deal with unions; some paying for close surveillance of the activities of unionists so that they could frustrate union efforts. Manufacturing remained unorganized, and industrialists supported efforts by unionized employers, especially in the building and printing trades, to abrogate their collective bargaining agreements. AFL membership fell from about 4 million in 1921 to 3 million in 1929, and the unions, in order to remain in existence, often resorted to wage-cutting and similar devices.[15] It was the first prolonged period of prosperity in which the unions did not expand. American business seemed to have won its battle to restrict unionism.[16]

In 1924 Gompers died and the presidency of the AFL passed to William Green, a Mine Workers official. Green held the position for 28 years, and at his death it went to George Meany. Green was not a strong leader like Gompers, however, and during his presidency the AFL was governed in practice by a small group of leaders of several of the larger national unions, who met periodically to play poker and to discuss AFL policy. It was this group that in 1940 chose George Meany to become secretary-treasurer of the AFL. It was not an imaginative or farseeing group, and under its leadership the AFL all but lost its first position in the American labor movement.

The twenties were the period in which mass production first came into its own in the American economy. The bulk of employees involved in mass production were not skilled workers and were not the targets of AFL organizers. Management spent considerable sums on industrial welfare work—housing, flower beds, parks and libraries, elementary schools, teachers, medical clinics and staff—to make workers' lives more pleasant. There were often also company unions; a subtle objective of this movement was undoubtedly to convey the sense that management would look out for workers without independent unions.[17] This sort of activity continued vigorously up until the stock market crash of 1929.

The great depression began late in 1929 and deepened without letup until 1933. By that year AFL membership had shrunk to about 2 million. The United Mine Workers, the AFL's largest affiliate, shrank from 500,000 to 150,000 in that period. For the first time since the depression of the 1890s there was cause to fear that the national unions would not survive.

---

[15]Vertrees S. Wyckoff, *Wage Policies of Labor Organizations in a Period of Industrial Depression* (New York: Arno, 1926).

[16]Robert N. Zieger, "Herbert Hoover, The Wage Earner and the New Economic System, 1919–1929," *Business History Review*, 51:2, Summer 1977, pp. 161–189.

[17]David Brody, "The Rise and Decline of Welfare Capitalism," in his *Workers in Industrial America: Essays on the Twentieth Century Struggle* (New York: Oxford, 1980).

In 1932, however, a Democratic presidential candidate, Franklin Roosevelt, was elected and in 1933 a slow economic recovery began.

EMERGENCE OF THE INDUSTRIAL UNIONS, 1932–1939

Formation of the CIO

The decade of the 1930s was the most turbulent in American labor history. In the economic turmoil that followed the great depression, the moral authority of American business was discredited and the seemingly stable industrial relations of the 1920s disappeared. Labor agitation increased as workers were recalled to factories in the aftermath of the depression. In 1934 the government began to sponsor collective bargaining as part of a program for national recovery. In 1935, when that program was declared unconstitutional by the Supreme Court, Congress passed the National Labor Relations Act to establish a mechanism by which workers could form unions.

Employers and investors generally opposed the passage of the National Labor Relations Act, and a recent study has demonstrated a key reason. Careful estimates show that the passage of the NLRA and the subsequent unionization of the work force of many large corporations reduced the wealth of shareholders in those firms by some 16 percent below what would have been their wealth had the law not been enacted.[18] The law was a key element in the process of a tremendous transfer of wealth from investors to employees in American industry.

By 1935 AFL membership had recovered to 3 million or so and total union membership (excluding company-dominated unions) to 4 million or so. But this was only the beginning.

Some labor leaders foresaw the possibility of enormous gains in the organization of workers in mass-production industries. John L. Lewis, president of the United Mine Workers, became an advocate of a major organizing campaign. The leaders of the AFL did not oppose an organizing campaign but did insist that workers be allocated by trade to the national union representing that occupation. Thus, carpenters working as maintenance employees in steel foundries were to be enrolled in the United Brotherhood of Carpenters, and so on. Lewis argued that this policy was so divisive and expensive that it would not work. Instead, Lewis proposed to organize workers on an industry basis (much as the Mine Workers themselves were organized). The AFL would not agree, and at one time Lewis and William Hutcheson, president of the Carpenters, came to blows over the issue on the floor of the AFL convention.

Lewis and several associates began to support organizing on an industrial basis late in 1935, acting as a committee on industrial organization (CIO).

---

[18]Craig A. Olson and Brian E. Becker, "The Effects of the NLRA on Stockholder Wealth in the 1930s," *Industrial and Labor Relations Review*, 44:1, October 1990, 116.

In 1936 the CIO began to organize the steel and motor vehicle industries, employing mine workers as organizers to supplement workers in the industries directly involved and using Mine Workers' funds. In December 1936, workers seized several General Motors plants in Flint, Michigan, beginning a 44-day sit-down strike. The tactic was an illegal seizure of private property (that of General Motors), but feelings were high, and the state government was now in hands friendly to the unions and did not intervene against the workers. Sit-ins spread to other industries and, unable to recapture their plants, corporations accepted the formation of industrial unions. (The sit-down was found illegal by the Supreme Court in 1939 after years of litigation and has largely been abandoned by organized labor since.)

Organizing Steel

The most dramatic events of the struggle were in the steel industry. In 1937 the highest officials of the United States Steel Corporation met with John L. Lewis to discuss recognition of the CIO's Steel Workers' Organizing Committee. Suddenly, and under no apparent duress, the corporation signed an agreement recognizing the union as the representative of its employees. There was no election and not even a sit-down strike. This peaceful recognition of the CIO by United States Steel must, in the words of one of the foremost historians of this period, "surely rank as one of the critical junctures of American economic history. Not only did it ensure the existence of unionism in basic steel, but it provided inestimable assistance to the CIO in its drive to organize other industries."[19]

Nonetheless, continuing the policy of most manufacturers,[20] other steel companies resisted the CIO, and on Memorial Day in 1937, police defending a Republic Steel plant in Chicago fired on union demonstrators, killing 4 and wounding 84. It was not until 1941 that the other steel companies recognized the union.

Similarly, an NLRB election in 1941 at Ford Motor Company was won by the CIO (though unsuccessfully contested by the AFL). The company did not accept defeat graciously. I. A. Capizzi, general counsel for Ford, stated, "The Ford Motor Company must now deal with a Communist-influenced and led organization. . . . The NLRB is an exact replica of the so-called courts by which Communist, Nazi, and Fascist partners purge the men who resist their tyrannies. It is a dictatorial concept imported from Europe."[21] There was little or no truth to these charges, but they indicate the bitterness and extreme feelings characteristic of the times.

[19]Walter Galenson, *The CIO Challenge to the AFL* (Cambridge, Mass.: Harvard University Press, 1960), p. 93.

[20]Edward Levinson, *I Break Strikes! The Technique of Pearl L. Bergoff* (New York: Arno, 1935). This book describes Bergoff's assembly of an organization of ruffians, which he leased to employers to defeat strikes.

[21]Galenson, *The CIO*, p. 183.

A New Federation

By 1941, the CIO had organized the steel, auto, rubber, and meat-packing industries on a virtually exclusive basis and was challenging the AFL in many other industries. In the process the CIO had broken completely with the AFL. In May 1938 the AFL expelled the CIO unions from membership, and they established a rival federation, the Congress of Industrial Organizations (also CIO), under the leadership of John L. Lewis and Sidney Hillman of the Amalgamated Clothing Workers. Lewis, meanwhile, had been successful in substantially increasing the membership of the United Mine Workers. Perhaps Lewis's success blinded him, because he now acted in a way that split the CIO and weakened it substantially. In 1940 Lewis opposed President Roosevelt's bid for election to a third term. When Roosevelt was reelected, Lewis resigned from the CIO and Philip Murray, a vice president of the Mine Workers, became CIO president. Lewis later engaged in disputes with Murray and withdrew the Mine Workers from the CIO in 1942. In 1946 he reaffiliated with the AFL but left it again 2 years later.[22] Lewis retired from the presidency of the Mine Workers in 1960 and died in 1969. Without its largest affiliate union and its strongest leader, the CIO after 1940 was a less dynamic organization than before.[23]

What were the causes of the success of labor's great organizing drives in the 1930s? The passage of the National Labor Relations Act is often credited with a substantial role,[24] but there were other factors as well. It must be remembered that in most major manufacturing industries CIO organizers were able to obtain NLRB-ordered elections only after sit-downs and other forms of strikes had opened the door to organization. Also, in some important instances, employers granted union recognition without a struggle and without NLRB compulsion, although perhaps in the belief that the law made resistance useless. Still, it cannot be imagined that the law alone would have brought about the rapid expansion of unionism that occurred. Instead, the law channeled labor agitation into a particular framework, helping to limit violence, and in the end, because the labor organizers exploited its provisions cleverly, helping to extend unionism in the 1930s to a greater degree than would probably otherwise have been possible.

EXPANSION AND RIVALRY, 1940–1955

What was happening to the AFL during the period of CIO growth? It was noticed so little by the public during much of this period that most observers of the labor-management relations scene were predicting its demise. Industrial unionism was to be the wave of the future and was ex-

---

[22]Saul Alinsky, *John L. Lewis* (New York: Putnam, 1949).

[23]Melvin Dubofsky, *John L. Lewis: A Biography* (New York: Quadrangle/New York Times Book Co., 1977).

[24]Neil Sheflin, Leo Troy, and C. Timothy Koeller, "Structural Stability in Models of American Trade Union Growth," *Quarterly Journal of Economics*, 96:1, February 1981, pp. 77–88.

TABLE 2-1 TRADE UNION MEMBERSHIP (in Thousands)

	AFL	CIO	Independent	Total
1934	3045	—	683	3,728
1938	3623	4038	604	8,265
1941	4569	5000	920	10,489
1943	6564	5285	1793	13,642

Source: U.S. Department of Labor, Bureau of Labor Statistics, *Handbook of Labor Statistics* (Washington, D.C.: U.S. Government Printing Office, December 1980), Bulletin No. 2070, p. 411.

pected to transplant the discredited craft union structure. The AFL's weak and failing attempts to challenge the CIO in several industries, especially autos, reinforced this view. But it was wrong.

In fact, the AFL emerged from World War II larger than the CIO. Using the threat of the CIO to persuade employers of the wisdom of dealing with the AFL and citing the NLRA to help persuade workers to join, the AFL unions expanded rapidly. Table 2-1 shows that in the 1940s the AFL added membership at a much more rapid rate than the CIO.

World War II brought a return of full employment to the economy and permitted the unions to consolidate their position. Yet throughout the war, rivalry continued as two national labor federations sought to represent trade unionism in the political and economic arenas. In the aftermath of the war, a wave of strikes brought substantial economic gains as the industrial conflict, which had been largely abandoned during the war, resumed. The Congress elected in 1946 was the first since 1930 with a Republican majority, and in 1947 it passed a law (the Taft-Hartley Act) amending the NLRA to place greater restrictions on unions' behavior. The AFL and the CIO both bitterly opposed the law but were unable to prevent its enactment. The period of labor's political ascendancy, which had accompanied President Roosevelt's New Deal, was at an end.

The great organizing period having ended, the two federations turned their attention inward. The CIO, particularly, had welcomed assistance from communist groups during its organizing campaigns. In consequence, many CIO unions were heavily influenced by radical groups.[25] With the onset of the cold war rivalry between the United States and the Soviet Union, the communist involvement became a liability. Congress in the Taft-Hartley Act required a noncommunist affidavit from labor union leaders, under penalty of denying to the union involved the protection of the law. The law alone did little to remove communists from union offices or influence—it simply drove them underground, that is, into secrecy and deception—but the noncommunist officials of the CIO seized it as an opportunity to wrest control of many unions from the communists.

[25]Benjamin Stolberg, *The Story of the CIO* (New York: Arno Press, 1938).

In some instances, noncommunist leadership within a national union was able to wrest control from the communists directly. For example, in the Transport Workers Union, Mike Quill used the communists' political support for the 1948 Presidential campaign of Henry A. Wallace (against Harry S. Truman, Democrat, and Thomas E. Dewey, Republican) to brand the communists as more interested in politics than in the needs of the workers. "So far as 42,000 transit workers are concerned, I say wages before Wallace," Quill argued in a bid for the presidency of the union. Winning office, Quill and his supporters stripped the union's high command of 19 supposed communists, and 16 national organizers were dismissed. Left-wing publicity people, secretaries, and clerks were fired. And the union's national convention adopted a constitution prohibiting communists and their supporters from holding office in the union. About the communists, Quill said, "We had a lot of help from the communists. They worked for us night and day. I'm sorry they didn't continue to help. I'm sorry they loused it up . . . but they showed allegiance to the Soviet Union and not to the American labor movement."[26]

In other national unions it was not possible to wrest control from within. In consequence, in 1949 and 1950 the CIO expelled 11 national unions with 900,000 members on grounds of communist control. After expulsion, the CIO chartered new national unions in the same industries and supported organizing campaigns in which the new CIO unions sought to capture the membership and collective bargaining rights held by the old unions. In most instances the CIO was successful in creating viable new, noncommunist unions to replace those expelled. But many of the communist-dominated organizations still exist today as remnants of their former selves.[27]

CONSOLIDATION, 1955–1972

In November 1952 both William Green, president of the AFL, and Philip Murray, president of the CIO, passed away. Since there had been considerable personal animosity between the two men, their deaths removed a barrier to better relations between the two labor federations. George Meany became president of the AFL, and Walter P. Reuther (the president of the UAW) became president of the CIO. Discussions about a merger between the two federations began in earnest. The passing of the men who had been participants in the early struggles between the two federations had removed a major impediment to merger. Another had been removed when the CIO destroyed the communist influence within its organizations.

[26]L. H. Whittemore, *The Man Who Ran the Subways: The Story of Mike Quill* (New York: Holt, 1968), p. 3.
[27]Bert Cochran, *Labor and Communism* (Princeton, N.J.: Princeton University Press, 1978). See also Thomas R. Brooks, "Rewriting History," *AFL-CIO Federationist*, 85:5, May 1978, pp. 11–15.

In 1955 the merger was completed, and the AFL-CIO was formed, a combination of the two federations with its own constitution. The AFL, the larger of the two federations, had absorbed its rival, but only by adopting features that it had rejected in expelling the CIO some 20 years earlier. The principle of exclusive jurisdiction was modified to accept the industrial unions and was now accompanied by a principle of respecting established bargaining units, whatever the conflicting claims of national unions to the jurisdiction might be. Furthermore, the new federation's constitution provided for considerable oversight of the affairs of national union affiliates. A strong provision against domination of unions by communists or other totalitarian groups was included, as well as provisions against corruption in the leadership of national union affiliates. The executive council of the Federation also bound itself to seek to remove overlapping or conflicting jurisdictions between affiliated national unions by encouraging mergers between former AFL and former CIO affiliates. In the years since 1955 there have been a number of such mergers, including unions in the metals, food, and paper industries.

The AFL-CIO has worked as a federation probably better than reasonably could have been expected. Conflict among the national unions in the Federation has been kept to tolerable levels. There has been no organizing surge of the type that occurred in the 1930s and 1940s, but millions of additional workers have been brought into the Federation.[28]

Perhaps what is most interesting in a human sense about the merger is that two groups of such different styles could be successfully combined. The CIO had been founded upon a core of idealistic organizers, largely leftist in political orientation, who sought to live among the workers. Pay scales for CIO officials tended to be considerably lower than those in the AFL. The AFL's propensity for holding conventions at such places as Miami Beach offended the CIO adherents strongly. The AFL, on the other hand, regarded most CIO representatives as impractical, radical individuals and reciprocated their disapproval. Despite these personal divisions, the merger has somehow worked, and the labor movement today is relatively united and without serious internal ideological or life-style cleavages. But the criticism from the left that the AFL is too conservative has continued even into the late 1980s.

DECLINE AND TRANSITION, 1972–1993

Beginning about 1972 (the date has not been exactly determined by researchers) the American labor movement began a profound transformation. Union organization among the blue-collar work force in manufacturing and construction declined substantially. But union organization in the public sector (i.e., among the employees of state, local, and federal govern-

[28]Joseph C. Goulden, *Meany* (New York: Atheneum, 1972), p. 173.

ments) continued a period of substantial growth that had begun in the 1960s.

The result was that the American labor movement began to shift away from its predominantly private-sector orientation. In the 1990s one in three union members is a government employee and public-sector unions continue to grow while those in the private sector generally are declining.

By comparison with union representation in other major industrial nations, the American unions were way behind, in both the private and public sectors. In 1985, for example (the latest year for which data are available), unions in America represented about 14 percent of employees in the private sector, while those in Germany represented 28 percent and those in Great Britain 38 percent. In the same year American unions represented some 36 percent of government employees, while those in Germany represented 58 percent and those in Great Britain 81 percent.[29]

George Meany headed the AFL-CIO for 24 years. In 1979 he resigned, and died soon after (on January 11, 1980). Lane Kirkland, the secretary-treasurer of the AFL-CIO, was selected to replace Meany as president, and Thomas R. Donahue, Meany's assistant, replaced Kirkland as secretary-treasurer. Kirkland was born in South Carolina and served in the merchant marines in World War II as a member of the International Organization of Masters, Mates, and Pilots, an AFL union. He studied foreign affairs at Georgetown University in Washington, D.C., and in the late 1940s became an assistant to George Meany. He was elected secretary-treasurer of the AFL-CIO in 1969.

In the years immediately following Kirkland's election to the AFL-CIO presidency, the American labor movement encountered very difficult times. Its membership eroded rapidly as workers lost jobs due to foreign and nonunion competition. By 1992 its proportion of the American work force had fallen to a post–World War II low, but there were signs of stabilization and renewed growth and influence; and in the mass-production industries—the ones hit hardest by competition from abroad—these signs seemed firmly rooted in a fundamental rethinking of shop floor relations and productivity that are described later in this book.

Several explanations are offered for the cycle of growth and decline, renewed growth and decline of the American labor movement. One view stresses the continual opposition of American employers to unions and their sometimes success and sometimes failure in containing unionism. In recent years, for example, court opinions and court decisions have been increasingly favorable to employers and less to unions. Another view sees long-term progress in the living standards of most workers causing a decline in the usefulness of unions. This view is often heard expressed when people say that many years ago unions were required to protect workers

[29]Leo Troy, "Is the U.S. Unique in the Decline of Private Sector Unionism?" *Journal of Labor Research*, 11:2, Spring 1990, p. 135.

from employers, but now companies provide better treatment for workers, and so unions are unnecessary. A third view stresses countervailing power: unions are said to have emerged as a reaction to excessive corporate power in the first half of this century and to have declined recently as government regulation protecting employees increasingly acts as a major counterweight to the corporations. "I would rather have a law than a union," Francis Perkins, secretary of labor for President Franklin Delano Roosevelt, said about the two methods of protecting workers from exploitation by business. After decades of increasing federal legislation on behalf of workers, unions appear to many observers to have given way to legal regulation as the nation's primary method of protecting workers. In later chapters the reader will encounter strands of evidence supporting one or another of these interpretations.

CHARACTERISTICS OF THE LABOR MOVEMENT IN AMERICA

The United States now has one of the largest organized labor movements in the world. American unionists are proudest of the freedom of their organizations from interference or control by the government. American unions are "free" trade unions, they point out, in that these organizations of workers were created by the workers themselves and are controlled by them. Workers have many interests, and unions in the United States reflect those interests, which include representing workers in their relations with employers, providing certain benefits and insurance for workers, assisting in educational activities, and serving as a mechanism to advance workers' desires through the political process.

The American labor movement is not homogeneous. Although it is possible to identify certain basic characteristics of American unions, especially as contrasted with those abroad, internally the American labor movement has many variations and divisions. These divisions include those between industrial, craft, and service unions, between skilled and unskilled workers, between large and small organizations, and between centralized and decentralized organizations. Periodically the movement is splintered into opposing factions, and although the 1980s have been, by comparison to other years, a period of relative unity in the labor movement, it is a fragile unity, possibly subject to sudden and substantial change.

The Two Faces of Unionism

Unions are both economic and social institutions. As economic institutions they attempt to develop a monopoly for their members, who can then sell their labor at a higher wage than would otherwise be possible. As economic institutions unions utilize strikes and the threat of strikes; they try to restrict work opportunities for persons not in the union; and they attempt to advance the interests of their members against those of others.

But unions are also social institutions that exist in large part to help their members have an effective voice in the world in which they live. They provide a mechanism for workers to express effectively their concerns about work, so that if things aren't right, the employee has some alternative to simply quitting his or her job.

So there are two faces of unionism: the economic, with its emphasis on monopoly and its pressure tactics, and the social, with its emphasis on providing a voice for workers and on mechanisms for participation.[30]

Principles of Structure

The basic structural principle of the American labor movement is that each major, identifiable group of workers is entitled to its own labor organization. This is in contrast to other principles of organization, such as the suggestion that all workers should be members of one big union. Instead, groups of American workers have ordinarily formed and governed their own independent organizations. These organizations are related to each other, if at all, through the device of a general federation.

In trade union doctrine, the right of each group of workers to its own union is accompanied by another principle: that there should be one and only one union for each group. There should not be "dual" unionism. Adherence to this principle is necessary to preserve the labor movement from what is felt would be excessive fragmentation, with corresponding rivalry and weakness. The group of jobs in which a union purports to have rights to represent workers is referred to as its "jurisdiction" (or "trade jurisdiction"). The term "jurisdiction" is also used with the preface "geographic" to indicate the geographic area to which a particular union lays claim or to refer to the geographic coverage of a collective bargaining agreement. The principle of only one union for each group of workers is referred to in trade union parlance as "exclusive jurisdiction," meaning that only one union has a right to represent workers doing a particular group of jobs.

The principle of exclusive jurisdiction has not been simple to apply. In an economy as complex and changing as that of the United States, there are always conflicts among workers and among unions as to who should be represented by what organization. Initially (in the nineteenth and early twentieth centuries), the American Federation of Labor tried to establish unions on a craft (or occupational) basis and was substantially successful in doing so. Among these craft unions were such groups as shoemakers, cigar wrappers, printers, and bricklayers. However, some crafts were too small to support unions and were combined with a paramount craft into a form of enlarged craft union. For example, the United Brotherhood of Carpenters and Joiners of America, for many years the largest union in the

---

[30]Richard B. Freeman and James L. Medoff, *What Do Unions Do?* (New York: Basic Books, 1984).

American Federation of Labor and generally referred to as a craft union, in fact includes in its trade jurisdiction not only carpenters (who are the paramount craft in the union) but also piledrivers, dock builders, mill-wrights (i.e., machinery installers), sheetrock installers (i.e., installers of gypsum wallboard), and soft-floor (i.e., carpet and linoleum) layers.[31] And in some industries, trades could not be distinguished fully enough without undue confusion and rivalry, so that the AFL established so-called craft unions that were largely industrial unions. Among these modified craft organizations were the United Association of Journeymen and Apprentices of the Plumbing and Pipefitting Industry, whose very name betrays an industrial basis,[32] as does that of the United Mine Workers (in the coal industry). In later years, it became apparent that in some industries not even a modified craft union could survive against employer resistance, and, over the objections of the AFL, unions were established on a strictly industrial basis in such manufacturing industries as automobiles, steel, and aluminum.

Thus, the result of a historical process has been that unions in America reflect craft, modified craft, and industrial orientations in defining their jurisdiction. Nonetheless, the principle that there should be only a single organization for each group, however defined, remains alive and in fact has, in a much modified form, been incorporated in federal labor legislation, as we shall see below. The resolution of disputes between contending unions over what organization is entitled to represent which workers remains a function of the central federation, the AFL-CIO.

What explains the structural principles of American unions? "It is the primacy of collective bargaining," say two American researchers. "Other goals that have been hypothesized as primary to unions include revolution, job consciousness, business union, maximizing (or satisficing), power accumulation, monopoly, organizational and a 'front for capitalism.'"[33] But other goals fail to explain American union structure as well as a theory of union behavior offered by Jack Barbash. In his theory the bargaining goal prevails in clashes with other goals. Historical evidence shows collective bargaining to be the basic working principle of union structural government and administration, and the concept of revolution as a union goal is invalid because of its fundamental inconsistency with collective bargaining.[34]

---

[31]Robert A. Christie, *Empire in Wood* (Ithaca, N.Y.: New York State School of Industrial Labor Relations, Cornell, 1956).

[32]Martin Segal, *The Rise of the United Association: National Unionism in the Pipe Trades, 1884–1924* (Cambridge, Mass.: Harvard University Press, 1970).

[33]Rudy Oswald and Rick Kraehevski, "Union Structure." In James L. Stein and Barbara D. Dennis, eds., *Trade Unionism in the United States* (Madison, Wis.: University of Wisconsin Industrial Relations Research Institute, 1981), pp. 5–6.

[34]Jack Barbash, "The Union as a Bargaining Organization," Proceedings of the 28th Annual Meeting of the Industrial Relations Records Association, Madison, Wis., 1975, pp. 145–153 (esp. pp. 149–150).

Principles of Administration

The American trade union movement is a decentralized movement. National unions, which have the jurisdiction to represent certain groups of workers, are "sovereign" bodies, meaning that they alone make policy for the union. National unions may choose to be affiliated with a central federation or not, or to participate in concerted activities with other unions or not. The central federation of national unions, the AFL-CIO, is more a place for cooperation than a governing body.

The national unions differ considerably as to how they organize themselves. Some national unions have a policy of "local autonomy," which grants to local unions considerable freedom from intervention in their affairs by the national union unless there are irregularities, generally of a financial nature, in the administration of the local. Local autonomy ordinarily extends to the financing of the local, to its activities in the political process in the state or city in which it is located, and to relations with local employers. In the national unions that operate in the printing industry, in local cartage trucking and warehousing, and in construction, for example, autonomy is a jealously guarded right of the local unions.

Other national unions grant far less discretion to their local unions. Instead, the constitutions of the national unions rather rigidly limit the authority of the locals, so that the national unions themselves may be said to be far more centralized. This is especially true of the United Steelworkers of America.

Nonetheless, in all national unions, at any time, a struggle continues as to the relative authority of the national union versus its local affiliates. Ordinarily this struggle is muted, but sometimes it breaks into open internal dissension (as, for example, in the unions in the paper manufacturing industry in the 1960s and in the United Mine Workers in the 1970s).

A Moderate Trade Unionism

The trade union movement in the United States has as its primary professed objective the improvement of the welfare of working people. This commitment it shares with labor movements abroad, except in some of the totalitarian states. Yet the American labor movement and those in Western Europe, in particular, differ considerably as to what direction improvement should take and how it can best be achieved. American unions have generally sought to obtain better wages and working conditions for workers in as direct and immediate a way as possible. Concerns about broadly based political and social change have been, if not forsworn, at least subordinated to attempts to ameliorate conditions as quickly as possible for the workers directly represented by the union.[35]

This emphasis on achieving improved wages and conditions as soon as possible, without regard to broader social aims, has been termed "business unionism" and is said to represent the central type of American trade union activity.[36] Its emphasis is on self-help, generally through collective bargaining with employers. It is often contrasted to revolutionary unionism, in which unions are perceived primarily as agencies in the attempt to alter substantially the form of government and economic society. This distinction is sometimes overdrawn. American labor's emphasis on business unionism should not obscure its use of other methods to improve the condition of working people. For example, the unions are deeply involved in political activity in the United States (as we will see below). Furthermore, unions engage in educational and social activities, the objective of which is to uplift the worker. To cite only a few examples, unions publish magazines with articles of general interest, send out special informational pamphlets on public issues, provide training programs, and sometimes provide scholarships to school.

The support of American unions for business unionism is in contrast to the philosophy of most labor movements abroad. Basically, European trade unions have sought to advance the entire working class by transforming the total society. The European labor movement developed country by country out of three sources: the trade unions, the socialist or communist political parties, and workers' cooperative movements. The resultant European labor movements place a much greater emphasis on achieving substantial change in the social system through political ends than does American labor. Where it has seemed impossible to achieve such change, elements of the European labor movement have sought a total substitute society made up of workers' organizations, a concept so remote from American labor philosophy that it is hard for an American to grasp.[37]

It is interesting to speculate on the reasons why the American trade union movement developed so differently from the one in Europe, despite historical ties between them. Probable reasons involve differences in basic characteristics of economic society on the two sides of the Atlantic and dif-

[35]Many studies support these generalizations. For example, a survey of the membership of five local unions in Ohio in the early 1960s demonstrated that a majority of the workers wished their union to concentrate its efforts on improving wages, benefits, and working conditions, and were less concerned or less enthusiastic about political or social objectives. Robert W. Miller, Frederick A. Zeller, and Glenn W. Miller, *The Practice of Local Union Leadership: A Study in Five Local Unions* (Columbus, Ohio: Ohio State, 1965).

[36]Robert F. Hoxie, *Trade Unionism in the United States* (New York: Appleton, 1921). Hoxie identifies four types of unionism: business, uplift (i.e., educational), revolutionary, and predatory (i.e., corrupt). A fifth type, reform unionism, may also be said to exist.

[37]Everett M. Kassalow, *Trade Unions and Industrial Relations: An International Comparison* (New York: Random House, 1969).

ferent historical experiences in different nations. Among the characteristics of American economic society that distinguished it, at formative stages in the development of the labor movement, from that of the European countries are:

1 The absence of previously existing feudalism with its rigid set of class attitudes and practices
2 The extension of full citizenship and voting rights for the white, male, urban working class at a relatively early date
3 Free public education
4 The possibility for workers to raise their standard of living and to move into managerial and entrepreneurial positions[38]

These characteristics of American society contributed to the development of a labor movement that was relatively free of class-consciousness, politically active within the existing system of government, somewhat less concerned with achieving social goals, and more concerned with obtaining immediate advances in wages and working conditions.

Perhaps the most generally recognized formulation of labor's overall goals is from a statement attributed to Samuel Gompers. But did he ever say it? As explained by AFL-CIO President Lane Kirkland to students at Dartmouth College, the matter is as follows:

> Let me address a canard that has dogged American labor for many years. It has found its way into textbooks, learned papers and baser prose, and may be no stranger here. That is the legend that our founder, Samuel Gompers, when asked what labor wanted responded simply: "More." That has become a synonym for our alleged innocence of ideals, if not unbridled avarice in the accepted wisdom.
>
> A university group from the University of Maryland recently completed the task of copying and indexing all of Gompers' recorded papers and works. I asked them to find that quote and was informed that it did not exist. The only source from which it could have been derived was an item dated 1893, when Gompers declared:
>
> "What does labor want? . . . We want more schoolhouses and less jails; more books and less arsenals; more learning and less vice; more constant work and less crime; more leisure and less greed; more justice and less revenge. . . ."[39]

The dominant philosophy of the American labor movement has traditionally gone beyond business unionism to a general defense of American free enterprise. Even when our political leaders occasionally warmed to the Soviet leadership, the AFL-CIO has stayed firm in its opposition to totalitarianism. "Today," read a statement of the top leadership of the AFL-

---

[38]Ibid. See also Walter Galenson, "Why the American Labor Movement Is Not Socialist," *American Review*, 1:2, Winter 1961, pp. 1–19.
[39]Lane Kirkland, remarks at Dartmouth College, October 4, 1982, text printed in *AFL-CIO News*, Oct. 16, 1982, p. 2.

CIO just before the collapse of the Soviet Union, "more than seventy years after the Communist experiment was launched, workers by the millions are pronouncing it a failure in economic, social, cultural and political terms . . ."[40]

The AFL-CIO has done more than merely denounce communism. It played an important role in the collapse of totalitarianism in Eastern Europe. When the Solidarity labor union in Poland was outlawed in the early 1980s by the Soviet-supported government, the AFL-CIO provided financial and organizational support to the union. The AFL-CIO's leadership worked closely with the American government, despite deep differences in domestic political philosophy with the Reagan Administration, to support Solidarity and destabilize the communist government. In the late 1980s the partnership between the AFL-CIO and the American government reached a successful conclusion when the communist government in Poland gave way to a reformist government run by former leaders of Solidarity.[41]

In its defense of American free enterprise, the American labor movement for many years distinguished itself from most trade union movements abroad, which were avowedly socialist or communist in ideology, and opened itself to considerable criticism from the left in the United States.[42] But the enthusiasm with which the American trade unions have supported American capitalism has been lessening in recent years.

In 1969 in a speech to the ministers of labor of the governments that make up the Organization of American States (an organization of most of the nations of the Western Hemisphere), George Meany endorsed American capitalism, saying in part:

> We accept without question the right of management to manage, with reasonable consideration, of course, for the rights of workers to a fair share of the wealth produced.
>   We accept without question the right of management to adequate compensation for its efforts.
>   We accept without question the right of the investor for a return on his investment in an enterprise.

But by 1980, the AFL-CIO was more cautious. In its proposals to the Democratic and Republican parties for their platforms in a presidential election year, the Federation chose not to endorse free enterprise, but to stress the democratic element of American society:

> The AFL-CIO believes the American dream has currency; workers have the right to continue to seek a better life. In a democratic society, it is wrong for one

---

[40]American Federation of Labor and Congress of Industrial Organizations, "Statements Adopted by the Executive Council," Chicago, Aug. 8–9, 1989.
    [41]Carl Bernstein, "The Holy Alliance," *Time*, February 24, 1992, 34.
    [42]Lawrence Lader, *Power on the Left: American Radical Movements Since 1946* (New York: Norton, 1979).

group to impose lower expectations on another group, to demand a degree of sacrifice not demanded of all, to permit exploitation of some for the profit of others. . . .

Resolving the inevitable conflicts between employer zeal for profits and the determination of workers for fair compensation is never easy in a democratic society. The quick solution, of course, is government compulsion, but democracy is not designed to be convenient; it is supposed to give the participants the opportunity to live their own lives.

Smarting under legislative defeats at the hands of the business community and frustrated by business opposition to union organization attempts,[43] the leaders of organized labor in the United States today have begun to shift slowly away from their previously largely unqualified support of American capitalism.

POLITICAL ACTIVITY OF AMERICAN LABOR

Only in a relative sense, that is, in comparison to some labor movements abroad, may American unions be said to have neglected political activity. Indeed, within the United States unions are credited with being one of the most active, and perhaps one of the most effective, political interest groups.

The AFL-CIO and the national unions are involved in politics and try to get local union leadership and members involved as well. Each year the AFL-CIO publishes a leadership manual, which provides information for union members and officials about the political status of current issues of concern to the labor movement, and suggests means of influencing the political process. But there are, as we will see, limits to labor's political success.

Labor's Political Goals

What do the unions seek to achieve through political activity? In general, unions may be said to have both positive and negative goals. Positive goals involve the enactment of legislation favorable to organized labor. Negative goals involve preventing the enactment of unfavorable legislation. In much of the history of the trade union movement, negative, or defensive, political activity has been the more important activity for the unions. Particularly in the case of the American Federation of Labor, unions have not ordinarily sought legislation that would affect the collective bargaining process. Instead, the unions have sought to keep the government outside the process. The major example of this political activity by unions was the long campaign, which began in the 1890s and ended with apparent success

[43]D. Quinn Mills, "Flawed Victory in Labor Law Reform," *Harvard Business Review*, 57:3, May–June 1979, pp. 92–102.

only in 1932, to relieve collective bargaining from the application of the antitrust statutes.

It should be noted that unions have a twin purpose in much of their defensive political activity: both to keep antiunion forces from using legislation to restrict union activity and to keep the government out of collective bargaining and out of the internal affairs of unions to as great a degree as possible. Labor often looks to the business community for support for the latter proposition. For example, reviewing the experience of the National War Labor Board of World War II, George Meany wrote, "There is a moral in this story of 'wage stabilization' by government that should appeal equally to American business and American labor—keep politicians out of the field of labor relations."[44]

In areas other than collective bargaining the unions have sought to make advances through political activity.[45] Unions have supported legislation on minimum wages, overtime provisions, equal employment opportunities, pension reform, national health insurance, and other such generally applicable social welfare measures, some of which have been enacted and others not. Unions have not been the only groups in support of such measures, but, because the unions are often more politically effective than other liberal groups, they have had an influence on American social welfare legislation out of proportion to their size and membership. "There is simply no avoiding the conclusion," one liberal observer has said, "that, considering its power as well as its views, labor has been the chief force for progressive domestic legislation in America."[46]

AFL-CIO Secretary-Treasurer Thomas R. Donahue has stressed that the labor movement "is literally in the business of assuring people fair and equitable treatment in the workplace."[47] But labor does not limit its methods to collective bargaining with employers. Instead, it turns to lobbying and other political activities as well.

Yet even here, in the opinion of some liberals, there is a paradox in the political objectives of organized labor. For reasons that are unclear to these liberals, the unions support certain progressive pieces of legislation, but not others. This behavior results in bitter denunciations of the unions as supporters of the status quo by the same liberal groups who rely upon union support to obtain passage of whatever liberal legislation is enacted. This pattern of political behavior was very characteristic of the AFL. In 1923 Mollie Ray Carroll studied the political attitudes of the AFL and found that

[44]George Meany, "The National War Labor Board," *American Federationist,* 53:4, April 1946, p. 4.
[45]John T. Dunlop, "Past and Future Tendencies in American Labor Organizations," *Daedalus,* 107:1, Winter 1978, pp. 79–96. See also Peter Gourevitch, Peter Lange, and Andrew Martin, "Industrial Relations and Politics," in Peter B. Doeringer, ed., *Industrial Relations in International Perspective* (New York: Macmillan, 1981), pp. 401–416.
[46]Andrew Levinson, *The Working Class Majority* (New York: Coward, McCann, 1974).
[47]Susan Dunlop, "Equity in Paychecks," *AFL-CIO News,* May 14, 1983, p. 3.

it supported proposals for workers' compensation legislation but steadfastly opposed campaigns for health and old-age insurance (i.e., Social Security legislation).[48] In the 1930s, partly because of the example set by the CIO, the AFL began to support a wider range of social legislation, a practice which the AFL-CIO continues today. Nevertheless, the Federation continues to favor reliance on collective bargaining to achieve many elements of security for workers, so that in the United States, unions have not supported, and Congress has not enacted, legislation dealing with layoffs, severance pay, discharges, vacations, holidays, and other such employment standards, which are generally subject to government regulation abroad.

There has been resistance to labor's political activities. In an important court case a person who was represented by a union in collective bargaining, and who had to pay dues as a result, but who was not a member of the union (for details on what membership entails see Chapter 19), objected to the union using his dues for political purposes. In 1988 the Supreme Court of the United States agreed and denied the union the right to spend dues from nonmembers on political activity. The union had argued that political activity was just as important to advancing the interests of workers, including the person who complained, as bargaining with employers—but the court was not persuaded. In 1992 President Bush indicated his intention to issue an executive order requiring companies doing business with the federal government to notify their employees of the rights of nonmembers of unions who are paying agency fees for union representation to refuse to allow their money to be spent for political purposes. The unions estimate that less than 10 percent of those whom they represent are agency-fee payers. Other estimates suggest that about 20 percent of agency fees are used by unions for political purposes. President Bush also directed the Department of Labor to require unions to report their expenditures to the government by category, including political expenditures. The unions have bitterly opposed this requirement, arguing that it will cost them substantial sums to prepare and file the reports, without any corresponding benefit to anyone.

Labor and American Political Parties

The American labor movement has tended since the 1930s to be considerably closer to the Democratic party in national, state, and local politics than to the Republican party. However, the labor movement is not a part of either political party. Unionists who serve in the councils of either party do so as individuals, not as representatives of trade unions. And in an important sense labor has built its own national political organization independently of the parties.

[48]Mollie Ray Carroll, *Labor and Politics: The Attitude of the American Federation of Labor toward Legislation and Politics* (New York: Arno, 1923).

The formal position of the AFL-CIO is, in the words of its president, Lane Kirkland, that "the only approach that makes sense [is] to support our friends, irrespective of party, on the basis of their records." Further, Kirkland said, "The American trade union movement . . . has no desire to be an integral part of the [political] parties as such, and we will not be influenced or guided in our role in society by party politics."[49]

The fundamental elements of this position, set forth in 1980, are the same as those enunciated by Samuel Gompers for the AFL three-quarters of a century earlier and expressed in the slogan "Reward our friends, and punish our enemies."[50] By this formulation, Gompers suggested that the labor movement would provide electoral support to public officials friendly to its interests and attempt to defeat others.

The political strategy of the AFL-CIO has three elements:

1 An independent and nonpartisan stance toward political parties
2 Active support to only a narrow set of legislative goals at any particular time
3 Utilization of the lobbying tactics of a special-interest group with the federal and state legislatures[51]

Perhaps the first of these elements is the most surprising to readers in light of the substantial degree of union support for the Democratic party that has been evidenced since the 1930s. In fact, the unions almost always endorse the Democratic candidate for President of the United States.

Also, at the state and local levels, unions continue to support Democratic candidates for office in far greater numbers than Republicans. There are exceptions, however, in which liberal Republicans receive union political support. If the labor movement were to become part of the Democratic party in a formal way, such alliances between labor and certain Republicans would be foreclosed. This is a result that the AFL-CIO does not want now.

Labor's Political Activity

Unions provide two major types of support to candidates for public office: financial contributions and direct campaigning. In 1936 the CIO made the first substantial financial commitment to a political party, a gift of $770,000 to the Democratic National Committee. By 1984 union contributions to candidates totaled many millions of dollars, and total election-oriented spending was considerably more. In defense of this practice, the unions cite even larger totals contributed by business people, bankers, and

[49]Lane Kirkland, quoted in *AFL-CIO News*, Dec. 13, 1980, p. 7.
[50]"Letter of Gompers to All Trade Unionists in America, Apr. 7, 1906," *The American Federationist*, vol. 13, 1906.
[51]John T. Dunlop and Derek Bok, *Labor and the American Community* (New York: Simon and Schuster, 1970), pp. 386–387.

corporations. Election law reform restricted union political contributions in 1976, but not expenditures for voter registration and similar purposes.

How does labor raise and spend money for political purposes? The unions, like employers, are prohibited by federal law from using members' dues (or corporate funds in the case of employers) for most political activities. Instead, the unions establish separate organizations, like the AFL-CIO's COPE, which solicit and collect contributions from individuals and are then free to use the money as they desire. National unions separately have similar organizations, such as the Machinists Non-Partisan Political League, the Railway Clerks' Political League, the Steelworkers' Voluntary Political Action Fund, and the Teamsters' DRIVE. These organizations as a whole supply more financial support for political activities than does COPE. Most of these funds are not used as contributions to candidates, however. Most are used to support such activities as registering voters and taking them to the polls.

What does labor receive for this political activity? Sometimes nothing. Labor often supports a candidate only to prevent him or her from being solely dependent on business support. In other instances, labor supports candidates who are friendly to organized labor's position on legislation, and who are susceptible to influence from the unions.[52] In still other instances, union leaders may expect special favors (sometimes illegal or unethical) from the politicians they have helped elect. However, organized labor is not alone in seeking to influence politicians in each of these three ways—business and professional societies do the same. Controlling the degree of influence exercised by interest groups through financial support for politicians is a persistent problem in all democracies, including our own.[53]

How Politically Effective Is Organized Labor?

Because of the unions' substantial political efforts, it is easy to overestimate their effectiveness. Unions do not control the American political process. They do not control a major political party. Despite union endorsements, the Democratic presidential candidates have failed to be elected in [six of the nine] national elections since the start of the 1950s, and in a seventh the AFL-CIO endorsed no candidate. At the congressional level, many senators and representatives are elected with labor support, but again, labor is often ineffective in influencing their actions. In 1974, for example, a Congress was elected with such large Democratic majorities that the AFL-CIO touted it as a "veto-proof" Congress and prepared to seek enactment of its own legislative program over the expected objections of the Republican President. The result was devastating to the unions. A whole

[52]Philip Taft, Labor Politics American Style: The California State Federation of Labor (Cambridge, Mass.: Harvard University Press, 1968).

[53]J. David Greenstone, Labor in American Politics (Chicago: University of Chicago Press, 1977).

series of union-backed measures were passed by Congress, vetoed by the President, and the vetoes sustained in the Congress.[54]

In recent years largely because of the control of the White House by Republicans, the AFL-CIO has failed repeatedly to get enacted laws that would support organized labor. It is easy to conclude from this that labor's political effectiveness is declining; and to a degree it is. But research shows that from 1978 through 1988 the proportion of candidates for the House of Representatives and the Senate endorsed by the AFL-CIO's Committee on Political Education (COPE) who were successfully elected has varied hardly at all. In 1978 COPE-endorsed candidates won 53.2 percent of the races; in 1980 (when Ronald Reagan was first elected President), 50.2 percent; in 1982, 55.5 percent; in 1984, 53.4 percent; in 1986, 56.7 percent; and in 1988 (when George Bush was elected President), 56.0 percent.[55]

What are the limitations on labor's political power? First, in election campaigns the unions are often unable to deliver the votes of union members for candidates whom the leadership endorses. Many public opinion polls over a long period have demonstrated that union members often ignore the suggestions of their leaders as to how to vote. However, the most careful research studies done on the matter of whether or not union members pay attention to union leaders' political endorsements shows that there is some positive effect.[56] Labor's own polls of its members as they left voting booths in the 1990 congressional elections showed that some 70 percent voted for union-recommended candidates.[57]

Second, in congressional lobbying (or in lobbying in the state legislatures) the disunity of labor organizations hinders their efforts. It is not uncommon for the AFL-CIO to be lobbying for a particular piece of legislation while its member unions are, in some cases, supporting alternative bills, or even opposing the measure altogether. In part, the frequent disunity of the labor movement reflects its complexity in terms of interests, with different unions having different industrial and occupational orientations. In part, also, the frequent disunity arises from conflicts between unions over jurisdiction, or internal politics and personality clashes. As a consequence of these factors, the labor movement (like the American business community) rarely operates cohesively and thereby exercises considerably less influence than might be imagined in light of its financial and organizational strength.

[54]See, for example, "Labor's Losing Battle on Capitol Hill," *Business Week*, July 14, 1975, p. 56.
[55]John Thomas Delaney and M. F. Masters, "Unions and Political Action," in George Strauss et. al., eds., *The State of the Unions* (Madison, Wis.: Industrial Relations Research Association, 1991), p. 326.
[56]John Thomas Delaney, Marick F. Masters, and Susan Schwochau, "Union Membership and Voting for COPE-Endorsed Candidates," *Industrial and Labor Relations Review*, 43:5, July 1990, pp. 621–635.
[57]*AFL-CIO News*, Nov. 12, 1990, p. 7.

Labor unions as a group are generally not cohesive in the political process, except perhaps in presidential elections. A study of the involvement of individual unions in the political process in 1978 to 1982 demonstrated the large extent of differences between unions in political activity. The study found that the demographic characteristics of its membership, its economic situation, and the union's own internal political processes affected its external political activity. Among the study's more interesting findings were that the higher the proportion of a union's members who were female, the greater its involvement in politics. Also, the more democratic the union, the greater its external political activity, suggesting that union leaders are not out of touch with their members' political preferences.[58]

In the 1980s and early 1990s American unions dealt at the national level with Presidents largely unsympathetic to them. Because the Democrats generally controlled the Congress during the Reagan and Bush presidencies, not a great deal of legislation unfavorable to the unions was passed. But conversely the unions were unable to get much legislation in their favor through Congress because many Democrats were insufficiently sympathetic to the unions' proposals and because of veto threats by Presidents Reagan and Bush.[59] In 1993 a President more favorably disposed to the unions took office. Will President Clinton assist the unions? Time will tell.

The most damage done to the unions in the political process came through the appointment by the Republican Presidents to federal regulatory agencies and to the federal courts of officials not favorably disposed to organized labor. After a sufficient number of such appointments had been made, regulatory and court decisions unfavorable to the unions became frequent.

As a result, the political power of organized labor has seemed to be at a low ebb. Yet a careful study of the union's record during the term of President Ronald Reagan indicates some substantial political successes.[60] This should remind us that the unions are an ongoing political influence in America with some reverses in what appear to be favorable settings (as in 1974–1975) and some successes in what appear to be unfavorable settings (as in 1981–1992).

The failure of the American people to elect a President friendly to organized labor in recent years, statements of dissatisfaction with the Democratic leadership, and increasing unhappiness among union leaders with the direction of American society suggest to some that the unions might be preparing to follow some of their European counterparts and form a labor

[58]John Thomas Delaney, Jack Fiorito, and Marick F. Masters, "The Effects of Union Organizational and Environmental Characteristics on Union Political Action," *American Journal of Political Science*, May 24, 1988, pp. 64ff.

[59]Kirk Victor, "Labor Pains," *The National Journal*, 23:23, June 8, 1991, pp. 1336–1339.

[60]Marick F. Masters and John Thomas Delaney, "Union Legislative Records during President Reagan's First Term," *Journal of Labor Research* 8:1, Winter 1987, pp. 14–17.

party separate from the Republicans or Democrats. By the year 2000, predicts one observer, "labor will take to politics, forming a pivotal third party in spite of all obstacles."[61]

Though the prediction seems very unlikely to occur, it reminds us that things could change drastically.

IS THE LABOR MOVEMENT CHANGING?

The American labor movement has been characterized as business unionism, to contrast it with the more political unionism of many labor movements abroad. The basic features of business unionism constitute an acceptance of the American free enterprise system and an emphasis in union activity on wages, hours, and procedures for handling disputes at the workplace. These characteristics of the American labor movement have had an important impact on American society, imparting to our political and social processes a degree of stability that would otherwise be absent.[62] It is, therefore, a question of major importance to American society what the direction of our labor movement will be.[63]

As America has changed, the private sector portion of the labor movement has lost ground. "The labor union can go in one of three directions," wrote an observer. "If it does nothing, it may disappear. . . . A second choice is to try to maintain itself by . . . political power . . . but that would require overwhelming voting power—and that the labor union has already lost. There is a third choice: that the union rethink its function."[64]

And so it is. Not for many years has the American labor movement taken so searching a look at itself. The AFL-CIO in the mid-1980s established the Committee on the Evolution of Work, and charged it with examining the status of workers and unions in America. Out of this effort there emerged in 1985 some startling recommendations.

First, the committee urged the unions to look beyond traditional issues of wages and conditions of work to new concerns of workers, especially those of women workers. Thus, when a unit of the American Federation of State, County and Municipal Employees negotiated its first contract with Harvard University—after winning in 1988 a 14-year effort to unionize clerical employees at the university—included with a wage increase were such items as joint labor-management problem-solving councils, more flexible work hours, expanded educational benefits, a joint union-manage-

[61]Michael Merrill, "Why There Will Be a U.S. Labor Party by the Year 2000," *Social Policy*, 20:4, pp. 43–55.
[62]Tim Bornstein, "Unions, Critics and Collective Bargaining," *Labor Law Journal*, 27:10, October 1976, pp. 614–622.
[63]John T. Dunlop, "Introduction," in John T. Dunlop and Walter Galenson, eds., *Labor in the Twentieth Century* (New York: Academic Press, 1978), pp. 1–10.
[64]Peter B. Drucker, *The New Realities* (New York: Harper and Row, 1989), pp. 193–194.

ment-run day-care center, and permission for clerical employees to use the university's athletic facilities.

Second, the committee urged unions to increase the opportunities for members to participate in their unions.[65]

Third, the committee recommended going beyond the tie between collective bargaining and union membership by establishing new categories for membership. For the first time, major American unions envisioned recruiting members for whom they would not do collective bargaining. Instead they would provide services and broader, political representation. The committee observed that 28 percent of all nonunion workers (about 27 million people) are former union members whom the unions might wish to regain as members even if they are unable to organize enough workers at the companies for which they work to obtain a collective bargaining relationship.

By 1990 the AFL-CIO was reporting some 300,000 associate members. For these members, for whom the unions do not bargain with employers, the AFL-CIO provides credit cards at low rates of interest, lower-cost buying programs for goods and services, a legal services program, and similar benefits.[66] In addition, the unions have been assisting employees in nonunion companies to bring lawsuits against their employers for alleged violations of the law. Nonunion firms have objected in the courts to unions' bringing suit on behalf of persons for whom they have no official representation rights, but various appeals courts have permitted the unions' actions. The issue has yet to reach the Supreme Court.

With the findings of the Committee on the Evolution of Work the AFL-CIO set its sight on the future, and the first dim outlines of a very different American labor movement became visible.

CHAPTER SUMMARY

Certain themes run throughout the history of American trade unionism. Both the cyclical expansion and depression of business and the long-term growth and development of the American economy have affected the size and strength of labor organizations. There has been a continuous and often dramatic struggle for control within the trade unions between the mainstream on one side, and Marxist and other radical groups on the other. At the same time, the moderate mainstream has grown steadily. Finally, government regulation of trade unionism has expanded despite the unions.

[65]AFL-CIO Committee on the Evolution of Work, *The Changing Situation of Workers and Their Unions* (Washington, D.C.: AFL-CIO, February 1985). See also Charles McDonald, "Progress Report on AFL-CIO Blueprint for the Future," in Bureau of National Affairs, *Daily Labor Report*, no. 6, Jan. 9, 1987, pp. E1–E2.

[66]Lane Kirkland, *AFL-CIO News*, Sept. 2, 1989, p. 10. See also, Paul Jarley and Jack Fiorito, "Associate Membership: Unionism or Consumerism?" *Industrial and Labor Relations Review*, 43:2, January 1990, pp. 209–224.

The first unions, in the early 1800s, were an outgrowth of the desire for workers to regulate and control the trades at which they made a living. As early as 1834, a National Trades Union had been formed, but depression in 1837 brought about its collapse. By the early 1870s, there were 30 national unions and a total union membership of 300,000, which dropped by 80 percent in the depression of the 1870s. The American Federation of Labor, which was committed to organization by trade and to business unionism, was established in 1886. Although it encountered strong opposition from manufacturers, it prospered and grew to nearly 2 million members by 1904. The period from 1905 to 1920 was characterized by violent struggles between employers intent on repressing unions and radicals who wanted to abolish capitalism. A recession in the early 1920s and employer opposition weakened the unions, and the great depression in the early 1930s devastated the labor movement.

The 1930s was the most turbulent decade in labor history. Labor agitation increased, and the government endorsed collective bargaining as part of the program for national recovery and industrial peace. Labor unions expanded rapidly, and there were great organizing drives in the steel, auto, rubber, and meat-packing industries. World War II and the return to full employment permitted the unions to make even greater organizing gains and to consolidate their position. In the late 1940s and early 1950s communist control and involvement in unions, particularly in the CIO, was largely ended, and in 1955 the AFL and the CIO formed a merged federation. The AFL-CIO has operated for the most part without serious internal ideological cleavages.

In the 1970s the labor movement entered a long transition, in which unions declined in manufacturing and construction and grew among government employees; this pattern has continued into the 1990s.

The U.S. labor movement, which is now one of the largest and best financed in the world, is very heterogeneous, involving many divisions and factions. There are, however, basic structural principles of American labor organization which are important in understanding labor relations. These include (1) the principle of exclusive jurisdiction, the doctrine that there should be one and only one union to represent each group of workers; (2) the principle of local autonomy, which gives local unions the right to run their own affairs with minimal control by the national union and thus contributes to strong local, or workplace, unions; and (3) the emphasis on business unionism, the concentration on obtaining better wages and working conditions for union members. The emphasis on business unionism is in contrast to the philosophy of labor movements abroad, which have sought the advancement of the working class through revolutionary transformation of the total social structure.

American unions have been active and effective political interest groups. They have tried to block antiunion forces from using legislation to restrict union activity, and they have tried to keep government out of collective bargaining and the internal affairs of unions. The political strategy of the AFL-CIO has been to remain independent in terms of party, although there has been fairly consistent support of Democratic party candidates. The unions have not been as politically effective as their financial and organizational strength warrants, largely because there is such a diversity of interests in the movement.

QUESTIONS FOR THOUGHT AND DISCUSSION

1 What impact did business cycles have on the labor movement before World War II? Why? Has the impact of recessions on the unions changed since World War II? Why or why not?

2 Why haven't socialists and communists been more influential in the American labor movement?

3 What were the advantages and disadvantages of industrial unionism? Of craft unionism?

4 Is the American trade unions' philosophy too conservative? Is it too liberal?

5 What are the traditional differences in philosophy between the AFL and the CIO? Which had a "better" platform and for whom?

6 Why has there been (and is still) such strong opposition to the trade union movement by American business management?

7 What are the goals, or objectives, of the labor movement? Were unions necessary to achieve better working conditions and fairer compensation for workers?

8 Were government support and protection necessary for the development of the American labor movement? Was government intervention appropriate?

9 What are the principal explanations for the cycle of growth and decline of the American labor movement?

10 What is the relationship of the trade union movement to the political parties and the political process? How much political influence would you say the trade unions have? What are the pros and cons of the political influence or involvement of the unions?

SELECTED READING

Draper, Alan, *A Rope of Sand: The AFL-CIO Committee on Political Education, 1855–1967* (New York: Greenwood Press, 1989).

Gompers, Samuel, *Seventy Years of Life and Labor,* 2 vols. (New York: E. P. Dutton, 1925).

Goulden, Joseph C., *Meany* (New York: Atheneum, 1972).

Larson, Simeon, and Bruce Nissen, eds., *Theories of the Labor Movement* (Detroit: Wayne State University Press, 1986).

Lens, Sidney, *The Labor Wars* (New York: Doubleday, 1974).

Lieberman, Sima, *Labor Movements and Labor Thought: Spain, France, Germany and the United States* (New York: Praeger, 1985).

Livesay, Harold C., *Samuel Gompers and Organized Labor in America* (Boston: Little, Brown, 1978).

Neufeld, Maurice, Daniel J. Leaband, and Dorothy Swanson, *American Working Class History: A Representative Bibliography* (New York: R. R. Bowker, 1983).

Schacht, John N., *The Making of Telephone Unionism, 1920–1947* (New Brunswick, N.J.: Rutgers University Press, 1985).

Stone, Irving, *Adversary in the House: The Life of Eugene V. Debs* (New York: Doubleday, 1947).

CHAPTER 3

MEMBERSHIP AND STRUCTURE IN THE AMERICAN LABOR MOVEMENT

MEMBERSHIP OF THE LABOR MOVEMENT

Statistics do not give a comprehensive picture of the labor movement, but they help to provide a framework in which an evaluation can be made. We are fortunate in the United States to have extensive and reasonably reliable data about labor unions, of which the federal government's Bureau of Labor Statistics is the principal source. These data are collected periodically by the government and permit us to assemble a quantitative portrait of unions in the United States. However, not all the relevant information is published regularly, and there is a lag time between data collection and the subsequent publication. Consequently, the most up-to-date information available may be several years old. The figures in these chapters represent the most current information available.

Membership of National Unions

There are some 190 major labor organizations headquartered in the United States. These organizations—most of which are unions and other employee associations—report a membership of almost 20 million, of whom almost 1.5 million are in Canada. Because of their Canadian membership, many American unions refer to themselves as "international" unions. Ordinarily, however, the terms "national" and "international" are used interchangeably in the United States. As a proportion of the total labor force in the United States (both employed and unemployed persons), union and employee association membership was 16.1 percent in 1991.

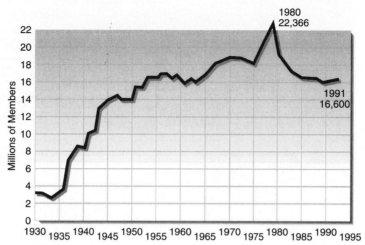

FIGURE 3-1   Membership of national unions, 1930–1991. (*Source:* From Bureau of Labor Statistics, *Directory of National Unions and Employee Associations, 1976,* Washington, D.C.: U.S. Government Printing Office, 1977. Data for 1977–1982: Bureau of National Affairs, *Directory of U.S. Labor Organizations, 1984–1985,* Washington, D.C.: p. 2. Data for 1983–1986: Bureau of Statistics, *Employment and Earnings*, 32–34:1, January 1985–1987, p. 219. Data for 1988–1989: from Courtney D. Gifford, *Directory of U.S. Labor Organizations,* Washington, D.C.: Bureau of National Affairs, 1990 1992.)

Figure 3-1 shows the membership of national unions in the United States from 1930 to 1991, the last year for which comprehensive data are available. The reader will note the steep growth of membership in the late 1930s and early 1940s, its moderate growth through the 1950s, its resumed growth in the 1960s, its rapid decline in the early 1980s, and its stability since.

Figure 3-2 shows membership as a proportion of the nonagricultural labor force through 1991. This chart tells a different story. Although total membership increased in the period from 1935 to 1980, the proportion of the labor force in unions has been declining irregularly since its last peak in the mid-1950s. Furthermore, in recent years union membership has declined in manufacturing, largely because of a general decline in manufacturing employment. However, union membership has grown among government employees until, by 1972, the proportion of public employees organized in unions was approximately the same as the percentage of all employees (private and public) who are union members. By 1982 the percentage of public employees in unions exceeded the percentage of private employees. In 1992 some 17 percent of private-sector employees were represented by unions and some 37 percent of those in the public sector were union-represented.

In recent years Canadian members of many U.S.-headquartered international unions have withdrawn to form separate unions for Canadians only.

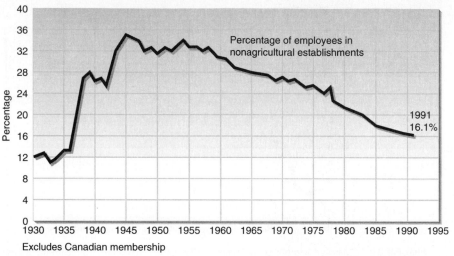

FIGURE 3-2   Union membership as a percentage of employees in nonagricultural establishments, 1930–1989. (*Source:* From Bureau of Labor Statistics, *Directory of National Unions and Employee Associations, 1976,* Washington, D.C.: U.S. Government Printing Office, 1977. Data for 1977–1982: Bureau of National Affairs, *Directory of U.S. Labor Organizations, 1984–1985,* Washington, D.C.: p. 2. Data for 1983–1986: Bureau of Statistics, *Employment and Earnings,* 32–34:1, January 1985–1987, p. 219. Data for 1988–1989: from Courtney D.Gifford, *Directory of U.S. Labor Organizations,* Washington, D.C.: Bureau of National Affairs, 1990–1992.)

In the major event in the 1970s, the Canadian members of the United Paperworkers left the international union. In the fall of 1984, the Canadian members of the United Automobile Workers withdrew to form their own organization. It appears that slowly the international character of American-based unions is disappearing.

There are numerous reasons for the exodus of Canadian members from what have been international unions. In part the Canadians feel that they are outnumbered in the internationals and that their concerns do not receive adequate attention. In part, Canadian nationalism plays a role—Canadians want their own organizations free of American domination or even influence. But the American-based international unions, which have done a careful calculation of the costs and revenues of their Canadian affiliates, maintain that more is spent by the internationals on Canadian members than is received in dues payments. As a result, many Americans argue that it is cost-effective to let the Canadians leave.

With such strong forces pulling the international unions apart it is surprising that so many unionists have resisted the divisive and nationalistic pressures and have maintained the ideal of labor unity across international boundaries. In part this has been accomplished by providing substantial autonomy in the international unions for the Canadian affiliates. As we will see in Chapter 11, the rise of the multinational corporation has given rise to pleas for labor to combine on an international scale to protect itself. In North America, for example, the free trade pact between Canada and the United States is steadily drawing the economies of the two countries into closer contact. Canada is the largest trading partner of the United States (larger even in volume than Japan), and the reverse is also true. However, the spectacle of the breakup of several international unions based in North America has given comfort to those who insist that labor is usually too xenophobic and shortsighted to be able to unite on an international—much less global—basis.

Employee Associations

In addition to the nation's 190 national labor unions, there are 30 major professional and state employee associations, which in 1989 had approximately 2.3 million members. These employee associations are not labor unions per se, and in the past they were generally reluctant to espouse union-like aims or to endorse union methods (such as strikes). In the 1960s, however, this changed, so that many of the employee associations are now very much like unions in their behavior and may fairly be considered "quasi-unions." The largest of these associations is the National Education Association (NEA), with a membership of 2 million. Interestingly, there also exists an AFL-CIO-affiliated union of teachers, the American Federation of Teachers (AFT), with a membership of 544,000. There have been merger discussions between the professional association, NEA, and the union, AFT, but without success to date. If the total membership of employee associations is added to that of labor unions, then in 1991 total membership was 16.7 million and constituted 16 percent of the total labor force in the United States.

Membership of the AFL-CIO

The AFL-CIO includes as affiliates most American national labor unions. In 1991, there were some 89 national unions affiliated with the AFL-CIO. AFL-CIO national unions affiliates (and a few directly affiliated locals where nationals had not yet absorbed them) included in 1991 a total of 13.9 million members (and about 83 percent of total union and association membership).

In recent years there has been a slow pace of mergers of national unions. Between 1978 and 1989, for example, the number of national unions affiliated with the AFL-CIO declined from 108 to 88, primarily through mergers. By and large mergers represented attempts of unions to consolidate resources as economic conditions deteriorated.

Women, Minority, and White-Collar Membership

Labor unions are often thought of as primarily organizations of blue-collar, male workers, and in fact many labor union members have these characteristics. Unions also include many female, minority, and white-collar members, however. After years of discrimination, and in some instances legal proceedings, these groups have formed an increasing proportion of union membership.[1] In 1989 women constituted 35 percent of union membership, a smaller proportion than they form of the work force as a whole. Minority workers constituted in 1989 some 22 percent of union membership, a larger proportion than they represented in the work force. A study has shown that blacks participate in local union activities at much the same rate and in the same form as whites.[2] Blue-collar workers constituted 47 percent of union membership in 1989—a far higher proportion than in the work force (30 percent).[3]

Women, minorities, and white-collar workers are not evenly distributed among national unions, but they reflect in their union affiliation their distribution among industries and geographic regions. The following unions have a substantial number of women members:

The Amalgamated Clothing and Textile Workers International Union
The International Ladies Garment Workers Union
The United Food and Commercial Workers
The International Brotherhood of Electrical Workers

Minority membership is especially large in the following unions:

The Laborers International Union
The United Steelworkers
The United Automobile Workers

White-collar membership is more diverse and includes substantial proportions of the memberships of unions of actors, musicians, retail clerks, office and professional employees, and government employees.

As the proportion of Hispanics in the work force has grown, the AFL-CIO has made special efforts to contact and interest them in unions. The AFL-CIO has a Hispanic advocacy arm called the Labor Council for Latin American Advancement. When the 1986 Immigration Act offered amnesty to persons who had been living in the country illegally, the Labor Council developed videotapes and other information in Spanish to inform Hispanics of their rights.

[1]Ray Marshall, *The Negro and Organized Labor* (New York: Wiley, 1965); and Marshall, *The Negro Worker* (New York: Random House, 1967).

[2]Michele M. Hoyman and Lamont Stallworth, "Participation in Local Unions: A Comparison of Black and White Members," *Industrial and Labor Relations Review*, 40:3, April 1987, pp. 323–335.

[3]Bureau of Labor Statistics data available in Bureau of National Affairs, *Daily Labor Report*, No. 27, Feb. 8, 1990, pp. B-8ff. See also Courtney D. Gifford, *Directory of U.S. Labor Organizations, 1990–1991* (Washington: Bureau of National Affairs, 1990).

Although some unions have long represented many women, others have been made up primarily of men. The leadership of the trade unions has also been largely male, as has been that of the business community.[4] Several years ago a group of women in trade unions formed an organization called the Coalition of Labor Union Women. The coalition supports the increased participation of women in unions and in political activity. Joyce Miller, vice president and social services director of the Amalgamated Clothing and Textile Workers Union, has been the president of the coalition. In 1980, Miller was elected to the executive council of the AFL-CIO, the first woman to serve on that body. By 1988, three women served on the 35-member executive council. In 1990 Lenore Miller was elected president of the Retail, Wholesale and Department Store Union, now the largest woman-led union in North America.

Large numbers of women are employed in American industry as clerical workers.[5] Unionization among these employees is relatively low. In recent years, however, several associations of clerical employees have emerged, and these groups are now developing relationships with various elements of the labor movement. Among these associations are Working Women, the National Association of Office Workers, and Nine to Five. Clerical employees of banking institutions and insurance companies play an especially important role in these organizations.[6] Several women's organizations have developed relationships with labor unions, and in the 1980s unions increased their efforts to organize large numbers of clerical workers, many of whom are women.[7]

Table 3-1 gives the occupational distribution of unionism for 1991. It will be seen that the clerical occupations in which women are so strongly represented are less unionized than the mechanical crafts and trades in which men predominate.

For a number of years there have been projections that union organizing among white-collar employees—most of whom are unorganized—would increase. This has not occurred, however. Instead, in the 1980s white-collar union election activity declined dramatically and the proportion of union victories in elections declined. Nonetheless, a substantial increase in union organizing among white-collar workers may be likely in the future, given the large numbers of potential members in white-collar jobs.

---

[4]James J. Kenneally, *Women and American Trade Unions* (Boston: Eden Press, 1978).

[5]Nancy S. Barrett, "Women in the Job Market; Occupations, Earnings and Career Opportunities," in Ralph E. Smith, ed., *The Subtle Revolution: Women at Work* (Washington, D.C.: The Urban Institute, 1979), pp. 31–62.

[6]Robert Jackall, *Workers in a Labyrinth: Jobs and Survival in a Bank Bureaucracy* (New York: Universe Books, 1978).

[7]See Linda McDonnell, "Women and Unions," a series of articles published by the *Minneapolis Star* in the summer of 1980. See also David Wagner, "Clerical Workers: How Organizable Are They?" *Labor Center Review*, 2:1, Spring–Summer 1979, pp. 20–50.

TABLE 3-1 EMPLOYED WAGE AND SALARY WORKERS BY OCCUPATION AND UNION AFFILIATION
(Numbers in thousands)

Occupation and industry / Occupation	1990					1991				
	Total employed	Members of unions[1]		Represented by unions[2]		Total employed	Members of unions[1]		Represented by unions[2]	
		Total	Percent of employed	Total	Percent of employed		Total	Percent of employed	Total	Percent of employed
Managerial and professional specialty	25,671	3,674	14.3	4,572	17.8	26,018	3,802	14.6	4,611	17.7
Executive, administrative, and managerial	11,805	709	6.0	963	8.2	11,977	762	6.4	971	8.1
Professional specialty	13,866	2,965	21.4	3,609	26.0	14,041	3,040	21.7	3,639	25.9
Technical, sales, and administrative support	33,292	3,462	10.4	4,122	12.4	32,649	3,395	10.4	4,035	12.4
Technicians and related support	3,744	431	11.5	535	14.3	3,696	432	11.7	527	14.2
Sales occupations	11,522	580	5.0	678	5.9	11,265	581	5.2	677	6.0
Administrative support, including clerical	18,026	2,451	13.6	2,909	16.1	17,688	2,382	13.5	2,832	16.0
Service occupations	14,400	1,989	13.8	2,241	15.6	14,649	2,037	13.9	2,261	15.4
Protective service	1,940	755	38.9	840	43.3	2,065	812	39.3	886	42.9
Service, except protective service	12,460	1,235	9.9	1,401	11.2	12,585	1,224	9.7	1,375	10.9
Precision production, craft and repair	11,616	3,011	25.9	3,227	27.8	11,189	2,899	25.9	3,105	27.8
Operators, fabricators, and laborers	17,114	4,514	26.4	4,795	28.0	16,492	4,345	26.3	4,619	28.0
Machine operators, assemblers, and inspectors	7,840	2,124	27.1	2,246	28.6	7,480	2,001	26.8	2,110	28.2
Transportation and material moving occupations	4,484	1,283	28.6	1,376	30.7	4,513	1,282	28.4	1,372	30.4
Handlers, equipment cleaners, helpers, and laborers	4,789	1,107	23.1	1,173	24.5	4,499	1,063	23.6	1,138	25.3
Farming, forestry, and fishing	1,812	89	4.9	100	5.5	1,790	90	5.0	103	5.7

[1]Data refer to members of a labor union or an employee association similar to a union.
[2]Data refer to members of a labor union or an employee association similar to a union as well as workers who report no union affiliation but whose jobs are covered by a union or an employee association contract.

Note: Data refer to the sole or principal job of full- and part-time workers. Excluded are self-employed workers whose businesses are incorporated although they technically qualify as wage and salary workers.

Source: Bureau of Labor Statistics, U.S. Department of Labor, *Employment of Earnings*, 39:1, Jan. 1992, p. 229.

Union Organization by Industry

The industrial distribution of union membership is also uneven. Table 3-2 shows union organization by broad industry classification.

Unions represent people who are not their members, and so the total number of persons in our society who are represented by unions is greater than the membership totals of the union. Employees who were covered by the provisions of a collective bargaining agreement, whether or not they were members of a union, made up 18.6 percent of all employees in 1989.

Researchers have shown that in the early 1970s the percentage of persons covered by a collective bargaining agreement who were union members was highest outside the South (94 percent) and lowest in the South (80 percent).[8] These data, though now over 20 years old, are the most recent available in published form.

Union membership in most of the manufacturing, transportation, and construction industries shown in Table 3-2 has been declining. For example, a recent study shows that union membership in construction declined from one-half in 1966 to less than one-third in 1983.[9]

Union Organization by Geographic Region

Union membership is also concentrated in certain geographic regions (see Figure 3-3). Generally, union membership as a proportion of the labor force is highest in the middle Atlantic, north central, and far western states. (The most recent data for all states are from 1982.) The most highly unionized states are New York (with 35.8 percent unionized, mainly in the manufacturing industry), Michigan (33.7 percent), Washington (32.9 percent, largely in lumber and milling), Hawaii (31.5 percent, mainly agricultural workers), Alaska (30.4 percent), and West Virginia (28.9 percent, largely in the bituminous coal industry).

Other states with a high proportion of union membership are Illinois, Oregon, Ohio, and Pennsylvania. The southeastern states are the least unionized. South Carolina has only 5.8 percent of its work force organized, North Carolina, 8.9 percent, and Mississippi, 9.3 percent. Some western and midwestern states also have little unionization, including South Dakota (10.3 percent), Texas (12.5 percent), and Oklahoma (12.9 percent). Over the past several years, unionization has been decreasing throughout the country.

[8]Richard B. Freeman and James L. Medoff, "New Estimates of Private Sector Unionism in the United States," *Industrial and Labor Relations Review*, 32:2, January 1979, pp. 143–174. See also A. J. Thieblot, Jr., *An Analysis of Data on Union Membership* (St. Louis: Washington University, Center for the Study of American Business, Working Paper 38, October 1978).

[9]Steven G. Allen, "Declining Unionization in Construction: The Facts and the Reasons," *Industrial and Labor Relations Review*, 41:3, April 1988, p. 343.

TABLE 3-2 EMPLOYED WAGE AND SALARY WORKERS BY INDUSTRY AND UNION AFFILIATION

Industry	1990					1991				
	Total employed	Members of unions[1]		Represented by unions[2]		Total employed	Members of unions[1]		Represented by unions[2]	
		Total	Percent of employed	Total	Percent of employed		Total	Percent of employed	Total	Percent of employed
Agricultural wage and salary workers	1,530	29	1.9	33	2.1	1,517	32	2.1	36	2.4
Private nonagricultural wage and salary workers	84,610	10,227	12.1	11,336	13.4	83,294	9,909	11.9	10,907	13.1
Mining	675	121	18.0	136	20.2	676	101	15.0	114	16.9
Construction	5,122	1,073	21.0	1,137	22.2	4,624	977	21.1	1,034	22.4
Manufacturing	20,339	4,197	20.6	4,514	22.2	19,590	3,976	20.3	4,269	21.8
Durable goods	12,089	2,667	22.1	2,864	23.7	11,424	2,503	21.9	2,683	23.5
Nondurable goods	8,249	1,531	18.6	1,650	20.0	8,166	1,472	18.0	1,586	19.4
Transportation and public utilities	6,124	1,934	31.6	2,091	34.1	6,082	1,895	31.2	2,036	33.5
Transportation	3,517	1,031	29.3	1,093	31.1	3,439	1,014	29.5	1,074	31.2
Communications and public utilities	2,608	903	34.6	998	38.3	2,643	881	33.3	962	36.4
Wholesale and retail trade	21,274	1,338	6.3	1,493	7.0	21,015	1,406	6.7	1,552	7.4
Wholesale trade	3,993	261	6.5	293	7.3	4,016	282	7.0	309	7.7
Retail trade	17,281	1,077	6.2	1,200	6.9	16,999	1,124	6.6	1,243	7.3
Finance, insurance, and real estate	6,835	173	2.5	233	3.4	6,694	161	2.4	221	3.3
Services	24,241	1,391	5.7	1,731	7.1	24,613	1,392	5.7	1,681	6.8
Government workers	17,765	6,484	36.5	7,689	43.3	17,975	6,627	36.9	7,791	43.3

[1]Data refer to members of a labor union or an employee association similar to a union.

[2]Data refer to members of a labor union or an employee association similar to a union as well as workers who report no union affiliation but whose jobs are covered by a union or an employee association contract.

Note: Data refer to the sole or principal job of full- and part-time workers. Excluded are self-employed workers whose businesses are incorporated although they technically qualify as wage and salary workers.

Source: Bureau of Labor Statistics, *Employment of Earnings,* Jan. 1992, p. 229 (Vol 39, No.1).

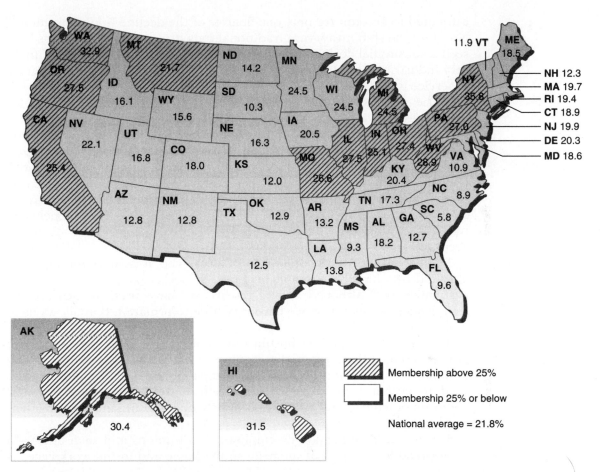

FIGURE 3-3   Union membership as a percent of states' total labor force, 1982. (*Source: U.S. Union Sourcebook, 1985,* West Orange, N.J.: Industrial Relations Information Services.)

Where Have All the Members Gone?

What have been the sources of the decline in membership in American unions? It should be recognized that the decline has not been in the number of people represented, which has continued to grow slowly, but in the proportion of all employees who are union members. Union membership has grown in relative size much more slowly than the overall work force has, so that the importance of unions has declined greatly. There is quite a controversy over the causes of this decline. Among those listed are:

1 The shift in the economy away from manufacturing, transportation, and construction—industries that have been heavily unionized—to services, which have not. This factor, while undoubtedly important, has been estimated to account for only one-quarter of the decline in unionization.[10] Nor does the shift away from traditional industry explain why unions have seen a substantial decline in their representation in what remains of those very industries. The shift doesn't explain the inability of unions to organize in service industries either.

2 The provision by government of many services and protection for employees that in the past were available primarily from unions. Since government now provides protection, the argument goes, why do employees need unions? A recent study indicated that government's increased protection of workers may have had a significant negative impact on the numbers of people represented by unions.[11] Because unions have by and large supported increased protection, they may be said to have contributed to their own decline.[12] This conclusion remains controversial, however, and research is continuing as to its accuracy.

3 The ineptitude of the unions themselves, who, it is alleged, in industry after industry have been unable to appeal to workers or to act in their own best interests.[13] Although several researchers have tried to measure the significance of this factor, we have very little information that allows us to evaluate it.[14]

4 Increased employer hostility to unions, possibly because with greater competition, especially from foreign firms, the cost of being unionized is now more difficult for companies to bear. Employers who used to accept a union organization effort, or at worst were neutral about its outcome, now openly and overtly opposed unionization by their employees.[15]

5 A loss of identification by employees with unions and each other—"a widespread localization of interest—in the home and in the workplace, as

[10]Richard B. Freeman, "Contraction and Expansion: The Divergence of Private and Public Sector Unionism in the United States," *Journal of Economic Perspectives*, 2:2, 1988, pp. 63–88. See also Daniel J. B. Mitchell, "Will Collective Bargaining Outcomes in the 1990's Look Like Those of the 1980's?" *Labor Law Journal*, August 1989, p. 491.

[11]William J. Moore, Robert J. Newman, and Loren C. Scott, "Welfare Expenditures and the Decline of Unions," *Review of Economics and Statistics*, 71:3, August 1989, pp. 538–542.

[12]George R. Neumann and Ellen R. Rissman, "Where Have All the Union Members Gone?" *Journal of Labor Economics*, 2:2, 1984, pp. 174, 192. See also "Unions in Decline: Causes and Consequences," *American Economic Review*, 76:2, May 1986, pp. 92–108; and Lee P. Stepina and Jack Fiorito, "Toward a Comprehensive Theory of Union Growth and Decline," *Industrial Relations*, 25:3, Fall 1986, pp. 248ff.

[13]Herbert R. Northrup, "From Union Hegemony to Union Disintegration: Collective Bargaining in Cement and Related Industries," *Journal of Labor Research*, 10:4, Fall 1989, pp. 337–376.

[14]Daniel C. Gallagher and George Strauss, "Union Attitudes and Participation," in George Strauss et. al., *The State of the Unions* (Madison, Wis.: Industrial Relations Research Association, 1991), pp. 166–167.

[15]Henry S. Farber, "The Decline of Unionization in the United States," *Journal of Labor Economics*, 8:1, 1990, p. S75.

against solidarity with fellow workers."[16] This view is bolstered by evidence that the decline of unions is occurring all over the industrialized world—in Europe, Japan, and Canada, as well as in the United States. But the decline has been more prolonged and dramatic in the United States than elsewhere (for a comparison to the Canadian experience, see Figure 3.4).

6 A greater degree of satisfaction by nonunion workers with their jobs and a decline in the confidence of employees that unions can improve their working lives. Also, "there seems to have been a decreased desire for unionization by nonunion workers who are . . . more satisfied with their jobs and have less faith that a union would benefit them." In support of this proposition, Henry Farber notes that two extensive surveys of American workers showed a dramatic increase in nonunion workers' satisfaction with their jobs between 1977 and 1984.[17]

The controversy about the cause of the decline of union membership in the United States is fed by continuing research. Richard Freeman and David Blanchflower have argued that American unions have been espe-

[16]Henry Phelps Brown, "The Counter-Revolution of Our Time," *Industrial Relations*, 29:1, Winter 1990, pp. 1–14.
[17]Henry S. Farber, "Trends in Worker Demand for Union Representation," MIT Department of Economics Working Paper No. 512, 1988.

FIGURE 3-4 Union density in North America, 1921–1989. (*Source:* United States, 1921–1984, Leo Troy and Neil Sheflin, *U.S. Union Sourcebook,* West Orange, N.J.: Industrial Relations Data Service, 1985, pp. 3–18. United States, 1985–1989: *Current Population Survey Membership Series,* U.S. Bureau of the Census, various years, U.S. Department of Labor, 1990; Canada, 1921–1988: *Labor Canada Series,* 1921–1989, Ottawa, Canada: Department of Labour, Labour Canada Series, 1990.)

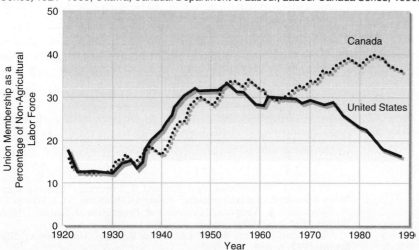

cially effective in generating wage rates for their members that are much higher than those received by nonunion workers in the same industries and occupations. Evidence from other countries is that unions have obtained much smaller pay advantage for their members. For example, American unions on average generated a 22 percent advantage for union employees over nonunion employees; in Britain the advantage was 10 percent, and in Germany 8 percent.[18]

But it is this very success of the American unions which is the cause of their downfall, according to the two researchers. For the unions success has given unionized companies a very strong financial incentive to be rid of the unions. As companies have become more expert at avoiding unions, and as legal tolerance for their actions has risen (due in large part to the appointment of conservative justices to the nation's courts by recent Republican administrations), unions have lost ground in membership.

Jonathan Leonard has generalized this argument by saying that in conditions of intense competition between union and nonunion firms (the setting in many industries in North America, but unusual abroad), successful unions in firms that try to maximize profits have the unintended consequence of destroying union members' jobs.[19]

This is an appealing explanation, but it is only part of the story. In fact, the causality involved is complex. Leo Troy has summarized the matter as follows: "The explanation [for union decline] lies in . . . structural changes in the American economy; . . . increased competition for the heavily unionized American manufacturing industries; and employee opposition to union organization."[20]

Is the causality primarily economic? If one looks abroad, there is the suggestion that it is not. Most other nations have very different legal and political settings than America has. As a result, the fact that there is a lower union-nonunion wage differential is less significant than it is in America. What is important about the different setting in Germany, for example, is not that the lower compensation differential is a lesser incentive for employers to be nonunion, but that the legal and institutional context does not permit many firms to be nonunion. That's why the differential is low—not the other way around. In other words, the causality is not economic but political and social.

Most American unionists hold to this view rather than that higher pay differentials cause employers to go nonunion and that employees fear that unionizing will cost them their jobs. For example, Charles McDonald, who

[18]David G. Blanchflower and Richard B. Freeman, "Unionism in the United States and Other Advanced OECD Countries," *Industrial Relations*, 31:1, Winter 1992, p. 64.

[19]Jonathan S. Leonard, "Unions and Employment Growth," *Industrial Relations*, 31:1, Winter 1992, pp. 80–94.

[20]Leo Troy, "Market Forces and Union Decline," *University of Chicago Law Review*, 50:2, Spring 1992, p. 688.

heads membership organizing for the AFL-CIO, suggests that should a few elements of American labor law be modified in the union's favor, then membership growth would be very substantial.[21]

In effect, McDonald is suggesting that the law ought to deprive most employers of the opportunity to be nonunion, as it does in Germany and many other nations abroad. (See Chapter 9 for McDonald's suggestions in detail.) If this occurred, then there would be two results: union representation would grow rapidly, and the union-nonunion differential would cease to be important economically and would probably decrease.

THE NATIONAL UNION

In the United States we often think that labor unions exist primarily to perform the functions of collective bargaining and contract administration for their members. And, of course, this is a very important part of their role. But each union also has an ongoing life as an institution or organization, with its own internal political affairs, procedures, financial structure, and concerns for its survival as an organization. In this section we will briefly examine unions as organizations. We begin with the national union, which is the sovereign body in the American labor movement. We then turn to the local union, closest of the organizational entities to the union member. Last, we examine the federation of national unions, the AFL-CIO.

Briefly, the vertical structure of unions in the United States may be described as follows:

Type	Example
Federation	AFL-CIO
National unions	United Auto Workers
Intermediate bodies	District Council
Local unions	Local 21
Individual member	Jane Doe

Organizational Structure of the National Union

A national union is composed of local unions, which it charters, and is ultimately governed by a national convention of the local unions. The functions of the national union, the duties of its officers, and the relationship between the national union and its local affiliates are set forth in a constitution of the national union. National conventions are held every 1 or 2 years by most unions, but a period of up to 5 years between conventions is common.

[21]Charles McDonald, "U.S. Union Membership in Future Decades," *Industrial Relations*, 31:1, Winter 1992, pp. 13–30.

At a convention, the constitution may be amended, resolutions proposed for adoption, officers elected, budgets reviewed, dues changed, and other similar business conducted. The conventions of some large unions are very elaborate and costly affairs, with invited speakers and entertainers, reports of resolution committees, speeches by officers, electioneering on behalf of candidates for office, and similar activities. In some national unions the locals pay the expenses of delegates to the conventions. In others, the national union defrays all or part of the cost in order to permit small locals to be represented.

When the convention is not in session, a national union is governed by its general president and general executive board, usually made up of the president, secretary-treasurer, and vice presidents of the national union.[22] The actions of the president and the board are subject to the provisions of the national union's constitution.

Figure 3-5 describes the governance of an idealized national union (the specific structure varies, of course). A department of benefits administers the various union funds, whether strike funds, pension or welfare funds, or death benefits, and tracks member eligibility for them (increasingly on computers); an organizing department prepares information for organizing activities; a legal department assists the union in litigation and inter-

---

[22]In at least one major union, the International Brotherhood of Electrical Workers (IBEW), the general executive board is made up of elected persons (other than the union's vice presidents) who represent the various industries in which the union has members.

FIGURE 3-5   Organizational structure of a national union.

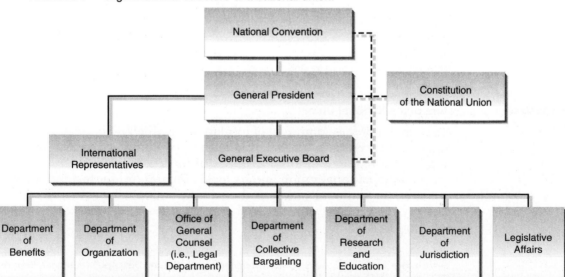

pretations of the law; a file of collective bargaining agreements and provisions is maintained; research and education programs are set up; the jurisdiction of the trade is overseen and defended (especially by the craft and modified craft unions); and lobbyists are employed to represent the union's views to government officials and legislators.

In addition to the various staff functions, attached to the office of the general president is a group of full-time salaried representatives of the national union. Generally, these representatives are hired, or appointed, by the general president (although in some unions they are elected by the convention). The function of these representatives is, in large part, to serve as intermediaries between the national and local unions. A "rep" assists the locals in collective bargaining negotiations and in handling grievances and renders assistance in the administration of the locals. Reps are also responsible for efforts to organize the unorganized workers in their area, and, in craft unions, for protecting the jurisdiction of the union. Furthermore, reps keep the national union informed about

TABLE 3-3 CHANGES IN EMPLOYMENT OF PROFESSIONAL UNION STAFF IN SELECTED NATIONAL UNIONS, 1961–1985

Union/year	Staff employed[1]	Union members[2]	Ratio of staff/10,000 members
Teamsters			
1961	41	1.489.000	.28/10,000
1973	104	1,931,000	.54/10,000
1985	223	1,611,000	1.38/10,000
Steelworkers (USWA)			
1961	877	851,000	10.31/10,000
1973	1141	1,248,000	9.14/10,000
1985	845	598,000	14.13/10,000
Railway and Airline Clerks (BRAC)			
1961	33	255,000	1.29/10,000
1973	80	185,000	4.32/10,000
1985	112	104,000	10.77/10,000
Rubber Workers (URW)			
1961	112	158,000	7.09/10,000
1973	149	189,000	7.88/10,000
1985	120	115,000	10.43/10,000
Iron Workers			
1961	61	141,000	4.33/10,000
1973	83	176,000	4.72/10,000
1985	87	169,000	5.15/10,000

[1]Staff employment figures are for professional, technical, and managerial employees of the national union, as reported in LM-2 reports.
[2]1961 and 1973 union membership figures include both U.S. and Canadian members as reported in Leo Troy and Neil Sheflin, *Union Sourcebook* (West Orange, N.J.: Industrial Relations Data and Information Services, 1985). 1985 figures provided on request by Troy and Sheflin.

developments in the locals.[23] The number of professional union staff and their proportion to the number of members has been rising rapidly, as Table 3–3 indicates.

National unions differ in the degree to which they are centralized, the size and function of local and regional bodies, and the manner in which they bargain with employers. Several researchers have proposed a model in which the external situation that a union faces—including the size and practices of the firms with which it bargains, the legal environment, the industries in which it operates, and its history and political environment—interacts with the union's goals to determine its strategies for collective bargaining, legislative action, and potential confrontations with employers, and thereby the characteristics of its structure. For example, a union facing large, aggressive employers and a hostile political environment is likely to pursue its goals through collective bargaining in a centralized fashion with a strong vertical structure and closely coordinated bargaining among its locals. A union facing employers who are many and fragmented and a favorable legal climate is likely to be more decentralized and to rely more on a horizontal structure than a vertical one.[24]

Financing

A national union is supported financially by a "tax" paid by each local on the basis of its membership size. The tax is generally referred to as the "per capita." Its amount is specified in the constitution of the national union and may be set in either dollar or percentage terms.

In some national unions (including the United Steelworkers, United Mine Workers, the Communication Workers, and the Airline Pilots Association) the national receives dues directly and remits a share to the locals. Ordinarily, the reverse occurs. The amount of money received by unions in the United States is large, by international standards, and the assets of American unions are substantial. For example, in 1976 (the most recent year for which data are available), U.S. unions reported $4 billion in assets, about evenly distributed among local unions and national unions. If the labor movement in the United States were to be conceived of as a corporation (Labor, Inc.), then in 1976 it would have ranked in assets as the thirty-third largest industrial corporation.

Union revenues are spent primarily on recurring operating expenses, especially salaries for officers and employees (43 percent in 1976). Strike benefit payments, pension benefit payments, and the like constituted 17

[23]See Morris A. Horowitz, *The Structure and Government of the Carpenters' Union* (New York: Wiley, 1962); Jack Stieber, *Governing the UAW* (New York: Wiley, 1962); and Lloyd Ulman, *The Government of the Steelworkers' Union* (New York: Wiley, 1962).

[24]Jack Fiorito et al., "Union Structural Choices," in George Strauss et al., eds., *The State of the Unions* (Madison, Wis.: Industrial Relations Research Association, 1991), pp. 103–138.

percent of expenditures in 1976.[25] It is unfortunate that these useful data have not been updated since the mid-1970's.

Selecting Leaders

The choosing of union leaders is a political process instead of a process of promotion through merit or selection by senior officers. National unions in the United States generally elect officers at their conventions. Since by federal law an election for national officers must be held at least once in a 5-year period, conventions must be held at least that frequently. A number of unions, however, elect national officers by a referendum of the membership. Elections ordinarily involve opposing candidates and are often between opposing slates of officers running as a group. There are, however, a significant number of instances in which officers are unopposed for reelection. Sometimes union general presidents serve for many years; in other instances they are defeated after only one or two terms.

The political process in national unions is not very much like that in the United States as a whole. Organized parties that contend for election to office exist only in the International Typographical Union.[26] National union leadership is rarely particularly tolerant of opposition, although both self-restraint and federal regulation limit the suppression of dissenting views. In most instances, the individuals who succeed in being elected general presidents of major unions are men 40 years of age or older who have become very skilled in the handling of people. They almost invariably have worked their way up through various local and national offices in the union and ordinarily began their careers as workers. This is in contrast to union leadership in many countries abroad, where lawyers or other professionals are officers of the unions.[27] There are exceptions, however, to this pattern of development of national union leaders. In some instances, especially in the building trades, general presidents have groomed their sons to follow them as general presidents, and the sons have been elected in turn. There are certain disadvantages to this process if the result is an inept and

---

[25]Leo Troy, "American Unions and Their Wealth," *Industrial Relations*, 14:2, May 1975, pp. 134–144. Also Leo Troy, "The Finances of American Unions, 1962–69," in National Bureau of Economic Research, *Explorations in Economic Research*, 2:2, 1975, pp. 217–251; and Neil Sheflin and Leo Troy, "Finances of American Unions in the Seventies," *Journal of Labor Research*, 4:2, Spring 1983, pp. 149–158.

[26]Seymour M. Lipset, Martin Trow, and James Coleman, *Union Democracy: The Internal Politics of the International Typographic Union* (Glencoe, Ill.: Free Press, 1956).

[27]A study in the United States of national union presidents, secretaries, and vice presidents showed that 17 percent had completed college, fewer than half had any college training, and more than 25 percent had not completed high school. Abraham Friedman, "Characteristics of National and International Union Leaders," unpublished manuscript, 1967, cited by John Dunlop and Derek Bok in *Labor and the American Community* (New York: Simon and Schuster, 1970), p. 181.

undemocratic leader. Generally, however, in recent decades at least, the quality of leadership so obtained has been high, and the unions involved have benefited from continuity of policy and from leaders carefully trained for the job.

Turnover among national union officers is low, and there have long been concerns that they may be too firmly entrenched in their positions to need to be responsive to the membership.[28] However, research indicates that the performance of union leaders in their positions affects the likelihood that they will retain their office.[29]

Updating the National Union

As times change, unions must also. But it is often a difficult and lengthy process for unions to change, just as it is for corporations or governments.

One of the most imaginative and far-reaching efforts to change a national union has been conducted in recent years by the International Union of Bricklayers and Allied Craftsmen. Speaking to a union audience the international president of the union described the change effort as

> a broad effort to remake the structure—not the character—of the Union, altering it from that of a building trades union consisting of an aggregation of local entities serving members and markets on a 19th century scale—which is to say a small city scale—loosely bound together . . . but more or less functioning independently; to that of a new Union framework, one suited to the emerging facts of the 21st century and, therefore, based on both a larger, or regionally-scaled unit and on a tighter, more cohesive, better integrated overall organization.[30]

This statement is remarkable both for its acknowledgment that the current structure of the union is fundamentally unchanged from its form in the nineteenth century, though many superficial alterations have been made, and for its articulation of what is required of the union in the twenty-first century. A great many of the AFL unions that emerged in the nineteenth century share a somewhat outdated structure based on many small, largely autonomous locals, but few national and international unions are making the significant efforts to modernize themselves, as reflected in the statement above.

[28]Shulamit Kahn, Kevin Lang, and Donna Kadev, "National Union Leader Performance and Turnover in Building Trades," *Industrial Relations*, 25:3, Fall 1986, pp. 276–291.

[29]See Seymour Martin Lipset, Martin Trow, and James Coleman, *Union Democracy* (New York: Doubleday, 1962); and J. David Edelstein and Malcolm Warner, *Comparative Union Democracy* (New York: Wiley, 1976).

[30]John T. Joyce, International Union of Bricklayers and Allied Crafts, February 1, 1992, communication to the author.

THE LOCAL UNION

Number and Size of Locals

We may summarize certain aspects of our review of the local union, since many characteristics of the nationals apply to the locals, though on a different scale. There are in the United States some 71,000 local unions, most of which are affiliated with national unions. Locals hold their charters at the pleasure of the national union, although some locals predate their national. Generally, locals guard their separate existence carefully, and union constitutional provisions limit the capacity of the national union to abolish or merge local unions.

Locals vary greatly in size, averaging about 200 members. But many are much larger. Some locals, with as many as 30,000 to 40,000 members, are larger than some national unions. In manufacturing and services, a local union ordinarily represents the workers in a single plant or facility. In other industries, however, a local ordinarily has a geographic jurisdiction and represents the employees of many employers and at many working places.

Administration of Locals

Locals are governed in much the same way as national unions. Membership meetings are the chief executive body, and the officers of the local union govern in accordance with bylaws adopted by the local. The officers of a local union ordinarily include a president, vice president, secretary, treasurer (sometimes these last two offices are described as recording secretary and financial secretary, respectively), and a sergeant at arms. Officers are chosen by election from the membership and are ordinarily not paid by the union. Stewards are also elected, or named by the officers, to represent the union in grievance handling and in the administration of collective bargaining agreements. Stewards are usually paid by the employer and are workers designated by the union and detailed on occasion from duty as workers to represent the union (see Figure 3-6).[31]

Women and minorities are gaining representation in local union leadership, although they remain significantly underrepresented in its top levels. A study of women's participation in local union leadership in Massachusetts showed that while women were represented in leadership positions in

---

[31]Eric Bastone, Ian Boraston, and Stephen Frenkel, *Shop Stewards in Action: The Organization of Workplace Conflict and Accommodation* (Forest Grove, Ore.: ISBS, 1977). See also Allan N. Nash, *The Union Steward: Duties, Rights, and Status* (Ithaca, N.Y.: New York State School of Industrial and Labor Relations, Cornell, 1977); and Tony DeAngelis, *Basic Steward Training*, rev. ed. (Minneapolis, Minn.: University of Minnesota Industrial Relations Center, 1983).

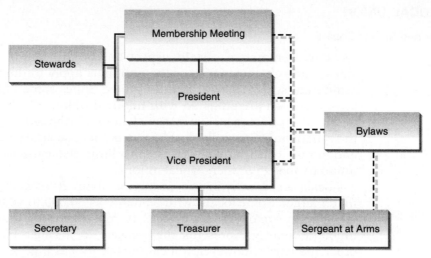

FIGURE 3-6   Organizational structure of a local union in manufacturing or services.

roughly their proportion in the locals' membership, they were rarely in the top elected positions.[32]

A local union ordinarily does not have the same staff structure that a national union has. Locals do not have research and education directors, general counsels, legislative aides, and so on, although most locals retain legal counsel from a law firm. A local union in the construction, retail trade, and transportation industries, for example, not only has the organizational structure shown in Figure 3-6, but has additional officials as well (see Figure 3-7).

The membership typically elects a business agent (or business representative) who is a full-time, salaried official of the local union (except in very small locals, where limited finances prevent engaging a salaried official). Larger locals will also elect (or allow the business agent to appoint) assistant business agents, who are also full-time, salaried officials of the local. Some of the largest construction locals hire as many as 35 assistant business agents.

The principal duty of the business agent is to enforce the local's collective bargaining agreements. He or she is expected to travel a great deal to visit the various workplaces where members of the local are employed (in fact, many years ago the business agent was called the "walking delegate" of the local).

Figure 3-7 also includes the position of "apprentice coordinator," which increasingly exists as a full-time salaried position of a skilled craft local union. Thus, the local has full- and part-time officers and salaried and non-

[32]Dale Melcher et al., "Women's Participation in Local Union Leadership: The Massachusetts Experience," *Industrial and Labor Relations Review*, 45: 2, January 1992, p. 267.

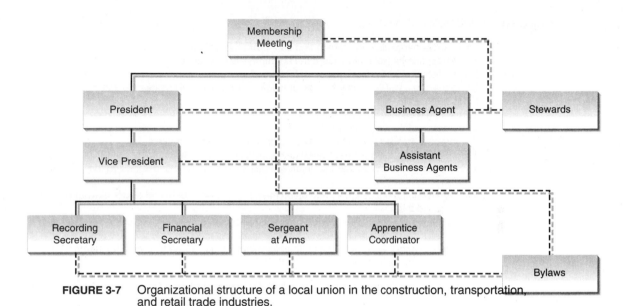

FIGURE 3-7   Organizational structure of a local union in the construction, transportation, and retail trade industries.

salaried officers. The whole structure is held together by a set of bylaws that define the duties of the various officers.[33]

Functions of Locals

The functions of a local union are remarkably varied. One list developed by the general secretary of a craft union included 13 items, and is given in Table 3-4. The key items are collective bargaining and contract administration. Collective bargaining as we shall see in later chapters is primarily conducted by the locals' officers and teams of negotiators, either elected by the membership or chosen by the locals' elected officers. Contract administration is first and foremost in the hands of union stewards who are also elected in some locals and appointed in others.

In addition to duties to its own membership, a local union has duties to its national union and to other locals of its national. An international officer of the United Steelworkers once described a "good" local union as one that

1 *Supports the political activities* of the national union
2 *Supports other steelworker locals* that are on strike
3 *Attends the convention* of the national union and participates in its activities[34]

---

[33]George Strauss, "Union Government in the United States: Research Past and Future," *Industrial Relations*, 16:2, May 1977, pp. 215–242.
[34]Statement of James Smith, assistant to the president, United Steelworkers of America, Oct. 25, 1974.

TABLE 3-4   FUNCTIONS OF A LOCAL UNION

1 Collective bargaining, the "bread and butter" of any local union
2 Contract administration to ensure the agreement is lived up to
3 Establishment and administration of fringe benefits
4 Organization, which is the life-blood of the union and ultimately makes the first three essential points possible
5 Ensuring a continuing supply of jobs
6 Protection of the union's supply of jobs
7 Apprentice training to ensure a steady supply of well-trained workers
8 Political action to protect negotiated gains, both locally and nationally
9 Community relations so that the union can help shape public attitudes toward the union
10 Information and education so that union members are up to date and aware of what is happening around them
11 Management of legal affairs, which have today become an integral part of every union
12 Maintenance of good relations with all other labor and management
13 Internal administration of the union to ensure that it runs efficiently, giving the members the most for their dues dollar

Source: General Secretary John T. Joyce, Bricklayers International Union, *St. Louis Labor Tribune,* Aug. 30, 1974, p. 7.

Election of Officers

Local union officials are elected for a period of 1, 2, or 3 years. Federal law requires elections at least every 3 years, but most locals hold them more frequently. In some local unions the political process is very stable, with few contests for office and with officials serving many terms. In others, factions exist that compete for office and turnover is very frequent.

Local union memberships are rarely homogeneous. Instead, a local union is a mixture of conflicting interest groups. For example, in an industrial local union these groups might be older versus younger workers or skilled versus unskilled or semiskilled workers. Conflicts arise because, for example, older workers might desire improvements in a pension plan or be very strong supporters of a seniority system as a method of allocating benefits, while younger workers might prefer a wage increase over improved pensions and might feel little loyalty to a seniority system.

Since local union officials must get elected frequently, they often tend to let their political interests overrule their better judgment.[35] This often occasions bitterness and anger in employers and national union officials about the behavior of local union leadership. Other observers, however,

[35]Address by General President Hunter P. Wharton, International Union of Operating Engineers, to the South Atlantic Conference of the International Union, Oct. 21, 1974 (mimeographed).

may applaud it as reflecting the changing will of the democratic majority of the local union.

Compensation of Officers

Compensation of local union officials varies greatly. Many local officials receive no compensation from the union, as we have seen. Others receive a salary. Ordinarily salary levels are commensurate with the earnings of the workers, although generally above the average level of earnings of the local's members. In some trades and large locals, however, salary levels may be much higher. Some large locals of the Teamsters, especially, pay substantial salaries to union officials. And there has developed in recent years the questionable practice of union officials receiving more than a single salary. It has even been reported that some union officials are able to collect more than three salaries.[36] Often there is nothing illegal about this process, but it does permit the establishment of substantial incomes for a few union officials through the pyramiding of salaries.

Participation of Members

The participation of members in the affairs of local unions has been investigated several times. Most studies indicate that there is both an active and an inactive segment of membership. Union meetings ordinarily attract only a small proportion of the local's total membership. However, if a major issue, such as a strike vote or a ratification vote on a proposed new collective bargaining agreement, is scheduled, a very high proportion of the membership may turn out.[37] While it may be regrettable that there is not ordinarily greater participation by members in local union affairs, it cannot be said to be unusual in our society. Voters often turn out in small numbers in governmental elections, town meetings are often conducted in virtually empty halls, and corporation stockholder meetings are often poorly attended. Union members are no different from the general public in this aspect of their behavior.

Unions try by various devices to encourage participation by members in the affairs of the local. Some unions distribute to local officers guides that describe methods of assisting union members in meeting family health and welfare needs. It is thought that if the union goes beyond the workplace to meet the needs of members, it will be likely to attract greater participation and loyalty from its members. The United Steelworkers once

[36]Jerry Landauer, "Wearing Many Hats," *Wall Street Journal*, Aug. 17, 1973, pp. 1, 19. Similar pyramiding sometimes occurs in the business and educational worlds. See also L. Applebaum and H. R. Blaire, "Compensation and Turnover of Union Officers," Industrial Relations, 14:2, May 1975, pp. 156–157.

[37]Arnold S. Tannenbaum and Robert L. Kahn, *Participation in Union Locals* (Evanston, Ill.: Row, Peterson, 1958).

had a rule that a member had to attend at least half of the local union's regular meetings for the 3 years prior to an election in order to be eligible to run for office in the local. But in 1977 the U.S. Supreme Court found that this was not a reasonable qualification for union officers. The Court pointed out that 96.5 percent of the membership of the local union that complained about the meeting attendance rule would have been ineligible to run for office if it had been enforced.

Financing of Local Unions

The financing of local unions is by dues paid by the membership. The amount of dues varies, but averages perhaps 1 percent of union members' annual income. A rule of thumb often used is that dues average 1 or 2 hours' pay per month per member. When a local union must collect monthly dues from each member, the administrative expense and loss of income from members who do not pay are substantial. While sanctions may be placed by the union on members who do not pay, such measures are sometimes ineffective (or even counterproductive). Unions often seek, therefore, to obtain the employers' agreement to deduct the dues of union members from their paychecks and forward the money directly to the union as a lump sum. This is called a "checkoff" and can be done only if (1) the employer agrees and (2) each worker individually signs a document authorizing the deduction to be made from his or her pay. Various local unions also handle their financial affairs, in terms of balancing revenues and expenditures and the amount of borrowing by the local, very differently. Some are conservative fiscal managers; others are not.[38]

Ordinarily unions establish dues as a fixed dollar amount to be paid each month. But some unions have recently begun to set dues as a percentage of a member's earnings. A complaint by some members of the Air Line Pilots Association went to court because of this. In 1980, a federal circuit court of appeals ruled that the union could lawfully set dues as a percent of a member's earnings (*Bagnall v. Air Line Pilots Association*, 1980).

THE FEDERATION

The American Federation of Labor-Congress of Industrial Organizations (AFL-CIO) is the central trade union federation in the United States. Its lengthy name is a result of its establishment by merger of the AFL and the CIO in 1955. Not only its name but also its organizational structure reflects

---

[38]Elisabeth Allison, "Financial Analysis of the Local Union," *Industrial Relations*, 14:2, May 1975, pp. 145–155. See also Gary N. Chaison, "Local Union Mergers," *Journal of Labor Research*, 4:4, Fall 1983, pp. 325–338.

the merger, as we will see. Since the merger, the Federation has achieved a degree of internal cohesion and external influence in American society unparalleled in labor's history, and perhaps never matched by any other single nongovernmental institution in the United States. Whether the influence of the AFL-CIO can remain at this high level is a matter we explore below.

Functions of the Federation

The Federation is a device by which national unions in the United States may cooperate with each other to pursue certain common objectives and to attempt to resolve certain problems internal to the affairs of organized labor. The most important of its functions are:

1 *Improving the image* of labor in American society
2 *Conducting political activity*, both by participating in elections and by lobbying with elected officials
3 *Resolving disputes* between national unions
4 *Strengthening weak links* in the labor movement
5 *Policing the internal affairs* of particular unions whose actions threaten the good name or influence of the labor movement as a whole[39]

The items not included on this list are as important to an understanding of the AFL-CIO as the points that are enumerated. Collective bargaining is the major omitted item. The Federation does not ordinarily become involved in negotiations with employers in the United States; collective bargaining is the province of the national and local unions.

Collective bargaining is at the heart of the concerns of "business unionism," and American trade unionism is characterized as the world's preeminent example of business unionism. Thus, the AFL-CIO's exclusion from collective bargaining suggests the substantial degree to which its role is limited in the activities of the American labor movement and demonstrates the primacy of the national union.

It would be difficult to distinguish among the five functions of the Federation listed above in terms of importance. But among the most difficult tasks of the Federation is the resolution of disputes among national unions. In 1962 concern about the potentially disruptive impact of internal disputes was so great that a special procedure was set up under article XX of the AFL-CIO constitution, which provided for the resolution of such disputes.

Complaints can be filed by one affiliated national union against another where a union thinks it has an established relationship with a group of

---

[39]Dunlop and Bok, *Labor*, p. 190. See also Victor Reisel, "Last Giant," Sept. 24, 1976, syndicated newspaper column.

workers and another union is trying to raid its members. There follows a process of mediation and eventual arbitration before an impartial umpire, in which a decision is rendered.[40] An appeal may then be filed by an affected union to the executive council of the AFL-CIO. Sanctions are provided against a national union that refuses to accept an award under article XX. On February 18, 1986, the Federation extended the article XX procedure to provide a mechanism to settle disputes between national or international unions that were attempting to organize the same workers—that is, where no established collective bargaining relationship yet existed.

This record of resolving disputes among national unions is remarkable in light of the history of bitter divisions within the American labor movement. It is even more remarkable as the achievement of a federation established by the merger of two groups of rival national unions. George Meany said that the plan was "working wonderfully . . . beyond my wildest dream."[41] Whether or not the article XX procedure will continue to compile such a record remains to be seen, but its current success is clearly a major contributor to the relative unity of the American labor movement.

In recent years the AFL-CIO has become concerned with what appears to be a decline in the public's opinion of unions. By doing public opinion polling the unions discovered that their members held a much more favorable view of unions than did nonmembers. This "image gap," as the union termed it, became a target for union advertising.[42] In an effort to enhance labor's image, the AFL-CIO in 1983 began a nationwide television series showing unions and their members at work and in community services.[43] In May 1988, the Federation launched its largest advertising campaign, "Union Yes." The goal of the presentations was to talk directly to American workers about the value of unions.

By the early 1990s labor's decline in public opinion polls seemed to be ending. For decades more Americans had reported to pollsters that they were more inclined to support a company during a strike than a union, but now the tilt was reversed, with the larger number leaning toward supporting a striking union.[44]

[40]"Mediation Proves Successful in Settling Internal Disputes," *AFL-CIO News*, Mar. 2, 1983, p. 3.

[41]"Most Internal Disputes Settled by Mediation," *AFL-CIO News*, Mar. 1, 1975, p. 2.

[42]James A. Craft and Suharl Abboushi, "The Union Image: Concept, Programs and Analysis," *Journal of Labor Research*, 4:4, Fall 1983, pp. 299–304; Carol Keegan, "How Union Members and Nonmembers View the Role of Unions," *Monthly Labor Review*, 111:8, August 1987, p. 50.

[43]"New Season Opens for TV Series of Labor," *AFL-CIO News*, Jan. 7, 1984, p. 6; and Lane Kirkland, "Using Television to Reach Workers," *AFL-CIO News*, 33:20, May 14, 1988, p. 3.

[44]"Public Support for Strikers Rises," Bureau of National Affairs, *Daily Labor Report*, No. 231 (Dec. 4, 1989), p. A-3.

Authority

How does the AFL-CIO compare with trade union central bodies abroad? Is it stronger or weaker, more centralized or less centralized? Most Western industrial countries have a federation of national unions. The number of nationals affiliated with the central body varies by country; there is a low of 16 in Germany (where the trade union movement has virtually no fragmentation) and a high of more than 100 in the United States and Britain. In all Western countries except Israel and Austria, the trade union central body is a federation of legally separate national unions; but in those two countries, the national unions are simply subdivisions of the central body, without separate legal identity.[45]

Table 3-5 presents estimates of the authority of central union bodies in certain selected Western European countries and the United States. It will be noted that the Federation in the United States is described as decentralized, with only a moderate authority to intervene in the internal affairs of national unions, and only low involvement in collective bargaining. The table also shows that the percentage of the industrial labor force that is unionized is

[45]John P. Windmuller, "The Authority of National Trade Union Confederations: A Comparative Analysis," in David B. Lipsky, ed., *Union Power and Public Policy* (Ithaca, N.Y.: Cornell University Press, 1975), pp. 91–108.

TABLE 3-5 ESTIMATE OF AUTHORITY OF CENTRAL UNION BODIES IN SELECTED COUNTRIES

	Percentage of total union revenues received by central bodies	Intervention in internal union affairs	Involvement in collective bargaining	Percentage of industrial labor force in unions
Highly centralized				
Austria	80	H*	H	65
Norway	18	M	H	65
Sweden	18	M	H	80
Moderately centralized				
Belgium	40	M	M	71
Denmark	9	M	M	58
France	21	M	M	22
Decentralized				
West Germany	12	L	L	38
Great Britain	2	L	M	48
United States	3	M	L	30

*H = high; M = moderate; L = low.
Source: John P. Windmuller, "The Authority of National Trade Union Confederations: A Comparative Analysis," in D. B. Lipsky, ed., *Union Power and Public Policy* (Ithaca, N.Y.: Cornell University Press, 1975), tables 2 and 3. Data are from various years in the period 1964–1973, and data for France are from the CFDT.

low in the United States (only France is lower) and that the Federation receives a relatively small percentage of total union revenues (only Britain is lower). This table does not suggest that the AFL-CIO is a weak or insignificant organization. It indicates only that the AFL-CIO's authority with respect to the national unions is relatively more limited than in many countries abroad. On an absolute scale, however, the AFL-CIO is wealthier and more influential in American society than many federations abroad.

Structure

The AFL-CIO is a federation of 89 national unions. Its supreme governing body is a national convention held every 2 years. At the convention each national union is represented according to the size of the membership for which it pays a per capita tax to the AFL-CIO. The convention elects two top officers, the president and the secretary-treasurer. The president interprets the AFL-CIO constitution and directs its staff (totaling more than 100 people) between conventions. The secretary-treasurer is responsible for financial matters. The Federation has an executive council of 33 vice presidents (who are ordinarily general presidents of national unions), which meets at least three times a year to adopt policy and oversee the internal operations of the Federation. In 1980 the AFL-CIO set aside 2 of the 33 seats on its executive council, one to go to a woman and one to a member of a minority group.

The unions that make up the AFL-CIO vary greatly in size. According to one careful estimate, in 1977–1978 some 70.7 percent of the total membership of the AFL-CIO was contributed by the 10 largest national unions affiliated with the Federation.[46] An important element of the AFL-CIO's function is to seek to bring about mergers that will strengthen the trade union movement as a whole. In recent years there have been several significant mergers, which created larger organizations and lessened competition among national unions.[47]

There is also a general board, consisting of the officers of the Federation, the executive council, and a principal officer of each affiliated national union and department. The general board meets only occasionally, at the request of the president, and acts on matters referred to it by the executive council.

The AFL-CIO has a very complex administrative structure. The Federation has central bodies in all 50 states and Puerto Rico, and over 700 local central bodies. It is a characteristic complexity of AFL-CIO structure that, although a national union may be an affiliate of the AFL-CIO, the national

---

[46]John P. Windmuller, "Concentration in the Union Structure: A Comparative Analysis," Cornell University, unpublished, 1980.

[47]Gideon Chitayat, *Trade Union Mergers and Labor Conglomerates* (New York: Praeger, 1979). See also John Freeman and Jack Brittain, "Union Merger Process and the Industrial Environment," *Industrial Relations*, 16:2, May 1977, pp. 173–185; "Union Mergers in the 1970's," *Monthly Labor Review*, 101:10, October 1978, pp. 13–23; and Gary N. Chaison, *When Unions Merge* (Lexington, Mass.: Lexington Books, 1986).

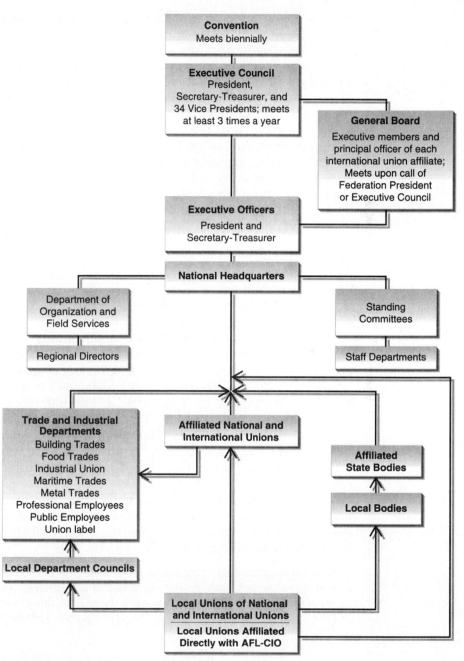

FIGURE 3-8   Structure of the AFL-CIO.

union's local unions in a particular state may not be affiliated with the state AFL-CIO body.

The Federation also has a group of nine trade and industrial departments (the most recent—covering transportation—was created in 1990). An industrial union department is composed of the national unions that were the old CIO. The national unions affiliate with the departments that represent their interests. The trade and industrial departments have local and state bodies also. The Federation also has staff departments, of which the most important is the department of organization and field services, which supervises regional offices of the AFL-CIO. This department was created in its present form at the 1973 convention of the Federation. Finally, the Federation maintains offices in 10 countries abroad. Figure 3-8 on page 99 depicts the structure and elements of the AFL-CIO.

Activities

The AFL-CIO attempts to organize craft and industrial unions, to assist its affiliated national unions in their organizing work, to supply legal assistance in some litigation, and to represent its affiliates in governmental and nongovernmental agencies. It maintains research, information, publicity, and educational services as well. AFL-CIO publications include a weekly newspaper, The *AFL-CIO News,* and pamphlets and organizing information. In civic affairs, the AFL-CIO encourages and promotes the involvement of union members in such community projects as campaigns for voter registration, better schools, more hospitals, and the elimination of slums.

The AFL-CIO has for a long time had an interest in the education of union members and officers. Many universities conduct labor education programs on a year-round basis.[48] But the labor movement has never developed the same close affiliation with the universities that the business community has evolved (reflected in part by the growth of graduate schools of business at the nation's universities and by the development of undergraduate business administration courses). Instead, the labor movement has grown more disenchanted with the universities. Meany voiced labor's disenchantment as follows:

> It is unfortunate that there seems to be a view in certain parts of the academic world that labor's problem is smugness and self-satisfaction, and that it needs a great deal of abrasive criticism to open its eyes. In this arrogant conviction, from time to time we see academic facilities turned over to labor's enemies to use as a forum for attacking labor.[49]

[48]Lois S. Gray, "Academic Degrees for Labor Studies," *Monthly Labor Review,* 100:6, June 1977, pp. 15–20.

[49]Remarks of AFL-CIO President George Meany at the 25th anniversary dinner of the New York State School of Industrial and Labor Relations, New York City, Dec. 11, 1970. The remarks were reprinted in Bureau of National Affairs, *Daily Labor Report,* No. 240, Dec. 11, 1970, pp. F1–F2.

(Incidentally, Meany's reference to "labor's enemies" was probably not directed to the business community, but to left-wing and radical critics of the unions.)

Reflecting this discontent with American universities, the AFL-CIO has established its own university at a suburban campus in Silver Spring, Maryland, just north of Washington, D.C. The AFL-CIO Labor Studies center is an incorporated, nonprofit educational institution governed by a board of trustees composed of labor and public members. It was established in 1969 at a cost of several million dollars. In 1974, a college degree program was established at the center, offering bachelor's degrees in labor studies.[50]

The AFL-CIO also takes a strong interest in American foreign policy. From the earliest days of the AFL under Samuel Gompers, and continuing through the period of the two federations (AFL and CIO), the American labor movement has remained substantially independent of governmental foreign policy.[51]

In recent decades, the position of the labor movement as expressed by the AFL-CIO has been strongly antitotalitarian, opposing both communist and fascist regimes. This position often places the American labor movement in opposition both to the position of foreign labor movements and to that of the U.S. government.

The AFL-CIO has consistently opposed the policy of the United States government to establish a detente (i.e., understanding) with the Soviet Union. For example, on October 1, 1974, Meany testified before the Senate Foreign Relations Committee. He quoted complimentary comments by Don Kendall, president of Pepsi-Cola Corporation, about Leonid Brezhnev, then chief of the Communist party of the Soviet Union, and then proceeded to reiterate the AFL-CIO's opposition to the detente policy, characterizing it as "building castles of sand on the watery foundations of petty greed, wishful thinking, irresponsibility, self-indulgence, and plain old ignorance . . . [as well as] the inability to . . . understand clearly the nature of freedom's enemies."[52]

These statements demonstrate the continuing threads of the AFL-CIO's foreign policy position: (1) opposition to totalitarianism and (2) fear that the American government and business community will reach accommodation with totalitarian regimes that will threaten the existence of free labor movements.[53]

[50]Carolyn J. Jacobson, "An Expanding Role for Labor's College," *American Federationist,* 81:10, October 1974, pp. 13–19.

[51]Arnold Beichman, "American Labor and U.S. Foreign Policy," *American Federationist,* 81:10, October 1974, pp. 20–24. Also, Lane Kirkland, "Free Trade Unions—Force for Democracy," *American Federationist,* 85:4, April 1978, pp. 1–5.

[52]Statement of AFL-CIO President George Meany to the Senate Foreign Relations Committee, Oct. 1, 1974. The text is the *AFL-CIO Free Trade Union News,* 29:9, October 1974, pp. 1–8.

[53]Roy Godson, *American Labor and European Politics* (New York: Crane, Russack, 1976).

So sensitive is the AFL-CIO to the threat of totalitarian advance that the U.S. Congress has repeatedly declared, in the Foreign Assistance Act, that aiding the development of free and democratic trade unions is an objective of U.S. foreign policy.[54] The AFL-CIO supports an organization named The American Institute for Free Labor Development, which has been active in Latin America in opposition to communist regimes or insurgencies.[55]

LABOR UNITED?

In 1955, at the time of the AFL-CIO merger, Steelworker general counsel Arthur J. Goldberg (later secretary of Labor, Supreme Court associate justice, and ambassador to the United Nations) wrote an account of the merger, entitled *AFL-CIO Labor United*.[56] Even then labor was not fully united, for the United Mineworkers were outside the Federation. And the AFL-CIO itself remained united only very briefly.

In 1957 the AFL-CIO expelled its largest affiliate, the Teamsters, after the Teamsters' leaders were accused of unethical practices and when an agreement to reform the practices could not be obtained.[57] In 1968 the United Automobile Workers, then the largest AFL-CIO affiliate, withdrew in a dispute with the Federation. (The Teamsters and the UAW briefly formed a rival federation, the American Labor Alliance, in the late 1960s, which did not survive.) In 1981, the UAW rejoined the AFL-CIO, and the Teamsters, the largest union in the United States, rejoined in 1987. The issue of unethical practices in the Teamsters had not been resolved, but the leadership of the AFL-CIO took the position that it was up to the government to clean up the Teamsters. The federal government did put the Teamsters under court oversight and in 1992 an election was held under government supervision. A reformer—Ron Carey—was elected national president of the union, and announced the formation of an internal ethics committee to investigate misconduct and corruption in the union and recommend disciplinary action.[58] In 1990 the United Mineworkers rejoined the Federation. The reaffiliation of the UAW, the Teamsters, and the Mineworkers means that today the

---

[54]Memorandum of the Secretaries of State and Labor to all U.S. Ambassadors, reprinted in *AFL-CIO News*, Aug. 12, 1978, p. 5.

[55]See Donald Robinson, "Bill Doherty's Blue-Collar Freedom Fighters," *Reader's Digest*, September 1985, pp. 141–144.

[56]Arthur J. Goldberg, *AFL-CIO Labor United* (New York: McGraw-Hill, 1956).

[57]Gary N. Chaison, "Federation Expulsions and Union Mergers in the United States," *Relations Industrielles*, 28:2, 1973, pp. 343–360.

[58]See Arthur A. Sloane, *Hoffa* (Cambridge, Mass.: MIT Press, 1991); Dan LaBotz, *Rank and File Rebellion: Teamsters for a Democratic Union* (London and New York: Verso Press, 1990); and John R. Oravec, "Carey Vision: 'New Teamster's Union,'" *AFL-CIO News*, Feb. 17, 1992, p. 9.

labor movement is as cohesive as it has been at virtually any time in its long hisory.

CHAPTER SUMMARY

In 1989, the most recent year for which data are available, there were some 190 major labor organizations in the United States with a total reported membership of almost 17 million, or 16.4 percent of the total labor force. Of these, 88 national unions, or about 82 percent of the total union membership, were affiliated with the AFL-CIO. Although total union membership has grown in the years since 1935, the proportion of the labor force in unions has been declining since the 1950s. Also, the number of women, minority, and white-collar workers in unions has been rising.

Each union has its own internal political affairs, procedures, financial structure, and concerns for survival. In the United States, there are local unions, national unions, and a federation of national unions—the AFL-CIO. A national union is composed of local unions and is governed by a national convention of the local unions, which is held every few years. Its functions, the duties of its officers, and its relationships to affiliates are set forth in a constitution. The national union has a general president and an executive board made up of the president, a secretary-treasurer, and several vice presidents. There is also a group of full-time salaried representatives attached to the general president's office who serve as intermediaries between the national and local unions.

Union leaders are elected to their posts, but the political process in national unions generally does not involve organized parties. Financial support for the national unions comes from taxes paid by the locals, and this revenue, which is substantial, is spent on officers' and employees' salaries, governmental lobbyists, a legal department, the national convention, strike benefit payments, pension and welfare plans, and many other functions.

There are some 65,000 local unions in the United States, most of which are affiliated with national unions. Locals vary greatly in size (from 200 to 40,000 members) and in the units of jurisdiction that they represent. Many of the organizational characteristics of the locals are similar to those of the national unions. They are governed through their membership meetings and financed by membership dues. The officers are elected to office, but not ordinarily paid by the unions. Some local unions elect full-time salaried business agents, or representatives, who enforce the local's collective bargaining agreements. In addition to its responsibilities to the national union, the local union's basic functions include collective bargaining, contract administration, union organizing and recruiting, apprentice training, education, political action, and management of legal affairs.

The AFL-CIO is the central trade union federation in the United States. Through the Federation, about 88 national unions cooperate with each other to pursue common objectives and resolve the internal disputes and problems of organized labor. The Federation does not engage in collective bargaining, which instead is the province of the national and local unions. In relation to the trade union federations in other countries, the AFL-CIO is considered to be decentralized, possessing only moderate authority to intervene in the affairs of national unions. Nevertheless, it has had a remarkable record for resolving disputes in national unions. The governing body of the Federation is a national convention, held every 2 years, which elects the president and secretary-treasurer. An executive council of 33 members meets at least three times a year to adopt policy and conduct other business. The administrative structure of the AFL-CIO is very complex and includes over 700 local central bodies and trade, industrial, and staff departments, which also have local and state offices. The Federation maintains legal, research, information, publicity, and educational services and has had a strong interest in American foreign policy as well.

QUESTIONS FOR THOUGHT AND DISCUSSION

1 How is a national union different from an employee association (e.g., the National Education Association)? Will the differences widen or narrow in coming years? Why?
2 Why are there not more women and minority members of labor unions? Are they too few now? Too many? Do businesses have a better record in treating women and minorities fairly than unions have? Does government have a better record?
3 Why are local unions in construction structured differently from those in manufacturing? Does the difference in structure make a difference in how effective they are in representing their members? Why or why not?
4 Does the AFL-CIO have enough authority with respect to its affiliate national unions? How should its role be expanded? Contracted? Should the AFL-CIO be involved in collective bargaining?
5 Do you believe that the size of the labor movement in general will expand or contract in the coming decade? What industries and areas are now most unionized? What industries or sectors of the economy will show increased unionization in the future?
6 How do people become leaders in national unions? Do you think the election of officers in local and national unions is better than selection by merit or professional expertise? Why? Is the union political process truly democratic? Why or why not?
7 What are some of the functions of a local union? Of the national union?
8 Why do you think the AFL-CIO has taken such a strong position against communist and fascist regimes abroad?
9 One of the functions of the AFL-CIO is to improve the image of labor. If you were in charge of publicity for the AFL-CIO, how would you approach this task? How would you promote "big labor"? How would you design a television advertising program for labor?

SELECTED READING

Cook, Alice, et al., eds., *Women and Trade Unions in Eleven Industrialized Countries* (Philadelphia: Temple University Press, 1984).

Dunlop, John T., *The Management of Labor Unions* (Lexington, Mass.: Lexington Books, 1990).

Marshall, Ray, *The Negro Worker* (New York: Random House, 1967).

Sayles, Leonard R., and George Strauss, *The Local Union* (New York: Harcourt, Brace & World, 1967).

C

MANAGEMENT AND EMPLOYEES

Since labor-management relations have a long tradition in the United States, it is not uncommon for some people to think that they are mired in established ways. But American society is changing, and so are its labor-management relations.

The key issues with which labor and management normally deal have been compensation, benefits, work practices, and the equitable treatment of employees. Each of these items remains significant, but changing times have added significant issues to the list of concerns.

Among the key topics that a changing economy is advancing for labor and management's attention are how to keep U.S. industries competitive internationally and thus preserve jobs; how to accommodate the needs of a more diverse work force, and how to adjust to a very different workplace.

In this chapter we will consider the new workplace. In Chapter 5 the increasing diversity of the work force will be described, and in Chapter 6 the nonunion employee relations process.

It would have been possible to have placed these chapters toward the end of the book as elements of a look at the future of labor-management relations. But that might have implied that these matters are somehow of lesser importance than traditional concerns. Instead, these issues are of great significance already, and therefore they belong at the outset of any discussion of labor-management relations. The new workplace is a crucial part of the context, and the diverse work force is central to the human dynamics of labor-management relations.

CHAPTER 4

UNIONS, MANAGEMENT, AND THE NEW WORKPLACE[1]

"NEW" WORKPLACE VERSUS "OLD"—WHAT IS CHANGING AND WHY?

The Traditional versus the New Workplace

A traditional workplace is marked by several features, among them sharp task specialization and extensive management hierarchy. Task specialization first came to the attention of industry when economists like Adam Smith (author of *The Wealth of Nations*) showed that separating the steps in a production process and assigning each one to a different person, rather than asking each person to perform all the steps as necessary, greatly enhanced total output. Management hierarchy, on the other hand, emerged in ancient China and Egypt as a device allowing small groups of army officers to command and coordinate the activities of large groups of soldiers and thereby impose unity of purpose on them.

As the tinkerers in turn-of-the-century Detroit developed the machinery necessary to make mass production techniques work in practice, they also found that they needed management methods by which to structure the supporting human infrastructure of their factories. They found what they were looking for in "scientific management," a set of concepts for governing industrial workplaces often associated with Frederick W. Taylor.[2]

---

[1]G. Bruce Friesen contributed substantial portions of this chapter.
[2]See Frederick W. Taylor, *The Principles of Scientific Management* (New York: Praeger 1967.)

Followers of scientific management believed in the virtue of applying time and motion studies to physical work of all kinds—a key function of industrial engineers. They felt that by breaking jobs into detailed components and studying them, wasted motions could be identified and removed, thus enhancing work efficiency. In one famous experiment, Taylor was able to get a worker to load pig iron at four times regular speed after analyzing and "correcting" his motions.[3]

Scientific management was expanded and adapted by its adherents from a theory of productivity improvement to a philosophy holding that

1 Workers tend to be "lazy" when unsupervised and so require close supervision at work; hence, supervisors arranged in hierarchies are needed to manage factories.

2 Asking workers to make conscious decisions about production work has the potential to disrupt preset machine routines; hence, decisions must be made by those away from the line—management.

3 Wages are the most powerful motivator of behavior, and, as they rise, people will work harder; hence, profits from productivity improvement should be shared with workers as increased pay.

Taken in the context of the early twentieth century—a period of limited public education and low living standards relative to today—the ideas of scientific management struck a chord among managers. Organizational structures designed to channel, control, and direct workers in accordance with its precepts became a standard feature of the industrial workplace.[4]

Over time, scientific management proved both beneficial and costly. It was beneficial in that it pushed firms to rigorously study their production processes—standardizing machines, jobs, and product designs as they did so. As machines and human labor were more fully integrated into a single whole, the tremendous potential of mass production was revealed. Wage levels rose to unprecedented levels, and the wealth of society greatly advanced. Scientific management became costly, however, when it led to work structures in which most jobs were narrowly specialized, repetitive, and deskilled, creating monotony and boredom among those required to perform them. Further, with machines pacing factories and most of the power and authority in the hands of management, there was little opportunity for workers to relieve the stresses of production except on themselves. Sociologist Emile Durkheim coined the term "anomie" or "alienation from work" to describe the resulting behavior, which included excessive drinking

---

[3]Ibid., pp. 41–47.

[4]It is important to note that Frederick Taylor himself did not hold to all of these views himself. See Robert Hayes, Steve Wheelwright, and Kim Clark, *Dynamic Manufacturing* (New York: Free Press, 1988), pp. 28–40.

and drug abuse, violence, even the occasional sabotage of equipment in the workplace.[5]

The eventual realization that few benefits of automation were flowing back to assembly workers except in higher wage rates, and that workers were absorbing the bulk of the psychological and physical punishment of monotonous work, generated a discontent that unions expressed. Bound by scientific management's dictates to channel work according to machine requirements, rather than according to the long-term psychological and social requirements of employees, managers refused to change practices until pushed to the brink by the challenges of unions to their authority.

But in recent decades changes in the business environment, in technology, and in the expectations of employees have compelled companies to begin moving away from the scientifically engineered workplace. As the trends—each of which is described in the next section—have gathered momentum, businesses have increasingly opted to abandon scientific management in favor of other methods for structuring their workplaces.

There has emerged a new concept for managing the workplace. Broad authority is delegated to employee teams, thereby empowering them to operate largely on their own and without direct supervision. This large-scale delegation of authority permits a reduced number of managers to successfully lead organizations without breaking themselves down with overwork. It also brings a new type of employee to the forefront, one capable of taking initiatives and working under minimal supervision, and skilled in many tasks instead of just one—nearly the exact opposite of the desired attributes of a worker under scientific management.

The new system is an attempt by management to improve competitiveness. At its center are programs to improve quality and productivity and to lower costs. These programs appear under various labels—including total quality management (TQM) and market-driven quality (MDQ)—but have certain elements in common. For example, they stress a transformation in management from directing work to leading employees; from supervising employees at narrow tasks to empowering them to utilize their own discretion in how to accomplish their missions in the firm; from having many layers of management to far fewer managers. They even allow teams of employees to largely manage themselves.[6] Workers are invited or required to participate in processes of continuous improvement through quality circles or employee involvement initiatives, which are described

---

[5]In the classic silent film *Modern Times,* the noted actor and filmmaker Charlie Chaplin sought to illustrate with humor some of the more destructive effects of machine-paced production on a hapless worker.

[6]Richard Walton, "From Control to Commitment in the Workplace," *Harvard Business Review,* 87 (March–April), 1985, pp. 45ff. Reprinted by the U.S. Department of Labor, Bureau of Labor-Management Relations and Cooperative Programs, Washington, D.C., 1991.

TABLE 4-1   THE CHANGING APPROACH TO ORGANIZING WORK

What management assumes about workers	
OLD WAY Worker wants nothing from the job except pay, avoids responsibility, and must be controlled and coerced	**NEW WAY** Worker desires challenging job and will seek responsibility and autonomy if management permits
How the job is designed	
OLD WAY Work is fragmented and deskilled. Worker is confined to narrow job. Doing and thinking are separated	**NEW WAY** Work is multiskilled and performed by teamwork where possible. Worker can upgrade whole system. Doing and thinking are combined
Management's organization and style	
OLD WAY Top-down military command with worker at bottom of many supervisory layers; worker is expected to obey orders and has no power	**NEW WAY** Relatively flat structure with few layers; worker makes suggestions and has power to implement changes
Job training and security	
OLD WAY Worker is regarded as a replaceable-part and is given little initial training or retraining for new jobs. Layoffs are routine when business declines	**NEW WAY** Worker is considered a valuable resource and is constantly retrained in new skills. Layoffs are avoided if possible in a downturn
How wages are determined	
OLD WAY Pay is geared to the job, not the person, and is determined by evaluation and job classification systems	**NEW WAY** Pay is linked to skills acquired. Group incentive and profit-sharing plans are used to enhance commitment
Labor relations	
OLD WAY Labor and management interests are considered incompatible. Conflict arises on the shop floor and in bargaining	**NEW WAY** Mutual interests are emphasized. Management shares information about the business. Labor shares responsibility for making it succeed

DATA: RICHARD E. WALTON, HARVARD UNIVERSITY

Source: Business Week, Sept. 29, 1986, p. 71.

later in this chapter. The idea of continuous improvement is for managers and employees to cooperate in continually improving the productivity (see Chapter 21 for a detailed discussion of productivity) and quality of work produced.

Table 4-1 summarizes briefly key elements of the transition from the old Taylorist, or "scientific," approach to management to the new system.

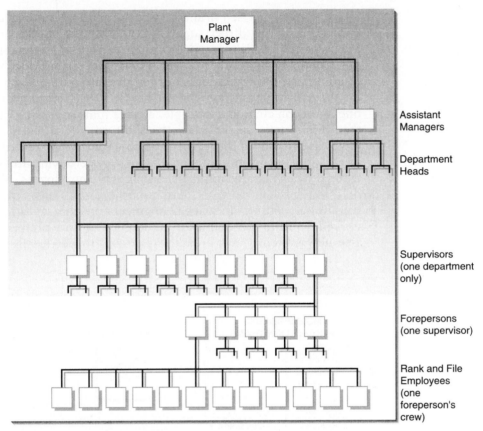

FIGURE 4-1   Traditional organization charts.

Figure 4-1 is an organization chart for a traditional factory (with changes in the titles of the managers it could apply equally well to a traditionally organized office, such as a bank or an insurance company, or even to a large retail store). Note that there are five layers of managers, and that each box represents a manager or supervisor. A line running up to the higher level of management represents a reporting relationship to that person's boss. A line running into the box from below represents the reporting relationship from the manager's "direct reports." Only the rank and file have no one reporting to them. This is a traditional organization chart depicting the typical chain of command. It represents a traditional hierarchy in which everyone has a boss (though here the plant manager's boss isn't shown). It is a system designed for direction and control.

Figure 4-2 shows a similar facility organized by self-managed teams. There are still managers, but far fewer than before (the ratio of employees to managers has risen dramatically over that in the traditional hierarchy), and there are no direct supervisors. Circles represent empowered teams that produce goods or services in the plant. The system requires considerable communication within and between teams but does not use the chain of command as a mechanism of communication, relying instead on more informal processes. The whole system is less complex and rigid than the one it is replacing. For example, a large manufacturing plant organized in the traditional way will often have 90 or 100 different carefully defined jobs—each with a different rate of pay—with complex rules for the transfer of employees among them. The new system will rarely have more than three or four classifications of rank-and-file employees, allowing people to do a much wider range of tasks on an ordinary basis than permitted in a traditional setting. Industrial engineers in the traditional system have viewed so little job definition as inefficient and preferred specialization. The new system views breadth as crucial to needed flexibility in a world

FIGURE 4-2 Team structure in a factory.

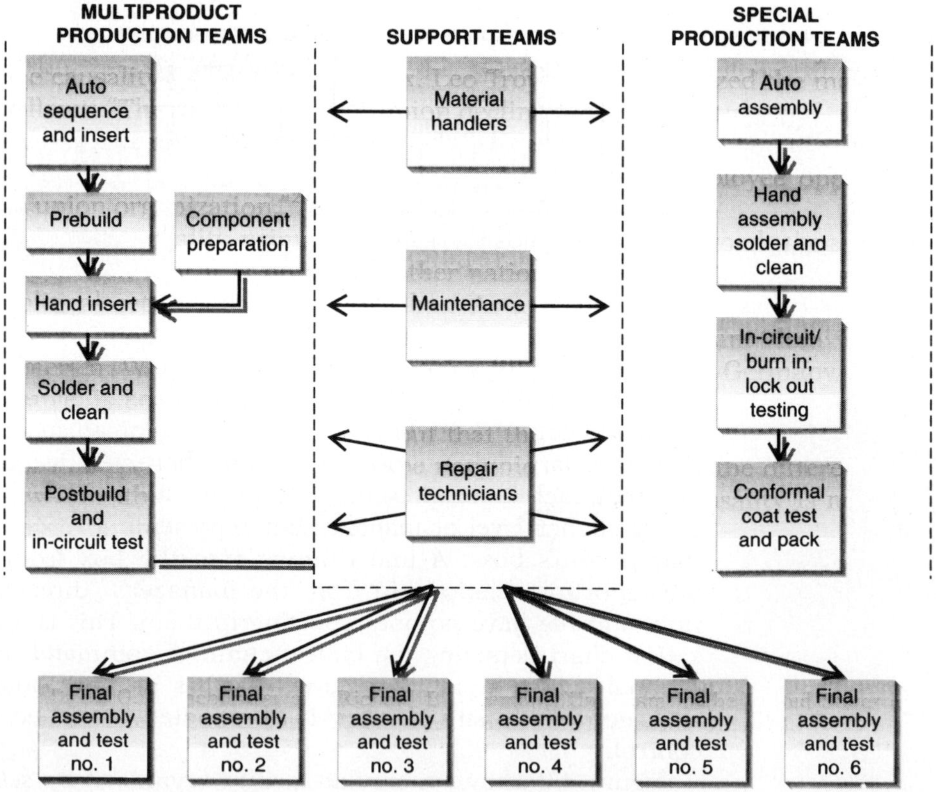

that changes too rapidly to wait for a reengineering of the work system each time key circumstances in the market alter.

Seeking to be flexible and adaptable, the new system is much less formal than the old and gives people much more discretion and independence in what they do. Since there is little direct supervision, the company must trust its employees much more than in the old system, where it could continually checkup on them. Hence, the need, really almost a requirement, for labor-management trust and cooperation in the new system.

This is not the place to spell out in detail new approaches to management and work. The old system remains in place in most American workplaces, but the new one is rapidly gaining adherents. Most major American firms now have facilities organized in the new fashion. Already the new systems are having an impact on labor-management relations generally. In the new system, the role of labor is enhanced by greater delegation of responsibility and management requires a more cooperative relationship with workers. In fact, trust and cooperation emerge as integral to the operation of the new system, so that it impels unions and management into a more intimate relationship than did the old ways.

CAUSES OF THE CHANGE

The Business Environment

In recent years the business environment has experienced much more rapid change and also much more intense competition. Economic conditions alter rapidly from growth to recession; new products and services are introduced into the marketplace much more frequently than previously; and competition has developed on a global scale so that firms must be much more responsive to their customers than before. These factors have put a premium on quality in production and the delivery of services, on controlling costs, and on being able to adapt quickly in the marketplace.

The traditional, or Taylorist, system of work and supervision often falls short on these new requirements. It is a system designed for a slower-moving world and one that is less competitive. It still works and in stable environments is often very effective, even more so than the new systems that are trying to replace it. But because it is slow, cumbersome, and costly—due to so many layers of management and so much rigidity and specialization in the design of jobs—it often seems a dinosaur in today's fast-moving business world.

Firms have been pressed to become competitive by doing more than just laying off employees when demand for their products or services declines, then waiting for sales to recover. They are now attempting to stay close to customers to anticipate needs and avoid such costly mistakes as faulty product designs and poor after-sales service. They are improving quality in their factories. They are also trying to improve agility, quickness, and innovation. How do these efforts affect the workplace?

Firms sticking to the standard approach of using layoffs to cut costs in recent recessions often found that this strategy didn't work as planned. As ex-employees hit the streets, the morale and loyalty of those staying on slumped. Orders from managers went half obeyed as people kept one eye on job opportunities and one eye on responsibilities. And sales volume never recovered fully, even when a recession ended, because competitors—often from abroad—had seized more of the market for good.

Many firms challenged the conventional layoff logic. They concluded that they had too many managers, professionals, and staff rather than too many workers; that new technology could enable workers to cover many tasks assigned to expensive managers; and that sales and service suffered when customers dealt through layers of management instead of directly with front-line employees. This thinking led to employment reductions in the middle of these firms rather than at the bottom. A result was the type of new and delayered organization described above.

Technological Pull

One technology—mass assembly—led to the application of scientific management in the workplace. Now, another—the computer—is eroding the work structures that were created under scientific management.

Today, computers capable of doing routine tasks with only human monitoring are being installed in factories and offices, mainly to enhance productivity. As the role of machines is expanding, human activity in organizations is shifting along with it. The focus is now on solving problems for which the computer is not programmed. Instead of employees being asked to do routinized tasks under close supervision, many are now encountering novel situations, whose resolutions call for initiative and imagination.

Solving novel problems requires flexibility and speed, which a traditional workplace hierarchy, complete with specialized tasks and institutionalized confrontation between supervisors and employees, cannot deliver. The more skilled, creative, and thinking employees are hired to monitor self-standing machines, review manuals, make adjustments, and document activities for senior managers, the more the duties of supervisors and managers blur with those of employees, calling for a new approach to labor relations.

For example, today's steel, oil refinery, and utility workers generally deal with highly capital-intensive, self-monitoring equipment. This means that they often receive most of the data they need to solve production problems directly from the equipment itself. Under such conditions it would cost hours of valuable production time for operators to note problems, collect data, call supervisors, describe problems, wait for answers, and then try management solutions. It is much easier to delegate responsibility to the workers, treat them like professionals, and pay them bonuses for keeping up quality.

An example of technological pull is General Electric's rescue of its circuit breaker business.[7] This GE subsidiary employed various new technologies to reduce elapsed time between customer order and delivery to 3 days from 3 weeks. For example, six manufacturing facilities were consolidated into one, reducing inventory storage, handling, and shipping time. An automated design system with 1200 interchangeable parts was created to replace a custom-design process supported by engineers with 28,000 parts. With the new systems in place, a salesperson could enter specifications into a computer at the main office and have the order flow through the plant for assembly automatically. These technology shifts produced 1 full week of the 2 1/2-week reduction that the business was looking for.

And where did the other 1 1/2 weeks come from? Because factory floor decision making and problem solving were slowing order processing down in spite of the new technology, senior management cut all line supervisors and quality inspectors out of the plant's ranks. All middle-management functions—vacation schedules, quality management, work rules—were handed to the 129 workers, who were divided into teams of 15 to 20. "And do you know? The more responsibility GE gave the workers, the faster problems got solved and decisions made," said a GE manager.[8]

The results of fully utilizing the new technology by applying a different set of organizational rules to the workplace? A 2-month backlog of orders dropped to 2 days. Productivity went up 20 percent. Manufacturing costs went down 30 percent. The 3-day target was achieved. Examples such as these reflect major changes in the role of employees in firms. When supervision disappears, employees work in teams, and the discretion of employees increases at work, then labor-management relations must adapt. Management and labor must develop means of working together, since the old system of close supervision is disappearing.

Changing Aspirations of People

The new workplace is also being encouraged by marked differences in the attitudes of the "baby boom" generation and those of its parent generation toward the authority of institutions and the meaning of work in people's lives.[9] Today's work force is full of baby boomers accustomed to de-

---

[7]Brian Dumaine, "How Managers Can Succeed through Speed," *Fortune*, Feb. 13, 1989, pp. 54–59.
[8]Ibid., p. 56.
[9]D. Quinn Mills, *Not Like Our Parents* (New York: Morrow, 1987), pp. 99–117, describes a number of these value differences.

manding and receiving freedom from institutional controls, and many of them have been insisting on a greater role in managing their own lives both on and off the job.

For companies running their workplaces under traditional scientific management, the result has been difficulty in recruiting the "brightest and best" of the new workers. As one head of a manufacturing company noted, "Don't give us your best and brightest. Give us the people who are average or mediocre and don't know what they want to do with their lives."[10] (The results for this company were rapid turnover, low productivity, high supervisory costs, and lack of quick responsiveness.)

Many companies are now trying to avoid the trap of low education/low motivation/low productivity/high costs by searching for more imaginative employees. There are still many competent people in the work force and there are others in whom an investment in training will pay off. The problem is to find them. The new workplace, with its delegative management style and emphasis on teamwork, is itself an attraction to such workers.

Caterpillar Inc., for example, now encourages its blue-collar employees to comment on subjects like product engineering, workplace layout, and quality improvement. "Five years ago the foreman wouldn't even listen to you, never mind the general foreman or the plant supervisor," says Gary Hatmaker, a 37-year-old assembly line worker in a factory that makes the D10 and other giant tractors. "Now everyone will listen." When Hatmaker installs hydraulic hoses, he, not a spot-checking quality inspector, makes sure they are put on right. "I know how these things are supposed to fit," he says with pride.[11]

CHANGING WORKPLACE—CHANGING LABOR RELATIONS

From the broad analytical perspective, then, businesses are being impelled toward a nontraditional workplace by three forces. The first is today's business environment, with its demand for quick responsiveness to customers and cost control (the economic push). The second is the sudden availability of technology to support delayered, flexible organizations (the technological pull). The third is the desire of employees for greater involvement in their work (changing aspirations).

As the workplace changes, the styles of labor relations are undergoing significant change as well. In particular, the antagonism and confrontation that traditionally marked supervisor-employee interaction on the factory floor are being reduced and replaced with cooperation. Cooperation between supervisors and employees, on the one hand, demands different attitudes and behaviors from unions and managements, on the

---

[10]Robert D. Hershey, Jr., "As Labor Pool Ebbs," *New York Times*, Dec. 22, 1989, p. D1.
[11]Ronald Henkoff, "This Cat Is Acting Like a Tiger," *Fortune*, Dec. 19, 1988, pp. 71–76.

other. It is hard for managers to make unilateral decisions when employees have a say in managing the workplace. It is harder for shop stewards to disagree with management when employees are involved in decision making.

The new roles being pressed on unions and managements are creating uncertainty for union officers, managers, even the legal institutions that were created to umpire conflict between the two sides. Both unions and managements have become comfortable with antagonism. Even the National Labor Relations Board has been known to favor confrontation.[12]

Nonetheless, there are a number of different vehicles that have been explored as means for bringing cooperation to life in the new workplace. The earliest of these were quality of work life (QWL) programs that resulted from application of "humanist" management philosophies that emerged in the 1960s. More advanced ideas include those of "employee involvement" (EI) in various forms, the most radical of which nearly completely eliminate differences in the roles of managers and employees in the workplace.

Quality of Work Life Programs (QWL)

Douglas McGregor and others from what has been called the humanist school of management philosophy[13] suggested that the patterns of ritual distrust and confrontation observed in the "old" workplace could be traced to the lack of control over work experienced by workers in a machine-paced environment. The humanists felt that workers needed more control and participation in such workplaces to enhance their sense of satisfaction and ultimate productivity. To provide forums for participation, the humanists suggested concepts like job rotation, job enlargement, and flexible work schedules, ideas later combined into broad QWL frameworks.

Although it has its modern beginning in the 1960s, QWL has deep roots in American history. According to one authority, "Labor Management Cooperation to improve quality of products, worklife and the effectiveness of companies can be traced to the early 19th century."[14]

The term "quality of work life" itself has been attributed to Professor Louis Davis of the University of California at Los Angeles, who introduced it in 1972. QWL was used in separate contracts between Chrysler, Ford, GM, and the United Automobile Workers in 1973.

[12]Wilford Johansen, talk given on Mar. 25, 1987, reported in Bureau of National Affairs, *Daily Labor Report*, No. 63, Apr. 3, 1987, pp. A9–A10.
[13]Douglas R. McGregor, *The Human Side of Enterprise* (New York: McGraw-Hill, 1960).
[14]Henry P. Guzda, "Industrial Democracy: Made in the USA," *Monthly Labor Review*, 107:5, May 1984, pp. 26–33, esp. p. 26.

Five major components may be found in QWL programs today:[15]

1 *Work redesign* job enlargement, job enrichment, job rotation, autonomous work teams
2 *Pay restructuring* salaried work force, pay for knowledge, unit productivity sharing
3 *Time rescheduling* flexible work hours, compressed week, job sharing
4 *Performance development* positive reinforcement, problem-solving quality circles, middle-range planning, physical redesign
5 *Administrative review* information sharing, procedural change, training

Michael Maccoby, who has assisted in the development of QWL programs in several industries, has defined quality of work life as "a means to move from the bureaucratic-industrial model of scientific management with its fragmentation of jobs and hierarchical control, to a flexible, broadly skilled participative team. This is a more effective way of managing market-driven technoservice work while protecting the rights and dignity of employees."

Employee Involvement

The term "employee involvement" (EI) first appeared in a 1979 agreement between Ford and the UAW. EI goes beyond QWL to address fundamental issues of power and control over work in the workplace. It represents a "next stage" in an ongoing evolution of management thought, holding that the more engaged people are in their work, the better they perform it.

Scientific management assigned control over work to management to ensure that factory machines ran efficiently; the evolution of unions forced a sharing of this control through ritualized conflict. QWL advocates suggested that this conflict could be mediated in a more cooperative fashion. EI's proponents suggest that workers will perform still more effectively if the two sides ultimately cease to be separate entities. In the very broadest examples of EI, therefore, the definitions of supervisor and employee blur as employees effectively become "self-managing" to a great degree.

Different vehicles for implementing EI have been tried. Among them are committee structures, quality circles, employee ownership programs, and, particularly in Europe, comanagement arrangements (see Chapter 12).

[15]Michael Maccoby. "Helping Labor and a Firm Set Up a Quality-of-Work-Life Program," *Monthly Labor Review,* 107:3, March 1984, pp. 28–32, esp. p. 29; and Walter J. Gershenfeld, "Employee Participation in Firm Decisions," in M. M. Kleiner et al., eds., *Human Resources and the Performance of the Firm* (Madison, Wis.: Industrial Relation Research Association, 1987), p. 125.

Employee Involvement through Committee Structures

In 1987, seven steel companies and the Steelworkers union established participation teams in which workers and management, with union involvement, attempt to improve productivity and working conditions.[16] A survey conducted by the Federal Mediation and Conciliation Service found unions and management generally satisfied with these joint labor-management committees and their approach to workplace management.[17]

Joint labor-management committees have appeared in other settings as well. Generally they are organized to deal with a specific subject. The two most frequently mentioned by management are safety and job evaluation. The problems of alcohol and drug abuse also receive attention from joint committees in some companies, involving a cooperative program by which a system is established for early identification of these problems, for referral of the employee for proper treatment, and for a concerned follow-up. Other areas of effort include quality of work life, labor relations training for supervisors and stewards, profit sharing, and start up of new facilities.[18]

The auto industry has made effective use of joint union-management committees in training employees. Unfortunately, much of the training provided is to enable those who have lost their jobs to find employment elsewhere in the economy.

Quality Circles

Quality circles are teams or committees of employees that meet before or after the work day to discuss production problems and to try to work out solutions. They are a significant device for involving workers in the improvement of the quality and efficiency of production. Conceived by American management theorists but long largely ignored in the United States, quality circles were adopted by Japanese manufacturers with excellent results. Under the pressure of Japanese competition many American firms are now using the circles.

But American unions have often opposed them. In part, because the circles meet before or after the regular work day and the workers are on their own time, unions have insisted that either employees be paid or the circles be abolished. Also, because the circles attempt to improve quality and pro-

---

[16]Aaron Bernstein and Matt Rothman, "Steelmakers Want to Make Teamwork an Institution," *Business Week*, May 11, 1987, p. 84.

[17]Bureau of National Affairs, *Daily Labor Report*, No. 107, June 5, 1987, pp. A8–A9.

[18]Joseph A. Loftus and Beatrice Walfish, eds., *Breakthroughs in Union-Management Cooperation* (Scarsdale, N.Y.: Work in America Institute, 1977); and National Center for Productivity and Quality of Working Life, *Directory of Labor-Management Committees* (Washington D.C.: U.S. Government Printing Office, 1978).

ductivity, unions have feared that jobs will be lost as a result, and so have opposed quality circles.

Nonunion companies, however, have made considerable use of the circles as a device for employee involvement. (They are also using employee committees to address such issues as health-care cost containment and the provision of child care for employees.) But a controversy has developed as to whether or not the circles and committees are legal. It happens this way. As we will see in Chapter 9, American law prohibits an employer from dominating and assisting a labor organization. A labor organization is any group of employees that meets for the purpose of dealing with the employer about wages, hours, or conditions of work. The origin of these provisions lies in the "company unions" of the 1920s by which employers tried to prevent their employees from joining independent unions (see Chapter 2).

A quality circle is a group of employees that deals with management about matters affecting conditions of work, including, for example, job design, task assignments, and pace of work. Also, an employee committee that is concerned with child care or attendance or health benefits is also considering conditions of work. When an employer dominates such a circle or a committee (i.e., sets it up and controls its agenda) and assists it (i.e., provides space and financial support for its meetings), then the employer is violating the law.

Cases of this nature are now making their way through the legal system of the United States. In 1988 an Indiana electronic components manufacturing firm, Electromation, set up employee "action committees" to address several issues of concern to employees including absenteeism, the plant no-smoking policy, and an attendance bonus program. Then the Teamsters union started to try to organize the plant's employees. The company withdrew management representatives but allowed employees to continue to meet in the committees. The Teamsters union complained to the National Labor Relations Board (see Chapter 8), and an administrative law judge ruled that the company had violated the law. The company appealed to the National Labor Relations Board itself, where the case has been under review.

In another such case a Phoenix, Arizona, attorney and a Southern Methodist University professor together brought suit against the general counsel of the NLRB (see Chapter 8) to compel it to issue a complaint charging that the grievance procedure established by a nonunion firm was an illegal company-dominated union. The grievance plan provides that an aggrieved employee will be assisted by trained counselors from the company's human resources department. The issue is whether this sort of assistance given employees by the company is an illegal company-dominated labor organization.[19]

---

[19]"Federal Judge in Arizona . . .," Bureau of National Affairs, *Daily Labor Report*, No. 174, September 1991, pp. A-5ff.

In yet another instance, company-sponsored employee-management safety committees at a DuPont plant passed out T-shirts, coolers, and driving gloves to employees. Receiving a complaint, the government has charged that these activities constitute a violation of federal law. Handing out gifts changed the terms and conditions of employment at the plant, without negotiations with the union in the plant.[20]

Decades ago Polaroid Corporation established employee committees that were then involved in company decision making. When in the early 1990s the government challenged the committees as illegal employer-dominated unions, the company disbanded them.[21]

Nonunion employers express concern that if quality circles, employee committees, and grievance procedures are determined to be illegal in nonunion companies, then quality, safety, and employee relations improvements needed in nonunion companies will be effectively blocked by the law. Those who oppose the companies' views reply simply that if a company wants to use such devices, it can simply recognize a union to represent its employees. Then, they add, the employees will have independent representation, not a company-dominated situation.

Empowered Teams

The most recent and dramatic of initiatives that change the workplace are those in which supervisory responsibilities are delegated to teams of employees. The teams have the authority to make decisions about work and to take action without review by management. It is this authority which distinguishes an empowered team from a committee or a quality circle. Committees and quality circles make recommendations to management, which then decides whether or not to implement them. Empowered teams have the authority to decide and act on their own. The teams are, of course, responsible to management for the success or failure of their actions.

Companies in many different industries are experimenting with empowered teams. They permit a firm to reduce its numbers and levels of supervision and management, and so obtain cost savings. Teams have also helped to improve quality and responsiveness to customers.

However, many managers fear that the firm will lose control of its business activities if employees work without close supervision. And many unionists believe that in empowered teams employees do more work for the same compensation as before, and so oppose them. Despite opposition,

[20]Janet Novak, "Make Them All Form Unions," *Forbes*, May 11, 1992, p. 174.
[21]Paul Hemp, "Labor Department Closes Book on 'Hallmark' Polaroid Committee," *Boston Globe*, June 20, 1992, p. 11.

however, empowered teams are becoming a more common aspect of our business landscape.[22]

Employee Involvement through Employee Ownership

Employee ownership of the stock of a corporation is often espoused as a means for increasing employee involvement. By 1987 there were about 9 million workers covered by employee ownership plans (ESOPs), which were favored by American tax laws until 1988. Some half million are believed to be in firms more than 50 percent owned by employees.[23] Both union and nonunion companies utilize employee ownership, but there have been no charges that it is illegal for a nonunion firm.

The record of ESOPs in encouraging involvement has been mixed. At one employee-owned firm a study showed local union leaders alternatively cooperating and contesting with managers over a 4-year period. Strikes have even occurred at plants owned by the workers. This is because even with worker ownership, managers remain and sometimes get into disagreements with employees and unions.[24]

Employee Involvement through "Comanagement"

Union officers are sometimes placed on a company's board of directors as a mechanism for enhancing cooperation. This is legally required in Germany (see Chapter 12), but unusual in America. In America there have been voluntary experiments with such representation, but they are very few in number.[25] Most American union leaders and top managers seem to believe that for a union leader to serve on a company's board involves too much of a conflict of interest. Labor-management cooperation in America doesn't go that far.[26] In the most publicized such experiment the president of the United Auto Workers Union sat for several years on the board of directors of Chrysler Corporation, then was not returned to the board when his term expired.

---

[22]D. Quinn Mills, *Rebirth of the Corporation* (New York: John Wiley and Sons, 1992).

[23]Joseph Raphael Blasi, "The Sociology of Worker Dimensions and Participation," *Proceedings of the Industrial Relations Research Association*, Dec. 28–30, 1984, pp. 360–369. See also "Employee Stock Ownership Plans," *Employee Relations Law Journal*, 11:1, Summer 1985, pp. 89–105; and Robert D. Hershey, Jr., "Including Labor in the Division of Capital," *New York Times*, Sunday, Apr. 24, 1988, p. E5.

[24]Tove H. Hammer and Robert N. Stern, "A Yo-Yo Model of Cooperation," *Industrial and Labor Relations Review*, 39:3, April 1986, pp. 337–349.

[25]Tove H. Hammer et al., "Worker Representation on Boards of Directors," *Industrial and Labor Relations Review*, 44:4, July 1991, pp. 661ff.

[26]Charles S. Loughran, "Union Officials as Corporate Directors," *Directors and Boards*, 10:1, Fall 1985, pp. 24ff. Also see Robert Kuttner, "Blue-Collar Boardrooms," *The New Republic*, 3:674, June 17, 1985, pp. 18–23.

The Record of QWL and Employee Involvement

Employee involvement initiatives have been most prevalent in the auto industry in America as firms try to increase quality and cut costs in order to compete with Japanese and European rivals. EI programs are credited with having been of value in many instances, but in some they were inadequate—perhaps because of too limited commitment by management or labor or both. For example, in 1990 the federal government published a report lauding an EI program between General Motors and the United Auto Workers at the company's Willow Run plant.[27] In February 1992, General Motors announced that the Willow Run plant would be closed. In this instance employee involvement did not save workers' jobs, and it would be understandable if employees were to feel that they had been misled.

Employee involvement also involves risks for management, however. At the core of employee involvement is the willingness of management to share much more information about costs, scheduling, productivity, and quality. At Ford, for example, management estimates that it now shares with production workers information reserved only a few years ago for managers at the level of the assistant plant manager. But a careful study has shown that releasing sensitive information to workers can reduce the firm's profits, either through production workers' taking advantage of it to gain pay increases or potential leakage of the information to competitors.[28] This finding suggests that employee involvement programs do not always work to the benefit of the firm, as is sometimes suggested by their opponents. Further evidence of the evenhandedness of these programs is provided by a study that finds QWL efforts associated with fewer accidents, reduced absenteeism, fewer grievances, and fewer quits.[29]

FROM QWL AND EI TO COOPERATION

How do QWL and EI programs contribute to cooperative relationships between labor and management? Because of diversity in the programs, an example may be helpful.

An automotive parts manufacturer with a history of acrimonious labor relations established a joint labor-management committee at the recommendation of the Federal Mediation and Conciliation Service. The firm had been through three changes in management in 8 years and was threatened with closing when its major customers announced a 10 per-

---

[27]Denise Hoyer Tanguay and Gregory E. Huszczi, *Forging a Partnership through Employee Involvement: The Case of the GM Hydra-Matic Willow Run Plant and UAW Local 735 Joint Activities,* BLMR No. 130 (Washington, D.C.: U.S. Department of Labor, Bureau of Labor-Management Relations, 1990).

[28]Morris M. Kleiner and Marvin L. Bouillon, "Information Sharing of Sensitive Business Data with Employees," *Industrial Relations,* 30:3, Fall 1991, p. 490.

[29]Stephen J. Havlovic, "Quality of Work Life and Human Resource Outcomes," *Industrial Relations,* 30:3, Fall 1991, p. 469.

cent reduction in the amount they were willing to pay for the firm's products.

The QWL committee meets each month for a frank discussion of problems at the plant, including quality control, cleanliness, safety, and productivity. The company shares all pertinent information about the financial status of the company with union representatives on the committee. The program has helped keep the firm operating and has improved relations between labor and management.[30]

Improved relations are not all that QWL programs envisage. In fact, Maccoby's definition cited above goes beyond attitudes and relationships to changes in the nature of jobs and increased participation for employees in what have been until now management responsibilities.

The distinction between these aspects of what is now called QWL was noticed early. Writing in 1965, Raymond Miles made a distinction between human relations and human resources as practiced by management. The former has as its key objective to make members of the organization "feel a useful and important part of the overall effort." The human resources concept, in contrast, is that "many decisions may actually be made more efficiently" at other than managerial levels.[31]

In the human resources or participative management model, employees participate in management via committees that consider business problems and opportunities. In the general discussion of worker participation in management, three types are distinguished. In America, employees usually participate via teamwork in labor-management committees and sometimes through broad responsibilities in their own jobs. In Europe, participation is often through work councils, which are established as required by law. Finally, participation may occur indirectly via union or employee representatives who are members of a company's board of directors. In some European countries worker representation on supervisory boards is required by law. In the United States there is no such legal requirement, and union membership on boards is uncommon.[32]

The little research that exists about reactions of union members to such cooperative efforts as QWL programs shows lukewarm support. One study published in 1988 of national data collected 11 years earlier showed that wages and benefits and internal communications between a union and its members were far more important than QWL issues (such as interest in

[30]Bureau of National Affairs, "Auto Supplier," *Daily Labor Report,* No. 203, Oct. 19, 1984, pp. A-2, A-3.

[31]Raymond E. Miles, "Human Relations or Human Resources?" *Harvard Business Review,* 43:4, July–August 1965, pp. 148–155, esp. pp. 149, 151.

[32]Alan Gladstone and Rose Marie Greve, "Workers' Participation in Management: A Framework for Discussion," *Labor and Society,* 9:3, July–Sept. 1984, pp. 217–234. See also William Foote Whyte, "Worker Participation: International and Historical Perspective," *Journal of Applied Behavioral Science,* 19:3, August 1983, pp. 395–407.

the job) in causing members to be satisfied with their unions.[33] A more recent study based on surveys of union members in four different bargaining units in the same local union found that those who participated in QWL programs were less likely to view the programs as threats to the union and were also more loyal to the union than those union members who hadn't participated in the programs.[34]

A NEED FOR COOPERATION

Today the workplace institutions of unions and managements, and the relationship between them, are demonstrating some substantial ability to adapt to change and to cope with an increasingly competitive environment. Still, there are major challenges. As the former research director of the United Steelworkers has said, "Unless unions can help preserve jobs, they will lose members. Workers want jobs with good benefits and satisfactory working conditions—but in any case they want jobs. If unions are associated with strikes and noncompetitive practices that cause plants to go out of business, ordinary working people are not likely to be union enthusiasts."[35]

As was noted earlier, many U.S. companies have come under intense economic pressure. In many instances the pressure was from foreign competitors. In others it was a result of deregulation, which removed government protection and permitted other firms to compete. In still other cases pressure came from domestic nonunion companies that grew to challenge existing unionized firms.

The question has arisen as to why U.S. firms seem unable to compete successfully with those from abroad. Many reasons are offered, including what many Americans view as unfair support from foreign governments for their own companies. But another critical element is said to be the low productivity and poor quality of American work. And for these problems American labor relations are held partly to blame.

The conflict-ridden state of labor-management relations in many American industries can be contrasted with the more highly productive and quality-conscious work abroad that seems to emerge from cooperative labor-management relations. It is said that American management and

[33]Jack Fiorito, Daniel G. Gallagher, and Cynthia V. Fukami, "Satisfaction with Union Representation," *Industrial and Labor Relations Review,* 41:2, January 1988, p. 294. See also Thomas A. Kochan, Harry L. Katz, and Nancy R. Mowen, "Worker Participation and American Unions," in Thomas A. Kochan, ed., *Challenges and Choices Facing American Labor* (Cambridge, Mass.: MIT Press, 1985), pp. 271–306.
[34]Adrienne E. Eaton et al., "The Impact of Quality of Work Life Programs and Grievance System Effectiveness on Union Commitment," *Industrial and Labor Relations Review,* 45:3, April 1992, pp. 521ff.
[35]Ben Fischer, "Labor Takes a Look at Itself," *Los Angeles Times,* Mar. 29, 1985, part II, p. 6.

labor are too busy blaming each other for declining competitiveness to get together to improve the situation.

A dramatic example of the significant impact that employee attitudes can have on competitiveness is offered by two General Motors plants. Each has about 5400 employees; each assembles automobiles. But one has considerable automation and more than 150 robots. The other uses much older and less effective technology. However, the quality levels and efficiency of production are much higher in the older plant, because employee-management cooperation is much advanced over the newer and better-equipped plant.[36]

Hence, one part of the solution to the problems of the U.S. economy is being sought in increased labor-management cooperation. In April 1988 Secretary of Labor Ann McLaughlin called for labor and management to improve American competitiveness and productivity. She criticized what she called "some astoundingly slow thinking on the part of American management about new initiatives in labor-management cooperation." She added that the United States "can no longer afford the dubious battle of adversarial relations." She cited a recent Gallup Poll in which a majority of the executives surveyed singled out workers as the primary cause of quality problems and called the prevailing attitude disclosed in the survey a "ridiculous" one.

"Workers are not part of the problem. They're the source of the solution," McLaughlin said. "Nobody knows more about a job, and how to improve it, than the person who's doing it. . . . Those firms that have established cooperative relationships have made dramatic productivity gains, because everyone involved has a stake in the success of the enterprise," the labor secretary explained.

McLaughlin cited another survey in which only 9 percent of American workers felt they would benefit from their companies' increased productivity compared to 93 percent of Japanese workers interviewed in a similar survey. "Productivity growth depends on a shared interest between management and labor," she concluded.[37]

Despite the labor secretary's apparent pessimism, there were grounds to believe that U.S. competitiveness was already increasing in 1988. The value of the dollar had declined so much that the volume of U.S. exports was rising quickly. There seemed a greater recognition among management, unions, and workers of the need to increase productivity, cut costs, and improve quality. By 1991 the World Economic Forum in Geneva, Switzerland, rated the countries of the world for competitiveness. The United States ranked second behind Japan.[38]

[36]Gregory A. Patterson, "Two GM Auto Plants . . . ," *Wall Street Journal,* Aug. 23, 1991, pp. 1ff.
[37]"Labor-Management Cooperation Stressed," Bureau of National Affairs, *Daily Labor Report,* No. 70, Apr. 12, 1988, p. 12.
[38]IMD International, Lausanne and World Economic Forum, Geneva, Switzerland, *World Competitiveness Report,* 1991.

Competitiveness remained a major issue in American politics, but the primary concern was competitiveness vis-à-vis Japan. The disappearance of the issue as the American trade balance improved could already be glimpsed. What then of the increased cooperation between labor and management that economic adversity had helped foster? Would it disappear as competitiveness improved? Possibly not. Managers, union leaders, and workers have learned a hard lesson about the consequences of letting productivity and quality slide. Cooperation to remain competitive may become a long-lasting feature of labor relations in U.S. companies.

In the attempt to respond to the threat of foreign competition and growing nonunion competition at home, unions and management are moving toward a more cooperative relationship. Pushed into the background are the contentious labor-management relations of the recent past. Brought to the forefront are joint labor-management efforts to provide employment security to union members and business success to companies. Thrust back on their own resources by a period of economic adversity, unions and management in many instances are responding with enhanced cooperation.

In these relationships the parties are able to resolve disagreements without major confrontations; the union shares responsibility for productivity, and the company shares responsibility for employment security and pay equity for employees.

Unions are learning how to help companies faced with intense competition to survive and prosper, yet continue to represent the interests of their members. It takes leadership qualities to do this: the ability to see potential, the willingness to take risks, and the desire to communicate with and persuade others of the opportunities.

Creating a trusting relationship between union and management requires recognition of the obligations that the other side has, a feeling that the other side shares certain basic values, and the personal integrity of the individuals involved. Progress on these dimensions is being made in American labor-management relations. It is good for labor, good for management, and good for the nation. Perhaps in response, the long slide in public approval of unions (which peaked in 1957 at 76 percent and reached bottom in 1977 at 48 percent) has reversed itself and by 1991 had climbed back to 62 percent.[39]

An excellent example of the effort of union and management to forge a cooperative relationship so that both can prosper in a very competitive world is provided by Magma Copper Company and the council of unions representing its employees. A joint union-management cooperation council developed in 1989 a statement of principles, as follows:

> Our vision is to create an economically viable, profitable company that provides job security . . . .

[39]*AFL-CIO News*, 36:9, Apr. 29, 1991, p. 14.

. . . the company and the union mutually recognize the link between productivity and job security. . . .

The company and the union recognize the role of collective bargaining but
are committed to moving more concerns into the area of joint problem solving. . . .

Each party must be open and honest about [its] objectives.[40]

The agreement provides for important modifications of traditional ways
of handling labor-management relations in America. For example, work redesign teams made up of management and labor representatives have been
set up to increase productivity and settle such questions as overtime scheduling and work assignments. The contract was reached only after both the
union and the company invested considerable amounts of time and money
in meetings to forge the new approach. If either side wants to change the
agreement in 1997, when it expires, a new agreement will be negotiated by
the problem-solving team. If they fail to reach agreement, a neutral person
will establish wages and benefits for a 2-year period. If at the end of that
period the terms of a new contract cannot be agreed upon, it will be canceled.[41]

Another example involves Ameritech, a large midwestern phone company, and the Communication Workers of America. In a presentation the
chairman of Ameritech pointed to the recommendations of the Labor-
Management Forum, a group of union and company leaders, who have
called on management to accept the validity of unions and an enlarged
role for worker and union participation in certain decisions of the enterprise. In return, labor has an obligation to work with management to improve the economic performance of businesses.[42]

Yet another example, which adds construction to the examples of manufacturing and service given above, involves the building trades unions and
a large construction firm, the Bechtel Construction Company. Under the
agreement reached in late 1992 the unions and the firm will cooperate on
many of the less traditional areas of the bargaining process, including
quality, safety, and compensation for injury. "Our aim," said a union
spokesperson, "is to develop a structure so that we can more effectively
find solutions to problems."[43]

[40]"100 Percent Commitment to Cooperation," American Productivity and Quality Center,
Houston, Texas, *Case*, Special Edition, February 1991.

[41]Marj Charlier, "Magma Copper's Workers Approve Pact," *Wall Street Journal*, Oct. 23,
1991, p. A-2.

[42]William L. Weiss, chairman of Ameritech, and Morton Bahr, president of the Communication Workers of America, Distinguished Lecture Series, School of Labor and Industrial Relations, Michigan State University, 1989.

See also, Peter Lazes et al., "Xerox and the ACTWU: Using Labor-Management
Teams to Remain Competitive," *National Productivity Review*, 10:3, Summer 1991, pp.
339–349.

[43]Sharolyn A. Rosier, "Building Trade, Bechtel Sign Innovative Pact," *AFL-CIO News*,
Oct. 12, 1992, p. 4.

WHY SOME UNIONS AND MANAGEMENTS RESIST COOPERATION

The above examples show that involvement and cooperation can be attained through a wide variety of vehicles. There is, however, still resistance to such efforts, in spite of their importance to the economy. Consider the experience of General Motors' Saturn Corporation subsidiary.

In 1985 GM decided to create a subsidiary, called Saturn Corporation, to develop, produce, and sell a new automobile. As part of the Saturn experiment, GM management agreed to let Saturn try a more cooperative approach to managing its laborers. Saturn and the United Automobile Workers worked out an agreement calling for very close cooperation in running the company. It begins: "We believe that all people want to be involved in decisions that affect them. . . ."

The contract calls for minimizing "differentiation among people," so that there are no time clocks for workers, no special parking places, entrances, identification, or dining rooms for management, and only one salary and benefits system (though rates of pay differ). Each Saturn employee belongs to a team or work unit. Management and union officials sit on a strategic advisory committee to top management and an operations committee. Decision making is by consensus. ("Consensus" is defined as joint problem solving, and, "voting, trading, and compromise are not part of this process.")

The agreement is controversial. Management-oriented observers say the union is too heavily involved in management decisions. For example, in 1991 the union was demanding from the company considerable involvement in quality control.[44] An employer's group went to the NLRB to try to block it, charging that it constitutes illegal support by the company for the union. The NLRB's general counsel, however, refused to file a complaint.[45] Some union-oriented observers have insisted that Saturn "is part of a nationwide corporate anti-union offensive."[46]

Saturn Corporation is certainly the most extensive partnership between a union and a corporation in America. Most business decisions are made by management and union together. The success of the partnership depends on an educational process that makes union leaders business-oriented persons and helps managers understand how employees feel about the business and the direction in which it is going. The Saturn Corporation has produced very high quality automobiles, but costs are also high and it doesn't seem that the firm has yet been profitable.[47]

[44]David Woodruff, "At Saturn, What Workers Want Is . . . Fewer Defects," *Business Week*, Dec. 2, 1991, pp. 117–118.
[45]John Hoerr, "The NLRB Strikes a Blow for Worker Participation," *Business Week*, June 16, 1986, p. 36.
[46]Andrew Remes, "The Saturn Contract," *Economic Notes*, 54:4–5, April–May 1986, pp. 12–13.
[47]Richard G. Lefauve and Arnoldo C. Hax, "Managerial and Technological Innovations at Saturn Corporation," *MIT Management*, Spring 1992, pp. 8–19.

A key question to be asked about this experience is a simple one: Why are some partisans of both management and labor very resistant to it?

Managers often resist allowing employees greater participation in responsibilities in an enterprise, stating in public that their employees lack the necessary expertise or loyalty to handle sensitive information. Underneath these more public concerns lie some less articulated but just as real fears about the loss of their own personal power or privileges, or even, in some cases, fears about continued employment.

Unions also have strong reasons for resisting participation, stating in public that it may only be a device to get employees to work harder for equal or less pay.[48] "Despite its public stance of cooperation, management appears to have all the bargaining table leverage—and is using it," wrote Michael Verespej, who entitled an article "The Illusion of Cooperation."[49] Underneath these concerns lie fears regarding the apparent loss of a union's role in the workplace.

Managers say that cooperation gives too much authority to the workers and so exposes the company to potential business trouble. Union proponents say cooperation gives too much authority to the company and so threatens the safety and livelihood of the employees. Yet Saturn produces a high-quality car, and employee health and safety are often not well protected in the traditional adversarial relationship between management and labor. In a lengthy study of the American chemical industry's safety record—one that recognizes that record as often inferior to that in Japan, where union and management are more cooperative[50]—the authors commented: "Management is unwilling to accept labor as a legitimate partner and share the information and decision-making power required to develop or sustain a truly effective and meaningful partnership. Labor, in turn, sees itself in a fight for survival in a hostile environment and continues to rely on traditional bargaining and political tactics rather than pursuing strategies that demonstrate its willingness and ability to sustain a partnership role."[51]

Union resistance to involvement programs also stems from management's increased resistance (since the 1940s) to organizing campaigns. AFL-CIO Secretary-Treasurer Thomas Donahue made the point in a speech in 1983:

> The position by employers is responsible for the current difficult labor-management climate in this country and continuing inability of the labor movement to

[48]See, for example, Michael Verespej, "The Illusion of Cooperation," *Industry Week*, Aug. 19, 1991, pp. 13–20.

[49]Ibid., p. 13.

[50]Richard E. Wokutch and Josetta S. McLaughlin, "The U.S. and Japanese Work Injury and Illness Experience," *Monthly Labor Review*, April 1992, pp. 3ff.

[51]Thomas A. Kochan, John C. Wells, and Michal Smith, "Consequences of a Failed Industrial Relations System: Contract Workers in the Petrochemical Industry," *Sloan Management Review*, 33:4, Summer 1992, p. 87.

embrace wholeheartedly some writers' views of "labor-management cooperation. . . . It is very hard to think about cooperating with the bear while you are
wrestling with him.

The fact is that the employers of this nation want to have labor-management
cooperation only after we have wrestled with them and pinned their shoulders
to the mat. At about that point when the referee counts to two, and just before
he tolls the final verdict, they start preaching "cooperation" to us and to all jour-
nalists and economists who will listen . . . .[52]

Yet many of the academics and neutrals in labor-management relations
who urge union and management to cooperate to improve workers' jobs
and enhance job security via more productive enterprises also urge management to recognize the legitimacy of unions.[53] And unions, on their part,
are urged to be selective in their view of worker participation.

Rather than adopting a uniform position for or against worker participation . . .
union leaders need to think . . . about the conditions that must exist for worker
participation to be in the interest of their members. . . .[54]

Some experts also point to the difference in interests that exists—labor's
interest being to raise pay levels and management's to improve profits—as
fundamental reasons against cooperation and involvement in the workplace, even insisting that both sides are better served by conflict.[55] Yet
there would seem to be no logically compelling reason to conclude that because interests differ the relationship must be adversarial. Diverse interests
can be accommodated by cooperation.

Others point to the adversarial nature of the legal system itself, in which
much modern labor relations tradition has been established, as a potential
source of conflict. Recently, however, the legal environment has been
changing.

The courts and the NLRB have been enlarging the range of management decisions about which there is no obligation to bargain with a union.
In particular, matters relating to the basic strategy of a company, including
what businesses to be in, plant closures, and transference of work, need
not be discussed with a union. Despite the direction of legal decisions,
however, some companies are choosing to include the unions in discussions of exactly this kind in order to gain union and employee support for
the company's efforts. Perhaps surprisingly, considering the efforts of some
unions to compel companies to bargain about such matters via litigation,
other unions will not participate when offered an opportunity. In these situations union leaders apparently fear that participation in management

[52]Thomas R. Donahue, "American Unions Continue Struggle as Worker's Voice," *Trowell*
(International Union of Bricklayers and Allied Craftsmen), Winter 1983, pp. 23–25.
[53]Wayne Horvitz, quoted in Bureau of National Affairs, *Daily Labor Report*, No. 237, Dec.
8, 1983, pp. A-10, A-11.
[54]Thomas A. Kochan, Harry C. Katz, and Nancy R. Mowen, *Workers Participation and
American Unions* (Kalamazoo, Mich.: W. E. Upjohn Institute, 1984).
[55]See Barbara Reisman and Lance Compa, "The Case for Adversarial Unions," *Harvard
Business Review*, 63:3, May–June 1985, pp. 22–24ff.

deliberations will coerce them into silence or overwhelm them with detail.[56]

Only under conditions of economic stress and renewal do these basic fears of unions and management seem to moderate to the point where involvement and cooperation become less of a threat. As the United States is currently in such a period, we may expect to see many more experiments in involvement and cooperation.

One study of labor-management cooperation in the 1920s stresses the importance of economic difficulties in forcing companies to work with unions.[57] The economic difficulties of the 1920s stimulated cooperation; the greater difficulties of the 1930s stimulated conflict; the intermediate problems of the late 1960s, 1970s, 1980s, and 1990s have again stimulated cooperation.

For the most part American employers and unions do not cooperate with one another on broad aspects of the labor-management process. Management does not make great efforts to provide employment security for employees, and employees, fearful for their jobs, resist productivity and quality improvements. Also, employees in most U.S. firms have little or no participation in decision making, no matter how directly it affects them. Studies show that people will not buy into corporate goals unless they've had some say in the decisions most directly affecting them. This is true of both managers and employees. But in the new workplace these things are beginning to change—and with it is coming a new set of issues and opportunities for labor-management relations in America.

CHAPTER SUMMARY

The American workplace is changing. A dominant mode of organizing work came out of the early 1900s—Taylorism, or "scientific management"—but today that system is being challenged by new forces that are economic, technological, and human in nature.

Among the most important workplace innovations arising from the interplay of the new forces and the old are quality of work life (QWL) and employee involvement (EI) schemes. The purpose of these programs is to encourage workers to become more involved in their job, to reduce their sense of alienation, and to improve productivity.

EI and QWL programs require both management and labor to replace confrontation with a more cooperative relationship. This is sometimes dif-

[56]Robert B. McKersie, "Union Involvement in Entrepreneurial Decisions of Businesses," in Thomas A. Kochan, ed., *Challenges and Choices Facing American Labor* (Cambridge, Mass.: MIT Press, 1985), pp. 149–166. See also Henry H. Perritt, Jr., "Aspects of Labor Law that Affect Labor Management Cooperation in the Railroad and Airline Industries," prepared for the U.S. Department of Labor, Villanova School of Law, Feb. 19, 1988.

[57]Sanford M. Jacoby, "Union-Management Cooperation in the United States: Lessons from the 1920s," *Industrial and Labor Relations Review*, 37:1, October 1983, pp. 18–33.

ficult because of institutional rigidities and the history of conflict between the two sides.

QUESTIONS FOR THOUGHT AND DISCUSSION

1 What are the basic features of the old workplace? Of the new? How do they differ?
2 How have workplace changes affected labor relations?
3 What are quality of work life programs?
4 What is employee involvement?
5 Do you think that labor-management cooperation is a good idea? Why? Why does the federal government promote labor-management cooperation? Do you think it should?
6 What objections might labor raise to cooperating with management? What objections might management raise to cooperating with labor?

SELECTED READING

Carnevale, Anthony Patrick, *America and the New Economy: How Competitive Standards Are Radically Changing American Workplaces* (San Francisco: Jossey-Bass, 1991).

Mills, D. Quinn, *Rebirth of the Corporation* (New York: John Wiley, 1991).

Parker, Mike, and Jane Slaughter, *Choosing Sides: Unions and the Team Concept* (Boston: South End Press, 1988).

Shuster, Michael H, *Union-Management Cooperation: Structure—Process—Impact* (Kalamazoo, Mich.: W. E. Upjohn Institute for Employment Research, 1984).

U.S. Department of Labor, Bureau of Labor-Management Relations and Cooperative Programs, *Labor-Management Cooperation: 1990*, BLMR No. 142 (Washington, D.C.: U.S. Government Printing Office, 1991).

Walton, Richard E., *Up and Running: Integrating Information Technology and the Organization* (Boston: Harvard Business School Press, 1989).

Zuboff, Shoshana, *In the Age of the Smart Machine: The Future of Work and Power* (New York: Basic Books, 1988).

CHAPTER 5

HUMAN DIVERSITY IN THE WORKPLACE[1]

DIVERSITY IN THE WORKPLACE

Labor-management relations are about the needs of people. In the United States the people who work have been changing. For many years America had a relatively young, predominantly white, male work force, most of whom were married with nonworking spouses and children. Today, minorities, women, and two-income families with and without children predominate. As a result, both unions and managements are having to meet the needs of a more highly diverse work force. The new demographics have brought new issues to the fore: child care, parental leave, flexible hours, new occupational ailments, safety concerns, sexual harassment, and employee assistance programs to supplement or replace the more traditional group medical and pension plans of the past.

Unions in particular have been grappling with the impact of diversity in their ranks. Under American law unions have obligations to represent everyone in a bargaining unit and to use democratic procedures to maintain representation rights; hence, they must effectively operate as coalitions of divergent groups in setting negotiating agendas and managing their internal activities. The large industrial unions were reasonably successful in building broad coalitions between those of different occupations and skill levels in such basic industries as steel and coal; the diverse work force challenges them to manage differences in race, age, and family situations, too.

The new demographic fissures have added complexity to the union coalition-building process. "There is a sharply different and more complex

[1]G. Bruce Friesen contributed substantial portions of this chapter.

work force," wrote the head of the AFL-CIO's organizing department, "one that docs not automatically assume that unions arc the answer to its problems. Today's workers do not typically have a homogeneous set of problems that a union organizer can readily identify and use to develop a mass movement in the workplace, resulting in an election victory."[2]

An Older Work Force

Figure 5-1 shows that the median age of the U.S. population has been rising since 1970 and that this will continue through the 1990s. While the population and work force are not identical, they are similar enough so that it can be said that in today's America, as the population ages, so does the work force.

The reasons for this aging trend can be found in declining U.S. birthrates after 1964. Between 1946 and 1964 inclusive, about 4 million babies were born each year, adding 70 million people to the population in the so-called postwar baby boom. As birthrates fell after 1964—the so-called baby bust—declining numbers entered the population, and the median age began to rise. Immigration may offset some of this tendency, of course, if the average age of immigrants is lower than that of the existing population. To a small degree, this seems to be the case.

Because birthrates fell many years ago, the number of young people available to take jobs for the first time has fallen greatly. This has created a shortage of workers in some areas of the country, leading to the continued employment of people after they might have retired. Also, the importance of the older work force has been magnified because many employers have expressed dismay at the lack of employment-related skills of many young

[2]Charles McDonald, "U.S. Union Membership in Future Decades," *Industrial Relations,* 31:1, Winter 1992, p. 19.

FIGURE 5-1   The U.S. population is growing older (median age). (*Source:* U.S. Bureau of the Census, "Current Population Reports," Series P-23, No. 138, Table 2-9.)

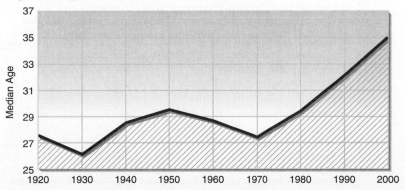

people. As a result, many people who have retired are being brought back into the work force as consultants to their previous employers or in entirely new employment situations.[3]

The effects of aging on the work force will be a powerful factor in the future. Many social and economic policies ranging from access to affordable medical care to pension policy reform to mandatory retirement will be shaped by the growing number of older workers. Not surprisingly, the concerns of older workers have begun receiving more attention from unions and employers. An especially important concern of this group involves discriminatory dismissals by companies that believe older workers are less productive and cost more than younger ones.[4]

An Increasing Number of Minorities, Women, and Immigrants

Tables 5-1 and 5-2 show that the ethnic and racial diversity of the work force is increasing. Table 5-1 shows the working-age population and work force in 1975, 1990, and projected to 2005. The nonwhite share increases over the 35-year span from 11.7 percent to an estimated 16.6 percent. The table also shows that the nonwhite share of growth in the labor force is even larger.

Just how significant will women and minorities be in the labor force in the year 2000? Table 5-2 indicates that by 2005 women will compose 47.4 percent of the total labor force and minorities (including minority women) 16.6 percent. This is the continuation of a trend that has been in the making for a long time. In 1960 the percentage of women in the work force stood at just 33 percent.

[3]Arnold Packer, "Skills Shortage Looms," *Human Resources Magazine*, April 1990, pp. 38–40. See also Joan L. Kelly, "What Went Wrong?" *Personnel Journal*, 69, January 1990, pp. 42–55.
[4]See American Association of Retired Persons, *Workers Over 50* (Washington, D.C.: AARP, 1988).

TABLE 5-1   NONWHITES ARE A GROWING SHARE OF THE WORK FORCE

	(In millions)		
	1975	1990	2005
Working-age population (16+)	157.3	193.6	223.6
Nonwhite share (%)	12.0	14.7	17.4
Labor force	93.8	124.8	150.7
Nonwhite share (%	11.7	14.1	16.6
Labor force increase			
Over previous period (%)	NA	33.0	20.8
Nonwhite share (%)	NA	21.6	28.0

Source: U.S. Bureau of Labor Statistics, *Monthly Labor Review,* November 1991, pp. 15, 33, 37.

TABLE 5-2   THE GROWING EMPLOYMENT SHARE OF WOMEN AND NONWHITES

	1960	1970	1980	1990	2005
Labor force (in millions)	69.6	82.8	106.9	124.8	150.7
% Female	33	38	43	45.3	47.4
% Nonwhite	NA	11	12	14.1	16.6

Source: U.S. Bureau of Labor Statistics, *Monthly Labor Review,* November 1991, p. 33.

Other data indicate that most new entrants to the work force between 1985 and 2005 will be nonwhite or female and/or immigrants. Only 15 percent of the net work force growth are likely to be native-born white males, fewer than the total of immigrant males and females.

Immigrants are increasing as an element of the labor force and are also coming from different places than in the past. Table 5-3 shows the area of birth of immigrants to the United States from 1961 through 1985. The proportion of immigrants from Europe fell dramatically from 37 percent to 11 percent over that time, and immigrants from Asia rose from 13 percent to 48 percent.

These data demonstrate the increasing diversity of the U.S. work force. With diversity will come the need to accommodate people in a variety of living situations. For example, in 1960, only 11 percent of women with children under the age of 5 were working; by 1990 that percentage was well above 60 percent. Further, 70 percent of working women have children between the ages of 6 and 17.[5] This is the basic reason why employers and unions are now spending time and attention on policies for childcare, flexible hours of work, and parental leave of absence.

[5]F. E. Winfield, *Work and Family Sourcebook* (New York: Panel Publishers, 1988).

TABLE 5-3   IMMIGRANTS, BY COUNTRY OF BIRTH: 1961–1985

Area of Origin	(In millions)					
	1961–1970	% of Total	1971–1980	% of Total	1981–1985	% of Total
Total	3.322		4.493		2.864	
Europe	1.239	37	.801	18	.322	11
Asia	.445	13	1.634	36	1.376	48
North America	1.351	41	1.645	37	.886	31
South America	.228	7	.284	6	.184	6
Africa	.039	1	.092	2	.077	3
Other	.019	1	.057	1	.020	1

Source: U.S. Immigration and Naturalization Service, *Statistical Yearbook,* various issues.

An Increasing Need for Education

At the beginning of this century the average worker had completed only 8 years of school. Only 20 percent of the work force held white-collar jobs. Most people earned their living as farmers or as craftspersons and laborers. Today, the average worker has completed more than 12 years of school and more than half of the work force is employed in a white-collar occupation of one type or another.[6] These trends are not changing.

Table 5-4 indicates that the occupations of the future will require more education than those of the past. Table 5-5 suggests that language, math, and reasoning skills will become still more significant in the workplace. For many employers and unions, therefore, the future will be one in which they will find themselves working with more highly educated employees, who are likely to be both more attuned to their personal circumstances and more articulate in demanding attention to them.

The Effect of Changes in the Work Force

The changes that have been occurring in the characteristics of the U.S. work force are profound ones. The married white male, whose job supported himself, a nonworking spouse, and their children, was the mainstay of the work force for many decades. Meeting the needs of this traditional employee for wages sufficient to support a family unit, health-care coverage for dependents, pension plans with benefit provisions for spouses, vacations, and protection against periods of unemployment was a principal objective of collective bargaining between unions and employers.

While traditional workers continue to receive attention from unions and management, they have long been a minority in the workplace. At the end of World War II about 40 percent of the work force could be described as "traditional." In 1960, it was about 30 percent. By 1992, only 12 percent

---

[6]Clark Kerr, "Introduction," in Clark Kerr and Jerome Rosow, eds., *Work in America: The Decade Ahead* (New York: Van Nostrand Reinhold, 1979), pp. ix–xxvii.

TABLE 5-4   THE OCCUPATIONS OF THE FUTURE WILL REQUIRE MORE EDUCATION

	Current jobs	New jobs
Total	100%	100%
8 years or less	6%	4%
1–3 years of high school	12%	10%
4 years of high school	40%	35%
1–3 years of college	20%	22%
4 years of college or more	22%	30%
Median years of school	12.8	13.5

Source: Bureau of Labor Statistics, Hudson Institute.

TABLE 5-5   FAST-GROWING JOBS REQUIRE MORE LANGUAGE, MATH, AND REASONING SKILLS

	Current jobs	Fast growing	Slowly growing	Declining
Language rating	3.1	3.8	2.7	1.9
Math rating	2.6	3.1	2.3	1.6
Reading rating	3.5	4.2	3.2	2.6

Source: Hudson Institute.

could be so described. The largest group by far in the 1992 work force consisted of people living in multiearner (i.e., two-income) families.

Changing demographics imply changing needs and aspirations on the part of the work force. For example, fringe benefits such as medical care offered to dependents of employees through collective bargaining are of limited value in a household where there are already two jobs: both wage earners will more than likely be covered under separate employer plans. Such households are more likely to require maternity and paternity leave and more effective child-care arrangements than presently exist. Flextime, which permits employees to adjust working schedules to take care of family members, is also a crucial benefit since it gives them the opportunity to care more effectively for their families.

Unfortunately, the history of the 1970s and 1980s has shown that neither managements nor unions are particularly effective in accommodating change in the existing patterns of the workplace. The slowness with which companies and unions are addressing family issues has brought political pressure to bear on Congress and the state legislatures to force the workplace to change through legislation.

Changing demographics have also brought new urgency to issues of fair treatment, long-standing concerns of labor-management relations. Among the most important concerns are equal opportunity for women and minorities, including discrimination and affirmative action, and for white males the question of reverse discrimination. When much of the work force growth is projected to come from the ranks of women and minorities, it is increasingly important for companies and unions to establish and enforce unbiased recruitment and promotion processes that eliminate discrimination against women and minority males while preventing reverse discrimination against white males from rising in its place. On a closely related topic, such traditions of the unionized workplace as seniority systems and grievance procedures are also being challenged for their effect in perpetuating past discrimination. These and related issues are discussed below.

EQUAL EMPLOYMENT—WHAT DOES IT MEAN?

The interaction between discrimination, affirmative action, and reverse discrimination might best be described by reference to both the "ideal" and "real" worlds. The philosophical ideals underpinning U.S. society hold that employees should be hired *only* on the basis of their potential to contribute to the employer, and once on the job, to be managed, compensated, and promoted based *only* on job performance.

In a world where hiring, compensation, and promotion decisions are based solely on potential and actual contributions by individuals to businesses, there can be no discrimination based on personal characteristics or attributes, no need for affirmative action to counter such discrimination, and finally, no complaints from individuals not favored under affirmative action programs about reverse discrimination practiced against them in the name of affirmative action in favor of others. Out in the real world, however, gender, skin color, national origin, ethnic background, religious beliefs, sexual orientation, and physical handicaps, among other attributes with little or no bearing on ability, have been used to exclude people of particular backgrounds from the workplace. Other attributes such as age, while often indirectly linked to an individual's ability to perform a job, have been used much more heavily than warranted to justify termination or refusal to hire.

U.S. businesses and unions have had difficulty in avoiding discrimination in the absence of formal law, and, accordingly, Congress and the courts have been forced to act. Congress has weighed in with Title VII of the Civil Rights Act to set forth statutory law in this area with special impact on labor relations; and in response to suits by blacks and women's groups, U.S. courts have found employers and unions, together and separately, discriminating against minority groups and/or women.[7]

Firms involved in discrimination suits have sometimes settled cases in advance of decisions by agreeing to certain conditions. At other times the courts have fashioned remedies to rectify past discrimination and prevent it in the future. Courts have sometimes established preferential hiring lists for minorities or have virtually taken control of apprenticeship programs to see that minorities are recruited and trained for skilled jobs. Courts have also forced employers to adjust their personnel practices to include written documentation of performance criteria.

Discrimination suits have led to substantial awards of back pay. For example, Norman Drake, a satellite controller for Lockheed Missiles and Space Company, complained to his superiors that he was being harassed by fellow workers because he was black. His supervisor transferred him to a job as security guard. Drake filed suit against Lockheed for retaliating against him for complaining, and a California jury awarded him a significant sum of money from the company.[8]

---

[7]Arthur B. Smith, Jr., "The Impact on Collective Bargaining of Equal Employment Opportunity Remedies," *Industrial and Labor Relations Review,* 28:3, April 1975, pp. 376–394.

[8]*Drake v. Lockheed Missiles and Space Co., Inc.,* California Superior Court, No. 656788, August 2, 1991 (see Bureau of National Affairs, *Daily Labor Report,* No. 155, Aug. 12, 1991, p. A-8).

Various groups affected by discrimination have urged the government and industry not to stop at prohibiting discrimination. They have argued that both the continuing effects of past discrimination (e.g., the failure of minorities to seek certain jobs because they've been denied work there before) and patterns of "institutionalized" discrimination (established practices that have the effect of excluding minorities and women) should be acted against by creating obligations for employers to seek out, identify, and employ minorities and women where there have been few before. These obligations go beyond nondiscrimination and so are labeled affirmative action.

The federal government and many state and local governments have established affirmative action policies. Some levels of government, including the federal level, have also imposed obligations of an affirmative nature on privately owned companies that do business with government. Employers with federal government contracts of $50,000 or more and 50 or more employees are obligated to prepare and maintain a written affirmative action program. The plans provide goals and timetables by which the employers will attempt to seek out minority and other target-group persons for hiring into job opportunities or for promotion, training, and similar advancement. Failure to meet the affirmative action obligations may cause companies to be barred from receiving federal contracts. (Table 5-6 shows the elements of a typical business affirmative action plan.)

There has been controversy in the law concerning discrimination. In 1971, the U.S. Supreme Court in *Griggs v. Duke Power Company* established that an employment practice having a disproportionate negative impact on racial minorities or women violates Title VII of the Civil Rights Act of 1964 unless the employer can demonstrate that the practice is significantly related to effective job performance or is supported by business necessity. Thereafter the courts decided that a plaintiff (the person or group bringing suit) need show no more than that an imbalance of employment exists in order to compel the defendant to show that its policies were related to job performance or business necessity. But as more conservative jurists were appointed by several Presidents, the courts took a different tack and decided that plaintiffs must show some discriminatory intent before a defendant had to prove job performance or business necessity. Also, more conservative courts, including the Supreme Court, in the 1980s severely limited the financial awards that plaintiffs could receive when they won discrimination cases.

These court decisions lessened the burden on employers of showing a relationship between job performance and business necessity and increased the burden on plaintiffs to show discriminatory impact. The Supreme Court reinforced this trend with *Wards Cove*, a decision in which the majority opinion held that "a plaintiff must demonstrate that it is the application of a specific or particular employment practice that has created the disparate impact under attack. Such a showing is an integral part of

TABLE 5-6   ELEMENTS OF AN AFFIRMATIVE ACTION PLAN

- Establishment of quantitative (statistical) objectives for representation of women and minorities in all jobs, levels, and functions
- Inclusion of equal opportunity issues in regular management training
- Specific training in equal opportunity, including:
  (a) Knowledge-focused training (i.e., legal issues, company policy, benefits, changes)
  (b) Attitude-focused training
  (c) Behavior-focused training (i.e., training dealing with managerial expectations of behavior with an emphasis on behavior changes in recruiting, selecting, training, work assignment, and career development of employees)

the plaintiff's prima facie case in a disparate-impact case suit under Title VII."[9]

Then Congress passed and the President signed into law the Civil Rights Act of 1991 intended to undo the string of court decisions and to lessen the legal burden on plaintiffs by returning to the original interpretations of the Court in the early 1970s. Potential financial awards to successful plaintiffs were also enlarged.

In a sense the Civil Rights Act of 1991 had little to do with affirmative action, focusing instead on discrimination. But opponents of the law insisted that it would create quotas for women and minority groups, rather like affirmative action—although proponents of the goals and timetables that characterize affirmative action plans insist that they are not quotas. Since quotas were not required, how did it happen that opponents saw them in the law? They argued that the only way an employer could protect itself from a lawsuit alleging discrimination was to use quotas to balance its work force by gender and race. In the 1992 presidential campaign some candidates denounced the new law as abandoning the ideal of a society free of any discrimination and instead establishing quotas in favor of certain favored groups.

There has also been important litigation about affirmative action plans. Do affirmative action plans actually discriminate in favor of minorities and women and against white males? If so, how should an employer and the union representing its employees act? A white male who was employed at a plant in the South raised this issue in a lawsuit that found its way to the Supreme Court.

The United Steelworkers (the union) and the company had negotiated a new on-the-job training program to replace a prior-experience requirement for entry to better-paying craft jobs in the plant. The plan's objective was to achieve a representation of blacks in craft jobs equal to the 39 percent representation of blacks in the labor force in the community surrounding the plant. To this end, union and company agreed to admit blacks and whites

[9]Bureau of National Affairs, *Current Developments,* No. 30 (Washington, D.C.: 1990), p. A9.

for training on a one-to-one basis. At the time the plan was implemented only 1.83 percent of the skilled crafts workers in the plant were minority group members. A white male who failed to be admitted to the program challenged its ratio for white-black admissions.

The Supreme Court found that even though neither the company nor the union had been found guilty of discriminating against minorities in regard to the skilled jobs, nonetheless, where goals and timetables for the purpose of eliminating racial imbalance were voluntarily adopted by the union and the company, the affirmative action plan was legal. In this case the Court seemed to say that goals and timetables for minority advancement were not illegal reverse discrimination, even though white male employees might thereby be passed over for training and promotion.[10]

The institutionalization of affirmative action led members of demographic groups not favored under such plans to question how their rights are being affected. Where all current employees at firms have been hired under effective equal employment standards and the nonfavored are denied advancement due to application of affirmative action criteria, reverse discrimination may be present.

Reverse discrimination occurs when a minority, woman, or member of another affected group is hired, promoted, or transferred in preference to another person, including a white male, solely on the grounds of gender, race, or age of the individual who receives the advantage. The Supreme Court has apparently held, in a decision involving preferences given to racial minorities in admission to medical school (the *Bakke* decision) that preference given solely on the basis of race is illegal.[11] This decision, among others, has been used to suggest that when an employer gives preferential treatment solely on the basis of gender, race, or other factor, he or she is in danger of violating the law.

The foregoing precedents on discrimination, affirmative action, and reverse discrimination suggest that in hiring practices, Congress and the courts are trying to steer between protecting the rights of minorities and females and those of the remaining members of the work force, who could be subjected to discrimination as past and present practices are "corrected."[12] What behavior by an employer or a union is illegal, what sort of evidence is necessary to prove guilt, and what kinds of remedies can be created by the courts are issues that are in continuing evolution.[13]

Racial minorities and women are not the only groups protected from discrimination under federal law. Table 5-7 lists the major protected groups and the principal statutes (and dates) that protect them. Many of

---

[10]*United Steelworkers of America v. Weber*, 443 U.S. 193 (1979).

[11]*Bakke v. Regents of the Univesity of California*, 438 U.S. 265 (1978).

[12]Kenneth T. Lopatka, "Developing Concepts in Title VII Law," in L. J. Hausman et al., eds., *Equal Rights and Industrial Relations*, pp. 31–70.

[13]Arthur B. Smith, Jr., "The Law and Equal Employment Opportunity: What's Past Should Not Be Prologue," *Industrial and Labor Relations Review*, 33:4, July 1980, pp. 493–505.

these statutes, or other policies of the federal government, require not only that an employer not discriminate against members of these groups, but that actions be taken to remedy continuing effects of past discrimination.[14]

Why is this continuing concern for protecting the rights of minorities still with us after nearly 30 years of the Civil Rights Act of 1964? The answer is that despite progress in racial relations in the United States, there is still serious ongoing discrimination.

In 1984, for example, the Michigan Civil Rights Commission issued a report describing in detail 9 years of harassment suffered by the first black person to be hired into a skilled job at a Michigan steel plant. The welder was ostracized and threatened and lived in constant stress and fear. When he complained to management about his treatment, he was told that nothing could be done about it. A complaint to government finally brought relief via state equal employment opportunity laws.[15]

EQUAL OPPORTUNITY AND LABOR-MANAGEMENT RELATIONS

Discrimination is not just a feature of hiring and promotion decisions. Several of the mechanisms that unions and management use to govern the workplace under their collective bargaining agreements have also been questioned; among them are seniority systems and grievance procedures.

Seniority Systems

Seniority systems are designed to reward workers on the basis of their length of service to an employer, or in some cases, to an industry (where firms have merged and the unions involved have organized across specific employers). Rewards attached to seniority usually include preferential ac-

---

[14]Phyllis A. Wallace, *Black Women in the Labor Force* (Cambridge, Mass.: MIT Press, 1980).
[15]*Michigan Dept. of Civil Rights v. Firestone Steel Products*, Nos. 12190-EM and 15378 EM, May 1984.

TABLE 5-7 PROTECTED GROUPS UNDER FEDERAL ANTIDISCRIMINATION LAW

• Persons over 40 years of age	Age Discrimination in Employment Act (1967)
• Racial and ethnic minorities	Equal Pay Act (1963)
	Civil Rights Act (1964)
	Equal Employment Opportunity Act (1972)
• Women	Civil Rights Act (1964)
	Equal Employment Opportunity Act (1972)
	Education Act Amendments (Title IX) (1972)
• Handicapped	Rehabilitation Act (1973), Americans with Disabilities Act (1990)
• Vietnam-era veterans	Vietnam-Era Veterans Readjustment Assistance Act (1974)
• Mentally Ill	Americans with Disabilities Act (1990)

cess to better paying or physically less taxing jobs, longer vacation periods, higher pay, promotions in grade in a current job, enhanced security from layoff, and even pension rights and recognition.

In theory at least, most industrial jobs are designed so that workers of varying ages and backgrounds can perform them to a similar standard. Once an initial period of training or apprenticeship is past, it should make little difference how much time an employee has put in at the job. Why then is the 20-year veteran typically worth so much more than a 2-year recruit to an employer? For an answer to this question, we must delve into the area of seniority systems. Such systems have evolved for various reasons.

First, they are a powerful device with which to cement worker loyalty. As benefits related to seniority accrue over the years (especially pensions), workers find it increasingly difficult to leave. Should they choose to do so, they would have to start accumulating seniority elsewhere; most careers are usually not long enough to gain complete seniority with two different employers.

From a company's perspective, loyalty in the work force has many benefits. One, it sharply reduces turnover among experienced employees, retaining this valuable knowledge for the future. Two, as workers become invested in an employer, they begin to change behavior to protect their investment. It is no accident that workers with larger investments in seniority rights are less prone to support employee activities, such as strikes, that run contrary to an employer's economic interests than are their less heavily invested colleagues; the economic interests of the two groups often differ substantially, which weakens worker solidarity and affects bargaining outcomes. Evidence to support this contention can be found in the recent history of the U.S. airline industry, where many "two-tier" wage structures were established in the early 1980s. Such schemes sought to reduce airline costs by cutting wages for future hires into selected jobs while maintaining an existing wage scale for those already in these jobs—who would have seniority over incoming colleagues. Union memberships often approved these schemes with large favorable votes.[16]

Second, seniority systems have become a powerful means of allocating the benefits negotiated through collective bargaining. In this guise, the systems are a vestige of the more paternalistic era of employment relations that prevailed before the advent of Social Security, Medicare, and unemployment insurance. From the 1930s through the 1950s, as bargaining for protection against layoffs, paid vacations, and job classification schemes took place, it was frequently agreed that older workers should be favored over younger workers. Why was this so?

One, older workers typically had more obligations to protect (children, spouses, mortgages) than did their younger colleagues. Their years of toil

---

[16]See "Human Resource Management at American Airlines," Harvard Business School case N1-491-097, p. 4, for a discussion of two-tier wages at American Airlines.

on behalf of the company were worth consideration as well. (This argument resonated with managers, as similar practices favored them.)

Two, seniority-linked benefits often appeared less costly than wage increases in the short run for firms with relatively youthful workers that were experiencing increasing productivity. Under such conditions, a firm could quite rationally bargain for small-percentage wage increases while offering large-percentage increases in seniority-linked benefits that would not come due until years later. Further, most U.S. firms found their seniority-linked obligations less than anticipated as many older or retiring workers died relatively young and without fully tapping their benefits.

Today, with longer average life spans and stagnant productivity, this economic rationale for seniority-linked benefits has disappeared. Such programs have even become a financial burden, leading sometimes to blatant age discrimination in the form of termination before the vesting of pension or other seniority-linked benefits.

In one such recent case, the United Steelworkers won a $415 million settlement from Continental Can Company. Continental Can had allegedly created a scheme to lay off workers just before they qualified for company pensions in an attempt to minimize benefit costs. By shifting work between various plants and forsaking customer orders, the firm was able to close key plants for "lack of work," thereby creating conditions for layoffs under its union contracts. Once layoffs were complete, plants would be reopened with new customer orders and workers with less seniority hired to do the work.[17]

Third, and perhaps most importantly, seniority offers a simple basis for both sides to distribute bargained benefits with minimal disruptions in the workplace. It is difficult to dispute the day a person began work, although changing job classifications, plant consolidations, or partial closures can make even establishing seniority complicated at times.

It is worth noting that there are other bases on which to award benefits. One might be productivity; another might be production output. However, such bases could present difficulties to unions, managements, or both. Consider the situation of a union reviewing a move to productivity from seniority as the basis for awarding benefits. It would have to agree to allow individual workers or teams to receive what might appear to be long-term "rate-busting" bonuses. Consider the situation of a management team reviewing a move to productivity; it would have to work harder at appraising individuals and work teams fairly in situations where the "facts" could never be as objective as seniority criteria. Both unions and managements gain relative ease of administration and some benefits from seniority-based systems, while both sides have to work much harder for potentially divisive results from a productivity-based system.

[17]Eric N. Berg, "$415 Million Settlement on Pensions, *New York Times*, Jan. 3, 1991, p. D1.

Seniority systems by their nature perpetuate past discrimination in hiring or promotion practices. Older employees (often disproportionately white and male) continue to receive disproportionate protection from layoff and preferential access to other benefits by virtue of their positions on the seniority list, while younger employees (often disproportionately women and minorities) become the first subject to layoff under the "reverse seniority" clauses in many union contracts. In 1977 the U.S. Supreme Court considered the degree to which Title VII required changes in seniority systems to counter such discrimination.

The specific case involved practices under collective bargaining agreements in the trucking industry. In that industry it has been common for many years, going back before passage of the Civil Rights Act in 1964, to have separate bargaining units for city and over-the-road, or long-distance, drivers. The over-the-road drivers ordinarily get better pay and benefits. As a result of the dual structure, a driver who wished to transfer from city driving to an over-the-road job had to give up his or her entire seniority and start at the bottom of the list in the over-the-road unit.

The U.S. government and a minority group challenged this practice, arguing that it perpetuated a pattern of racial discrimination by causing minority employees in city-driver units to stay out of largely nonminority over-the-road units so as not to give up their seniority. The Court, however, found that dual seniority was not illegal, even though it did, indeed, perpetuate past discrimination. The Court reached this conclusion by finding that when it passed the Civil Rights Act in 1964, Congress had intended to leave existing seniority systems untouched, even "where the employer's pre-Act discrimination resulted in whites having greater existing seniority rights than [blacks]."[18]

In 1982, the Supreme Court broadened immunity for bona fide seniority systems (those without an intent to discriminate). It ruled that the exemption from Title VII of the Civil Rights Act was not limited to systems in place prior to the effective date of the statute. Instead it extends to seniority systems established since the act.[19]

In 1984, Memphis, Tennessee, attempted to ignore a bona fide seniority system in its agreement with its firefighters' union to preserve the employment of black firefighters with less seniority than their white counterparts. The Supreme Court determined that Memphis had done so illegally, saying that only individual identifiable victims of discrimination are entitled to special consideration, not classes of people.[20]

On the other hand, maintenance of separate seniority lists for blacks and whites in the same firm has been found illegal, and separate depart-

---

[18]*T.I.M.E.—D.C., Inc. v. United States, International Brotherhood of Teamsters v. United States* 431 U.S. 324 (1977), and *East Texas Motor Freight System, Inc. v. Rodriguez,* 97 S. Ct. 1891 (1977).
[19]*American Tobacco Company v. Patterson,* No. 80-1199, Apr. 5, 1982.
[20]*Fire Fighters Local 1784 v. Stotts,* 1984.

mental seniority rules, under which blacks are confined to certain departments, have in some cases been found to restrict minorities to lower-paying jobs. Rearrangement or merger of seniority districts in the basic steel industry to eliminate this has been an important result of rights legislation.[21] In subsequent cases, the Court has permitted unions and firms to negotiate affirmative action plans to override seniority when determining who should be laid off if a company has to reduce its work force.[22]

Grievance Procedures

A further set of problems with which the courts are now grappling in the context of discrimination is the effect of civil rights legislation on collective bargaining in the area of grievances. Grievance procedures lie at the heart of union-management relations in the workplace, and challenges to them raise fundamental issues of fairness in representation. (See Chapter 20 for a thorough discussion of grievance procedures.)

For example, if minority employees decide to disregard a grievance process in the collective bargaining agreement and strike in a dispute over alleged discrimination, does the law protect them from discipline by the employer? A federal appeals court has said that it does: "Concerted activity regarding racial discrimination enjoys a special status." The court was reading the Civil Rights Act with the National Labor Relations Act to reach this conclusion. But the Supreme Court disagreed. If the union was fairly representing minority employees, it said, then they could not go outside the grievance procedure with impunity.[23]

EQUAL COMPENSATION

The Logic of Comparable Worth

Women receive about 65 percent of the earnings men do from their jobs in the United States;[24] this number has increased by an average of about 1 percent per year over the last 5 years. (See Chapter 18 for further informa-

---

[21]David Ziskind, "Retroactive Seniority: A Remedy for Hiring Discrimination," Industrial Relations Research Association, *Proceedings of the Spring Meetings*, May 1976, pp. 480–489.

[22]*Tangren v. Wackenhut Services, Inc.*, 81 U.S. 1540 (1982).

[23]*Emporium Capwell Co. v. Western Addition Community Organization*, 420 U.S. 50 (1975).

[24]James P. Smith and Michael P. Ward, *Women's Wages and Work in the Twentieth Century* (Santa Monica, Calif.: Rand Corp. Publications Division, 1984). According to these authors, the increase in the percentage of women's hourly wages as a percent of men's from 60 to 64 percent (1980 to 1983) was the largest and swiftest gain in this century. See also Bureau of National Affairs, *Daily Labor Report*, No. 121, June 22, 1984, p. A-8, where Janet Norwood, commissioner of the Bureau of Labor Statistics, describes the trend of women's relative pay as up; and U.S. Bureau of the Census, *Statistical Abstract of the United States 1987*, 107th ed. (Washington, D.C.: U.S. Government Printing Office, 1986).

tion on this topic.) Two factors are at work in explaining the difference between male and female rates of pay.

First, women sometimes receive less pay for the same jobs than men. This is illegal under both the Equal Pay Act and the Civil Rights Act, Title VII, and appears to be declining in frequency as the laws are more closely respected.

Second, women have been concentrated in jobs and careers that often pay less than those of men. It is often argued that the pay differential reflects the choice by women of careers that permit them to move readily in and out of the labor force for reasons having to do with the bearing and raising of children. As women entered and left the work force, they lost training opportunities, promotions, and the accumulation of seniority rights. Also, many young women, believing that they would work only a short time before starting families, did not look for jobs with long-term potential or did not undertake the lengthy training required for careers in the professions to the degree men did.[25]

The result has been an uneven distribution of women and men in occupations. In 1982 women made up approximately 43 percent of all employees in the United States.[26] However, they were concentrated in occupations paying less than those that men dominated. For example, clerical workers were 78 percent female, service workers were 52 percent female, teachers were 67 percent female, and textile workers were 72 percent female.

During the 1970s the American labor force grew rapidly and women made up 57 percent of the growth. The most striking shift in the distribution of the sexes among occupations occurred among managers, where women held 18.5 percent of managerial positions in 1970 and 30.5 percent of managerial positions in 1980.[27] During the 1980s a small further increase in the proportion of managerial positions held by women occurred.

Despite this progress, however, most of the occupations in which women are disproportionately represented are among the lower-paying jobs in the country. The result is that, on average, women earn considerably less than men.[28] Some studies show that as much as 35 to 40 percent of the wage gap between men and women is due to occupational differences.[29] Historical evidence suggests that movement of black women,

[25]Nancy S. Barrett, "Women in the Job Market: Occupations, Earnings and Career Opportunities," in Ralph E. Smith, ed., *The Subtle Revolution: Women at Work* (Washington, D.C.: The Urban Institute, 1979), pp. 31–62.

[26]Earl F. Mellor, "Investigating Earning Differences in Weekly Earnings of Women and Men," *Monthly Labor Review*, 107:6, June 1984, pp. 20–23.

[27]See N. F. Rytina and S. Bianchi, "Occupational Reclassification and Distribution by Gender," *Monthly Labor Review*, 107:3, March 1984, pp. 11–17 (esp. pp. 14 and 13) for the data cited in the text.

[28]Edward P. Lazear and Sherwin Rosen, "Male-Female Wage Differential in Job Ladders," *Journal of Labor Economics*, 8:1, p. S106.

[29]Mary C. King, "Occupational Segregation by Race and Sex, 1940–1988," *Monthly Labor Review*, April 1992, pp. 30ff.

in particular, into jobs they hadn't previously held has accounted for much of the improvement in their earnings compared to other Americans since 1940. About this the authors of one major study comment: "Black women's improved [relative and absolute] economic status after 1940 was largely due to decreases in racial discrimination by occupation and industry."[30]

Are women's jobs paid less than men's, on average, not because of differences in jobs or skill content of the work, nor because of working conditions, nor because of availability or nonavailability of persons who can do the work, but simply because most of the people in the jobs are women? This is the question behind the controversial theory of comparable worth. Increasingly, women's organizations insist that there is discrimination that must be remedied, and some judges have found merit to their arguments.

According to the theory, jobs should be compensated according to their value to the business, not according to who holds them. Thus, in firms where floor sweepers (predominantly male) are paid more than clerks (predominantly female), the rates of pay should be realigned—clerks might then actually receive more money than sweepers. As a practical matter, it often happens that male sweepers in manufacturing plants are represented by unions and receive higher pay than clerical workers, who are often not unionized, but it is hard to argue that the sweepers' jobs are more highly skilled, more valuable to the company, or more difficult to fill than the clerks' jobs.

Comparable worth becomes legal doctrine when it is the basis for assertions that jobs in which women predominate are undervalued because women are in those jobs and that this is discrimination in violation of the law. When this has been put to federal courts, the courts have given contradictory answers. Some federal courts have dismissed comparable worth as being without merit. But others have not agreed.

In August 1980, the Third Circuit Court of Appeals ruled that gender-based wage discrimination is illegal under Title VII of the Civil Rights Act even when the jobs in question are different from one another. The suit involved was brought not by a women's organization per se, but by the International Union of Electrical Workers against Westinghouse.[31]

Other litigation has involved public employees. In a case involving some 15,000 employees of Washington State, the Ninth Circuit Court of Appeals in effect required the state to equalize pay among men and women in jobs requiring equivalent skill, education, and effort, even where the jobs were different.[32] Other precedents have not been as favorable. The Supreme Court held that nursing teachers complaining that they were paid less than other

[30]James S. Cunningham and Nadja Zalokar, "The Economic Progress of Black Women," *Industrial and Labor Relations Review*, 45:3, April 1992, pp. 540ff.

[31]*IUE v. Westinghouse*, 631 F.2d 1094 (1980).

[32]"Washington State Employees to Get First Comparable Worth Pay Raises," Bureau of National Affairs, *Daily Labor Report*, No. 114, June 13, 1984, pp. A6–A7.

teachers at the University of Washington had to show they were victims of gender discrimination, not simply paid less because of market forces.[33]

In recent years a few localities have adopted comparable worth legislation. Opponents of such laws argued that if pay was raised in jobs dominated by women, then the number of such jobs would decline, causing unemployment. They also asserted that work would be shifted from jobs affected by comparable worth legislation to other jobs, further reducing employment in women-dominated jobs. So far the evidence doesn't support these arguments. For example, San Jose, California, was one of the first cities in the nation to implement comparable worth wage adjustments. A study of the consequences found that employment went up in the affected jobs, and that employment was not shifted to nonaffected jobs.[34]

It appears that litigation and legislative contests over comparable worth are continuing. In November 1984, six U.S. senators and representatives asked the General Accounting Office to study the federal pay system to determine if there is pay equity among jobs held predominantly by women and among those held predominantly by men. About 40 percent of the 2 million federal workers are women. Women earn an average of 60 percent of men's earnings in federal jobs.[35] This action by Congress is significant because an issue like comparable worth often gets significant push to action at the federal level, which sets informal standards for other employers, both state and local governments, and private companies.

Family-Oriented Benefits

It was noted earlier that the largest group of workers in the American work force in 1986 lived in dual-income families. This phenomenon arises from various economic and social factors.

First, women have been increasingly liberated from doing only traditional and nonpaid work in the home.[36] It is now deemed socially acceptable for women to seek careers in all occupations and at all levels in society, although some barriers—the so-called glass ceiling—still remain to be breached in some executive suites.

Second, as American productivity growth has stagnated in the past 15 years, real standards of living have remained at roughly their 1973 averages, adjusted for inflation, across the economy. For large parts of America, the illusion of further gains in material prosperity since have been generated by increasing numbers of second incomes provided by working spouses.

[33]Stephen Wermiel, "High Limit," *Wall Street Journal*, Nov. 27, 1984, p. 12.
[34]Shulamit Kahn, "Economic Implications of Public-Sector Comparable Worth: The Case of San Jose, California," *Industrial Relations*, 31:2, Spring 1992, pp. 270ff.
[35]Bureau of National Affairs, *Daily Labor Report*, No. 226, Nov. 23, 1984, pp. A8–A9.
[36]Barbara R. Bergmann, *The Economic Emergence of Women* (New York: Basic Books, 1986).

The benefit needs of dual-income families are considerably different from the needs of a "traditional" employee. For example, both earners usually qualify for health coverage when it is offered by both employers; neither needs the spousal option offered by most plans. Both earners will generate pension credits—assuming both employers offer pension plans—and neither should need the spousal options available in qualified pension plans. What dual-income families do need, and often do not get, are basic "family benefits"; child-care plans, flexible parental leave policies, and, particularly for women, recognition for both men and women that being a parent can require them to be away from work for periods as long as several years to get their children off to a healthy and happy start in life.

America is still coming to grips with the problems posed by the children of dual-income families. Social policy appears to have escaped from the trap of forcing women to become stay-at-home mothers, only to fall short of the goal of supporting parents in their attempts to raise children while they retain their jobs. The problems of such children, and their even worse-off single-parent counterparts, are legion. Accounts of poorly paid and badly motivated babysitters losing children to accidents occur in the newspapers nearly every day. Child abuse in poorly regulated and maintained day-care and child-care centers is of national proportions. The alienation and lack of social skill building that such children experience from lack of contact with their parents promises future difficulties for the public school and justice systems.

Many employers are reluctant to get out in front in providing child care and flexible parental leave, arguing that it is not their responsibility to spend the billions of dollars needed to handle a social problem. The federal government, on the other hand, points to excessive deficits in existing programs and fails to move beyond limited tax credits for child-care expenses, leaving the matter in the hands of various state governments.

As of 1989, only about one-third of employees working in medium and large private businesses were covered by benefit plans that included unpaid maternity leave. Paid parental leave was uncommon, with only about 2 percent of employees surveyed in 1988 having paid maternity leave, and 1 percent having plans calling for paid paternity leave.

Protection from Sexual Harassment at Work

One of the most difficult problems that many women (and also some men) face in the workplace is the unwelcome attention of coworkers or supervisors. For many years the problem was largely hidden. But in recent years several surveys, and a generally more candid public discussion of such matters, have brought it into the open. In particular, an allegation by a former employee of sexual harassment by Supreme Court nominee Clarence Thomas was the subject of hearings before a panel of the U.S. Senate in the summer of 1991 and brought the issue dramatically before the American public.

In the spring of 1980, the Equal Employment Opportunity Commission issued guidelines specifying that sexual harassment at work is, in many instances, a violation of Title VII of the Civil Rights Act. Specifically, unwelcome sexual advances become a matter of illegality when the employee's acquiescence is a condition of employment or becomes a basis for employment decisions by the employer or the employer's agent. The guidelines apply to men as well as to women, although it is expected that the primary application will be to women. Complaints by injured parties can be made to the commission, and if the matter cannot be worked out with the employer, the commission may go to court against the employer. In subsequent years many American employers adopted policies against sexual harassment. More recently other nations have begun to do the same.

CHAPTER SUMMARY

The American work force is changing in many ways. Workers are getting older on average; there are more women and minorities and foreign-born. There is an increasing need for education for the jobs of the future.

A changing work force raises the suggestion as to whether all people are being treated fairly. Equal employment opportunity attempts to see that all people are treated without discrimination. Affirmative action creates preferences for certain groups to rectify past or present discrimination; reverse discrimination results when members of groups not given preferences are held back.

Unions affect equal opportunity in numerous ways. Seniority systems reward and promote those first in a job. They assist the older worker, but may disadvantage recently hired minority or female employees.

Some groups of people fare better than others in compensation. Comparable worth attempts to rectify the differences by being sure that people of all sorts are paid equally for work of the same worth.

Since most parents now work, firms have to provide benefits that help employees with the care of their children. This is an emerging area in which labor-management relations is directly affected by the new work force.

QUESTIONS FOR THOUGHT AND DISCUSSION

1 How is the American work force changing?
2 What does equal employment mean? Affirmative action? Reverse discrimination?
3 How do seniority systems affect equal employment opportunity?
4 Explain the theory of comparable worth.
5 What are the important family-oriented benefits employers provide?

SELECTED READING

Blum, Linda M., *Between Feminism and Labor: The Significance of the Comparable Worth Movement* (Berkeley, Calif.: University of California Press, 1991).

Borus Michael, et al eds., *The Older Worker*, Industrial Relations Research Association Series (Madison, Wis.: Industrial Relations Research Association, 1988).

Brown, Clair, and Joseph A. Peachman, eds., *Gender in the Workplace.* (The Brookings Institution, Washington, D.C., 1987).

Fernandez, John P., *Managing a Diverse Work Force.* (Lexington, Mass.: Lexington Books, 1991).

Koziara, Michael, et al, *Working Women: Past, Present, Future,* Industrial Relations Research Association Series (Washington, D.C.: Bureau of National Affairs, 1987).

Melendez, Edwin, ed., *Hispanics in the Labor Force: Issues and Policies* (New York, Plenum, 1991).

Thomas, Roosevelt R., *Beyond Race and Gender: Unleashing the Power of Your Total Workforce by Managing Diversity* (New York: AMACOM, 1991).

Wilkinson, Carroll Wetzel, *Women Working in Non-traditional Fields: References and Resources* (Boston: G. K. Hall, 1991).

6

THE NONUNION EMPLOYER

In the United States labor organizations have not organized most employees. Instead the substantial majority of people continue to work for companies that set labor relations policies unilaterally. This is a surprising fact. In the 1930s and 1940s unions made rapid headway in organizing the employees of private firms. Since that time, there has been stagnation in union growth. There are undoubtedly many reasons why this has occurred, but among them has been the development of sophisticated policies with respect to labor relations by many nonuninized firms. In the first section of this chapter we study the nature of those policies.

The employment relationship confers authority on the employer. The employer may discipline or discharge workers; the employer may decide what to pay workers and what benefits to provide. In the absence of a union, the only limitations on the employer's authority are those imposed by law or by the marketplace. In the United States, the limits imposed by law are relatively few (as compared with other industrialized countries). The limits imposed by the marketplace vary with the availability of workers and are often few because many people are unemployed and seeking work.

Many American employers value highly the freedom of action that they are allowed as a result of limited government regulation and slack labor markets. But companies behave in many different ways in the use of this freedom. Some establish policies that provide high wages, good benefits, and a generally good working environment for their employees. Others do the opposite. It is to a degree a matter of management choice. Management has the power and exercises it.

TWO EXTREMES OF NONUNIONIZED EMPLOYERS

There are many different types of nonunion employers. Some are very small companies; some are very large. They operate in many different industries and regions of the country. They follow many different kinds of labor policies. Often the only characteristic they seem to have in common is that their employees are not represented by labor organizations. For this reason it is perhaps not appropriate to lump them together into one category; referring to them all as nonunionized employers may seem to imply that their most important characteristic is the one they have in common. But this is too negative and too narrow a view. The labor policies of many of these firms are much more positive than is suggested simply by referring to them as nonunionized. For some of these firms, remaining nonunion is less an objective of their labor relations policies than it is a result of the policies they pursue. But there are also other firms that do not provide good employment standards and whose major labor relations objective is simply to avoid unionization at any cost and by virtually any means.

It is useful to examine the labor relations policies of nonunionized firms at these two extremes, even though most firms would fall somewhere in between. At one extreme we may place the low-standards nonunionized employer. At the other extreme we may place the better-standards nonunionized employer. What labor relations policies characterize the former? The latter? We will see that it is a fairly simple task to describe the low-standards employer, but that the operations of the employers with higher standards are complicated and require considerable study.

The Low-Standards Employer

The low-standards employer is a firm that survives primarily because of low labor costs. Generally, labor costs are kept down by paying low wage rates, providing few fringe benefits or none, and spending as little as possible on amenities at the workplace. In the garment trades, the operations run by such employers have been known as "sweatshops," a term that has been extended to include all low-standards employers.

Low-standards employers are often poorly managed firms. They not only pay low wages but also make inefficient use of labor. Thus, low labor costs are necessary to keep them in business, by permitting them to compete against more efficient firms. Low-standards employers rarely seek to train employees, to provide for their participation in their jobs in a constructive fashion, or to provide competent supervision. They employ extremely authoritarian management techniques and use discharge as a device to discipline the work force. Ordinarily, they experience high levels of labor turnover. Their personnel practices are haphazard, resulting in a crazy-quilt pattern of wage rates, job assignments, and work loads. They ordinarily give no thought to grievance procedures or communications mechanisms.[1]

The Better-Standards Employer

The better-standards nonunionized employer may be described as a firm that pays wages and fringe benefits comparable to or better than those paid by similarly situated unionized firms (i.e., firms in the same industry and geographic area). Such a firm ordinarily remains competitive in its product market by virtue of efficient management, advanced technology, resource control, an effective sales force, or other such advantages. Better-standards firms generally conduct employee relations with great care. Hiring, training, disciplining, and discharging are administered in accordance with carefully prepared policies. Employee attitudes are monitored often, two-way communication is encouraged, and grievances are attended to. Managerial direction, although often authoritarian, is applied with a paternalistic concern for the welfare of employees.[2]

Better-standards employers are generally as firmly opposed to the unionization of their employees as are low-standards employers. However, better-standards employers usually respond to union-organizing attempts in a more sophisticated fashion and generally do not employ overtly illegal methods in opposition to unionization. Instead, reliance is placed on persuasion of employees, generous wage and benefit policies, and legal action that delays an organization campaign. Some employers do not resist unionization itself, but insist on freedom to operate an "open shop," involving both union and nonunion employees. But the considerable legal restrictions that apply to unionization and to collective bargaining narrowly circumscribe this alternative.

HOW THE BETTER-STANDARDS EMPLOYER OPERATES

The Psychological Contract

The absence of a union means that employees will not have a collective bargaining agreement with their employer. Nonetheless, a contract of one sort or another may exist between the individual employee and the employer. In some industries there is a document, legally binding to a degree, setting forth the agreement between an employee and the firm for which he or she works. The procedure is especially common in radio and televi-

---

[1]The labor relations practices of low-standards employers are described in a number of studies of the high-turnover, low-wage sector of the labor market, the so-called secondary labor market. See, for example, Peter B. Doeringer and Michael J. Piore, *Internal Labor Markets and Manpower Analysis* (Lexington, Mass.: D. C. Heath, 1971), esp. chap. 8.

[2]For an extensive review of the labor policies of large nonunion firms, see Fred K. Foulkes, *Effective Personnel Policies: A Study of Large Nonunion Employers* (Englewood Cliffs, N.J.: Prentice-Hall, 1980).

sion broadcasting. Under the terms of the contract a broadcast station ordinarily agrees to a term of employment (e.g., 2 years) at a specified salary, and the employee agrees to accept whatever assignments are given and not to work for another station for some set period (e.g., during the term of the contract).

Most industries do not have a written contract between each employee and the employer, however. Instead, there exists what may be termed a "psychological contract."[3] This contract is in the form of an understanding between the employee and the employer about the respective rights and obligations of each. It includes more than the wage rate and fringe benefit payments the employee and the firm agree on. It also involves the expectations of both sides about the employee's performance, the working conditions provided by the employer, and other factors. Because the contract is not in written form, it is not legally enforceable, but it is nonetheless real and significant. If one party believes the other has violated the agreement substantially (psychologists employ the term "cognitive dissonance" to describe this sort of dissatisfaction), difficulties may be expected to arise.[4]

Better-standards employers recognize the importance of the psychological contract and devote care to its content and administration. They attempt to see that the employee's expectations of the job are consistent with their own as employers. They identify possible problem areas. And they hold the employer to his or her understanding with the company and themselves to their commitments to the employee. Thus, while there are no formal, legally binding obligations placed on the employer by a psychological contract, as there are by a collective bargaining agreement, nonetheless better-standards employers are not free to simply do whatever they want in dealing with employees. In fact, self-imposed restraints of the type accepted by an employer under the psychological contract are often as well respected as (or in some cases better than) those imposed from outside with the force of law.

Misunderstandings and disputes arise between management and employees in all firms. The low-standards employer imposes its will on employees; the better-standards firm provides employees with an opportunity to present their side of a controversy. In many firms there are procedures

[3]M. H. Dunahee and L. A. Wrangler, "The Psychological Contract," *Personnel Journal*, 53:7, July 1974, pp. 518–526. See also John J. Beach and William A. Murray, "The Career Contract," *Management Review*, 68:10, October 1979, pp. 20–28; and Daniel Yankelovich, "The New Psychological Contract at Work," in Clark Kerr and Jerome Rosow, eds., *Work in America: The Decade Ahead* (New York: Van Nostrand Reinhold, 1979).

[4]J. S. Adams and W. B. Rosenbaum, "The Relationship of Worker Productivity to Cognitive Dissonance about Wage Inequities," *Journal of Applied Psychology*, 46, 1962, pp. 161–164. Incidentally, a psychological contract between the individual employee and the firm might be said to exist even when a collective bargaining agreement is in force. In this case the psychological contract might be said to include the provisions of the formal agreement and whatever additional understandings exist between the employee and employer.

like the skip-level interview—in which employees regularly meet with their supervisor's boss so that complaints against a supervisor can be aired—or the "open door"—in which an employee can ask to have a meeting with the top executive of the firm. At Federal Express Corporation an employee can take his or her case to an appeals panel composed of senior executives of the firm.[5]

These procedures do not give an employee access to a neutral—that is, nonmanagement—person to make a final decision about a controversy as is ordinarily done in a union-management grievance procedure (see Chapter 20). Some nonunion firms do, however, provide for a final decision by a neutral person in the case of an employee complaint.

A Supportive Climate

Better-standards employers recognize that employees may perform better and have greater job satisfaction in a workplace climate that is supportive. In consequence, personnel procedures and supervisors' behavior may be established in order to provide support for employees, as well as impose discipline. To a substantial degree, the procedures and behavior of an employer establish the tone of the employee-employer relationship and have less to do with what is done than with how it is done. Thus, a supportive climate need not imply a weak management or low productivity. Instead, profit-conscious managers may believe that a supportive climate is most efficient at the workplace.

A supportive managerial climate may be contrasted to one that generates defensive, often antagonistic, behavior in employees. The supportive climate exists when the employer adopts such attitudes as problem orientation and provisional views and when he or she permits a degree of equality and spontaneity in the working relationship. A problem orientation means that the employer shows concern for resolving difficulties that arise in the course of the job, rather than requiring the blind carrying out of orders. An employee is thereby made to feel part of a team, to whose mission he or she is expected to contribute. Provisional views set forth by the supervisor often truthfully reflect uncertainty about how a problem should be handled, instead of the supervisor insisting that absolute certainty exists. Provisional views permit the supervisor to learn how to deal with a problem in cooperation with employees and thereby may elicit a more productive result. Finally, a degree of equality in the manager-employee relationship permits better communication, facilitates an employee's constructive involvement in his or her job, and may increase harmony at the workplace.

[5]Martin Everett, "Court of Last Resort," *Across the Board*, 28:11, November 1991, pp. 49–53.

Applied Behavioral Science

The twentieth century has seen considerable development of formal methods of surveying the attitudes and behavior of groups of people. To a large degree this work has been done by psychologists studying the activities of people within organizations, especially work organizations, such as business firms or governmental agencies. Various designations have been given to the academic disciplines involved, including "industrial psychology," "organizational psychology," "administrative sciences," and "organizational development." What they all have in common is the attempt to apply behavioral science techniques to the workplace. Since World War II there has been a great outpouring of analysis and suggestions by academic researchers as to how managers should manage, especially with respect to the relationships between supervisory style, the work environment, and worker satisfaction and productivity.

The impact of this research and effort on the management of the average, or representative, firm in the United States has been substantial. Some firms, which include many of the large nonunionized companies, have developed ongoing programs of research into the attitudes and behavior of their employees, undertaken by staffs specially hired for this purpose. These monitoring programs, carried out by questionnaires and interviews, have permitted the companies to be much more aware of the full range of employee contents and discontents and of the changes that are taking place. "An attitude survey allows for a detailed comparison of the attitudes held by the employees of the firm taking the survey with the attitudes held by employees at all the other firms who took the survey previously."[6]

The usefulness of these programs has persuaded many companies to expand their communication programs. When these surveys by behavioral science researchers are contrasted with the massive industrial spying that many large firms employed in the 1920s and 1930s as a method of monitoring employee discontent, one can see to what a large degree managerial practices have improved.[7]

Often survey results suggest changes in particular management practices. Sometimes these changes are made and sometimes they are not. But in either case application of behavioral research techniques does tend to generate a greater commitment to good communication, flexibility, and creativity in the managerial response to employee concerns.

---

[6]Thomas J. Burns, "Learning What Workers Think," *Nation's Business*, August 1988, p. 32. Burns is quoting here an employee of a firm which sells attitude surveys.
[7]Sanford M. Jacoby, "Worker Attitude Testing at Sears, Roebuck and Company, 1938–1960," Institute of Industrial Relations, University of California at Los Angeles, Working Paper No. 112, June 1986.

The Policies as a Whole

Figure 6-1 describes in diagrammatic form the overall structure of the policies and practices of a better-standards nonunion firm. The approach begins at the top with certain beliefs or principles about behavior in the firm that are stated by top management. For example, in IBM's case there are three principles: the best service to customers, respect for the individual in the firm, and the pursuit of excellence in all that's done.

Managers and the human resources staff in the firm then turn beliefs into policies such as employment security (i.e., no layoffs unless as a last resort), promotions from within instead of hiring people from outside the firm (in order to make available promotion opportunities for the firm's employees), communication and feedback programs, and so on. These policies are intended to create a climate of trust, cooperation, and confidence between the firm and its employees and among employees. Out of this climate emerge characteristics of the organization that are desirable, includ-

FIGURE 6-1 Top management's stated beliefs in a nonunion firm. (*Source:* Adapted from Fred K. Foulkes, *Personnel Policies in Large Non-Union Companies,* Englewood Cliffs, N.J.: Prentice-Hall, 1980.)

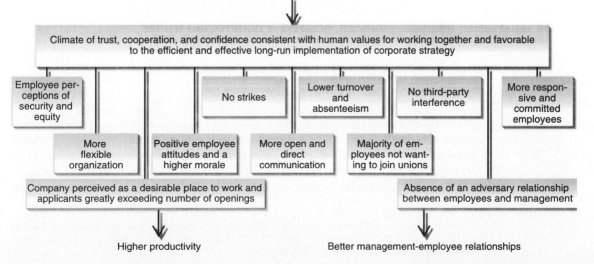

ing flexibility, positive attitudes, no strikes, and lower absenteeism. Finally, these favorable characteristics are expected to provide the firm with higher productivity and better management-employee relations than its competitors. In this way, better standards for the employee are intended to generate higher sales, lower costs, and more profitability for the firm. Better standards are not simply about being more generous to employees; they have a business purpose as well.

THE NONUNION SECTOR IN AN OTHERWISE UNION FIRM

In the past several years many industrial firms that were once largely unionized have developed a substantial nonunion sector. Several major companies that in the early 1950s had 80 percent or more of their production and maintenance employees unionized now have less than 50 percent unionized.

Researchers Thomas A. Kochan and Anil Verma studied the nonunion sector in a large industrial company. They concluded:

• The development and expansion of the nonunion part of the firm is "an articulation of managements' long-term philosophical opposition to unions";
• The nonunion strategy is driven by philosophical opposition to unions and by differences in labor costs that are lower in the nonunion plants;
• The nonunion strategy is carried out by opening new plants in low labor cost regions, keeping their size small, and using an "alternative human resource management system";
• The alternative system is based on
  Wages and benefits based on the local labor market, not industry averages or union levels,
  Relatively few job classifications, or all-salary programs,
  Emphasis on flexibility in assigning people to tasks,
  Extension of management communications to employees via small groups.[8]

Response to Union Organization Attempts

All nonunionized companies are conscious of the possibility of union organization of their employees and most wish to avoid it. Less sophisticated managements respond to a union organizing attempt by trying to repress it. Union activists are fired, union organizers are expelled, and the employer does whatever else seems expedient to prevent unionization. Often in

---

[8]Anil Verma and Thomas A. Kochan, "The Growth and Nature of the Nonunion Sector within a Firm," in Thomas A. Kochan, ed., *Challenges and Choices Facing American Labor* (Cambridge, Mass.: MIT Press, 1985), pp. 89–121.

this process employers violate the labor laws of the United States and find themselves with substantial legal problems. In addition, the employers have probably offended or alienated many of their employees by their action and have therefore created a poor industrial relations climate at the workplace.[9]

The better-standards nonunionized employers do not ordinarily behave in this fashion. Instead, they pay careful attention to how they may most effectively defeat a union-organizing campaign without violating the law or offending employees. Seminars are offered periodically by such organizations as the American Management Association and the National Association of Manufacturers that explain to managers how to oppose an organizing campaign. Also, newsletters and books that explain how to respond to union drives have been prepared by management-oriented writers. For example, Herbert Rothenberg and Steven Silverman list four major labor relations standards that help an employer avoid unionization:

1 The employee has the right to know the conditions under which he works.

2 The employee has a right to reasonable job security, including seniority standards.

3 The employee should have readily available a practical grievance mechanism.

4 The employee should receive a reasonable level of compensation, not the cheapest possible.[10]

Using enlightened personnel policies, often borrowed from unionized firms, many companies have been able to remain largely or completely nonunion. According to one study, firms using enlightened policies to avoid unions were able to reduce the probability that the companies' new facilities would be unionized from 15 percent to less than 1 percent.[11] There is also statistical evidence that in the period 1977 to 1983 there was a substantial shift among large American companies from an objective of trying to get the best bargain with a union to one of trying to keep unions out.[12]

There are various opportunities for a company to consider what strategy it wishes to follow with respect to unionization. For example, when a firm considers expanding its capacity, it has three alternatives: to expand an ex-

---

[9]Aaron Berstein, "Busting Unions Can Backfire," *Business Week*, Mar. 18, 1991, p. 108.

[10]Herbert I. Rothenberg and Steven B. Silverman, *Labor Unions, How to Avert Them, Beat Them, Out-Negotiate Them, Live with Them, Unload Them* (Elkins Park, Pa.: Management Relations, Inc., 1973), pp. 163–170.

[11]Thomas A. Kochan, Robert B. McKersie, and John Chalykoff, "The Effects of Corporate Strategy and Workplace Innovations on Union Representation," *Industrial and Labor Relations Review*, 39:4, July 1986, pp. 487ff. See also David Wessel, "Fighting Off Unions," *Wall Street Journal*, May 12, 1985, pp. 1, 22.

[12]Peter Cappelli and John Chalykoff, as cited in Bureau of National Affairs, *Daily Labor Report*, No. 4, Jan. 7, 1986, pp. A4–A5.

isting unionized facility, to negotiate with a union over the opening of a new facility, or to open a nonunion plant. Each alternative has advantages and disadvantages. Expanding an existing facility may offer greater efficiencies of scale, but there may also be expensive union work rules. Opening a new plant with union representation may provide an opportunity to negotiate a better contract for the company, but the advantage may not last long. Opening a nonunion plant may let the company implement a flexible work system like those described in Chapter 5, but the location may be smaller, less efficient, and sometimes in a less desirable geographic location.[13] So many American companies have chosen the final option that the areas of the nation that are least supportive of unions have grown much more rapidly than those that are heavily unionized.

Three important lessons may be learned from this review of employer policy toward unionization attempts.

1. *Ordinarily opposition to unionization is taken, without question, to be the proper course for management.* There is little or no discussion about whether to accept unionization or not, or even if some type of unionization might be appropriate. Instead, nonunion employers in the United States tend to look on unionization as an unwarranted interference with management and seek to learn how best to avoid unionization.

Following is a paraphrase of a description by a manager of his view of the reason a company would not want to deal with some particular unions:

> Those of us who have had the opportunity to directly manage a union work force (or to work as a union member) have experienced the debilitating effects of inflexible work rules, bureaucratic systems and political in-fighting. . . . The union's inert work rules stifle creativity and promote worker apathy. Furthermore, rigid job classifications and bumping procedures needlessly complicate training and educational programs within the company.
>
> Here is an example. My corporation had three separate unions: a maintenance union, a toolmakers' union, and a machine operators' union. A particular product line which required precise machining also required a simple but frequent readjustment which entailed removing a plate and resetting a dial. The adjustment process did not require any special skill and could be accomplished in less that twenty seconds. However, a machinist was required to call for a maintenance worker to make the adjustment to remove the plate which covered the dial. Then the maintenance worker was required to call for a tooling employee to reset the dial. Once the maintenance worker replaced the plate, the machinist could resume working. Since the area maintenance and tool workers were rarely immediately available, the adjustment process often took over an hour. When the company and the workers involved agreed to let the machining workers reset the dials themselves, the maintenance and tooling unions invoked their contracts with management and enforced the rigid separation of the work.[14]

[13]Robert J. Flanagan, "The Economics of Unions and Collective Bargaining," *Industrial Relations*, 29:2, Spring 1990, pp. 305–306.

[14]Joe Saldutti, "The U.S. Can't Afford Unions," *Harbus News*, Mar. 15, 1991, 45:2, p. 3. Jan. 22, 1991, p.3.

We do not know if this is the entire story; nor even if it is, whether or not such practices are common. But the conviction that unions operate in the manner described and impose unwarranted inefficiencies on management is very widespread in America and accounts to a large degree for much of American management's strong opposition to unions.

2. *Management uses the threat of unionization to encourage itself, and especially its more authoritarian elements, to improve working conditions and personnel practices, with the argument that better practices will prevent unionization.*[15] Often nonunion management borrows its policies directly from unionized firms and may even improve on them. Some nonunion firms thus tend to become more unionlike than many unionized firms.

3. *The influence of the unions in improving conditions in nonunionized firms can be seen clearly in the process by which nonunionized firms imitate the policies of unionized firms.* Because of this behavior, the impact of unions on industrial relations in the United States goes far beyond the firms that are organized by unions. That is, the secondary impact of unions is substantially broader than their primary impact.

It is also important that the reader avoid certain unwarranted assumptions about unionization, including the following:

1. *A company that follows enlightened personnel policies can always remain nonunionized.* This is not so. Plants or companies in some industries and geographic areas are likely to be organized no matter what policies the employer follows. This is because strong unions that will always mount an organizing campaign exist and because union identification among employees, even new employees, is high.

2. *A company that follows poor personnel policies will always be unionized at some point.* This is not so, either. In some industries and geographic areas, companies can continue to operate much as they did in the 1930s without serious risk of unionization. This is because some firms are so small, or the unions in the area are so weak, and the employees have so little union consciousness, that organization is unlikely. This situation exists in many service industries in much of the United States (including, e.g., laundries, retail shops, and restaurants).

3. *Companies that profess to have good labor relations policies actually have them.* Often companies know what they should do and have policies that commit them to good practices. Yet the press of business activities, the desire to make profits and to control costs, and other factors cause better-standards labor relations policies to be ignored.

---

[15]Marvin S. Myers, *Managing without Unions* (Reading, Mass.: Addison-Wesley, 1976). Myers maintains that if management provides conditions that result in employees having a joint-stake concern with the goals of the company, the reasons people join unions will be eliminated.

MANAGING LABOR RELATIONS

Corporate Organization in Industrial Relations

Unionized companies must manage their labor relations. Managers of various responsibilities are involved in industrial relations. Line managers direct the work force. Staff managers have specialized responsibilities for personnel and labor relations functions, such as compensation, hiring, affirmative action, and collective bargaining, to name but a few. General managers have overall responsibility for setting policies and coordinating line and staff personnel, and for the results.

General managers in different companies structure the line and staff relationships very differently. In some companies corporate staff is kept small, providing primarily advice and overall policy direction. Organization of large corporations by semiautonomous divisions under central controls is now pervasive in American business.[16] Line managers in the divisions have industrial relations and personnel staff reporting to them. In other companies, staff at the divisional or plant level have a dual reporting responsibility—partly to plant or divisional line management and partly to corporate staff. Much of what appears in the literature on personnel as an appeal for more "power" for the personnel function is an argument for reporting by plant and division staff directly to corporate staff, rather than to plant or division top managers.

Companies also organize the various personnel and labor relations functions differently. Some companies combine all functions. Others separate labor relations from personnel. General Motors, for example, has corporate vice presidents for both labor relations and personnel. General Electric, however, includes all such functions under a single corporate vice president for employee relations. Nor is the industrial relations–personnel function always at the level of corporate vice president. Some companies have only directors of personnel or of labor relations. The labels "personnel," "labor relations," "employee relations," and "industrial relations," when used in corporate organization by different firms, do not always have the same meaning. The detailed list of personnel and labor relations functions may be distributed differently in different companies between personnel and labor relations, for example.

In corporations, staff executives in labor relations have tended to spend their careers in the function. By 1979, according to the National Industrial Conference Board, "fully four out of five top labor relations executives . . . spent their whole corporate life in the industrial relations or personnel function."[17] The large number of employee relations staff and the longevity of managers in this specialty suggest that a high degree of professionalism has been achieved by management.

---

[16]Richard F. Vancil, *Decentralization: Managerial Ambiguity by Design* (Homewook, Ill.: Dow Jones-Irwin, 1979), p. 3.

[17]Audrey Freedman, *Managing Labor Relations*, Report No. 765 (New York: The Conference Board, 1979), p. 29.

Labor Relations Policies of Individual Companies

There is a range of labor relations policies followed by American corporations that can be described as a spectrum (see Figure 6-2). At one end are companies that adamantly oppose unionization with whatever weapons are at hand. The Kohler Company, a plumbing fixture manufacturer in Wisconsin, typified this policy for many years. The company engaged the United Auto Workers in a lengthy and often violent contest, ending in the early 1970s in a renewal collective bargaining agreement between the company and the union.

Other companies do not resist unionization to the last breath but do take a hard line in attempting to remain as free of union interference as possible. Until 1973 a prime exponent of this policy of strong opposition to unions was the General Electric Company. As described by the company, GE's approach emphasized complete and timely communication with all employees, unionized and nonunionized, and treating all employees as individuals first, not as members of a union or other group.[18] In effect, the company attempted to establish compensation and other industrial relations policies for its employees, both union and nonunion, with as little regard for the unions as possible.

In the middle of the spectrum in Figure 6-2 is the policy of neutrality. Many companies leave their individual divisions and plants to work out labor relations matters largely without central corporate direction, unless the financial performance of the division or plant draws attention to failures due in part to poor labor relations. Other companies actively cooperate with labor unions on many matters.

Finally, a few American companies have become overly cooperative with unions and have failed to control costs adequately. In the end, these companies have either gone out of business or been acquired by other concerns.

Organizations of Employers

In most European countries business concerns have formed central, nationwide associations of employers. These associations represent the interests of employers in discussions with the government and with the central

---

[18]See "Our Employee Relations Philosophy and Union Bargaining Approach," Supplement to General Electric Company's Relations Reviews, 1969; and Herbert R. Northrup, *Boulwarism* (Ann Arbor, Mich.: Bureau of Industrial Relations, University of Michigan, 1964).

FIGURE 6–2   The spectrum of labor relations policies of American companies.

Adamant opposition to unions	Strong opposition	Neutrality	Cooperation	Close cooperation

federation (or federations) of labor unions. In the United States there is no such central employer association. This is surprising because there exists a single major labor union federation, the AFL-CIO, with which a business association might be expected to have dealings.

American employers—usually on an industry or sector (e.g., manufacturing or construction) basis—have established many sometimes overlapping associations, however, that have some labor relations responsibilities. Among their activities are data collection, assistance to member firms in collective bargaining, and lobbying with the government. The largest of these include the U.S. Chamber of Commerce and the National Association of Manufacturers (NAM). Other groups of a more ad hoc nature exist, including the Business Roundtable. The Roundtable, formed in 1972, is composed of the chief executive officers of the largest corporations. Each of these associations has much broader responsibilities than labor relations, and none is really a counterpart to the AFL-CIO. In 1976 the Chamber of Commerce and the NAM agreed to merge, with the support of the Roundtable. The merger plan collapsed, however. In part the explanation of the failure of American employers to create a national association is to be found in the wide range of labor policies followed by American companies. Rather than pool their efforts, American companies have preferred to pursue independent courses.

There have been three major efforts in the history of this country to persuade American management to voluntarily accept unionization and form a centralized policy-making body, somewhat akin to European models. First, the National Civic Federation in 1900 under Marcus Hanna, a major Republican party figure, urged such a course. In 1920 President Wilson sought, through the Industrial Conference and the leadership of Herbert Hoover, to perpetuate the development of collective bargaining, which had begun in World War I. Finally, in 1934–1935, under section 7A of the National Industrial Recovery Act, the federal government proclaimed the right of workers to form unions and urged management to voluntarily accept them. All three efforts failed. The result was that American unions developed in a hostile environment and that government intervention ultimately occurred. American business still finds itself without central coordination when dealing with government and labor in labor relations matters.

WHAT PROCESSES ARE ASSOCIATED WITH LABOR-MANAGEMENT RELATIONS?

In the United States the existence of a union means that management and the union must do certain things together. Broadly speaking, they must negotiate a contract with each other at periodic intervals; they must administer the contract while it is in effect; and they must cooperate, or compete, with each other in a variety of other activities.

Negotiation of an agreement is a process that we refer to as collective bargaining, and about which we will have much to say in later chapters. Briefly speaking, it means that management and labor each select a team of representatives who will meet with each other to work out the provisions of a contract. If an impasse develops, a strike or lockout may occur.

Contract administration involves the implementation and application of the contract. When disputes develop over the meaning of the contract, management and labor must have some method of resolving the disputes. Ordinarily, they find a way to work out the problem. When this is not possible, there may be a work stoppage, or, much more commonly, some neutral person is asked to decide the issue and both sides agree to accept the decision.

Finally, management and the union both exist in a broader community, in which they are concerned about government, living conditions, social services, and similar matters. They may choose to cooperate with each other on such issues or to be in conflict. Often unions and management try to cooperate at the local level but are in disagreement at the state or national levels. Regardless of what is actually done, it is important to realize that the relationship of management and unions is not confined exclusively to the workplace, but inevitably overflows into the wider society of which both are members.

Nonunion companies and employees do not engage in these processes. There is no collective bargaining, no contract, and no contract administration. Because employees do not have their own organization, they are not involved in issues as a group, though individual employees, like individual managers, may be personally involved in politics or social activities.

CHAPTER SUMMARY

In the United States, most employees are not unionized and many employers do not deal with unions. There are many different types of nonunion employers with a wide range of employment standards. At one extreme are the low-standards employers, who keep costs down by paying low wages, providing few benefits, and spending little on workplace amenities. At the other end of the spectrum are better-standards employers, whose labor relations policies are as good as, if not better than, those in unionized companies.

Better-standards nonunionized firms pay wages and benefits comparable to, or better than, those paid by unionized firms and conduct their employee relations with great care. Although they generally oppose unionization, they do so by legal means and by generous wage and benefit plans. Sound employment policies are their best defense against a union. In better-standards nonunionized firms, a kind of psychological contract exists between employee and employer about the rights and obligations of each, rather than a written contract. Personnel procedures and supervisory attitudes attempt to provide support for employees and promote team spirit and loyalty. Some firms consciously use behavioral science knowledge and techniques with their employees, and many have developed practical grievance, or complaint, procedures.

The various personnel and labor relations functions are organized very differently in different companies. Some companies combine all functions, others clearly separate labor relations from personnel, and still others delegate labor and personnel functions in individualized ways. Specialists in personnel and labor relations have, in the last few decades, established their importance at the corporate level, and professionalism is beginning to characterize staff functions in labor relations.

American companies follow a wide range of labor relations policies, from adamant opposition to unions to close cooperation. The diversity in part results from the fact that there have been no comprehensive nationwide business associations to represent the interest of employers in discussions with government and the AFL-CIO.

When a company has to deal with union representatives rather than directly with its employees as individuals, it needs to be much more careful and consistent in its actions and in how it develops policies. Its actions will be scrutinized and subject to review, its discretion limited by a contract. This is an important reason companies prefer not to have unions. Furthermore, a union is more than just a group of employees. It is a separate institution with its own objectives and claims to the loyalty and involvement of workers.

Where a union exists, management and the union must negotiate a contract through collective bargaining, then administer the contract and resolve disputes that develop over its meaning. They may also cooperate or oppose each other on more general social issues involving the local community or the government.

QUESTIONS FOR THOUGHT AND DISCUSSION

1 What is included in the psychological contract between the employer and the employee? What is excluded?

2 What are the advantages to a company of remaining nonunionized? What are the advantages of unionization? Can you quantify the advantages? The disadvantages?

3 How do companies manage their labor relations? Should managers who deal with unions be separated from those who do not? Why or why not?

4 Should personnel functions in management be separate from labor relations functions? Why or why not? If you had a company, how would you structure the personnel and labor relations functions?

5 How has the existence of unions improved employment conditions for nonunionized employees? Do you think employers would provide high standards of employment even if there were no threat of unionization? Why?

6 In what ways does having a union affect a company?

7 What type of labor-management relationship is best? Why? What circumstances affect your choice?

SELECTED READING

Bakke, E. Wight, *Mutual Survival: The Goals of Unions and Management*, 2d ed. (Hamden, Conn.: Archon, 1966).

Beer, Michael, and D. Quinn Mills et al., *Managing Human Assets* (New York: Macmillan/The Free Press, 1984).

Foulkes, Fred K., *Effective Personnel Policies: A Study of Large Nonunion Employers* (Englewood Cliffs, N.J.: Prentice-Hall, 1980).

Myers, Marvin S., *Managing without Unions* (Reading, Mass.: Addison-Wesley, 1976).

D

LABOR-MANAGEMENT RELATIONS AND THE LEGAL SETTING

Work is performed in our society by persons who are specialized by function into different occupations and industries, permitting us to accomplish work more efficiently. With specialization, however, come differences in the status and authority of people in the workplace. In consequence, work is ordinarily performed by some persons under the supervision or direction of others.

Labor-management relations are concerned with the relationships that exist between those persons who perform work and those who direct and supervise it. Supervisory relations involve the exercise of authority and the use of power. Therefore, labor-management relations involve the use of power by managers and employees.

When there are disagreements and disputes, the unrestrained use of power can result in disruptive conflicts. In some instances, the conflict imposes harm only on the employer and the workers immediately involved. In other instances, the broader community may also suffer losses. As a result, the broader community often restricts the use of power through law.

Matters that might otherwise result in conflicts involving a contest of power are often settled by the creation of legal rights for individuals, companies, and unions. Also, companies and unions often jointly agree to establish rights for each other so that work may proceed unhindered by disputes. Rights place limits on the unbridled use of power.

Labor-management relations in the United States involve both the exercise of power by employers and unions and the limitations which the creation of rights places on the use of power.

CHAPTER 7

STATUTORY AND JUDICIAL REGULATION

LAW AND LABOR RELATIONS

Citizens of the United States live in a free country. However, in the area of labor relations the activities of workers, unions, and employers are very much regulated and restricted by law. This has not always been the case. Many years ago there was little government interference in labor relations. However, disputes between labor and management were often taken to the courts or the legislatures by one side or the other in an attempt to gain some advantage. Other disputes threatened to disrupt society through violence or through interrupting vital public services, and these, too, brought about government intervention. As a result, there has developed a network of law and regulatory agencies that oversees most aspects of labor relations.

American labor law has certain fundamental characteristics that make it different from labor law in other countries. Some of these characteristics it shares with American law generally, and these we explore below; but others are unique to labor law itself. Perhaps the two most distinctive features of American labor law are these:

1 *Different procedures and standards* exist for different sectors of the economy.

2 *Most American law* regulates the procedures followed in the relations of labor and management but leaves the substantive rules of the workplace (e.g., the amount of wages, fringe benefits, layoff provisions) to the action of management alone or management and labor jointly.

American labor law is now very extensive and complex. When Congress published the texts of the federal statutes that pertained to labor relations, labor standards, and employee benefits, the complete text consumed 3 volumes and 1060 pages.[1] In addition to the statutory language, there are thousands of pages of administrative regulations issued by government agencies applying the laws and even more pages of court decisions interpreting them. The result is that labor law has become a field for experts. Many lawyers specialize in the practice of labor law, and most large law firms now have labor lawyers on their staffs. In most major cities a number of smaller law firms practice in this branch of the law exclusively. Union organization campaigns, collective bargaining negotiations, and the handling of grievances all find labor and management increasingly bringing lawyers in to represent or advise them. Major law schools provide courses in labor law and even permit students to specialize in the area. A wide variety of textbooks in labor law are also now available.[2]

The result of the growth of labor law is that the average business person, worker, or labor leader is not ordinarily able to comprehend fully his or her own rights and responsibilities. Instead, he or she must rely on expert legal advice. It is common for articles or books about labor relations to begin by advising the reader to see a labor lawyer, and this is sound advice. Nonetheless, there is much about the law that the nonlawyer must know, including its basic features, how it has developed, and some of its major provisions. Detailed questions, however, cannot be answered except by specialists.

CHARACTERISTICS OF AMERICAN LAW

What Is Justice?

A primary function of law is the settlement of disputes between citizens. When such a dispute exists, for example, between a union and a company, the complaining parties want either to win the dispute or at least to receive justice. The law has the function, it may be said, of dispensing justice. Unfortunately, justice is not a simple concept or one that all of us define in the same way. As a result, laws that appear to some to be fully just appear to others as the height of injustice. Such division of opinion has been especially common with respect to labor disputes.

In order to provide a framework for the evaluation of labor law as it has developed in this country, it is useful to begin with a brief examination of the concept of justice. In essence, different theories of justice devolve into different rules for deciding whether to do one thing or another, that is,

---

[1] U.S. Congress, Senate Committee on Labor and Public Welfare, Subcommittee on Labor, Compilation of Selected Labor Laws Pertaining to Labor Relations, 3 vols. (Washington, D.C.: U.S. Government Printing Office, committee print, Sept. 6, 1974).

[2] See, for example, Julius G. Getman and John D. Blackburn, *Labor Relations: Law, Practice and Policy*, 2d ed. (Mineola. N.Y.: Foundation Press, 1982).

TABLE 7-1   THEORIES OF JUSTICE

Justice is found in serving.
• The greatest good for the greatest number
• The needs of the disadvantaged
• A balancing of various principles of fairness

how to make a choice. A study of justice[3] lists three different principles of justice (Table 7-1).

• *The greatest good (utilitarianism)* Justice is the greatest good for the greatest number.
• *Equality or fairness (egalitarianism)* Justice is equality in duty and rights among individuals, and inequality is justified only if its existence causes all, especially the least favored (i.e., the disadvantaged), to benefit.
• *Balancing among principles (intuitionism)* Justice involves the accommodation of several diverse principles of justice, including equality, liberty, property rights, and human rights.

These three different theories of justice may lead to very different conceptions of what the law ought to be as it applies to conflicts between labor and management. The first theory suggests that the law ought to favor the interests of society as a whole; the second suggests that the law ought to favor the weak, poor, and disadvantaged; the third theory suggests trying to find a balance between the other two. The history of American labor relations law is full of the debate among proponents of each of these theories.

Types of Law

The United States has four distinct types of law (Table 7-2), and all are involved in labor relations.

• *Constitutional law* The Constitution of the United States is a written document that is our highest form of law. All other law must conform to its provisions.

[3]John Rawls, *A Theory of Justice* (Cambridge, Mass.: Harvard University Press, 1971).

TABLE 7-2   TYPES OF LAW

• Constitutional
• Statutory
• Common
• Administrative

• *Statutory law* Congress, state legislatures, and other representative bodies may enact laws, or statutes.

• *Common law* The actions of courts and the customs of the people constitute a body of law that is called common law. Common law rests primarily on decisions of courts and on the willingness of one court to follow what another has done (i.e., to follow precedent). Common law is especially important in the area of procedure.

• *Administrative law* Agencies of government are often set up to apply particular statutes, and the regulations and decisions issued by these agencies constitute administrative law.

The following examples of each type of law may be found in the field of labor relations:

Constitutional

• The Fourteenth Amendment to the U.S. Constitution prohibits involuntary servitude and so rules out certain types of relationships between companies and workers. The First Amendment to the U.S. Constitution guarantees freedom of speech and so ensures that both union and management have a high degree of latitude in voicing their opinions in labor union organizing drives.

• The First Amendment does not protect employees of a private company from discharge or other disciplinary action if they complain to supervisors. A union contract may protect them, or in some instances, the National Labor Relations Act (which is described later in this chapter and in the two chapters following) may protect them; but the freedom of speech guarantee in the U.S. Constitution does not. However, the First Amendment prohibits government from abridging freedom of speech, and so does apply to public agencies acting as employers. Therefore, if a public employee complains to a supervisor about working conditions, that employee is protected from discipline by the First Amendment to the Constitution.[4]

Statutory

• The National Labor Relations Act establishes rules and procedures for unions and management in most of the private sector of our economy. The Employees Retirement and Income Security Act establishes certain standards that employers must meet in providing pension coverage for workers, if any coverage is provided at all.

Common

• Courts in various states, operating under different statutes, will still often honor decisions of courts in other states when the same or a similar

[4]*Givhan v. Western Line Consolidated School District,* 77 U.S. 1051 (1979).

issue was in dispute. The practice of labor and management in an area, unless clearly contrary to statutory law, will often be upheld by a court simply because it is the prevailing practice.

Administrative

• The National Labor Relations Board hears and issues rulings in disputes arising under the National Labor Relations Act. The Labor-Management Services Administration of the U.S. Department of Labor acts on cases arising under the Landrum-Griffin Act.

Functions of Labor Law

Law as it is applied to labor relations in this country has three primary functions:

1 *To facilitate and protect private voluntary arrangements*, such as private contracts.
2 *To resolve disputes.*
3 *To establish minimum standards* for employment, as, for example, the minimum wage and health and safety standards.

The Federal Court System

The federal government, by passing statutes about labor relations, has directed most litigation involving private companies and unions into the federal court system. Briefly, there are three levels of courts: district, appeals, and the Supreme Court.

Efforts to enforce contractual provisions between a company and a union are made in federal district courts. (Complaints about violations of various statutes are taken first to federal administrative agencies. Thus, an unfair labor practice charge goes first to the National Labor Relations Board. A charge of racial discrimination in employment goes first to the Equal Employment Opportunity Commission.)

Appeals from decisions of the district courts and from actions of the administrative agencies are taken to the courts of appeals. Finally, appeals from decisions of the courts of appeals are made to the Supreme Court. The Supreme Court is unlike the other two levels of the federal court system in that it does not have to consider cases filed with it, but uses its own discretion to decide which cases to hear (a process involving the issuance of a writ of certiorari).[5]

The Supreme Court ordinarily receives many appeals each term involving labor relations cases and usually accepts several for decision. It is in-

---

[5]Alvin L. Goldman, *The Supreme Court and Labor Management Relations Law* (Lexington, Mass.: Lexington Books/D.C. Heath, 1976).

teresting that labor relations cases are sometimes of such significance as to receive special treatment. For example, only three cases have been accepted by the Supreme Court for its own decision without first having been decided by a court of appeals. Two of these cases involved labor relations. The first involved the 1947 Mine Workers strike. The second involved President Truman's seizure of the basic steel industry from its owners in 1952 as part of the President's efforts to settle the steel strike of that year. The third instance involved the special prosecutor's subpoena of the Watergate tapes from President Nixon.[6]

THE NATURE OF LAW

Whether it be labor or another form of law, there are certain basic characteristics of the legal process in this country. Among the most important are the following:

1 *The law is a result of a process of historical evolution.* It is changing constantly, but it also contains many vestiges of the past.

2 *The law is an often paradoxical combination of unchanging principles and common-sense adjustments to changing conditions.*[7]

3 *The role of judges in making the law what it really is at any given time is very important.* In fact, judges may read into the law very different meanings than those of the parties who sought or even drafted the legislation itself.[8] Archibald Cox, an eminent legal scholar who began his career specializing in labor law and later was special prosecutor during the Watergate affair, commented on the role of judges in American society:

A judge, in order to preserve his authority and the authority of his decisions, must wrap himself in the mantle of the past, must keep a continuity of principle. But at the same time, he must find an accommodation with the dominant needs of his times, must shape the law so as to meet the changes in society. . . . What is it that leads people to comply with Supreme Court decisions? James Madison said that the Court was to be an impenetrable bulwark against executive or legislative overreaching. Well, the president has the army, the Congress has the money, how can the Supreme Court be an impenetrable bulwark? . . . Only if the people believe in law and the rule of law. An essential ingredient of law is that the judges be seen to be deciding according to law, and not just according to their druthers [preferences] like a bunch of politicians.[9]

---

[6]Leon Jaworski, *The Right and the Power* (New York: Simon and Schuster, 1977), p. 175.

[7]Oliver Wendell Holmes, Jr., *The Common Law* (Boston: Little, Brown, 1938, first published 1881).

[8]John R. Commons, *Legal Foundations of Capitalism* (Madison, Wis.: University of Wisconsin Press, 1957, first published 1922).

[9]Peter Costa, "A Conversation with Archibald Cox," *Harvard Gazette*, Sept. 20, 1991, p. 5.

4 *Legal thinking is essentially classification (i.e., a process of inclusion and exclusion) and analogy.* What may be legal behavior for one type of organization (like a union) may be illegal behavior for another (like a corporation). Alternatively, what may be legal in one industry may be illegal in another. Much of the practice of law involves determining into what category a particular event falls and then looking up the rule that applies to it. When there is a question regarding classification, the issue is likely to be settled by argument using analogy (i.e., this situation is very like another situation and should therefore be treated as the other was treated).[10]

5 *Our system of law places considerable reliance on advocacy, or the adversary system, as a method of jurisprudence.* Rather than the court itself (i.e., the government) investigating a dispute or alleged violation of the law (in order to determine the truth), each side brings its own advocates (usually attorneys, lawyers) and witnesses. The court hears each side and attempts to determine the case on the record that is compiled. Elsewhere in the world much more reliance is placed on active investigation by officers of the court to get at the facts. Surprisingly, in the United States many federal administrative agencies, especially the NLRB, operate much like courts abroad, in that the agency investigates the dispute itself.

6 *Law may be divided into two categories: substantive and procedural.* Substantive law involves rules about topics, such as what the minimum wage is to be. Procedural law includes rules about how things are to be done. Procedural law includes such matters as rules of pleadings, process, evidence, jurisdiction, rulings, and appeals. Ordinarily we are much more interested in substantive law than in procedural law, but the latter can be very important, as when cases are dismissed because of procedural irregularities (so-called technicalities). An undue regard for the niceties of procedure is called "legalism," a term that suggests a legal system more interested in its own activities than in justice for citizens.[11] In recent years charges have been made that labor law has become increasingly legalistic.[12]

7 *There are two broad standards in American law: (1) specific rules and (2) equity (i.e., adherence to generally accepted principles).* Detailed rules arise from legislation and court decisions. The equity standard is applied by courts where rules are lacking. Most labor litigation is decided via detailed rules, but issues of equity sometimes arise.

---

[10]Harold J. Berman and William R. Greiner, *The Nature and Functions of Law,* 3d ed. (New York: Foundation Press, 1972).

[11]Judity N. Shklar, *Legalism* (Cambridge, Mass.: Harvard University Press, 1964).

[12]Douglas V. Brown, "Legalism and Industrial Relations in the United States," *Proceedings of the Industrial Relations Research Association,* 1970, pp. 2–11.

THE DEVELOPMENT OF LABOR LAW

Unions as Conspiracies As early as the first decade of the 1800s, unions had gained enough importance in some trades to cause employers to go to courts for relief from union activities. In 1806 Philadelphia shoemakers' employers charged that unions were conspiracies to do them harm, and as such, that unions were illegal combinations. The court agreed and was followed by other courts in some 17 trials between 1806 and 1842. While unions continued to operate in this period, the courts, employing the common law doctrine of conspiracy (imported from Great Britain), often found the unions' very existence to be in violation of law.[13]

In 1842 a Massachusetts case changed this. Chief Justice Lemuel Shaw of the Massachusetts Supreme Judicial Court ruled that a union was not per se an illegal conspiracy. For a union to be in violation of the law, the court ruled that it must be shown that the union's objectives or the means it was employing were illegal *(Commonwealth v. Hunt)*. This decision did not put an end to conspiracy trials against labor unions,[14] but it did begin the process of legalizing their existence and activities. Furthermore, as the nineteenth century continued, juries became less willing to convict unions of conspiracy charges, and the value of the legal doctrine of conspiracy to employers declined.[15]

The Labor Injunction In 1895 the Supreme Court of the United States upheld the issuance of an injunction by a federal court against Eugene Debs and the American Railway Union in the Pullman strike. The injunction had been sought by the attorney general of the United States on grounds of interference with the delivery of the mail by train. In the years thereafter, labor injunctions were commonly issued. Prior to 1931, some 1845 injunctions were issued by state and federal courts in labor disputes.[16]

The injunction was a court order to an individual or an organization to cease certain activities (or, conversely, but much less frequently in practice, to perform certain activities). Failure to obey the order rendered the person or organization subject to summary punishment for contempt of court. The labor injunction was, therefore, a very powerful legal tool, and one that, unlike the conspiracy charges, involved no need for a lengthy, and possibly unsuccessful, trial by jury.

[13]John R. Commons and Eugene A. Gilmore, *A Documentary History of American Industrial Society* (Cleveland: A. H. Clark, 1910).

[14]Edwin E. Witte, "Early American Labor Cases," *Yale Law Journal*, 35, 1926, p. 827.

[15]Benjamin J. Taylor and Fred Whitney, *Labor-Relations Law*, 3d ed. (Englewood Cliffs, N.J.: Prentice-Hall, 1979), pp. 22–23.

[16]Edwin E. Witte, *The Government in Labor Disputes* (New York: McGraw-Hill, 1932), p. 234.

When union organizers appeared at a plant, or a strike was threatened, employers would send lawyers to a court seeking an injunction. The employers argued that irreparable harm was threatened to the company as a result of the union activity, and they sought an order to the union and its activists to cease their efforts. Often the process of seeking an injunction was full of abuses. For example, injunctions were issued on a "John Doe" basis, that is, against no one in particular but anyone in general, even persons not involved in the dispute itself. Injunctions also sometimes made acts illegal that otherwise were legal. Finally, injunctions were commonly issued by judges without giving their objects a chance to be heard before issuance.

The Yellow-Dog Contract   The labor injunction was not the only legal tool used by management to oppose unions. Another such tool was a contract between the workers and the employer, by which the workers bound themselves not to become members of a union while they worked for the company. This sort of contract was labeled by the unions a "yellow-dog" contract, because, they said, only a yellow dog would sign it. The combination of the labor injunction and the yellow-dog contract became a virtually insurmountable barrier for the unions.

In 1917 the U.S. Supreme Court not only upheld the legality of the yellow-dog contract, but permitted federal courts to issue injunctions to enforce it *(Hitchman Coal Company v. Mitchell)*. The result was that employers could insist that workers sign a contract not to join a union, or they would be fired, and the federal courts would enforce the contract by issuing injunctions against union organizers who tried to persuade workers to join the union and thereby violate the contract.

The Antitrust Laws   In 1980 Congress passed the Sherman Antitrust Act, and employers found in this statute a new weapon against union activity. The law made combination in restraint of trade illegal. Presumably aimed against big corporations, the "trusts," the Sherman Act was soon applied against union activities. The advantage of the act was that it provided for the issuance of injunctions for enforcement, with additional provisions for fines, jail terms, and treble (i.e., tripled) damages for violations of the act.

In 1902 the United Hatters, an AFL union, undertook to organize Loewe and Company, a hat manufacturer located in Danbury, Connecticut. A strike against the company failed, and so the union turned to a product boycott. The boycott was effective enough to cause the company to file suit under the Sherman Act. In 1908 the U.S. Supreme Court found against the union and ordered a judgment of $252,000 against the union and its members, an enormous sum for those days (*Loewe v. Lawlor,* or, more commonly, *Danbury Hatters*).

This and the *Hitchman* decision constituted the high-water mark of the federal courts' intervention against union activities. During World War I the unions, with presidential support, gained members and mounted a counterattack against the courts and the application of the antitrust laws to union activities. In 1914 the Clayton Antitrust Act amended the Sherman Act and provided specifically that "the labor or a human being is not a commodity or article of commerce; nothing contained in the antitrust laws shall be construed to the existence and operation of labor . . . organizations . . . nor shall such organizations or the members thereof be held or construed to be illegal combinations in restraint of trade under the antitrust laws." The act also made strikes, boycotts, and peaceful picketing legal under federal jurisdiction.

Samuel Gompers hailed the Clayton Act as labor's Magna Carta. But soon the Supreme Court weakened its provisions. In 1921, in its first pronouncement on the labor provisions of the act, the Court held that secondary boycotts could still be enjoined by the courts despite the anti-injunction provisions of the Clayton Act. In consequence, the unions lost many of their legal gains, and soon membership began to decline as well. The 1920s were largely an antiunion period, buttressed by the courts.

MAJOR LABOR LAWS

After the First World War, Congress became increasingly involved in labor relations through the passage of legislation. Table 7-3 lists the major pieces of legislation that have affected the private sector in the United States. These statutes regulate union organization and collective bargaining. It is interesting that the last three acts listed were passed in 1935, 1947, and 1959, at 12-year intervals from each other. The year 1971 passed without a major piece of legislation, and more than two decades later there is no indication of the immediate likelihood of further comprehensive legislation.

Table 7-3 lists the acts by their general description and includes the designation of the congressional sponsors of the bill where the designation is widely used. Thus, the Labor Management Relations Act of 1947 was cosponsored by Senator Taft and Representative Hartley and is customarily referred to as the Taft-Hartley Act. Of the five acts listed in Table 7-3, only the Norris-LaGuardia Act applies to all private industry. The Railway Labor Act applies to the railway and airline industries. The National Labor

TABLE 7-3   MAJOR FEDERAL LEGISLATION DEALING WITH LABOR RELATIONS

1926	Railway Labor Act
1932	Anti-Injunction Act (Norris-LaGuardia Act)
1935	National Labor Relations Act (Wagner Act)
1947	Labor Management Relations Act (Taft-Hartley Act)
1959	Labor Management Reporting and Disclosure Act (Landrum-Griffin Act)

Relations Act (NLRA) and the acts that amended it (Taft-Hartley and Lan-drum-Griffin) apply to the private sector excluding airlines and railways.

The Railway Labor Act

Following a particularly difficult strike, railway unions and the carriers co-operated in developing legislation that was enacted by Congress in 1926. This and the passage of the health-care amendments to the Taft-Hartley Act in 1974 are the only times in U.S. history when such cooperation has occurred. Ordinarily, labor legislation has been passed in an atmosphere of extreme conflict. For example, in 1935 employers bitterly opposed the NLRA, and in 1947 the unions labeled the Taft-Hartley Act a "slave labor bill" and vowed to get it repealed.

Collective bargaining under the Railway Labor Act differs in several important respects from that which was later to be established under the National Labor Relations Act. There are three fundamental differences. First, whether or not an obligation exists between the employer and the union to bargain about a specific issue is determined on a matter-by-matter basis, not, as under the National Labor Relations Act, on the basis of a broad statement (specifically, "wages, hours, and conditions of work") in the law. Second, arbitration of grievances is statutory rather than on the basis of the collective bargaining agreement between the employer and the union. Third, policies under the Railway Labor Act are interpreted not by an administrative agency of government (like the National Labor Relations Board) but by the federal courts. State courts may also be involved in deciding disputes between airlines or railways and the unions, but only in order to apply the federal law.[17]

The Railway Labor Act is an extensive piece of legislation. Among its major provisions are mechanisms for dealing with labor disputes. Grievances can be submitted to the National Railway Adjustment Board. An unresolved grievance may go to an arbitrator appointed by the National Mediation Board. Under the act, therefore, arbitration is paid for by the government. Elsewhere in American labor relations, the parties bear this financial cost. As a partial result of the parties' facing no costs, the arbitration mechanism of the Railway Labor Act has had tremendous backlogs.

Disputes over the negotiation of collective bargaining agreements are subject to a different set of procedures. These provisions may best be presented in the fashion of an outline:

[17]Henry H. Perritt, Jr., "Control of Economic Activity under the Railway Labor Act," in *Strikes, Stoppages and Boycotts 1980* (New York: Practicing Law Institute, 1980). See also National Mediation Board, *The National Mediation Board at Fifty* (Washington, D.C.: U.S. Government Printing Office, 1985).

Collective Bargaining Under the Railway Labor Act

Scope

1 Since 1926, all railroads and subsidiaries; since 1936, all U.S. flag air carriers that operate within or from the United States.
2 All employees and subordinate officials as defined by the Interstate Commerce Commission.
3 Airline pilots specifically included.

Purposes

1 Avoid interruptions to interstate commerce.
2 Protect employee and employer freedom of self-organization and representation.
3 Provide prompt, peaceful settlement of major and minor disputes.

Negotiation

1 30 days' written notice of intended changes required.
2 Conferences to be held within 10 days after notice.
3 Strikes not permitted during these conferences or for 10 days after conferences are terminated.

Mediation

1 Either party may request mediation from the National Mediation Board after direct negotiations have begun and failed or there is a refusal to negotiate.
2 NMB may impose mediation in the case of a "labor emergency" without a request from either party.
3 The status quo (no strike and no change in conditions) is preserved during mediation.
4 No prescribed time limit or cutoff for mediation.

Arbitration

1 If mediation fails, NMB must proffer voluntary arbitration.
2 If arbitration is accepted, the award made is final and binding.
3 If either party refuses, NMB withdraws from the case and the status quo is preserved for a 30-day "cooling-off" period.

Emergency

Statutory Provisions

1 President of United States may set up an Emergency Board if:
  a No settlement is reached under the foregoing provisions.
  b The NMB judges the dispute could "threaten substantially to interrupt interstate commerce to a degree such as to deprive any section of the country of essential transportation service" and so informs the President.
2 Emergency Board investigates and makes recommendation only—not binding.
3 Creation preserves status quo for up to 60 days:
  a 30 days maximum for board to submit report.
  b 30 days after report.

Presidential Action (Nonstatutory)

1 Convince parties to accept Emergency Board recommendations or his own recommendations.
2 Seek special legislation from Congress.

Some provisions of the Railway Labor Act anticipated those of the NLRA. For example, management was not to interfere with labor in its choice of representatives and vice versa. Also, "the majority of any craft or class of employees" was to determine a representative for all that craft or class. Finally, the determination of which union should represent a class of workers is the responsibility of the National Mediation Board, by means of a secret ballot election or other appropriate method. But this does not mean that the law promotes union organization.

For example, in 1987, Delta Air Lines, which is largely nonunion, purchased Western Airlines, which was largely unionized. The unions at Western attempted to block the acquisition by charging that it would extinguish the unions' representation rights and nullify their contracts with Western. But Supreme Court Justice Sandra Day O'Connor permitted the acquisition to go ahead.[18]

Unlike the later NLRA, however, the Railway Labor Act permitted penalties to be assessed against carriers or unions not following the requirements of the act. Under the NLRA the courts have held for only remedial, not punitive, actions. Thus, a company that violates the NLRA (or Taft-Hartley, which amended the NLRA) can be ordered to make restitution of damages caused others by its acts, but cannot be fined for its illegal actions as a punishment. Under the NLRA, the only time a penalty may be

---

[18]*Teamsters v. Western Airlines, Inc.*, U.S. Supreme Court, A-716, Apr. 1, 1987.

assessed is for a willful failure to cooperate in investigations or proceedings under the act.

Under the Railway Labor Act unions are granted a wider range of activities directed against employers than under the NLRA. For example, unions are allowed by the Railway Labor Act to picket employers who are not directly involved in a labor dispute in order to try to force the noninvolved companies to bring pressure on directly involved employers to settle the dispute. When the Maine Central Railroad decided to abolish the jobs of 300 of the 400 members of the Brotherhood of Maintenance of Ways Employees (BMWE), the union decided to picket other railways that interchanged traffic with the Maine Central. This action, labeled secondary picketing, would be illegal under the NLRA, but the Supreme Court found it to be legal under the Railway Labor Act.[19]

The Norris-LaGuardia Act   The Norris-LaGuardia Act was the first of several statutes enacted in the 1930s in which Congress actively favored union organization and collective bargaining. The act began with a statement by which the public policy of the United States was declared as follows:

> Whereas under prevailing economic conditions, developed with the aid of governmental authority for owners of property to organize in corporate . . . forms of ownership association, the individual unorganized worker is commonly helpless . . . wherefore . . . it is necessary that he have full freedom of association . . . for the purpose of collective bargaining or other mutual aid or protection. . . .

Therefore, the law established a series of limitations on the rights of federal courts to issue injunctions and provided a series of procedural steps that must be followed prior to issuing an injunction. The most important procedural requirement was that a hearing be held to determine whether or not an injunction should be issued. At this hearing the union could challenge the alleged need for an injunction. The procedure has been especially effective in reducing the use of the labor injunction in the years since 1932. The act also made unenforceable in the federal courts the yellow-dog contract, which then passed from the labor relations scene.

The National Labor Relations Act (the Wagner Act)   The National Labor Relations Act was passed in 1935. It is the most important single piece of labor-management relations legislation. It established the basic obligations of companies in dealing with unions and also established the National Labor Relations Board, a federal administrative agency, to adjudicate and enforce the law. The major amendments to the Act occurred in 1947 via the Labor-Management Relations Act, also known as the Taft-Hartley Act. So significant is this statute and its various amendments that the following two chapters deal with it in detail.

---

[19]*Burlington Northern Railway Company v. Brotherhood of Maintenance of Way Employees,* U.S. Supreme Court, No. 86-39, Apr. 28, 1987.

The Landrum-Griffin Act A union exercises considerable power, potentially, over the persons it represents, both its members and nonmembers. The legal source of this power is the provision of the National Labor Relations Act which provides that a union selected by the majority of employees in a bargaining unit will be the sole, or exclusive, representative of all the employees. An American union, therefore, does not legally represent only its own members. The right, or obligation, of a union to represent all employees in a bargaining unit delegates to the union the authority to take actions that will substantially affect the welfare of individual employees. Among these actions are such things as processing or not processing grievances, calling strikes, and deciding to accept one type of wage-and-benefit offer in collective bargaining rather than another.

Because a union can and does exercise authority over employees, there has grown up in the United States a substantial body of law about how that authority can be exercised. Underlying this body of law is an analogy that seems to view the relation of an employee to the union that represents him or her as similar to the relation of a citizen to the government. The rights conveyed by law to the individual with respect to the union are therefore somewhat similar to those conveyed to the citizen with respect to the government.

In 1959 the Landrum-Griffin Act was passed as an amendment to the Taft-Hartley Act. The Landrum-Griffin Act made some changes in the provisions of Taft-Hartley that applied to the relations of employers and unions, but it also placed restrictions on the activities of unions with respect to the people they represent. These provisions of the act are the result of a public debate and a congressional review of the internal affairs of unions in which the central issue was the impact of the union on the freedom of the worker. Title I of the act is entitled a "Bill of Rights" for union members. It provides that every member of a labor organization is to have certain enumerated rights and privileges. Included are the following:

- Equal rights to nominate candidates for union elections, attend membership meetings, and vote on union business
  - Freedom of speech and assembly in and out of union meeting
  - Right to sue in court against the union (but prior to initiating a suit union members must exhaust reasonable hearing procedures within the union)
  - Right to have a copy of the collective bargaining agreement with the employer that directly affects the union member

Furthermore, the law provides that dues and initiation fees of a local union can be increased only by a secret ballot of the members.[20]

---

[20]Janice R. Bellace and Alan D. Berkowitz, *The Landrum-Griffin Act: Twenty Years of Federal Protection of Union Members' Rights* (Philadelphia: The Wharton School, University of Pennsylvania, 1979). See also Clark Kerr, "Unions and Union Leaders of Their Own Choosing," in *The Next Twenty Years in Industrial Relations* (Cambridge, Mass.: MIT, 1958).

The law also establishes procedural safeguards for union members. No member may be disciplined by a union without being served with specific written charges, given a reasonable time to prepare a defense, and afforded a full and fair hearing by the union. Final judgment remains, however, within the union. Usually the final step in an internal disciplinary procedure in a union is an appeal by the member to the general president of the national union or to its general executive board. The United Auto Workers, virtually alone among American unions, provides for a final appeal to an outside, independent panel.[21] In about one-fourth of cases, the panel, called the public review board, has overruled the union's decision. This provision of the law has generated some interesting court cases. One in particular found its way to the Supreme Court.

George Hardeman, a boilermaker, was a member of the International Brotherhood of Boilermakers Local Lodge 112. On October 3, 1960, he went to the union hiring hall to see Herman Wise, business manager of the local lodge and the official responsible for referring workers for jobs. Hardeman had talked to a friend of his, an employer who had promised to ask for him by name for a job in the vicinity. He sought assurance from Wise that he would be referred for the job. When Wise refused to make a definite commitment, Hardeman threatened violence if no work was forthcoming in the next few days.

On October 4 Hardeman returned to the hiring hall and waited for a referral. None was forthcoming. The next day, in his words, he "went to the hall . . . and waited from the time the hall opened until we had the trouble. I tried to make up my mind what to do, whether to sue the local or Wise or beat hell out of Wise, and then I made up my mind." When Wise came out of his office to go to a local job site, as required by his duties as business manager, Hardeman handed him a copy of a telegram asking for Hardeman by name. As Wise was reading the telegram, Hardeman began punching him in the face.

Hardeman was tried for this conduct on charges of creating dissension and working against the interest and harmony of the local lodge and of threatening and using force to restrain an officer of the local lodge from properly discharging the duties of his office. The trial committee found him guilty as charged, and the local lodge sustained the finding and voted his expulsion for an indefinite period. Internal union review of this action, instituted by Hardeman, modified neither the verdict nor the penalty.

Five years later, Hardeman sued the union, alleging that it had violated the Landrum-Griffin Act by denying him a full and fair hearing in the union's disciplinary proceedings. A federal district court in Alabama found

[21]Jack Stieber, *Democracy and Public Review: An Analysis of the UAW Public Review Board* (Santa Barbara, Calif.: Center for the Study of Democratic Institutions, 1960). See also "Union Power to Discipline Members who Resign," *Harvard Law Review*, 86:8, 1973, pp. 1536–1569.

the union guilty and a jury awarded Hardeman damages of $152,150. The Supreme Court reversed the decision. The question, said the Court, was "whether the evidence in the union disciplinary proceeding was sufficient to support a finding of guilt." And, the Court concluded, "We think there is no question that the charges were adequately supported."[22]

In the Hardeman case, the courts ultimately upheld the validity of the union's actions. But in other instances, violations of the law have been found. For example, on December 2, 1976, Dave Newman, a steward in Local 1101 of the Communication Workers, was removed from his post after he had condemned the leadership's tactics at a membership meeting.

Newman called for a nationwide strike unless the telephone company agreed to a 32-hour work week at 40 hours' pay and no layoffs. This position by an official of the union was at variance with the official position of the union, and so Newman was removed from his position as a union official, but not as an employee of the telephone company. Newman sued the union, seeking reinstatement. After lengthy litigation a federal district court ordered Newman reinstated as a steward. The judge held that the views of the local union's president—that no member could serve as a union steward without renouncing the right to express opposition to the local's policies—constituted a violation of the Landrum-Griffin Act.[23]

In yet another example, Linda Nixon was hired in November 1987 as an organizer for United Food and Commercial Workers local union 7. She became an outspoken critic of Charles Mercer, the president of the local. When Mercer sought reelection, Nixon actively campaigned for his opponent. Mercer ultimately won reelection and fired Nixon, citing her dissension from his policies as the reason for the discharge. Nixon sued the local and Mercer, alleging that her discharge violated the free speech guarantees afforded union members under the Landrum-Griffin Act.

At trial, the union and Mercer argued that the will of the membership, as expressed in periodic elections, is served by permitting union leaders to choose staff whose views are compatible with their own, as the Supreme Court has found (*Finnegan v. Leu*). Nixon countered that her discharge was part of a purposeful and deliberate attempt to suppress dissent within the local, and therefore went beyond the protection of *Finnegan*. A jury found in favor of Nixon and ordered the local and its president to pay her back pay as well as benefits and damages for emotional distress.[24]

Other sections of the Landrum-Griffin Act deal with trusteeships and union elections. A trusteeship involves a process by which a national union sets aside the duly elected officers of a local union and appoints trustees to administer the local's affairs and finances. Ordinarily, the trusteeship

[22]*Boilermakers v. Hardeman*, 123 U.S. 516 (1971).
[23]*Newman et al. v. Communication Workers Local 1101*, 597 F. 2d 833 (1979).
[24]"Federal Jury Awards . . .," Bureau of National Affairs, *Daily Labor Report*, No. 172, Sept. 5, 1991, p. A-5.

power is vested in the general president of a national union (or the general executive board) by the constitution of the union. The trusteeship provision of the constitution of one major national union reads as follows:

> For the purpose of correcting corruption or financial malpractice, assuring the performance of collective bargaining agreements or other duties of a bargaining representative, restoring democratic procedures, or otherwise carrying out the legitimate objectives of the international union, including the observances of the ritual, obligation, laws, rules or decisions of the organization or its duly constituted authorities, [the general president] shall have full power to suspend or remove such local officers, suspend or revoke charters of such local unions or place such local unions and their officers and members under international supervision.

There was evidence submitted to Congress of the abuse of this procedure by certain national unions. They were accused of looting the treasuries of local unions and suppressing democracy in the locals. To prevent such abuses, Congress included in the act limitations on the application of the trusteeship's power.

The act requires national unions to hold elections at intervals of not more than 5 years and locals to hold them at not more than 3-year intervals. These provisions were intended to see that union officers did not perpetuate themselves in office indefinitely, as a few had done, by not calling elections. Incidentally, when the law was passed, many local union officials who ran for election annually successfully persuaded their members to extend their terms of office to 3 years on the grounds that Congress favored a 3-year term.

The act also provides safeguards regarding the fair conduct of elections. Charges that union elections were unfairly conducted can be filed with the secretary of labor of the United States. If an investigation indicates that the election was improper, the secretary may invalidate the election and cause a new one to be held. There has not been great use of this power by the secretary. Only a relatively few national elections have been rerun. By far the largest case of a court-ordered rerun was the election in the United Mine Workers in 1972, in which hundreds of government personnel supervised balloting in 1200 local unions at a cost of several million dollars to the government.

In 1989 leaders of the Teamsters Union, America's largest, signed an agreement with the U. S. Department of Justice, which had been investigating alleged corruption in the union. The agreement allowed the union to avoid a lawsuit brought by the government, and more than a hundred of the union's officers were forced from their positions because of associations with organized crime. In 1991 the Teamsters held a convention under the supervision of the federal government. At the convention candidates were nominated for the top positions in the union, and an election was held thereafter in which members voted freely for the union's leadership—a president and 17-member executive board.

The act provides safeguards for the handling of union funds by union officers, including bonding requirements. Unions are required to file periodic reports with the Bureau of Labor-Management Reports of the Department of Labor regarding their internal operations and finances. These files are open to the public and have become an excellent source of information and research data about unions.

The law as it applies to the relationship of employees and unions makes some important distinctions. One is that although the union represents all employees in a bargaining unit, it may apply discipline under its bylaws only to those employees who are members of the union. Thus, if union members decide to work during a strike called by the union or to violate a rule against banking too much in extra earnings under an incentive pay plan, the union may take action against them according to its own internal procedures. The courts will, of course, look over the union's shoulder, so to speak, to be sure that the procedures used are legal. But some researchers believe that allowing the union to discipline its members unduly restricts the freedom of the individual. In particular, some observers wish to permit employees to resign from union membership when the employees are in substantial disagreement with a union policy and thereby avoid fines or other possible disciplinary action by the union.[25]

Further, the union member is in a sense subject to two sets of rules, both of which the union is involved in enforcing. One set involves the bylaws of the local union and the constitution of the national union of which it is a part, if any. A second set of rules encompasses those created by the collective bargaining agreement between the union and the employer. This twofold system of rules has been referred to as the process of "dual governance" in unions.[26]

Are unions democratic enough? It is sometimes said that unions are probably less democratic than governmental units. But this view ignores important differences between unions and governmental units. For example, an employee who wishes to escape union discipline may resign from the union. A citizen cannot escape the law of a municipality by resigning from it. Even where there is a union security clause in the collective bargaining agreement (see Chapter 17), an employee's obligations to the union do not ordinarily extend beyond a willingness to pay dues and assessments as uniformly levied on all members of the union. Thus, it is possible to be represented by a union and yet be free of obligations to it to a greater extent than to governmental units.

On the other hand, the internal processes of unions are not subject to the full range of procedural safeguards that exist for citizens in their dealings

---

[25]Harry H. Wellington, "Union Fines and Workers' Rights," *Yale Law Journal*, 85:8, July 1976, pp. 1022–1059.

[26]Alice H. Cook, "Dual Governance in Unions: A Tool for Analysis," *Industrial and Labor Relations Review*, 15:3, April 1962, pp. 323–349.

with government, nor are the processes under a collective bargaining agreement (e.g., the grievance arbitration procedure, see Chapter 20) subject to the full requirements of due process as present in our courts.

The internal decision-making procedures of unions are subject to considerable regulation and therefore compare favorably with democratic procedures in government units. Elections must be held at specified times and conducted in a specified manner. This does not prevent abuses from sometimes occurring, just as abuses of the governmental political process occur that sometimes require redress in court or in Congress.

Other Legislation

The legislation listed in Table 7-3 is the major federal legislation dealing with labor relations. It is not the only legislation that has an effect on labor and management; there are many such statutes and it is not possible to list them all here. However, to provide some familiarity with these laws, the following several pages list the dates of enactment, titles, and brief descriptions of the more significant pieces of legislation:

• *The Antikickback Law (Copeland Act)* makes it a crime to induce or accept payments from workers ("kickbacks") for getting them jobs on construction financed with federal funds. (1934)

• *The Interstate Transportation of Strikebreakers Act (Byrnes Act)* makes it a crime to transport or travel in interstate commerce for the purpose of interfering by force or threats with peaceful picketing by employees or with other rights of employees. (1936)

• *The Prevailing Wages Law (Davis-Bacon Act)* requires that on all federal and federally assisted construction (of above a certain size) the wages and fringe benefits paid to workers shall not be less than those found by the secretary of labor to be prevailing in the area. (1936)

• *The Overtime Law (Walsh-Healy Act)* requires payment of overtime at one and a half times the base hourly rate for all work in excess of 8 hours a day on federal nonconstruction contracts. (1936)

• *The Fair Labor Standards Act* requires all private employers subject to federal law (and above a certain small size) to pay at least a minimum level of wages ($4.35 an hour in 1992) to employees and to pay one and a half times the worker's regular hourly wage for work beyond 40 hours in a week to certain categories of employees. Employees subject to the overtime provision are called "nonexempt" employees, and those not covered are called "exempt" employees.[27] (1938)

• *The Farm Labor Contractor Registration Act* requires persons serving as contractors for migrant farm laborers to register with the federal government and to meet certain standards. (1963)

[27]Rudolf A. Oswald, "Fair Labor Standards," in Joseph P. Goldberg et al., *Federal Policies and Worker Status Since the Thirties* (Madison, Wis.: Industrial Relations Research Association, 1976), pp. 107–134.

• *The Equal Pay Act* provides that employers cannot pay different rates of pay for the same job on the basis of gender or race. (1963)

• *The Civil Rights Act, Title VII,* concerns employment practices and makes it illegal for an employer to discriminate against any person because of race, color, religion, gender, or national origin. Similar provisions apply to unions and employment agencies. The Equal Employment Opportunity Commission (EEOC) is established by the act to enforce Title VII. (1964) (Substantial amendments were made in 1972, and Title VII was renamed the Equal Employment Opportunity Act of 1972.)

• *The Services Contract Act (McNamara-O'Hara Act)* requires payment of one and a half times base hourly rate for all hours of work in excess of either 8 hours per day or 40 hours per week in any federal contract for services not covered by Walsh-Healy. (1965)

• *The Age Discrimination in Employment Act* makes it illegal for an employer to discriminate in employment practices among employees for reasons of age. It is intended to protect the rights of older workers. In 1978, the act was amended to make it unlawful for a private employer to force workers to retire before age 70; and it was amended again in 1986 to prohibit any mandatory retirement age. (1968)

• *The Health Industry Amendments to Taft-Hartley* extend coverage of the Taft-Hartley Act to approximately 1.4 million employees working in private nonprofit hospitals and apply special notice and mediation procedures designed to minimize work stoppages in contract disputes at all health-care institutions (except publicly operated hospitals). (1974)

• *The Employees Retirement Income Security Act (ERISA)* protects the pensions of employees of private concerns, in part by insuring pensions against business failure. (1974)

• *The Labor-Management Cooperation Act* encourages the formation of labor-management problem-solving groups. It also amends Taft-Hartley to permit such joint programs to be funded by employer payments made pursuant to a collective bargaining agreement. Previously, U.S. courts, citing Taft-Hartley, had barred unions from the management of such funds. (1978)

The Labor-Management Cooperation Act reflects the increasing emphasis being placed on cooperation between management and labor, rather than the emphasis of previous statutes on settling disputes. The purposes of the law are:

(1) to improve communication between representatives of labor and management;

(2) to provide workers and employers with opportunities to study and explore new and innovative joint approaches to achieving organizational effectiveness;

(3) to assist workers and employers in solving problems of mutual concern not susceptible to resolution within the collective bargaining process;

(4) to study and explore ways of eliminating potential problems which reduce the competitiveness and inhibit the economic development of plant area or industry;

(5) to enhance the involvement of workers in making decisions that affect their working lives;

(6) to expand and improve working relationships between workers and managers; and

(7) to encourage free collective bargaining by establishing continuing mechanisms for communication between employers and their employees through federal assistance to the formation and operation of labor-management committees.

• *Bankruptcy legislation* was passed by Congress to preserve collective bargaining agreements from being set aside by the courts when a company declared bankruptcy. The Supreme Court had permitted a company to cancel its agreement with a union as soon as it filed for reorganization under the bankruptcy laws. Soon several companies had availed themselves of the opportunity afforded by bankruptcy to avoid collective bargaining contract obligations. Congress then passed a law requiring a company that files for bankruptcy to bargain with a union over any changes it wants to make in the contract. (1984)

• *Americans with Disabilities Act* provides access to and protection in the workplace for the handicapped. This law prohibits discrimination in employment opportunities against disabled people; requires equal accessibility to all services provided by state and local government, including transportation; and prohibits discrimination in public accommodations and services—including hotels, retail stores, and recreational facilities—against the disabled. Much of the law became effective in 1992. (1990)

Plant Closings

In recent years, plant closings have had serious consequences on individuals who have lost their jobs, and on communities which were largely abandoned as their economic bases disappeared. The number of such closings increased dramatically during the 1981–1982 recession. This led to a search for alternatives to closings and the development of programs for displaced workers.[28] Some collective bargaining agreements anticipate and provide some measure of protection for workers who lose their jobs due to plant closure.[29] In other cases, income support for qualified

[28]Paul F. Gerhard, "Finding Alternatives to Plant Closings," *Proceedings of the Industrial Relations Research Association,* spring meeting, May 2–4, 1984, pp. 469–474.6

[29]U.S. Bureau of Labor Statistics, *Major Collective Bargaining Agreements: Plant Movement, Interplant Transfer, and Relocation, Allowances* (Washington, D.C.: U.S. Government Printing Office, Bulletin No. 1425-20 July 1981).

workers through state-administered unemployment insurance programs is the major protection afforded workers. States and municipalities began to enact legislation to mitigate the adverse effects of plant closings.[30]

The lack of regulation in the United States regarding plant closings stood in sharp contrast to the legislative requirements of European countries. There, prenotification is legislated in almost every country; the longest, 12 months, in Germany, is a requirement introduced as part of the 1976 Co-Determination Act.[31] In 1988 the federal government enacted legislation requiring advance 60-day notice of major layoffs or complete shutdowns. A study of advance notice found that it was effective in reducing the loss of income of those who were laid off and permitting them to find jobs only when it was given at least 2 months in advance.[32] Thus, the 60-day period in the law seems appropriate.

Impact of Civil Rights Legislation on the NLRA

To what degree should the National Labor Relations Board consider equal employment opportunity in the application of the National Labor Relations Act? For example, should an employer's objection that a union discriminates against women and/or minorities be investigated by the board before it certifies the union as an exclusive collective bargaining representative for the company's employees? In several cases decided in 1977 and 1978, the NLRB held that the U.S. Constitution does not require and the NLRA does not permit the NLRB to withhold certification from unions that allegedly practice racial, sexual, or other discrimination.

A second question involves the obligation that the NLRA imposes on unions to represent all employees fairly. Does this obligation entitle the unions to insist that employers furnish the union with detailed data concerning the demographic composition of the employer's work force? In a series of recent decisions, the NLRB has said that the employers must give the unions otherwise confidential data about hiring practices, applicants for jobs, employees, and the employer's status with respect to the Equal Employment Opportunities Commission.[33]

---

[30]Bennett Harrison, "The International Movement for Prenotification of Plant Closures," *Industrial Relations,* 23:3, Fall 1984, pp. 387–409.

[31]Ibid.

[32]Stephen Nord and Yuan Ting, "Impact of Advance Notice of Plant Closings on Earnings and the Probability of Unemployment," *Industrial and Labor Relations Review,* 44:4, July 1991, pp. 681ff. See also, Ronald G. Ehrenberg and George H. Jakubson, *Advance Notice Provisions in Plant Closing Legislation* (Kalamazoo, Mich.: W. E. Upjohn Institute for Employment Research, 1988).

[33]Betty Southard Murphy, "Today's Concerns," *Proceedings of the Thirty-Second National Conference on Labor* (New York: New York University Press, 1980). The cases cited are Handy Andy, Inc., Bell and Howell, Co., and Murcel Manufacturing Corp. with respect to the issue of certification; and Westinghouse Electric Corp. and East Dayton Tool and Die Co. with respect to the employer's obligation to provide data.

Finally, can a union violate the law by not objecting vigorously enough to racial discrimination? The answer is apparently yes. Federal courts have held that where a union was aware of racial harassment in a firm and did not file a grievance against it, the union had failed in its duty to represent fairly all employees. "While the union did not ignore Woods [an employee subjected to racial harassment] altogether," the court wrote, "its treatment of his harassment grievances never rose above the most informal level. Knowing failure to file grievances on behalf of Woods concerning racial harassment . . . was racial discrimination in grievance processing which constitutes a primary violation of the law."[34]

Occupational Health and Safety Act

Injuries, illness, and death are all too common in the workplace. Although much progress has been made over the years, many hazards remain. In all private industry in the United States there are some 8.6 cases of injury and illness per thousand workers per year.[35]

The Occupational Safety and Health Act (OSHA) attempts to protect the safety and health of workers employed by private industry. It is the most comprehensive piece of industrial safety and health legislation passed anywhere. OSHA's enactment followed decades of cooperative effort between some managements and some unions to improve occupational health and safety. But it largely replaced the cooperative efforts with a generalized process of regulation by a government agency.

Under OSHA the government establishes standards for workplace health and safety. Section 8(f)1 of OSHA gives any employee or union the right to complain to the secretary of labor when the employee or the union believes there is a violation of a safety or health standard that threatens physical harm. If the labor secretary believes there are reasonable grounds for the complaint, he or she is required to order a special inspection for the alleged hazard as soon as possible.

These provisions of the act sometimes conflict with employee desires and union behavior on the job. One company tried to comply with OSHA regulations that required persons working over water to wear life jackets by disciplining employees who refused to wear jackets. But the employees did not like the jackets and struck in refusal to wear them. The employer then asked a federal court to order the employees to return to work.[36]

[34]*Woods v. Graphic Communications Union Local 747*, Seventh Circuit Court of Appeals, Feb. 20, 1991 (see Bureau of National Affairs, *Daily Labor Report*, No. 46, Mar. 8, 1991, pp. A-7–A-9).

[35]Melissa K. Hackey, "Injuries and Illnesses in the Workplace, 1989," *Monthly Labor Review*, May 1991, p. 34.

[36]Leo Teplow, "Comprehensive Safety and Health Measures in the Workplace," in Joseph P. Goldberg et al., eds., *Federal Policies and Worker Status Since the Thirties* (Madison, Wis.: Industrial Relations Research Association, 1976), pp. 209–242.

A matter of increasing concern about employee safety involves alleged hazards of using computer (video display) terminals. VDTs first appeared in the American workplace in the 1960s and in 1991 numbered more than 40 million. By the year 2000 half of all American workers are expected to be operating terminals.[37] As the use of VDTs has increased in the workplace, there have been more and more complaints that employees are suffering vision problems and disabling hand, wrist, and arm conditions. There is also concern that low-level radiation from terminals may help cause cancer, birth defects, and miscarriages. Careful research has not proved a connection of VDTs to most of these conditions, except where the equipment is used in inappropriate conditions.

In December 1990 the San Francisco Board of Supervisors voted to approve the nation's first law regulating the use of VDTs in the workplace. It calls for companies to provide proper lighting and adjustable computer equipment and furniture, allow VDT workers to take regular paid breaks, and implement education and training programs on proper VDT use. Fines are provided for employers violating the ordinance.

Many industries in the United States have a long tradition of joint management-labor safety committees. In Europe, safety legislation in many countries requires such committees generally and encourages resolution of workplace health and safety problems by these committees. But the American law, OSHA, makes no provision for such committees. The AFL-CIO has recently asked employers to support such committees as an alternative to the excessive government regulation of which the employers complain.[38] The employers have not yet supported that position, however.

The Return of the Antitrust Laws

As was pointed out above, the first part of the twentieth century saw the high-water mark of the use of the antitrust laws against unions. In the 1940s a series of decisions by the Supreme Court virtually granted the unions an exception from the application of the antitrust statutes. But in the 1970s employers again sought to restrict union activities through suits filed under the antitrust laws, and the courts received the suits with considerable sympathy.

In 1975 the Supreme Court considered a case involving the plumbers' union in Dallas, Texas. The union had picketed a general construction contractor, Connel Construction Company, for the purpose of obtaining an agreement that the contractor would subcontract all plumbing and mechanical work only to firms having an agreement with the plumbers' union. The appellate court had upheld the union's action on the grounds

---

[37]"VDTs," *Labor Relations Today,* 6:1, January–February 1991, p. 1.
[38]Matt Witt, "Learning Job-Safety and Health from Europe," *New York Times,* May 5, 1979.

that it advanced a legitimate union interest in organizing nonunion subcontractors. But the Supreme Court reversed the appellate court. The
Court held that this effort by the plumbers went beyond legitimate union
goals and had the effect of restraining competition. Therefore, it was in violation of the antitrust laws, the Court said.[39] In consequence, as the 1980s
continue, it has again become common for employers to file antitrust suits
against unions, and litigation continues in an effort to define how far the
courts will now go in restricting union activity by application of the antitrust laws.

Smarting under the renewed application of the antitrust laws to prohibit certain of their activities, the unions tried to turn the antitrust weapon
against employers. In 1974 the Associated General Contractors of California, an employer association with collective bargaining agreements with
the carpenters' union, held a seminar in which member companies were
told how to operate nonunion. Soon thereafter, the carpenters' unions in
California brought suit under the antitrust laws against the AGC charging
that AGC was engaged in a conspiracy to undermine and destroy the
union. The Ninth Circuit Court of Appeals upheld the unions' complaint,
saying that it was virtually the reverse image of the situation that confronted the Supreme Court in the Connel Construction case. Yet the Supreme
Court in reviewing the California carpenters' allegations held that "the
union's most specific claims of injury involve matters that are not subject
to review under the antitrust laws."[40]

THEORIES OF THE LEGISLATIVE PROCESS

In the preceding pages we charted the development of the major features
of American labor relations law. But how should we attempt to understand
the process as a whole? Has legal regulation evolved as a logical response
to the developing problems of our industrial society? Or does it represent
instead a series of historical accidents? There is a surprising degree of dispute among the country's most outstanding scholars with respect to these
issues. With respect to labor law, it may be said that the more fundamental
the question that is asked, the more uncertain the answer.

Law as the Perfection of Reason

The development of American labor law may be viewed as the adjustment
of the rules of society to the experience of management and labor in the

---

[39]*Connell Construction Company v. Plumbers Local 100*, 421 U.S. 616 (1975).
[40]*Associated General Constructors of California, Inc. v. California State Council of Carpenters*, U.S. Supreme Court No. 81-334, Feb. 22, 1983. See also Bureau of National Affairs, *Daily
Labor Report*, No. 36, Feb. 22, 1983, pp. AA1–AA2.

context of changing economic, social, and political circumstances. Thus, in the 1930s, when companies exploited the workers too much, the government intervened on behalf of the unions by passing first the Norris-La-Guardia Act and then the National Labor Relations Act. Later, when a wave of strikes following World War II demonstrated that unions had become too powerful, Congress enacted Taft-Hartley to restore the balance. When revelations in the late 1950s demonstrated corruption in unions, Congress responded by placing controls on the internal behavior of unions (the Landrum-Griffin Act).

Labor legislation is viewed by the proponents of this theory as the vehicle by which a national labor policy is devised. They believe the process to be largely rational and characterized by public debate and by decisions based on the preponderance of the testimony placed before Congress. The legislative process is conceived as a quasi-judicial process, in which advocates for management and labor make their case and Congress, influenced by an intelligent and informed citizenry, makes its own decision on how best to proceed in the national interest. The procedure is legitimate because it is democratic in nature and is one by which problems are met and solved.[41]

The proponents of this view do not deny that the system has imperfections. They admit that it sometimes is very slow to react, that crises may be necessary to stimulate action,[42] and that as a result the pendulum of the law may swing too far in one direction for a time. But as the nation becomes aware of an imbalance, the legislative process will respond, and the passage of new statutes will cause the pendulum to return to a moderate position.

The imperfections that exist are believed to be short-term and subject to correction. They do not gainsay the essential rationality of the process. For example, Taylor and Whitney conclude their text on labor law with the observation: "Repeated examination of government regulation of the collective bargaining process is evident. . . . The policies forthcoming depend and have depended largely upon the public's view of the type of economic system it desires. . . . The citizen should become more informed . . . since he will determine the ultimate status of unions."[43] In this observation, written in the 1970s, one can hear the echo of Sir Edward Coke, writing in the early 1600s: "Reason is the life of the law, nay the common law is nothing else but reason. . . . The law, which is perfection of reason."[44]

---

[41]David Ziskind, "Standards for Evaluating Labor Legislation," *Cornell Law Quarterly*, 51:3, Spring 1966, pp. 517–518.

[42]Archibald Cox, *Law and the National Labor Policy* (Los Angeles: University of California Press, Institute of Industrial Relations Monograph Series, No. 5, 1960).

[43]Taylor and Whitney, *Labor-Relations Law*, pp. 582, 586.

[44]Sir Edward Coke, *Institutes*, Commentary upon Littleton, First Institute, Section 138.

Law as the Reflection of the Society

What is most characteristic of the view of the legislative process as one of reason is a rather uncritical attitude toward its results. This view tends to presume that if a problem exists, it will eventually be dealt with in a constructive fashion. But others do not hold this view. Instead, it may be argued that the law is not so much a method of correcting the abuses in society as it is a reflection of those abuses. Legislation is still viewed as a process of reason, but not as one that necessarily results in benign outcomes.

For example, Derek Bok contrasted American labor law with that of several European countries, asking the question "[how did] our labor laws come to take . . . a shape that is so different from the labor laws in other industrial democracies?" The answer, he concludes, has to do "with the nature of our unions, our employers, and our working people and the peculiar ways in which they organize and deal with one another." The result is a system of law that "permits great flexibility . . . and provides abundant opportunities for initiative." But "these national traits have also produced a system of labor law that is uniquely hard on the weak, the uneducated, the unorganized and the unlucky."

But these are not, in Bok's view, "haphazard oversights." Instead, "they are part of a long series of . . . choices that weigh against the weak and the unorganized."[45] Thus, the system is rational but deeply imperfect.

Furthermore, the system is paradoxical. "The pressures engendered by a decentralized, competitive system of labor relations have led to a web of regulation that is highly complex and extremely litigious. As a result, the United States—so identified with free enterprise and so skeptical of bureaucracy—paradoxically emerges with a regulatory system that is much more intricate and burdensome than that of Sweden, home of welfare socialism."[46] In this view, the legislative process and the law itself are not fundamental devices by which wrongs are righted in society and the weak protected, although law sometimes performs this function. Law is rather a further process, in addition to economic and political means, by which the powerful institutions of society, including business and labor unions, conduct their relations with each other.[47] Labor relations law, rather than establishing the rules of the game, is itself a part of the game.

Law as Accommodation to Pressure Groups

There is yet another theory of legislation and law that departs still further from the conception of law as the perfection of reason. In the place of a ra-

---

[45]Derek C. Bok, "Reflections on the Distinctive Character of American Labor Laws," *Harvard Law Review*, 84:6, April 1971, pp. 1458–1460.

[46]Ibid., p. 1460.

[47]John R. Commons and J. B. Andrews, *Principles of Labor Legislation* (New York: Harper, 1927).

tional choice among alternatives, each designed to resolve a problem, this view substitutes the largely political and expedient response to the clash of narrow and parochial interests.

The legislation that results is subject to inordinate influence by current events, although the legislation itself may endure for decades. It is often inconsistent with itself, a result of impulsive congressional action.[48] It reflects no underlying consensus about how the country should conduct its labor relations and so is characterized by formal compromises in statutory language, when no underlying agreement exists, a process that "assures unending litigation."[49]

Far from being a process in which management and labor jointly influence Congress to a set of views consistent with their own objectives, "the responsibility of organized management and labor in shaping the legislative framework and in the administration of the statutes is virtually nil; it is confined to making formal and highly extreme public statements."[50] The legislative framework of collective bargaining is now regulated by a highly partisan political process. Politicians enact legislation with little regard for its relation to the needs of business and labor, but with great regard for its political consequences.[51] The result is not an intelligent structure of law adapted to the resolution of real problems, but instead a crazy-quilt pattern of regulation that creates as many problems as it solves, and serves little or no constructive function on the whole. "The government is seeking to impose on parties to collective bargaining by statute and administrative rulings a set of standards of conduct which in many respects is highly unrealistic . . . and leads to impractical and unreal policies and to mass evasion and disrespect."[52] Labor relations law, rather than establishing the rules of the game, or even being a part of the game, is, in this theory of law, an alien imposition that hampers the performance of the players.

Are the Laws Enforced?

If a person is to understand American labor-management relations, he or she must be willing to consider the possibility that Congress passes laws it does not intend to have enforced. This is a highly controversial matter, but to the extent that it is true, it explains why even when laws exist, workers may wish to be represented by unions. After observing the process of government regulation for years, John T. Dunlop concluded that except where

---

[48]Douglas V. Brown and Charles A. Myers, "Historical Evolution," in Joseph Shister, Benjamin Aaron, and Clyde Summers, eds., *Public Policy and Collective Bargaining* (New York: Harper & Row, 1962), pp. 1–27.

[49]John T. Dunlop, "Consensus and National Labor Policy," *Proceedings of the Industrial Relations Research Association*, 1960, p. 6.

[50]Ibid., p. 5.

[51]David R. Mayhew, *Congress: The Electoral Connection* (New Haven, Conn.: Yale University Press, 1974).

[52]Dunlop, "Consensus," pp. 6–7.

unions exist, laws "are not generally enforced, save in larger enterprises. . . . The Congress will never appropriate the money and staff required [for] enforcement . . . and the inevitable game between the regulator and the regulatee goes to the persistent and the well-heeled."[53]

Unions complain that laws against management interfering with the rights of workers to join unions are often not enforced, and cite such examples as the J. P. Stevens textile company, which for years resisted unionization despite being repeatedly found guilty of labor law violations. In another instance a fire at a poultry-processing plant in North Carolina in 1991 caused the death of 25 workers because the doors of the plant had been padlocked in violation of OSHA regulations, and there had been insufficient government investigations to identify the violation.

CHAPTER SUMMARY

American labor law is extensive and complex. Increasingly, both labor and management depend on legal specialists for guidance in their disputes and negotiations. Nonetheless, it is very important for managers, employees, and intelligent citizens to know some of the basic characteristics of the law in general and, in particular, how labor law developed and some of its major statutes and provisions.

Within the general legal framework, there are three different theories of what type of justice the law should seek: utilitarian, egalitarian, or a balance of principles. There are also three conflicting theories of the nature of the legislative process: (1) that the law is a product of the rational, intelligent adjustment of the rules to social changes; (2) that the law reflects, rather than corrects, the attitudes and abuses of society; and (3) that the law has developed haphazardly in accommodation to pressure groups. Each theory of the legislative process leads us to view labor legislation in a very different way.

Labor relations exist within the province of four types of law: constitutional law; statutory, or legislative, law; common law; and administrative law. Labor laws function basically to protect collective bargaining contracts, to resolve disputes, and to establish minimum standards for employment. American labor laws involve different procedures and standards for different sectors of the economy.

Labor law developed from an antiunion position in the early 1800s toward the search for peaceful means of settling disputes to an active support for union organizing in the years after the great depression of the 1930s. Legal tools that were used against emerging unions in the nineteenth and early twentieth centuries included the labor injunction, yellow-dog contracts requiring workers not to join unions, and antitrust laws. The

---

[53]John T. Dunlop, "The Legal Framework of Industrial Relations in the United States," Bureau of National Affairs, *Daily Labor Report*, No. 194, Oct. 7, 1985, p. E1.

Railway Act of 1926 was the first major piece of legislation that established procedures for collective bargaining. It was enacted with the cooperation of both unions and carriers. The Norris-LaGuardia Anti-Injunction Act was enacted in 1932. It was followed by the National Labor Relations Act of 1935, also called the Wagner Act, which has been the most important single piece of labor-management relations regulation. The Taft-Hartley Act of 1947 modified the NLRA. The Landrum-Griffin Act in 1959 regulated the internal workings of unions and established a bill of rights for union members.

In addition to major federal legislation there are many other statutes which affect labor-management relations. The more significant legislative acts include the Fair Labor Standards Act, which establishes the minimum wage; the Equal Employment Opportunity Act of 1972; and the Age Discrimination Act.

QUESTIONS FOR THOUGHT AND DISCUSSION

1 What are the major types of law in the United States? How does each apply to labor relations? Give examples.

2 What were the major stages in the development of labor law in the United States?

3 What is the labor injunction? How was the injunction used to control union activities? What impact did the Norris-LaGuardia Act have on the labor injunction?

4 What are the major features of the Landrum-Griffin Act? Think about and discuss some aspect of the Landrum-Griffin Act from the perspective of a manager, a union member or official, or a citizen/consumer.

5 What are the implications of the courts again applying the antitrust laws to some union activities? Should this be done?

6 Which theory of the legislative process do you think is most applicable to labor law? Why?

7 Why is it important to understand the legal setting of labor-management relations, not only the major pieces of labor legislation but also the nature and characteristics of the legal process in which they are rooted (e.g., the evolving nature of the law)?

8 What is distinctive about American labor law and in what ways could these characteristics have importance for management and union officials?

SELECTED READING

Bellace, Janice R., and Alan D. Berkowitz, *The Landrum-Griffin Act: Twenty Years of Federal Protection of Union Members' Rights* (Philadelphia: Industrial Research Unit, Wharton School, University of Pennsylvania, 1979).

Berman, Harold J., and William R. Greiner, *The Nature and Functions of Law*, 3d ed. (New York: Foundation Press, 1972).

Cox, Archibald, *Law and the National Labor Policy*, Monograph Series No. 5 (Los Angeles: University of California Institute of Industrial Relations, 1960).

Gohmann, John W., ed., *Air and Rail Labor Relations: The Railway Labor Act* (Dubuque, Iowa: Kendall/Hunt Publishing, 1979).

Goldberg, Joseph P., et al., eds., *Federal Policies and Worker Status Since the Thirties* (Madison, Wis.: Industrial Relations Research Association, 1976).

Gould, William B., *A Primer on American Labor Law* (Cambridge, Mass.: MIT Press, 1984).

Justice, Betty W., *Unions, Workers and the Law* (Washington, D.C.: BNA Books, 1983).

Keeline, Thomas J., *NLRB and Judicial Control of Union Discipline* (Philadelphia: Industrial Research Unit, Wharton School, University of Pennsylvania, 1976).

McAdams, Alan K., *Power and Politics in Labor Legislation* (New York: Columbia University Press, 1964).

Morris, Charles, *The Developing Labor Law,* rev. ed. (Washington, D.C.: The Bureau of National Affairs, 1981).

The Railway Labor Act at Fifty; Collective Bargaining in the Railroad and Airline Industries (Washington, D.C.: U.S. Government Printing Office, 1977).

Summers, Clyde W., and Robert J. Rabin, *The Rights of Union Members* (New York: American Civil Liberties Union, 1980).

Taylor, Benjamin J., and Fred Whitney, *Labor Relations Law* (Englewood Cliffs, N.J.: Prentice-Hall, 1992).

CHAPTER 8

THE NLRB AND UNFAIR LABOR PRACTICES

THE NATIONAL LABOR RELATIONS BOARD

The National Relations Board (NLRB) is an independent federal agency. It was created in 1935 by Congress to administer the basic law governing relations between labor unions and business enterprises in the private sector. It was established by the National Labor Relations Act (NLRA) and administers that act as it has been amended. The law bestows on employees certain rights, which are set forth primarily in section 7 of the act. Section 7, entitled "Rights of Employees," reads as follows:

> Employees shall have the right to self-organization, to form, join or assist labor organizations, to bargain collectively through representatives of their own choosing, and to engage in other concerted activities for the purpose of collective bargaining or other mutual aid/or protection, and shall also have the right to refrain from any or all such activities. . . .

These rights of employees are not self-enforcing. It was to ensure that employees could exercise these rights and to protect them and the public from certain unfair labor practices (which are spelled out in section 8 of the act) that Congress established the NLRB.

The stated purpose of the nation's labor law is to serve the public interest by reducing interruptions in commerce arising from industrial strife. It seeks to do this by providing orderly process for protecting and implementing the respective rights of employees, employers, and unions in their relations with each other. The NLRB has been given two principal functions by the law: (1) to determine through secret-ballot elections the free, democratic choice by employees of whether they wish to be represented by a union in dealing with their employer, and if so, by which union; and (2) to prevent unlawful acts, that is, unfair labor practices, by employers or unions and to remedy the unlawful acts. The board does not act on its own initiative in either function; it processes charges of unfair labor practices and petitions for employee elections that are filed in the board's various regional offices.

ORGANIZATION AND STRUCTURE

The National Labor Relations Board consists of two parts: a five-member board that has quasi-judicial functions and an administrative agency. The five-member board itself acts as a judicial body in deciding cases submitted to it. There is also an office of the general counsel of the board that is largely independent of the five-member board. The general counsel is responsible for the issuance and prosecution of formal complaints about violation of the law. The general counsel has supervision of the NLRB's regional offices. The board's chairperson is the chief executive officer of the NLRB as a whole and is a member of the board.

Each of the five members of the board is appointed by the President for a term of 5 years, and the appointment must be confirmed by the Senate. The 5-year terms are staggered, so that one member's term expires each year. The President appoints one of the five members of the board as chairperson.

Figure 8-1 describes some aspects of the structure of the NLRB. It shows the five-member board as separate and distinct from the office of the general counsel. The general counsel's office has several divisions, including a division of litigation, which handles court cases; a division of operations, which administers the regional offices; and a division of administration, which handles personnel, budgetary, and similar functions. The board itself is shown to include the staffs of administrative law judges. Administrative law judges hear cases and issue decisions. They are attached to the board for administrative purposes, but are stationed in either San Francisco or Washington, D.C. They are assigned cases, conduct hearings, and issue decisions. ALJs, as they are called, are appointed under the Civil Service regulations of the federal government. They are not subject to removal by the board. In the process of hearing cases and making decisions, they are fully independent of the board. There are some 95 ALJs, headed by a chief administrative law judge.

The arrangement between the board itself and the general counsel's office is somewhat unusual for agencies of government. Ordinarily, the general counsel's office is simply the legal department (so to speak) of an agency. But at the NLRB the general counsel exercises a substantial degree of independent, in fact, separate, judgment regarding matters that come before the agency. Why is this so? In the period from 1935 to 1947 the organization of the agency was not as it is now. In that period the general counsel's office was an agent of the three-member board, taking its direc-

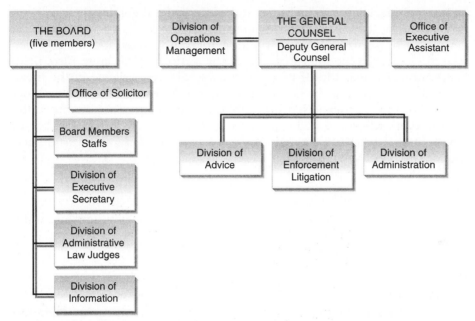

FIGURE 8-1   NLRB organization chart (simplified). (*Source:* Chairman's Office, National Labor Relations Board.)

tion from the chairperson of the board. But employers complained about this arrangement. The NLRB was, they said, both prosecutor and judge. With respect to unfair labor practices, the board investigated charges, issued complaints when it thought the law had been violated, and prosecuted the employers (until 1947 only an employer could commit an unfair labor practice). The five-member board was the tribunal, that is, the judge, before whom the case was heard. Agents of the board were thus both the prosecutor and the judge. This, the companies argued, was contrary to American judicial tradition and was unfair.

In 1947 Congress, in the Taft-Hartley amendments to the Wagner Act, separated the office of the general counsel from the board. Because of this organizational change, the role of prosecutor was separated from that of judge in the activities of the NLRB. The Taft-Hartley Act also established unfair labor practices as they applied to unions. These two reforms—the separation of the functions of the agency and the establishment of union unfair labor practice categories—were viewed as major factors increasing the impartiality of the board. The unions unsuccessfully opposed these reforms, believing they would weaken the board in its capacity to promote collective bargaining and to protect the rights of employees.[1]

[1]James A. Gross, *The Reshaping of the National Labor Relations Board: National Labor Policy in Transition, 1937–1947* (Albany: State University of New York Press, 1982).

Through decisions of the board and of the federal courts, the law as administered by the NLRB has become very complex. As a result, there has developed a group of lawyers working for both labor and management who are expert in the interpretation of the nation's labor laws. Also, membership on the board itself requires considerable experience in the meaning and application of the law. As a result, the NLRB is filled not with persons who have had experience in labor-management relations but rather with lawyers who have had experience in the federal government. For example, in 1980 the average length of service in the federal government of the members of the NLRB was 35 years.

OPERATIONS

The NLRB handles two types of cases: representation petitions and unfair labor practice charges. We consider each in turn.

Representation Cases

In 1990 the NLRB conducted 3981 representation elections.

The NLRB can conduct an election only when a petition has been filed requesting one. A petition for the certification by the board of a bargaining representative can be filed by an employee or a group of employees or a union, or it can be filed by an employer. The petition must be signed, sworn to, or affirmed under oath and filed with the NLRB's regional office in the area involved. If filed by or on behalf of employees, the petition must be supported by a showing that a substantial number (30 percent or more) of employees wish to be represented by a bargaining representative, and the petition must state that the employer refuses to recognize their representative for the purposes of collective bargaining. If an employer files the petition, it must state that employees or a union have made a claim for recognition as the exclusive representative of the particular group of employees involved.

When a petition is filed, a regional office of the board must investigate to see if a question of representation actually exists. If a question is found to exist, then the regional office may hold a hearing if necessary, at which the employer and the persons seeking the representation appear to present their respective positions. The investigation is to determine

1 *If the board has jurisdiction to conduct an election.* Some employees and employers are outside the coverage of the NLRA. Among groups not covered are agricultural laborers, domestic servants, government employees, supervisors, and independent contractors.

2 *Whether there is enough showing of employee interest* in a collective bargaining representative to justify an election.

3 *Whether there actually is a question about representation.*

4 *Whether the election is sought in an appropriate unit of employees.* (This is an especially important question, to which we will return later.)

5 *Whether the representative (ordinarily a union) named in the petition is qualified.* (This is also an important matter to be discussed later.)

6 *Whether there are any legal barriers to an election.* Often such a barrier takes the form of a bona fide existing collective bargaining agreement covering the employees in question. Such an agreement may constitute a contract bar to an election. Another legal impediment involves the certification by the NLRB of a bargaining unit within the previous year. Such a certification bars an election, as does a previous election held within the prior 12 months.

If the regional office of the board finds that the circumstances with respect to these six matters are such as to permit a question of representation to be resolved, then the board must conduct a secret-ballot election. If a union wins a majority of the votes in the election, it will be certified by the board as the exclusive collective bargaining representative of the employees in the bargaining unit, which was found by the board to be appropriate. A union that is certified is entitled to be recognized by the employer. If the employer fails to bargain with the union it commits an unfair labor practice.

The board has delegated much of its authority in representation cases to the regional directors of the NLRB. Appeals from decisions of the regional directors with respect to bargaining unit determinations and objections on how elections are conducted can be taken to the five-member board, however.

Unfair Labor Practice Cases

The basic procedures in cases involving charges of unfair labor practices are described in Figure 8-2. These procedures are initiated by the filing of a charge. A charge may be filed by an employee, an employer, a labor organization, or any person other than a board employee. Like representation petitions, charge forms are available from regional offices of the NLRB and must be signed, sworn to, or affirmed under oath and filed with the regional office in the geographic area in which the alleged unfair labor practice was committed. The regional office must investigate the charge, ordinarily by sending a representative to interview the person complaining and the company or union against which the charge was brought. The regional office, with such guidance from the general counsel's office in Washington as is appropriate, may issue a complaint if its investigation shows that there is cause to believe a violation of the law has occurred.

The issuance of a complaint by the general counsel's office is a formal legal act, in which charges of violation of the law are set forth and the charged party is informed of a hearing to be held regarding the complaint.

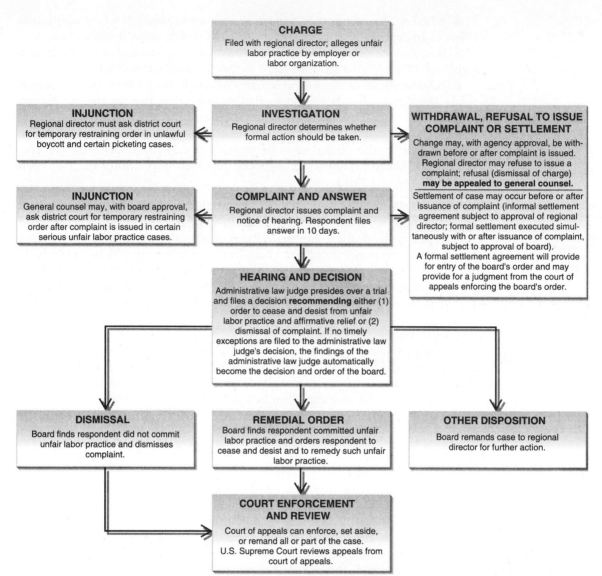

FIGURE 8-2   NLRB basic procedures in cases involving charges of unfair labor practice. (*Source:* Chairman's Office, *National Labor Relations Board.*)

Once a formal complaint is issued, the office of the general counsel becomes the prosecutor and the government bears the costs of the further legal proceedings. The person or organization that initially filed a charge is usually not formally involved except perhaps to give evidence. Occasionally a charging party may have its own lawyer, but the general counsel's office plays the major prosecuting role. The party against which the complaint was filed (either a union or an employer) must defend itself with its own legal counsel against the allegations of the government (i.e., the office of the general counsel) that it has violated the law.

The regional director may refuse to issue a formal complaint after investigating the charges filed. The director would refuse to issue a complaint if no merit were found to the accusation that a company or a union had violated the labor law. If the regional director refuses to issue a complaint in any case, the person who originally filed the charge is entitled to (1) a statement of findings and reasons from the regional director, (2) a decision not to issue a complaint, which shows precedents for the decision, (3) a right to take an appeal to Washington to the office of appeals in the general counsel's office and to people who are wholly independent of the officers in the regional office. The general counsel may choose to issue a complaint or not to do so. If the decision is not to do so, the office of appeals issues a letter setting forth the reasons why a complaint was not issued. This lengthy procedure provides as complete a review and response to a charge filed with the board as any federal agency provides in any matter before it. Ordinarily, if the agency decides to take no action on a charge or a matter of any nature brought to it, the charging party is unlikely to be successful in any court appeal of that decision or an opinion giving the reasons for it.[2]

When a formal complaint is issued, a hearing is held before an administrative law judge. The representatives of the regional office of the NLRB serve as prosecutors, and counsel for the company or union defends it. The regional office, on behalf of the board, has power to examine and copy any evidence of any person being investigated that relates to the matter under review and may issue subpoenas and obtain federal court orders to compel the production of evidence or giving of testimony. Based on the record of the hearing, the judge makes findings and recommendations. All parties to the hearing may appeal the decision of the ALJ to the five-member board.

The five-member board, on appeal, reviews the decisions of the ALJs and may affirm, alter, or amend their decisions. However, approximately 80 percent of the decisions are issued by three-member panels, with only the more difficult cases going to the full five-member board.

The National Labor Relations Act is not a criminal statute, but a civil one, and it is entirely remedial. It is intended to prevent and remedy unfair labor practices, not to punish the people responsible for them. Therefore, if a company or union is convicted of an unfair labor practice, it is not

---

[2]J. Davis, *Discretionary Justice: A Preliminary Inquiry* (Baton Rouge, Louisiana State University Press, 1969). The advice given to NLRB regional offices by the general counsel's office in Washington is generally available publicly as a result of a Supreme Court decision (*Sears Roebuck,* 1975) and is published by Labor Relations Press at Fort Washington, Pa. NLRB decisions are published by the board and are circulated by several reporting agencies, including the Bureau of National Affairs and the Commerce Clearing House, both in Washington, D.C.

fined nor are its officers jailed. The board fashions a remedial order that attempts to make up for the infraction of the law. In determining the remedy in any particular case, the board has considerable discretion.

If an employer created a union that it dominated, a violation of the law, the board might order the company to disestablish the union. If a union illegally collected dues from employees, the board might order the union to refund the dues, plus interest. If a company refused to bargain with a union, in violation of the law, the board would issue an order compelling the company to bargain with the union.

In fashioning remedial orders, the NLRB often requires companies to make restitution to employees for wages lost as a result of the employer's action in violation of the law. Thus, companies sometimes are required by the board to pay sums of money to employees against whom they have taken action found by the board to be illegal. But these payments are not technically penalties. For example, if employees were unlawfully discharged by an employer, the board would require the employer to reinstate the employees and pay them for working time missed plus interest. In one of the largest such payments required by the NLRB, a major American chemical company agreed in December 1979 to pay $12 million in back pay to 405 Louisiana chemical plant workers unlawfully locked out of their jobs by the company for 3 years. Such a financial requirement may seem to the company like a penalty, but it is legally different from the award of damages by a court. The NLRB's remedial power, for example, is limited to the financial losses which the workers can be shown to have actually sustained. Back pay for time lost at work is reduced by the amount an employee earned at any job he or she was able to get during the time the employer denied the employee the right to work. Damages would not be limited in this fashion.

COURT ACTIONS

Appeals

If a company or union fails to comply with an order of the NLRB, the board may petition a U.S. circuit court of appeals for a court order enforcing the board's directive. Thus, the NLRB cannot enforce its own orders, but must make application to a federal court to do so (see Figure 8-3). An employer or a union against which the NLRB's order was issued may oppose the NLRB's request for a court order. This is one method by which an employer or a union may obtain court review of NLRB actions.[3]

A company or union may also simply petition a circuit court of appeals to review any decision or final order of the board. The court of appeals

[3]Douglas S. McDowell et al., *NLRB Remedies for Unfair Labor Practices* (Philadelphia: Industrial Research Unit, Wharton School, University of Pennsylvania, 1976).

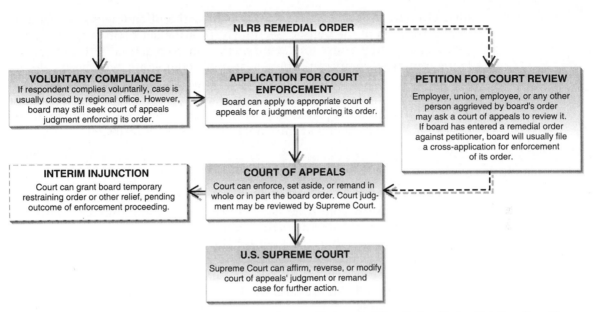

FIGURE 8-3   NLRB order-enforcement chart. (*Source:* Chairman's Office, National Labor Relations Board.)

may approve the board's order and enforce it, or it may remand the order to the board for reconsideration. It may also change the board's order or even set it aside entirely. If the court enforces a board order, failure by a company or union to comply with the order may be punished by fine or imprisonment for contempt of court. In some cases the U.S. Supreme Court is asked to review decisions of the circuit courts about NLRB orders. The Supreme Court decides on its own which cases it will hear and which it will not hear, looking for a substantial question of law or a conflict between the decisions of circuit courts of appeal in deciding to hear a case.

Enforcement in District Courts

In certain instances the law requires the NLRB to ask federal district courts to grant injunctions against certain types of activities. Section 10(1) of the act requires that whenever a charge is filed alleging a violation of certain sections of the act relating to boycotts, picketing, and work stoppages, the preliminary investigation of the charge must be given priority over all other types of cases in the regional office where it was filed. A second priority must be given to charges alleging violations by employers or unions that involve discrimination against employees with respect to membership in a union. If the preliminary investigation of the first-priority cases shows there is reasonable cause to believe that the charge is true and that a complaint should be issued, the board is required to ask a federal district court to grant an injunction against the offending party, pending final resolution of the matter. Section 10(j) of the act permits the board to petition a district court for an injunction in connection with any unfair labor practice complaint after a formal complaint has been issued. Through these provisions of the law, as well as in other ways, the injunction, issued by a federal district court, has found its way back into labor relations. But in these procedures at least, the injunction is granted at the behest of a governmental agency, not of the employer or union.[4]

A Contrast with Practice Abroad

The United States is unusual in that it does not have a specialized set of labor courts. Most countries have courts that handle only cases arising under the law that determines the rights of employees and employers. In the United States, labor cases either find their way into the NLRB and thereafter into general-purpose federal courts, or go directly into the general-purpose courts. America does have courts specialized to some areas; for example, there are bankruptcy courts that deal only with bankruptcy filings.

Should America have labor courts? Those who favor such a system believe that cases would be better decided by judges who are expert in the subtle matters of employment law. They believe that the general-purpose courts have judges whose training and experience are generally in commercial contract law and who then inappropriately apply those concepts to employment law. Also, they argue that the general courts are delayed by heavy case loads and that a system of specialized labor courts would reduce delays. In effect, supporters believe that labor courts would be quicker and give better decisions than general-purpose courts.

Those who oppose the idea of labor courts do so because they believe that either unions or management will have undue influence on them and thereby pervert the system. They argue that this has happened abroad. In the European democracies, they say, the labor courts are unfairly on the side of workers and unions, while in countries with totalitarian governments they are unfairly on the side of employers. Nowhere, it is said, is there a fair balancing of rights.

UNFAIR LABOR PRACTICES BY EMPLOYERS

American labor law is not greatly concerned with the substantive results of collective bargaining (i.e., with what wage levels are established, how long the workday is, and so on) in the private sector, but it is very much concerned with the procedures of the parties in labor relations. The NLRB

[4]Frank W. McCulloch and Tim Bornstein, *The National Labor Relations Board* (New York: Praeger, 1974).

closely regulates activities of unions and employers with respect to each other and with respect to employees. The NLRB has the authority to issue general rules or regulations to implement the provisions of the labor laws but rarely does so; it prefers to decide individual cases. These case decisions provide guidance to employers and unions involved in a similar situation concerning what is legal and what is illegal activity.

There is a body of NLRB and court decisions with respect to unfair labor practices that is very large. Furthermore, the absence of generally promulgated rules prevents a simple listing of what is and is not legal. All that can reasonably be done in a text is to discuss some of the more significant matters that have arisen under the labor laws.

Types

Section 8(a) of the National Labor Relations Act proscribes certain activities by employers. Specifically, employers are prohibited by the act from

- Interfering with, coercing, or restraining employees in exercise of their rights to join or assist labor organizations, or not to join or assist [section 8(a)(1)]
- Assisting, dominating, or contributing financially to labor unions [section 8(a)(2)]
- Discriminating against employees to discourage or encourage union membership, except as provided by a valid union security clause in a collective bargaining agreement [section 8(a)(3)]
- Discriminating against employees because they have filed charges or given testimony to the NLRB [section 8(a)(4)]
- Refusing to bargain in good faith with the representatives of employees [section 8(a)(5)]

Interference with the Rights of Employees

Section 8(a)(1) involves a broad prohibition on employer interference with employees exercising their rights under the labor laws. The prohibition is so broad that whenever the NLRB finds that an employer has committed any other unfair labor practice by virtue of violating sections 8(a)(2) or 8(a)(5) of the act, it also finds a violation of section 8(a)(1). Employer conduct that is in violation of this section of the act can occur at any time in the course of the relationship between an employer and its employees and their union(s), if any. However, section 8(a)(1) violations are especially common in the course of a union organization campaign. Some examples of what an employer legally can and cannot do under section 8(a)(1) in an election campaign were given in the previous chapter.

Violations of section 8(a)(1), which are not also violations of other parts of section 8(a), include such actions as

- Threatening employees with loss of jobs or benefits if they should join or vote for a union
- Threatening to close down a plant if a union should be organized in it
- Questioning employees about union membership or activities in a situation that tends to restrain or coerce the employees
- Spying or pretending to spy on union meetings
- Granting wage increases intentionally timed to discourage employees from joining a union

UNFAIR LABOR PRACTICES BY UNIONS

Types

Section 8(b) of the National Labor Relations Act proscribes certain activities by labor organizations. Specifically, unions are prohibited by the act from

- Coercing or restraining employees in their choice of a bargaining representative [section 8(b)(1)(A)]
- Coercing or restraining employers in their choice of a bargaining representative in collective bargaining [section 8(b)(1)(B)]
- Causing an employer to discriminate against employees illegally [section 8(b)(2)]
- Refusing to bargain in good faith with an employer [section 8(b)(3)]
- Engaging in secondary boycotts or jurisdictional strikes [section 8(b)(4)]
- Charging excessive or discriminatory initiation fees [section 8(b)(5)]
- Engaging in featherbedding [section 8(b)(6)]
- Engaging in organizational or recognition picketing [section 8(b)(7)]

Finally, the law prohibits both unions and employers from entering into so-called hot-cargo agreements.

What do the terms used in some of these prohibitions mean? Each is encrusted with substantial legal interpretation, but we can briefly explain.

Jurisdictional strikes are efforts by unions to compel an employer to assign work to members of one of two or more competing unions. For example, if the pipefitters were to quit work to try to compel a contractor to assign work to a pipefitter rather than a laborer (represented by a different union), that would be a jurisdictional strike.

Featherbedding is defined in the law to mean a union's trying to force an employer to pay its members for work not done. For example, it is illegal for a union to require an employer to pay plasterers when wallboard is installed (wallboard is prefabricated plaster installed by carpenters rather than plasterers), when the plasterers do no work even though the carpenters are now doing what arguably used to be plasterers' work. But as the unions quickly determined, the legal prohibition against featherbedding does not prevent compelling an employer to pay for work done but not needed. For example, if a fire stoker rides on a diesel locomotive, even though there is no fire to stoke, and watches out to see that the train doesn't hit anything, it isn't prohibited for the employer to be required to pay him or her, even though the work seems to the employer not to be needed. Another example involves workers at the union's insistence setting type by hand for a printing company when the company isn't going to use the hand-set type to print, but instead will use automated printing equipment. The work, so-called bogus type, isn't needed, but since the work was done, the employer can legally be compelled to pay for it.

Secondary boycotts are strikes (in the past "boycott" and "strike" were synonymous) by a union aimed at one employer to force it to stop doing business with another, with whom the union has its real dispute. That is, the union puts pressure on one employer to cause it to put pressure on another. Employers bitterly oppose such strikes, insisting that they involve them in disputes to which they are not party.

The secondary boycott is a very strong union weapon, and its being made illegal in the Taft-Hartley Act of 1947 (when union unfair labor practices were added to the nation's law) was a significant setback for them. But in 1988 the Supreme Court restored to the unions a portion of the right to stage secondary boycotts, finding that prohibitions against unions leafletting at secondary employers' premises were unlawful restrictions on unions' freedom of speech. The case in which this decision was made is interesting.

In 1979 the DeBartolo Company hired H. J. Wilson Company to build a store in a shopping center in Tampa, Florida, owned by Debartolo. Wilson then hired a contractor to do some work on the store. A construction union thought that the contractor was paying too little in wages, and so it passed out handbills at the mall asking customers not to shop at any of the mall's 85 stores. This was a classic secondary boycott and illegal until 9 years later, when the Supreme Court reversed the law and held the distribution of handbills to be lawful.

THE ROLE OF EMPLOYERS IN AN ELECTION CAMPAIGN

There has been a great deal of litigation before the board about what employers may and may not do in the course of an NLRB election campaign. The process of elections to determine whether or not employees want to be represented by unions is described in the next chapter. But here we will consider the standards under the law to determine if unfair labor practices are being committed in an election campaign.

Originally the NLRB tried to require employers to remain outside the election process. However, in the Taft-Hartley Act of 1947 Congress provided that

[t]he expressing of any view, argument, or opinion, or the dissemination thereof, whether in written, printed, graphic, or visual form, shall not constitute or be evidence of an unfair labor practice under any of the provisions of this Act, if such expression contains no threat of reprisal or force or promise of benefit.

This provision was intended to ensure that the right of employers to express their views was not unduly restricted by the NLRB. As a practical matter, this statutory language had the effect of putting the employer back into the matter of union organization—usually in opposition to unionization.

In the spring of 1988 a group of technical and clerical workers at Harvard University, who were affiliated with the American Federation of State, County and Municipal Employees (AFSCME), petitioned for and obtained an NLRB election among several thousand Harvard employees. When the union asked Harvard's president to remain neutral during the campaign, and students at Harvard College joined the request, the university's president wrote the following letter to employees and students of the university. Since President Bok of Harvard taught labor law before becoming an administrator, the letter represents a particularly knowledgeable response from an employer. It is reproduced below from the *Harvard Gazette*, May 6, 1988, page 4.

Should the Harvard administration be "neutral" toward the efforts of the American Federation of State, County and Municipal Employees (AFSCME) to organize our support staff? In other words, Should Harvard feel obliged not to disclose its views on the union election nor to present its reasons for opposing union representation?

Since Harvard is an institution dedicated to the free exchange of ideas, it seems odd to suggest that the administration keep silent on an issue that clearly affects the University and the welfare of those who live and work here. Yet this is the view advanced in a petition signed by 3000 students and endorsed by a number of student organizations, including [the student newspaper]. With such backing, the proposition merits a thoughtful response.

Apparently, the argument for neutrality is that the administration is not an ordinary party to the debate over union representation, since Harvard employs the staff members and hence controls the livelihood of those who will vote in the election. As a result, it is said, an expression of Harvard's opposition carries an inevitable threat that dire consequences may befall those who vote in favor of the union.

In weighing this argument, it is important to bear in mind that staff members will decide on representation by secret ballot so that Harvard need never know how any individual votes. Hence, the notion that Harvard's opposition will intimidate staff members and coerce them into voting against the union reflects surprisingly little respect for their independence of mind and seems implausible on its face.

The argument for neutrality also finds no support in the system of legal rules worked out over many years under the National Labor Relations Act to guarantee fair union elections. In order to insure a free and informed choice, the Act expressly guarantees to the employer a right to communicate to employees about the election and has done so for four decades, through Democratic as well as Republican administrations. The law protects employees against coercion and manipulation by prohibiting acts of intimidation, such as firing or penalizing union supporters; it likewise bans specific kinds of speech that could prejudice a free and informed choice; notably, employer threats, promises of benefits if the union loses, and interrogations. But the law in no way seeks to silence employers from presenting accurate facts and reasoned arguments in opposition to the union.

This framework of rules is not only well established but based on sound democratic principles. In a democracy that guarantees free speech, employers should have a right to communicate on a subject of obvious importance to their organization. In addition, if employees are to make an informed choice on whether or not to be represented by a union, they need to hear relevant facts and arguments on both sides of the issue and not merely listen to views in favor of the union. In order to learn the arguments and facts against as well as for the union, they will normally need to hear from the employer. For though individual employees may choose to argue against representation, they cannot begin to match the union's financial resources and organizing expertise. At Harvard, for example, numerous staff members have expressed opposition to the union, but they can hardly muster the hundreds of thousands of dollars, the paid organizers, the legal staff, and the other resources that AFSCME has poured into this campaign.

Some students have argued, nevertheless, that Harvard has an unfair advantage in presenting its case because it can call meetings of the staff during working hours. Yet Harvard has not exercised its legal right to compel attendance at these meetings and the record shows that many staff members do not choose to attend. Moreover, it would be hard to argue that the union has been placed at an overall disadvantage in this campaign. The union has had three years to communicate its message in countless different settings, while the University has confined its campaign to less than three months. In addition, the law gives the union various advantages not granted to Harvard, such as the opportunity to decide when to call for an election, the right to promise any gains in wages, benefits or terms of employment, and the right to question employees about their views on union representation. Under the law, employers cannot do any of these things.

Since most people who urge neutrality strongly favor the union, they may feel that employers need not speak since they have no important arguments to make. Such sentiments often animate arguments against free speech. But there is no support for this notion generally nor is there in this case. In fact, there are many legitimate reasons why employees might oppose a union. To mention but a few, employees may find that they are already receiving higher wages and benefits than the union has typically been able to achieve; they may resent the possibility of being compelled to pay substantial dues or agency fees; they often dislike union efforts to abolish merit pay or to secure less flexible work rules; and they may fear that collective bargaining will lead to strikes, resulting in losses of pay and conceivably even the loss of jobs. In no small part because of reasons such as these, unions regularly lose more contested elections than they win.

As is so often the case, then, there are two sides to the question whether to be represented by a union. Before our staff members enter the polling booth to make a decision important to their lives and welfare, they deserve the opportunity to inform themselves fully on all aspects of the subject. Hence, it is not only in keeping with Harvard's commitment to free expression but a matter of fairness to our staff that they be made aware of all the pertinent facts and considerations rather than merely listening to the views of one side. In this spirit, we have done our best to present information and arguments and decide the issue of representation when they cast their ballots on May 17.

An employer that oversteps the limits of the statutory language may find itself convicted of an unfair labor practice. But what is illegal and what is not? Specifically, with respect to statements by employers in the course of a union organizing drive, there is a bewildering complexity of NLRB rulings:

• An employer told employees that if they went on strike, they could lose their jobs and be permanently replaced by other workers.

The NLRB held this to be a violation of the law because it was a threat of reprisal if the employees voted to join a union. But the board indicated that if the employer had merely predicted that if there was a strike, it might replace the strikers, and that in certain circumstances the workers might have a right to reinstatement, that would have been legal (Badour, Inc., 1991).

• An employer predicted in a speech to employees that if the union came into the plant, the company would face economic disaster.

The NLRB held this not to be a "threat of reprisal" and therefore found the employer's action did not violate the law (Agar Packing and Provision Corporation, 1949).

• An employer in a speech and mailing to employees said that if the union was voted in, the annual wage increases the company ordinarily provided for employees would be delayed.

The NLRB found the employer guilty of an unfair labor practice: a threat not to pay employees a benefit ordinarily provided (Peterson Builders, Inc. v. Boilermakers, 1974).

• Two supervisors for a company suggested to employees about to vote in an NLRB election that the company would be likely to provide more and better job opportunities in the plant if it were nonunion.

The NLRB found the employer guilty of a thinly veiled threat of reprisal (General Electric v. International Union of Electrical Workers Local 676, 1974).

• A representative of the Catholic diocese of Gary, Indiana, read a Bible text to union leaders before an election by lay teachers to choose, or not choose, a bargaining representative. The text read in part, "Cleanse your hands, ye sinners."

The NLRB's general counsel issued an unfair labor practice complaint (Diocese of Gary, Indiana, 1976).

• An employer held a meeting with supervisors, floorladies, and working foremen, instructing them on their proper roles in a current union organizational campaign. Among other things, the employees were told not to talk to NLRB agents outside the presence of company attorneys.

The NLRB found no violation of the law, saying that at the time of the meeting the employer "honestly regarded the floorladies and working foremen" as part of supervision (Cato Show Printing Co., 1975).

• During a union campaign a meeting was held between employees and the employer at the employees' request. A spokesperson for the employees told the employer that all the employees had decided that they did not want to join the union. The employer asked, "Nobody wants to join the union?" The employees said no. "Well, fine. That's excellent. Is this everybody here? Nobody wants to join the union?"

The NLRB found that there was no violation of the law, since the employer polled the employees only after the employees had openly stated their position to him. The employer merely verified what they had told him (Jerome J. Jacomet et al., 1976).

• An election was scheduled from 2:45 to 4:45 p.m. On the day of the election, the company president spoke individually to every employee on the first shift—approximately half of the eligible voters—urging them to vote against union representation. The talks lasted a few minutes at each employee's work station. The union lost the vote.

The NLRB held that the talks were informal and individual, and as such did not tend to develop a mass psychology and therefore were lawful. The election results were allowed to stand (Electro-Wire Products et al., 1979).

• An employer responded to employee dissatisfaction with a union by initiating a proposal to terminate the collective bargaining agreement and assisting employees to circulate an antiunion petition.

The NLRB held that the company had violated the law. On appeal a federal court held that the employer must maintain neutrality of action, though it can express its views, about unionization of its employees. This the company had not done (Texaco, Inc. v. NLRB, Fifth Circuit Court of Appeals, No. 82-4454, 1984).

• An employer met with workers who were considering forming a union. He was asked if a rumor that the plant would be closed if the union won an election was true. "What would you do in my shoes?" the employer replied.

The NLRB held that in the context of threats by other supervisors, the response was coercive and in violation of the law (Rosewood Manufacturing Inc., 269 NLRB no. 140, 1984).

• An employer sent a letter to all employees during a union organizing effort. The letter read in part, "We have been able to work on an informal and person-to-person basis. If the union comes in this will change. We will have to run things by the book, with a stranger, and will not be able to handle personal requests as we have been doing." The NLRB's regional director found that these statements were misrepresentations of employees' rights under section 9(a) of the act, under which employees retain the right to present individual grievances to their employer. The regional director reasoned that these statements posed a threat to take away existing rights.

The board itself disagreed. It found that the employer's statements in the letter were not threats, but permissible campaign rhetoric (TriCast Inc., 274 NLRB no. 59, 1985).

• A Pennsylvania company distributed a letter during a Teamsters organizing campaign to employees saying in part: "The second point I would like to address directly concerns the reports I have been receiving about the manner in which employees are being approached to sign a union card. If you are threatened or subjected to abusive treatment to sign a union authorization card by anyone, please notify your supervisor or the personnel department. Steps will be taken to see that such actions are immediately stopped." The union filed an unfair labor practice charge. The company contended that its letter was solely to assure its work force freedom from coercion at the hands of union organizers.

The NLRB disagreed. It held that the employer's request to report abusive treatment could be interpreted by some employees to be broad enough to cover lawful attempts by union supporters to persuade employees to sign union cards during their nonworking time and off the employer's premises. "Therefore," continued the board's decision, "we find that such a statement is tantamount to a request that the employees report persistent attempts to persuade and would therefore tend to restrain the union proponent from attempting to persuade any employee through fear that his conduct would be reported to management" (Arcata Graphics/Fairfield Inc., 304 NLRB no. 68, 1991).

The examples just cited indicate actions that management can take in a union organization campaign without violating the law. But the unions maintain that management in many instances knowingly violates the requirements of federal law in order to defeat union organization campaigns. Academic research supports the proposition that companies may have something to gain by violation of the law if they are thereby successful in thwarting union organization of their employees.[5] This research does not prove that managements do sometimes knowingly violate the law, since to have an incentive to do something does not necessarily imply that an action is taken.

Is Management Playing Unfairly?

In 1990 the NLRB held 3423 elections in which 214,880 employees were eligible to vote. Unions won 47.6 percent of the elections covering some

[5]Charles R. Greer and Stanley A. Martin, "Calculative Strategy Decisions During Union Organization Campaigns," *Sloan Management Review,* 19:2, Winter 1978, pp. 61–74.

TABLE 8-1 UNION VICTORY RATE IN NLRB ELECTIONS AND FRACTION OF LABOR FORCE IN UNION VICTORIES

	Union victory rate in NLRB elections
1950	74
1955	68
1960	59
1965	61
1970	56
1975	50
1980	48
1985	47
1990	48
1992	49

Source: 1950–1980, Paul Weiler, "Promises to Keep," *Harvard Law Review,* 96:8 (June, 1983), p. 1792. Data for 1985, 1990, 1992, from various Annual Reports of the NLRB, Washington DC: 6PO, Annual.

77,689 employees. Preliminary data for 1991 suggest that the unions won approximately 44 percent of elections. The unions are now winning a larger proportion of elections than in the mid-1980s, but over the past two decades the percentage of elections won by unions has fallen from 57 percent in 1968 to 44 percent in 1991.

Table 8-1 shows the percentage of union victories in NLRB elections every 5 years since 1950. The substantial decline in union victories is evident. As a result, unions are adding only very small increases to the total number of employees they represent. The reason is that unions lose members in a variety of ways, including plant closings and resignations. As the proportion of elections won by unions has fallen, the net increase annually in union membership has dwindled to very little. Researchers estimate that in the 1980s the unions gained on balance only some 43,000 members a year, far less than a 1 percent gain per year.[6]

Why are unions losing more and more representation elections? The unions maintain that the NLRB has tipped the scales in favor of management. Management is now increasingly free to oppose unions and to do so actively and with legal impunity. As a result, unions lose elections. When unions win elections, employers often engage in surface bargaining, that is, bargaining without any serious intent to reach agreement, so that the union cannot obtain a contract. The effect is to demonstrate the futility of union organization to employees.[7] Finally, the unions charge, the board has imposed unreasonable legal restrictions on the organizing

[6]Gary N. Chaison and Dileep G. Dhavle, "A Note on the Severity of the Decline in Union Organizing Activity," *Industrial and Labor Relations Review,* 43:4, April 1990, pp. 366, 369.
[7]*AFL-CIO News,* Oct. 30, 1976, p. 8.

activities of unions. One major example that the unions cite involves the repeated denial by the board of the right of nonemployee (or "outside") union organizers to go onto the employers' property to talk with employees.[8]

In 1955 the Supreme Court ruled that when employees are physically "beyond the reach of reasonable union efforts to communicate with them," an employer might be required to permit union organizers onto its property (*NLRB v. Babcock and Wilcox*, U.S. Supreme Court, 1955). Over the ensuing years the NLRB and the courts interpreted this to mean that a balance ought to be reached between the employer's rights to keep its property private and the rights of the union to communicate with the workers.

However, in 1992 the Supreme Court ruled in another case that the NLRB had gone too far when it adopted in 1988 a rule allowing union organizers to go into shopping center parking lots and factories. The Court held that "only in the rare case" when the union faced "unique obstacles" should organizers be given access to private property to try to persuade employees to choose a union. In fact, the Court ruled, this is what it had meant in the 1955 case (*Lechmere v. NLRB*, U.S. Supreme Court, 1992).

Some researchers agree with the unions' claims that employers are abusing the law and thereby preventing people from joining unions. "There is no question that the number of people fired for organizing activity went up in the 1970s and continued to go up in the 1980s," Professor Thomas Kochan of MIT told the *New York Times*. He said that on average one worker active in recruiting was discharged for every 20 workers who voted on whether or not they wanted union representation.[9] Other scholars dispute Kochan's conclusion.[10]

Richard B. Freeman has made quantitative estimates of the importance of various factors in the decline of union successes in NLRB elections. In 1950 unions won representation rights for 84 percent of the employees eligible to vote in NLRB elections. By 1980, unions won representation rights for only 37 percent.

- 40 percent of the decline was a result of increased management opposition

[8]Max Zimmy, "Access of Union Organizers to 'Private' Property," *Labor Law Journal*, 25:10, October 1974, pp. 618–624. See also Stephen I. Schlossberg, *Organizing and the Law* (Washington, D.C.: Bureau of National Affairs, 1967). This board policy was established by decision of the Supreme Court in 1956 *(Babcock & Wilcox Co.)*.

[9]Alan Finder, "Dismissals of Key Workers Said to Slow Union-Building," *New York Times*, Sept. 28, 1991, p. 24.

[10]Robert J. LaLonde and Bernard D. Meltzer, "Hard Times for Unions: Another Look at the Significance of Employer Illegalities," *University of Chicago Law Review*, 58:3, Summer 1991, pp. 953–1014. See in rebuttal, Paul C. Weiler, "Hard Times for Unions, Challenging Times for Scholars," *University of Chicago Law Review*, 58:3, Summer 1991, pp. 1015–1032.

- 20 percent was due to reduced union organizing efforts
- 40 percent was due to changes in the economy and other factors[11]

Management opposition to unions takes many forms, some of which are more positive than others. Many companies encourage employee communication and participation programs, including nonunion grievance procedures. In effect, they provide employees with a substitute for unions, and appear to be more successful in avoiding unions than are other companies.[12]

One of the most difficult NLRB policies for the unions to accept involves the question of what the law requires when an employer has by unfair labor practices prevented a union from gaining a majority. Should the board order the employer to bargain with the union despite the union's never having won an election?

Conair Corporation is a manufacturer of hair care and grooming products with a plant at Edison, New Jersey. A local of the International Ladies Garment Workers Union tried to organize the plant and received authorization cards from 46 percent of 380 production and maintenance employees. The company acted quickly. The top management threatened to close the plant and move production to Hong Kong if the union won an election. Managers threatened to end benefits if employees voted for the union. Many employees were so afraid of losing their jobs that they went to the union and sought return of the authorization cards. The union then called a strike. The company fired all strikers and promised benefit increases and improved working conditions to employees if they would not strike. The union gave up the strike after 5 months. Meanwhile an NLRB election had been held. The company contributed to profit sharing for nonunion members only and promised other improvements if the employees would abandon the union. In an election held on December 7, 1977, some 9 months after the start of the organizing effort, the union got one-third of the ballots cast.

The NLRB in 1982 held that the management's violations of the labor law were so "outrageous" and "pervasive" that it would be ordered to bargain with the union regardless of the election's outcome, and it issued an order to the company to recognize the union.[13] The Supreme Court had suggested that in an exceptional case marked by flagrant employer violations that preclude a fair election, the NLRB might issue a bargaining

---

[11]Richard B. Freeman, "Why Are Unions Faring Poorly in NLRB Representation Elections?" in Thomas A. Kochan, ed., *Challenges and Choices Facing American Labor* (Cambridge, Mass.: MIT Press, 1985), pp. 45–64.

[12]Jack Fiorito, Christopher Lowman, and Forrest D. Nelson, "The Impact of Human Resource Policies on Union Organizing," *Industrial Relations*, 26:2, Spring 1987, pp. 113ff. See also Kenneth Gilberg and Nancy Abrams, "Countering Unions' New Organizing Techniques," *Personnel*, 64:6, June 1987, pp. 12ff.

[13]"Divided NLRB," Bureau of National Affairs, *Daily Labor Report*, No. 106, June 2, 1982, pp. AA-1, AA-2. The case is *Conair Corporation*, 1982.

order even if the union could not and even if the union had never shown majority support.[14] In 1983 the District of Columbia Circuit Court of Appeals struck down the NLRB order against Conair. In 1984 the NLRB returned to the same question and announced that it would "under no circumstances" issue a bargaining order where the union had not demonstrated majority support.[15]

To the unions it appears that the policy of the NLRB and the courts means simply that an employer who flagrantly and successfully violates the labor laws will be allowed to enjoy its success. It is this situation, perhaps more than any other, that in the mid-1980s caused union officials to publicly question whether or not the nation's labor laws are of any benefit to workers who wish to organize a union.

Is the NLRB Thwarting Unions?

There is today considerable ambivalence in opinion about the NLRA. Professor Paul C. Weiler of Harvard Law School has commented:

> If there is any one observation that one can make with some degree of confidence during this, the fiftieth anniversary year of the National Labor Relations Act, it is that the authors of the Act would be mightily surprised to hear who is saying what about their offspring. The business community, which excoriated the Wagner Act as the most radical feature of the New Deal, now praises the balanced and constructive character of our legislation. "The '. . .'-damned Labor Board," to use Fortune Magazine's sobriquet of 1938, is now applauded by management attorneys for its moderate and even-handed jurisprudence. Meanwhile, the Democratic supporters of the union movement in Congress have just issued a report entitled "Has Labor Law Failed?": their answer to their question is most emphatically, "Yes!" [16]

In essence, those who support unions believe the NLRA was enacted to foster union organization, and that it has been perverted in recent years. Jay Siegel, a management attorney, described the law's posture in the mid-1980s as follows:

> Fifty years after the passage of the National Labor Relations Act, U.S. labor policy is precisely where the sense of the nation wants it to be: conservative toward the unionization of workers but supportive of their individual rights. However

---

[14]*Gissell Packing Co.,* 71 LRRM 2481, 1969.

[15]"Board Rejects Bargaining Order," Bureau of National Affairs, *Daily Labor Report,* No. 97, May 18, 1984, pp. AA-1, AA-2. The case is *Gourmet Foods, Inc. and Teamsters Local 503,* May 14, 1984.

[16]Paul C. Weiler, "Reflections on the NLRA at 50," Bureau of National Affairs, *Daily Labor Report,* No. 112, June 11, 1985, pp. E1–E11. See also Weiler, *Governing the Workplace: The Future of Labor and Employment Law* (Cambridge, Mass.: Harvard University Press, 1990); and James A. Gross, "Conflicting Statutory Purposes," *Industrial Labor Relations Review,* 39:1, October 1985, pp. 7–18.

distressful to organized labor this may be, it is a classic example of the democratic process at work.[17]

He writes elsewhere,

The collectivist approach runs counter to the individualistic trends that have marked our way of life beginning in the 1970s, particularly among the younger people entering the workforce for the first time. Their way of life is to "do their own thing." Thus, they are restless in a work environment that does not allow for easy expression. They recognize, however, that there is a price to be paid for the wages and benefits they receive from a company and so tolerate, in most instances, the employer's rules for conduct and job performance. But they do not see a need for additional structure in the form of a union for which they may not get any direct or immediate benefit and have to pay a dues charge, which is simply lost money to them.[18]

In 1987 a personnel consultant studied whether political bias influences decisions by the NLRB. He found a sharp difference between voting of appointees of the two political parties. "Republican members originally appointed by Republican Presidents appear to be staunch party-liners who make decisions which are influenced by political party philosophy," he said, adding that such appointees were less likely to decide in favor of unions over employers than nominees of other political stripes.

According to him, the same cannot be said of nominees selected by Democratic Presidents. "Results also suggest," he said, "that Democratic members originally appointed by Democratic Presidents are no more likely to decide in favor of employers or unions, but play by the rules and render decisions in an evenhanded manner."[19]

These observers agree that the NLRA has tilted away from unions, but disagree whether this is good or bad. This is a question for the American people to answer.

Finally, despite the unions' unhappiness with the NLRB and their low rate of election victories, they continue to make the effort to organize workers. In 1990, after a 12-year battle, the United Food and Commercial Workers Union won a representation vote at Seafirst Bank in Seattle; Seafirst became the first large bank in the United States to have union representation of its employees.

Unions also have studied the causes of their defeats and their victories in campaigns. Interestingly, according to an AFL-CIO inquiry unions won only one-third of elections in which wages were a primary issue. But unions won 62 percent of elections where the union had the support of a

[17]Jay S. Siegel, "A New Labor Policy Consensus," *Wall Street Journal*, Sept. 4, 1985, p. 18.

[18]Jay S. Siegel, "Has Labor's Day Passed?" *Boston Globe*, Sept. 3, 1985, p. 25.

[19]"Consultant . . .," Bureau of National Affairs, *Daily Labor Report*, No. 2, Jan. 5, 1988, p. A-10.

rank-and-file committee among employees. In response, unions are stressing rank-and-file committees in organizing and placing less stress on wages as an issue.

LEGAL REGULATION: IS IT AN ANACHRONISM?

The current body of American labor law is not well suited in a technical sense to our changing economy. Current law presumes a manufacturing-type employment environment—one in which the employee has a stable job, in which the employer has substantial capital invested and cannot move its facility or change its employees readily, and in which the employer has substantial net worth in a particular corporate identity and cannot readily abandon it for another corporate identity. Yet service firms, which are increasing in importance as manufacturing employment declines, often lack these characteristics. Hence, law intended to provide employees a free choice about unionism has come to the unions and some observers to seem biased against union organization.[20] Manufacturing employers are increasingly able to avoid unionization of new facilities, while service employers readily change corporate identities, move locations, and replace employees as necessary to avoid unions.

The result is that top union leaders now are calling for the reform or abolition of the nation's labor laws—a major reversal of position for them. Lane Kirkland, president of the AFL-CIO, broached the idea publicly in 1984 in newspaper interviews.[21] Union leaders testifying to Congress describe the laws as hindering the advancement of organized workers.[22]

Historically, it was not the unions but employers who argued for the weakening or abolition of the National Labor Relations Act. A first argument was that it made unions monopolists, and thereby damaged the interests of firms and customers. But this position assumes that the act provides superior outcomes for labor—something that is increasingly unclear.[23]

Management spokespersons, accustomed to decades of protest that the nation's labor laws unfairly favor unions,[24] have apparently been caught off guard by the unions' sudden attack on the labor laws. Few management voices have been raised in defense of the laws. If the unions are committed, perhaps the nation's labor laws will be repealed. A more sig-

---

[20]Paul Weiler, "Promises to Keep," *Harvard Law Review*, 96:8, June 1983, pp. 1788ff.

[21]Leonard M. Apcar, "Kirkland's Call to Void Labor Laws," *Wall Street Journal*, Nov. 6, 1984, p. 31.

[22]Richard L. Trumka, president, United Mine Workers, statement before House Labor Subcommittee on Labor-Management Relations, *Daily Labor Report*, No. 121, June 22, 1984, pp. F1–F4.

[23]Robert J. Flanagan, "The Economics of Unions and Collective Bargaining," *Industrial Relations*, 29:2, Spring 1990, p. 308.

[24]Morgan D. Roberts, *Power and Privilege: Labor Unions in America* (New York: Universe, 1984).

nificant modification of the industrial relations system would be difficult to imagine.

Why would the unions want the labor laws repealed? The answer is to be found in the declining success rate that unions have in NLRB elections. The law provides predictability, orderliness, and the potential for delay. These characteristics may be seen as favorable to management, which, in a stable and predictable environment, may bring its greater resources into play against a union.

What would labor relations be like without the labor laws? There would be no NLRB elections, no unfair labor practices. Unions would be free to strike employers and related companies (suppliers or customers). The potential power of the strike would be used whenever employees were prepared to support a work stoppage.

On the other hand, employers would be free to discharge union activists, to threaten employees favorable to a union, and to promise benefits to those who oppose unionization.

On balance, who would benefit? Would employers break unions, or would unions have a more effective strike weapon? Would union membership rise or fall?

We do not know the answers to these questions today. But as the discussion about repeal of the nation's labor laws sparked by Kirkland's comment continues, answers may emerge.

CHAPTER SUMMARY

The National Labor Relations Board is a federal agency that administers the law governing labor relations. It was created by Congress in 1935 and has two principal functions: (1) to determine through elections whether employees wish to be represented by a union and, if so, what union; and (2) to prevent unfair (i.e., unlawful) labor practices by either employers or unions.

The organization and the structure of the NLRB are complex. The board consists of a five-member board, which acts as a judicial body in deciding cases submitted to it, and as an administrative agency, which has about 95 administrative law judges (ALJs) who hear cases and issue decisions. There is also an independent general counsel's office, which is responsible for the issuance and prosecution of formal complaints. The Taft-Hartley Act amendments of 1947 separated the role of prosecutor (the general counsel) from that of judge (the ALJs and the board) in the structure of the NLRB.

The board does not act on its own initiative, but processes petitions for employee elections and charges of unfair labor practices. In a recent year, the NLRB received more than 50,000 cases, about 75 percent of which involved charges of unfair labor practices. An unfair labor practice proceeding is initiated by the filing of a charge with a regional office of the NLRB, which investigates the charge. If a formal complaint is issued, the office of the general counsel becomes the prosecutor, the government bears the costs, and an ALJ hears the case. Appeals of board decisions go to various federal circuit courts of appeal, and some ultimately find their way to the U.S. Supreme Court. The NLRB has the largest volume of federal court appeals of any federal administrative agency.

An important aspect of unfair labor practice proceedings is that there are no provisions for the issuing of penalties for violations—only remedial orders intended to prevent and remedy unfair labor practices.

Enforcement of NLRB decisions can also be complicated. In the face of union or employer compliance, the board must ask a federal district court to issue an order enforcing the board's decision. The union or company may, in turn, ask the federal district court not to enforce the decision and thus tie up the matter in further litigation and review.

The NLRB regulates what the unions and employers may say and do in election campaigns. Representation elections ordinarily involve extensive campaigns conducted by both the employer and the union. In the past two decades, the proportion of NLRB elections won by unions has steadily declined, and the unions claim that management has been increasingly free to oppose unions and to defeat union attempts to obtain bargaining rights.

American labor law is very much concerned with the procedures used in labor relations. The NLRB closely regulates activities of unions and employers with respect to each other and to employees, and there is a substantial body of decisions on unfair labor practices. Significant matters that are regularly dealt with include prohibiting employers from (1) interfering with employee rights to join or not to join labor organizations (by threats of job loss or plant closings if employees vote for a union, by interrogation of employees and solicitation to discourage union activity, and by unlawful surveillance of union organizers and employees) and (2) discriminating against employees through plant closings, employer lockouts, and refusals to bargain that are motivated by antiunion bias.

The NLRB also proscribes certain activities on the part of labor unions. These include (1) restraint and coercion of employees (e.g., by physical assaults or threats of violence), (2) coercion or inducing of employers to discriminate against employees, (3) refusal to bargain in good faith (e.g., by including illegal provisions in a contract, terminating a contract, or striking against an employer who is willing to bargain), and (4) engagement in strikes or boycotts (especially secondary boycotts) to accomplish certain objectives.

QUESTIONS FOR THOUGHT AND DISCUSSION

1 Why is the general counsel's office separated from the five-member NLRB? Does this organizational arrangement help ensure the board's fairness? Why or why not?

2 What should be the role of an employer when its employees are going to vote in an NLRB election? Should the employer be neutral? Should it be prounion or antiunion? Does the NLRB let the employer take part in the election campaign? Should it do so?

3 Should an employer be free to close a plant to avoid unionization? Under what circumstances may it do so now? Should the law be modified? How?

4 Do you think there are general underlying problems in labor relations that lead both employers and unions to commit unfair labor practices?

5 The Supreme Court has said that the NLRB can reverse its previous decisions or precedents since there is a responsibility to adapt the NLRA to changing patterns of industrial life. What are the pros and cons of this position?

6 It is sometimes suggested that the NLRB be abolished. Do you agree? Why or why not?

SELECTED READING

Gould, William B., IV, "Fifty years under the National Labor Relations Act: A Retrospective View," *Labor Law Journal*, 37:4, April 1986, pp. 235–243.

Gross, James A., *The Making of the NLRB*, 2 vols. (Albany: State University of New York, 1974) and *The Reshaping of the NLRB* (Albany: State University of New York, 1982).

Murphy, Betty Southard, and Elliot S. Azoff, *Practice and Procedure before the National Labor Relations Board*, Corporate Practice Series No. 41 (Washington, D.C.: Bureau of National Affairs, 1985).

Weiler, Paul, *Governing the Workplace: The Future of Labor and Employment Law* (Cambridge, Mass.: Harvard University Press, 1990).

CHAPTER 9

UNION ORGANIZATION AND REPRESENTATION ELECTIONS

THE DECISION TO JOIN A UNION

Most employees do not actively participate in determining the conditions under which they work. Instead, they accept whatever rules and benefits are established for them. They may grumble at things they don't like and may even quit if they are dissatisfied enough, but they are essentially passive in the relationship. Why is this? In part it is simply apathy. In part it is because an employee does not feel that he or she alone can affect the conditions of the job. In part it is because the employee lacks a method, or a vehicle, for getting his or her message across.

In many instances, both in the United States and abroad, employees form or join organizations that represent them as a group. Employees may call these organizations by many names: associations, benevolent societies, unions, brotherhoods, and so on. Generally, we refer to such organizations by the generic term "union." In the United States employee organizations are given certain rights and responsibilities by law, again under the general term "union."

There is no single reason why employees join unions. Interestingly, recent research suggests that blacks have the most favorable attitudes toward unions, but that there is no difference in the propensity of Americans to join unions that is attributable to ethnicity.[1] So why do people join unions? There appear to be several reasons, each of which may be operative at any one time, although some have been of special significance at certain periods of our history. Here are the major ones.

---

[1]Ronnie Silverblatt and Robert J. Amann, "Race, Ethnicity, Union Attitudes and Voting Predilictions," *Industrial Relations*, 30:2, Spring 1991, pp. 271ff.

To Obtain an Instrument in Opposition to Management

Employees often join unions in order to have a method of collectively resisting actions of management. When employers cut wages or pay low wages, when employers arbitrarily discipline or dismiss employees, when working conditions are unsafe or too unpleasant, or when managers interfere in employees' personal lives, employees may resist by joining unions. Through the union employees may petition management for changes, and, if unsuccessful, they may resort to a concerted work stoppage—a strike.

Often an employee's initial interest in unionization is a result of dissatisfaction with some aspects of his or her employment. Perhaps the employee believes that wages are too low, or that too much overtime work is being required by management. But dissatisfaction alone will not result in the formation of a union unless the employees are willing to work together as a group. Many employees in this country have reservations about collective action against their employers and so resist joining unions even though they may experience dissatisfaction about aspects of their work life. But where employees accept the concept of collective action, they must take yet a further step, conceptually, in order to be prepared to join a union. They must believe that the union is a device that can yield advantages for them.

Research by behavioral scientists in recent decades has stressed the role of unions as instruments for obtaining the objectives of workers. According to this view, employees differ as individuals, having different objectives with respect to their jobs.[2] Some objectives are common to large numbers of employees, such as dissatisfaction with low pay levels and a desire for wage increases. Research indicates that lower-paid workers are likely to be more committed to a union and to be stronger in their opposition to management than better-paid employees.[3] Other objectives than raising pay levels may be unique to certain employees, such as a desire to improve working conditions in a particular part of a plant. But for employees to unionize, they must see the union as a potential method of achieving better pay and/or improving working conditions in their particular areas of the plant.

The manner in which employees view unions as an instrumentality has been explored by many survey questionnaires. One study involved interviewing employees who voted in NLRB-conducted union representative elections. Voters were interviewed twice: once before voting and once after. Some 31 elections were surveyed, and 1239 employees were interviewed. Data were collected as to the attitudes of the employees and how they had voted in the election. Statistical analysis of the data revealed that employees who were dissatisfied with wage levels, the behavior of company super-

---

[2]Victor H. Vroom, *Work and Motivation* (New York: John Wiley, 1964).
[3]Peter D. Sherer and Motohiro Morishima, "Roads and Roadblocks to Dual Commitment," *Journal of Labor Research*, 10:3, Summer 1989, p. 325.

visors, the type of work they were doing, fringe benefits, and their opportunities for promotion were most likely to vote in favor of union representation.[4]

Another study involved 200 randomly selected members of a public employees' union who were asked about their reasons for joining the union. The researchers made a distinction between extrinsic and intrinsic reasons for joining a union. Extrinsic reasons involve obtaining wage and benefit increases, job security, and protection against unfair action by management. Intrinsic reasons include gaining greater influence over day-to-day decisions made about the individual's job, both in terms of its quality and in terms of its relation to the organization as a whole and to the persons served by the organization (e.g., the clients of a government agency providing social and rehabilitative services). The researchers found that even though the union members surveyed were professional employees, the extrinsic motives for union membership took precedence. Thus, they concluded that this group of white-collar employees joined a union for reasons quite similar to those found in the major studies of the reasons for which blue-collar workers joined unions: in order to obtain an instrument (the union) by which to better their pay and working conditions.

Union leaders are aware that many workers view unions primarily as instruments by which to attempt to achieve their own personal goals, whether intrinsic or extrinsic. But union leaders are often somewhat hesitant about endorsing this view of unions too completely. Unions cannot always deliver improvements in pay and other aspects of employment. Sometimes conditions do not permit improvements. And employees who have become union members only for short-term benefits may not prove loyal in difficult times.

Union leaders have a somewhat disparaging term for the concept of a union that sees itself only as an instrument for obtaining better conditions for each individual member. They describe such a concept as one of "vending-machine unionism." In the same way that an employee who deposits several coins in a cigarette machine expects to receive a package of cigarettes in return, a union member who pays dues may expect to receive an improvement in pay or working conditions. But a union is not as simple a device as a vending machine, nor is it necessarily as reliable in the short term. There has always been a strain of thought in American unionism that objected to the instrumentalist view, where the objectives of the union were too closely set to the employee's own job satisfaction. "The only way people will see a union as important to their lives," wrote one unionist, "is if they see the union . . . as an agency that could not only affect wages and working conditions, but also their environment,

[4]Jeanne M. Brett, "Why Employees Join Unions," *Organizational Dynamics*, 8:4, Spring 1980, pp. 47–59.

their children's education and health care, and their prospects for racial justice."[5]

To Participate in Union Activities

Unions are self-help organizations. Employees may join them to obtain certain health or insurance benefits, to participate in educational programs, or to learn about their own business and occupation. They may also join to engage in social or community activities. Through these activities unions constitute a form of employee self-government that has nothing to do with relations to the employer.

In some skilled trades and professions, unions are the primary organization through which the occupation is regulated, and relationships with employers are a secondary function of the union. In the past, people applying for jobs sometimes had to join a union first in order to be referred to an employer. An arrangement between a union and employers that requires union membership in order for a person to be hired is now illegal in the United States (since 1947), but in some occupations arrangements that have virtually the same effect continue.

To Exercise Leadership

Certain individual employees join unions as an outlet for their own ambitions. They may aspire to leadership and find that the union offers a convenient vehicle. They may hope to get ahead by obtaining an office in the union. Also, employers often notice employees who are leaders in the union, and it is not uncommon to have union officials hired directly into managerial ranks as supervisors or superintendents.

Because of Social Pressure

Many employees join unions simply because other employees urge them to do so. They may be made to feel that they are traitors or malingerers if they do not join. Or they may simply become the object of a friendly but persistent campaign to get them to join the union. Such social pressures are hard to resist, whether their subject be hair styles, personal behavior, or union membership. Many people belong to unions probably for no other reason than an inability to resist social pressure.

Compulsory Unionism

There is no law in the United States that requires an employee to join a union. But in most states the law permits an employer to agree with a

[5]Frank Kashner, "A Rank and File Strike," *Radical America*, 12:6, November–December 1978, p. 60.

union that after a certain period (generally 30 days except in the construction industry, where the period is 7 days) an employee must join the union or be fired. Joining the union ordinarily entails a ceremony and membership pledge and paying dues or assessments. We do not know how many employees are union members solely because of agreements that compel union membership.

WHY EMPLOYEES FAIL TO JOIN UNIONS

Most American employees are not members of labor unions. There are several reasons for this.

Antiunion Attitudes   Many employees believe that unions are either inappropriate or unnecessary. They are suspicious of union leaders and of what they, as members, might be asked to do. Also, many employees hope to be promoted to better jobs and believe membership in a union would restrict their opportunities.

Social Pressures   Employees working in a nonunionized place may be under considerable social pressure not to join a union. They may be made to feel disloyal if they do so. Employees who do not want a union, often aided and abetted by management (although some forms of management involvement are illegal), are likely to exert considerable pressure on other employees not to join a union.

Job Satisfaction   Some employees are generally satisfied with their jobs and have no substantial grievances against management. They may believe that management would consider formation of a union a hostile act by employees, and they see no reason to take such action.

Fear of Reprisal   Some employees do not join unions simply because they are afraid of reprisals by management. Although reprisals for union-related activity are illegal in the United States, the employees may fear that they will occur nonetheless. Fear of being fired because of union activity certainly remains a factor in keeping workers from joining unions, although we do not know how many people are intimidated in this way.

Cost   Unions cost money. An employee who joins a union must pay an initiation fee (generally less than $100, but considerably higher in certain trades) and pay dues on a periodic basis. Dues average about 1 or 2 hours' pay per month, or about 1 or 2 percent of before-tax pay. Whether or not the amount seems large, many workers prefer not to pay it and do not join unions for this reason.

Union Hostility or Indifference   Some people do not join unions because the unions won't accept them. There are many possible reasons why this might occur. Some unions have excluded people on grounds of race, ethnic background, or gender. It is now illegal for unions to refuse membership to anyone on these grounds (as it is illegal for employers to refuse to hire on these grounds), but, unfortunately, such instances do still occur. Also, some skilled craft unions refuse to accept people who do not have the skills required of a member.

Unions may also simply fail to assist in the unionization of groups of workers. The union may decide that the workers involved are too few or are located at too remote a place to be serviced at a reasonable cost to the union. The union may also decide that there are too few job opportunities for the already-existing union membership or that the workers involved will not make good union members. Finally, a union contacted by a group of employees might decide that the employees seeking membership actually belong to the jurisdiction of a different union and might therefore refuse to accept their application for membership.

Conscientious Objection   Some employees have religious or moral scruples against joining organizations, including unions. For this reason, some employees refuse to become members of labor unions.

A diagrammatic representation of three alternative models by which a person may be said to decide whether or not to support a union is given in Figure 9-1. In Model A dissatisfaction leads a person to embrace a union as a means to improve his or her situation. In Model B a person need not be dissatisfied, but simply thinks he or she can do better through a union. In Model C a person's political or ideological beliefs incline him or her to support a union, if it espouses the same beliefs.

FIGURE 9-1   Models of the decision to support a union. (*Source:* Adapted from Hoyt N. Wheeler and John A. McClendon, "The Individual Decision to Unionize," in George Strauss et al., *The State of the Unions,* Madison, Wis.: IRRA, 1991, p. 51.)

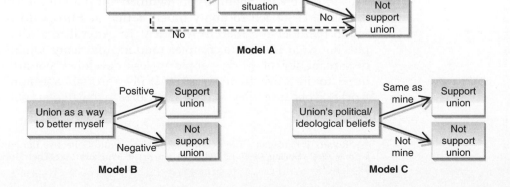

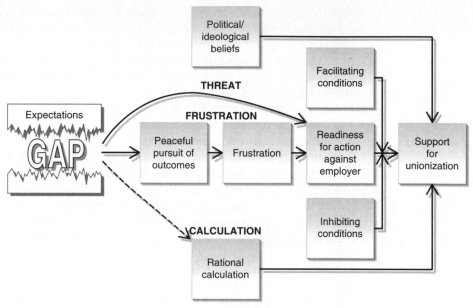

FIGURE 9-2   The decision to support unionization. (*Source:* Adapted from Hoyt N. Wheeler and John A. McClendon, "The Individual Decision to Unionize," in George Strauss et al., *The State of the Unions,* Madison, Wis.: IRRA, 1991, p. 51.)

It is widely thought that Model A best represents what happens in America: that is, workers turn to unions if they are dissatisfied with their jobs. In support of this view is offered the evidence that surveys indicate that the fraction of the American work force which is satisfied with its jobs has grown over the last several decades, and that the fraction of nonunion workers desiring union representation has decreased. This is often cited as another reason for the decline in union membership in the United States.[6]

Model B is often viewed as applying much better in less developed countries to the choice about union membership than in the United States; and Model C is judged to apply much better in Europe to the choice about union membership than in America. To generalize at the risk of oversimplifying what is surely a complex matter: Americans join unions because of dissatisfaction at work; people in less developed countries because they hope to improve their lives generally through a union; and European workers because they want to advance a particular political and social agenda.

[6]Robert J. Flanagan, "The Economics of Unions and Collective Bargaining," *Industrial Relations,* 29:2, Spring 1990, p. 308; and "Surprise! Workers Like Their Jobs," *Training,* March 1989, p. 74.

An elaboration of Model A is given in Figure 9-2. It shows dissatisfaction as less a matter of the actual conditions of work than as the difference between the expectations of workers and the reality in which they live. This conforms to the often observed situation in which some workers who have very difficult conditions are less likely to take union-related action than others who seem more favorably situated. The model in Figure 9.2 also incorporates elements of Models B and C from Figure 9.1, which is appropriate since they also play some role in American workers' decisions about joining unions.

WHAT DOES IT MEAN TO HAVE A UNION?

To a Company

The existence of a union has many implications for a company. Probably the most obvious is that the employer must deal with employees as a group and not simply as individuals. In many instances, this may not be as major a difference as it seems, however, because many companies are so large that they already have personnel policies designed to treat employees as members of a group. But what is different is that the company must deal with the union, which represents the workers. And dealing with representatives of a group of people is not at all like dealing with them as individuals.

Managers often complain about this. They distinguish between the union and the employees and then comment on how reasonable the employees are and how irresponsible and difficult their union representatives are. Yet the union is ordinarily another manifestation of the employees' needs and desires. In part, the employees are able to be reasonable with management because they know the union is there to be more difficult in their behalf.

A company that deals with a union must be very careful in its policies, for the union is always observing what it does and looking for inconsistencies. When a company is inconsistent, treating one employee differently from another in the same situation, then the union will try to get the better treatment for both, and this may be costly and inefficient from the company's viewpoint.

In a union-management relationship the day-to-day activities of both are measured against a contract. The contract is an agreement between the union and the company that sets forth the rights and obligations of each. Actions that management takes with respect to an employee or a group of employees may be judged in light of the contract and found to be permissible or not. The contract is a more rigid form of control on managerial discretion than ordinarily exists in a nonunion situation.

When management is said by the union to have violated provisions of the agreement, it may even have to defend itself before a third and neutral party, an arbitrator, who will decide if there has been a violation. In the United States companies without a union do not ordinarily have their actions subject to review by neutral persons. In other countries, however, there are often laws about labor-management relations at the plant and courts that handle disputes between workers and management, even where a union does not exist. This is one of the reasons that companies in the United States prefer so strongly not to have a union representing their employees. In the absence of a union, American managers have much more discretion in their actions than is the case abroad because there are fewer laws about management-employee relations in the United States.

Finally, when a union exists it is ordinarily more than just a group of employees who band together to deal with an employer. Instead, a union is a human institution separate and independent from the company. The union has its own internal political life; its own objectives, officers, and activities; and its own financial status. It may also be affiliated with other unions in a national body. Whatever the formal organizational characteristics, however, the union is for workers a separate source of involvement and loyalty, apart from the company and often in conflict with it. In this sense, managers often resent unions for reducing the loyalty of company employees.

Each reader may have his or her own view as to whether these results of the existence of a union are for the better or worse. Some think unions are an inappropriate interference with the lives of managers and workers. Others believe unions are a necessary device to protect and assist workers in dealings with management. Whatever a person's view, however, it is obvious that having a union in a company will tend to make a considerable difference in the company's relations with its employees. Whether this difference leads to a good or a bad situation depends on factors we will examine below.

To Employees

Employees who are represented by unions find in the union an advocate in their dealings with management. A union is primarily a service organization that attempts to assist and defend the people it represents. Employees who feel they are not being treated fairly by management may take their questions or complaints to the union, which should investigate their problem and report back to them. In nonunion companies employees are often afraid to press their problems with managers. They may fear for their jobs if they are too persistent in asserting their rights or if they appear to managers to be malcontents. Even though well-managed nonunion firms encourage employees to bring complaints to their supervisors, the inherent suspicion that employees have of their supervisors may make such a procedure of limited value.

Unfortunately, unions do not always treat employees fairly either. Sometimes union officials are too busy to handle problems for certain employees. Sometimes union officials give in to the human temptation to serve union members better than other employees, although they have a legal obligation to represent all employees in a bargaining unit equally. Generally, however, union officials attempt to represent employees equally and well and do provide an independent channel for employees to use in dealing with management.

One way to look at the role of a union in representing employees is in terms of power relationships. An individual employee dealing directly with management is plainly at a great disadvantage if power plays a role in settling his or her problem or complaint. A union, however, exercises power of its own, arising from the collective weight of the employees as a group. Therefore, when an employee encounters management through the instrumentality of a union, the power balance is much more even.

The existence of a union confronts an employee with the decision of whether to participate in the activities of the union or not.[7] In some instances the employee is free to pay dues or not, as he or she decides. In other instances, the employee must pay dues by virtue of a provision in the collective bargaining agreement. But whether an employee pays dues voluntarily or involuntarily, he or she is not obliged to participate in union activities. Unions have meetings, elect officers, and have social occasions. Sometimes unions conduct strikes or participate in boycotts. The individual must determine whether or not to take part in these activities. Usually a union acts by majority vote of the members who attend meetings. An employee must decide whether to go to the meetings and whether to be bound in his or her own actions by the majority rule. Ordinarily, the decisions involved are not difficult, but crises and conflicts arise in which such decisions can be very hard to make.

An employee who actively takes part in the union will also be drawn into the internal life of a broader movement, involving other local unions and the national union. This involvement may make demands on the employee's time and energy outside the workplace. Again, some people welcome such involvements, while others do not.

Finally, the existence of a union presents both management and employees with the possibility that a conflict may develop that cannot be resolved, so that a work stoppage occurs. One major reason why managements object to unions is the fear that if a union exists, it is certain to call a strike at some time or other. Many employees also fear loss of their pay during strikes. But a union does not guarantee that strikes will occur. Most companies and unions reach agreements without work stoppages. Nor does the absence of a union ensure that if a dispute develops, a strike won't occur.

[7]Michael G. Kolchin and Thomas Hychak, "Participation in Union Activities," *Journal of Labor Research*, 5:3, Summer 1984, pp. 259–261.

REPRESENTATION PROCEEDINGS

The National Labor Relations Act requires that an employer bargain with the representative of its employees, but it does not require that the representative be selected in any particular fashion, as long as the representative is clearly the choice of the majority of the employees. The act also provides that the employees' representative for collective bargaining can be any individual or labor organization. A supervisor or any other management representative cannot be an employee representative.

UNIT DETERMINATIONS

How Determinations Are Made

Section 9(b) of the NLRA authorizes the NLRB to decide in each representation case whether "in order to assure to employees the fullest freedom in exercising the rights guaranteed by this Act, the unit appropriate for the purposes of collective bargaining shall be the employer unit, craft unit, plant unit, or subdivision thereof." This section of the NLRA is regarded as one of the broadest grants of discretion that Congress has entrusted to any federal administrative agency.[8]

A unit can thus be all the employees of a company in however many plants it has, all the employees in a single plant, or even separate groups of employees within a plant. The board will certify a multiemployer unit if the employers and the union agree to set up such a unit, but it will not establish a multiemployer unit in any other case.[9]

There are certain limitations placed on this grant of discretion by the act itself. Among the most important limitations are:

1 *The board is not permitted* to approve a unit that includes both professional and nonprofessional employees unless a majority of the professional employees involved vote to be included in a mixed unit.

2 *The board is prohibited* from including plant guards in the same unit with other employees.

3 *Supervisors are excluded* from the coverage of the act, and therefore from inclusion in a bargaining unit, by virtue of not being included in the term "employee" to which the act applies. Whether an individual is a supervisor in the board's view depends on his or her authority over employees and not merely on the person's formal title.[10]

The exclusion of supervisors from coverage by the act is important. The exclusion was entered into the act by the Taft-Hartley amendment of 1947.

---

[8]Ibid., p. 125.

[9]John E. Abodeely, *The NLRB and the Appropriate Bargaining Unit* (Philadelphia: Industrial Research Unit, Wharton School, University of Pennsylvania, 1971).

[10]Robert B. Allen, "Status of Supervisors under NLRA," *Louisiana Law Review*, 35:4, Summer 1975, pp. 800–812.

Prior to that time there was a national union of foremen (the Foremen's Association of America) that was active in many industries, especially in the automobile industry. The passage of the Taft-Hartley Act removed the prohibitions against employers discharging supervisors for union activity. Thereafter, in the face of overt employer opposition, the foremen's unions declined.

How has the board exercised its discretion in establishing bargaining units? The board has generally sought to determine the appropriateness of a bargaining unit on the ground of the common employment interests of the employees involved. Those who have the same or substantially similar interests concerning wages, hours, and working conditions are grouped by the board into a bargaining unit. The following factors are also considered:

1 *Any history* of collective bargaining by the employees involved
2 *The desires* of the employees
3 *The extent* to which the employees are organized into a union

Section 9(c)5 of the act prohibits the board from giving the third factor controlling weight. That is, the board cannot determine that an appropriate unit is simply whoever the union has gotten to support it.[11]

The determination of bargaining units can have a major impact on the likelihood of the unionization of a group of employees. For example, until the early 1970s the employees of one subsidiary of a major corporation were represented by an independent union. The independent union began to lose its support, however, and several national unions became interested in seeking recognition rights. The company employed some 40,000 persons in several states at 200 or so facilities. The unions sought NLRB decisions establishing several separate units, involving each major facility or the major facilities in each metropolitan area. So defined, the cost to the unions of the election campaigns would be minimized and the unions would not incur the cost of servicing small, isolated facilities with few employees, since they would not be in the established units. The company, however, sought a unit consisting of all its nonsupervisory personnel in all states in which it operated and in all its facilities. The company argued that since it used a single personnel system for all employees, the unit should conform to its administrative procedures.

The NLRB's regional office held hearings to determine the appropriate unit and decided in favor of the employer's proposal. The unit was established to cover all the company's nonsupervisory employees. The subsequent election campaign was beyond the financial capability of all but one of the interested unions. That union assigned more than 100 full-time organizers and spent several million dollars in the election campaign (which it ultimately won). In a similar instance involving another company, the

---

[11]Editors, "The Board and Section 9(c) (5) . . .," *Harvard Law Review*, 79:5, February 1966, pp. 811–840.

union obtained authorization cards from about 70 percent of the employees at one of the employer's major facilities. When the NLRB decided that the appropriate unit was companywide the union abandoned the effort to organize the employees as too costly.

The employer and the union may, of course, agree on the appropriate unit and thereby expedite an election, but when there is a dispute over the appropriate unit, the delay involved in scheduling an election can be substantial. Hearings must be held and a decision prepared by the NLRB's regional director. Then either side, union or management, may appeal to the five-member board, which may at its discretion review the regional director's unit determination. The unions object to the delay often involved in this process, maintaining that it weakens their ability to get a favorable vote from the employees.

The NLRB usually sets bargaining units on a case-by-case basis. But it has the legal authority to establish bargaining units through what is termed a "rule-making" process. Rule making means that the board holds hearings about a general issue rather than a specific case, and then issues regulations that apply to many situations rather than to only one at hand.

Recently the NLRB has—for the first time in its history—made use of its rule-making power to set bargaining units for an entire industry. The industry is health care, and the reason for the NLRB's departure from its previous case-by-case approach was said to be unprecedented confusion. From 1947 until 1974 private, nonprofit hospitals, which number about 4000 and constitute 83 percent of all private (i.e., not government) hospitals in the United States, were not covered by the NLRA. In 1974 Congress added private, nonprofit hospitals to the NLRB's jurisdiction. For more than a decade after 1974 there were sharp disagreements between hospitals and unions over how to organize workers into bargaining units, and the federal courts of appeal were also in disagreement about the question. Unions generally favored smaller, craft-oriented units; management favored fewer, larger units.

In 1987 the NLRB began 2 years of hearings about the question and in 1989 issued industrywide rules supporting smaller, craft-oriented units. Specifically, the rules provided for eight different bargaining units in each hospital, including, for example, registered nurses, physicians, skilled maintenance workers, and technicians. The American Hospital Association immediately sued to block the NLRB's action on behalf of the employers. After 2 years of litigation the U.S. Supreme Court ruled on April 23, 1991, in favor of the NLRB; so the employees of all private, nonprofit hospitals in the United States are now available for organization by unions into eight different bargaining units.[12]

---

[12]See "NLRB Votes to Complete Rulemaking," Bureau of National Affairs, *Daily Labor Report*, No. 56 (Mar. 24, 1989), pp. A-1–A-3; and Steven Wermiel and Albert R. Karr, "Supreme Court, in Victory of Unions, Rules NLRB Can Set Bargaining Units," *Wall Street Journal*, Apr. 24, 1991, p. B-11.

Bargaining Units versus Bargaining Structure

The law requires the NLRB to establish bargaining units, but it does not require unions and employers to utilize the units as the actual elements of the bargaining process. Many do not. In the oil industry, for example, NLRB certifications are issued to locals of the Oil, Chemical, and Atomic Workers union at particular refineries belonging to the various oil companies. But bargaining itself is very much centralized and coordinated among the locals and companies. Similarly, in much of the electric manufacturing industry, NLRB certifications are issued on a single-union, single-plant basis, while bargaining takes place on a companywide, multiunion basis. Thus, the NLRB may be said to make decisions about bargaining units but not about certain important aspects of bargaining structure. To put it differently, the NLRB tells unions and management if they must bargain but does not necessarily specify the form in which negotiations occur. If the union and the employer agree to negotiations on a broader basis than the NLRB has certified, the board will permit it. But if either party refuses to agree, the NLRB will require that bargaining be on the basis of the board-certified unit.

Should the NLRB be more concerned with bargaining structure? Certainly the NLRB has concerned itself with a major aspect of bargaining structure in its decisions with respect to the craft severance issue. With respect to the other aspects of bargaining structure, it has been less direct. NLRB decisions often affect bargaining structure, but ordinarily those decisions have been made on the basis of other considerations.[13] An important aspect of bargaining structure involves the level at which various issues are negotiated. In the auto industry, for example (see Chapter 10), economic issues are negotiated at the companywide level, but many working conditions are negotiated at the plant level and are included in local supplements to the national agreements. The NLRB does not normally recognize such matters in unit determinations. The board's reluctance to involve itself in many questions of bargaining structure is probably appropriate, since it leaves the parties free to develop such arrangements as they wish.

HOW AN ELECTION IS CONDUCTED

When the NLRB finds that a question of representation exists, it must, by law, hold a secret-ballot election among employees to see if the employees want to have a bargaining representative. In such an election, employees who are in the bargaining unit are given a choice of one or more bargaining representatives or of no representative at all. To be certified as a bargaining representative, an individual or a labor union must receive a ma-

---

[13]Douglas V. Brown and George Schultz, "Public Policy and the Structure of Collective Bargaining," in Arnold R. Weber, ed., *The Structure of Collective Bargaining* (Chicago: Graduate School of Business, University of Chicago, 1961), pp. 300–324.

jority of the valid votes cast. If a majority of employees votes for a bargaining representative, that representative is certified as the exclusive bargaining agent for all employees in the unit. This is a critical aspect of American labor law. It prevents more than one union from having the right to speak for a single group of employees (i.e., a single bargaining unit). It adds great stability to our labor relations but continues to seem to some people to be an unreasonable infringement of the freedom of individuals.[14]

Elections are usually conducted within 30 days after the regional director of the board directs that an election is to be held. To be entitled to vote, an employee must have worked in the bargaining unit during an eligibility period set by the board and must be employed in the unit on the date of the election. Sometimes elections are conducted while a strike is under way. If the strike is legal, strikers may vote in the election. If the strikers have been permanently replaced, they may nevertheless vote up to 12 months after the strike began; but their permanent replacements may also vote.

The NLRB prepares ballots, selects voting places, and has representatives who observe the election and tabulate the votes (see Figure 9-3). A ballot may say:

Do you wish to be represented for the purpose of collective bargaining by:

	YES	NO
The United Metalworkers	_____	_____
The Union of Workers	_____	_____
No union	_____	_____

If any category gets a majority of ballots cast, no runoff is held. If no category gets a majority, there is a runoff between the two categories receiving the largest number of ballots. The category getting the majority of votes cast in the two-way election prevails.

NLRB elections are conducted in accordance with strict standards designed to give the employees an opportunity to make a free choice. For example, it is unlawful for either employers or unions to make any election speeches, statements, or comments during working time to massed assemblies of staff members within 24 hours before the scheduled time for conducting an election. These speeches, statements, and comments constitute "captive audience speeches," and the making of any such speech is grounds for setting aside an election. A manager or a union official may speak to groups during the 24-hour period before the election only so long as attendance at the meeting or gathering is voluntary and it occurs on employees' own time.

[14]George Schatzki, "Majority Rule, Exclusive Representation, and the Interests of Individual Workers: Should Exclusivity Be Abolished?" *University of Pennsylvania Law Review*, 123:4, April 1975, pp. 897–938.

1 You see sitting at a desk union representatives, the U.S. government's NLRB agents who conduct the election, and a company representative.	**6** After you have marked your ballot, you fold it so no one can see how it is marked, and you leave the voting booth.
2 You give your name and employee identification number.	**7** You drop the folded-up ballot into a locked ballot box that no one but the government agents can open. Your ballot is mixed in with all the other ballots cast by your fellow workers.
3 The representatives check your name off the official list of eligible voters so no one else can vote under your name and no one can vote twice.	**8** After the polls are closed, the government agents open the ballot box and the counting begins.
4 A government agent gives you a ballot. It does not list your name or number or have any other means of identification.	**9** The government agents count the ballots while union and company representatives watch.
5 You go into the voting booth, which is curtained to give you privacy and to prevent anyone from seeing how you mark your ballot.	**10** After announcing the results, the government agents seal up the ballots.

FIGURE 9-3   You are ready to vote in an NLRB election. (*Source:* Adapted from a pamphlet issued by the United Steelworkers of America.)

Prior to the last 24 hours before an election, an employer may legally attempt to persuade employees not to vote for a union, just as a union may attempt to persuade them to vote for a union. But should an employer act in this fashion? If the employer or a union doesn't believe the standards for a fair election were met, it may file an objection with the regional director and thereafter may appeal any decision to the board in Washington.

An election will be set aside if it was accompanied by conduct that the NLRB considers created an atmosphere of confusion or fear of reprisals and thus interfered with the employees' freedom of choice. In any particular case the NLRB does not attempt to determine whether the conduct actually interfered with the employees' expression of free choice, but rather asks whether the conduct tended to do so. If it is reasonable to believe that the conduct would tend to interfere with the free expression of the employees' choice, the election may be set aside. Examples of conduct the board considers to interfere with employee free choice are

- Threats of loss of jobs or benefits by an employer or a union to influence the votes or union activities of employees.
- Misstatements of important facts in the election campaign by an employer or a union when the other party does not have a fair chance to reply.
- An employer's firing employees to discourage or encourage their union activities or a union's causing an employer to take such action.
- An employer's or a union's making campaign speeches to assembled groups of employees on company time within the 24-hour period before the election.
- The incitement of racial or religious prejudice by inflammatory campaign appeals made by either an employer or a union.
- Threats or the use of physical force or violence against employees by an employer or a union to influence their votes.
- The occurrence of extensive violence or trouble or widespread fear of job losses that prevents the holding of a fair election, whether or not caused by an employer or a union.
- The union is endorsed as a "strong and honest" union by the Commissioner of Labor of the state in which the balloting is conducted. The endorsement is made by a letter written on official stationery to the workers who are to vote in the election and is sent the day before the election is scheduled to take place.

Do Campaign Tactics Affect the Outcome of NLRB Elections?

Representation elections conducted by the NLRB ordinarily involve an extensive campaign carried on both by the union or unions seeking to represent the workers and by the company. In the election campaign, both the unions and the company try to persuade the workers to vote a certain way. The NLRB has, for most of its history, regulated what the unions and employers say and do in the midst of election campaigns. If either side oversteps what the NLRB thinks are appropriate limits under the law, then the election may be postponed or set aside by the board. Thus, a union or employer that wins an election may be deprived of victory if its election tactics were illegal.

It is now common for employers to express their opposition to unionization of their employees by conducting a campaign to persuade employees not to join unions. A substantial group of lawyers and consultants, who offer their services to employers threatened by a union organizing campaign, has grown up. These advisers sometimes offer a preplanned strategy for the employer to follow in opposing unions.[15]

---

[15]Lyman Powell, *How to Handle a Union Organizing Drive* (Los Angeles: Libby's, 1968); Louis Jackson and Robert Lewis, *Winning NLRB Elections: Management Strategy and Preventative Programs* (New York: Practising Law Institute, 1972).

Some of the tactics used are very imaginative. For example, in 1974 Dean Witter and Company, a New York stock brokerage firm, was faced with a campaign to organize its employees. The firm distributed to its employees listings of strikes that local affiliates of the national union involved had conducted in the last year and a half. At another time during the campaign the company paid employees with two checks—one amounting only to union dues that employees would pay if the union won the election and the other check amounting to the employees' regular pay less the union dues. The union lost that particular election by a vote of 469 to 154.[16]

Researchers have investigated whether or not employer opposition to union organizing efforts is often effective. One study found that strong management opposition was most likely when the firm had relatively low wages, poor working conditions, and supervisory problems; when the likelihood of union victory was uncertain; and when the potential effect on firm profits was significant. Opposition by supervisors was found to be particularly effective in defeating union drives. The same study included a survey of employers which showed that 41 percent of companies had used consultants to try to defeat union drives and that unfair labor practice charges had been filed against 24 percent of companies and 15 percent of the companies had been found guilty.[17]

The NLRB and its agents spend considerable effort overseeing the conduct of elections. But it is not certain that this effort contributes substantially to the outcome of elections.

A study of elections conducted by researchers and published in 1976 indicates that the statements made by union or management representatives in an election campaign, even where these statements were misleading or false, did not substantially affect the outcome of the election. In effect, the researchers argued, employees had their minds made up about how they would vote independently of statements by the union or company.[18] Previously, however, we have reviewed other research which indicates that employer opposition to unions has been effective in limiting union election victories. It is possible to reconcile these two findings to a degree by arguing that employer opposition is communicated effectively to employees in ways which cause the particular language used to be unimportant.

In recent years, the question of what an employer may do in a union organization campaign has moved beyond the issue of individual actions or statements and has dealt with broad patterns of behavior. In particular, the unions charge that there has grown up an industry of consultants whose

[16]Bureau of National Affairs, *Daily Labor Report*, No. 246, Dec. 20, 1974, p. A1.

[17]Richard B. Freeman and Morris M. Kleiner, "Employer Behavior in the Face of Union Organizing Drives," *Industrial and Labor Relations Review*, 43:4, April 1990, pp. 351, 355.

[18]Julius G. Getman et al., *Union Representation Elections: Law and Reality* (New York: Basic Books, 1976).

purpose is to help corporations prevent organization of their employees by unions. Since 1979, a subcommittee of the U.S. House of Representatives concerned with labor-management relations has held hearings in which the unions have argued that federal laws should be tightened to prevent management from using "union-busting" consultants.

In a study of 130 NLRB elections held in retail grocery stores, researcher John J. Lawler found that management consultants did help to turn close votes against the unions. But he also found that other aspects of the election, including the size of the potential bargaining unit and the shortage or oversupply of labor in the area, were more important in determining the election outcome than the involvement of management consultants.[19]

The unions' response has not been limited to seeking congressional support for restrictive legislation about such consultants. In collective bargaining negotiations the unions have sought to get management to agree not to oppose unionization by their members in union representation elections. In 1976, the United Auto Workers obtained from General Motors a pledge "to neither discourage nor encourage the Union's efforts in organizing production and maintenance employees traditionally represented by the union elsewhere in General Motors, but [to] observe a posture of neutrality in these matters." In turn, the UAW pledged "to conduct itself in a manner which neither demeans the Corporation as an organization nor its representatives as individuals." This so-called neutrality pledge by General Motors has been an important factor in preserving the very high degree of unionization that exists among the company's employees.

Thus, despite the provisions of the National Labor Relations Act that attempt to provide for a full and fair opportunity for employees to express their preferences about union representation, both labor and management have developed the practice of mounting elaborate campaigns designed to influence these preferences. So widespread has this practice become that now both labor and management must attempt in the collective bargaining process to establish limitations on each other's actions in order to ensure a fair opportunity for workers to express their desires.

There is also evidence that union tactics affect the outcome of an election campaign. A study by Kate Bronfenbrenner of some 261 representation elections in 1986 and 1987 found that union tactics were the most important determinant of the outcome of the elections. Unions fared best, she found, when they ran "rank-and-file intensive" campaigns involving house calls, small group meetings, and committees of employees. Less effective techniques included mass mailings, phone calls, videos, and hand-

---

[19]John J. Lawler, "The Influence of Management Consultants on the Outcome of Union Certification Elections," *Industrial and Labor Relations Review*, 38:1, October 1984, pp. 38–51.

bills. She also found that unions won most often when women or minorities were a majority of the employees voting.[20]

The several studies of the factors which determine the outcome of NLRB elections which have been cited in this text seem to be in conflict with one another in some particulars. Recent scholarship has accepted the conflicts as evidence that we lack a thorough understanding of the factors which determine election results. In a 1990 summary of the issue, John J. Lawler contends that union and management strategies and tactics in a campaign matter, and so do contextual influences such as employee demographics, market conditions, social support, and politics.[21]

Decertification Elections

The NLRB conducts elections not only to see if workers who are not presently represented by a union wish to be represented but also to determine if workers who are presently represented by a union wish to continue to be represented. An election for union representation ordinarily begins with a petition (called an RC petition) filed by workers or by a union seeking an election. Similarly, an election to determine if workers want to get rid of a union, called a decertification election, ordinarily begins with a petition filed by employees (called an RD petition) or by an employer (called an RM petition).

Elections to decertify a union are much less common than elections to see if presently unrepresented employees wish to have a union. But decertification elections have been increasing.[22] In 1966, the NLRB conducted about 200 decertification elections. By 1983 the NLRB conducted some 922 such elections. But in the late 1980s the number of decertification elections declined dramatically. In 1990 the board conducted only 558 such elections. Unions ordinarily lose these elections. In 1990, for example, unions lost 73 percent. Approximately 15,200 employees gave up union representation as a result of these elections.

---

[20]"Union Tactics Found Key Factor," Bureau of National Affairs, *Daily Labor Report*, No. 232, Dec. 12, 1991, pp. A7–A10.

[21]John J. Lawler, *Unionization and Deunionization: Strategy, Tactics and Outcomes* (Columbia: University of South Carolina Press, 1990). See also, Julian Barling, E. Kevin Kelloway, and Eric H. Bremermann, "Preemployment Predictors of Union Attitudes: The Role of Family Socialization and Work Beliefs," *Journal of Applied Psychology*, 76:5, October 1991, pp. 725–731.

[22]William E. Fulmer, "When Employees Want to Oust Their Union," *Harvard Business Review*, 56:2, March–April 1978, pp. 163–171. See also John J. Lawler and Greg Hundley, "Determinants of Certification and Decertification Activity," *Industrial Relations*, 22:3, Fall 1983, pp. 335–348.

How Labor Wants the Law Modified

In most developed industrial countries union membership is accomplished with little formality and no real contest. Instead, of an informal process, "union organizing in the United States is "a high-stakes game. . . . Employees risk a lot of time, money and emotional energy. Their jobs are on the line throughout the process and a victory is not so much a money proposition as significant leverage for bargaining for major improvements."[23]

If union organization were the sort of informal process it is abroad, the unions say, their membership would be much greater. Even without such a free and unencumbered opportunity, some observers suggest, unions would have many more members in this country if a few modifications were made to labor law.

Charles McDonald has provided a list of the major changes in the nation's labor laws desired by the unions. If these few changes were made, he suggests, then union membership would rise dramatically. "Given a supportive political climate," he wrote, "unions are calling for

- legislated card-check recognition (i.e., without an election)
- immediate or five-day elections (if they are held)
- employer neutrality in organizing efforts (which was once the law)
- first-contract arbitration (i.e., that if union and company can't agree on a first contract, then an arbitrator could establish its terms)
- severe and immediate penalties for antiunion discrimination (the law currently provides only remedies, not penalties, so that an illegally discharged employee might get reinstated with lost pay, but there is no fine or criminal prosecution of the employer which discriminated against the employee)
- elimination of the permanent replacement of strikers by an employer. (The majority of these proposals were included in proposed labor law reform legislation that was narrowly defeated in 1978.)"[24]

Unions are taking dramatic approaches in organizing: putting aside old rivalries and working together, and bringing new people into the movement. The AFL-CIO now has an organizing department and in 1989 created the Organizing Institute for education of organizers. "Twenty years ago," writes Charles McDonald, head of organizing for the AFL-CIO, "the proposition that unions would accept, let alone eagerly solicit, recruits from non-labor sources and allow them to be training by participation in other unions' campaigns would have been ridiculed."[25]

[23]Charles McDonald, "U.S. Union Membership in Future Decades," *Industrial Relations*, 31:1, Winter 1992, p. 25.
[24]Ibid., p. 27.
[25]Ibid., p. 21.

The unions are even considering proposing a minority representation system under which unions could organize members without an election and without a majority, but the employer would not be required to negotiate a comprehensive collective bargaining agreement.[26]

CHAPTER SUMMARY

There is no single reason why employees join unions. Some of the major reasons are to have a means of effectively resisting unfair or unpleasant working conditions, to get better pay, to be able to participate in benefits and activities sponsored by unions, and, sometimes, to respond to social or union pressure. Employees choose not to join unions, in general, because they are satisfied with their jobs or because they believe unions are unnecessary. They also do not join unions when there are social pressures not to join, when they fear reprisals from management, when unions are not open or available to them, and, sometimes, just because union membership costs money.

Employees who are represented by a union have a much more substantial power base in their dealings with management, whether they are union members or not. But the employee is faced with the decision of the extent to which he or she will become involved in the union and support its goals and activities. Both employees and employers fear that if a union comes into a company, strikes will occur. However, strikes are not an inevitable outcome of unionization.

The question of whether a group of employees should be represented by a union is legally determined by majority rule. Usually, this entails an election conducted by the NLRB after a petition has been filed requesting one. First, however, an investigation must determine the appropriate unit in which to conduct the election. The choice of a bargaining unit can have a major impact on the likelihood of unionization of an employee group and frequently involves the question of craft versus industrial units. Through the years, the board has taken (and sometimes rescinded) various positions on this issue.

Employers and unions are strictly regulated in what they can say in a representation election campaign. Nonetheless, there is a considerable controversy about whether or not campaign tactics affect the outcome of elections. The unions apparently believe they do and are suggesting changes in the NLRA that would make organizing simpler and faster.

QUESTIONS FOR THOUGHT AND DISCUSSION

1 Do employees want to join unions only if the employer is doing something wrong? Why or why not? Why might employees in better-standards companies join unions?

---

[26]Ibid., p. 27.

2 Why do some employees join unions? Why do other employees decline to join unions?

3 What are the most important ways that a union affects employees?

4 Should union leaders limit themselves to "instrumental objectives" if this is what union members want, or should they be concerned with broader social issues, such as the environment, discrimination, and even corporate ethics?

5 How does the NLRB's handling of representation cases differ from its handling of unfair labor practice cases? Do you have ideas on how either procedure could be improved?

6 Why are unit determinations important? What factors are involved in judging the appropriate size and type of unit? Do you feel that the NLRB has too much discretionary power in making these determinations? What would be a better method?

7 Do campaign tactics affect the outcome of NLRB elections? What evidence is there to support your answer?

8 Do you agree with the unions' proposals to modify the election provisions of the NLRA? Why or why not?

SELECTED READING

Gagoula, Kenneth, *Union Organizing and Staying Organized* (Reston, Va.: Reston Publishing Company, 1983).

Purcell, Theodore V., *Blue-Collar Man: Patterns of Dual Allegiance in Industry* (Cambridge, Mass.: Harvard University Press, 1960).

BARGAINING STRUCTURE

The way in which collective bargaining is conducted differs dramatically among industries. Some industries utilize national-level bargaining between large companies and industrywide unions. Other industries rely on plant-by-plant bargaining or on bargaining by localities. At one extreme, General Motors and the United Automobile Workers negotiate one bargain, covering several hundred thousand unionized employees. At the other extreme, the building trades unions and their employers negotiate about 6000 separate bargains, locality by locality, to cover 1.5 million workers.

The structure of bargaining differs dramatically as well in the public sector of the economy, where millions of people work and a large proportion belong to unions. Finally, it is very different in other countries, but practices abroad are having an increasingly significant influence in this country.

CHAPTER 10

DIFFERENT PATTERNS OF RELATIONS IN THE PRIVATE SECTOR

CENTRALIZATION AND DECENTRALIZATION OF BARGAINING

The degree of centralization and other aspects of bargaining structure and practice affect the relative power of unions and employers. Also, bargaining structure affects what can actually be accomplished in collective bargaining. In some instances, the parties can act almost without regard to economic, political, and other conditions; in other instances, the parties are virtually forced to act as economic, political, and other conditions dictate.

The various forms of bargaining relationships that exist may be referred to as the "structure" of bargaining. There are several ways to describe the bargaining structure of the American economy, and we review several of them here. But this review, or any review, is necessarily largely by example, because the actual structure is far too complex to be represented on paper. There are millions of places of work, hundreds of thousands of separate firms, almost 200,000 collective bargaining agreements, tens of thousands of local unions, and, therefore, too many bargaining relationships to describe except by summary and example.

Bargaining structure is important because it affects other aspects of the bargaining relationship. Economists suggest that bargaining structure affects bargaining outcomes such as wage inflation, job satisfaction, and the relative wage levels set for different jobs. Decentralized bargaining structures may lead to greater strike activity. Bargaining structure may also affect the balance of power by influencing the economic leverage each side possesses.[1]

---

[1]Wallace E. Hendricks and Lawrence M. Kahn, "The Determinants of Bargaining Structure," *Industrial and Labor Relations Review*, 35:2, January 1982, pp. 181–195.

An Overall View of Bargaining Structure

Table 10-1 summarizes the bargaining structure of 42 industries or sectors of the U.S. economy.[2] The classification is by type of employer negotiating unit and by relationships between bargaining units. The majority of the industries listed involve privately owned companies, but some governmental agencies are included. The table does not reflect the type of union negotiating unit or other aspects of bargaining structure, which will be mentioned later.

The table has 18 categories, only two of which (IC and IVC) are without entries. The absence of entry IC indicates that no major industry is characterized as having negotiations with individual companies at the plant level but also having industrywide bargaining. In fact, the two concepts are substantially inconsistent. Thus, we see that industrywide negotiations with a multiemployer bargaining unit take place in such industries as over-the-road trucking (IA). Alternatively, an industrywide agreement is negotiated by a single company (IB). In the case of the U.S. Postal Service, the agreement is industrywide because the Postal Service has a legal monopoly on moving the mail.

The table suggests by the frequency of entries in column B that negotiations by individual employers on a companywide basis are most common in the United States, but that the relations among negotiating units vary across the entire spectrum from a strong national pattern in the settlement to no pattern (or local patterns). Negotiations on a plant basis and negotiations on a multiemployer basis are both less common.

Additional Perspectives on Bargaining Structure

Table 10-1 has certain limitations. It does not indicate whether in the industries identified a single union or several unions exist. Nor does the table indicate whether a single union bargains with one employer or several, or whether a national union or the locals alone are engaged in negotiations. Nor does the table indicate where a single corporation is involved in several industries, rather than only one. Finally, the table fails to describe whether bargaining occurs at a single level or at multiple levels. Each of these items is an additional, important aspect of bargaining structure.

Table 10-2 reclassifies the 42 industries from Table 10-1, indicating the characteristic size of employers and the number of the national unions with which the employers negotiate. Nine categories are given in the table and at least one industry is identified in each category.

---

[2]The size of the list is dictated by convenience. It could be expanded considerably, although without significant additional value in providing examples.

TABLE 10-1 STRUCTURE OF BARGAINING

| Relations among negotiating units | Type of employer negotiating unit | | |
| | | Individual employer | |
	Multiemployer A	Companywide B	Company subunit (plant) C
I An industrywide agreement for unionized companies	Trucking (not local cartage) Professional baseball, football	Postal Service Bituminous coal	
II Strong national pattern	Glass containers Fur	Nonferrous metals Meat packing Aluminum Cigarettes Containers, metal Automobiles Basic steel	Oil refining Cement
III Middle national pattern	Apparel	Shoes Railings Airlines Rubber Textiles	Plumbing manufacture Telephones
IV Weak national pattern	Longshoring Maritime	Electrical machinery Cement	
V Regional pattern	Farm workers	Supermarkets Shipbuilding Lumber Furniture	Paper converting Pulp and paper
VI Local pattern	Hotels Building construction	Local transit Utilities Public education Health Newspapers and printing	Chemicals

Source: Updated and adapted from David H. Greenberg, "The Structure of Collective Bargaining and Some of Its Determinants," *Proceedings of the Industrial Relations Research Association,* 1966, p. 345.

TABLE 10-2   INDUSTRIES CLASSIFIED BY NUMBER OF NATIONAL UNIONS AND BY CHARACTERISTICS OF EMPLOYERS

Characteristics of employers	Number of national unions representing workers		
	Single national union (primarily) A	Few unions B	Many unions C
Large companies primarily	Petroleum refining Automobiles Basic steel Rubber Containers, metal	Railways Meat packing Textiles Utilities Cigarettes Telephones Chemicals Electrical machinery Airlines Glass containers Postal Service Aluminum	Supermarkets Nonferrous metals Plumbing manufacture
II Small companies primarily	Trucking Fur Shoes	Longshoring Apparel Furniture Farm workers	Building construction Newspapers and printing
III Both large and small companies	Bituminous coal Professional baseball, football Paper converting	Cement Lumber Pulp and paper Hotels Public education	Maritime Local transit Health

The table shows, for example, that in petroleum refining, automobiles, and basic steel and rubber manufacturing, a single national union negotiates with several large companies (IA). In contrast, in interstate (or over-the-road) trucking, a single national union (the Teamsters) negotiates with many small companies (IIA). The table suggests that industries usually do not have a single union, or many unions, but instead, a small group of national unions (column B). Once again, the table demonstrates the wide range of bargaining structures that different industries have.

Individual companies that possess subsidiaries in several industries may negotiate with different unions. The rise of conglomerates has made this more common in recent years, but multi-industry companies are not new; USX, for example, through its various subsidiaries, negotiates agreements in not only basic steel, but also steel fabrication, bituminous coal, cement, petroleum, and construction. The total complexity of bargaining structure becomes apparent as one examines it from various perspectives.

Students should not expect to absorb all the material contained in these tables. Rather, they should study the tables as examples of the variety and complexity of the nation's collective bargaining structure. The tables should also be of use as reference points in the discussion of the specific form and development of collective bargaining in various sectors of the economy.

Multilevel Bargaining

Bargaining structure is not only a matter of who bargains with whom. In addition, there may be different methods of bargaining about different issues. Often, bargaining occurs at different levels with respect to different issues. When this occurs, certain major items (including wages and grievance procedures, for example) may be included in the primary contract between the parties, but there may also be negotiated supplemental agreements. Supplemental agreements are ordinarily of two types.

First, special agreements may be negotiated by the primary parties (for example, a national union and an automobile company) to deal with certain specific issues, such as pensions, benefit plans, wage incentives, or job evaluation. For instance, General Motors and the United Automobile Workers negotiate a 6-year pension agreement while the national contract between the parties is only for 3 years.

Second, when there are companywide negotiations, plant-level supplements dealing with such matters as working conditions at individual facilities may also be negotiated between local unions and plant managers. Strikes are common when impasses occur in these negotiations. Supplements are commonly negotiated in automobiles, basic steel, and similar industries involving multiplant firms and companywide or industrywide negotiations.

In general, particular arrangements in different industries seem to be increasing and add markedly to the complexity of the bargaining process. The existence of such arrangements also makes it very difficult to generalize about the degree to which bargaining in an industry is centralized.[3]

Centralized Bargaining

Centralized, or industrywide, bargaining used to be standard in many basic manufacturing industries. Always, it has been subject to considerable criticism. It is argued that centralized bargaining has two major disadvantages.

First, it is said that by eliminating competition from other unions or unorganized workers, centralized bargaining allows a union to negotiate a

[3]E. Robert Livernash, "Special and Local Negotiations," in John T. Dunlop and N. W. Chamberlain, eds., *Frontiers of Collective Bargaining* (New York: Harper & Row, 1967), pp. 27–49.

monopoly wage. This wage is alleged to be higher than would otherwise be the case, and to be paid not out of profits but out of price increases passed on to consumers.[4]

Second, centralized bargaining is alleged to reduce the influence of individual employees on negotiations and to destroy democratic participation in trade unions. George Brooks, once a trade union official and later a professor at Cornell University, has been especially forceful in presenting this point of view. He argues that the most important characteristic of collective bargaining structure is the locus of decision making and authority.

Brooks suggests that for years there have been moves toward centralized bargaining in manufacturing and the result has been a decline of the energy and vitality of local unions. Brooks favors plant-centered unionism with collective bargaining at the plant level only.[5] Several studies in the mid-1960s confirmed the tendency toward centralized negotiations cited by Brooks. In the agricultural implements industry (involving firms like International Harvester and John Deere), for example, Arlyn Melcher categorized bargaining structure as follows:

Physical location of negotiations	Contract results		
	Master contract	Master and local supplements	Local supplements
Central	1	2	3
Central and local	4	5	6
Local	7	8	9

This classification yields nine different possible combinations of physical location of negotiations and contract results. Melcher found a trend toward the category marked 1, central negotiations and a master contract.[6]

Congress for many years debated amending the Taft-Hartley Act to prohibit industrywide bargaining (the Ball amendment). At one point, this amendment failed to pass by a single vote in the U.S. Senate. Had it passed, bargaining might have been restricted to the company level by law.

Events in the 1980s and 1990s have moderated concern about centralized bargaining somewhat. In many industries the emergence of important bargaining about local supplements to industrywide or companywide

[4]Fritz Machlup, "Monopolistic Wage Determination," In *Wage Determination and the Economics of Liberalism* (Washington, D.C.: Chamber of Commerce of the United States, 1974), pp. 49–82.

[5]George W. Brooks, "Unions and the Structure of Collective Bargaining," in Arnold Weber, ed., *The Structure of Collective Bargaining* (Glencoe, Ill.: Free Press, 1960), pp. 123–140.

[6]Arlyn S. Melcher, "Central Negotiations and the Master Contract: An Analysis of Their Implications for Collective Bargaining," *Labor Law Journal*, 16:6, June 1965, p. 353.

agreements has caused bargaining to become more like Melcher's category 5 (central and local negotiations for a master agreement and local supplements) instead of the highly centralized category 1.

For example, in 1985 the major companies in the basic steel industry ended a 30-year practice of joint national negotiations with the United Steelworkers of America. Major economic problems have also arisen in industries with highly decentralized bargaining, such as supermarkets and construction. Thus, it no longer appears to many managers that they would have more difficult labor relations if the bargaining were centralized.

VARIETIES OF BARGAINING PATTERNS

The following discussion of bargaining illustrates the variety of arrangements that exist in various industries. Chapter 1 pointed out that although the image most people have of union-management relations is that of one company dealing with one union, in fact most relationships are more complicated. In addition to the one-to-one situation, the major types of union-management relationships are

- Several companies dealing with a single union
- Several unions dealing with a single company
- Several companies dealing with several unions

Nor does this list exhaust the variety of arrangements. For example, a single company may negotiate with one or more unions on a plant-by-plant basis, or in a single negotiation at the company level, or it may do both. If it does both, one level of negotiation may precede the other or they may occur simultaneously.

Whatever form a bargaining relationship takes, it is likely to have some relation to certain other employers and unions. In a sense, all collective bargaining relationships—indeed, all circumstances by which wages and conditions of employment are established—are related to each other because each is part of the economic and social system as a whole. In the overall system, all elements are subject to influence from each other. For example, in economics there exists a special area of study in which the interactions of all wages and prices are studied for their impact on each other. (It is called general equilibrium analysis.) There is no such formal name for the study of the interactions of companies and unions in collective bargaining, but we speak of certain interrelationships as involving "patterns" in negotiations.

Why do employers and unions follow patterns at all? Many don't, of course, but those that do have the following primary reasons. Employers will follow a pattern ordinarily because they do not want to have higher labor costs than their competitors. Although the company might like to pay less, perhaps, than the pattern, the union would probably strike to resist that. The union follows a pattern because it can show its members that they receive as much as other people in their line of work and because it can show the company that its labor costs are comparable with those of its competitors. The union might like to receive more than the pattern allows, but the company is likely to resist this strongly. Thus, a pattern is followed because neither side objects strongly to following it, but each objects strongly to not following it: the union objects to receiving less and management objects to giving more.

BASIC FEATURES OF MANUFACTURING

Manufacturing enterprises are at the core of an industrial society and are the type of economic activity most often brought up in discussions of labor relations. Manufacturing is an important sector of our economy, now involving some 17 percent of total employment (see Table 10-3).

Manufacturing ordinarily involves a factory at a fixed location, in which machinery is installed. Materials are delivered to the factory and products are shipped from it. The work force reports on a fixed schedule for work and is usually closely supervised by managerial personnel. These characteristics of manufacturing employment are not exactly like those in other sectors of the economy, and they should be carefully noted by the reader (see Table 10-4). While other sectors of the economy possess some of these attributes, no other sector combines them all.

TABLE 10-3 DISTRIBUTION OF EMPLOYMENT BY SECTOR OF THE ECONOMY, 1992

	Percentage of total employment
Total employment (nonagricultural establishments)	100.0
Private, total	82.5
Mining	.6
Contract construction	3.8
Manufacturing	16.8
Transportation and public utilities	5.3
Wholesale and retail trade	23.9
Finance, insurance, and real estate	6.2
Services	26.8
Government, total	17.5
Federal	2.8
State and local	14.7

Source: Bureau of Labor Statistics, U.S. Department of Labor, Bureau of Labor Statistics, *Employment and Earnings,* 39:3, March 1992, pp. 98–108. Percentages calculated by author.

TABLE 10-4   CHARACTERISTICS OF EMPLOYMENT IN MANUFACTURING

- A fixed place of production
- A relatively stable work force
- A close identification of workers with the company
- A relatively regular working schedule
- A relatively well-defined set of tasks for each worker
- A relatively closely supervised work environment
- Repetitive output of a product or a product line, as opposed to custom-designed items

Many important features of labor relations in manufacturing derive from the basic characteristics of employment in the manufacturing sector. For example, collective bargaining agreements commonly involve only a single company (although there are exceptions in certain industries). Also, agreements must include provisions relating to working conditions specific to each particular plant, although there may be a more general agreement with a company that covers items common to all its facilities.

Great concern is expressed in labor negotiations in manufacturing about the competitive status of employees (including, for example, which employees are to be laid off first and which are to be given first chance at recalls, promotions, or transfers). But there is almost no concern about hiring decisions—these are left to management. These concerns are in dramatic contrast to the concerns of workers and unions in construction, for example.

In construction, employers negotiate as a group (in associations) and agreements cover all the work sites in a geographic area. It is very uncommon to negotiate specific standards for a single job site (unless it is a very large project). Also, since projects open and close continually and there is no job security in construction, there is little concern among workers about who is laid off or who is eligible for recall or promotion. However, there is great concern about how companies conduct hiring. Thus, the characteristics of employment in different sectors of the economy determine what issues are of importance in bargaining and even the manner in which bargaining is conducted.

Manufacturing is not a homogeneous group of activities (although all manufacturing shares the characteristics identified in Table 10-3). Some manufacturing industries are very large, some quite small. Some are located in a single geographic region, others are nationwide. Some involve very profitable firms, some do not. Some industries are expanding rapidly, some are stagnant, and some are declining. Some industries produce a wide range of products, some very few. Some production processes involve a relatively large input of labor, others involve a relatively large input of machinery and/or materials. All these differences in manufacturing industries are reflected in variations in the labor relations of the industries.

In manufacturing, as elsewhere in the economy, labor relations defy simple description or explanation. The most likely suppositions are often incorrect. For example, very large, nationwide, multicompany industries (like autos or steel) often have a simpler bargaining structure than far smaller industries with fewer companies (like some building materials industries). Furthermore, in some industries bargaining occurs at the plant level, so that employees are able to take an active, direct role in negotiations.

Single plant bargaining has the advantage that it is closest to the worker, so that he or she is most likely to feel that the union and the company are being responsive to his or her own concerns. But because a single plant is usually involved in a web of interactions with other plants, the overall interest of people may not be as well served as by bargaining on a larger, multiplant scale. For example, the plant involved may be part of a large corporation which can shift production among plants. In this case, if the union in one plant negotiates a big wage increase or more restrictive work rules, even though the members want those things, then the corporation may shift work to another plant and employees may lose their jobs. Also, when local unions don't coordinate bargaining, a large company can use its economic strength to force a bad settlement on one local and then apply it as a pattern to other locals. By not cooperating, the locals could all see their situations worsened, even though each is trying to do its best for itself. The strategy of playing one local against another is called "whipsawing."

Unions can also whipsaw, but only if they represent many plants in the same or multiple companies. A union whipsaws employers by negotiating a sizable agreement where it has strength and then using it as a pattern at other plants. In effect, whipsawing is a divide-and-conquer strategy which can be used by either management or labor and to which local unions or plants which negotiate on a single-site basis are especially vulnerable.

In other industries negotiations occur through representatives at the national level, and the individual employee, although consulted as part of a group and kept informed, ordinarily has no direct role in the negotiations process. Yet, generally in the United States, wages and conditions of work are better for workers in the latter than the former case. Can one conclude that there is a trade-off between economic gain and personal participation for the individual worker? Probably not. But the question points out the difficulty of generalizing from a group of labor relations systems that vary so greatly.

In the following pages we will review briefly the labor relations structure and experience of the automobile manufacturing industry. It is chosen for its intrinsic interest and because it exemplifies a form of labor-management structure. While the particular arrangements in an industry do reflect a historical adjustment to the conditions of that industry and therefore cannot be said to be random, particular arrangements are not inflexible either.

THE AUTOMOBILE INDUSTRY

The Companies

Three large American companies have traditionally dominated the production of automobiles in the United States: General Motors, Ford, and

Chrysler. In total sales, GM is the largest, but Ford and Chrysler are both giants by the standards of most industries. GM has recently been losing market share: down from 45 percent in the early 1980s to just over 33 percent in 1992.

Each American automaker is not just an automobile manufacturer; each is at the hub of a broadly diversified group of enterprises earning revenues from the sale of products and services other than automobiles. Each operates in a web of domestic and foreign operations, joint ventures, co-production arrangements, parts sourcing, and other alliances on a global basis. In a significant long-range development, Japanese auto companies have begun locating manufacturing plants in the United States. In 1993, Honda, Nissan, Toyota, Mitsubishi, Subaru-Isuzu, and Mazda all had significant U.S. production. These companies operated a total of eight assembly plants with a capacity of 1,815,000 vehicles per year. Three of the plants were unionized; five were not. Some 100,000 workers are employed in the Japanese-operated plants in America, but only some 8000 are in the union. Despite the movement into the United States of Japanese auto producers, total employment in the American auto industry had declined from 1,050,000 in 1979 to 760,000 in 1990. The decline was due in part to the larger share that imports were taking of total vehicle sales in the United States, and also to improvements in the productivity of manufacturing, so that vehicles were produced with less labor.[7]

The Union

The production employees of the American automobile companies are members of the United Automobile Workers (UAW). Two Japanese companies have UAW representation in their American plants (Toyota and Mazda) and two do not (Honda and Nissan). The union is headquartered in Detroit (see Table 10-5) and has more than 1 million members.

The UAW is not confined to employees of the auto companies. Many other firms operate as suppliers to the automobile companies, manufacturing and selling parts. The UAW has organized the employees of many of these companies as well. The UAW also represents the employees of the

[7]Christopher J. Singleton, "Auto Industry Jobs in the 1980's: A Decade of Transition," *Monthly Labor Review,* February 1992, pp. 18ff.

TABLE 10-5   THE UNITED AUTOMOBILE WORKERS (UAW)

Headquarters	Detroit, Mich.
Membership	922,000
Local unions (number)	1231

Source: Bureau of National Affairs, *Directory of U.S. Labor Organizations, 1990–1991* (Washington, D.C., 1990), pp. 38–39.

major companies that manufacture trucks, agricultural implements and machinery, and construction machinery. Further, the UAW represents employees in the manufacture of aircraft and plumbing fixtures and even some public employees in the state of Michigan.

Collective Bargaining

The UAW has a department for each of the automobile companies. The departments are composed of the locals at the plants of each company and a staff that is knowledgeable about the company involved. Each company has a national agreement with the UAW, with local supplements, negotiated at the plant level, to the national agreement. The national agreement establishes the economic package and certain nationally applicable working conditions and dispute procedures. Local supplements deal with conditions of work, grievances, and the like at each facility.

There is no industrywide bargaining in autos, but there are company-wide negotiations. The national contracts between the UAW and Ford and General Motors expire on a single date, usually after a 3-year term. The UAW does not seek to bargain simultaneously with all three companies, however. It picks a target company, announces its choice publicly, and seeks to settle an agreement with that company. Once a settlement is reached with the target company, the union will try to obtain an agreement on similar terms with the remaining companies. (The Chrysler settlement is made a year after the Ford and GM contracts.)

The selection of a target company carries with it the identification of the company that will be struck if an agreement is not reached before the expiration date of the contract. Much of the strategy involved in the choice of a target involves the determination of which company the UAW may hope to strike most successfully. But the union must also seek a company that is profitable enough to give a good settlement and one that is not so profitable that the other companies would not meet the terms of the pattern settlement.

Table 10-6 lists the UAW's target companies from 1955 to 1990. Ford was selected six times; General Motors, four times; and Chrysler, twice. The company selected as the UAW's target in any given year is in a difficult position. It faces the unpleasant likelihood of being shut down by a strike while its competitors are producing. Yet it has the opportunity to seek a settlement on grounds more favorable to it than to its competitors.

After the national agreement is reached with a company, local negotiations go ahead. Strikes often occur at certain plants. These strikes are supposed to be about local issues only but sometimes are instead about the application of national concerns to a local plant. For example, in 1992 the UAW sequentially struck a series of plants of the General Motors Corporation in an effort to prevent the company from reducing its work force. Because of the great integration of production within the firm, when a parts

TABLE 10-6   THE UAW'S TARGET COMPANY IN NATIONAL AUTOMOBILE NEGOTIATIONS, 1955–1991

1955	Ford
1958	Ford
1961	American
1964	Chrysler
1967	Ford
1970	General Motors
1973	Chrysler
1976	Ford
1979	General Motors
1982	Ford
1984	General Motors
1987	Ford
1990	General Motors

manufacturing plant is on strike, much of the company may come to a standstill because of the lack of parts produced by that plant. From the company's point of view, a general shutdown brought on by a few local strikes is very expensive. This has been occurring more frequently in recent years and has made the companies increasingly dissatisfied with the entire bargaining procedure. The company was forced by the series of strikes to modify its planned reduction in force. In the 1990 contract the firm had contributed some $3.35 billion to guarantee incomes for UAW workers displaced by factory closings and efficiency gains, and was disturbed when the strikes nonetheless disrupted its work force reduction programs.

Work Standards and Skilled Workers

An important peculiarity of automobile labor relations is that the companies (GM in particular) refuse to include certain areas of dispute in the coverage of the grievance and arbitration procedures of the national contract. The establishment of production standards (such as the speed of an assembly line) and health and safety standards and the setting of wages on new jobs are excluded under the GM agreement. The union retains its right to strike in disputes over these issues and exercises it in some instances.

The position of skilled workers in automobile industry negotiations is unique. The UAW is an industrial union, including in its membership unskilled, semiskilled, and skilled workers. Skilled workers are a well-organized numerical minority in the union (making up perhaps 20 percent of the UAW's automobile industry membership). The NLRB has effectively prevented skilled workers from leaving the UAW by insisting that such a secession (called "craft severance") can take place only through a companywide election. This procedure has proved too costly for the skilled tradespeople to attempt, but still the skilled trades have formed a separate caucus in the UAW and have sought a degree of independence.

In 1966 the UAW's constitution was amended to permit the skilled trades to vote separately on a contract offer. In 1973 the skilled trades rejected the national-level settlement with Ford. The UAW, however, did not permit the skilled trades to strike, nor did it declare the Ford settlement rejected (since the majority of all Ford employees had voted in favor of the contract). But the union did go back to the bargaining table with Ford to seek certain adjustments in the new contract on behalf of the skilled workers. The UAW's experience with the discontent of skilled workers demonstrates that industrial unionism does not resolve the conflict between skilled and other workers but just makes it internal to one union.

Pattern Bargaining beyond the Big Three

After the national settlement is reached with the big three automakers, the UAW negotiates with many parts manufacturers and other suppliers to the automobile industry normally seeking settlements similar to the agreements with the Big Three. Often, however, smaller companies cannot afford the automobile package, and an agreement less favorable to the union is negotiated. A study of the UAW's bargaining in the period from 1946 to 1957, for example, showed that only 26 percent of the companies (employing 40 percent of the employees in the sample) followed the auto pattern closely. The rest obtained agreements below the auto pattern.[8]

MINING

Mining industries are not very large in terms of employment or revenues, but they have a strategic spot in the economy and have figured largely in American labor relations. In 1991 mining employed some 685,000 people in the United States, approximately 0.6 percent of total nonagricultural employment. Coal, employing some 150,000 people, was one of the larger of the mining industries.

Coal production is currently concentrated east of the Mississippi but is growing in the West. The labor relations of the industry are scarred with violence. It is characterized by industrywide bargaining and a single national union.

Employment in mining has certain distinguishing characteristics. Perhaps the most important of these is the isolation of the workplace and liv-

---

[8]Harold M. Levinson, "Pattern Bargaining: A Case Study of the Automobile Workers," *Quarterly Journal of Economics*, 74:2, May 1960, pp. 296–317.

ing quarters of the miners from the places where a majority of the population lives. Living in small communities made up primarily of miners, and at a distance from other citizens, miners have developed a strong sense of their own identity and a sense of separation from the broader society around them. These attributes have helped to create strong loyalties among miners to their unions.

The Employers

Companies in the coal industry are widely diversified in size and type. Independent coal companies, many of them small operations, mine about half of U.S. coal. The rest comes from subsidiaries of noncoal companies, including some known as "captive suppliers" to coal users. Important groups are subsidiaries of oil companies, steel companies, and electric utilities. Both steel companies and electric utilities use coal as fuel and are heavily dependent on independent producers as well as on their own mines.

Different economic interests exist among the major ownership groups. First, the steel companies are concerned with the impact of the price of coal on the price of steel. Second, the oil companies are not committed to coal itself and may move their investment out of coal if returns are not adequate. Third, the independent coal operators are tied to coal as their primary business. Thus, some companies are fully committed to coal, while for others it is at least partly a sideline.

The Bituminous Coal Operators Association (BCOA) represents the industry in national collective bargaining. Within the BCOA, attitudes toward labor relations are as diverse as the economic interests of the producers. The independent coal operators tend to view labor primarily as part of the production process. Few of these firms have labor relations professionals. The steel companies' need for cheap coal to help them make steel produced in the United States competitively leads them to press for low wage settlements. They are also influenced by their relationships with the sophisticated and fairly cooperative United Steelworkers, who represented employees in the steel production process. The oil companies consider themselves enlightened in industrial relations, and are concerned to be grouped in bargaining with the steel companies and independent operators. The BCOA's internal governance system gives the few large companies the greatest influence—despite the fact that the BCOA is overwhelmingly composed of small companies. In recent years several large companies have tried to break out of the industrywide negotiations to make their own arrangements with the union, and though the union resists the fragmentation of the national agreement, it has sometimes had to go along. Even with increasingly divergent interests, however, there are powerful incentives holding the BCOA together—in particular the desire not to be whipsawed by the union—and many companies prefer a joint negotiation with the union.

The Union

The United Mine Workers of America (UMW) represents employees in the coal industry. An industrial rather than a crafts union, it represents all workers at the mines, both skilled and unskilled. The UMW also includes building and construction workers who are employed by contractors to do construction work at the mines. The UMW's membership is approximately 60,000 active miners and 110,000 retired workers. UMW membership is virtually confined to the coal industry.

The UMW was formed from the merger in 1890 of two earlier unions. Poor leadership and intense internal strife characterized its early history. Chronic excess production capacity and cutthroat price competition plagued the industry. Collective bargaining contracts were often violated by owners. Illegal wage cuts and strikebreaking were common.

The union grew strong and united under the leadership of John L. Lewis. Lewis was president of the UMW from 1920 to 1959 and was one of the most prominent people in the U.S. labor movement. At the peak of coal production in the United States the union had some 600,000 members.

During the 1950s employment declined in coal mining. The union sought peaceful contract settlements and constant meetings with coal operators in order to sustain smooth, continuous production. The union also established stiff penalties for wildcat strikes. Union policy endorsed mechanization of coal production and the closing of smaller, inefficient mines even at the cost of increased unemployment. This policy was an effort to protect the industry from cheaper alternative energy sources, and thereby to preserve employment opportunities for miners.

Lewis retired in December 1959. In his 40 years of leadership, he stamped union loyalty deep in the hearts of the miners. He left a legacy of union solidarity and absolute respect for a picket line.

Collective Bargaining

Ordinarily the UMW and the BCOA negotiate a national contract every 3 years. The contract is complex. The 1978 agreement had 30 major articles and covered 101 general job classifications and almost 1000 job titles. Health insurance and pension benefits for miners were provided by a series of special trusts. The trusts were funded by contributions made by employers for each hour worked and for each ton of coal mined. Operators also made contributions to the trusts for each ton of coal mined by non-UMW workers.

Prior to the 1974 contract negotiations, all health and pension benefits were paid for by a single fund, to which employers paid a royalty on each ton of coal produced. Surface mines produced far more coal per worker day than underground mines, and yet employees of each type of mine drew equally on the benefits. This meant that surface mine operators were paying substantially more to cover each employee's benefits than underground operators. A dispute over this issue almost broke apart the BCOA before 1974.

As part of the 1974 negotiations, the employers developed a plan to restructure the trusts, and the union accepted the plan. The 1950 pension trust would provide pensions for miners who retired prior to 1976. The 1950 benefit trust would provide health benefits to the same group. (About 82,000 miners and surviving spouses were covered under these plans.) The 1950 trusts would be funded by royalty payments as in the past.

Pension and health benefits for current miners and their families and for miners who retired after 1976 would be funded by employer contributions made for each hour worked. These were the 1974 pension trust and 1974 benefit trust. Over a period of years, the new funds would replace the old ones, with benefits costs being tied to employee hours worked.[9]

The late 1970s and early 1980s saw substantial unemployment among the UMW's members and the growth of nonunion coal production. After an especially long and bitter strike in 1977–1978, the union and the companies slowly began to improve their relationship[10]—leading to a 40-month agreement signed in September 1984—the first settlement without a strike in many years. But the growth of nonunion production continued. By 1990 about 65 percent of all coal mined in the United States was by nonunion labor.

Though industrywide strikes ceased, bitter struggles continued with individual companies. In 1989 the UMW struck Pittston Coal Group, Inc., in a dispute over the company's plans to cut back on its health insurance coverage for retired and disabled miners. Pittston argued that with intense competition in the coal industry it could no longer afford to cover all the health care costs of people who were no longer working. The strike continued for months and involved shutdowns at other coal companies and picketing by miners in the communities—far from the coal fields—in which corporate executives lived. Ultimately the federal government intervened and brought about a settlement. The union survived but its situation remained precarious.

CONSTRUCTION

Construction is not an industry (like autos, for example), but a sector of the economy (like manufacturing or mining). It is not as large a sector as manufacturing but still employs some 4 to 5 million people and includes several hundred thousand firms. The sector may be subdivided either by type of construction product or by specialization of firms.

---

[9]William Miernyk, "Coal," in Gerald G. Somers, ed., *Collective Bargaining: Contemporary American Experience* (Madison, Wis.: Industrial Relation Research Association, 1980), p. 32.
[10]Charles R. Perry, *Collective Bargaining and the Decline of the United Mine Workers* (Philadelphia: Industrial Research Unit, Wharton School, University of Pennsylvania, 1984).

The major branches of construction by type of product are residential buildings, nonresidential buildings, highways, dams and other engineering projects, pipelines, electrical transmission lines, and industrial and power plants. If the specialization of contractors is used to categorize firms, the major divisions are general contracting, heavy and highway contracting, and specialty trades contracting (e.g., electrical, plumbing, and masonry contracting).[11]

Construction is a sector of the economy which has many unique features. A physical product is produced, as in manufacturing, but instead of being produced at a plant and shipped to a customer, it is produced at a site selected by the purchaser. Nor is the product standardized. Instead, each facility is designed to order, on a custom basis. The product is not priced and advertised for sale, but instead a unique price is determined for each project. Rather than the customer's buying a completed product, the customer contracts with a particular construction firm to build the project for a fixed price or on a cost-incurred basis.

These characteristics of the product and its pricing have a major effect on the characteristics of employment in construction.[12] Table 10-7 lists several aspects of construction employment which, taken as a whole, cause the sector to have a unique place in the American economy. Especially important is the assembling of contractors and subcontractors with various specializations to build a particular project. This results in specialization of the work force and intermixing of the employees of different employers.[13]

---

[11]Government statisticians use the classification by constructor specialization in reporting employment and earning data, and by type of product in reporting expenditures and output.

[12]See "Strategic Factors in Industrial Relations in the Construction Industry," *Labor and Society*, 4:4, October 1979, pp. 415–432.

[13]For a discussion of the management problems caused by subcontracting, see J. A. Grimes, "Personnel Management in the Building Trade," *Personal Journal*, 47:1, January 1968, pp. 37–47.

TABLE 10-7 CHARACTERISTICS OF EMPLOYMENT IN CONSTRUCTION

Considerable shifting of employees between work sites
Considerable shifting of employees between employers
Identification by the employee with a craft or occupation, not with an employer
A relatively large portion of skilled workers
Much self-supervision
Very unstable employment opportunities
Dangerous and often difficult work conditions
Intermixing of employees of different employers at a single project site
Construction of nonstandard (i.e., custom-designed) products
Intermixing of members of different unions at a single project site

The Employers

Construction firms range from very large to very small and are very numerous. General contractors take responsibility for an entire project but subcontract most of the actual construction work. Most firms operate in a particular locality or region but some are national in scope. Those that operate nationally are generally specialized to a particular branch of the industry.

Most firms hire employees in only one or two trades, although general contractors may hire in as many as five or six trades. The average firm in construction has fewer than 10 employees, and of these most are temporary in that they do not work for a single employer for a full year but move from employer to employer as the availability of work dictates.

In order to deal with the union that represents the workers (or "mechanics") in a trade, the employers ordinarily join together in an association. The association is governed by its bylaws and ordinarily negotiates an agreement with a local union. The associations are not limited to labor relations activities, but also lobby with governmental agencies on behalf of their members, provide legal services, promote construction, and handle public relations and similar functions. Local employer associations are often affiliated with national bodies.[14]

Because of the peculiar conditions and characteristics of employment in construction, employers and unions are placed in a much more intimate relationship than that usually found in other industries. Contractors and unions must negotiate not only wages and working conditions but hiring and training practices as well. The development and retention of a skilled labor force require that employers and unions agree to practices to preserve the job opportunities of craftspeople.

The problem, of course, is to adopt policies that are effective in protecting employment opportunities without either unduly restricting needed expansion of the labor force or promoting uneconomic practices. A special provision of the National Labor Relations Act [section 8(f)] permits unions and contractors in construction to sign prehire agreements, by which an employer agrees to recognize a union to represent its employees before it hires employees and without an election being held.

Not all crafts, branches of construction, or geographic areas are unionized at all or to the same degree. But all contractors, union or nonunion, are influenced by the labor relations policies of the others. Wages in the union segment influence what nonunion contractors must pay. Frequently, nonunion scales are below union scales, but union workers are often considered better mechanics. Many contractors feel that the wage rate paid employees is less important than the productivity of the workers. Because of higher productivity, union employers can sometimes pay higher

---

[14]Daniel Quinn Mills, "Labor Relations and Collective Bargaining," in Julian E. Lange and Daniel Quinn Mills, eds., *The Construction Industry: Balance Wheel of the Economy* (Lexington, Mass.: Lexington Books, 1979), pp. 59–82.

wage rates but nonetheless have lower labor costs than nonunion contractors.[15]

The industrial relations arrangements of construction now operate in three forms, which are in stiff competition for dominance in the future: (1) the system under collective bargaining agreements, (2) open shop (i.e., nonunion) arrangements under national or local policies of contractor associations (the "merit shop"), and (3) the sector of individual enterprises pursuing policies apart from either collective bargaining or a formal organization of contractors (the truly "unorganized" sector). In a sense, the merit shop associations have adopted many of the substantive industrial relations policies and procedures of collective bargaining (such as apprenticeship programs, health and welfare plans, and even, in some few instances, the hiring hall). But decision making is under the control of a local or national employers' association without union involvement or participation.

We do not know what proportion of construction activity or employment is open shop. There are no reliable statistics on the degree of organization in construction, although superficial surveys are sometimes taken. However, a number of indicators of the importance of the nonunion sector are available.[16] According to the best information within the industry, a relatively larger proportion of contractors than of employees is in the nonunion sector (i.e., the average number of workers employed by nonunion contractors is smaller than the average number employed by union contractors). For example, in the housing industry, a major employer association estimates that more than half of the employers are nonunion and some 70 percent or so of all housing is constructed by nonunion builders. Nonetheless, many large metropolitan areas have a majority of housing done by union builders. Much industrial and power plant construction is unionized, while commercial and office building is more often nonunion. On balance, by 1992 less than half of all construction employees were represented by unions.

For many years the nonunion construction firms have stressed what they see as the advantages to customers of using nonunion firms. First, they describe themselves as free from costly restrictive work practices imposed by unions; second, they argue that nonunion construction is cheaper and of better quality; third, they stress the absence of strikes from nonunion work. Recently, the building and construction unions and their employers have begun to answer these claims by advertising the advantages, as they see them, of union construction compared to nonunion. They stress the greater degree of training provided union workers, the

[15]Steven G. Allen, *Unionized Construction Workers Are More Productive* (Washington, D.C.: Center to Protect Workers' Rights, November 1979).

[16]Howard G. Foster and Herbert R. Northrup, *Open Shop Construction* (Philadelphia: Industrial Research Unit, Wharton School, University of Pennsylvania, 1975).

higher productivity and better quality due to more skilled workers, and the infrequency of strikes.[17]

The Unions

The building and construction labor force comprises more than 20 crafts and many more specialties. In the union sector, a group of 18 or 20 national unions represent workers. It is customary to speak of these unions as crafts unions, but most represent more than a single craft or specialty. For example, the United Brotherhood of Carpenters and Joiners of America represents not only carpenters and joiners but also pile drivers, millwrights, soft-floor layers, and dock builders. Outside construction, the union represents workers engaged in maintenance of industrial plants and production workers in sawmilling, lumbering, cabinetmaking, and similar endeavors. Other major construction unions are also agglomerations of specialists around a central, or main, craft. Thus, while construction unions may be generally described as crafts unions, they are more accurately considered to be a form of crafts-industrial unionism.

Collective Bargaining

The structure of collective bargaining in construction is extraordinarily complex. There is considerable variation by branch of the industry, geographic location, and craft. In consequence, only a very general description can be given. There are some 5000 to 7000 collective bargaining agreements in the industry, most negotiated between local unions and employer associations. The agreements run for 1 to 5 years and average about 18 months. Each year, therefore, 2000 to 3000 agreements are negotiated.[18]

Table 10-8 summarizes bargaining structure in various branches of the industry. The only branch in which all the trades are involved in negotiations is building construction, and this branch is described in detail in Table 10-9 and Table 10-10. In the pipeline industry each of the four trades listed negotiates a national agreement with the Pipeline Contractors Association, and the four unions and the association maintain a policy committee to resolve disputes. In the industrial construction industry, the individual companies and an association (the National Constructors Association) negotiate national agreements with the unions listed, but the companies also apply, in most instances, many terms of the building agreements generally in effect where a project is located.

[17]Construction Industry Labor-Management 1990's Committee, *The Unionized Construction Industry: Myth vs. Reality* (Washington, D.C.: 1991).
[18]D. Quinn Mills, "Construction," in Somers, ed., *Collective Bargaining*, pp. 49–98.

TABLE 10-8   BRANCHES OF THE CONSTRUCTION INDUSTRY, PRINCIPAL UNIONS,
AND GEOGRAPHIC COVERAGE OF AGREEMENTS

Branch	Principal unions	Geographic cover age of agreements
Highway construction	Carpenters Laborers Operating engineers Cement masons Teamsters	Local
Pipeline construction	Pipefitters Operating engineers Laborers Teamsters	National
Electric transmission lines	Electricians (IBEW)	Local
Industrial and power plant construction	Pipefitters Ironworkers Electricians (IBEW) Boilermakers Millwrights (United Brotherhood of Carpenters) Carpenters Laborers	National and local

Note: For building construction, see Table 10-9.

HEALTH CARE

Health care is a huge, fragmented, and rapidly growing business in the United States; one consuming about 12 percent of the gross national product. In 1988, nearly 7.1 million people worked in private health care—about 1 in every 15 wage and salary workers in the economy—up from 4.6 million in 1977. (Adding employment in government hospitals increases this total by about another 1 million workers.) Like construction, health care is an economic sector rather than an industry; unlike construction, it delivers services rather than products to consumers.

Health care employment can be classified according to facility type. In 1988, hospitals employed 46.2 percent of health care workers, outpatient facilities 3.2 percent, nursing home/personal care facilities 18.5 percent, physician's office 15.6 percent, dentist's offices 6.8 percent, and other areas such as medical and dental labs and the offices of optometrists, chiropractors, and podiatrists 9.7 percent.

Health care employment can also be classified according to occupation. In 1988, the 7.1 million employees were listed as follows: 700,000 managerial or supervisory staff, 550,000 medical practitioners, 1,600,000 registered nurses, 625,000 licensed practical nurses, 1,400,000 allied health per-

TABLE 10-9   BARGAINING STRUCTURE IN BUILDING CONSTRUCTION: MAJOR EMPLOYER ASSOCIATIONS AND UNIONS

Employer association	Principal unions	Geographic coverage of agreements
Associated General Contractors (AGC)	Carpenters Laborers Operating engineers Teamsters Ironworkers (rod workers)	Local or state
National Association of Homebuilders (NAHB)	Carpenters Laborers Bricklayers	Local or state
Mason Contractors Association of America (MCAA)	Bricklayers	Local
National Electrical Contractors Association (NECA)	Electricians (IBEW)	Local
Elevator Constructors Employers Association	Elevator constructors	National (except New York City)
Mechanical Constructors of America (MCA)	Pipefitters	Local
Sheet Metal and Air Conditioning Contractors National Association (SMACNA)	Sheet metal workers	Local
National Erectors Association	Ironworkers (structural)	Local
International Association of Wall and Ceiling Contractors (IAWCC)	Plasterers	Local
National Insulation Contractors Association (NICA)	Asbestos workers	Local
Painting and Decorating Contractors Association (PDCA)	Painters	Local
National Roofing Contractors Association (NRCA)	Roofers	Local
Plumbing, Heating, and Cooling Contractors National Association (PHCCNA)	Plumbers	Local

sonnel, whose jobs complement those of the practitioners, and about 2,200,000 office, clerical, accounting, custodial, and other nonmedical administrative and support personnel. Just under 90 percent of these workers held nonmanagerial and nonsupervisory positions and were thus eligible to join unions.

The structure of collective bargaining in health care is very complex. Both employers and employees are significantly fragmented.

On the employee side, these splits have prevented movement toward large multisite industrial unions and have encouraged development of smaller and less powerful craft-oriented unions and associations in health care. Even groups aimed at specific crafts in health care have historically left significant numbers of health care workers unrepresented, while those who do enjoy representation are often represented by different labor orga-

TABLE 10-10   BUILDING TRADES RANKED BY AVERAGE WAGE AND BENEFITS COMPENSATION
PER HOUR 1950* AND 1980

1950		1980	
Trade	Hourly rate	Trade	Hourly rate
Bricklayers	$2.83	Electricians	$16.80
Plasterers	2.80	Plumbers and pipefitters	16.28
Painters	2.62	Carpenters	15.28
Plumbers and pipefitters	2.57	Bricklayers	15.26
Electricians	2.54	Plasterers	14.53
Carpenters	2.37	Painters	14.25
Laborers	1.65	Laborers	12.26

Note: All data are building construction rates only.
*In 1950, benefits were not a significant part of compensation.
Source : Bureau of Labor Statistics and Construction Services Division, U.S. Department of Labor. For 1980
data, see *Current Wage Development*, 32.9, September 1980, p. 44. In the early 1980s the government ceased
to collect these data, and no information is available for the period following 1980.

nizations in different areas of the country, leading to further fragmentation
at the bargaining table.

On the employer side, the splits are multifold. First, management authority within a typical health care facility is normally fragmented as government bureaucrats, insurance firm personnel, facility administrators,
and medical practitioners all take partial responsibility for establishing
staffing levels and other key aspects of bargainable conditions of work.
Second, management authority at the industry level is split. The four
groups previously mentioned must also share authority with elected officials because of the strong public perception that health care is an essential service not to be subjected to bargaining tactics such as strikes or lockouts that could conceivably cut patient services in emergency situations.
Third, management authority is affected by different sets of labor laws; a
significant portion of health care is in the public sector, and is organized
by public sector unions under public-sector labor law, which usually
specifically forbids the use of strikes or lockouts and relies on arbitration
to settle contract negotiations in the event of impasse at the bargaining
table (see Chapter 11 for a discussion of U.S. public sector labor law).

The Employers

There are three overlapping sources of health care management: facility
administrators, who are nominally in charge of health care facilities and
their budgets; licensed practitioners, who, with nurses and technologists,
provide patient care, both in hospitals and private offices; and government bureaucrats and insurance company staff, who manage health care

bills and exert cost control on behalf of taxpayers or insurers. No one group effectively controls the health care workplace in isolation from the others.

Facility administrators, while having budgetary authority in their own institutions, cannot control practitioners when they practice medicine in their private offices or clinics. Nor can they control wages and conditions offered nurses, technologists, and nonmedical support staff outside facility settings. This significantly fragments the workplace. In 1988, for example, practitioners collectively employed nearly 23 percent of all health care workers (mainly nurses and technologists) in their private offices and clinics.

Practitioner influence extends even further. With their formal admitting privileges and indirect control over accreditation procedures, practitioners can affect conditions of work for the 67 percent of health care workers who are nominally under the control of the administrators in hospitals, outpatient, and personal care facilities. Nearly all of the conditions of employment in a facility can be subject to the judgment of practitioners over whom the administrators and employees have little direct influence in return. For example, if a facility becomes understaffed because an administrator is trying to compensate for high wage rates with fewer staff, it can lose its accreditation; if there are not enough nurses or technologists on certain shifts because an administrator does not want to pay collectively bargained shift premiums, accreditation can be threatened, and so on.

On the other hand, administrators and practitioners are "employees" of insurance firms and government bureaucrats who set fee schedules and pay for their services through Medicare, Medicaid, or private insurance. Both payors have been exerting pressure on administrators and practitioners to keep health care costs down, placing strains on the system.

Sometimes the bureaucrats may become administrators as well as accountants. A large chunk of health care employment falls in the public sector. Examples include the Veterans Administration (VA), other military hospitals, and even state, county, and city hospitals and clinics. Workers in such facilities tend to be under the rules and provisions of public-sector labor law and are organized by public-sector unions (see Chapter 11 for a discussion of public-sector labor law and unions).

The Employees

If the structure of management in health care is confused, the structure of employees in this sector is equally so. There are vast disparities in educational attainment, duties, and job locations among the various health care occupations. The extremes can be illustrated by contrasting medical practitioners with support staff such as janitors.

Medical practitioners must obtain considerable training before they practice on patients. They use billions of dollars in sophisticated technology. They are asked to make life-and-death judgment calls on a daily basis.

Relatively few people can fill these positions, and those who do have commanded relatively high wages from the rest of society

Janitors require minimal training and often do not graduate from high school. They use unsophisticated equipment like mops and buckets. They are asked to perform physical labor requiring limited judgment. There are large numbers of people who can fill such positions, and they have traditionally commanded relatively low wages from the rest of society.

As we saw earlier in the auto industry, keeping groups of individuals with sharply divergent skills and interests together in a single union is difficult. Although two groups might share common work space, perform interdependent tasks, and share a history of working for a common employer, the underlying divergence in background still drives them apart. This occurs even though collective agreements can be negotiated that include multiple job classifications or pay schedules to reflect differences in skills and abilities, and aggregate settlements may be much better than could be negotiated for either group on its own with greater economic leverage.

It should be no surprise to discover that it has been nearly impossible to create broad bargaining units in health care. This has occurred although the leverage that comes from unity has been aptly and repeatedly demonstrated by the practitioners and their association—the American Medical Association (AMA).

The AMA acts as a powerful craft union would, although it vehemently refuses to call itself one. It has been successful in limiting the supply of entrants to medical schools, and thus the supply of doctors, attempting to maintain the earnings of its members. It has also been active in discouraging development of "non–fee for service" forms of health care, in which doctors move from fee-based payments and independent to salaried jobs and negotiated contracts setting hours and other conditions of work. With recent pressures for cost control, such as moves to impose fee schedules on doctors, peer reviews on medical practices to curb unnecessary tests and procedures, and endless rounds of paperwork to justify insurance claims, the AMA is gradually yielding its control over procedures in health care to bureaucrats and insurance company personnel, but it still retains considerable strength; at least 50 percent of all practitioners continue as members.[19]

Despite the AMA example, and changes in U.S. labor law in 1974 designed to bring hospital workers under the National Labor Relations Act to encourage collective bargaining, the employee side of the bargaining structure continues to be one of smaller, less-encompassing craft unions and associations. It has even been hard to decide who actually ought to belong to which occupation or craft for representation in collective bargaining.

[19]Sar A. Levitan and Frank Gallo, "Collective Bargaining and Private Sector Professionals," *Monthly Labor Review*, September 1989, pp. 24–33, esp. pp. 26–27.

The 1974 labor law changes ushered in litigation over the composition of bargaining units that, years later, is still under way. The issues are twofold. From the union perspective, the employers, knowing that large multicraft bargaining units are difficult to establish through representation elections, and seeing their own power enhanced by employee disunity, insist that they will only recognize broad units. From the employer perspective, recognizing many separate bargaining units (for nurses, skilled maintenance workers, technologists, doctors, and others) would create chaotic conditions in their facilities; bargaining would never cease.

Are the employers correct in thinking that multiple bargaining units in a single hospital will create rapidly escalating wages, frequent strikes, and interunion disputes over work assignments? A study of several hospitals in 1988 suggests that this has not happened. The hospitals had from zero to 10 bargaining units, but strikes, pay increases, and jurisdictional disputes were not more common in the hospitals with multiple bargaining units.[20]

In 1989 the National Labor Relations Board (NLRB) sought to break the logjam by issuing a set of rules creating eight recognized bargaining units: registered nurses, physicians, all other professionals, technical employees, skilled maintenance workers, office and clerical employees, and all other nonprofessionals and guards. The courts, petitioned by the employers, promptly issued an injunction to prevent this classification scheme from being used, pending an appeal on its validity by the employers.[21]

The nurses are a good example of the turmoil on the employee side of the bargaining table in health care. With nearly 1.5 million nurses in the United States, nursing has become a battleground for union organizing in the last 15 years, after having been largely left to associations in the past.

The American Nurses Association (ANA) was founded in 1896, an era when nurses were self-employed just like doctors. For many years, the ANA acted to discourage collective bargaining for reasons similar to those offered by the AMA.

As health care shifted to institutional settings, nursing became an industrial profession; by 1950 half of all nurses were employed in hospitals. Away from the cottage setting, wages and conditions for nurses began to decline relative to other trades. Relatively low pay and onerous working conditions during World War II, and the emergence of several AFL-CIO affiliates (the Service Employees International Union and the National Union of Hospital and Health Care Employees), stimulated the ANA to reverse its opposition to collective bargaining in 1946.[22]

---

[20]Joshua L. Schwarz and Karen S. Koziara, "The Effect of Hospital Bargaining Unit Structure on Industrial Relations Outcomes," *Industrial and Labor Relations Review*, 45:3, April 1992, pp. 573ff.

[21]Gene Zack, "Health Care Workers Turn to Unions," *AFL-CIO NEWS*, Apr. 2, 1990, pp. 6–7.

[22]Ibid.

Organizing proceeded very slowly however. Nonprofit hospitals were excluded from the protection of the Taft-Hartley Act in 1947 (see Chapter 9 for a discussion of labor law on organizing), and many states refused to pass the necessary legislation authority to allow bargaining to take place with nurses. By 1956 only 5900 members out of 181,400 total ANA members were covered by contracts. In 1974, when the law was changed to recognize health care workers, 21 unions, including AFSCME, AFT/FNHP, SEIU, CWA, Teamsters, RWDSU, and FCW, jumped into the organizing struggle. The result has been one of confusion and overlapping jurisdictions.

PROFESSIONAL SPORTS

Professional sports, although employing relatively few people, have considerable influence on society through their close relationship with the media, which have come to rely on sports programming.

Enhanced media exposure has increasingly given professional athletes the status and compensation levels of other public entertainers. Like entertainment, there are structural and economic factors at work that make employment relations in some professional sports subject to quite vigorous collective bargaining. As a result, sports fans are often very much aware of labor relations in the sports they follow, especially when a strike looms.

In determining pay and benefits of employees, the most important factor is the relative scarcity of the talent required to play a professional sport to pro standards. The physical gifts of stars are those of a select few. Because their abilities are scarce, outstanding athletes can command high compensation. But this situation is limited to a degree by the many potential replacements playing organized sports in public schools, colleges, and even in semiprofessional leagues. While the ranks of top players remain limited, the sifting of literally millions of potential professionals by scouts, agents, coaches, and others allows a relatively large pool of high-caliber athletes to be assembled for staffing professional sports teams, a factor tending to curb the market power of any individual in the pool. For this reason, even top athletes may have an interest in cooperating with other athletes in a union.

Individual and team sports exhibit different patterns of collective bargaining and bargaining outcomes, mainly because of the different requirements they place on those who play them. These differences are explored below.

Team Sports

Team sports such as hockey, baseball, football, and basketball operate in a much different fashion than the individual sports. Team sports exhibit features that give them well-structured, and sometimes quite militant, patterns of collective bargaining.

First, all of the professional team sports are franchised activities. Each has created a league structure that limits the number of teams participating in league play and the number of players that each team may have under contract at any time. Ostensibly done to enhance quality and equity of play and thus improve marketability of the sport to fans and media, the franchise and roster limit concepts have had major implications for collective bargaining patterns and bargaining outcomes.

Tight limits on franchises have encouraged the development of a highly concentrated ownership structure on the employer side of the bargaining table in every professional sports league. Indeed, visibility and concentration are so high that all existing franchise sports have received exemptions from antitrust statutes to allow their franchise holders to gather in closed meetings to discuss league business, an activity that could be construed as restraint of trade if practiced in virtually any other industry. The organization of owners to run league affairs has encouraged the emergence of leaguewide employer associations for purposes of bargaining with the players.

Restrictions on roster size at the professional league level have also had significant effects on collective bargaining patterns. On one hand, these restrictions have increased competition among would-be professional players for positions in the league, reducing individual bargaining power. On the other hand, roster size restrictions have created heavy economic incentives for individual franchise holders to sign the very best players they can find to their rosters. The increased economic value of franchises that field consistent winners—which comes from increased fan support at the ticket office, merchandise purchases, and larger television contracts—is usually far greater than the salaries of even the best individual players.

Second, the dynamics of competition in team sports, which pit two groups of athletes in head-to-head competition, give the players considerable leverage in collective bargaining. Achieving a winning record in team sports requires the athletes to work with coaches and trainers to create consistent team play. It would be difficult to achieve consistency in the face of constant player turnover; as a result, team sports require greater stability of employment among athletes than do individual sports, leading to player contracts that may be multiyear affairs. The need for roster stability also makes it difficult to replace a large number of team members and maintain the standards of regular play. As a result, the strike weapon has teeth; if regular players refuse to play, the quality of games declines, fans lose interest, and lucrative media contracts will be in jeopardy.

Economic incentives, league structures, and the dynamics of play all combine to give labor relations in team sports a distinctly industrial feel despite the large salaries and perks now granted to many players. The National Football League (NFL) endured a 3-week strike in 1987. Major league baseball has endured seven potential strike situations in the 17 years between 1973 and 1990 inclusive. In 1991 and 1992, the National Hockey League went through an extended period of labor unrest.

Bargaining Patterns in Team Sports:
The Example of Professional Baseball

As perhaps the oldest professional sport, major league baseball has had many decades in which to evolve its collective bargaining pattern. Baseball has a very strong industrywide employers' association (the Owners Association), and a very strong craft labor union (the Major League Baseball Players Association), which sometimes work together and sometimes conduct acrimonious negotiations and hurl lawsuits at each other.

The organization of professional baseball players got off to an early start. The first incarnation of the Players Association (known as the Brotherhood of Professional Baseball Players) began signing members in 1885—just 9 years after the formation of the National League in 1876. The issues propelling the players to organize have a remarkably contemporary ring: a reserve rule preventing free agency for players, salary caps on player contracts, the unrestricted sale and assignment of player contracts between teams, and the provision of postcontract benefits such as pensions or medical care for retired players. But other issues have long since been resolved. For example, a hundred years ago some players were required to do ticket taking and sweeping up after games, something now ended.[23]

The reserve rule, and the restrictions on player mobility that it created, provided the first real test of wills between owners and players. The conflict began in 1879, when the owners, who had initially allowed players to change teams between seasons, realized that continuing this practice might well destroy the league. The problem was one of ensuring equal competition in play to maintain fan interest and support even though some franchises could command larger audiences and thus had more money to spend on players. As long as teams were free to hire whomever they chose, unrestricted free agency would soon see the best players playing for the teams that could afford to pay them the highest salaries. Financially weaker teams, which could not compete for the best players, would then begin consistently losing games and fans; eventually they would fold, leaving the best teams with no one else to play. To head off this eventuality, each club pledged not to employ any player reserved by another team, even though that player's contract had expired.

The players, quickly realizing the impact of the reserve rule on their incomes, began to protest. When these protests went unheeded, they began to organize. The early leadership of the Brotherhood, however, was unwilling to use the strike weapon to address the subject of reserve rules and free agency, and thus progress in addressing player grievances was slow.

A number of players broke from the Brotherhood's stance in 1889 and took matters into their own hands by forming another league—the National Brotherhood League. This organization was noteworthy both for

---

[23]See Kenneth M. Jennings, *Balls and Strikes* (New York: Praeger, 1990) for a detailed history of labor relations in Major League Baseball.

its ownership structure and its player contracts. Each franchise was run as a corporation with players holding shares in individual teams. Each franchise was allowed to sign contracts with individual players for periods as long as 3 years that could be raised as time progressed, but not lowered.

The internal collective bargaining patterns of the new league were complicated by the presence of players as part-owners; on the one hand, the players began voting for such practices as the compulsory transfer of players between teams (without contract changes) to equalize playing strength, and on the other hand, the owners acceded to multiyear contracts that were relatively independent of interim performance on the part of the players.

Rivalry between the two leagues led to falling ticket prices in 1890, and the limited financial resources of the Brotherhood League relative to those of the more established National League eventually saw the new league's demise after just one season. The collapse of the players' league signaled the loss of negotiating power on the players' side of the bargaining table, and with it the effective end of the Brotherhood itself.

The controversy between owners and players continued for several decades with rival leagues driving up salaries and then collapsing, and with the repeated formation of player associations, which also subsequently collapsed. For example, the Players Protective Association came into existence in 1900. Again, none of the members believed in striking, and its negotiating power with the National League was relatively weak. Creation of the American League—also in 1900—enhanced the Protective Association's negotiating power, but this was short-lived as the National and American leagues merged in 1903, creating the present format of Major League Baseball, Inc. with its separate National and American leagues and the World Series playoff format.

Finally, in 1946 a player's organization supported by regular organized labor came into being. Robert C. Murphy, a lawyer and former examiner for the National Labor Relations Board, became concerned with working conditions and the poverty status of some retiring baseball players. His American Baseball Guild was registered as an independent union and applied to the National Labor Relations Board for certification to represent all of the players in major league baseball. The NLRB refused to hold the necessary balloting, and Murphy decided to concentrate on unionizing one team, the Pittsburgh Pirates in a state (Pennsylvania) with a labor relations act and agency equivalent to the NLRB.

The state union representation election was lost, but Murphy was successful in increasing player power through the threat of strikes and actions during 1946. The Owners Association responded with reforms in an attempt to exclude outside union representation. It was at this time that the owners established the Major League Baseball Players Benefit Plan. It pays a pension to players based entirely on their length of service in the league, disregarding salary levels. As a result, the inequity between those who played the game years ago and earned relatively small salaries, and today's often very well compensated players is partially offset by the pensions paid.[24]

In recent years the proportion of baseball revenues that goes to players has been increasing. In the mid-1980s, to try to stop this escalation, the owners decided to stop bidding for free agents (those players who with 6 or more years' service in the game can sell their services to the highest bidder). The effort worked, and salaries as a proportion of total revenues fell from a peak of 38 percent to about 31 percent in 1989.

However, arbitrators ruled that the owners' actions were a violation of the collective bargaining contract and granted the players about the same share of revenue as they had before the owners' actions. The owners had to pay large sums to the players involved to make up the difference.[25]

As the realization that the owners were in fact still working together to keep salaries in check sunk home, the players association filed conspiracy charges in 1984 and 1985. Twice the owners were found guilty in court of restrictive practices, and in 1985 were forced to agree to a new system utilizing player contract arbitration to settle player's association charges. The presence of arbitration in the contracting process forces both club managements and player agents to table salary demands with a neutral choosing between the competing numbers based on trends and patterns observed in other clubs, taking performance into account. Sharply escalating player salaries have been associated with arbitration.

In the 1991–1992 season, for example, 12 of the 19 players going into arbitration received in excess of $1 million for the subsequent season. Several received in excess of $3 million. Interestingly enough, the old issue of equality on the playing field among teams from small and large markets that first propelled labor relations in baseball has resurfaced with the advent of less restricted free agency. As Andy MacPhail, the general manager of the Minnesota Twins, says, "Right now when a guy is a free agent, he's 31 years old or so . . . [so] at least a small market can hold onto players longer. If you start turning the real young players loose and let the [Los Angeles] Dodgers or whoever have those guys, you're going to make the [im]balance of power issue worse."[26]

Individual Sports

Sports such as golf, tennis, and marathon running exhibit the following features: first, they pit individual athletes against fields of peers; second, the competition takes place in a framework of independently organized

[24]Charles W. Bevis, "Baseball Players' Pension Plan: A Home Run by Any Measure," *Employee Benefits Journal,* 16:3, September 1991, pp. 5–10.

[25]Aaron Bernstein, "The Baseball Owners Get Beaned," *Business Week,* Oct. 15, 1990, p. 122.

[26]"Owners Know It's Spring When Chilling Arbitration Process Hibernates," *New York Times,* Feb. 23, 1992, p. 53.

and operated tournaments; third, the focus of marketing to the public is on the event, rather than the athletes.

Individuality and relative anonymity of athletes and sponsors in golf, tennis, and marathon running diffuses bargaining power on both sides of the table. However, tournament sponsors do retain a relative advantage, given their control over purse strings, marketing activities, and media access. An asymmetrical distribution of power has a distinct effect on bargaining outcomes between players and sponsors.

In general, athletes playing individual sports must act much like private contractors in their dealings with the tournament sponsors. They have relatively limited influence over the size of prizes or working conditions. They seldom, if ever, hold long-term playing contracts. There are few, if any, development programs beyond those available in colleges or private camps for them. There are few pension or disability programs.

The various individual sports do not have the same degree of asymmetry in bargaining patterns. The marked differences in how the tennis and golf professionals handle the issue of tournament entry is a good example.

Invitations to play in professional tennis tournaments (known as seedings) are given out according to the Association of Tournament Players (ATP) computer rankings. These rankings are based on immediate past performance against ranked opponents; failure to play for even a limited time can drop even a top-ranked player in the overall standings and hamper entry to later events. Low-ranked players have to compete in preliminary rounds for qualifier berths in the main draw of an event and then play well enough to move up and avoid the preliminary draw.

Historically, invitations to play in professional golf tournaments also relied on performance with openings held for qualifiers who won practice rounds held prior to a main draw—much like tennis. However, in recent years, as the Professional Golf Association (PGA) tour has gained visibility through televised tournaments,[27] distinct changes have occurred in bargaining dynamics. Today, while there are still no long-term contracts, the PGA tour has been able to establish "touring cards" allowing holders to compete in PGA-sanctioned events over a season, regardless of the player's specific finish in any one of them. These cards are earned by finishing in the top 120 on the previous year's earnings list, by winning in a PGA qualifying school, or by finishing near the top of the junior Hogan tour. Qualifying rounds at major tournaments have been eliminated.[28] It appears that higher media profiles are giving greater power to the existing professional golfers; as a result, they are now able to exert some degree of control over their working conditions.

---

[27]Complete with a commissioner equivalent to those responsible for major league baseball, football, basketball, and hockey.

[28]The similarity of Hogan tour and qualifying school to baseball's minor leagues is more than coincidental. Players must now serve an apprenticeship to get their union cards.

CHAPTER SUMMARY

The various forms of bargaining relationships that exist are referred to as the structure of bargaining. There are several different ways to describe the bargaining structure of the American economy. One classification is by the type of employer negotiating unit (multiemployer, individual employer, etc.) related to the relationships between negotiating units (e.g., whether there is an industrywide agreement or only local agreements). There are a number of other important dimensions that could be added to these two factors. Bargaining structure is not only a matter of who bargains with whom. There are also different methods of bargaining about different issues.

The characteristics of employment in different sectors of the economy determine what problems or issues are of importance in collective bargaining, even the manner in which bargaining is conducted. Manufacturing is a very important sector of the economy. Its characteristics of employment are not exactly like those in other sectors. Manufacturing usually involves a factory at a fixed location in which machinery is installed. The work force is relatively stable and made up of a large proportion of unskilled and semiskilled workers who identify closely with the company. The work force reports for work on a fixed schedule and is usually closely supervised by managerial personnel.

Collective bargaining agreements in manufacturing commonly involve only a single company. A general agreement covers items common to all facilities of the company, but there may be supplemental provisions relating to working conditions specific to each particular plant. There is great concern in labor negotiations about the competitive status of employees but little about hiring decisions. However, there is no single or simple form of labor relations in manufacturing. There are different practices with respect to bargaining format, issues, and results.

The automobile industry illustrates a different form of labor-management structure. Large companies dominate the production of automobiles in the United States. Most negotiate with the United Auto Workers, and most of the employees of the auto companies are members of the UAW. Several companies have national agreements with the UAW, and local supplements to the national agreements are negotiated at the plant level. The national agreement establishes the economic package and certain nationally applicable working conditions and dispute procedures. The local supplement deals with conditions of work and grievances at a particular plant. There is no industrywide bargaining in autos.

There are a variety of bargaining arrangements that exist in other industries. In addition to one company bargaining with one union, there are several other major types of bargaining relationships. For example, several companies may deal with a single union or vice versa. Other variations include negotiations that occur on the plant level or at the company level.

In negotiations, certain stable kinds of interrelationships are called patterns. When a number of negotiations are very closely related, pattern bargaining is said to occur. A particular union and employer settle their negotiations on the basis of a pattern established elsewhere.

The coal industry has been significant in American labor relations. It has had industrywide bargaining (though this is now weakening) and a single national union. The most distinguishing characteristic of employment in mining is that the workplace and living quarters of the miners are isolated from population centers. As a result, the miners have a strong sense of identity and separateness that creates strong loyalties to the unions and distrust of the mining companies.

Companies in the coal industry are widely diversified in size and type. Independent coal companies produce about half the coal mined. The rest is produced by companies that are subsidiaries of the heavy users of coal— the oil, steel, and electric companies. The Bituminous Coal Operators Association (BCOA) represents the industry in collective bargaining and embodies the economic interests that characterize the producers. Despite divergent interests, the companies prefer a joint negotiation with the miners' union. The United Mine Workers of America (UMW) represents the workers in the coal industry. It is an industrial union and represents both skilled and unskilled mine workers.

Construction is a sector of the economy that includes several hundred thousand firms. Construction can be divided by type of construction project (e.g., housing), or it can be divided by the specialization of the firms (e.g., highway contracting). Employment in construction has many unique features. The product is custom-built, individually priced, and produced on a site chosen by the purchaser. Each project involves an assemblage of various specializations. Employees shift among work sites and employers and identify with their craft or occupation. Employment is unstable, often dangerous, and nonstandardized. Construction firms vary greatly in size and are very numerous. In order to deal with unions, employers ordinarily join together in an association that negotiates with the union. The building and construction labor force is represented by a group of 18 or 20 national unions that are crafts-industrial in form. The nonunion segment of the construction industry appears to be growing rapidly. Its labor relations are being formalized by the policies of nonunion employer associations. These are called open shop or merit shop arrangements.

The structure of collective bargaining in union construction is extraordinarily complex. There is considerable variation by branch of the industry, by geographic location, and by craft. There are between 5000 and 7000 local, national, and state collective bargaining agreements in the industry. Occupations negotiate separately, and the relative position of each in wages and benefits is an important aspect of negotiations.

Health care is the fastest growing sector of the economy and now employs more people than auto manufacturing, coal mining, and construction combined. The employers are very fragmented, being primarily hospitals, clinics, and nursing homes, some of which are nonprofit and others for-profit. In the major cities the hospitals often join into associations to bargain with the unions. On their part the unions are primarily organized by occupation. Medical doctors, who are in many respects the key managers in the industry, do not think of themselves as managers and are organized into a professional association (the American Medical Association), which functions in many respects as if it were a union.

Professional sports have become increasingly unionized in recent decades and now feature collective bargaining between players' unions and associations of the clubs. There are significant differences between professional sports and other industries with respect to labor-management relations, including the free-agency concept and individual salary arbitration in baseball.

QUESTIONS FOR THOUGHT AND DISCUSSION

1 Why is the structure of collective bargaining so complicated in the United States? Is this a strength or a weakness of the industrial relations system?

2 Is centralized bargaining better than plant-level bargaining? Better for whom? Why?

3 Should the automobile companies bargain as a group? What would be the results if they did?

4 What is pattern bargaining? How does it work? Give examples. Where does pattern bargaining occur in the auto industry?

5 How does the industrial-versus-craft-union conflict enter into labor relations in the auto industry? Why do you think this occurs?

6 Many major coal companies are owned by larger companies from the steel and oil industries. What difference does this circumstance make to labor relations in the coal industry? Why?

7 Construction has a very decentralized structure of bargaining. What are the advantages of such a structure? What are the disadvantages? Why?

8 In what ways are construction labor relations different from those in various manufacturing industries you have studied? What are the causes of these differences?

9 There are three forms of industrial relations arrangements in the construction industry that are in stiff competition for dominance in the future. What are they? Do you think one form will come to predominate? Why or why not?

10 What are the key features of labor-management relations in the health care industry? Do you think unionization and collective bargaining increase the quality or care, or not? Why?

11 Should professional sports be unionized? Why or why not?

SELECTED READING

Alinsky, Saul, *John L. Lewis* (New York: Putnam, 1949).

Barnard, John, *Walter Reuther and the Rise of the Auto Workers* (Boston: Little, Brown, 1983).

Bourden, Clint, and Ray Leavitt, *Union and Open Shop Construction: Compensation, Work Practices and Labor Markets* (Lexington, Mass.: Lexington Books, 1980).

Jensen, Vernon H., *Heritage of Conflict: Labor Relations in the Nonferrous Metals Industry up to 1930* (Ithaca, N.Y.: Cornell University Press, 1950).

Katz, Harry C., *Shifting Gears: Labor Relations in the U.S. Automobile Industry* (Cambridge, Mass.: MIT Press, 1985).

Lipsky, David B., and Clifford B. Donn, *Collective Bargaining in American Industry* (Lexington, Mass.: Lexington Books/D. C. Heath, 1987).

Mills, Daniel Quinn, *Industrial Relations and Manpower in Construction* (Cambridge, Mass.: MIT Press, 1972).

Northrup, Herbert R., *Open Shop Construction Revisited* (Philadelphia: Industrial Research Unit, Wharton School, University of Pennsylvania, 1985).

Weber, Arnold, ed., *The Structure of Collective Bargaining* (Glencoe, Ill.: Free Press, 1960).

CHAPTER 11

LABOR-MANAGEMENT RELATIONS IN THE PUBLIC SECTOR

Almost 17 percent of all employees in America work for federal, state, or local governments. Of these, about one-sixth are employed by the federal government in civilian occupations, about one-quarter by state governments, and about seven-twelfths by local governments. Thus, about as many Americans work for government as for all manufacturing companies combined (roughly 18.5 million in each in 1992).

There are important differences between labor-management relations in private business and those that exist in the public sector. Among the most apparent differences are those that are created by the application of different laws. The National Labor Relations Act does not apply to employees of federal, state, and local governments. Instead, there are many different laws passed by the federal government, state governments, and municipalities, each covering employees in their own jurisdictions. A common characteristic of these laws is that they usually deny employees the right to strike.

Despite the absence of a legal right to strike in most states and municipalities, public employees have joined unions to a larger proportion than have private employees. (In 1991, 45.4 percent of all government employees were represented by unions.) And public employees, by virtue of their close familiarity with law, generally are very conscious of their rights and obligations. In public employment, therefore, the power balance and the procedures and topics of bargaining are often quite different from those found in the private sector of our economy. The situation that exists in the public sector is one of confusion, complexity, and evolution.

STATE AND LOCAL GOVERNMENT

Growth in State and Local Government Employment and Unionization

In the period since the end of World War II, the number of employees of state and local government has grown from 3.5 million to some 15.5 million and increased from 8.2 percent of nonagricultural employment to 14.2 percent (as of 1992). Today roughly one employed person in seven in the United States is an employee of some state or local governmental agency.

Employees of state and local governments serve in a variety of capacities. Among public employees are police, firefighters, sanitation workers, nurses, health aides, engineers, clerks, prison guards, and utility workers. This is a substantial range of occupations, demonstrating the wide variety of matters with which public employee relations are concerned. Slightly more than half of all public employees are involved in education, primarily as teachers. Hospitals and police protection account for the next largest groups, followed by highway maintenance.

Employee Organizations

About half of state and local government employees belong to unions or employee associations. This is a much larger degree of organization than exists in the private sector (about 13 percent in 1992) and is the result of substantial growth in recent years. About half of organized state and local government employees belong to unions, and about half belong to employee associations.

What is the difference between a union and an employee association? It has been common to think of unions as principally concerned with wages, benefits, work rules, and similar aspects of the employment relationship. Associations, in contrast, are said to have a greater concern for the professional aspects of employment, including the quality of public service and of the people performing it. These distinctions have never been fully accurate. Before laws permitting collective bargaining became common among the states (Wisconsin passed the first such law in 1959) even public-sector unions focused not on wages and benefits but on other concerns. Today unions that represent public employees share with employee associations interest in both professional standards and the economic aspects of employment. So much have employee associations embraced collective bargaining that some even engage in strikes, activities normally associated with unions only.

The Bureau of Labor Statistics classifies organizations of public employees as unions or associations on the basis of how the organization describes itself. Some differences do still exist between the two. Most public employee unions are affiliated with the AFL-CIO and take part in the activities of organized labor. Most employee associations do not wish to have this identification with working people from other sectors of the economy. This difference reflects the tendency of public employees in urbanized and industrialized states to belong to unions, whereas public employees from suburban, rural, and less industrialized areas tend to belong to associations. Too much should not be made of the union versus association dichotomy, however, for the groups are behaving more and more alike with regard to their employers and the public in general. The issues that divide organized public employees into unions and associations are primarily internal ones and are not reflected in external behavior.

There are many organizations representing state and local government employees. Several are unions and several are associations. The largest organization is formally not a union, but rather an association (the National Education Association). The larger unions are the American Federation of State, County and Municipal Employees (AFSCME), which represents public employees across a wide spectrum of occupations, including police in some localities, and the American Federation of Teachers, which represents public school teachers, especially in larger cities and towns. The firefighters' union represents most nonvolunteer firefighters and is affiliated with the AFL-CIO. The International Conference of Police Associations does not have as complete representation of police as the firefighters union does of firefighters. The Police Association affiliated with the AFL-CIO only recently, having been outside the Federation partly because of a jurisdictional dispute that caused opposition from other police employee unions already in the Federation. Another large group of police is represented by the Fraternal Order of Police, not affiliated with the AFL-CIO. The Teamsters also represent some police officers.

Other unions that are not primarily representative of public employees, but nonetheless represent substantial numbers of them in various geographic areas, include the Service Employees, the Laborers, and the UAW.

Association membership continues to outnumber union membership among public employees. Among public school teachers, for example, the National Education Association outnumbers the American Federation of Teachers by three to one. But in many geographic areas NEA units bargain collectively just as do AFT local unions, so that both may be said to be fully engaged in labor-management relations.[1]

What is the likelihood of a resumption of rapid growth among public-sector unions and associations? About half of public-sector employees remain unorganized, so that there is ample potential for growth. But the growth of unionization of public employees in the 1960s and 1970s was in large part due to the absorption of existing employee associations into unions, or the adoption of overtly unionlike behavior by associations. This process has now largely been completed. Additional members will have to

---

[1]Sar A. Levitan and Frank Gallo, "Can Employee Associations Negotiate New Growth?" *Monthly Labor Review,* 112: 7, July 1989, pp. 30ff.

come from the ranks of those not members of any group, and this is likely to be harder to accomplish.

Unions could get a boost from a federal law that would provide for collective bargaining in all states and localities. Such a law now appears to be constitutional since the Supreme Court in 1985 upheld the right of Congress to regulate employment practices by states and localities.[2] But there is little likelihood that Congress would pass such a law in the near future.

Finally, many public-sector unions represent some people who are not members, but are nonmembers for whom the union or association serves as an agent in collective bargaining. Yet the union charges an agency fee to these people, just as it charges dues to its members. What activities of the union or association can an agency fee cover? In 1991 the Supreme Court decided that only expenses associated with collective bargaining can be charged in agency fees. Included are not only actual bargaining expenses, but the costs of conventions that adopt bargaining goals and strategies and the costs of preparing for a strike, even if the strike is illegal under applicable state law or municipal ordinance.

However, expenses of the union for lobbying, political activities, litigation not directly related to a person's own bargaining unit, and literature about such litigation are not permitted to be charged to agency fee payers.[3]

The Employers

State and local government employees work for a variety of different agencies of government. There are so many agencies, in fact, that the federal government takes a census in order to find out how many agencies of government exist. In recent years the count has been over 78,000 separate units of government, including towns, school districts, and water conservation districts. Some 13,375 of these agencies have bargaining units.[4] These agencies have various degrees of authority under the laws of the state or municipality that created them. In some cases an agency is simply an administrative organ of a state or municipal government, but in others, especially in school districts, the agency may be a quasi-independent branch of government.

This multiplicity of agencies raises the question of who is really the employer of state and local government workers. Is it the immediate agency? Is it the chief executive officer of the municipality, or county, or state (e.g., the mayor of a city or governor of a state)? Or, since in our republican form of government considerable authority rests in the legislature, is the employer the legislative body, whether city council or state legislature? Labor relations in the public sector are very much complicated by this

---

[2]*Garcia v. San Antonio Metropolitan Transit Authority,* 496 U.S. 528, 1985.
[3]*Lehnert v. Ferris Faculty Association,* U.S. Supreme Court, No. 89-1217, May 30, 1991.
[4]Ibid.

issue, which has no exact parallel in the private sector. It is not uncommon for a union or an association to reach an agreement in collective bargaining with an agency of government, only to have another agency or legislative body refuse to honor it. Many difficult disputes have been created in this manner.[5]

Collective Bargaining

The structure of collective bargaining in state and local government has many similarities to that in the private sector. Unions or employee associations meet with their employers (either the managers of agencies or officials of the municipality or state) to negotiate agreements that are binding on the two parties for a specified term. Ordinarily the union is the exclusive representative of a certain unit of employees and negotiates wages, benefits, and working conditions on their behalf. These features of state and local government labor relations are much like those of the private sector. But there are important differences.

First, the strike is usually illegal for public employees, a matter to which we will return later in this chapter. Second, labor negotiations involving public employees sometimes have a very pronounced political aspect. Union and association leaders may conduct negotiations on three fronts simultaneously: by meeting directly with public managers, by lobbying with the legislative body involved, and by attempting to influence the voters. Public managers often complain that the unions go around them to the legislature and the voters, thereby frustrating true collective bargaining. The unions, on the other hand, charge that public managers often are not authorized to make a commitment for the legislative body, so that the unions must lobby in order to gain their objectives.[6]

Third, many governmental bodies possess civil service systems that regulate employee relations. These systems were established on a widespread basis in American municipalities and states in the late nineteenth and early twentieth centuries. Their purpose was to limit political influence and corruption in public employment. They utilized commissions, expert staffs, and regulations to control the processes of hiring, promoting, compensating, and dismissing government employees. Methods of instituting and investigating complaints by employees about allegedly unfair practices were also included.

Collective bargaining has as one of its objectives the establishment of rules and procedures of a similar nature, but collective bargaining uses different methods. To establish rules, it employs a process of negotiation, not

[5]David T. Stanley, *Managing Local Government under Union Pressure* (Washington, D.C.: Brookings, 1972).
[6]R. Theodore Clark, Jr., "Politics and Public Employee Unionism: Some Recommendations for an Emerging Problem," *University of Cincinnati Law Review*, 44, 1975, pp. 680–689.

enactment by a legislative body or promulgation by a commission; and to enforce rules, it relies on a grievance procedure that generally ends in a decision by a neutral instead of an investigatory process that ends in a decision by a commission.[7] Thus, civil service and collective bargaining stand as potential rivals.

The Structure of Bargaining

The structure of bargaining in state and municipal governments is surprisingly complex. Some cities and states bargain with many separate unions and associations. Others negotiate with only a few. When there is a multiplicity of bargaining units, it is because employees are organized by occupation or public agency (or department). When there are few units, it is because large, broadly representative groups exist (somewhat analogous to industrial unions in the private sector).

Until recently the number of bargaining units with which a municipality or state dealt was largely a matter of historical accident,[8] but in the past few years some cities and states have passed laws that allow public employee relations agencies to establish new, and fewer, bargaining units and to conduct elections to determine union representation. This process is creating a rationalized and simplified bargaining structure in many areas.

A study examined the establishment of public employee bargaining units in seven jurisdictions—Hawaii, Massachusetts, Michigan, New Jersey, New York City, Minnesota, and Wisconsin. These places were selected because they vary with respect to the laws and procedures they use to regulate and conduct public employee collective bargaining. The experiences in these jurisdictions were compared with each other and with those in the federal government. They covered such topics as unit determination procedures; criteria; treatment of special employees, such as supervisors, confidential employees, and guards; and bargaining unit structure. The study concluded that the use of broad bargaining units tended to improve the operation of collective bargaining arrangements involving large public employers.[9]

How the Difference between Profit and Nonprofit Organizations Affects Collective Bargaining

It is common to group organizations in the United States into three very general classifications:

---

[7]Stephen L. Hayford and Richard Pegnetter, "Grievance Adjudication for Public Employees," *The Arbitration Journal*, 35:3, September 1980, pp. 22–29.

[8]New York City, for example, negotiates with several hundred bargaining units, while Philadelphia has only about five. See Derek C. Bok and John T. Dunlop, *Labor and the American Community* (New York: Simon and Schuster, 1970), p. 324.

[9]Richard S. Rubin, Public Sector Unit Determination, Administrative Procedures and Case Law (Washington, D.C.: U.S. Government Printing Office, 1979).

- Private, profit-making businesses
- Private, nonprofit concerns
- Governmental agencies

Let us cite just a few examples. Private, profit-making businesses include not only large corporations like General Motors and General Electric, but also the corner grocery or drugstore. For this classification it doesn't matter whether or not the business makes a profit; what matters is whether or not it intends (or hopes) to do so. Private, nonprofit concerns include such organizations as hospitals and schools run by religious or charitable groups (e.g., a Baptist hospital or a Roman Catholic parochial school). Governmental organizations include various agencies of federal, state, and municipal governments, such as public school systems, water departments, and the unemployment insurance office. It is characteristic of governmental organizations that they profess to exist and function for the public good. Often the public good is offered as an excuse for poor financial performance. But it should not be forgotten that private business also professes to serve the public good and that the corporate charters issued to private business originally, and still today to a degree, were for the purpose of allowing a business organization to meet a public need.

These three groups of organizations can be split into two different two-way classifications. Thus, one may speak of the private versus the public sector, in which classifications 1 and 2 are lumped together and contrasted against 3. For many purposes this is a useful classification, for federal laws apply to labor relations very differently in the private versus the public sector. Alternatively, one might stress the importance of the distinction between for-profit organizations and not-for-profit organizations, in which classification 1 is contrasted with 2 and 3 together. To evaluate the usefulness of this classification, we must ask how important the role of profit is to the way in which labor relations are handled. Put another way, does the objective of making a profit cause managers in for-profit organizations to behave very differently in labor relations from the way managers in not-for-profit organizations do?

What is profit? Essentially, profit is a surplus—what remains after expenses are subtracted from revenues. Profits are used for two major purposes. They may be reinvested in the enterprise in order to expand its facilities or to make it more efficient. Or profits may be used to provide dividends to stockholders (or, in some cases, to provide bonuses to management and/or workers). When a company has no profits or negative profits (i.e., expenses exceed revenues), it is said to have losses. Generally high profit levels are an indication of success in a business, while losses will result in bankruptcy or a change in management, or both. The purpose of business is often defined as making the largest possible profit. Some companies probably do operate this way. But often companies try to maximize profits only after other objectives are met, including product quality, employee compensation, and community citizenship. This does not mean that businesses are good-hearted organizations that are concerned first about the public and only then about profits. On the contrary, there is much range of dispute over whether particular business policies are appropriate for the public good. But business corporations do not constantly seek higher profits regardless of other considerations. Most business executives do not behave that way, especially in labor relations.

Because business seeks to make as much profit as possible, subject to its other policies, a business is often at odds with its employees or labor unions over how much additional employee compensation is appropriate. Thus, business has a motivation to resist employee demands at some point. But do not-for-profit organizations, both private and governmental, have this motivation?

The answer is almost certainly yes. While not-for-profit organizations may not calculate and report profits, they are nonetheless cost-conscious. The level of costs cannot ordinarily be allowed to exceed budget limits without either a cutback or a change in management. Thus, it is clear that not-for-profit organizations have an incentive not to suffer persistent budget deficits, and this is analogous to a profit-making firm's desire to avoid losses. But does a not-for-profit organization have any incentive to generate budget surpluses? Yes, it does. A mayor may use a surplus to reduce taxes, or to initiate new programs, or to provide salary increases. A public official is probably not as surplus-conscious as a business executive is profit-conscious. Still, the same motivation exists for both.

Some readers will object that public agencies and other nonprofit organizations are notoriously wasteful and persistently overrun their budgets. Furthermore, when tax revenues are high, public employers sometimes appear simply to throw money away on salary increases, additional hiring, and other superfluous activities. This also is true. But private business is not immune to this behavior. Some business corporations continue year after year with substantial losses (e.g., certain railways). And in periods of economic boom private business often spends money in ways later shown to have been profligate. Where then is the difference?

The difference between profit-making and not-for-profit organizations is primarily one of degree. Private profit-making business is far more cost-conscious, on the average, than not-for-profit organizations. Profit-making firms are better managed; their control and accounting practices are better developed to accurately reflect expenses and to keep up a continual monitoring of revenues and expenses.[10] The managers of profit-making enterprises usually know more about their organizations, their objectives, and the constraints they face. But this is changing, and the managerial revolution that has improved management in the profit sector in this century is

---

[10]Joseph L. Bower, "Effective Public Management," *Harvard Business Review*, 55:2, March–April 1977, pp. 131–140.

now reaching the not-for-profit sector. As not-for-profit organizations become more cost-conscious, we may expect them to behave increasingly like profit-making enterprises. For labor relations analysis, therefore, the difference between profit-making and not-for-profit organizations is less significant than one might have thought at first glance.

This is not to say that there are not large differences between collective bargaining in the public and private sectors; there are large differences. But the differences tend to stem from causes other than the fact that the public sector is made up of not-for-profit organizations. The factors that cause public-sector labor relations to be different from those in the private sector have to do with the role of politics in the public sector, the division of the employer side into several different decision-making bodies, and the differences in laws governing labor relations in the public and private sectors.

State Regulation of Labor Relations

At present there is wide variability in the manner by which states regulate their own labor relations and those of their municipalities. Collective bargaining may be permitted by any of a number of legal devices, including statute, civil service law, state constitution, charter, executive law, and decisions of state and municipal courts. Approximately 42 states permit collective bargaining for some or all state and local government employees. The others have no explicit authorization for the process, but often have de facto bargaining in some areas and functions (like school teachers or sanitation workers). The states that lack formal authorization are primarily in the deep south (Arkansas, Louisiana, North Carolina, and South Carolina), the border states (Virginia and West Virginia), or the southwest (Arizona and Colorado).

Collective bargaining is permitted in 38 states for public employees. Four states have so-called meet-and-confer laws. Some states permit collective bargaining for some public employees, but have only meet-and-confer provisions for others. For example, Texas permits collective bargaining for police and firefighters in cities and towns in which collective bargaining has been approved by a majority of voters, but has only meet-and-confer allowances for teachers. California, in contrast, permits collective bargaining only for employees of school and community college districts; meet and confer is provided for state civil service and department of education employees, but in practice, despite the law, employees have collective bargaining rights. Also, in California some cities and counties have enacted comprehensive collective bargaining ordinances that provide for an independent administrative agency to oversee labor relations and a procedure to resolve impasses.

Many states permit bargaining for some public employees but not all and have a different scope of subjects for which bargaining is permitted for different groups of employees.

Twelve states permit some or all public employees to strike, but usually under limited circumstances; 30 states prohibit strikes altogether, while 8 states are virtually silent on the matter.[11] Where strikes are permitted, they are usually coupled with extensive dispute settlement procedures; if those fail and a strike looms, the public employer may sometimes receive a court injunction against the strike if a threat exists to public health and safety. Further, in most states the right to strike is simply not extended to cover police, fire, and security employees (e.g., at a prison).

Several states have fairly broad statutes dealing with public employee relations. They ordinarily permit collective bargaining for all public employees covering wages, hours, and conditions of employment.[12] Statutes of this nature provide

- The right of employees to join unions or associations[13]
- A method of establishing bargaining units and of determining union representation
- Collective bargaining when a union or association is selected by employees in a bargaining unit
- Issues about which bargaining may take place
- Prohibition of strikes (or permission for them in limited instances)
- Procedures for resolving disputes

Such statutes exist in Hawaii, Iowa, Massachusetts, Minnesota, Montana, New Hampshire, New Jersey, New Mexico (fully effective as of April 1, 1993), New York, Ohio, Oregon, Pennsylvania, and South Dakota. Where comprehensive statutes do not exist, labor relations are governed by ad hoc acts of the state legislature, by common law, or by municipal ordinance. The state laws that now exist are not at all uniform.

What causes states to enact laws requiring public-sector agencies to bargain with unions that represent their employees? There has been a debate as to whether already-established unions cause such laws to be enacted (i.e., simply make legal what already is occurring) or whether the passage of collective bargaining laws causes unions to grow. Gregory Saltzman has investigated this issue. He found that during the period 1959 to 1978, enactment of the laws caused growth in the number of teachers covered by union contracts, rather than the other way around.[14]

---

[11] Based on a study done by the American Federation of State, County and Municipal Employees, March 1992.

[12] For an up-to-date survey of state and local bargaining arrangements, see Donald S. Wasserman, Director of Research, American Federation of State, County and Municipal Employees, Washington, D.C.

[13] In *AFSCME v. Milton Underward*, the Eighth Circuit Court of Appeals of the United States held that the right of free association guaranteed by the First and Fourteenth Amendments to the Constitution extends to membership in a labor organization and denies municipalities the privilege of prohibiting membership in unions by their employees.

[14] Gregory M. Saltzman, "Bargaining Laws as a Cause and Consequence of the Growth of Teacher Unionism," *Industrial and Labor Relations Review*, 38:3, April 1985, pp. 335ff.

What do public employees bargain about? In contrast to the common practice in private industry, public employee unions do not hesitate to negotiate about policy issues as well as about wages, hours, and conditions of work. Teachers' unions, for example, raise questions of educational policy in collective bargaining. One study found that 46 percent of teacher agreements regulated the curriculum, 59 percent regulated student placement; and 96 percent regulated teacher placement.[15]

THE FEDERAL GOVERNMENT[16]

In 1992 the federal government employed some 2,990,000 people in civilian occupations (up from 1,892,000 in 1947). These employees ranged from construction mechanics in naval shipyards to aeronautical engineers employed by NASA. While a considerable amount of federal employment is concentrated in the Washington, D.C., metropolitan area, other federal employees are located throughout the nation.

Unionization and collective bargaining among federal employees are not recent. In fact, federal employees were among the first in the nation to organize. Crafts unions of workers in federal printing plants, naval yards, and arsenals were active in obtaining a reduction in the workday from 12 hours to 10 in 1840. By 1868 these unions had achieved, through lobbying and legislation, a reduction in the workday to 8 hours. So effective did the unions become in influencing Congress that in 1902 President Theodore Roosevelt issued an executive order forbidding federal employees from petitioning Congress in their own behalf. This so-called gag rule was affirmed and strengthened by President William Howard Taft in 1909. In turn, Congress, in 1912, in an act written specifically for postal employees (the Lloyd-LaFollette Act), provided the right to federal employees to organize unions and petition Congress.

Presidents continued to refuse to recognize the unions of federal employees. Presidents Herbert Hoover and Franklin Roosevelt made strong statements that collective bargaining as practiced in the private sector could not belong to federal employees. It was not until President John F. Kennedy's administration that actions favoring collective bargaining began. But collective bargaining for federal employees stops far short of what is done in the private sector, or even in many state and local governments. Federal employees are not permitted, by law, to bargain over wages, salaries, or pensions.

Among the most important federal labor organizations historically have been the unions in the Postal Service. For years their unions bargained with management over issues of work conditions and work load and lob-

---

[15]Steven M. Goldschmidt and Leland E. Stuart, "The Extent and Impact of Educational Policy Bargaining," *Industrial and Labor Relations Review*, 39:3, April 1986, pp. 350ff.

[16]Jon Brock and Richard Martin of the John F. Kennedy School of Government at Harvard University assisted in the preparation of this material.

TABLE 11-1   Selected Unions Representing Employees of the U.S. Postal Service

	Membership
American Postal Workers Union	365,000
National Association of Postal Supervisors	39,000
National Association of Letter Carriers	314,214
National Association of Rural Letter Carriers	77,000
Laborers International Union (mail handlers)	45,000
National League of Postmasters	N.A.
National Alliance of Postal and Federal Employees	20,000

Source: Courtney D. Gifford, *Directory of U.S. Labor Organizations, 1990–1991* (Washington, D.C.: Bureau of National Affairs, 1990).

bied with considerable success in Congress for pay raises. Other federal employees thereafter generally received similar increases, also by congressional action. In 1971 the U.S. Postal Service was reorganized as an independent agency of the federal government with authority to negotiate its own labor agreements. The unions and the Postal Service negotiated a collective bargaining agreement in 1973, including wage rates and benefits, and the postal employees were cut off from the federal employment system. Table 11-1 lists the major postal unions. Each of the organizations listed is primarily a postal employee union except the Laborers International Union, which in 1968 absorbed the Mail Handlers Union.

Extent of Unionization in the Federal Government

Unions currently represent about 60 percent of all civilian federal employees (excluding the Postal Service), and about 80 percent of all Postal Service employees. Non–Postal Service employees are grouped into two primary classifications: wage board and general schedule. Wage board employees are generally blue-collar workers, and general schedule employees are primarily white-collar workers. Wage board employees are paid an hourly rate; general schedule employees are salaried. Wage board employees number approximately 500,000 and work primarily at government installations, such as shipyards. General schedule employees number about 1.5 million and include most other federal government workers. (There is also a senior executive service of top managers.) Some 80 percent of wage board employees and 55 percent of general schedule employees are represented by unions that have the authority to be the exclusive representatives of employees in designated units (this is analogous to the situation in the private sector).

Exclusive recognition occurs when a majority of the employees in an "appropriate unit" have elected the union as their representative in a secret-ballot election. The Federal Labor Relations Authority (FLRA) is responsible for making appropriate unit determinations. The authority specifies that the determination that a group of employees constitutes an appropriate unit will be based on specific criteria: community of interest among the employees, promotion of effective dealings with the agency concerned, and promotion of efficiency of operations in the agency. Once exclusive recognition is conferred on a union, that union becomes the sole representative of the employees for collective bargaining purposes. Consequently, competition among rival unions for exclusive recognition is frequently intense.

Short of exclusive recognition, the union seeks the right to "consultation." The Civil Service Reform Act (CSRA) specifies that if "no labor organization has been accorded exclusive recognition on an agency basis, a labor organization that is the exclusive representative of a substantial number of the employees of the agency" will be granted "national consultation rights." The union's right to consultation requires management to inform the union "of any substantive change in conditions of employment." Additionally, the union must be given time to present its "views and recommendations" on the proposed changes. Management must then consider the union's response before reaching a final decision and provide the union with a written explanation of the action taken. The FLRA establishes criteria and resolves questions involving the right to consultation and exclusive recognition.[17]

The Scope of Bargaining

A major area of contention between labor and management is in the defining of the appropriate range of negotiable issues. In the federal sector the scope of bargaining is legally restricted by two factors that do not operate in the private sector. First, no bargaining outcome is permitted to change federal law. Since the legislative branch is entrusted with the sole authority to make laws, representatives of the executive branch are not allowed to change the law through bargaining.

The second limitation on bargaining in the federal sector is the merit system, designed to eliminate political and other inappropriate influences from personnel actions in the federal civil service. This concept requires that hiring, transfers, and promotions in the federal sector be based solely on merit considerations and leaves relatively little room for bargaining over such issues as job rights and access. Merit requirements for personnel actions are administered by statute and by regulations promulgated by the central Office of Personnel Management. The strong congressional endorsement of the merit system is apparent in the CSRA's creation of the independent Merit Systems Protection Board.

As labor has sought the right and opportunity to bargain collectively with management over matters of mutual interest, a fundamental concern

[17]Federal Labor Relations Authority, "The Federal Service Labor-Management Relations Statute (Chapter 71 of Title 5 of the U.S. Code and Related Amendments to 5 USC 5596 (b)— the Back Pay Act)," FLRA Document 1071, January 1980, pp. 20–22.

of management has been the formal safeguarding of management rights. Management rights are areas in which management has retained, through statute, the exclusive right to make the final decision and which are not, therefore, within the scope of bargaining. In the tradition of the executive orders, the CSRA identifies specific areas as management rights. Bargaining on these areas, including the agency's mission, budget, number of employees, and procedures for internal security, is therefore prohibited. Bargaining is permitted, but not required, in such areas as the technology, means, and methods of performing the agency mission. Bargaining is mandatory for such areas as procedures for resolving grievances.

PUBLIC EMPLOYEE IMPASSES AND THEIR RESOLUTION

Legal Prohibitions Against the Strike

All federal and most state and local employees are currently legally denied the use of the strike. Not only are the unions or associations prohibited from calling work stoppages, but individual employees are often prohibited from joining or participating in organizations that advocate or assert the right to strike against the government. Thus, in an action amending the Taft-Hartley Act, adopted on August 9, 1955, Congress established that

> No person shall accept or hold office or employment in the Government of the United States who participates in any strike or asserts the right to strike against the Government of the United States. . . . or is a member of an organization of Governmental employees that asserts the right to strike against the Government of the United States . . . knowing that such organization asserts such rights.

Yet strikes by public employees are not unusual and have also occurred in the past. Perhaps the most famous such strike occurred in 1919, when the Boston police quit work because of the refusal of the city police commissioner to permit police officers to form a union affiliated with the AFL. On Sunday, September 8, a strike vote was taken among the city's 1544 police officers; 1134 voted to strike, 2 were opposed, and others did not vote. At 5:45 p.m. on Monday, September 9, 1127 police quit work. The result was a night of violence and crime in the city in which 9 people were killed and 23 wounded. The situation was finally brought under control by the militia. The strike collapsed on September 10. Commenting on the strike, Massachusetts Governor Calvin Coolidge (later President of the United States) said, "There is no right to strike against the public safety by anybody, anywhere, anytime." Seventy years later police strikes are generally no more successful at getting a union. A study of 600 nonunion police departments found that strikes have not helped police gain union representation.[18]

---

[18]Ray Richard, "Police Strike Boston in 1919," *Boston Globe*, Sept. 16, 1969, p. 22; and Casey Ichniowski, "Police Recognition Strikes," *Journal of Labor Research*, 9:2, Spring 1988, pp. 194ff.

In the aftermath of the Boston police strike, public employee unionism was checked and strikes by public employees were halted. Nonetheless, strikes did sometimes occur. During the 1930s work stoppages on public employment projects were not uncommon. One author, writing in 1940, titled a study *One Thousand Strikes of Government Employees.*[19] Since the end of World War II data have been compiled on the frequency of work stoppages by public employees and the number of persons involved. There were relatively few stoppages until the mid-1960s, but the number of stoppages was high in 1969, 1970, and 1975. Throughout the rest of the 1970s and into the 1980s, the number of strikes by public employees remained at a relatively high level (by historical standards). In 1980, for example, there were some 502 strikes by employees of state and local governments.[20] The frequency of strikes by public employees has declined significantly since 1980, but when one considers that virtually all these work stoppages were illegal, interesting questions are raised concerning the effectiveness of legal prohibitions in avoiding stoppages.

On August 3, 1981, approximately 11,500 federally employed air traffic controllers, members of the Professional Air Traffic Controllers Union (PATCO), went on strike. President Ronald Reagan, declaring the strike to be illegal, immediately announced that any striking controller who failed to report back to work within 48 hours would be dismissed. Three days later, approximately 12,000 dismissal notices were mailed, and the secretary of transportation announced, "It's over. Our concern is rebuilding the system." The government proceeded to hire replacements for the strikers. The strikers sued to regain their jobs. On November 14, 1984, the Supreme Court refused to hear an appeal by 34 former air traffic controllers fired after the 1981 walkout. The Court let stand lower court rulings that President Reagan did not exceed his authority by ordering the firings because the controllers—all federal employees—broke the law when they struck and refused to return to work.[21]

So ended the most dramatic and widely publicized strike of public employees in the United States since the Boston police strike of 1919. And the PATCO strike of 1981 ended just as the police strike of 1919 ended: the strike collapsed and the strikers lost their jobs.

---

[19]David Ziskind, *One Thousand Strikes of Government Employees* (New York: Columbia, 1940). For current data, see U.S. Bureau of the Census and U.S. Labor-Management Services Administration, *Labor-Management Relations in State and Local Governments: 1978,* State and Local Government Special Studies No. 95 (Washington, D.C.: U.S. Government Printing Office, July 1980).

[20]U.S. Bureau of the Census, *Labor-Management Relations in State and Local Governments: 1980,* Special Studies No. 102 (Washington, D.C.: U.S. Government Printing Office).

[21]Bureau of National Affairs, *Daily Labor Report,* No. 220, Nov. 14, 1984, p. A8. See also David B. Bowers, "What Would Make 11,500 People Quit Their Jobs?" *Organizational Dynamics,* 3, Winter 1983, pp. 5–19; and Herbert R. Northrup, "The Rise and Demise of Patco," *Industrial and Labor Relations Review,* 37:2, January 1984, pp. 167–184.

Surprisingly, perhaps, the ultimate outcomes of the Boston police strike and the air traffic controllers' strike were similar. Years after the strike the Boston police unionized and today bargain with the city. In the fall of 1986, 5 years after the PATCO strike, air traffic controllers, many of whom were originally hired to replace strikers, began to form a new union. Nine months later, the National Air Traffic Controllers Association (NATCA) supplanted PATCO as bargaining agent via an election held in the spring of 1987. According to reports, controllers were upset over what were said to be insensitive, authoritarian supervisors and the unwillingness of the Federal Aviation Administration to take remedial action. NATCA, however, has pledged not to strike.[22] Finally, in 1989, a new director of the Federal Aviation Administration began an effort to straighten out problems with controller training and to improve relations with the union. Some of the personnel management changes introduced by the FAA have received praise from the union.

The PATCO strike was dramatic and had far-reaching consequences—some observers believe it triggered a decade of aggressive hostility to unions by American management. When in 1986 Trans World Airlines hired 2350 permanent replacements for its striking flight attendants, effectively breaking the union, and the Supreme Court of the United States upheld the action (in 1988), many saw in TWA's action the long shadow of the federal government's handling of the PATCO strike. That the point had been understood by organized labor was made evident when United Airlines' flight attendants worked for some 5 years without a contract—and without striking—because they feared that if they struck, the airline would replace them with new employees.

The PATCO strike was of great consequence, but it was not typical. It was too large, too visible, and occurred in the federal government. Most strikes of public employees occur at the local level and involve far fewer people. Each year, for example, scores of teachers' strikes occur around the country, generally at the opening of school in the fall, because then a strike exercises a maximum disruption and therefore gives striking teachers what they often believe to be maximum leverage in bargaining. Strikes occur over many different issues, but pay increases and threatened layoffs are major causes. Since teachers' strikes are generally prohibited by law, courts are drawn into the struggle by local school boards and striking teachers soon face injunctions against staying away from work and their unions often face fines. Most teachers' strikes are resolved by bargaining; sometimes the union is forced back to work without a contract; sometimes some strikers go to jail

---

[22]"New Air Controllers' Union Forms," Bureau of National Affairs, *Daily Labor Report*, No. 188, Sept. 29, 1986, pp. A3–A4; "Air Controllers Choose Union by More Than 2-1 Margin," Bureau of National Affairs, *Daily Labor Report*, No. 112, June 112, 1987, pp. A9–A10. See also Arthur Shostak and David Skocik, *The Air Controllers' Controversy: Lessons from the PATCO Strike* (New York: Human Sciences Press, 1986).

briefly and they and their union are fined. In some few instances replacement teachers are hired and the strikers lose their jobs.

Not all public employee work stoppages are strikes, of course. In contrast to the private sector, where strikes are generally legal, unions and associations in the public sector have an interest in avoiding the semblance of a strike. Therefore quasi-strikes, or "job actions," are common, but are only occasionally included in strike statistics. These actions include sick-outs, slowdowns, demonstrations, "blue flu" (so called because of its use by police as an excuse for mass sick calls), and mass resignations.

When strikes do occur, public authorities are often quick to respond. For example, under the law of New York State public employees are denied the right to strike, and those who take part in illegal walkouts not only are not paid for the time on strike but are required to forfeit an additional day's pay for each day spent on strike. As a result of a brief strike in the spring of 1980 by the employees of New York City's transit system, the employees lost pay equal to double the amount of time they were out on strike. In some instances, it is now said, public agencies count on some savings due to strikes as a way to balance their budgets. Also, union leaders who encourage illegal walkouts are subject to jail terms, and it is not uncommon for leaders of strikes to be sent to jail. For example, in 1992 18 school teachers in Warwick, Rhode Island, were sent to jail for refusing to obey a judge's order to stop striking and return to work.[23]

Nonetheless, workers sometimes ignore the prohibition and conduct illegal strikes. What conditions make strike prohibitions effective? The success of a prohibition against strikes is likely to depend on the following factors:

1 The weight of public opinion against strikers is a strong weapon to prevent, or to bring to an end, illegal strikes. However, when strikers live in isolated communities and have a strong sense of grievance against outsiders, public opinion in the society as a whole may have no restraining impact.

2 The degree to which strikers can be replaced by other workers who can effectively perform their jobs is a major determinant of whether an illegal strike can be halted. Small groups of highly skilled employees may be virtually impossible to replace and so may strike successfully despite legal sanctions.

3 The degree of internal disagreement within the union is an important factor. If the union is united, the threat of legal compulsion to end a strike may only increase the strikers' determination to persevere, but a disunited group may easily be induced to return to work.

4 The threat of the arrest or forced dispersion of strikers by police, whether to free property or to prevent illegal picketing, is sometimes, but not always, effective. Elected public officials are often unwilling to risk violence by ordering police to disperse strikers.

---

[23]"Rhode Island Teachers Are Jailed for Striking," *New York Times*, Sept. 12, 1992, p. 8.

SHOULD PUBLIC EMPLOYEES BE ALLOWED TO STRIKE?

Some commentators believe public employees should be allowed to strike. They cite the following principal arguments in support of a right to strike for public employees:

- A right to strike is necessary to make collective bargaining work; without the threat of a work stoppage the employer has no incentive to bargain.
- All employees should have the right to undertake concerted activities to better their working conditions.
- Strike prohibitions are not necessarily effective.
- Jail terms and fines are unreasonably punitive as a response to a work stoppage.

Those who advocate continuing the prohibitions against public employee strikes offer the following arguments:

- The public is the government, and the government is the sovereign (i.e., the lawful authority). A strike, which is force or compulsion, directed against the public is intolerable—no such right can be said to exist.
- Public services are too important to be disrupted by strikes.

There are ways other than strikes to settle public-employee disputes. Those who oppose public-employee strikes insist that a strike against the government is not like a strike against a private employer. George Taylor, coauthor of New York State's Taylor Law and one of the nation's foremost labor relations experts, said:

> The right to strike has not been accorded to employees in the public sector. The wherewithal to pay wages does not derive from a competitive marketplace, but through taxes levied and budgets enacted by elected government officials. In a representative government the elected officials are responsible for determining the amount of taxes we pay and how the total revenue is to be allocated among claimants so as to maintain a viable society. In some respects, the legislative body may be looked upon as the counterpart of competitive forces or the market in private industry.[24]

Thus, in public-sector employment, there does not exist a product marketplace to determine whether wages and other labor costs are raised too high, or set too low, through competition.[25]

---

[24]George W. Taylor, "Using Factfinding, and Recommendations in Impasses," *Monthly Labor Review*, 92:7, July 1969, pp. 63–64.

[25]The argument is that if compensation is set too high, the product will not sell, or other workers will seek the jobs at lower pay scales; and if compensation is set too low, workers will leave for other jobs. Thus, the marketplace is argued to establish an appropriate level of compensation among firms and occupations in the private sector. "In the private sector . . . negotiators are typically limited by such restraints as the entry of nonunion competitors, the impact of foreign goods, substitution of capital for higher-priced labor, the shift of operations to lower-cost areas, the contracting out of high-cost operations to other enterprises, slowdown of unprofitable plants and operations. . . ." D. Bok and J. T. Dunlop, *Labor in American Community* (New York: Simon and Schuster, 1970), pp. 334–335.

In consequence, the use of a strike by public employees to raise compensation or increase other benefits cannot be constrained except by a legislative procedure. Further, in the private sector a strike is directed against the employer—to cause it to lose money—and harm to customers or to the public is incidental. In the public sector the objective of the strike is to do harm to the public, the taxpayer, the citizenry.[26]

Some observers have tried to discover a middle way between the prohibition of strikes by public employees and the legalization of all walkouts. A distinction is made between those work stoppages that potentially endanger the public health and safety (e.g., those by police or firefighters) and those by other public employees that may inconvenience the public but do not threaten its wellbeing (e.g., walkouts by municipal office workers or by public-works employees). Employees performing so-called nonessential services for government can, it is argued, be permitted to strike legally.[27] In further support of this position, state laws that permit collective bargaining by public employees have been studied to determine how effective such laws are in discouraging illegal strikes. State laws that prohibit bargaining as well as strikes were also studied. These studies indicate that laws permitting bargaining had only a mild tendency to encourage strikes, whereas laws prohibiting bargaining were not effective in preventing illegal strikes.[28] Thus, some observers have concluded, since strikes cannot be effectively prohibited, and since many public services are not essential to the public health and safety, large numbers of public employees in the nonessential areas can be permitted the right to strike, although it must be denied to workers performing essential functions.

The debate about the advisability of a legal right to strike for some or all public employees has been conducted actively in the United States since the mid-1960s. In the 1990s, public employees continued to be generally denied any right to strike (although Hawaii, Minnesota, Pennsylvania, and Ohio permitted strikes by nonessential public employees).[29] It would appear that for the foreseeable future the advocates of a complete or partial right to strike for public employees will not be successful in achieving such a right in any appreciable number of political jurisdictions. Nonetheless, polls of the American public show that from the 1970s forward the proportion of people supporting a right to strike for public employees such as firefighters and police has risen (e.g., in 1978 some 35 percent of Ameri-

[26]Harry Wellington and Ralph K. Winter, Jr., *The Unions and the Cities* (Washington, D.C.: Brookings, 1971).

[27]John F. Burton, "Can Public Employees Be Given the Right to Strike?" *Labor Law Journal,* 21, August 1970, p. 472.

[28]John F. Burton, Jr., and Charles E. Krider, "The Incidence of Strikes in the Public Employment," in Daniel S. Hammermesh, ed., *Labor in the Public and Nonprofit Sectors* (Princeton, N.J.: Princeton University Press, 1975), pp. 161–170.

[29]Richard A. Lester, *Labor Arbitration in State and Local Government* (Princeton N. J.: Industrial Relations Section, Department of Economics, Princeton University, 1984), pp. 209–210.

cans supported a right to strike for police, and in 1989 the percentage had grown to 45).[30]

Strikes can often be avoided by other means than legal prohibitions, however. A study has shown that strikes are more likely to occur where negotiators for either management or labor are inexperienced.[31] Thus, the increasing maturity of public-sector bargaining may help to lessen the frequency of strikes.

RESOLVING LABOR-MANAGEMENT DISPUTES IN THE PUBLIC SECTOR

In the absence of a legal right to strike for public employees, there is a tendency for disputes between management and labor to continue indefinitely without resolution. Without the strike or threat of a strike, neither side is under substantial pressure to settle matters in dispute. In this circumstance, how can disputes be resolved?

There has been considerable experimentation in the public sector with alternative methods of dispute resolution. Most states and the federal government now specify various procedures that management and labor are to use in an effort to resolve disputes without recourse by the unions to illegal strikes. There is not enough space in this text for a comprehensive description of these various procedures and the experience that has occurred with them. However, several of the more important procedures are described below.

Dispute Resolution at the State and Local Government Level

State and local governments have a greater need for effective disputes resolution machinery than does the federal government. This is because bargaining at the state and local government level ordinarily includes important subjects excluded from federal government bargaining (in particular, compensation). It has been common, therefore, for state and local governments to require that disputes over the terms of collective bargaining agreements be submitted to various procedures designed to resolve such conflicts. The most important such procedures involve mediation by a neutral party, fact-finding, and binding arbitration. Mediation will be described in a later chapter. In a fact-finding procedure, the parties to a dispute submit whatever information they believe relevant to a potential resolution of the dispute. A neutral fact-finder then makes a study of the evidence and prepares a report on the facts. This procedure is often quite

---

[30]Report of polls conducted by the Roper Poll, *AFL-CIO News*, Jan. 8, 1990, p. 10.
[31]Edward Montgomery and Mary Ellen Benedict, "The Impact of Bargainer Experience on Teacher Strikes," *Industrial and Labor Relations Review*, 42:3, April 1989, pp. 380ff.

useful where there are important disagreements between unions and employers over the truthfulness of the information each is using. In collective bargaining, comparisons with rates of pay and working conditions of groups of employees other than those involved in the immediate negotiations are common, but it is often difficult to determine the exact pay scales and conditions of work of other employee groups. A fact-finding procedure helps to dispel uncertainty over these matters and thereby helps the parties reach agreement.

Fact-finding ordinarily goes beyond fact-finding, however. There is therefore a sense in which the name is a misnomer.[32] Instead of limiting themselves to the determination of matters of fact, most fact-finders proceed, often with statutory authority, to prepare a set of recommendations as a suggested basis of settlement of the dispute by the union and public employer involved. In this way, fact-finding assumes the character of a mediation process. In some states the law explicitly authorizes either management or labor or both to ask the fact-finder to attempt to mediate the dispute to a peaceful resolution.

Neither fact-finding nor mediation necessarily results in a contract between management and labor. Consequently, binding arbitration of a dispute is often resorted to, either as a matter of law (so-called compulsory arbitration) or by agreement between union and management. This sort of arbitration is described in a later chapter and is commonly referred to as "interest arbitration."[33]

Interest arbitration of collective bargaining disputes has become a controversial matter.[34] Many municipal employers apparently feel that arbitrators have been too generous in the awards made to public employee unions in the interest arbitration process.[35] As a result, some states now specify the factors arbitrators must consider in making their awards. Cost-of-living and comparable wage rates, items favored by the unions, are ordinarily specified; but productivity and the ability of the employer to pay, items favored by management, also are now often specified.

Arbitrators as a rule do not, understandably, feel that their awards have been more favorable to the unions than to the public employers. Instead,

[32]Thomas A. Kochan, "Dynamics of Dispute Resolution in the Public Sector," in B. Aaron et al., eds., *Public-Sector Bargaining* (Washington, D.C.: Bureau of National Affairs, 1979), p. 182.

[33]Charles J. Morris, "The Role of Interest Arbitration in a Collective Bargaining System," *Industrial Relations Law Journal*, 1:3, Fall 1976, pp. 427–531.

[34]Peter Feuille, "Selected Benefits and Costs of Compulsory Arbitration," *Industrial and Labor Relations Review*, 33:1, October 1979, pp. 64–76. See also David E. Bloom, "Collective Bargaining, Compulsory Arbitration and Salary Settlements in the Public Sector: The Case of New Jersey Municipal Police Officers," *Journal of Labor Research*, 2:2, Fall 1981, pp. 369–384.

[35]Thomas A. Kochan et al., *Dispute Resolution under Fact-Finding and Arbitration: Am Empirical Evaluation* (New York: American Arbitration Association, 1979). See also Patricia Compton-Forbes, "Interest Arbitration Hasn't Worked Well in the Public Sector, *Personnel Administration*, 29:2, February 1984, pp. 99–104.

arbitrators argue that they have had a difficult time fashioning contracts where there is little experience to guide them.[36]

One arbitrator has prepared a list of the most important qualities of an arbitrator:

- A sense of constructive relationships between people and organizations of the value of facts and how to identify them
  - A sense of the criteria that are relevant to a particular case[37]

Whatever the merits of this controversy, the search for substitutes for the strike in settling public-sector disputes has been long and imaginative and is continuing. Many types of arrangements have been developed, and experimentation is continuing.

One basic feature of disputes procedures that seems to be standing the test of time is that the settlement of economic disputes must be somehow related to the legislative and budgetary process.[38] That is, the school committee, city council, or state legislature, as the case may be, must somehow be bound, either by participation in negotiations or by a separate act of approval of a negotiated settlement, to what the public manager and union establish as the terms of a contract.

On other matters there is less clarity. Some participants in public-sector impasse procedures prefer open-ended mediation and fact-finding, which permit the parties to devise methods to resolve disputes on an ad hoc basis. Others prefer clearly delineated procedures ending in binding arbitration or some other method of finally resolving the issues between the parties.[39] At this stage, all that is certain is that the questions of the role of the strike in public-sector labor relations and of alternatives to the strike involving various methods of dispute settlement remain in a state of transition and flux.

FINAL OFFER ARBITRATION

In an effort to minimize resort to binding arbitration of contract disputes, several variations of binding interest arbitration have been developed. Professor Richard A. Lester studied interest arbitration in nine states and cities and reached the following conclusions:

1 The systems of interest arbitration analyzed have tended to receive increased acceptance, and performance under them has improved as the

[36]Jean T. McKelvey et al., "Interest Arbitration in the Public Sector," *Arbitration Journal*, 37:4, December 1982, pp. 3–31.

[37]Tim Bornstein, "Interest Arbitration in Public Employment," *Labor Law Journal*, 29:2, February 1978, pp. 77–86.

[38]See *Report of the Governor's Committee on Public Employee Relations*, State of New York, Mar. 31, 1966, p. 33, where this proposition was first set forth.

[39]Joseph R. Grodin, "Political Aspects of Public Sector Interest Arbitration," *California Law Review*, 64:3, May 1976, pp. 678–702. See also D. S. Chauhan, "The Political and Legal Issues of Binding Arbitration in Government," *Monthly Labor Review*, 102:9, September 1979, pp. 35–41.

parties and the neutrals have had the benefit of experience over an extended period of time. . . .

2 Over an extended period in many jurisdictions (for example, Michigan, Wisconsin, New Jersey, and New York City), more and more of the arbitration awards have actually been agreed upon by the negotiating parties. Essentially, they are collectively bargained contracts. . . .

3 A public-sector arbitration program works more satisfactorily where (a) the parties (management and union) participate extensively in the process and (b) representation of the parties in negotiations and arbitration proceedings is approximately equal in sophistication and advocacy, including the marshaling of supporting material. Participation includes such items as choice of the form of arbitration, selection of an arbitrator or arbitration panel, influence on the arbitration proceedings, and a role in shaping the award. . . .

4 Experience has shown that no one form of arbitration or set of procedures is best suited for application in every state; instead, different forms (or combinations of forms) and various procedures have worked well over time in particular states, due partly to the education-adaptation process. To illustrate, this study shows that the following forms of arbitration have worked effectively in the named states: (a) last-offer-by-package in New Jersey and in Wisconsin; (b) last-offer-issue-by-issue with a tripartite panel in Michigan and combined with fact-finder recommendations serving as a third offer with a single arbitrator in Iowa; and (c) conventional arbitration with a tripartite panel in New York State and with the right to strike as an alternative to arbitration in less essential employment in Minnesota.[40]

One of the most interesting of these variations is final offer arbitration. Proposed in 1966 by Carl M. Stevens, a professor, the notion had its roots in the jury process of ancient Athens. Under Athenian law the jury could not decide a penalty of its own; it had to choose between the penalty proposed by the prosecution or that proposed by the defense. It was not allowed to find a middle course—or "split the difference"—between them.[41]

Final offer arbitration was designed in theory to prevent frequent recourse to binding interest arbitration for the settlement of bargaining impasses, particularly, but not exclusively, in the public sector.[42] Final offer

[40]Richard A. Lester, "Lessons from Experience," *The Arbitration Journal,* 41:2, June 1986, pp. 34–37. See also Richard A. Lester, *Labor Arbitration in State and Local Government* (Princeton, N.J.: Industrial Relations Section, Princeton University, 1984).

[41]Robert J. Flanagan, "Socrates Confronts Final-Offer Selection," *Industrial Relations,* 30: 1, Winter 1991, pp. 163ff. Flanagan attributes the information about ancient Athenian juries to the journalist I. F. Stone.

[42]Use of final offer arbitration in the private sector has occurred primarily in the construction industry. In southern Nevada, final offer procedures exist in collective bargaining agreements between various employer associations and Laborers, Bricklayers, Hod Carriers, Teamsters' concrete truck drivers, and Teamsters' lumber industry workers. There is also a final offer procedure in the contract between the Oregon-Columbia chapter of the Associated General Contractors and the Operating Engineers.

arbitration was proposed as a response to the criticisms of conventional arbitration, especially its alleged "chilling," or deterrent, effect on the bargaining process.

The chilling effect argument states that if either party anticipates, for whatever reasons, that it will receive more from the arbitrator than from the negotiated settlement, it will have an incentive to avoid the trade-offs of good-faith bargaining and cling to excessive or unrealistic positions in the anticipation of tilting the arbitration outcome in its favor. In such a case, "The compromising nature of the conventional arbitration award—i.e., the arbitrator gives more than the employer has offered and less than the union has asked for—significantly reduces the costs tied to the uncertainties associated with continued disagreement."[43] Therefore, given its availability, conventional arbitration usage will increase as an alternative to bargaining. The available evidence shows that though conventional arbitration "does not immediately and inevitably destroy collective bargaining, there is evidence that conventional arbitration has often reduced the incentive to bargain."[44]

The purpose of interest arbitration is to resolve disputes, not to create them. Unfortunately, when the parties to collective bargaining are aware that if they do not reach agreement, the dispute will be submitted to an arbitrator for decision, this knowledge may affect their behavior in negotiations. Specifically, union or management negotiators, or both, may decide not to try to reach agreement, but rather to take their chances in arbitration. The existence of an arbitration procedure thereby stimulates disputes by having a sort of "narcotic effect" on bargaining.[45]

Final offer arbitration is a binding mechanism that requires an arbitrator to select, without modification, one of the final offers from the parties in a bargaining impasse. This procedure is intended to increase the parties' incentive to bargain by retaining the more equal distribution of costs of disagreement between union and management provided through any binding dispute resolution procedure, but eliminating the reduction of disagreement costs that produce the chilling effect of conventional arbitration. Since the arbitrator is not allowed to compromise between the parties' positions, the parties will be induced to develop ever more reasonable positions prior to the arbitrator's decision, in hope of winning the award. These mutual attempts to win neutral approval should result in the parties' being so close together that they will create their own settlement. Thus, "the final offer procedure was purposefully designed to contain the seeds of its own destruction. However, even if the procedure does not self-destruct, i.e., if an award does become necessary—the parties would have

[43]Peter Feuille, *Final Offer Arbitration* (Chicago: International Personnel Management Association, 1975), p. 12.

[44]Gary Long and Peter Feuille, "Final Offer Arbitration: 'Sudden Death' in Eugene," *Industrial and Labor Relations Review*, 27:2, January 1974, p. 189.

[45]Henry S. Farber and Harry C. Katz, "Interest Arbitration: Outcomes and the Incentive to Bargain," *Industrial and Labor Relations Review*, 33:1, October 1979, pp. 36–54.

narrowed the area of disagreement enough, that whatever the arbitrator's choice, the award would be reasonable."[46]

Final offer arbitration may be used in many different variants. For example, an arbitrator might be required to select a final offer on all terms of the contract, but he or she could be allowed to use final offer only on certain issues; alternatively, the arbitrator might be allowed to use final offer only as a fact-finder recommends. These variations introduce flexibility into a process that is otherwise quite rigid.

CHAPTER SUMMARY

In recent decades, unionization and collective bargaining have expanded in the public sector. Elaborate procedures for representation elections and for mediation and arbitration have been established to resolve public employee disputes. In the federal government, a statute now governs labor relations, providing a framework for union representation and collective bargaining. But there is no federal law that applies uniform regulations to labor relations of states and municipalities. Towns and states are free to regulate their labor relations with their own employees as they see fit.

The number of employees of state and local government has grown considerably in the last 45 years, and there is a substantial range of occupations. Employee organization has also grown substantially. About half of the organized state and local government employees belong to unions and to employee associations. Combined unions and associations are becoming more alike with regard to their employers and the public in general, and there is little clear difference between the two. Most public employee unions are affiliated with the AFL-CIO and identify with organized labor. Employee associations do not. The largest unions are the American Federation of State, County, and Municipal Employees (AFSCME) and the American Federation of Teachers (AFT). The largest public employee association is the National Education Association.

The employers in state and local government are more difficult to identify than private employers. It is possible to identify the employer as the agency head, the mayor, the city council, the state legislature, or the governor. There is often considerable uncertainty as to who has the authority to commit the government to a particular wage settlement in collective bargaining negotiations. Many of the complications and disputes that accompany public employee bargaining arise out of the lack of structure on the employer's side.

Collective bargaining in state and local government has many similarities to that in the private sector, but there are important differences. The

---

[46]Feuille, *Final Offer Arbitration*, p. 13. See also Hoyt N. Wheeler, "Compulsory Arbitration: A 'Narcotic Effect'?" *Industrial Relations*, 14:1, February 1975, pp. 117–120.

strike is usually illegal for public employees. Labor negotiations have a definite political aspect to them, which involves lobbying and influencing voters. Many governmental bodies already possess civil service systems that regulate employee relations by methods other than collective bargaining. An important question is when collective bargaining can supersede provisions of civil service codes.

Unionization and collective bargaining are extensive in the federal government. Federal employees were among the first workers in the nation to organize. The federal government has a much more complete format structure for dealing with labor relations than exists in state and local government. The current framework of labor-management relations in the federal sector is defined by the Civil Service Reform Act of 1978, which codified decades of evolving federal labor-management policies. The CSRA established a federal labor-management program and authorized the structural reorganization of the federal agencies responsible for personnel management and labor relations.

All federal and most state and local employees are currently legally denied the right to strike. Yet strikes by public employees have occurred in the past and are becoming more frequent. Financial loss and jail sentences have been used to enforce the strike prohibition. When in the 1970s strikes by public employees reached an all-time high level, the effectiveness of legal prohibitions against strikes was called into question. The effectiveness of the legal prohibition depends on the degree of public opinion against the strike, the degree of internal disagreement in the union, the extent to which the strikers are replaceable, and the willingness of public officials to risk public censure by using force against strikers.

Whether public employees should be allowed to strike is still an open question. On the one hand, strikes seem necessary because without the threat of a work stoppage the employer has no incentive to bargain. On the other hand, a strike against the government is not like a strike against a private employer. Some public services are too important to be disrupted by strikes. In the private sector, the employer is harmed. In the public sector, the public in general is harmed. One alternative that has been considered is to distinguish work stoppages which potentially endanger the public health and safety and those which do not. Large numbers of public employees in nonessential services could be permitted the right to strike, although it would be denied to others.

State and local governments have a greater need for effective dispute settlement machinery than does the federal government. They therefore require the submission of disputes to various types of procedures designed to resolve the conflict. The most important procedures of this type involved mediation by a neutral party, fact-finding, and binding arbitration. Fact-finding involves the submission by disputing parties of whatever information they believe to be relevant to resolution of the disputed issue. The fact-finder then prepares a set of recommendations as a suggested basis of settlement.

Arbitration of collective bargaining disputes is controversial because many municipal employers feel that arbitrators have been too generous with awards made to public employee unions. Furthermore, the knowledge that a dispute will be submitted to an arbitrator for a decision is alleged to reduce the incentive for good-faith bargaining. One party or the other may anticipate that it will receive more from the arbitrator than from a negotiated settlement and so will cling to unrealistic positions. Final offer arbitration was designed to prevent frequent recourse to binding interest arbitration. It requires the neutral arbitrator to select, without modification or compromise, one of the final offers from the parties in a bargaining impasse. Ideally, it induces the parties to develop very reasonable positions in hope of winning the award. However, final offer arbitration has also been criticized for reducing the incentive of parties to reach a settlement.

QUESTIONS FOR THOUGHT AND DISCUSSION

1 Should government employees be able to have unions? Why or why not?
2 How do labor relations in the public sector differ from those in the private sector?
3 How does the difference between profit and nonprofit organizations affect collective bargaining? What differences would you expect to find and why?
4 What are the differences between a union and an employee association? How important are the differences? In the future will unions and employee associations become more alike or less alike?
5 What matters are subject to collective bargaining in the federal government? Should there be a wider scope of bargaining? Why or why not?
6 Do you think public employees should have the right to strike? Why or why not?
7 Should police be treated differently with respect to the right to strike than other public employees? Should firefighters be treated differently?
8 What is the best method for resolving disputes in the public sector? Why?
9 How does final offer arbitration work and why was it developed?

SELECTED READING

Aaron, Benjamin, Joyce M. Majita, and James L. Stern, eds., *Public-Sector Bargaining*, 2d ed. (Washington, D.C.: Bureau of National Affairs, 1988).

Blackburn, Jack, and G. Busman, *Understanding Unions in the Public Sector* (Los Angeles: Institute of Industrial Relations, University of California, 1977).

Coleman, Charles J., "Grievance Arbitration in the Public Sector," *Journal of Collective Negotiations in the Public Sector*, 17:2, pp. 89–103.

Freeman, Richard B., "Unionism Comes to the Public Sector," *Journal of Economic Literature*, 24:1, March 1986, pp. 41–86.

Salerno, Charles A., *Police at the Bargaining Table* (Springfield, Ill.: Charles C Thomas, 1981).

CHAPTER 12

INDUSTRIAL RELATIONS ABROAD

INFLUENCE FROM ABROAD

Improved communications are making the world a much smaller place than it used to be. There is more economic interchange between nations, and developments abroad seem to affect the U.S. economy to a greater degree than they used to. The evidence for this is substantial. In the past 15 years the volume of U.S. foreign trade has grown from about 5 percent to more than 15 percent of total U.S. economic activity.

In an effort to further expand trade among nations, the United States concluded a free-trade agreement with Canada in 1988. In 1991 U.S. diplomats broadened this agreement to include Mexico, raising concerns in some quarters that American jobs will be lost to workers in other countries. These concerns are also being fueled by the intense competition being encountered by American firms, both in the United States and abroad, from firms headquartered in other countries. In 1993 a vigorous debate was conducted in the Congress about whether or not to ratify the argument with Mexico.

In an effort to improve their competitiveness, American firms and unions are studying the production, finance, and labor relations practices of other countries. The recent advantages of Japanese and European (especially German) firms in competition with American firms has focused attention on the reasons for their success. Among the factors often pointed out as contributing to this success are the significant differences that exist between the systems of industrial relations in Europe, Japan, and the United States.

Some authors suggest that American firms should borrow Japanese and European practices to improve productivity. As a result, many groups of

American managers, union officials, and workers have traveled to Japan in recent years to study Japanese manufacturing techniques. Similarly, American unions and government officials are curious about how unions and governments operate elsewhere. In particular, northern Europe has developed systems for providing participation and protection to workers which are of great interest to some Americans.

Union membership in major trading partners is generally much higher than in the United States. For example, in 1989, the last year for which data adjusted to account for differences in definition among the nations are available, American unions represented 16 percent of the nation's work force; Japanese unions represented 26 percent, German unions 33 percent, Canadian unions 33 percent, and British unions 41 percent.[1]

INDUSTRIAL RELATIONS SYSTEMS IN JAPAN AND EUROPE

Chapter 1 described the industrial relations system of the United States and suggested that each nation has some such system of its own, involving aspects of its legal, social, and economic life. In this section we will examine certain salient features of the industrial relations systems of Japan, Canada, Germany, and the emerging system of the European Economic Community (EEC). Each of these topics could comprise a book in itself, so it is necessary to be very concise here, picking out only those points which are most significant and most unusual to Americans.

Japan

Japan, an island nation like Great Britain, has a population of some 125 million. It is a major industrial power which since World War II has had a very high rate of economic growth. For many years Japanese products were known in the United States for low quality and low cost. Both these characteristics were based in part on very low wages paid to Japanese employees. But these conditions are far less prevalent now. Today Japan sells many high-quality products in the United States, including televisions, radios, and phonographic equipment from such makers as Sony and Panasonic and automobiles from Toyota, Nissan, and Honda. Japanese workers have received considerable wage increases in recent years, so that the difference between American and Japanese wage levels has been narrowed appreciably.

The Japanese industrial relations system is an interesting one for an American to study. In some ways the Japanese system is much like ours. For example, the Japanese have a diversified industrial economy, employ very modern technology, and have a largely free enterprise system. Govern-

[1] U.S. Bureau of Labor Statistics estimates, *Monthly Labor Review,* December 1991, p. 51.

ment regulation of business and labor takes much the same form as in the United States, partly because after World War II the Japanese remodeled their labor laws on the American statutes. However, Japanese industrial relations are also different in profound ways from those in the United States.[2] The dual economic system and the lifetime employment system have no exact American counterparts, and the result is a different role for unions and employers than in the United States.

The most unique characteristics of the Japanese industrial relations system arise from the duality of the Japanese economy. In the mid-1800s the Japanese discovered that they had fallen behind the Western nations in military and industrial development. Fearing for its future as an independent nation, Japan began to stimulate economic advancement through the agency of certain private trading companies. Over the years, these companies grew into very large and modern industrial enterprises.[3] Other elements of the Japanese economy did not grow as much or progress as rapidly. The result is that Japan's economy has two sectors: one made up of large firms that are technically advanced and another made up of many small firms, often with very inefficient production processes. As one might expect, the larger firms pay higher wages and provide better working conditions for their employees than do the less advanced firms.

The connection between the two sectors is through subcontracting. When large firms have more orders than they can fill, they subcontract them to small firms. But when there is a recession and orders decline, the subcontractors are cut off. This procedure allows the big firms to provide stable employment for their own employees and is a basic component of the lifetime employment system.

The lifetime employment system is practiced by large Japanese firms. Employees are hired when they finish school, and they remain with the same company all their lives. These workers are called "standard workers." They receive many benefits and are paid higher salaries as their length of time with the company increases.[4] Nonstandard workers are hired by the company to supplement its standard work force, but they have fewer benefits and may be laid off if business declines. A company may also hire temporary workers and may utilize the services of outside contractors' employees. Figure 12-1 is a diagrammatic representation of the employment structure of a large Japanese firm, showing the various categories of workers. The lifetime employment system applies primarily to standard workers. These workers are laid off only if the company has a major reduction

---

[2]Taishiro Shirai, ed., *Contemporary Industrial Relations in Japan* (Madison, Wis.: University of Wisconsin Press, 1983).

[3]Chie Nakane, *Japanese Society* (Berkeley: University of California Press, 1970).

[4]Makotu Sakurabayashi, "How a Japanese Firm Sets Salaries for Its Clerical Employees," *Compensation Review*, 7:2, 1975, pp. 42–49. Also, Nan Weiner, "The Japanese Wage System," *Compensation Review*, 14:1, 1982, pp. 45–56.

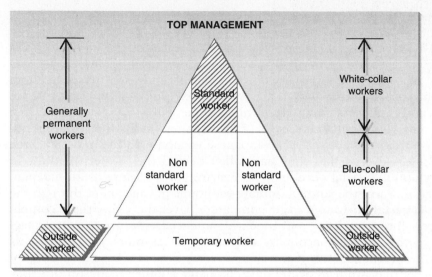

FIGURE 12-1 Employment structure of a large Japanese firm.

in business. Nonstandard, temporary, and outside workers (who total approximately one-half of the firm's workers) are readily laid off. Deep recessions can require layoffs even of standard workers so that the agreements must be modified. In 1974, for example, the head of a Japanese union at a camera manufacturing plant agreed to a new contract that permitted layoffs. Then, when people actually lost their jobs, he tried to commit suicide, since he felt responsible for their misfortune.[5]

In order to make lifetime employment possible Japanese firms keep hiring to a minimum and try to keep growing. They rely on employee adaptability to respond to shifting demand without incremental hiring and layoffs. Japanese firms rarely use what they refer to as the "Euro-North American" system of highly specialized job categories. Therefore," says a Toyota memorandum to supervisors, "new employees are not hired to do only specific jobs, and decisions concerning workshop and job assignments are made during the training period according to manpower needs and employee aptitudes and wishes."

Japanese firms also invest much more in the formal training of workers than is common in the West. Recent estimates by an American firm—which declines to be cited—suggest that Japanese workers in the auto industry receive an average of 150 hours of formal training per year, German workers 75 hours, and American workers 5 hours. It should be noted that

[5]Fox Butterfield, "Economic Woes Imperil Lifetime Jobs in Japan," *New York Times*, Oct. 24, 1974, p. 1.

these practices of Toyota and other Japanese firms in Japan are continued for the most part by those companies in their American factories.

During the early 1990s Japan's economy entered a period of slowing growth and potential recession, which put severe strains on the full employment practice in many firms. By early 1993 several Japanese firms had begun substantial reductions in force, initially by dispensing with subcontractor's employees, then by reducing hiring and letting attrition reduce the overall work force, then by early retirements, and finally, if absolutely necessary, by actual layoffs. Some commentators forecast the end of the lifetime employment system, but that was most likely an exaggeration.

The lifetime employment system has created among Japanese employees a degree of loyalty to the firm that is much envied by American managers.[6] The labor relations of Japanese firms also reflect this loyalty. Japanese unions are organized primarily among the permanent employees of a firm and exhibit considerable personal identification with their company, rather than with an occupation or an industry. Plant unions usually belong to a companywide federation of unions.

There are also national unions, of course, some of which are affiliated with national federations. These federations provide general guidance to constituent national unions, but they rarely intervene in day-to-day industrial relations. The labor movement as a whole continues to be divided on ideological grounds. The largest central federation, Sohyo, is essentially Marxist in orientation. It was formed in 1950 and identifies with the Japanese Socialist party. The second largest central federation, Domei, is anticommunist and supports the moderate Democratic Socialist party. Surprisingly to an American, the largest proportion of the membership of Sohyo, the more radical federation, is made up of government employees. Private employees are the larger group in Domei, the more moderate federation. As in the United States, Japanese unions have been losing ground. The unionization rate fell from 34 percent in 1975 to 26 percent in 1989. Also, as in the United States, the sectors of the economy most unionized have changed from manufacturing to public services, while services are weakly organized.[7]

In the spring of each year the unions conduct a wage offensive, called Shunto. A single union is selected to try to reach an agreement with its employers, which will then become a pattern that other unions and employers can follow. Through this process, collective bargaining negotiations and strikes are concentrated in the spring months.

---

[6]Richard T. Johnson and William G. Ouchi, "Made in America (under Japanese Management)," *Harvard Business Review*, 52:5, September–October 1974, pp. 61–69. See also Kazutoshi Koshiro, "Lifetime Employment in Japan," *Monthly Labor Review*, 107:8, August 1984, pp. 34–35.

[7]Susan Chira, "Bitter Days for Japan's Unions," *New York Times*, Jan. 14, 1987, pp. D1, D5.

Employers are well organized in Japan.[8] The Japanese Federation of Employers Association (Nikkeiren) is concerned exclusively with labor relations. It coordinates labor policies among its members, expresses an employer view on labor issues and public policy in general, and disseminates information to its members. Another organization of firms that is very influential in expressing a management viewpoint on the development of national economic policy in Japan is the Federation of Economic Organizations (Keidenren). There are no comparable organizations of employers in the United States, where there are several competing employer associations, each seeking to speak for various elements of the business community. The sort of centralized and coordinated action by employers that occurs in Japan with respect to labor relations and economic policy does not occur in the United States.

Recent years have seen a decline in the membership of Japanese trade unions which is being attributed to the inability of the unions to organize new industrial plants. Employers seem to resist unionization more than they did in the past, and workers to have less interest in the unions.[9] Japanese workers put in long hours in comparison to the workers of other industrialized nations, and appear to have lower living standards. Because the economy has grown greatly in recent decades and because Japan now has a reputation for wealth, there is increasing criticism of the companies and the unions for not doing enough for the workers. Writing about Japan recently an American reported:

> Unions are regarded as part of the problem. This is because almost all unions for private companies in Japan are company unions. Their officers are company employees who can expect to be rewarded by the company if they do a good job in curbing union militancy. A Nissan auto worker, for instance, said that at the height of car production in 1987, the company speeded up the work and the unions did nothing. . . . "The workers were totally uninterested in what the union does, because the union is useless and powerless," said the worker . . . "They just do whatever management wants."[10]

The unions deny that they are so powerless and unconcerned for the welfare of the worker. They point to decades of growth in employment and improvement in living standards, and to very low unemployment rates in Japan as a whole. They ask if American unions, which say they are so much for the workers, can point to such a positive record. Instead, the

---

[8]Taishiro Shirai and Haruo Shimada, "Japan," in John T. Dunlop and Walter Galenson, eds., *Labor in the Twentieth Century* (New York: Academic Press, 1978), pp. 241–322. See also William B. Gould, *Japan's Reshaping of American Labor Law* (Cambridge, Mass.: MIT Press, 1984).

[9]Richard B. Freeman and Marcus E. Rebick, "Crumbling Pillar? Declining Union Density in Japan," Working Paper No. 2963 (Cambridge, Mass: National Bureau of Economic Research, May, 1989).

[10]Steven R. Weisman, "More Japanese Workers Demanding Shorter Hours and Less Hectic Work," *New York Times*, Mar. 3, 1992, p. A6.

record in American manufacturing as a whole is one of declining employment, rising unemployment, and stagnating living standards. Americans, they say, may criticize the approach of Japanese unions, and American reporters may find some Japanese workers who also criticize it, but the record of accomplishment in Japan speaks for itself.

There are firm-specific unions in the United States that are similar to those in Japan, though the American ones are not many in number or in membership. They generally pursue a largely cooperative relationship with the companies, but do obtain a premium in compensation above that of nonunion plants in the same companies.[11]

The European Community

In the aftermath of World War II six nations in Western Europe (West Germany, France, Italy, and the three Benelux countries) formed the European Economic Community (EEC) to facilitate trade among themselves as a spur to economic growth. Over the years six additional member-states have signed on, giving the Community a total population presently 15 percent larger than America's and a combined economy almost as large.

In 1992 major steps were taken to extend economic integration in Europe. The EEC concluded a free-trade agreement with the six nations of the European Free Trade Area (EFTA). Seven Eastern European countries, four of whom were applying for EEC associate status, also concluded interim Community trade agreements. Finally, the Euro-Asian state of Turkey, already an associate member of the Community, was contemplating filing an application for full membership.

While primarily an economic community, the EEC also has political insitutions, including executive and legislative branches. The nation-states are still supreme, but there are plans for increasing the political unity of Europe. As part of this ongoing integration effort, officers of the European Commission (the Community's executive arm) have been drafting a social charter or protocol that will define certain of the rights of workers and responsibilities of management and governments in the future.

The proposed social charter's provisions will be discussed below. But the process of its development is also significant. Unions and management are referred to in European parlance as the "social partners" and under the Maastricht Treaty are given expanded responsibilities. The European Commission, the executive arm of the European Economic Community, will promote consultation of management and labor at the Community level—that is, at the multinational level. The commission is to consult the social partners before social policy proposals. If the commission then wishes to

---

[11]Sanford M. Jacoby and Anil Verma, "Enterpr:se Unions in the United States," *Industrial Relations*, 31:1, Winter 1992, pp. 137–158.

take action, it will consult the social partners, who have the option of commenting on the proposals. Most importantly perhaps, if the social parties
desire, the dialogue between them, sponsored by the European Commission, could lead to "contractual relations, including agreements" (article
4(1) of the Maastricht Treaty). Further, the social parties may, upon being
consulted by the European Commission on a proposed social policy proposal, indicate their desire to have the matter handled not by regulation
but by collective bargaining agreement, and if so, the social partners have
9 months to negotiate such an agreement.[12] Some observers are noting
that these provisions of the treaty seem to envision Communitywide
bargaining—Euro-bargaining—between labor and management.

It should be noted that the Maastricht Treaty faces an uncertain future. It
may be modified or even rejected by the nations of Europe. But the social
dialogue that the treaty envisions has been developing for many years under
the European Economic Community and is almost certain to proceed in
some substantial form, whatever the fate of the Maastricht Treaty itself.

The proposed social charter will provide protections for young workers
(under age 18) and bans most work situations entirely for those under 15.
It attempts to provide so-called transparency for wages, meaning increased
quantity, quality, and distribution of information about pay and benefits in
different jobs and countries. Although virtually all aspects of the proposed
charter have been somewhat controversial, many have been largely accepted by the different governments, including those that specify minimum
terms and conditions of work (such as health and safety, information and
consultation, standard working conditions, and equal treatment of different groups of people). The Europeanization of labor-management relations
may be seen in the financial subsidies that the EEC already gives to the
union movements in member countries. For example, the EEC gave some
$12 million in subsidies to the British trade unions in 1992, a small part of
the unions total expenditures (some 2 percent) and one used largely on European matters, rather than matters of primarily British interest.[13] In the
future, as the Euro-social dialogue between the European Commission
and the social partners grows, financial support of the unions from the
EEC may also become more important.

What is at issue behind the charter is a problem similar to that being
encountered in the North American free-trade negotiations between the
United States, Mexico, and Canada. The northern European countries,
such as Germany, Denmark, and the Netherlands, are concerned that the
safety and working conditions of their workers will be undermined as
competition for jobs from countries with lesser conditions such as Spain,
Portugal, and Greece, increases. In part the social charter is an effort to

[12]"The Social Dialogue—Euro-Bargaining in the Making?" *European Industrial Relations
Review,* No. 220, May 1992, p. 26.
    [13]"Leaders Say UK Unions Winning Increasing Share of EC Funding," *The Financial Times*
(London), Sept. 16, 1992, p. 8.

improve the quality of life for workers in Europe. In part it is an attempt to standardize elements of labor costs and practices across the Community as a way of minimizing the flight of employers from northern to southern Europe in search of regulatory relief. There is no expectation that flight can be eliminated entirely. It is already under way. Nor does the social protocol include requlations about at what levels pay can be set, the right to form unions, and the right to strike or lockout—although each EEC country protects workers' rights to some degree.[14]

The most controversial elements of the social charter have to do with provisions for the representation of workers in companies. Here the majority view of those proposing the social charter is to incorporate substantial elements of the practices of worker representation and union consultation that are required by law in northern Europe. The British government, under control of the Conservative Party for many years, has been very much opposed to these elements of the charter. So much so that in early December 1991, the heads of government of the EEC countries decided to let Britain refuse to accept these parts of the social charter if it decided to do so.[15]

What so offends the Conservatives in Britain about the proposed worker representation provisions of the charter? The British argue that it gives too much power to the unions and would bring to Britain "managed capitalism" or "social democracy," something Britain has rejected in the past in favor of a more Anglo-American focus on free competition and individualism. American conservatives and most business executives share these reservations. While the specific provisions of worker representation laws differ in the northern EEC countries, the German provisions are roughly representative. Germany is also the largest of the EEC countries and the strongest economically. Hence, we review below the German industrial relations system.

Germany

We may identify two types of labor relations innovations that have been the subject of experimentation in Germany since World War II. These arrangements have sometimes been grouped together and referred to as developments involving "industrial democracy" or greater "worker participation in management." Discussion about which term, if either, is more appropriate need not detain us. Nor are these developments confined to Germany; counterparts exist for many of them in other European countries. However, their evolution has been carried further in Germany than elsewhere.

---

[14]"Two-Tier Social Policy . . . .," *Industrial Relations Europe*, 20:229, January 1992, pp. 1–3.
[15]See, for example, "What's in a Deal: How Maastricht Will Change Europeans' Lives," *The Economist*, Dec. 14, 1992, p. 53.

1 *Codetermination* involves the appointment of workers' representatives to the boards of directors of corporations. A broader definition of codetermination would stress providing workers a role in the decision-making processes of an enterprise.

2 *Works councils* are a method of providing representation for workers in the workplace and a chance for cooperation between workers and management on matters affecting the enterprise.

Codetermination on Supervisory Boards   "Codetermination" may be defined as a partnership of owners and labor in the operation of an enterprise. In 1947, after World War II, the British occupation forces in the Ruhr Valley of Germany introduced codetermination into the German steel industry. In 1951 it was extended to coal also. In practice codetermination means that workers have representatives on the boards that have responsibility for the enterprise. A European firm, unlike an American enterprise, has a two-level structure of boards.[16] One level, the supervisory board, meets only a few times a year and has general responsibility for policy decisions about the enterprise. For example, the question of whether or not to acquire another company would be a matter for action by the supervisory board. There is also a management board, consisting of top management of the enterprise, which conducts its day-to-day business. Codetermination in the German steel and coal industries affects both boards.

The supervisory boards of large companies in the steel and coal industries consist of five representatives of stockholders, 5 representatives of the firm's employees, and one neutral person nominated by majority vote of the other 10 members of the board. Employee members of the board, or the "worker directors," are two nominees of the works councils and three nominees of the unions. (If the board has more than 11 members, the parity principle between worker and stockholder representatives applies.)[17] One member of the management board of the companies must be a labor relations manager, who cannot be chosen against the majority vote of the employee members of the supervisory board. Thus, the employees (and the unions) are represented on both the supervisory and the management boards. On the supervisory boards the structure is truly codeterminational (*mitbestimmung* in German), in that stockholders and employees have acquired an equal number of directors.

Elsewhere in German industry employees are entitled by law to just less than equal representation on the supervisory boards of corporations.

German unions support codetermination as providing for the participation of workers in managerial decision making and also for a greater social awareness by business. German business people have not been opposed to

---

[16]William H. McPherson, "Codetermination in Practice," *Industrial and Labor Relations Review,* 8:4, July 1955, pp. 499–519.

[17]Bernard Wilpert, "Research on Industrial Democracy and the German Case," *Industrial Relations Journal,* 6:1, Spring 1975, pp. 53–64.

worker representation on boards of directors.[18] They credit codetermination with helping to develop Germany's reasonably stable labor relations climate. However, they have bitterly opposed *mitbestimmung* (i.e., a board split equally between employees' and shareholders' directors).

Other European countries are now experimenting with codetermination. And there have been proposals for a Western European statute under which businesses would be incorporated and which would include codetermination provisions.[19]

Works Councils   Works councils are committees, ordinarily made up of management and employee representatives, that have certain functions in the governance of a workplace. Employee representatives are generally elected by the employees in a particular plant. If the plant is part of a larger enterprise, the plant-level works councils send delegates to a central, or enterprise, works council.

Germany has experimented with joint labor-management committees, the precursors of works councils, since 1848.[20] The most recent comprehensive legislation affecting works councils is the Works Constitution Act of 1972. The act establishes works councils as all employees' permanent representative bodies and gives them specific rights.

Works councils generally have one of four types of powers. About certain issues the council has the legal right to be informed. Management has a duty, in this instance, to provide information regarding certain matters to the works council. About other issues the works council has the right to be consulted (i.e., to offer advice to the company's management). About still other issues the council members may have the right to investigate matters on their own initiative. The company must cooperate in their investigation. Finally, in some instances the council has the right of codetermination; that is, management cannot act without the agreement of the works council.

The types of matters about which works councils may have rights are often divided in Germany into economic and social matters. Economic matters include mergers, transfers, closure of the firm, expansion or contraction of operations, relocation, organizational structure, and the general trend of business and financing decisions. Social matters include layoffs, wage payment systems, methods of training, pensions, distribution of profits, safety and health, and holiday arrangements.[21]

Figure 12-2 shows how the process of working out a lay off would occur in Germany. The employer plans to layoff 25 workers. The employer then

[18]David Clutterbuck, "How Worker Directors Are Working Out," *Management Review,* 63:6, June 1974, pp. 32–34.
[19]Robert J. Kuhne, *Co-Determination in Business* (New York: Praeger, 1979).
[20]Friedrich Furstenberg, "Workers' Participation in Germany," *International Institute for Labor Studies Bulletin,* No. 6, June 1979, pp. 1–55.
[21]Walter Kolvenbach, *Employee Councils in European Companies* (Deventer, Germany: Kluwer, 1978).

informs the works council of its intention and formally consults the council about its opinion. The council may approve, or object, or propose changes in the employer's plan. If there is a dispute a conciliation board enters the discussion. Figure 12-3 depicts such a board, composed of employer's representatives, works council's (not union's) representatives, and a neutral chairperson. The result of the consultation between management and works council will be a social plan setting forth the number of layoffs (if any), the benefits those laid off will receive, and other relevant matters. Note that in social (that is, labor- or personnel-related) matters and the social plan, the conciliation board has the final say. In a sense this is negotiations between employer and works council with a neutral to determine the outcome. This system goes much further in limiting the employer's authority to lay off than occurs in the United States.

The reader will note that many matters that involving the works councils are ordinarily handled by collective bargaining in the United States. But in Germany it is the works council that negotiates arrangements with management about such issues.

The works council's relationship to the unions is complex. The two have carefully delineated—by law—responsibilities, and are not supposed to interfere in each other's areas of responsibility. The unions usually nominate candidates for election to the works councils. But works council members who are also union members are apparently free to act on the council as they wish.

The works councils normally do not have the right to strike, but the unions do. It is apparently not uncommon for works council members to coordinate activities with the unions and in some instances to arrange for

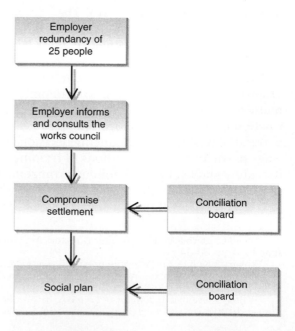

FIGURE 12-2   Model of a layoff in Germany.

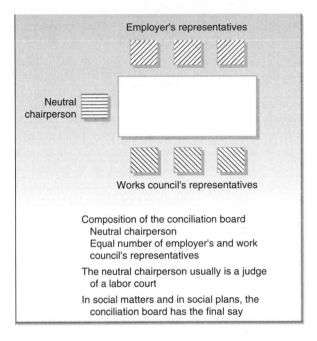

Employer's representatives

Neutral chairperson

Works council's representatives

Composition of the conciliation board
Neutral chairperson
Equal number of employer's and work council's representatives

The neutral chairperson usually is a judge of a labor court

In social matters and in social plans, the conciliation board has the final say

FIGURE 12-3   Composition of a German conciliation board (example).

the unions to strike in support of employee members of a works council when there is a difference of opinion with management.[22]

The unions are further removed from the workplace in Germany than in the United States, in the sense that full-time union representatives in a plant are uncommon. The unions operate primarily at the industry level, negotiating broad agreements covering wages and working conditions. The specific application of national agreements to a particular company are worked out by the works councils.

This dual structure of labor relations, the unions and the works councils, has no counterpart in the United States (or in Britain for that matter). The existence of works councils in all large firms is required by law in Germany. The national collective bargaining agreements apply to all firms in an industry, unless they are specifically replaced by an agreement between a particular firm and the union(s) involved. As a result, there is no such thing as the nonunion firm in the way it exists in the United States. All major firms are involved in the structure that establishes the representation rights of employees, both through works councils and through unions. In the United States, in contrast, a firm that is nonunion has no collective bargaining agreement and probably has no elected representation of its employees. (Some American nonunion firms do have elected employee staff associations, which are something like a works council, but with no rights or responsibilities established by law.)

[22]Catherine Coffin Lindsay, "Works Councils in the Federal Republic of Germany," unpublished master's degree thesis, MIT, 1976.

The relationship between the unions and works councils is highly complex. Some observers see the unions losing ground to works councils. A survey of the attitudes of German employees taken in the mid-1980s found that works councils are believed most valuable to the individual worker, unions next significant, and the labor director(s) on corporate supervisory boards least important.[23]

MULTINATIONAL FIRMS

What Is a Multinational Firm?

An important characteristic of human societies in general and of industrial relations systems in particular is that new forces for change are constantly emerging. Some of these new forces grow until they are effective in causing major modifications in the entire industrial relations system. Others emerge, then disappear. Among the most important force now emerging with the potential to greatly affect our industrial relations system is the growing activity of multinational firms. Will this force become an engine of change, or will it simply dissipate over time? How have the unions responded to the challenge? What will be the impact of multinationals on the shape of the future?

Multinational companies operate in more than a single nation. Often they have sales facilities, and sometimes manufacturing plants as well, in many nations. Or they may operate through subsidiary corporations in nations other than their home country. The multinationals include some of the most common names in business—General Motors, Ford, and Exxon, to name a few. Many multinationals are American-based companies, but not all are. These companies employ many thousands of people in many different countries.

Two of the most important questions raised by the emergence of multinational firms are: First, what is the current impact of multinationals on the economic and labor relations systems of various countries, including our own? Second, will the multinationals, operating as centralized units in many different countries, cause the industrial relations system in the United States to become more like that in certain countries abroad?

Economic Impact of the Multinationals

Do multinational firms[24] shift production abroad, and so lower employment opportunities in the United States?[25] Many people think so, giving

[23]Charles J. Hobson and James B. Dworkin, "West German Labor Unrest," *Monthly Labor Review,* 69:2, February 1986, pp. 46–48.

[24]Mira Wilkins, *The Emergence of Multinational Enterprise,* 2 vols. (Cambridge, Mass.: Harvard University Press, 1974).

[25]Hans Gunter, "An Overview of Some Recent Research on Multinational Corporations and Labour," *Institute for International Labour Studies Bulletin,* 12, 1974, pp. 37–46.

estimates of jobs lost and citing examples involving certain corporations.[26] Others disagree, citing the difficulty of comparing jobs created abroad by multinational firms with those created in the United States. The balance is hard to identify quantitatively.[27] To a degree the shift of production jobs abroad has been balanced by the creation of more jobs in headquarters, service, and technical areas in the United States.[28] A recent study of a particular group of overseas investments by American firms concluded that

- U.S. concerns tend to build manufacturing plants abroad when they cannot profitably serve markets from plants in the United States.
- Their main foreign competitors in those markets are not local firms, but rather subsidiaries of European or Japanese multinationals.
- The net effects of the U.S. investments are, on the average, favorable to the U.S. economy.
- Employment created in the United States as a result of U.S. foreign direct investment is of a higher skill level than exists on the average in U.S. manufacturing industries.[29] However, an interesting counterpoint to this study was provided by another observer of multinationals, who commented, "In the home countries (especially the United States), management and stockholders (of multinationals) benefit more directly than labor."[30]

Exporting American jobs is not the only criticism directed at United States–based multinationals. They are also accused of avoiding taxes and increasing imports, thereby weakening the U.S. balance of payments. Business people have attempted to refute these allegations by pointing to the advantages that foreign trade provides for the United States, especially by allowing us access to raw materials from abroad and by creating jobs at home producing goods for export.

The impact of multinationals on the U.S. economy through foreign trade and foreign investment is a complicated matter that will not soon be free from controversy. As we will see below, the unions are particularly opposed to much that the multinationals do and are attempting to have the activities curbed both by legislation and by direct trade union action.

When operating plants abroad, the multinationals sometimes seem to be little enclaves of their home country. In the case of American firms, this

[26]See *Multinational Corporations*, a compendium of papers submitted to the Subcommittee on Trade, Committee on Finance, U.S. Senate (Washington, D.C.: U.S. Government Printing Office, 1973).

[27]Roger G. Hawkins, *Job Displacement and the Multinational Firm: A Methodological Review* (Washington, D.C.: Center for Multinational Studies, 1972).

[28]Robert B. Stobaugh et al., *The Effects of U.S. Foreign Direct Investment* (Washington, D.C.: Center for Multinational Studies, 1973); and Daniel J. B. Mitchell, *Labor Issues of American International Trade and Investment*, Policy Studies in Employment and Welfare No. 24 (Baltimore: Johns Hopkins, 1976).

[29]Robert B. Stobaugh, ed., *Nine Investments Abroad and Their Impact at Home* (Cambridge, Mass.: Harvard University Press, 1976).

[30]Raymond Vernon, "A Decade of Studying Multinational Enterprises," *Harvard Business School Bulletin*, 52:5, September–October 1976, p. 27.

involves paying American wage levels and providing close approximations to American working conditions. More often, however, American firms abroad adapt to the local labor-market conditions and pay wages and provide working conditions commensurate with local practice. Local wages and conditions are in many cases, but not all, below American levels.

Labor Relations Impact

The industrial relations systems of various countries differ considerably. How does a multinational firm adapt to these differences? Does an American firm operating abroad try to operate everywhere as if it were in America, or does it try to adapt to local conditions?

Apparently, most American multinational firms attempt to adapt to local practices in the countries in which they operate.[31] In some instances the attempt to adapt goes so far that American firms that are strictly nonunion at home recognize and deal with unions abroad. Often, however, attempts to adapt to local practices do not seem to be altogether successful, especially when management direction is centralized in the home office of the corporation, or when American managers are sent to direct foreign subsidiaries. In these instances the American managers are often ignorant of local practices, and this may cause difficulties. The fewest problems of adjustment occur when the multinational has its foreign subsidiaries directed by foreign managers who understand local practices. This may be possible where a foreign subsidiary is profitably and efficiently managed. But inefficiency and losses inevitably occasion the intervention of American management and often the attempt to import American labor relations practices in the interest, it is believed, of greater efficiency of production.

Operating subsidiaries in several countries on a basis adapted to each country can be a severe strain for a corporation. Managers must become familiar with many ways of doing things if they are to be active in the corporation as a whole. And the corporation itself must be able to pursue simultaneously quite different personnel and labor relations policies in different countries. The rapid development of multinationals in recent years has largely been based on decentralized management and considerable autonomy for foreign subsidiaries, especially in the labor relations area. Whether this pattern of development can be continued remains to be seen.

The Response of the Unions

Unions have not generally responded favorably to the expansion of the multinational firms. In the United States the labor movement has criticized the multinationals for shifting jobs to lower-paid workers abroad,

---

[31]Duane Kujawa, "The Labor Relations of United States Multinationals Abroad," *Labour and Society*, 4:1, January 1979, pp. 3–25.

thus creating unemployment in the United States.[32] Since the oil crisis of 1973, the union attack on the multinationals has grown more strident. "By 1974," said an AFL-CIO economist, "published business reports, government and academic sources began to suggest that multinationals, in fact, were guilty as charged of profiteering, tax avoidance and other impacts on the U.S. economy and labor."[33]

For years the AFL-CIO had supported a national policy of free trade, that is, allowing companies to export and import with little government restriction. But opposition to the multinationals has caused the unions now to support legislative restrictions both on trade as a whole and on the multinational firms in particular. A high official of the AFL-CIO wrote:

> As we in the AFL-CIO see it, there is urgent need for an adequate U.S. trade and investment policy—for the orderly expansion of trade, including the prevention of growing adverse impacts on American workers and communities; for effective measures to regulate the operations of multinational companies; for curbs on runaway plant developments; for elimination of U.S. tax and other concessions that subsidize the foreign operations of U.S.-based multinationals; for regulations and curbs on the export of American capital and technology.[34]

Nor were American unionists alone in criticizing the multinationals. A leading European trade unionist wrote, "It is . . . a question of the abuse of power which is exerted by the multinational corporations—disguised as an interest in profit. . . ."[35]

The unions today have only a limited capacity to respond to the multinationals. In order to restrict the activities of the firms, unions in various countries are seeking legislation to regulate the companies' activities. And, in collective bargaining, the unions are seeking to deal directly with the multinationals.

Trade union cooperation to deal collectively with the multinational firms in collective bargaining in different countries is much talked about, but as yet amounts to little. Some international trade union secretariats, cooperative bodies operating primarily in Europe, have attempted to coordinate activities, including strikes, against certain multinational companies (especially European-owned companies). Such coordination is made necessary by the alleged potential ability of a multinational corporation to

---

[32]Gus Tyler, "Multinationals: A Global Menace," *AFL-CIO American Federationist*, 79:7, July 1972, pp. 1–7; and Andrew C. McLellan and M. C. Boggs, "Multinationals: How Quick They Jump," *AFL-CIO American Federationist*, 80:9, September 1973, pp. 21–25.

[33]Elizabeth R. Jager, "The Changing World of Multinationals," *AFL-CIO American Federationist*, 81:9, September 1974, pp. 3–4.

[34]Lane Kirkland, "Multinationals: Impact on U.S.," *International Herald Tribune*, May 17, 1974, p. 6. See also Stanley H. Ruttenberg, "The Union View of Multinationals: An Interpretation," in Robert J. Flanagan and Arnold R. Weber, eds., *Bargaining without Boundaries: The Multinational Corporation and International Labor Relations* (Chicago: University of Chicago Press, 1974), pp. 179–201.

[35]Gunter Kupke, "Union Responses in Continental Europe," in Flanagan and Weber, eds., *Bargaining without Boundaries*, pp. 203–217.

shift production from a struck plant in one country to a plant that is operating in another country. If a multinational firm can effectively shift production in this way, it can very much lessen the impact of a strike against it in any single country. The unions, by international cooperation, would like to prevent this sort of transfer of production. More positively, the unions through cooperation would like to raise the standards of employment for workers in each country in which the company operates, rather than allow the company to shift production by new capital investment to the lower-wage countries.

For example, in an effort to address the increasing importance of transnational companies in the telecommunications industry, the American and Canadian unions most involved have signed an alliance promising to cooperate in organizing and bargaining efforts not only in the two countries but wherever in the world telecommunications companies operate. According to the president of the American union, transnational companies "will have no place to flee. Wherever they go around the world, there will be a union waiting, and support from others."[36]

And in August 1990 a 2-day convention was held in Washington, D.C., of union officials from 20 countries to discuss practical, cooperative steps that labor groups can take in dealing with specific transnational firms. Yet examples of effective cooperation among international unions against multinational firms are still quite limited.[37]

The factors that have constrained the ability of unions in different countries to cooperate successfully in dealing with the multinationals include

- Lack of financial and human resources needed to organize information exchange, meetings, training, and coordination of action
- Different philosophical outlooks of the trade unions in different countries, pursuing different goals
- Weakness of the trade union movement in certain areas, especially in developing countries
- Different legal obstacles hampering coordinated industrial action
- Conflict of interests between employees in the different countries in their efforts to protect employment, as shown by the difficulties encountered between the United Auto Workers in the United States and the automobile workers in Japan in seeking an agreement to reduce Japanese auto exports to the United States

---

[36]"Union Effort to Deal with Transnational Firms," Bureau of National Affairs, *Daily Labor Report*, No. 113, June 12, 1990, p. A-6.

[37]Richard L. Rowan, Herbert R. Northrup, and Rae Ann O'Brien, *Multinational Union Organization in the Manufacturing and Processing Industries* (Philadelphia: Industrial Research Unit, Wharton School, University of Pennsylvania, 1980). Also, Rowan and Northrup, *Multinational Collective Bargaining Attempts* (Philadelphia: University of Pennsylvania Press, 1979). See also Richard L. Rowan, Kenneth J. Pitterle, and Philip A. Miscimarra, *Multinational Union Organizations in the White Collar, Service, and Communication Industries* (Philadelphia: Industrial Research Unit, Wharton School, University of Pennsylvania, 1983).

Foreign-Owned Firms in the United States

There are hundreds of manufacturing plants and other facilities now owned and operated by foreign firms in the United States. The Japanese alone have more than 200 manufacturing plants, and in some industries have become a major force on the American scene. For example, four Japanese auto companies now have assembly plants in the United States, and each has a different sort of labor relations.

In California, Toyota has a joint venture with General Motors to operate an automobile assembly factory at Fremont that Toyota manages. There the Japanese firm has a very unusual agreement with the United Auto Workers that gives the company much greater freedom in work assignments for employees than is common in American plants. In Tennessee, Nissan is nonunion, and its workers have voted against the UAW in an NLRB election. In Ohio, Honda is nonunion and has repulsed efforts by the UAW to get an election. In Michigan, Mazda and the UAW conducted a non-NLRB election, the union won, and the company has an agreement with the UAW that follows the pattern of the American auto companies' agreements with the union.

Harmonious labor-management relations and high productivity are central to the Japanese style of management. The American plants of these Japanese companies have high productivity and quality in production, and are serving as a model for the American companies in how to improve both.

How have American unions responded to the increasing number of foreign firms which operate in the United States? They've been surprisingly slow to adapt. A study of the perceptions of American trade union officials about foreign-owned firms revealed that they did not distinguish between foreign and domestic firms when trying to organize workers, had only very limited cooperation with their counterparts in foreign trade unions, and had found that foreign firms were generally (there are exceptions, such as Mazda) as determined in their opposition to unions as most American firms.[38]

Future Impact of the Multinationals

"The year 2000," wrote a supporter of the labor movement, "will see employment, wages and the conditions of work in every country shaped by forces that are international in character and increasingly beyond the control of the collective bargaining that goes on in any one firm, industry or nation."[39]

The expansion of multinational business is likely to continue, despite possible temporary setbacks in periods of economic recession. As the multinationals grow in significance, their struggle with the trade unions

[38]Rajib N. Sanyal, "Unionizing Foreign-Owned Firms: Perceptions of American Union Officials," *Labor Studies Journal*, 14:4, pp. 66–81.
[39]Jeff Faux, "Labor in the New Global Economy: Mobile Capital, Multinationals, Working Standards," *Dissent*, 37:3, Summer 1990, pp. 376–382.

will assume broader proportions. A recent study by a private consulting firm in Europe included a diagram of the impact of unions on various areas of concern to multinational companies, from which Figure 12-4 is adapted. It can be seen from the figure that the union objectives are to influence a very wide range of company policies in addition to traditional concerns regarding wages and working conditions. Other policies the unions seek to affect are capital expenditures, company planning, finance, and business strategy. Tactically, the unions rely on influencing government regulation, collective bargaining, and influencing works councils and supervisory boards to obtain their objectives. The unions rely on their influence on governmental regulations as a device to control the multinationals' activities. One form of governmental intervention sought by the unions will be the laws that give workers a right to participate through representatives (union or otherwise) in corporate decisions. In dealing not with government, but directly with the companies, collective bargaining

FIGURE 12-4   Union impact on multinational companies. (*Source*: Adapted from *European Industrial Relations in the 1970s*, Brussels: Industrial Relations Counsellors, 1972, p. 71.)

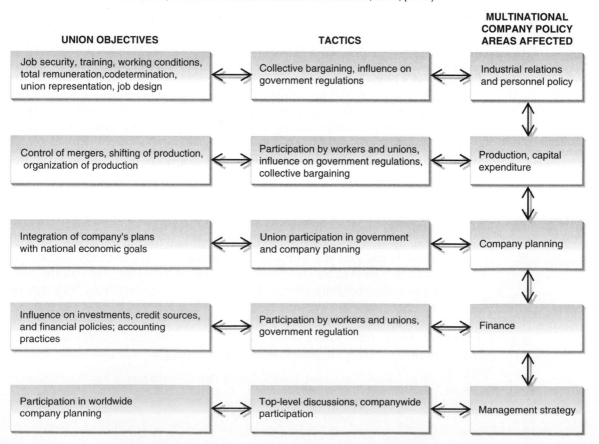

will also be expanded, if possible, by unions to cover a range of company policies now generally outside its scope.

For many years European unions have been attempting to obtain a code of conduct from the European Commission (the Common Market) for multinational firms in Europe. The purpose of the proposed code, called the Vredeling Plan, is to give workers rights to balance the growth of multinational companies. The plan requires multinational companies to give information about the company to union officials and to give notice in advance of business decisions, such as plant closures or work transfers, that would have a substantial effect on the interests of employees within the Common Market. An intensely controversial proposal, the plan continues under debate in Europe.[40]

Will there be transnational collective bargaining? Will unions from different countries join in single or coordinated negotiations with and perhaps conduct strikes against, the multinationals? There has been much discussion of this possibility,[41] but actual transnational bargaining remains very rare. One example had been the coverage of all North American operations (i.e., the United States and Canada) by agreements between the large American automobile companies and the United Auto Workers in both the United States and Canada.[42] These agreements, truly transnational in scope and operation, were each between one international union and a multinational company. The agreements did not require cooperation between totally separate unions in different countries. Then in 1984 the Canadian division of the UAW left the international union to found its own national union. Whether or not the two separate national unions will bargain together in the future is uncertain.

Transnational bargaining is only at the infant stage. Whether it will progress slowly or rapidly will depend on the ability of unionists from different countries, and often with different philosophies, to cooperate and the degree to which multinationals resist the idea. These factors are not yet clear enough to be assessed.

Multinationals: Force for Change in the World's Industrial Relations System

Because of the interdependency between the elements of each nation's industrial relations system, it used to be believed that it was not possible to export practices from one system to another. That would be like taking a

---

[40]*Industrial Relations Europe*, Common Market Special Report, 1982, pp. S-1–S-4, and *Industrial Relations Europe*, 11:127, July 1983, p. 1. Also, Duncan C. Campbell and Richard L. Rowan, *Muiltinational Enterprises and the OECD Industrial Relations Guidelines* (Philadelphia: Industrial Relations Unit, Wharton School, University of Pennsylvania, 1983).

[41]Lloyd Ulman, "The Rise of the International Trade Union?" in Flanagan and Weber, eds., *Bargaining without Boundaries*, pp. 37–70. Also, "Will Unions Win International Bargaining?" *Nation's Business*, 63:6, June 1975, pp. 36ff.

[42]Malcolm Denise, "Industrial Relations and the Multinational Corporation: The Ford Experience," in Flanagan and Weber, eds., *Bargaining without Boundaries*, pp. 135–146.

fish out of water, it was argued, and the fish would die. Japanese labor-management practices could not flourish in America or Europe, it was said, nor American practices in Japan or Europe. To a degree this is true. If a company or a union simply tries to export its own practices to another nation without modification, they are unlikely to work. For example, the attempts of Walt Disney Company to impose American dress and behavior codes on the French work force of its new theme park in France caused much consternation and opposition in France. Also, when Japanese companies tried to discriminate in hiring against minorities and women in the United States, arguing that they had a treaty-given right to do so, they were condemned in the press and ultimately required by the courts to conform to American antidiscrimination statutes.

But to a surprising degree, key elements of the Japanese and European industrial relations systems have been exported by their companies to operations in America, and key elements of American practice have been exported by American firms. For example, Japanese firms have brought employee participation in management via quality circles to their American plants, and in some instances have tried to develop the kind of union-management partnership at the firm level that exists in Japan. IBM, in contrast, successfully took its practice of paying employees according to individual performance, not seniority, to its Japanese subsidiary. Some American firms have successfully taken their individually oriented employee relations, with its opposition to unionization, to highly unionized European nations such as England and France.

The result of all this is a much more complex situation worldwide in which multinational companies are able to design labor relations practices that depart from those traditional in a nation. Thus, the multinational firm has become an engine of change in the industrial relations systems of many countries in the world. The likelihood is that this process is just beginning and will go much further in the years ahead.

However, despite their attempts to adapt to local conditions wherever they operate, multinationals do carry across international frontiers certain patterns of management behavior.[43] They serve, therefore, to extend labor relations practices to many nations and to cause a merging of practices.[44] Over the years, the multinationals will tend to lessen diversity among the industrial relations systems in the countries in which they operate. In this sense, the multinationals may serve to bring greater similarity to many countries, and perhaps to encourage the import of some foreign labor relations practices to the United States.

[43]Richard D. Robinson, *International Business Management: A Guide to Decision-Making* (Ninsdale, Ill.: Dryden Press, 1975).

[44]This is probably so. However, companies from different nations approach problems differently in the short run. See B. C. Roberts and Jonathan May, "The Response of Multinational Enterprises to International Trade Union Pressures," *British Journal of Industrial Relations*, 12:3, November 1974, pp. 403–416. See also John Gennard, *Multinational Corporations and British Labor* (Washington, D.C.: British-American Committee, 1972).

THE NORTH AMERICAN FREE-TRADE AGREEMENT

While the European Community has engaged in the broadening and deepening of trade links across Europe, North America's three major nations have embarked on a similar process among themselves. Not surprisingly, these negotiations have encountered many of the same difficulties as their European counterparts. A study of the history of trade relations between the United States and Canada may help students shed a greater light on the broader questions now being addressed by these partners and Mexico in the North American context.

Trade between the United States (the world's largest economy) and Canada (the world's seventh largest economy) is the largest bilateral exchange of goods and services in the world. Both nations are each other's single largest trading partner, with Canada consuming about 20 percent of U.S. exports and the United States taking about 80 percent of Canadian exports.[45] In 1991, the total volume of bilateral trade in goods and services between the two countires was more than $200 billion U.S.[46]

Trading between the United States and Canada

Free trade and protectionism have been recurrent themes in bilateral relations between the two nations. At certain periods, the political calculus on both sides has favored attempts to realize the economic gains of free trade with formal bilateral treaty agreements; at other times, the balance of interests (on one side or both sides) has favored the maintenance of protective tariffs and harsh domestic rhetoric about the economic practices of the other party.

The balance between free trade and protectionism in the relationship between Canada and the United States seems to move in swings lasting for several decades at a time. Typically, periods dominated by the spirit of free trade are followed by periods of protectionism and vice versa. Particularly important high-water marks for free trade occurred in the early 1870s, 1911, and the early 1960s, prior to the landmark agreement of 1988. Important high-water marks for protectionism occurred in the 1880s (a period of transcontinental railway building), the 1930s (the time of the Smoot-Hawley tariffs), and the early 1970s (the time of the first oil shock and Canada's national energy policy).

In 1872, spurred by the process of U.S. reunification following the Civil War and the unification of several major British North American colonies into the nation of Canada in 1867, the two sides almost concluded an unrestricted free-trade arrangement. The talks collapsed at the last minute and became mired in protectionistic wrangling. Influenced in part by the

[45]To place the scope of the relationship in context, one Canadian province (Ontario) does more two-way trade with the United States than the entire nation of Japan.
[46]Office of the U.S. Trade Representative, *1992 Trade Policy Agenda and 1991 Annual Report* (Washington, D.C.: 1992), pp. 13–14.

mercantilism then breaking out in Europe in the wake of a global recession that had begun in 1870, manufacturers, farmers, and others on both sides sought to protect what markets they already enjoyed. Canadian business interests in particular refused to press the British government to grant perferences to American manufacturers, a move that would have given them access on an equal basis with their Canadian counterparts to the large British markets, which Canada then enjoyed as a British dominion. The failure of these talks and some subsequent saber-rattling about "manifest destiny" and the location of boundaries between Canada and the United States across western North America prompted both nations to embark on a surge of high-tariff policies. An economic race to the northwestern regions of North America, chiefly manifested in an orgy of railroad building, subsequently took place in the 1880s and 1890s.

In 1911, following several decades of solid prosperity and consolidation of east-west trading patterns in both economies, diplomats in Ottawa and Washington, D.C., once again turned their attention to a comprehensive north-south trade deal. Both sides could see then see the troubles rising in pre–World War I Europe and sought to avoid the ensuing economic difficulties.

The free-trade discussions of 1911 were complicated when the governing Liberal party split over the issue in the Canadian House of Commons. A significant faction of the party, mainly from industrialized Ontario, was concerned that Canada's manufacturers could not compete effectively with their U.S. counterparts. (This "infant industry" argument has been used by countless industrialists throughout history when faced with the prospect of open trading.) The Ontario faction combined with the opposition Conservative party during the subsequent national elections and defeated Prime Minister Wilfred Laurier; with the defeat of Laurier came an effective end to free-trade discussions.

The economic dislocation of the 1930s was a trying time for both countries. Canada, facing life yoked to a Britain severely weakened by World War I and anxious to preserve its own wealth, lost many of its imperial preferences. Meanwhile, the United States had withdrawn into a profound economic and diplomatic isolationism, marked by passage of some of the severest trade protections then in use—the Smoot-Hawley tariffs.

It was not until after World War II forced the two nations to resume extensive trading for defense production purposes (the "neutral" United States was forced to ship its British-bound goods through Canada until it entered the war in 1942) that the political calculus again favored freer trade between the two nations. Passage of the Bretton Woods agreement linking the world's major currencies, the stunning success of the Marshall Plan, and the General Agreement on Trade and Tariffs' Kennedy round all pointed in favor of more open trading. In Canada, reelection of the freer-trade-favoring Liberal Party in 1963 complemented the return of Democrats to the White House in 1960, and prepared the way for further free-trade bargaining between the countries.

The climate of openness led to completion and ratification of a major sector trade deal in 1964. Known as the U.S.-Canada Auto Pact, it covered vehicle and related parts production in both countries. It allowed tariff-free trade in new vehicles and parts across the border provided that the American automakers who ran the plants in both countries would assemble at least one vehicle in Canada for every vehicle they sold there and that the vehicles and parts traded between the countries had at least 50 percent content sourced from either one.

The pact allowed the three Detroit-based automakers to rationalize the production of vehicles and parts across their U.S. and Canadian operations with several positive effects. There was a boost in overall efficiency that cut the cost of vehicles in both countries, a substantial rise in Canadian employment in vehicle assembly and parts manufacturing, and finally, a sharp increase in sales and profits for the automakers. However, the agreement was not without its political downside. It quickly became a lightning rod for nationalistic politicians in both countries, who alternately praised or condemned it depending on which side was enjoying a trade surplus with the other at the time of the comments. Both countries clearly felt some loss of sovereignty, particularly Canada, because of the relative sizes of the two economies.

The free traders managed to maintain their dominance from the mid-1960s through to the early 1970s, by which time nearly 80 percent of transborder trade was tariff-free. The events of the 1972–1973 oil shock, however, proved how tenuous international harmony can be in the face of crisis.

Canada, long self-sufficient in petroleum, had developed an economic strategy that saw it move its surplus western oil into Ontario and the United States via the Trans-Canada Pipeline, which crossed northern Michigan and Wisconsin on its way to Ontario, while importing foreign oil into Quebec and its Maritime provinces, via a trans-Maine pipeline. The 1973 Arab oil embargo and subsequent price surge disrupted this trading pattern. The American oil company subsidiaries who largely controlled western Canadian oil production at that time received orders from their U.S. parents to increase production substantially and sell the oil into the United States at existing prices. The Canadian government, acting in its own interest, curbed this increase in production and imposed a national tax on exported oil to prevent the American companies from generating windfall profits, depleting Canadian reserves, and staddling its own economy with higher oil prices. In the diplomatic crossfire, U.S. politicians threatened publicly to close both the Trans-Canada and trans-Maine pipelines at their border crossings until Canada resumed honoring existing contracts. Ultimately, the crisis saw Canada create its own national petroleum company (PetroCanada) and begin "Canadianizing" its oil industry on a wave of nationalism.

The election of a less nationalistic government in 1984 saw a return to prominence of free traders in Canada once again. Recurring trade disputes between the two governments had convinced the Canadians that they had to do something to ensure their continued access to the U.S. market. The United States, on the other hand, viewing events in Europe and its own large trade deficit with Japan and Asia, was seeking to create its own equivalent of the "common market." As in 1964–1965, the confluence of interests favored a trading agreement, and by 1988 the two sides had managed to do what had been politically impossible in the past; they signed and ratified an agreement to reduce tariffs on fixed schedules of 5 and 10 years on almost all economic sectors still affected by tariffs.

In the process of negotiating the agreement, the United States gave up its unilateral power to apply its domestic trade laws to disputes with Canada, agreeing to the creation of binding binational dispute settlement panels under the free-trade Agreement. This was seen as a significant curtailment of sovereignty and nearly caused the deal to fail to clear the U.S. Senate foreign relations committee. In Canada, concerns about the effects of losing further sovereignty in areas such as energy, agriculture, and media industries precipitated a national election, which the governing party won, but only by splitting the anti-free-trade vote between two opposition parties.

Given this climate, it is not surprising that there has been considerable concern on both sides of the border that the trade agreement would result in disadvantage. Throughout the negotiations, elements in both countries were concerned that jobs would migrate to the other country. Subsequent studies of the impact of free trade have been clouded by the recession of the late 1980s–early 1990s, the volatility of the exchange rate between U.S. and Canadian dollars, the fact that many of the tariffs negotiated away are still in the process of being removed, and finally the fact that industries are still adjusting to a tariff-free environment. It is quite probable that the true effects of the deal will not be known for some time to come. However, Canadian unions in particular are already claiming that over 250,000 Canadian jobs have been lost and that the country's social "net"—its welfare and comprehensive medical care programs—are being threatened by the lower standards and taxes prevalent south of the border. Their concern, that Canada will be forced to "harmonize" its policies with those of the United States to compete effectively in American markets, is putting considerable pressure on the Canadian government to exercise the abrogation clause in the agreement. In the United States, on the other hand, there have been political pressures to adopt Canadian-style medical care and other social policies, in effect moving it in the reverse direction.

On the broader front, the 1990s have opened with trade disputes on lumber, beer, automobile parts, and agricultural products between the two nations. These disputes, coming as they do in the wake of a severe recession, suggest that the traditional shift between "free trade" and "protection," powered by economic adversity, is once again under way. How this turning of the tide on trade will ultimately affect the new free-trading framework that has been established between the two countries is, of course, still open to debate.

Broadening the Arrangement to Include Mexico

Soon after the completion of the American-Canadian pact in 1988, negotiations began in earnest for a pact to include Mexico as well. The issue is highly controversial in the United States because Mexican wages and working conditions are generally much lower than those in Canada. American fears of the loss of jobs to Mexico are very great among certain politicians and trade unions.

The American government negotiated a free-trade pact with Mexico in 1991. "The fundamental goal of the United States," said the 1992 *Economic Report of the President*, "is the removal of all tariffs and the removal or reduction of nontariff trade barriers (the latter include, for example, quotas and import licenses)."[47] The Reagan administration argued that increased trade will improve living standards in both countries and that an improving economy in Mexico will reduce illegal immigration to America from Mexico by persons looking for work. Estimates differ, but there are apparently a million or more Mexicans illegally in the United States employed or seeking employment. The Clinton administration has expressed concern about the treaty which are similar to those of its opponents.

Opponents of the proposed free-trade pact point out that American jobs have already been traveling to Mexico in large numbers. The Mexican government has established the "maquiladora" program to permit American firms to wholly own subsidiary assembly and manufacturing plants in Mexico near the American border. Machinery and parts can be brought into Mexico by foreign firms duty-free so long as a plant's output is sent out of Mexico. The employees in the plants are Mexican, though often with foreign supervision. In areas like southern Arizona, many American managers live in the United States and go to work each day in Mexico supervising Mexican workers.

In 1982 the maquiladora plants employed some 100,000 workers. By 1990 some estimates are that 500,000 people were employed. In addition, American firms have other facilities in Mexico, not in the border areas, which employ thousands of Mexican workers.[48]

In the view of some Americans, these jobs have been exported by American firms to lower-paid Mexican labor, leaving Americans unemployed at home. There is much evidence of this. Many of the maquiladora plants assemble electric harnesses and electronic boards, work that used to be done

---

[47]*The Economic Report of the President, 1992* (Washington, D.C.: U.S. Government Printing Office, 1992), p. 221.
[48]John R. Oravec, "Mexican Trade Proposal Seen Draining More Jobs," *AFL-CIO News,* 37:3, Feb. 3, 1992, p. 8.

in America, for companies that used to employ Americans to do the work. The AFL-CIO has been very active in opposing the free-trade pact and in insisting that if it were to be approved by Congress, there must be provisions to protect American labor from low-wage Mexican competition.

American unions also object to the poor treatment that union organizers in Mexico are alleged to receive from employers and the government. According to the AFL-CIO, for example, Mexican police in early 1992 arrested a Mexican union leader who had called strikes against certain maquiladora plants and had negotiated large wage increases on behalf of the workers. The AFL-CIO wants to see protection of rights for workers and unions in Mexico included in any trade pact with Mexico.[49]

The companies argue, however, that as this sort of work has been refined it can be done by less skilled labor at much lower cost abroad. If American firms don't cut their costs to have it done by taking it abroad, foreign firms will simply gain the market, say the firms.

CHAPTER SUMMARY

American business has become more conscious of foreign industrial relations practices as a result of the recent successes of Japanese and German firms. Union leadership has also begun to look abroad for new models of labor-management relations. The Japanese industrial relations system is an interesting contrast to the American system. Like the United States, Japan has a diversified industrial economy, employs very modern technology, and has a largely free enterprise system. However, Japanese industrial relations are profoundly different from those in the United States. A unique characteristic of the Japanese system is lifetime employment. Standard workers stay in a Japanese firm all their lives and receive many benefits and high salaries. A great deal of personal responsibility and loyalty characterizes the relationship between management, standard workers, and the company. The labor relations of Japanese firms reflect these relations of loyalty. Japanese unions show considerable identification with their companies rather than with the occupation or industry.

Two types of labor relations innovations involving "industrial democracy" have been the subject of experimentation in Germany. Codetermination involves the appointment of workers' representatives to the boards of directors of corporations. The intent is to provide workers a role or even a partnership in the decision making of an enterprise. On the supervisory or policy-making boards of some large companies in the steel and coal industries, stockholders and employees have acquired an equal number of directors. Elsewhere in German industry, employees are entitled by law to just less than equal representation.

[49]Michael Byrne, "Mexican Disregard for Worker Rights . . . ," *AFL-CIO News*, 37:4, Feb. 17, 1992, p. 2.

Works councils are committees ordinarily involving management and employee representatives that have functions in the governance of the workplace. They were established by law in 1972 as permanent representative bodies with specific rights. The types of rights that works councils may have are complex. They are often divided into economic and social matters and may include the right to be informed, the right to be consulted, the right to investigate, and the right to codetermine. The works councils' relationship to the unions is also complex. The unions and works councils form a kind of dual structure of labor relations that has no counterpart in the United States. All major firms in Germany are involved in the structure.

The growing activities of multinational firms are one of the most important developments now affecting industrial relations systems in many countries. Multinational firms have been criticized for exporting American jobs, avoiding taxes, and increasing imports. Unions have been particularly opposed to the expansion of the multinational firms and are attempting to have their activities curbed both by legislation and by direct trade union activity. Trade union cooperation to deal collectively with multinational firms is much talked about but as yet amounts to little. There are a number of factors that limit the ability of unions in different countries to cooperate successfully in dealing with multinationals, not least of which is the lack of financial and human resources needed to organize such an effort.

The expansion of multinational business is likely to continue, and as it does the struggle with trade unions will assume broader proportions. Transnational bargaining is a possible response, but one still in its infancy. It is likely that as multinational firms expand, they will tend to lessen the diversity between industrial relations systems.

QUESTIONS FOR THOUGHT AND DISCUSSION

1 Compare labor relations in the United States, Japan, and Germany. What are the major similarities? The major differences? What factors cause similarities? What factors cause differences?

2 What aspects of the Japanese labor relations system do you think would be worthwhile for the American industrial relations system? What aspects could never work here and why?

3 Why do the British oppose the employee-representation provisions of the proposed European social charter?

4 What is codetermination? How does it operate?

5 What are works councils? How do they operate?

6 Should the United States have codetermination? Works councils? Why or why not?

7 Should the United States negotiate a free-trade pact with Mexico? Why or why not?

8 Imagine that you have been given the task of organizing an effective worldwide strategy for developing international union cooperation in order to cope with

multinational firms. What issues would you be most concerned about? What are the major problems with which you would have to deal? How would you do it?

9 How do multinational companies affect the U.S. economy? Should the United States favor multinationals or restrict their activities? How?

10 Will multinational companies bring about the formation of multinational unions? Why or why not?

SELECTED READING

Blanpain, R., ed., *Comparative Labor Law and Industrial Relations* (Washington, D.C.: BNA Books, 1982).

Flanagan, Robert J., and Arnold R. Weber, eds., *Bargaining without Boundaries: The Multinational Corporation and International Labor Relations* (Chicago: University of Chicago Press, 1974).

Hershfield, David C., *The Multinational Union Challenges the Multinational Company*, Report No. 658 (New York: The Conference Board, 1975).

Kendall, Walter, *The Labour Movement in Europe* (London: Allen Lane, 1975).

Okuchi, Kazuo, Bernard Karsh, and Solomon B. Levine, *Workers and Employers in Japan* (Princeton, N.J.: Princeton University Press, 1974).

Stobaugh, Robert B., ed., *Nine Investments Abroad and Their Impact at Home* (Cambridge, Mass.: Harvard University Press, 1976).

Vogel, Ezra, *Japan as Number One* (New York: Random House, 1979).

F

THE COLLECTIVE BARGAINING PROCESS

At the heart of labor-management relations in the United States is the process of collective bargaining. The term "collective bargaining" is used to distinguish the effort of a union on behalf of a group of employees from the bargaining of an individual employee for himself or herself. Through a union, the employees try to develop a counterweight to the power of the corporation. Through collective bargaining, a contract is created between management and the union which sets forth the rights and obligations of each.

Collective bargaining is sometimes a test of the power of the union against that of management. The relative strength of each side is called bargaining power. But collective bargaining is not only a test of strength—it is also a process of problem solving that involves the concerns of workers and of employers at the workplace

CHAPTER 13

THE NEGOTIATIONS PROCESS

WHAT IS COLLECTIVE BARGAINING?

Collective bargaining is a process by which management and unions establish terms and conditions of employment. The process is described as "collective" because workers are involved in it as a group and are represented by individuals chosen for that purpose. The process is "bargaining" because it involves give-and-take and, ordinarily, the making of a contract. The contract that results is called a collective bargaining agreement, and it regulates the relationship between the employer and the employees involved.

The bargaining process has been caricatured in a variety of ways: (1) as a poker game combining deception, bluff, luck, and ability; (2) as a debating society with long-winded speeches to impress one's colleagues and possibly have some effect on the opposition; (3) as power politics or pure brute strength in forcing terms of settlement on the weaker party; and, finally, (4) as a rational process in which appeal to facts and to logic reconciles conflicting interests in the light of common interests. All these elements are involved in some degree and combination in the bargaining process.[1] While "mature" collective bargaining no doubt implies enlargement of the rational process, there can be no such thing as complete escape from the other elements.

In the industrial relations system of the United States, collective bargaining has three major functions:

---

[1]John T. Dunlop and James J. Healy, *Collective Bargaining* (Homewood, Ill.: Irwin, 1953), pp. 53–68.

• It is a formal procedure to establish, revise, and administer many of the rules of the workplace.

• It is an informal process by which labor and management deal with each other about many matters of joint concern.

• It is a method for the settlement of disputes during the lifetime of agreements and on their expiration or reopening.[2]

These are basic processes that every industrial society and economy must somehow carry out. However, not all companies and workers are involved in the collective bargaining process in our country. Many workers are not represented by unions. In these instances the employer unilaterally determines the matters that otherwise are the subject of collective bargaining. But all employers and all employees in our society are much affected by collective bargaining, since the rules and standards established through collective bargaining have an important impact on the nonunionized sector of our economy.

Collective bargaining means many different things. A prominent neutral in the disputes between labor and management described it as follows:

> The term "collective bargaining" sometimes means an amicable exploration of joint problems resulting in friendly agreement; sometimes it means a difficult, suspicious, unfriendly relationship out of which a meeting of minds occurs only after pressure, threats of economic conflict, or strikes or lockouts.[3]

The Setting of Negotiations

Collective bargaining is a broader term than negotiations. But negotiations are often at its core. We will spend much of this chapter on negotiations. But first a word about what can and cannot be done in negotiations.

Negotiations usually occur between groups of individuals, one group representing the employer and another group representing the employees. The two groups meet at a chosen place, usually a conference room at some neutral site (i.e., neither the company's offices nor the union's meeting hall), such as a hotel. The two sides are called the "parties" to the negotiations. Each party designates a chairperson.

In some situations the parties begin negotiations on an ad hoc basis. One side usually opens the proceedings by identifying itself and asking the other side to do the same.

The first session of negotiations normally opens with a discussion in which the parties determine guidelines for their interaction, including place, time, process, and the role of committee meetings or problem solving. A presentation of the union's proposals, usually called "demands," fol-

[2]John T. Dunlop, "The Social Utility of Collective Bargaining," in Lloyd Ulman, ed., *Challenges to Collective Bargaining* (Englewood Cliffs, N.J.: Prentice-Hall, 1967), p. 169.

[3]Saul Wallen, quoted in Byron Yaffe, ed., *The Saul Wallen Papers: A Neutral's Contribution to Industrial Peace* (Ithaca, N.Y.: Cornell University Press, 1974), p. 41.

lows. The following session is devoted to the presentation of management's counterproposals. The parties thereafter schedule sessions and their agendas as they desire.

A negotiation has not only a physical setting, but one in time. Rarely do the parties enter a negotiation free of the encumbrances of their past relations with each other. In some instances the burden of the past is stifling. Some years ago George P. Shultz investigated industrial relations in the Massachusetts shoe manufacturing industry. The industry was declining, yet the companies and the unions were seemingly unable to come to grips with the problem successfully, although all knew it to be serious. Shultz concluded that the critics of the industry's behavior were

> wrong in placing the blame on the individual businessman, worker, or union leader. An individual may do a capable or even an outstanding job and yet fail to move ahead. Why? Because the local environment which no one person can control binds him to an inflexible pattern of action. . . . Individuals often struggle in an awkward institutional setting, created by the problems of years past. They are limited to an inflexible pattern of action in the making of today's decisions, and the limits cannot be waved or wished away.[4]

Distributive versus Integrative Bargaining

Collective bargaining is often thought of as a struggle between management and labor in which labor seeks to obtain concessions from management. Management is thought of as possessing economic advantages (such as profits) that labor seeks to wrest from it in the form of wage and benefit increases. Management is also thought of as possessing rights or prerogatives that labor seeks to limit or infringe on by increasing the rights of the workers. In both cases, collective bargaining is thought of as a dispute over the division of authority and of economic gains. This type of bargaining may be described as distributive, since it involves the distribution of financial and noneconomic privileges that are thought to be fixed in total amount.

But this is not all that is involved in negotiations. In fact, when one thinks of negotiating outside of the labor relations process, as, for example, between two business people over a possible sale, then bargaining is conceived as a process that results in a gain for both the buyer and the seller. Bargaining occurs over the terms of the transaction, and if the terms are sufficiently unattractive to either side, the transaction need not be made. Collective bargaining also involves this aspect of bargaining. Conflict is minimal, and both sides stand to gain from the bargain that is struck. This type of bargaining may be described as integrative bargaining. As defined by its proponents, integrative bargaining

---

[4]George P. Shultz, "Decision-Making: A Case Study in Industrial Relations," *Harvard Business Review*, 30:3, May–June 1952, pp. 105, 113. Shultz was later to be U.S. secretary of labor, and then secretary of the treasury and secretary of state.

refers to the system of activities which is instrumental to the attainment of objectives which are not in fundamental conflict with those of the other party and which therefore can be integrated to some degree. . . . Integrative bargaining and distributive bargaining are both joint decision-making processes. However, these processes are quite dissimilar and yet are rational responses to different situations. Integrative potential exists when the nature of a problem permits solutions which benefit both parties, or at least when the gains of one party do not represent equal sacrifices by the other.[5]

Many people think of integrative bargaining as involving the cooperation of labor and management in solving problems. In contrast, labor-management conflict is viewed as distributive bargaining. This is probably a confusion of ends and means, however. It is possible for labor and management to approach the resolution of distributive issues with cooperation, not conflict. In fact, it happens often, even though one party is making concessions to the other. Distributive issues need not involve conflict. Alternatively, labor and management are occasionally in conflict over issues that are integrative in nature, and the solution to which, after the conflict is resolved, benefits both parties. We may say, therefore, that there are both types of issues, integrative and distributive, and both types of bargaining, cooperative and conflict-ridden. We may also adopt Walton and McKersie's terminology and describe cooperative bargaining over integrative issues as *integrative bargaining* and conflict-ridden bargaining over distributive issues as *distributive bargaining*. But it should not be forgotten that cooperative bargaining over distributive issues also occurs, as does conflict-ridden bargaining over integrative issues. But we have no special terms for those two situations.

Walton and McKersie differentiate between different strategies and tactics in bargaining, calling them either distributive or integrative. By distributive tactics they mean those generating conflict between labor and management. By integrative tactics they mean those leading to cooperation between labor and management. Other persons make somewhat similar distinctions.

Union and management officials often try to distinguish between ordinary negotiations over an agreement (in which they assume a stance as adversaries) and quality of work life or other employee participation efforts (in which they try to be cooperative with one another). Yet another distinction is made between the period of negotiations prior to a contract in which labor and management battle with one another, and the period after the contract is concluded in which they cooperate to make it work.

Yet human relations are not so easily compartmentalized. In practice, labor and management negotiations blend the various types of tactics to fit the circumstances they confront. For this reason, the separation of negoti-

[5]Richard E. Walton and Robert B. McKersie, *A Behavioral Theory of Labor Negotiations*, 2d ed. (Ithaca, N.Y.: Industrial Relations Press, 1991), p. 5.

ation tactics and strategies into integrative and distributive categories is not done in the next section.

THE QUALITY OF A LABOR-MANAGEMENT RELATIONSHIP

There are many types of labor-management relationship. The public hears or reads primarily about strikes or threatened strikes in the news media and often presumes that all labor-management relations are antagonistic and strike-prone. The violent language of union leaders and management officials in the context of a dispute is especially attractive as a news item, and the average citizen hearing this language must think poorly of the people using it. Labor-management relations often appear, therefore, as a particularly difficult and unpleasant area.

One of the most glaring examples recently of the continuation of highly publicized labor-management conflict involves Eastern Airlines. In 1986 Eastern, a highly unionized carrier, was purchased by Texas Air Corp., which operates nonunion Continental Airlines. Continental had been unionized when Texas Air acquired it in the early 1980s, but after a strike that failed, bankruptcy proceedings, and the company's hiring of permanent replacements for strikers, Continental emerged from bankruptcy as a nonunion airline.

Apparently fearing that Texas Air would try to eliminate them, Eastern's unions began a bitter fight against Texas Air and its chairman, Frank Lorenzo. Smarting from adverse publicity, Texas Air filed a lawsuit on May 6, 1988, against two of Eastern's unions, charging them with an illegal "smear campaign" intended to ruin Eastern's business reputation. In a response, the president of one of the unions commented that Texas Air's lawsuit was like "Al Capone suing Elliot Ness"; that is, like the 1920s-era Chicago gangster Capone suing the federal agent Elliot Ness, who sought to convict Capone of various crimes.[6] The ending of this well-publicized labor-management conflict was unhappy. Eastern Airlines went out of business in 1990. Continental Airlines was forced into bankruptcy and Frank Lorenzo was forced out as its chairman. This unfortunate story shows that even when both sides have a great deal to lose from not working together they still will sometimes be unable to cooperate.

One often hears when labor and management do cooperate that it's nothing very important—"They had to do it," it is said, "because they both had a lot to lose." By saying this, people suggest that we really shouldn't admire people who set aside differences and work together for the common good because it is just to their advantage and should be expected. But that isn't true. People will often fight until everything is destroyed, just as

---

[6]"Eastern," Bureau of National Affairs, *Daily Labor Report*, No. 89, May 9, 1988, p. A-12. See also Jack Barbash, "Collective Bargaining and the Theory of Conflict," *British Journal of Industrial Relations*, 18:1, March 1980, pp. 82–90.

happened at Eastern Airlines. And therefore there is something to admire when labor and management rise above mere enmity to accomplish something together.

Fortunately, labor-management relations are not always of the Eastern Airlines type. Most relations between union and management take place in a reasonably quiet and responsible atmosphere, which is marked at times by disagreement but rarely by open strife. The people involved in labor-management relations generally are there because they believe in the importance of what they do. A survey of several hundred national and local union leaders in 1983 and 1985 found that 53 percent described their relationship with management as cooperative, and 71 percent said management accepts the union.[7] The noisy publicity seekers, the violent and abusive persons in whom the press delights, are a minority.

It is useful to examine a spectrum of labor-management relationships that describes their quality. It is possible for a particular company and union to be assigned to one category, but over time to move to another. The spectrum, therefore, may be interpreted statically (i.e., assigning different companies and unions to a certain category at the same time) or dynamically (i.e., assigning the same company and union to different categories at different periods of time).

Figure 13-1 shows a spectrum of the quality of labor-management relations. At one extreme is a situation in which the union and the employer are in open conflict. Each challenges the other's actions and motivations, cooperation is nonexistent, and work stoppages are frequent and bitter. Next is shown a situation of armed truce. The two sides view each other as antagonists and are prepared for open conflict (which sometimes occurs), but nonetheless each tries to limit the rivalry so that undue damage is not done to either. Next is placed a situation of working harmony, in which each side respects the other and conflict is limited because of a willingness to engage in give-and-take to settle disagreements. Finally, at the other extreme, is indicated labor-management cooperation. In this situation each side not only respects the other but looks to the other to help resolve common problems. Conflict is strictly limited, so that the overall quality of the cooperative relationship is not undermined.

[7]Brian P. Heshizer, "Labor's Perspective on Labor," *Personnel*, June 1986, pp. 58ff.

FIGURE 13-1 Types of labor-management relations. (*Source:* Adapted from Frederick M. Harbison and John R. Coleman, *Goals and Strategy in Collective Bargaining*, New York: Harper, 1951. See also, Benjamin M. Selekman, "Varieties of Labor Relations," *Harvard Business Review*, 27:2, March 1949, p. 125.)

Open conflict	Armed truce	Working harmony	Labor-management cooperation

We may characterize cooperation and perhaps working harmony as types of "good" labor relations. What do we mean in detail by the term "good labor relations"? Good labor relations include

- *A substantial degree of industrial peace* (i.e., absence of work stoppages).
- *Acceptance by each side* of the needs of the other as an ongoing institution (i.e., the company isn't trying to destroy the union, nor is the union trying to cause the company to lose profits).
- *Both the company* and the union believe the relationship is equitable (i.e., it is not only peaceful, but fair).
- *The net effect* of the good relationship is not detrimental to consumers or to the public (i.e., the relationship is not at the expense of other people or institutions).

In contrast, poor labor relations involve a situation in which there are frequent work stoppages, one or both sides are out to destroy the other, the relationship is not believed to be fair by one or both sides, and the net effect on customers and the public is detrimental

Figure 13-2 summarizes some of the factors facilitating the development of a cooperative and working relationship between management and labor. The external environment is critically important. Further, the necessary atmosphere cannot develop where the parties are grossly unequal in power or where either side does not accept the fundamental legitimacy of the other. A survey of management and labor negotiators indicated that labor representatives felt that they had more bargaining power than management, but that they accord more respect and acknowledge greater legitimacy to the management side. Management representatives acknowledge less legitimacy to the union and are more sensitive to criticism from the union.[8] Finally, the development of a group of representatives of the company and the union who trust each other, and may resort to outside neutrals and experts on certain matters, makes it possible to approach what could otherwise be divisive issues in a problem-solving way, so that each side has accomplishments and the relationships between the participants are strengthened.

Finally, as Figure 13-2 indicates, there is feedback from the successful accomplishment of difficult tasks to the union and the company that encourages them to deal with each other further in a cooperative fashion. Successful resolution of problems in a cooperative manner helps to create a climate in which future problems can be successfully addressed in a joint fashion. The key to cooperative industrial relations is not the total elimination of conflict, which is an unattainable ideal, but the reduction of the

---

[8]L. N. Tracey and Richard B. Peterson, "Differences in Reactions of Union and Management Negotiators to the Problem-Solving Process," *Industrial Relations Journal*, 8:4, Winter 1977–1978, pp. 43–53.

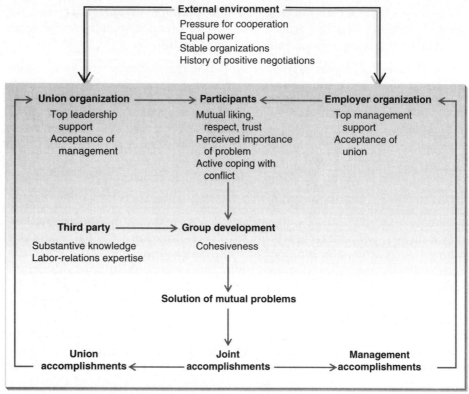

External environment
Pressure for cooperation
Equal power
Stable organizations
History of positive negotiations

→ **Union organization** ——————→ **Participants** ←—————— **Employer organization** ←

Top leadership
  support
Acceptance of
  management

Mutual liking,
  respect, trust
Perceived importance
  of problem
Active coping with
  conflict

Top management
  support
Acceptance of
  union

Third party ——————→ **Group development**

Substantive knowledge
Labor-relations expertise

Cohesiveness

Solution of mutual problems

Union
accomplishments ←—————— **Joint**
accomplishments ——————→ **Management**
accomplishments

FIGURE 13-2   Factors affecting the development of a cooperative relationship between management and labor. (*Source:* Adapted from James W. Driscoll, "Problem-solving between Union and Management," unpublished paper, MIT, 1979. See also, Michael Schuster, "Models of Cooperation and Charge in Union Settings," *Industrial Relations,* 34:3, Fall 1985, pp. 382–394.)

area of conflict to the minimum and the identification of the greatest possible area of common purpose.[9]

There is a sense in which a labor-management relationship can be compared to a marriage. As in a marriage, the two parties are bound to each other indefinitely. They are not like two unrelated individuals who meet once or twice to conclude a transaction or a contract and then are separated. Instead, labor and management must reach an agreement and then live with each other daily according to its terms. And, as in a marriage, what matters most is whether the two parties are trying to make it work or are trying to pick it to pieces. If they are trying to make it work, we may expect a good relationship. If the opposite, then the marriage will be likely to end in divorce and the labor-management relationship in continual, disruptive conflict.

[9]Trevor Owen, *The Manager and Industrial Relations* (Oxford: Pergamon Press, 1979), p. 16.

Yet even in a personal relationship some conflict may be desirable, and this is certainly so in labor-management relations. There are differences to be resolved. The issue is not whether or not there should be conflict, but how much and what form it takes. The issue for the relationship as a whole is whether or not the parties can keep periods and areas of conflict from preventing them for cooperating more generally. A good relationship is one in which conflict does not ruin interaction on a cooperative basis.

An important development in recent years has involved the degree to which the quality of a labor-management relationship is affected by the efforts of management to keep as much of its operations nonunion as possible. By the end of the 1970s a majority of the larger corporations in the United States that dealt with unions (in at least some of their facilities) also had a program to keep unions out of their unorganized plants. Others were prepared permanently replace striking workers to, so that the union would effectively be eliminated if it struck. Also, surprisingly, the corporations centralized responsibility both for keeping good relations with the unions and for keeping the unions out of the companies' nonunion plants in the same corporate officer: the vice president for labor relations (or personnel, or human resources, depending on the title used in each company).[10] Periodically unions complain that a company cannot have good relations with unions and at the same time actively try to keep them away or to destroy those with whom it deals. Yet with only a few exceptions corporations have been able to keep working relationships with the unions while opposing further organization of their employees by unions and even replacing workers when a strike occurs.

In 1947 a public-spirited nonprofit organization, the National Planning Association, decided to study not the causes of labor-management conflict, but the causes of industrial peace. They commissioned a set of studies of particular companies and unions to be made by a group of professional researchers. The studies were first published in 1949 and served as the raw material for a group of critical evaluations of the causes of labor peace.[11] The studies concluded that the environmental conditions conducive to industrial peace were more widespread in the economy than was industrial peace itself, so that there was much room for improvement. The authors stressed as important factors the development of positive attitudes by management and labor toward each other and the use of problem-solving, nonlegalistic procedures in dealing with each other.[12]

---

[10]Audrey Freedman, *Managing Labor Relations*, Report No. 765 (New York: The Conference Board, 1979), p. 12.

[11]C. S. Goldin and V. D. Parker, eds., *The Causes of Industrial Peace under Collective Bargaining* (New York: Harper, 1949).

[12]Herbert Northrup and H. A. Young have since criticized the original study as being strongly influenced by the favorable economic climate of the time and for having given platitudes as research results. Northrup and Young suggest that several of the companies involved in the study purchased peaceful labor relations at the cost of inefficient practices and unduly generous compensation. Herbert R. Northrup and H. A. Young, "The Causes of Industrial Peace Revisited," *Industrial and Labor Relations Review*, 22:1, October 1968, pp. 31–47.

The National Planning Association study was a milestone in American labor relations. The issue that had concerned the researchers was that of industrial strife—strikes, lockouts, and their impact on those involved and the public generally. By the 1990s the volume of industrial strife had declined sharply. Year after year the nation reported fewer work stoppages and less time loss due to strikes than before (see Chapter 16). Attention had shifted to another aspect of the quality of a labor-management relationship.

Most American labor-management relations remained adversarial. The two sides were locked in a bargaining rather than a problem-solving mode. There was peace, but little cooperation. But the new workplace and the pressures of international competition seemed to require a more affirmative response from management and labor than simply fewer strikes (see the discussion in Chapter 4). In consequence, efforts to build cooperation by constructive bargaining developed.

CONSTRUCTIVE BARGAINING

Planning Strategy

Labor-management negotiations have become far more complex in recent years. The image of union bargainers banging a table demanding increased wages, and company negotiators refusing with icy faces, is generally out of date. In recent years negotiators have come to the table accompanied by experts in benefit plans and in drafting legally binding language. Even more recently unions have brought investment bankers and consultants able to analyze the company's business situation in great detail.[13] This increasing complexity requires both sides to prepare more carefully for bargaining.

Good negotiators, whether for management or labor, prepare mentally for negotiations.[14] First, they organize the points they want to present in a natural order. Second, they prepare all major alternatives with the reasons for accepting one and rejecting the others. Third, they relate all the points they intend to make to the interests, needs, and wants of the other side in the negotiations. These are basic methods of preparing to attempt to persuade others, whether in collective bargaining, sales, or other types of human interactions.[15] Experienced negotiators are able to go several steps beyond these.

[13]Elizabeth Kaplan, "Labor Borrows the Tools of Capital from Wall Street," *Dun's Business Review,* October 1985, pp. 60–62.

[14]George E. Constantino, Jr., "The Negotiator in Collective Bargaining," *Personnel Journal,* 54:8, August 1975, pp. 445–447.

[15]Lee H. Hill and Charles R. Hook, Jr., *Management at the Bargaining Table* (New York: McGraw-Hill, 1945), p. 243. This book, now nearly five decades old, remains one of the best available on how to conduct negotiations.

Understanding the Other Group[16]

A negotiator should not expect himself to deal with another organization without having first developed a thorough working knowledge of that organization. He should find answers to the following questions: What is the formal leadership structure of the other organization? Who are its executives or officers? What are their personal backgrounds, their work histories, and their outside affiliations? Is there a struggle for leadership internally, or is there internal stability? What are the informal lines of communication and influence in the organization? What are the objectives—and the history of success or failure—of the organization? How will the other organization approach our own group? Will they expect cooperation or a confrontation? What do they regard as our strengths and weaknesses? Are they anxious for action or patient? How will they react to frustration—and to success? Are they able to deliver on commitments they might make or not?

There are various sources of such information. Most unions publish their constitutions or bylaws, and they often hold meetings, which in many instances the public is free to attend. Recently a representative of a major company involved in labor negotiations in the coal industry decided he needed to know more about the changing leadership and procedures of the United Mine Workers. So he attended their 1973 convention. He was, as a result, in a far better position to understand the union's behavior in the 1974 coal negotiations than other management representatives. And he used his knowledge to help settle the strike.

Research indicates that most negotiators enter negotiations expecting the other party's interests to be completely opposed to their own; and it is often only in the negotiations process itself that negotiators learn about the possibility of joint gains. Accurate perception of the other party before negotiations start can help advance common interests.[17]

Organizing Objectives

It is most important to analyze priorities thoroughly. And the best way to do it is to combine various options and hypothetically choose among them. This permits the negotiator's own organization to establish priorities in a systematic way. The results are often surprising to negotiators who thought, incorrectly, that they understood their organization's priorities.

A further advantage of this process to a company is to reveal how difficult it will be to mobilize internally all the related elements of the company that must deal with the problem at hand. Challenges from another organization rarely fit neatly into the corporation's internal structure, so considerable effort is required by a corporation in assigning responsibility for a response. The process of organizing objectives helps to resolve these issues.

---

[16]See D. Q. Mills, "Managing Human Relationships among Organizations," *Organizational Dynamics*, 3:4, Spring 1975, pp. 35–50.

[17]Leigh Thompson and Reid Hastle, "Social Perception in Negotiation," *Organizational Behavior and Human Decision Processes*, 47:1, October 1990, pp. 98–123.

Thinking Procedurally

Next, it is necessary to think about how these issues are to be addressed. Which should come first? Should ultimate priorities be revealed at the outset? Is there a logical step-by-step process to be followed, or would it be best to do everything at once? Initially, should the negotiator appear to be well prepared for meetings or simply to be in attendance?

It is often difficult for people who have certain objectives to think not about the objectives themselves but how to attain them. Yet it is critical to structure a particular approach, and it must be done, to a substantial degree, in advance.

Walton and McKersie also distinguish two other subsystems of the general process of negotiations in addition to integrative and distributive bargaining. One of these processes is referred to as *attitudinal structuring*. This refers to the activities and efforts of a management team or union officials to influence the attitudes of the other. Attitudinal structuring is an attempt to change someone else's opinion about something or someone. It is directed at the relationships between the people involved in bargaining.

The final subprocess of negotiations is identified as *intraorganizational bargaining*. Because both companies and unions are ordinarily large organizations, there is a necessity on both sides to work out a consensus internally. In a sense, in collective bargaining it always takes three agreements to reach one. There must be an agreement within the union on the final contract. There must be an agreement within the company on the final contract. And there must be an agreement between the union and the company on the contract. Often negotiators say that the internal negotiations are as complex and difficult as those with the other side.

Formal Proposals

Should formal, written proposals be exchanged by the union and the employer in negotiations? Many observers of collective bargaining think that formal proposals assist in bringing negotiations to a constructive conclusion. They suggest that written proposals should be exchanged well in advance of the actual expiration of a collective bargaining agreement. The advantages of this procedure are several. First, the preparation of formal, written proposals requires each side to be specific about what it desires and also to be comprehensive. It will be difficult to alter a proposal or introduce a new one later in negotiations. Second, the advance presentation of written proposals allows each side considerable convenience in analyzing, understanding, and preparing a reply. In this way written proposals may help to avoid the misunderstandings that can develop in verbal communications.

However, there are certain drawbacks to written proposals, especially in the course of negotiations (i.e., after presentation of initial positions):

1 *Written proposals force each side into fixed positions from which they may be reluctant to move, fearing loss of face with their constituents.* To the extent that written proposals tend to lock negotiators into certain positions, they interfere with the give-and-take necessary to successful bargaining.

2 *Written proposals also provide the opportunity for each side to characterize the other's position.* For example, in the 1976 negotiations between Ford Motor Company and the UAW, the company gave the union its first formal, written offer on September 1. The union leadership took the written offer and described it to the press in the following terms: "This is the most regressive offer in all my years of bargaining," said Leonard Woodcock, president of the UAW. "It is entirely unresponsive to any of our problems." On the other side, Ford spokespeople characterized the union's demands as expensive and unreasonable. Such public denunciations have become a common part of auto industry bargaining. In fact, it is not clear what purpose the initial written offers of both sides serve except to be the focus of denunciation by the other side. In the auto industry, as negotiations become more serious, formal, comprehensive proposals are abandoned in favor of a more flexible negotiations posture.

3 *The existence of written demands and responses makes it likely that the final settlement will be compared with initial positions and a judgment made as to which side won and which lost.* This win-lose mentality, given credence by written statements, can interfere with a problem-solving approach to negotiations.

Factual Studies

Writing in 1964, William E. Simkin, former director of the Federal Mediation and Conciliation Service, put great stress on factual studies by labor and management as a procedure that offered great hope for improving the likelihood of peaceful resolution of labor disputes.[18] Factual studies involve a joint effort by labor and management, at a time well before actual negotiations, to ascertain the facts about a particular problem. This procedure, which emphasizes the review of a particular item, or items, of concern to the parties in a noncrisis atmosphere, is also referred to as "continuous negotiations."

The advantages of factual studies lie in two areas. First, the likelihood is that the parties will be better able to agree on a solution to a problem if both accept the same set of facts about it. To a surprising degree, disputes between labor and management arise because of basic inadequacies of factual information about certain situations. Both sides believe they know the facts, but in reality they do not.

A classic case of a dispute in which the facts were not clear occurred in the 1959 negotiations in the steel industry. Many years before, the companies had proposed inclusion in the collective bargaining agreement of lan-

[18]William E. Simkin, "The Trend to Maturity in Industrial Relations," *Industrial Relations,* 3:1, February 1964, pp. 1–4.

guage regarding the establishment and change of local working conditions (this was section IIB of the agreement between United States Steel Corporation and the Steelworkers). Some people in U.S. Steel's management had opposed the company's decision to propose this language. By 1959 there had been a change in U.S. Steel's management, and the company's new negotiators wanted to take this language out of the agreement. The other steel companies were not sure that the matter was very important but went along with U.S. Steel. The union decided to oppose the companies' proposal to delete IIB from the agreement. No one really knew its significance. The result was a strike of 116 days in 1959. The companies were unsuccessful in getting the clause removed, and it remains in the steel agreements to this day.

Certain matters have proved especially susceptible to the factual studies approach. These are matters that are unusually complex. Among them are adjustment to technological change and provisions of pension and health and welfare plans. For the joint study approach to work, certain conditions are needed. Among them are

1 A joint will to solve the problems
2 Complete flexibility in discussion for both sides
3 Competent and sophisticated staffs on both sides

The great hopes for the factual studies approach that Simkin voiced in 1964 have receded somewhat in recent years. But joint study remains one of the most constructive procedures available to participants in collective bargaining.

Good Procedures

A list of suggested good bargaining procedures was developed in 1975 by the Joint Labor Management Committee of the Retail Food Industry. After reviewing bargaining procedures in American industry, the committee emphasized that the lack of agreement on basic procedures for bargaining was causing strife in the industry. In the interest of improving bargaining, the committee suggested the following procedures of general applicability:

1 *Contract proposals should be exchanged well in advance of contract expiration.* All proposals should be in writing and easily understood. If either side does not understand the proposals, the parties should meet promptly to clarify all the demands in detail. There must be ample time for joint or separate research and costing and for both parties to secure necessary clearances prior to negotiation.

2 *"Eleventh-hour" bargaining should be avoided.* Experience in other industries has demonstrated that this style of bargaining is counterproductive, frequently causes strikes, and almost never ensures a fair settlement for either labor or management.

3 *The use of the Federal Mediation and Conciliation Service* and appropriate state, local, and private mediation agencies and individuals is a cornerstone of rational collective bargaining.

4 *Negotiations should be conducted at the table, not in the press.* "Negotiating in the press" is damaging to achieving rational results in collective bargaining and leads inevitably to emotional confrontations caused by coverage that is too often inaccurate. If necessary, there should be joint agreement on a news blackout or joint releases to the press.

5 *The strike issues should be fully understood by both parties prior to strike or lockout action.* Contrary to popular belief, the parties often discover after the strike has started that the issues were not fully understood on both sides. The committee recommends that in the event one party or the other believes that the communication needed to clarify strike issues is blocked or broken down, a third party, a mediator, for example, if one is not already in the picture, be asked to clarify the issues for the parties before strike or lockout action is taken by either side.

6 *All possible alternatives should be considered before a strike occurs.*

A further point, not mentioned by the committee but raised in other discussions of collective bargaining, is the advantage of a problem-solving approach to negotiations (what Walton and McKersie called "integrative bargaining"). A contrast can be drawn between the behavioral scientist's paradigm of problem solving by small groups and the often conflict-ridden nature of collective bargaining negotiations.[19] Table 13-1 identifies three ideal types of labor-management interaction: open conflict, adversarial bargaining, and problem solving. The first is often characterized as "lose-lose" because in open conflict both sides usually get hurt. The second is characterized as "win-lose" because one or the other side ordinarily recognizes that it has prevailed. The approach creates a winner and a loser on some, if not all, issues. The third approach presumes that there are common problems to be tackled, and that if they are successfully resolved then both sides win.

Collective bargaining involves several stages, and different approaches to negotiation sometimes characterize them. Thus, in the stage of identifying problems, there is considerable use of the problem-solving approach. In the stage of developing alternative possibilities for agreement, there is some use of the problem-solving approach. But in making decisions about what the contract will entail, collective bargaining negotiations are often very conflictual.[20] It is at the stage of decision making that collective bargaining is, as one manager described it, "a kind of fist-fight."

---

[19]Lawrence E. Susskind and Elaine M. Landry, "Implementing a Mutual Gains Approach to Collective Bargaining," *Negotiation Journal*, 7:1, January 1991, pp. 5–10.

[20]James W. Driscoll, "A Behavioral-Science View of the Future of Collective Bargaining in the United States," Working Paper, Sloan School of Management, MIT, Mar. 3, 1979. See also Ian E. Morley and Geoffrey M. Stephenson, *The Social Psychology of Bargaining* (London: Allen and Unwin, 1977).

TABLE 13-1   THREE IDEAL TYPES OF LABOR-MANAGEMENT INTERACTION

Open Conflict

"*Lose-lose*"

Declining Sum

Each side:

Insists on its own way
Sticks to principles at all costs
Exhibits emnity toward the other side
Grasps for dominance

Adversarial Bargaining

"*Win-lose*"

Zero Sum

One or both sides:

Set forth demands
Hide reaction to the other's proposals
Conceal critical information
Threaten work stoppages or other action
Conceal priorities while attempting to ferret out those of the other side
Agree to nothing the other side suggests without lengthy consideration
Wait until the "eleventh hour" to make an agreement
Exhibit mistrust of the other side
Spread disinformation
Have a hidden agenda
Search for the other side's weaknesses
Insist on intragroup adhesion

Problem-Solving

"*Win-win*"

Positive, Non-zero sum

Both sides:

Identify issues and opportunities
Exhibit flexibility among alternatives
Are open in communication
Exchange relevant facts
Trust and cooperate with the other side
Work on intergroup teamwork
Are willing to see the other side's point of view
Share objectives and priorities
Address real concerns of the two sides, not just positions
Value the other side's contributions
Address the other side's concerns

It seems to many people that a well-intentioned person would always approach negotiations from a problem-solving perspective, resorting to an adversarial approach only when the other side proves untrustworthy. But this can be a very risky approach. For example, sharing information openly with the other side is a major element of the problem-solving approach.

But what if the other side isn't well disposed; couldn't they use the information against you?

Yes, they could. A study of information sharing in the United States and Japan showed very different results. "In Japan," wrote the researcher, "firms often attempt to influence the process and outcomes of wage negotiation by sharing confidential business information with their unions and employees through the joint consultation system. . . . [When this happened], negotiation processes were shorter and easier, and unions tended to demand and accept lower wage increases."

What about the United States? Did increased information sharing improve the bargaining process? In contrast to Japan, a similar study done in America found that information sharing increased labor's bargaining power.[21]

Why the different result? The authors of the studies don't tell us, but the probable reason is that American unions disposed to be adversaries of the companies simply used confidential business information provided by the firms to support the union's positions—that is, the unions used the information against the companies. Hence, if a union is an adversary of a company, then it is hazardous for the firm to share information openly.

Nonetheless, wherever possible, a problem-centered approach should be used—a "let's sit down and talk it over" attitude.[22] When discussion centers on problems to be solved, rather than on demands or on rights, the chances are much better that solutions compatible with the needs of both parties will be found.

HOW NEGOTIATIONS ARE CONDUCTED

The Physical Setting

Labor-management negotiations usually take place in a room with two tables facing each other, with labor seated behind one table, management behind the other. This is the customary format for negotiations, but not the only one available. Many times negotiators give no thought to the physical format, but it can be of psychological importance. For example, the table-facing-table arrangement implies an adversarial relationship, in that it appears set up for a contest between opposing teams.

An arrangement more congenial to cooperative problem solving would have the participants from labor and management seated around the same table, or even in a circular arrangement. In such a format, the distinction between the two sides is not so clearly drawn. Also, conversations can take place between various individuals, so that the role of the spokespersons for the two sides is minimized.

---

[21]Motohiro Morishima, "Information Sharing and Collective Bargaining in Japan: Effects on Wage Negotiation," *Industrial and Labor Relations Review*, 44:3, April 1991, pp. 469–485.

[22]F. H. Harbison and Robert Dubin, Patterns of Union-Management Relations (Chicago: Science Research Associates, 1947), p. 152.

The physical format of a negotiation can be manipulated to the disadvantage of one side by the other. In one instance, the company negotiators arranged the room. There was a single table; chairs for the management people were placed on one side of the table, and chairs for the union people were placed on the other side. When the union representatives entered the room, they were pleased by the apparent equality of treatment they had been given and the informality of the arrangements. However, when the two sides were seated, the union people discovered that the company negotiators had placed low chairs on the union's side of the table, so that the union representatives were looking across the table and up at the management people. The union representatives felt uncomfortable and distinctly at a disadvantage.

What Is Happening at the Bargaining Table

There is a way in which all negotiations appear very similar to an outside observer. A group of people, the negotiators, are seen to be engaged in a lively discussion. They are very involved in what they are doing. But is something significant occurring or not?

Often something important is happening. The two sides are engaged in give-and-take, or they are exploring alternatives for resolving a difficult problem.

But in some instances not much is happening at all. The negotiators in the bargaining room are only ratifying the results of struggles that have occurred elsewhere. Sometimes the really difficult problem was to get all the people on the same side—management's side or labor's—into agreement on what position to take. Reaching agreement with the other side was relatively easy. Sometimes, the two sides are rigidly tied to conflicting positions, and a strike is occurring that will determine which side, if either, prevails.

For a negotiator it is important to know whether the negotiations process itself is the center of the action or merely a sideshow.

Rituals in Negotiations

Labor negotiations sometimes seem to assume the ritualized character of religious or marriage rites. Negotiations are accompanied by the observance of certain set forms and procedures. Like rituals in other areas of human conduct, those involved in collective bargaining have a purpose. They have evolved for two primary reasons. The first is that observance of rituals imposes a certain order and predictability on what would otherwise be a very uncertain process. Second, rituals help the sides to come to an agreement, in part by limiting the hazards involved for both sides. This latter point is often misunderstood. Because certain things are rituals in negotiations, outside observers often believe them to be archaic and unnecessary appendages to the bargaining process. This is ordinarily not so.[23]

Major rituals involved in collective bargaining are the following:

• The first offer of management is usually a low offer. The first demands of the union are high. Both sides recognize that the offers are not intended to be acceptable, but both sides nevertheless make them. Why?

There are several reasons. First, both management and labor negotiators have constituents to serve who are likely to have high expectations. Employees may want big wage increases and the union negotiator doesn't want to be the one to tell them no. "Let management do that," the unionist muses, "I'll just present the demands no matter how high and unrealistic they are." And management negotiators may face just as unrealistic expectations from top executives or investors. "Don't give the union anything," the management representative may be told, "take something away." So management starts with little or nothing on the table and waits for labor to force the offer higher.

Also, the initial presentation of somewhat unrealistic offers allows each side to feel out the other without the danger of being unable to retreat from an initial position. High and low offers allow room for later bargaining.

• Normally, no agreement is reached in collective bargaining before the expiration date of the existing collective bargaining agreement. There is almost always, therefore, some eleventh-hour bargaining agreement. Why don't the parties just wrap it up early when they can, rather than waiting until the last minute?

The ritual of the last-minute settlement tends to protect the negotiators on each side from charges by their own constituents that they sold out. In bargaining, neither side gets all it hoped for. When the settlement and the concessions involved in achieving it occur at the last moment, then concessions appear necessary in order to avoid the costs of a strike or lockout. But when concessions are made in advance, the negotiators may be accused of having given in on certain issues without good reason.

In many instances, negotiators are criticized for eleventh-hour bargaining. It is said that this ritual involves the threat of unwarranted work stoppages because the parties too often simply run out of time and don't reach agreement on all issues before a strike deadline passes. This is a significant criticism of the ritual of settling at the last minute.

• A degree of acrimony, name-calling, and other verbal abuse is a ritual in certain negotiations. This is a particularly unpleasant ritual and one that is very difficult to justify or explain to outside observers. This book

---

[23]John T. Dunlop, "The Negotiations Alternative to Markets and Regulations," unpublished manuscript, 1977.

does not countenance this, but the reader may still see that the practice has certain functions in some instances.

Overt controversy is intended to demonstrate to the constituents of both sides that their advocates are loyal and prepared to do battle for their constituents' interests. It also reminds participants that the bargaining process is a serious matter, undertaken on behalf of others and not for the comfort of the negotiators. Finally, it tends to cause more timid souls to leave the bargaining before the truly serious and stress-producing issues are confronted.

Tactics in Negotiations

Labor negotiations involve two general types of tactics. One type includes those tactics intended to gain an advantage for the person or side who employs them. Tactics of the other type are intended to help persuade the other side to accept a point of view. Both are used in negotiations, often interchangeably. Bargaining has much in common with the methods of salespeople in this regard. Many books and articles about bargaining tactics stress methods developed in selling products. Some observers believe that tactics of persuasion are morally defensible, while tactics of advantage are not. This judgment is perhaps best left to the reader. It is made a judgment of even greater complexity by the question of whether the objective to which the tactics are applied is a moral one, and if so, whether this should affect the tactics employed.

Collective bargaining negotiations assume to a degree the aspect of a very complex human game. The stakes for which the game is played are high. The best players of the game are very sophisticated. At the center of the game is the psychology of the situation and of the other players. Such a contest between people is often a very complicated process and one of infinite variety. It is virtually impossible to summarize. A mere list of tactics, of potential moves and countermoves, would far exceed the space allotted to this book. Indeed, the bargaining aspect of labor relations is something that attracts certain people, who find it exciting and psychologically interesting. Below we list and briefly describe some of the tactics employed in collective bargaining. This list is not at all exhaustive, nor is it intended as an endorsement of all the items listed.

Tactics used to gain an advantage:

- Bogey tactics
- "This is all I've got to concede"—holding something back
- Bluffing—insisting that you have, or don't have, something, when the opposite is true
- Prevarication
- Decoys—suggesting for negotiation matters of no real importance

- Contrived emotional outbursts—acting very pleased or very upset about something
- Deliberate errors
- Good-guy-bad-guy—causing one negotiator on a team to pose as friendly and well disposed to the other side while another negotiator on the team is actively hostile

As described by one student of negotiations tactics, good-guy-bad-guy works in negotiations as follows. One person takes a tough stand, making demands and acting in a rough manner. "Next to him is friendly old Smiley who says little during the discussion. After a while the bad guy shuts up and the good guy takes over. When he makes his demands, they seem reasonable by comparison. Why not? It seems a pleasure dealing with such a nice man after being worked over by that mean one. You can't help feeling that things could have been worse."[24]

Bad guys come in nonhuman form sometimes. The bad guy is "company policy" or "union policy," which won't permit something to be done. About the good-guy-bad-guy tactic, the observer quoted above has said, "It works better than it should."

Tactics used to persuade:

- Anticipate objections to a proposal and answer them before they are voiced
- Agree, then refute—"Yes, but. . ."
- Stress similarities of position, not differences
- Offer a problem, not a solution. Wait until the other side recognizes that there is a problem before trying to persuade them to accept a proposed solution
- Provide information that helps the other side understand your position
- Present your own favorite viewpoint last, not first. If someone else announces it before you, let that person have the credit

Bruce Henderson has described the tactics used by business negotiators in the following way:

The negotiator's skill lies in being as arbitrary as necessary to obtain the best possible compromise without actually destroying the basis for voluntary mutual cooperation or self-restraint. There are some common-sense rules for success in such an endeavor:

1 Be sure that your rival is fully aware of what he can gain if he cooperates and what it will cost him if he does not.
2 Avoid any action which will arouse your competitor's emotions, since it is essential that he behave in a logical, reasonable fashion.

[24]Chester Karass, *Give and Take: The Complete Guide to Negotiating Strategies and Tactics* (New York: Crowell, 1974), p. 79. See also Roger Fisher and William Ury, *Getting to Yes* (Boston: Houghton Mifflin Company, 1981).

3 Convince your opponent that you are emotionally dedicated to your position and are completely convinced that it is reasonable.

It is worth emphasizing that your competitor is under the maximum handicap if he or she acts in a completely rational, objective, and logical fashion. For then he or she will cooperate as long as he or she thinks they can benefit. In fact, if he or she is completely logical, they will not forgo the profit of cooperation as long as there is any net benefit.[25]

Negotiations are fraught with opportunity for conflict. If one negotiator criticizes another, it is easy for the second to reply in kind. But this need not be done. A smart negotiator can keep the talks on a problem-solving track by turning aside antagonistic remarks. Recently some of the newer interpersonal-relations approaches have been turned to this topic. Transactional analysis (TA) figured importantly in one study in which the authors described the interchanges between negotiators (see Table 13-2).[26]

Unsound Attitudes

Negotiations make some people uneasy. Rather than admitting they are uneasy, being patient, and trying to work things out, these people often adopt unsound attitudes. These attitudes often result in damage to their own side of the bargaining table and sometimes in damage to the bargaining process as a whole. Some of these are expressed as follows:

- "Give them what they want."
- "Better make a trade."
- "Frankly, I'm bewildered."

[25]Bruce Henderson, *On Corporate Strategy* (Cambridge, Mass.: Abt Books, 1979), p. 28.
[26]Frank L. Acuff and Maurice F. Villere, "Games Negotiators Play," *Business Horizons*, 19:1, February. 1976, p. 76.

TABLE 13-2   SOME INTERCHANGES BETWEEN NEGOTIATORS

A comment causing controversy	A response continuing controversy	A response ending controversy
	"What's the use of arguing with you? You're going to get your way anyway."	"Any suggestions for getting us back on the track?"
"I know you're not prepared only because you've had a lot of other problems at the office."	"I've got so many other things on my mind that I'm no good to anybody today."	"Based on the information I brought with me, let's see in what areas we can move forward."
"Your demands are unrealistic!"	"You're the one who's unrealistic."	"Why?"

Source: Frank L. Acuff and Maurice F. Villere, "Games Negotiators Play," *Business Horizons*, 19:1, February 1976, p. 76.

These attitudes have in common a fatalism about the bargaining process that represents withdrawal from the attempt to get any useful result from it. They are a signal of serious danger for the side whose negotiator(s) professes them and sometimes for the collective bargaining process generally.

In the late 1960s economic and other conditions were such that collective bargaining in the construction industry was very much in favor of the unions. Employer associations took strike after strike over matters they thought were important, only to lose ingloriously. Attempts to get the intervention of outside parties were a failure for a prolonged period (although in the early 1970s both government and the broader business community intervened to stabilize bargaining in construction for a few years). By 1969 and 1970 many employers had simply given up. In their view nothing could be achieved in bargaining. The unions were too strong. A great bitterness crept into the relations between management and labor in the industry.

Attitudes of the type listed above became common. And by the early 1970s a substantial movement to operate construction firms nonunion, without the necessity for collective bargaining, was under way. Many factors caused these changing conditions in construction, but the attitudes generated by years of one-sided bargaining were an important element.

On the other side, some negotiators adopt positions of unreasonable confidence. Some examples are:

- "We're right and we won't budge."
- "We don't have to worry."
- "Stick it to them."

These attitudes reflect a stubbornness and a single-mindedness more appropriate to a military conflict than to collective bargaining. Sometimes it is necessary to be very firm, as all good negotiators know. But rigidity and vindictiveness are danger signals.

Ethical Issues in Negotiations

Negotiations potentially raise a number of ethical issues for those involved. Three of the most important are:

- To what degree, if any, is a negotiator justified in misleading the other party about his or her position, or objectives, or the facts of a matter being discussed?
- Is the outcome fair to both parties? If one side has greater power or skill in negotiations, how far should it press its advantage?
- Are the interests, welfare, and concern of others affected by a negotiation, but not party to it, adequately considered and provided for by the parties to the negotiation? For example, is the public adequately considered in negotiations involving public employees? Or, are customers adequately considered in negotiations by a union and a company?[27]

---

[27]David A. Lax and James K. Sebenius, "Three Ethical Issues in Negotiation," *Negotiation Journal,* 2:4, October 1986, pp. 363–370.

These issues are inherent in most labor-management negotiations. Sometimes they are considered, and sometimes not. As collective bargaining matures, perhaps unions and managements will increasingly try to resolve such questions in an ethical manner.

The Outcome of Negotiations

No general summary of the outcome of negotiations can be given. All situations are different. It is possible, however, to list the major factors that affect the outcome of negotiations.[28]

Economic Conditions   General business conditions in the economy, favorable or unfavorable trends in a particular industry, and the financial condition of particular companies influence both company and union positions in negotiations. Recession and unemployment considerably dampen a union's willingness to strike. But it is important to remember that economic conditions do not necessarily determine, in any absolute or a priori sense, the outcome of negotiations. Bargaining behavior and circumstances of bargaining have been shown in empirical tests to have as much effect on bargaining outcomes as do economic variables.[29]

Company Policies   Especially with respect to the noneconomic clauses in contracts, the extent to which companies have developed policies and taken firm positions with respect to achieving them has drastically influenced the outcome of negotiations. While collective bargaining always limits management rights and prerogatives, the character and degree of limitation vary widely from contract to contract.

Union Policies   Unions have varied considerably in both their militancy and their objectives. The Die Sinkers Conference, a small, strong craft union, has had little concern for pensions, health and welfare plans, and other such "frills." The union wants money in the pay envelope and an 8-year apprentice program. The UAW, in contrast, has been strongly interested in "social breakthroughs." Socially oriented, innovative demands and achievements have characterized the UAW over the years.

Union Politics   While union politics are in some way related to union policies, the political variations among unions deserve separate mention. A union torn by internal factionalism, such as previously existed in the United Mine Workers, presents a difficult problem for management. Some such

---

[28]E. Robert Livernash, "Note on Collective Bargaining in the United States," 1-676-171 (Boston: Intercollegiate Case Clearing House, 1976).

[29]Richard B. Peterson and Lane Tracy, "Testing a Behavioral Model of Labor Negotiations," *Industrial Relations*, 16:1, February 1977, pp. 35–50.

unions are virtually leaderless and have great difficulty conducting and concluding negotiations. Unions also vary in the degree of "democracy" they exhibit. Political stability is frequently associated with "responsible" behavior.

Union-Management Relations Benjamin M. Selekman identified nine types of union-management relations, and his list included conflict, containment-aggression, accommodation, and cooperation.[30] Over the years more and more relationships can appropriately be described as characterized by a significant degree of accommodation. Some negotiating situations have developed sufficient mutual confidence so that neither party seriously considers the possibility of a strike. The United Steelworkers and the basic steel industry have achieved a high degree of accommodation with respect to very difficult issues.

The Conduct of Negotiations The preparation for negotiations, the art of communicating during negotiations, the timing of proposals, the degree of management initiative, and other elements that might be listed as part of the "technique" of negotiation influence the outcome. Experienced negotiators rarely get boxed into an untenable position or stumble into a strike.

Other Variables Pattern-setting negotiations are normally more tense than pattern-following situations. Union rivalries play their part. Public pronouncements by participants may commit one or both parties to a rigid position. Government policies and official statements may give aid or comfort to one or the other party in major disputes.

MODELS OF BARGAINING

Collective bargaining is such a complex, human, and indeterminate process that it may be surprising to learn that some theorists have attempted to develop formal models of the bargaining process. Certain aspects of collective bargaining seem to invite a rigorously logical treatment.

First, economists have long since developed models to analyze and explain the process of price determination in a situation of bilateral monopoly and oligopoly. These models take strategic calculations into explicit account. Bargaining between a union and employer over wage rates has many characteristics of the bilateral monopoly situation and so has invited the extension of those theories to collective bargaining.

Second, the transactions between labor and management are often financial in nature (such as wage and fringe benefits increases) and are therefore easily quantified. Since the outcome of the process can be mea-

[30]Benjamin M. Selekman et al., *Problems in Labor Relations* (New York: McGraw-Hill, 1964), pp. 1–11.

sured, it seems that some quantitative treatment of the factors producing the result is also appropriate. Furthermore, the expression in a formal, logical manner (i.e., a model) of ideas about what factors affect bargaining and in what ways is a useful procedure for clarifying thought.

Bargaining Power

Much discussion of labor relations is and has been couched in the terminology of "bargaining power." In testimony before the Senate Education and Labor Committee in 1935, William Green, then president of the AFL, used this common phraseology: "The economic conditions which exist today can be corrected only when the bargaining power of the employees is made equal to that of the employers." And to the House Committee on Labor in that same year Green said, "The fundamental necessity [is] for establishment of equality of bargaining power between employer and employee."[31]

The idea of bargaining power as a fundamental determinant of the results of collective bargaining was thus blessed by organized labor. What the unions were seeking, Green was arguing, was not special treatment from Congress, but a mere equalization of bargaining power between workers and employers. In the Wagner Act, Congress accepted this notion and embodied it in the preamble to the act: "The inequality of bargaining power between employees . . . and employers . . . substantially burdens and affects the flow of commerce," reads section 1 of the National Labor Relations Act.

Thereafter, with bargaining power thus given legislative sanction as an important concept in American labor relations (it has no exact counterpart elsewhere), employers began to argue that the balance of power had shifted in labor's favor. By the mid-1950s employer complaints about the growth of union power in mass-production industries became frequent. And in the 1960s complaints about union bargaining power in the construction, maritime, and retail food industries increased.

It is not surprising that scholars should have attempted to base models of bargaining on the formulation of a theory of bargaining power. The initial problem was to formulate a careful definition of bargaining power. As used colloquially, the concept is somewhat slippery. Unfortunately, when formulated carefully, the concept tended to become a tautology. A settlement favorable to the company was said to result from the company's bargaining power. But how was the company's bargaining power to be measured? If bargaining power was measured by the degree to which the settlement was favorable to management, then the definition was circular; that is, bargaining power was bargaining power because it was bargaining

[31]Quoted in Marion Sadler, "Who Speaks for the People in Collective Bargaining?" *Columbia Journal of World Business*, 4, March–April 1968, pp. 21–26.

power. To attempt to escape this circularity, scholars developed a definition of bargaining power that stressed the concept of ability to compel the other party to do something: "Power is defined as the capacity of one subject to carry through its will against the will of another subject."[32] Alternatively,

> Bargaining power can be defined as the capacity to effect an agreement on one's own terms; operationally, one's bargaining power is another's inducement to agree. If X and Y are in a contest over the terms of their cooperation, X's bargaining power is represented by Y's inducement to agree . . . while Y's bargaining power is X's inducement to agree.[33]

These two definitions have a superficial similarity but may, in fact, be substantially different. The first definition envisages a substantial element of coercion of one side by the other—"carry through its will against the will of another subject." The second definition envisages the result of circumstances broadly affecting both parties. When one party is compelled to seek an agreement by circumstances, the other party is said to have bargaining power. For example, if a company is in difficult financial straits and cannot afford a work stoppage, the union is said to have bargaining power as a consequence of this circumstance.

Figure 13-3 is a depiction of bargaining power. It is useful because it systematically portrays the many elements which are involved in the development, application, and use of power in negotiations. The figure shows three sources of collective bargaining power: those that originate in the external environment and are uncontrollable by union and management in the specific situation; those that are "controllable"—that is, result from the actions of one or both parties—in the long term; and those that are controllable in the short run. There are also transformational factors, those attitudes and commitments that can enable management and labor to fundamentally alter a relationship. These several sources of power yield to both management and labor actual power in the relationship—the total power derived from all sources, expressed both absolutely (what can be accomplished) and relatively (compared to the other partner). The employment of power results in various manifestations that are its outcomes—settlements (whether forced—a win-lose outcome—or congenial—a win-win outcome), or conflict. From all this emerges the changes that ocurr in compensation, hours, and working conditions.

In recent years attention has been devoted to identifying and measuring components of bargaining power. The Illini City studies by Milton Derber

---

[32]Jan Pen, "A General Theory of Bargaining," *American Economic Review,* 42, 1952, pp. 24–42.
[33]Neil W. Chamberlain, *A General Theory of Economic Process* (New York: Harper & Row, 1955), pp. 80–82.

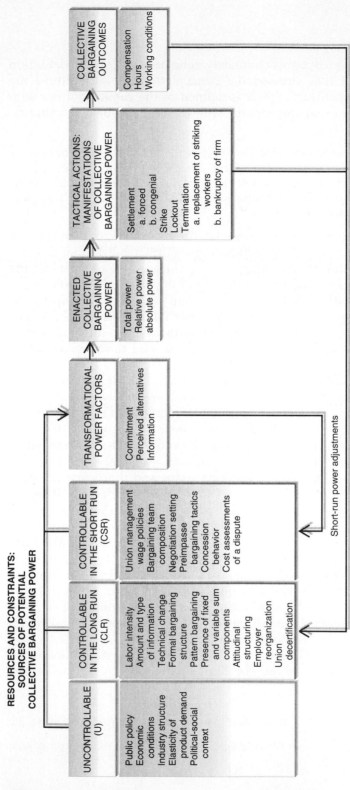

FIGURE 13-3 Collective bargaining power. (*Source:* Terry L. Leap and David W. Grisby, "A Conceptualization of Collective Bargaining Power," *Industrial and Labor Relations Review,* 39:2, January 1986, p. 209.)

and others attempted to evaluate the relative impact of environmental and volitional forces on various aspects of bargaining and its outcomes.[34] Other researchers have tried to identify separate categories of bargaining power: legal, political, social, and economic.[35]

Formal Models

Not all theorizing about bargaining employs the concept of bargaining power. Another line of theoretical development attempts to structure the bargaining process in terms of offers and counteroffers.

The analysis begins with a situation in which each party demands an outcome highly favorable to itself. This may be seen in Figure 13-4. In the diagram the two axes (labeled U_1 and U_2, respectively) represent the total amount of "utility" gained by each side. Utility is a concept that covers all benefits, both pecuniary (i.e., directly measurable) and nonpecuniary. It is not directly observable or measurable, as a wage rate or the cost of a wage and fringe benefit package would be. In Figure 13-4, party number 2 starts at demand position 2, which has a high utility to party number 2 and a low utility to party number 1. At position 2, party number 2 gets U_{22} utility for itself; party number 1 gets only U_{12} for itself. Party number 1, however, begins by insisting on point 1, which is more favorable to it than to party number 2. The curve that connects points 1 and 2 may be described as a "utility frontier" and includes the set of points that yields the *highest avail-*

[34]Milton Derber, W. E. Chalmers, and Milton Edelman, *Plant Union Management Relations* (Urbana: University of Illinois Press, 1965).

[35]D. J. Armstrong, D. Bowers, and B. Burkitt, "The Measurement of Trade Union Bargaining Power," *British Journal of Industrial Relations*, 15:1, March 1977, pp. 91–100; Christine Edwards, "Measuring Union Power," *British Journal of Industrial Relations*, 16:1, March 1978, pp. 1–15; Hervey A. Juris and Peter Feuille, *Police Unionism: Power and Impact* (Lexington, Mass.: D. C. Heath, 1973).

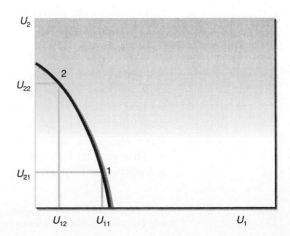

FIGURE 13-4

able utility to one side that can be obtained, given a *certain amount* of utility for the other side. All points inside the curve are less efficient than those on the curve—outside the curve points are not available because of financial or other constraints.

Then suppose each bargainer deliberates between accepting the other's offer and holding out for his or her own, in the hope that the other will accept it. From the first bargainer's point of view, for example, immediate capitulation would bring about the utility U_{12}, while stubbornness would bring either the greater utility U_{11} if the other surrendered or zero utility if the other proved equally adamant. What is the maximum subjective probability of conflict (C_1) that the first bargainer can rationally stand in holding out for his or her own demand? The answer is, that value of C_1 that will make it a matter of indifference to the bargainer, as a matter of expected utilities, whether he or she capitulates or holds out indefinitely—that is, the value of C_1 that satisfies the equation $U_{12} = (1 - C_1)U_{11}$. Hence the desired value of C1 and the corresponding value of C2 for the second bargainer are:

$$C_1 = \frac{U_{11} - U_{12}}{U_{11}} \qquad C_2 = \frac{U_{22} - U_{21}}{U_{22}}$$

Now specify (and this is the critical part of the theory)[36] that the first bargainer will make at least some concession, and the second will not, if $C_1 < C_2$ (i.e., if the first cannot stand as great a probability of conflict as the second); or the second bargainer will be the one to make a concession if $C_1 > C_2$; or they will both make simultaneous concessions if $C_1 = C_2 > 0$. Typically, however, neither makes a complete concession to the other's current demand, but rather concedes only enough to make it the other bargainer's turn to concede, at least a little, whether unilaterally or simultaneously with a corresponding further concession by the first bargainer. In other words, the first bargainer makes a concession when $C_1 \leq C_2$, or when (with reference to the above two equations):

$$U_{11}U_{21} \leq U_{22}U_{22}$$

Hence, each concession by the first bargainer raises the utility product that he or she proposes ($U_{11}U_{22}$), and similarly, each concession by the second raises $U_{22}U_{12}$. Accordingly, these utility products are maximized and equated to one another when an agreement is finally reached, with $U_{11} - U_{22} = U_{21}$ at a single point on the utility frontier, and with $C_1 = C_2 = 0$.

This model has been termed a "split-the-difference" model, in that it suggests that, by bargaining, the final position reached between two nego-

---

[36]This model was developed by Zeuthen and is reprinted and discussed in Oran R. Young, ed., *Bargaining: Formal Theories of Negotiations* (Urbana: University of Illinois Press, 1975).

tiators is somewhere between the initial positions of the sides. In recent years, researchers have begun to use such models to test the results of actual negotiations to see how well the empirical results can be explained by the theories. In one recent study the researchers concluded that the management and the union did not follow bargaining curves that were symmetrical, so that a split-the-difference model was not altogether appropriate as a measure of the union's wins or losses.[37] The most recent models investigate bargaining that occurs in stages during which different parties have different degrees of bargaining power.[38]

Such models of bargaining are useful in providing insights and conceptual stimulation. They are, however, subject to very significant limitations in their current form. None of these models will produce good predictions or satisfactory explanations concerning bargaining in actual situations. Different models result in different and often contradictory results even when applied to idealized situations, and the resultant lack of agreement among theorists of bargaining is increasing, not decreasing. Also, these models all omit various interesting phenomena that are commonly thought of as important features of bargaining. Among these are the multiplicity of issues and their possible incomparability. This circumstance the utility theorists simply assume away by the invention of "utility" itself, which is said to encompass all aspects of a possible bargain into a single, quantitative measure. The fact that negotiations take place drawn out over time and in an atmosphere of considerable uncertainty about what each side can really afford or tolerate also has no place in these analyses. They give no hint, for example, why strikes ever occur.[39]

Attempts have been made to develop formal models of the bargaining process that draw their inspiration from the behavioral sciences, rather than from economics. One study of this nature presented a conceptual model derived largely from the Walton and McKersie formulation. The model treated the four elements of bargaining as identified by Walton and McKersie as goals in the bargaining process for each side. A questionnaire was sent to negotiators in selected private-sector collective bargaining negotiations that occurred in 1973. The negotiators were asked how well they had achieved their economic goals (distributive bargaining) and their problem-solving goals (integrative bargaining). Negotiators were also asked how successful they had been at improving the working relationship between the two sides (attitudinal structuring) and how successful they

[37]Gary A. Hall and William R. Schriver, "Bluffing in the Bargaining Process: An Empirical Test," *Proceedings* of the Industrial Relations Research Association, December 1977, pp. 286–293.

[38]A. Manning, "An Integration of Trade Union Models in a Sequential Bargaining Framework," *The Economic Journal*, 97:385, March 1987, pp. 121–139.

[39]A positive analytical literature pursuing these themes has begun to appear. For a clear if somewhat technical introduction to its methods, see John Sutton, "Non-Cooperative Bargaining Theory: An Introduction," *Review of Economic Studies*, October 1986, pp. 709–724. See also Oran R. Young, "The Analysis of Bargaining: Problems and Prospects," in Young ed., *Theories of Negotiations*, p. 391.

had been in getting their constituents to agree to their own decisions during the negotiations (intraorganizational bargaining). The researchers concluded that bargaining behavior and conditions had as much effect on bargaining success as did the economic (distributive) variables.[40]

The basic insights that appear in behavioral models of negotiations can be summarized as follows. In the beginning each side to a negotiation faces a given set of economic facts and circumstances. These are similar, but involve differences, for management and labor. As a result of different contexts and different interests, the two sides will differ on the meaning of the current situation and how to deal with it. Thus, a threshold step in the behavioral analysis of a negotiation involves the parties' different perceptions of the situation and expectations as to the outcome of negotiations.

For example, considering a possible wage settlement only, the company and the union's positions may be characterized as having upper and lower limits. In Figure 13-5 the company expects a wage increase in the range of 3 to 6 percent, with the upper figure as high as it is willing to go. The union, in contrast, expects from 9 to 12 percent, with the lower figure its minimum. The result is that with no region of overlap, the most likely outcome of bargaining is a strike. However, in Figure 13-6 the initial situation is different. The company is prepared to settle between 3 and 6 percent, and the union between 5 and 9 percent. Here an agreement is possible without the parties reevaluating the circumstances and changing their positions. Effective negotiators will discover that an area of agreement exists. If the management negotiator is more skilled than the union counterpart, the agreement will be closer to 5 percent than to 6 percent. If the union negotiator is more skilled, the agreement will be closer to 6 percent. If one or both negotiators are unskilled, there may be no agreement at all, as one or both sides may fail to discover the range of possible agreement.

[40]R. B. Peterson and L. N. Tracy, "A Behavioral Model of Problem-Solving in Labor Negotiations," *British Journal of Industrial Relations,* 14:2, July 1976, pp. 159–173; and Peterson and Tracy, "Testing a Behavioral Theory Model," op. cit.

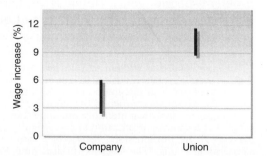

FIGURE 13-5

FIGURE 13-6

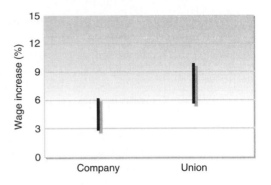

Returning to Figure 13-5, if an agreement is not possible, a strike or lockout is likely to occur. The strike has a function, in that it imposes costs on the two parties that force them to change their positions. Ideally and most often, the parties reevaluate their positions and the union lowers its expected increase while the company raises its offer until overlap occurs and an agreement results.

CHAPTER SUMMARY

Collective bargaining is the process by which management and unions negotiate the terms and conditions of employment and produce a contract. The major functions of collective bargaining are to establish the rules of the workplace, especially the amount of compensation for employees, and to settle disputes. The negotiation process can be approached to varying degrees as a poker game, a contest of power and wills, or a rational process for reconciling conflicting interests in order to support common goals.

Two types of collective bargaining have been identified. In distributive bargaining a struggle occurs between labor and management for a limited amount of economic and noneconomic advantage (whether profits, rights, or authority) that one party possesses and the other tries to obtain. Integrative bargaining, on the other hand, involves finding solutions to problems that benefit both parties or benefit one but not at the expense of the other. In practice, labor-management relations involve both types of bargaining.

There are many types of labor-management relationships, ranging from open conflict to close cooperation. In a cooperative relationship, each side respects the other and they work together to resolve common problems. Labor relations are most likely to be peaceful and equitable when a company is profitable and its market strong so that employees can be paid well and when the corporate owners and the national union are responsible and socially sensitive. A good relationship cannot develop where the parties are grossly unequal in power or where either side does not accept the needs and legitimacy of the other.

Good negotiators use methods which are positive and constructive rather than destructive. These methods include (1) the systematic establishment of priorities and the relating of all points to the interests, needs, and wants of the other side in the negotiation; (2) the detailed understanding of the other group—personally, historically, and organizationally; (3) the presentation of formal written proposals; (4) the mutual conducting of studies to establish the facts; and (5) the use of a problem-solving approach.

Negotiations are conducted in somewhat ritualized ways. The employer and union representatives usually meet at a neutral place, such as a hotel. In the first session the union presents its demands; in the second session management presents its counterproposals. Usually little thought is given to the physical setting, but it can be of importance in influencing the psychological climate. Major rituals in collective bargaining include a low first offer by management and high demands by labor to set the stage for bargaining; "eleventh hour" bargaining, or not reaching an agreement until the expiration of the existing contract is imminent; and acrimony and name-calling, which remind the involved parties that the situation is a serious matter. Two types of general tactics are used—tactics intended to gain an advantage for the side that uses them and tactics intended to persuade the other side to accept a point of view.

Negotiations are such a complex and indeterminate process that theorists have attempted to develop formal models of the factors that affect bargaining and the ways they do so. Bargaining power has been suggested as an important determinant in negotiations, and scholars have tried to formulate theories, models, and precise definitions for it. One definition emphasizes coercion of one party by the other. Another definition stresses the circumstances affecting both parties which give one an advantage over the other. Mathematical and other formal models of collective bargaining give clarification, insight, and stimulation, but none can provide good predictions or satisfactory explanations of actual bargaining. An aspect of the situation that is important but not easy to take into account in mathematical models is the history of the relationship of the negotiators and their established attitudes and expectations.

QUESTIONS FOR THOUGHT AND DISCUSSION

1 What are the major functions of collective bargaining in the industrial relations system? How well does it perform these functions?
2 What is distributive bargaining? Integrative bargaining? How are they different?
3 What role do rituals play in negotiations? Do you think rituals are necessary? Why or why not? Do you think they contribute to good collective bargaining? What model of collective bargaining is most useful to you? Why?
4 What model of collective bargaining is most useful to you? Why?

5 What is bargaining power? How has the concept been used to understand the results of collective bargaining? Do you think a precise definition of bargaining power is possible or useful? What do you personally think it consists of?
6 Do you think the attitudes and bargaining behaviors of the participants in collective bargaining negotiations are more or less important in the final outcome than economic conditions and factors? Why?
7 In what ways would jointly conducted factual studies of labor problems improve negotiations? In what situations would they be unlikely to help very much?
8 What is intraorganizational bargaining? How does it affect collective negotiations?

SELECTED READING

Gold, Charlotte, *Labor-Management Committees: Confrontation, Co-optation, or Cooperation* (Ithaca, N.Y.: Industrial and Labor Relations Press, Cornell University, 1986).

Peterson, Richard B., and Lane Tracy, *Models of the Bargaining Process: With Special Reference to Collective Bargaining* (Baltimore: Johns Hopkins University Press, 1977).

U.S. Department of Labor, Bureau of Labor-Management Relations and Cooperation Programs, *U.S. Labor Law and the Future of Labor-Management Cooperation*, BLMR No. 104 (Washington, D.C.: U.S. Government Printing Office, 1986).

Walton, Richard E., and Robert B. McKersie, *A Behavioral Theory of Labor Negotiations,* 2d ed. (Ithaca, N.Y.: Industrial and Labor Relations Press, 1991).

Young, Oran R., ed., *Bargaining: Formal Theories of Negotiations* (Urbana: University of Illinois Press, 1975).

CHAPTER 14

UNION ORGANIZATION
FOR BARGAINING

Both union and management must organize themselves to conduct negotiations. In this chapter we examine how unions decide what demands to make on employers for changes in a labor agreement, how unions select their negotiating team, and the role of union officers in these processes. We also examine how unions decide whether or not to strike an employer and the factors on which this decision depends. Finally, we review the process of ratification of a proposed agreement by the rank-and-file membership of a union. In Chapter 15 we will see how management prepares for negotiations and what its objectives are.

THE UNION AND ITS RELATION TO MEMBERS
AND TO MANAGEMENT

Labor-management negotiations involve three major actors: the union, management, and the employees. A union must determine its desired relationship to each of the other two. The employees are its members, but its officers may think of them in various ways. While there are a variety of potential relationships between a union's officials and its members, it is useful to think of a dichotomy. Union leaders may think of their members as either associates or clients. What is the difference? An associate is invited to be involved in the negotiations process and to receive considerable information about its progress. A client is given less involvement and information, and is hoped to be satisfied with the result.

A union may also approach management in different ways. The union may view management as an adversary or as a partner, a distinction we discussed in earlier chapters.

Over time there has been an evolution in how members and management are treated by union officials that affects the bargaining process. Figure 14-1 depicts the change. Originally many unions saw management as an adversary, their members as associates. They were in the upper left-hand cell of the matrix in Figure 14-1. Then many union leaders drew away from their members, becoming more professional. Members were at greater distance from the leadership, becoming clients, not associates. This was common in the 1970s. In the 1980s many unions made an effort to deal on more of a partnership basis with management; but members were still clients to be served and placated, not associates to be involved. By the 1990s the process had completed the diagram as unions sought to involve their members as associates and management as members.

THE UNION CHOOSES A NEGOTIATING TEAM

Whether a local union negotiates an entire collective bargaining agreement or only a local supplement to a national agreement with its employer, it still must do certain things to prepare for negotiations. At the outset, it must select a committee to represent it in negotiations. How does a local make this choice? Who are the persons ordinarily chosen to represent it, and why?

The local itself ordinarily selects its bargaining committee at a meeting of the membership. Sometimes the committee is made up of the officers of the local union. More often, some officers serve on the committee, but they are supplemented by rank-and-file members elected specifically for this purpose.

Factors in Choosing a Negotiating Committee

What are the factors that influence the selection of a bargaining committee? First, the choice of bargaining representatives is of political significance in the local union. If an officer fails to be included on the bargaining committee, it may be a signal that he or she is on the way to defeat at the next election or to retirement. A major reason for this is that a position on

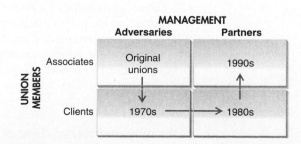

FIGURE 14-1   How union leaders view their members and managers.

the bargaining committee gives a potential candidate for office in the local union a good position from which to initiate a political campaign.

Thus, *the choice of a bargaining committee is part of the ongoing political process within a local union.*

It should be noted that employers often resent this intrusion of union politics into collective bargaining. Employers generally believe the political factor to be extraneous and disruptive. They do not like being asked to deal with certain union representatives in preference to others for political reasons or being asked to concede certain issues in order to facilitate the political career of a particular union officer or candidate for office. Yet a union is inherently a political body in which the leadership is chosen by election and, because bargaining is a primary function of the union, internal politics cannot be excluded from negotiations. In some instances, the internal political situation in a union is very stable, so that the incumbent officers have no challengers and the impact of political considerations on collective bargaining is minimized. This situation is unusual, however.

Second, a bargaining committee is usually selected to represent in some way the range of interests among members of the local. An industrial union, for example, needs to include on its committee representatives of both the numerous production workers and the less numerous skilled tradespeople. Sometimes one person is considered sufficiently knowledgeable and trustworthy to be acceptable to all groups. Generally this is not the case. When it is not, it is important that different interest groups, including minority groups, be represented on the negotiating team.

Thus, *the choice of a negotiating committee ordinarily involves making provisions for the representation of the more important interest groups of the local.*

Third, a negotiating committee requires persons with expertise in negotiations and the writing of contracts. These persons may be long-service union officials or union negotiators, or they may be representatives of the national union. Increasingly, professional expertise is provided by lawyers who are chosen by the local union and advise the negotiators on the legal technicalities of the negotiations. In some instances, union lawyers serve as chief negotiators for the union. As collective bargaining agreements have become more complex, and as federal regulation of the terms of contracts has been expanded, the need of union committees for technical and legal expertise has risen.

Thus, *the choice of a negotiating committee requires obtaining expertise in negotiating techniques and legal matters.*

Not all negotiating committees are chosen on the basis of these three principles. But when committees are not so chosen, the collective bargaining process is generally negatively affected.

Functions of a Negotiating Committee

We may understand these principles of the selection of a negotiating committee better if we ask, "What is the principal function of a union negotiating committee?" A first impression would be that its function is to convey to management the demands of the workers. But any of a number of other devices would serve this purpose, including a mass meeting with management or a letter listing demands. Rather, the function of a bargaining committee is to work out an agreement. This is not just a communication task, but one of creativity and compromise.

The real task of a committee is to develop and obtain solutions to the problems raised by the union's membership. After an agreement is reached, the negotiating committee must present it to the workers and sell its provisions so that it will be accepted. Yet this requires explaining to the members not only what was obtained in the negotiations, but what was not obtained, and the reasons why these things were not obtained. Often this is the most difficult task the committee faces, far more difficult than the negotiations with the employer.

Why is this so? Why is it so often difficult for union negotiators to sell a proposed agreement to the members? The major reason is that the workers have not been party to the discussions in the negotiations that convince the union's committee members that some demands were impractical, others too costly, and that still others should be traded off against gains elsewhere. The union committee members have probably spent many hours becoming convinced of these things, but the average worker has not. The worker knows only that in the union's list of demands were many that are not included in the proposed contract, and he or she looks to the negotiating committee for an explanation of their omission. It is very important that *it is not the employer who explains to the rank-and-file workers why they obtained some advances and not others in the agreement; it is the union negotiators' job.*

It is almost impossible to stress too strongly the importance of the responsibility of a union negotiating committee to sell the agreement it has reached to the membership. If it does not do so, the proposed agreement may be rejected by the membership, so that negotiations must resume. Employers, fearing rejection of an agreement, often insist on a commitment from the union negotiators to recommend approval of the proposed agreement to the union membership. This is a way of insisting that the union negotiators meet their responsibility to sell the agreement. When union negotiators avoid this responsibility, the negotiations process becomes one of union negotiators running back and forth between the workers and the employers' negotiating committee. In the meantime, confusion reigns and if a strike is in progress, it is prolonged.

The selling of an agreement by union leadership to the membership does not occur only after the agreement is fully negotiated. Instead, it involves an ongoing communication process during negotiations through meetings and newsletters. If this is done, when the agreement is reached, it offers fewer surprises to the membership and is likely to be more easily ratified.

Thus, there are three functions of a union negotiating committee:

- To present the union's demands to the employer
- To negotiate a tentative contract
- To explain the proposed settlement, both what was gained and what was not, to the rank and file and obtain their approval of its terms

FORMULATING DEMANDS

Unions have several methods of formulating demands. Generally, however, all methods begin with mass meetings of the rank and file at which lists of desired contract modifications are made up. Any worker can make his or her suggestion, and it will be included on these lists. In some instances, suggestions made in such meetings are allowed to become very impractical, with different persons arguing with each other to see to what extremes demands can be carried. For example, one worker may propose a 10 percent wage increase, another 15 percent, another 25 percent, and so on. The process may end only when its absurdity has become clear to all.

Some unions either dispense with a membership meeting altogether in favor of a bargaining council or use a council to supplement membership meetings. A bargaining council is made up of elected stewards and other elected bargaining council members. The council helps determine bargaining objectives by surveying members, developing proposals, and making recommendations to the union's negotiators. When an agreement is reached, the bargaining council reviews it and makes a recommendation to accept or not. If the recommendation is to accept, the bargaining council helps to persuade the membership to vote to approve the agreement.

Despite the apparently wide-open process of generating demands, unions are often very predictable in what they seek in negotiations. For example, listed below are the types of demands unions typically make about compensation. Among the most common are

- To raise pay rates above those of nonunion workers
- To add benefits
- To press for equal pay for equal work
- To apply automatic progression to increases
- To reduce the size of pay differentials among job classes (especially between skilled and unskilled workers)
- To avoid individual performance ("merit") reviews
- To avoid individual incentive systems
- To avoid group incentive plans
- To play a role in promotion decisions (which usually involve a pay increase)[1]

---

[1]David B. Balkin, "Union Influences on Pay Policy," *Journal of Labor Research,* 10:3, Summer 1989 pp. 295–307.

The range of issues that a union may wish a company to address in collective bargaining certainly isn't restricted to compensation. In later chapters the key issues of bargaining are discussed. The unions seem proud of the scope of their concerns. When a critic suggested that the unions may suffer from constriction of the areas in which they bargain, Douglas Fraser, former president of the United Autoworkers, responded:

> The fact is that unions have expanded the issues on which they bargain more in the last ten years than in the previous forty years. What were formerly the exclusive prerogatives of management are now bargainable issues. Among such issues are the ratio of supervisors to workers; the percentage of wages paid to nonunion salary personnel limited by a specific percentage of wages paid to the hourly workers; an effective voice . . . in areas such as outsourcing, health and safety and product quality; and administering employee assistance programs and employee training programs.[2]

Wish Lists

In some instances, suggestion lists (sometimes referred to as wish lists) compiled at mass meetings are taken directly into negotiations with the employer. When this happens, there are several consequences. First, considerable time may be spent by the two sides in narrowing down the list to one from which negotiations can reasonably commence. Second, there is the danger that the two sides may fall into adamant disagreement on one or more extreme demands presented by the union. This is very likely to occur if the employers' representatives insist on characterizing the unions' demands. "This is the most insane thing I ever saw," a management representative might say of a particularly unreasonable union demand. But the union bargainers, in order to save face after such a challenge, may feel obligated to defend that very demand. The result is an impasse that need not have occurred. Third, by taking extreme demands into the negotiations process the union committee may have raised unreasonable expectations in the rank and file. This may result in an unwillingness by the membership to accept the agreement that results from the give-and-take of negotiations.

Winnowing the List

These dangers have persuaded most union representatives to find some method of winnowing the demands put forward by the rank and file into a more restrained package for negotiations with the employer. There are many means by which this may be done. In some cases of local bargaining the negotiating committee treats the list compiled by the membership as a document from which to select a limited number of points as higher-

---

[2]Douglas Fraser, "Inside the 'Monolith,'" in George Strauss, ed., *The State of the Unions* (Madison, Wis.: Industrial Relations Research Association, 1991), p. 417.

priority items for presentation to management. The more limited list is then presented to the rank and file for approval at another meeting, and items that were omitted are identified and their omission explained. In cases in which negotiations occurred at a regional or national level, involving many locals, a bargaining council ordinarily receives lists of demands from each local and from these lists prepares a more limited package for submission to management. Finally, in some cases, the officers or staff of a union (either local or national) will prepare a list of demands in the course of the administration of an existing contract and present these demands to the membership for amendment and approval. Demands prepared in this way are usually more comprehensive (less oriented to exclusively economic items) and more realistic in terms of economic items than those gathered at a rank-and-file meeting.

There has been some research into the priorities of union members. Are economic or noneconomic goals more important? For the most part the studies confirm a strong focus among American workers on such goals as wages, benefits, and job security. Job content and quality of work life issues come in lower, and political goals lowest of all.

Interestingly, research also shows that union leaders are sometimes out of touch with members' bargaining goals. One reason is that union leaders may assume that what they want is what members want, when actually there are differences. In general, union leaders seem to be more liberal politically than members and more conservative in terms of bargaining expectations—perhaps reflecting their better understanding of management's position.[3]

There is always a political risk for a union leader or committee in attempting to limit or rationalize a list of demands. Dissident members of the union or politically ambitious rank and filers may charge that the leadership—not the employer—is denying benefits to the workers. Because of this risk, a politically expedient path for union leaders is to collect demands from the rank and file, give them to the employer, and let the employer take the onus for failure to grant them.

Since there is a political risk involved in winnowing demands, it is to the credit of union leaders that they often modify irresponsible lists of demands in an effort to make the bargaining process with management proceed more effectively.

Keeping Demands Separate

A final characteristic of the union's process of compiling demands should be noted. There is, generally, at no point in the process an attempt to cost out the package of demands as a whole. Rather, each issue

---

[3]Daniel C. Gallagher and George Strauss, "Membership," in Strauss, ed., *State of the Unions,* p. 143.

is considered on its own merits, without regard to the group of demands as a whole. A demand would ordinarily be modified as too extreme only because of its own characteristics, not because it, combined with many other demands, made too large a total cost. Employers, in contrast, often start their preparation from a definite position on what total cost they can afford and are less concerned with its distribution among items. It is, therefore, a characteristic of most negotiations that the union wants to discuss individual items, and the employer, the total cost of a package of items.

Why do unions pay so little attention to total package cost? There are three major reasons. First, unions often lack the financial information and skill to develop cost estimates. Second, workers and unions are not concerned with costs, but rather with benefits, each on an individual basis. Analysis of working conditions and benefits as cost items is foreign to their way of thinking. Third, unions perceive cost control as a managerial function. Consequently, the unions are prepared to leave the problems of estimating costs and their impact on the business to management. They are confident that if a particular demand or package of demands is really too expensive, the employer will not agree to it.

Applying Pressure to Management

Unions know that often managers will resist their demands. Hence, they must consider whether or not to use pressure to try to persuade managers to agree. The most common pressure tactic is the strike, which is discussed below. Another is the boycott, by which the union tries to persuade customers not to buy the products or services of the firm with which it has a dispute. In recent years the unions have developed new tactics, including

- Pressuring a company's bank and creditors, especially with the help of religious and community groups
- Challenging company applications for industrial revenue bonds, zoning variances, and the like
- Embarrassing directors and officers by picketing their homes, mounting unusually strong personal attacks, opposing management in proxy battles, and communicating directly with stockholders
- Suing the company or individual officers for breach of fiduciary duty, fraud, or racketeering
- Extending boycotts to nontraditional areas: health and life insurance, bank accounts, stock purchases[4]

[4]Aaron Bernstein and Michael A. Pollock, "The Unions Are Learning to Hit Where It Hurts," *Business Week,* Mar. 17, 1986, pp. 112, 114. See also Charles R. Perry, *Union Corporate Campaigns* (Philadelphia: Wharton School, University of Pennsylvania, 1987).

THE DECISION TO STRIKE

No decision that a union leader or negotiating committee makes is of greater importance than the decision to call a strike. While it is not unusual for union leaders to threaten to strike in support of their bargaining position and to imply that they have no hesitation about calling a strike, this bravado generally conceals serious foreboding. No responsible union leader ever embarks on a strike in a cavalier fashion, because the inherent dangers are too great.

Members are often hesitant about a strike, recognizing the sacrifices it may entail. Studies suggest that higher-paid workers are generally more militant than those who are lower paid. Perhaps this is because higher-paid workers—ordinarily the skilled—are more difficult for an employer to replace during a strike; perhaps they have a higher stake in their jobs and so are militant in protecting those gains. Also, the more members believe they are paid less than others of comparable skills, the more militant they become.[5]

Dangers of a Strike

A strike has its own dynamics. It may be called simply to support a bargaining demand, but it can readily get out of hand. Violence may develop on picket lines. The local police and the courts may become involved in the dispute. The union may incur substantial legal costs protecting itself. In addition, the union leadership will be confronted with the problems of assisting the members of the union who are out of work. If the strike is a long one, union strike benefits may be exhausted and assistance will have to be sought from the public welfare program or unemployment insurance (where legally permitted). A long strike will cause hardship in varying degrees for the strikers, and as difficulties increase, pressure from the families and dependents of the strikers for a return to work will increase. The intelligent union leader knows that while it may be easy to whip up enthusiasm for a strike at the outset, a long strike will see the erosion of that enthusiasm and the union will be increasingly blamed for the hardship involved.

However, in America collective bargaining can legally become a test of economic power, and the key power which a union wields is the strike. A union that never strikes may discover that management believes that it never will, so that the union has forfeited a great deal of its bargaining power.

The issues of power and the role of the strike are primarily associated with adversarial bargaining, however. In a cooperative labor-management relationship that uses problem solving, neither the strike nor the threat of

[5]Daniel C. Gallagher and George Strauss, "Membership," in Strauss, ed., *State of the Unions*, p. 152.

a strike has any significant role to play. If a union wishes to demonstrate to a doubting management that the membership cares greatly about an issue, an hour's demonstration via a work stoppage would be sufficient. In fact this occurs frequently both in the United States and abroad, but gets little attention from the news media, so that most people are unaware of this aspect of labor-management relations.

Why Strikes Occur

It has been pointed out that often a strike costs the strikers more in lost wages and benefits than they gain in the new contract when the strike ends. Since this is the case in many instances, why do strikes occur at all? Wouldn't it be more rational for the union to settle for less and avoid a strike (and may not the same be said of management)? We must leave a full discussion of the role of the strike in collective bargaining for Chapter 16, but we can give a partial answer here to this question. In most cases, a strike is provoked by a clash of wills. The costs incurred in the struggle seem of less significance than the humiliation that would be the consequence of a concession. In other instances, unions often embark on strikes without realizing their ultimate consequences. In the initial enthusiasm, union members and their leaders often believe that a work stoppage will quickly bring the company to acceptance of their terms for a settlement. It is only later that it becomes clear that the company has more staying power against the strike than the union had thought. In these cases, if the union had correctly foreseen the cost of the strike, it might have made concessions to avoid it.

Still, most experienced union leaders do calculate the probable length, cost, and outcome of a strike in advance. They recognize that there is little point in leading the rank and file into a strike which the union is unlikely to win. Their own position may be undermined in the process. They estimate the results of the strike by weighing a series of factors, just as their management counterparts do.

Factors Affecting the Results of a Strike

The union leader must assess four major factors in evaluating the potential success of a strike.

1. *What is the capacity of the company to operate without the union members?* In some instances highly automated facilities, such as telephone switching stations, power plants, and oil refineries, can be operated for long periods by supervisory personnel only. In other instances, a plant can operate without certain groups of workers if they are the only ones on strike, such as maintenance workers or janitorial personnel. In yet other instances, plants can be operated with the use of temporary employees, so-called strikebreakers. Whatever the specific method by which the facility

continues to operate, a long and perhaps ineffective strike is the likely result.

2. *What will the strike cost the union, and how long can strikers be assisted by the union or the public?* Even though a union may ordinarily provide benefits to its members who are on strike, existing funds cannot support a strike indefinitely. The larger the strike fund, the longer will be the period of support, and the more likely it will be that other local or national union groups will contribute to support the strikers. In some states, welfare assistance may be available to strikers who fall into very severe financial circumstances, and in a few states unemployment insurance may be available to support strikers after a waiting period. The greater the degree of support that can be obtained from private and public sources for the strikers, the more likely a strike is to be effective. Finally, in some industries (especially construction) it is often possible for a union to find jobs for strikers with employers who are not being struck, either in the same or in an adjacent geographic area. In extreme cases, local construction unions are sometimes on strike and every member is still fully employed. The ability of a union to conduct a successful strike in such a circumstance is clearly unlimited.

3. *What will be the role and attitude of public officials toward the strike?* In some areas of the United States, when there is a strike, public officials will order plants shut down to avoid picket-line violence, thereby preventing employers from operating during a strike. Such action is, of course, of great value to a striking union. In other areas of the country, however, local public officials will take the opposite attitude and fully protect employers in their attempts to operate their plants with supervisory or temporary personnel. Such action is, clearly, detrimental to the capacity of a union to conduct a successful strike.

4. *What will be the attitude of the local community?* In many instances a strike can fail simply because the local community is persuaded that the work stoppage is inappropriate. Strikers may be denied assistance from public authorities, denied credit by local merchants, or otherwise discriminated against. Conversely, when the community supports the strike, it may give considerable assistance to the strikers and apply pressure to the employer to reach a settlement. Community attitudes therefore may also affect the success or failure of a strike.

Because of the importance of community support to strikers, the AFL-CIO is considering the establishment of a permanent strike support center. The goal of the center, according to Steelworkers President (and AFL-CIO Vice President) Lynn R. Williams, is to "prevent the avoidable strikes and win the winnable strikes." Among the key things that need to be done to support striking workers is to provide health care coverage for them. The center would also urge member unions to allow time to explore tactics to be used in a strike. During the 1986 strike of the Steelworkers against a major steel company, the AFL-CIO set up a Steelworkers support committee to bring the dispute to the public's attention and to provide moral support for the workers. The proposed strike support center would provide such help for all striking workers, not only on an ad hoc basis.[6]

Experienced union leaders will weigh these four factors before risking a strike, and when conditions are unfavorable, the leaders will avoid work stoppages if possible. Unfortunately, it is not unusual for union leaders (or their management counterparts) to be mistaken in their judgment of the status of these factors and their implication as to whether or not a strike should be called. In consequence, strikes occur that might have been avoided.

CONDUCTING A STRIKE

Once a strike has been called, there are many things which a local union must do. Generally, however, these things may be grouped under two broad categories. First, the union must conduct the strike against the employer. Persons must be chosen to picket the gates of the employer's plant, and these picketers must be given instructions and assignments. Picket signs must be prepared. Union officials must be placed in charge of the picket lines to see that legal requirements are observed. Spokespersons must be identified to handle relations with the news media.

Second, the union must organize assistance for strikers. When employees go on strike, their paychecks stop. Often health insurance also stops. Some form of financial assistance is necessary for strikers, and the longer the strike, the greater will be the need. There are several sources of assistance for strikers. Many unions maintain strike benefit funds, especially at the national level. A portion of the dues which a member pays to a union goes into a fund to provide financial support to members when they are on strike. Some funds accumulate large sums of money, but when the amount is measured against wages lost in a strike, it often is not really very much. Therefore, strike benefits from the national union are ordinarily made available to locals only under the following conditions: that the strike is approved by the national union as being for a legitimate purpose and that the strikers are shown to have need of the financial assistance. Generally, where strike benefit funds are paid, they average some 20 to 30 percent of the regular earnings of the strikers when they are on the job.

A second source of strike assistance is from public sources. In some states strikers are eligible to receive unemployment insurance benefits from the government, and in some states strikers may receive food stamps or general relief payments. But eligibility for benefits and amounts of assistance depend on the laws of each state. Therefore, in putting together a strike assistance program, union officials must contact public agencies, de-

[6]"Panel Proposes a Permanent Strike Support Center," *AFL-CIO News*, Feb. 28, 1987, p. 3.

termine eligibility rules, then inform the union members who are on strike as to how to apply for benefits.

Finally, assistance for strikers may be available from private agencies, or even from shopkeepers. To obtain such assistance, union officials must meet with the representatives of private charitable agencies in order to notify them of the strike and explain its purpose and the hardship it may cause. If assistance is available, then a method by which the strikers can receive assistance must be set up. Sometimes merchants will extend credit to strikers during the strike. Sometimes local health facilities, such as hospitals or clinics, will also extend credit. Also, other unions or church groups may take up collections for distribution to the strikers and families most in need of aid.

RATIFYING THE AGREEMENT

Many, but not all, unions require formal ratification of a new contract by vote of the membership.[7] Until majority approval of those voting in a ratification election is received, the proposed contract is not final. Union negotiators whose agreement is subject to ratification by the membership are in a position of negotiating without final authority. They may reach an agreement with management on the terms of a new contract and may actually sign the document, but their agreement is not final. It is contingent on a favorable vote of the bargaining unit. Some unions that delegate authority to their negotiators to make a binding agreement nevertheless also have a ratification vote, a procedure that makes the negotiators' authority somewhat irrelevant.

How Ratification Operates

Ratification votes are required in a high proportion of contract negotiations, although they are not required by law. The Taft-Hartley Act did, however, impose on unions a legal duty to represent all members of the bargaining unit fairly, both in negotiations and in the administration of the agreement. Many unions have seized on the ratification vote as a method of demonstrating membership support for the actions of the bargaining committee and as an indication that the union has represented its members fairly.

Ratification elections are held in a wide variety of circumstances. When a local union negotiates an agreement with the employer, the ratification vote may take the form of a ballot in the union hall held after a meeting in which the negotiating committee has explained the terms of the proposed contract. These are relatively simple procedures. In other cases, a ratifica-

---

[7]Clyde Summers, "Ratification of Agreements," in John T. Dunlop and N. W. Chamberlain, eds., *Frontiers of Collective Bargaining* (New York: Harper & Row, 1957), pp. 75–102.

tion vote may be required for a nationwide agreement covering hundreds of thousands of workers. Normally, the vote will be scheduled a week or 10 days in advance, polling places established, and a campaign waged for and against the proposed contract. Just counting the votes may take days following the election, and meanwhile speculation about the fate of the contract proposal is rife.

In some industries a ratification vote is required, but not from the membership itself. Instead, a committee selected by the local unions must ratify the agreement. In steel, for example, the national union's wage policy committee must ratify the agreement, but this form of ratification by delegates is unusual.

What factors cause workers to vote for ratification of a contract and what factors cause them to oppose it? Two researchers studied plant-level data relevant to the 1982 and 1984 auto industry agreements with the UAW. As described by the researchers,

> the results strongly suggest that the more vulnerable workers are to layoff, the more likely they are to vote for ratification of proposed agreements. The results also show, however, that workers tend to vote against ratification in plants in which, other things equal, the labor relations climate is poor. In addition, comparisons across contracts indicate how voting patterns associated with various plant and worker characteristics change when contract proposals shift toward greater job security and away from increases.

Another study, also of the 1982 automobile negotiations, found that workers in plants with large layoffs will vote in favor of a wage concession only if they believe that a concession will save their jobs. Surprisingly, workers in plants with growing or stable employment are actually more likely to vote yes. Finally, the yes vote is smallest in plants with the most adversarial labor relations.[8]

Impact of Ratification Procedures on Collective Bargaining

The ratification procedure introduces some subtle considerations into the negotiations process for both union and management. For the union committee members, it means that their duty to explain and sell the agreement to the membership is given a rigid form. They are forced to take one of three possible positions about the merits of the agreement. First, they may support the agreement by recommending its approval and campaigning for it. Second, they may oppose the agreement and recommend its defeat. Ordinarily, a committee would not recommend rejection

---

[8]Peter Cappelli and W. P. Sterling, "Union Bargaining Decisions and Contracts Ratifications: The 1982 and 1984 Auto Agreements," *Industrial and Labor Relations Review,* 41:2, January 1988, p. 195; and Bruce E. Kaufman and Jorge Martinez-Vazquez, "Voting for Wage Concessions: The Case of the 1982 GM-UAW Negotiations," *Industrial and Labor Relations Review,* 41:2, January 1988, p. 183.

of an agreement unless the employer had asked them to submit an agreement with which they were not in accord. Employers do sometimes ask this, however, because they may believe the rank and file will accept the proposed contract although the union negotiating committee will not. In most cases, but not all, proposals submitted at the employer's request without a recommendation for approval by the union committee are defeated. There is one other instance in which a union committee may recommend against ratification. This occurs when the union committee has negotiated the agreement but then is unwilling to support it. From the employer's viewpoint, this is tantamount to a betrayal. Nonetheless, it does happen. Third, the union committee may assume a position of neutrality on the question of a favorable ratification vote. Again, for this position to be taken after an agreement was reached in supposedly good faith with the employer would seem dishonest. *The behavior of union representatives with respect to the ratification process can either destroy good collective bargaining relations with the employer or strengthen them.*

When a ratification vote is required, both union and management conduct negotiations with a view toward the ratification process. If management anticipates an unfavorable ratification vote, perhaps on the basis of past behavior by the union, it will attempt to withhold its best offer until after a tentative agreement has been reached and rejected by the membership. If the union suspects management of this strategy, a negative ratification vote is a virtual certainty. When this happens, the ratification procedure may be said to have become merely another hurdle the parties must pass in a *pro forma* way on the path to negotiating a final settlement.

Apparently, the ratification process generally does not follow so predictable a sequence. There does not always exist the temptation for workers to refuse to ratify the first settlement brought to them in hopes of getting more in renewed negotiations ("another bite at the apple," as this process is described by negotiators). Most proposed contracts are ratified on the first ballot by the rank and file. The Federal Mediation and Conciliation Service keeps statistics on ratification votes in many negotiations. These statistics show that ordinarily only about 10 percent of votes result in a rejection of the proposed agreement. But there has been a definite cycle in the behavior of ratification votes over time. The percentage of contract rejections reached a peak in the late 1960s and declined thereafter. The reasons for this peak are unclear, but they may have had to do with the generally unsettled environment of the late 1960s and with the especially low unemployment rates of the period.[9] Low unemployment raised workers' expectations for salary

---

[9]William E. Simkin, "Refusals to Ratify Contracts," *Industrial and Labor Relations Review,* 21:4, July 1968. See also Donald R. Burke and Lester Rubin, "Is Contract Rejection a Major Collective Bargaining Problem?" *Industrial and Labor Relations Review,* 26:3, January 1973.

increases and allowed them considerable ease of locating new jobs during work stoppages.

HOW BARGAINING STRUCTURE AFFECTS ORGANIZATION FOR BARGAINING

Superficially, all unions may appear to bargain in the same way. Initially, the local selects a bargaining committee and establishes a procedure to review the proposed terms of a new contract. Then the bargaining committee sits down to negotiate with the employer. Thus, it would appear that bargaining is essentially a process conducted by local unions and employers, who decide what the terms of employment will be. This is what actually occurs in some situations in which a local union is independent (i.e., not part of a national union) or has considerable autonomy. But bargaining by independent or autonomous locals is not the most common situation, so that the view of collective bargaining as depending most on the locals is, as we have said, superficial. *In many instances, the local union is controlled, influenced, or constrained in important ways by the national union with which it is affiliated.* There are four basic structures of collective bargaining on the union side:

1 *Bargaining by the national union* with a limited role for the local unions
2 *Bargaining by locals*, but with national union coordination or control, so-called pattern bargaining
3 *Bargaining by councils of locals* under national union supervision
4 *Independent or autonomous bargaining* by locals (discussed above)

National Negotiations

The national union becomes most intimately involved in negotiations when it is itself party to major aspects of the agreement with an employer (or employers), as, for example, in the steel and automobile industries. In these industries, the national union itself negotiates the economic package (i.e., wages and fringe benefits) with the employers. In industries in which national negotiations do not occur, the role of the national union is reduced and that of the local correspondingly enhanced. Yet even in this situation, the national union may be deeply involved in the bargaining process at the local level. The national union may provide assistance in negotiations at the request of the local union, or it may require the local to submit its proposed agreement to the national union for approval. This latter procedure is especially common when some form of pattern bargaining exists. The national will then insist upon coordinating the activities of the local unions in negotiation in order to obtain the best agreements possible and to prevent undue concessions to the employers. When individual plants of a multiplant corporation are involved, the employer will be doing the same thing, of course.

Pattern Bargaining

Pattern bargaining involving local unions in a single company or industry is an important and widespread form of collective bargaining in this country. It is important to know when and where it exists because the individual collective bargaining agreements may give no hint of it. Each agreement may be signed by a local union and the individual plant or company, and may not make reference to the national union, to other plants of the company, or to other employers. It may therefore appear to an uninformed observer to be the result of autonomous or unconstrained bargaining by local parties. This mistaken view of collective bargaining in many industries is often conveyed by discussions of bargaining that stress the organization and behavior of the local union, as if it operated as an independent body. This is usually not the case at all. As we discuss the ways that local unions organize themselves for bargaining, this word of caution needs to be remembered.

Council Bargaining

When several local unions negotiate through a council structure, there is no need for each local to pick a negotiating committee or to establish a contract review procedure. Each local's officers participate in a selection process through which a bargaining team for the council is assembled. In some instances all the locals involved are represented on the bargaining team; in others, only a few locals are represented. There is a major distinction to be made, however, between the case in which several locals of the same national union negotiate through a council and the case in which several locals of different national unions negotiate together. In the first case, the national union will exert great influence on the council and its activities, even to the extent, sometimes, of appointing the chief officers of the council. In the second case, however, the nationals involved exert less influence and the council structure itself is inherently less stable. Each local involved is likely to demand a voice on the negotiating team, and failing to receive it, may resign from the council. As a practical matter, the larger locals, or those made up of skilled tradespeople, will seek to dominate the council and probably will succeed to a substantial degree. The council of locals from various national unions is, therefore, probably the most fragile of the four structures listed above. In some instances, however, it has endured and operated for many years, especially in shipbuilding and construction in some cities (Detroit, Cleveland, New Orleans, and Dallas among them).

In general, union organization for bargaining is affected by bargaining structure. The relative authority and responsibility of the local union and the national union are very much a matter of how agreements are actually reached, not of the protocol of who signs specific agreements. Organization for bargaining on the union side is a very complex picture in which a generalization can be made only at the risk of oversimplification. Still, brevity requires generalization, so that in the pages that follow we describe matters as they affect the greatest number of workers and their employers.

BARGAINING AND THE UNION LEADERSHIP

Unions do much more than negotiate collective bargaining agreements. The bargaining process must, therefore, be integrated in some manner into a union's overall functioning. How is this to be done, and by whom?

Primarily, the task of integrating bargaining with other aspects of the union's activities is the responsibility of the union's full-time officers. These officers are elected by the membership for specific terms, as was described in Chapter 3. Union leaders always have a dual responsibility:

1 Responsibility to the desire of the rank-and-file workers who are members of the union
2 Responsibility to the needs of the union as an ongoing organization

In the area of collective bargaining, these two roles of union officers may come into conflict. For this reason it cannot simply be said that the function of union officers in bargaining is to try to get their members what they want. They must also think ahead to the long-term health of the union itself.

Representing Desires of the Membership

An example may help to clarify how the conflict between an officer's duties to the rank and file and to the union itself may arise. Suppose that in a local union there are many young workers and few older workers. In anticipation of upcoming negotiations with the employer, the young workers decide to demand a reduction in pension benefits in order to bring about increased wage levels. "After all," the young workers may say, "we're not likely to be here years from now to collect our pension benefits, so let's take the money now." Since there is a majority of young workers in the bargaining unit, they are in a position to insist that the union negotiators follow their preferences. Yet union officers will see that if the young workers obtain their desires, then the older workers will be embittered, and there will exist the threat of a deep split in the local. With the passage of time such a split could make the local ineffective or even destroy it. Their obligation to the union as a whole, as distinct from any particular majority of its rank and file, requires them to oppose this initiative by the young workers.

Another example involves a situation that is not so obvious, but one that occurs frequently. Suppose the majority of the members of a local union decides to seek a very large wage increase. The union officials, or national union representatives, may be certain that the increase will bankrupt the employer within a year or so. When the employer explains this to the union membership, they profess not to care; after all, they can always get work elsewhere, they say, and in the meantime they will live well. Since this is what the workers want, should the union officials support them? The answer most union leaders would probably give is no, even though they might be voted out of their positions at the next election if they refused. Instead, the union officials have an obligation to attempt to preserve the local union as an institution. This obligation is canceled, many union leaders would say, only if the company cannot support the minimum standards of employment that the national union recognizes in the industry and/or area involved.

Ignoring Desires of the Membership

Some union leaders err at the opposite extreme in negotiations. They pay little or no attention to the views of the union membership, imposing their own views on what should be included in the labor agreement. Employers, who sometimes unfortunately allow themselves to become very isolated from the views of their employees, charge union leaders with ignoring the desires of the membership more often than is justified. Still, it does occur.

In the end, whether a union leader is a demagogue, a tyrant, or simply a responsible union official is largely a matter of judgment. The answer depends on what are believed to be the legitimate interests of the union membership. Legitimate interests may be characterized as honest self-interest, as opposed to greed. One's own individual opinion on what constitutes the appropriate self-interest of union members will determine one's opinion of the fairness of leaders in defending that self-interest.

Unfortunately, in our society there are not many disinterested, knowledgeable third parties to make these judgments (although people who are not qualified by neutrality or knowledge do offer their views). Most union officials must make judgments about their own behavior and follow their own conscience. *In the United States our system of largely free, unregulated collective bargaining means that we as a nation must live with the results of these individuals' decisions on how they should act in positions of responsibility.* This is, of course, just as true of the judgments and behavior of business people as of labor leaders.

Duties of a Responsible Union Leader

What may be said about the duties of a leader who attempts to be responsible in the bargaining process? What should such a person bring to the negotiating process that rank-and-file members of a union negotiating committee are unlikely to offer?

There are three major contributions that responsible union officials can make. They should provide

1 A concern for the future against the needs of the present
2 A concern for broader interests than those of the bargaining unit directly involved, including the interests of other local unions, of the national union, and perhaps of the industry as a whole
3 A concern for the health of collective bargaining as a process against the short-term interests of either union or management.

CHAPTER SUMMARY

The organization for bargaining in a local union involves various stages and considerations. The initial choice of a bargaining committee is very much part of the internal politics of the union and involves balancing the interests of different groups. The choice also has implications for political careers within the union. The function of the bargaining committee is to bring about an agreement between the company and the union and thus involves expertise in negotiating and the ability to justify the agreement to union members. Many unions have characteristic ways of formulating demands. Sometimes a wish list is compiled at a mass meeting, then presented to an employer. More frequently, demands are presented in a carefully pared-down form. In most negotiations the union wants to discuss its demands as separate items, whereas the employer first considers the cost of the total package.

To strike or not to strike is a serious decision for a union. A strike is dangerous because there may be unforeseeable consequences such as violence, substantial legal costs, hardship, and loss of morale for union members. Several factors affect the outcome of a strike and are not always correctly weighed by union and management leaders. These include the cost to the union and the availability of assistance, as well as the support or opposition of public officials and the local community.

Many unions require formal ratification of a new contract by vote of the membership. The union negotiator is thus in a position of negotiating without final authority and must explain and sell the agreement to the membership. Once an agreement has been reached in good faith with an employer, it is important that the negotiator sincerely support the agreement, but this does not always happen. Ratification is an unpredictable process. There may be problems of membership division over a contract.

At its simplest, bargaining is a process conducted between local unions and employers to decide the terms of employment. However, in many instances, local unions are very much controlled or constrained by the national union with which they are affiliated. Different bargaining structures or arrangements give the national union and other local unions varying degrees of influence. Pattern bargaining and bargaining by a local union with behind-the-scenes national union control are important and widespread forms of negotiating.

Union leaders have responsibility both to the rank-and-file members of the union and to the needs of the union as an ongoing organization. Sometimes these responsibilities conflict. The union membership is often impatient and may tend to give priority to short-term benefits over the long-term health of the union or of the collective bargaining process itself.

QUESTIONS FOR THOUGHT AND DISCUSSION

1 What relationship should a union want with its members? With management?

2 What strategy should a union follow in negotiations? Should it ask for a lot or only what it expects to get? Why?

3 "A good labor leader never gets into a position in which it is necessary to have a strike." Do you agree or disagree with this statement? Why?

4 "If union leaders do not get the members to ratify a proposed agreement, they can always go back to the company for a better deal." Is this statement right or wrong? Why?

5 What is a union official's proper role in labor negotiations? Should the official simply represent the wishes of union members? Does the official have a leadership function? Does the official have any responsibility to the employer?

6 In your own words, what does it mean that choice of a bargaining committee and the process of bargaining are very much part of the political process of a union?

7 Why, in formulating demands, do unions pay so little attention to working out the total package cost? Would it be in the union's interest to do so?

8 Is having a strike evidence that union leadership has failed in bargaining? Why or why not?

9 Why do workers vote to ratify a proposed contract settlement? To oppose it?

10 Should strikers receive public assistance: unemployment insurance payments, food stamps? Why or why not?

11 What are the various forms of bargaining structure? How does the bargaining structure affect the local union's organization for bargaining? Why is the form of the bargaining structure not always apparent to outside observers?

SELECTED READING

Estey, Martin, *The Unions: Structure, Development and Management,* 3d ed. (New York: Harcourt Brace Jovanovich, 1981).

Sayles, Leonard R., and George Strauss, *The Local Union: Its Place in the Industrial Plant* (New York: Harper, 1953).

MANAGEMENT PREPARATIONS FOR NEGOTIATIONS

WHAT DOES MANAGEMENT WANT?

A common view is that management has no other purpose than to maximize profits. As a corollary of this view, many believe that in collective bargaining management simply seeks to obtain the least expensive settlement. In fact, the objectives of management are usually more complicated than these commonly held views suggest. Fletcher L. Byron, then chairman of the board of Koppers Company, Inc., once responded to those who described business as nothing more than profit maximization in the following way:

> I do not believe that my mission is solely to make a profit. Any fool can do that—for a while.
>
> I don't even believe that we should seek to maximize profits . . . . Companies whose profits are out of line with market conditions . . . . are only inviting us to come in and compete . . . . with them.
>
> . . . . Profits are to a corporation what breathing is to a human being. We cannot live without breathing, and a corporation cannot live without profits. But breathing is not the sole purpose of life . . . . and profits are not the sole purpose of . . . . business management.[1]

Business executives pay attention to profits, but their motivations are more complex than profit maximization. Other general objectives (sometimes related to profit maximization but sometimes diverging from it) include the survival of the firm for the long term, development of the capaci-

---

[1]Fletcher L. Byron, "Let's Close the Gap," a speech before the American Assembly of Collegiate Schools of Business, Apr. 24, 1975 (mimeographed).

ties of the firm's management and its employees, and community service. Not all business representatives express these various objectives in the same way, nor do all firms give equal weight to each. As a result, a lively controversy is continually waged over the motivations of business.

Views such as those expressed by Byron are less commonly stated today than when Byron uttered them almost 20 years ago. They are not less widely held, just less often articulated. The reason is that the United States has been going through a period of militancy by shareholders and their representatives in which profitability has been endorsed as the sole legitimate purpose of a business. Managers rarely share that view, because they know that many other people than investors contribute to the success of a business and must feel that it is also responsive to their needs.

In collective bargaining, firms have the following primary objectives:

Not to Be Put at a Disadvantage vis-à-vis Their Competitors   A firm does not want to have higher labor costs than its competitors. This goal is generally consistent with profit maximization, but it is not the same thing as seeking the cheapest possible collective bargaining agreement.

Firms would often like to pay lower wages than their competitors, if possible. But obtaining such an advantage over competition is not as significant as *not being put at a disadvantage*. The former would assist the firm's profitability, but being put at a disadvantage would threaten its very existence. The two are not of equal importance.

Many companies which negotiate with unions today have nonunion competitors. This was not as common in many industries in the past. But as we saw in earlier chapters there has been a significant decline in degree of union organization. As a result, many unionized firms are now very conscious of the labor costs of their nonunion competitors and are determined if possible to keep their own costs down. Generally unionized firms have higher labor costs than nonunionized firms. For example, in manufacturing unionized firms not only pay higher wages, generally, but provide more and costly benefits. For example, unionized manufacturing firms devote 33.6 percent of total payroll to benefits, against 29.3 percent for nonunion firms.[2] So a unionized firm tries to keep its wages and benefits from getting so far ahead of nonunion competitors that the company gets into financial difficulty.

A company may also have a different objective: simply to preserve management prerogatives against the union. The director of corporate industrial relations of a large paper company listed the five worst things, in his view, a company could agree to with a union: joint union-management administration of pension and health care plans, cost-of-living allowances, increased paid time off (holidays, vacations, etc.), specific work assign-

---

[2] Kay E. Anderson, Philip M. Doyle, and Albert E. Schwenk, "Measuring Union-Nonunion Earnings Differentials, " *Monthly Labor Review,* 114:6, June 1990, p. 36.

ments to individual unions, and union representation on corporate boards of directors.[3] (Each of these topics is considered later in this book.)

Why does management wish to preserve management prerogatives? There are several reasons. One is to preserve flexibility to meet changing conditions. Union agreements may limit flexibility in two ways: directly, by prohibiting management from taking certain actions; and indirectly, by forcing management to go through a lengthy process of discussion or negotiations before making changes, even though management eventually gets to make them. A second reason is that by preserving its prerogatives management retains more power in the workplace than otherwise, and power is often an end in itself in human relations. Finally, management may wish to preserve prerogatives for what are essentially philosophical reasons: the view that management's role in the workplace is to make decisions and supervise their being carried out, and that union agreements improperly limit management in its role. This executive's list includes items which other managers think should be negotiated with a union.

To Keep Shareholders Happy   When we speak of the objectives of a firm, we blur the distinction between the managers and the owners. In some circumstances, shareholders are not concerned with the details of labor negotiations. But sometimes—for example, in industries in which labor costs are quite a substantial part of overall costs—shareholders will be sensitive. A high wage settlement might cause the return on invested capital to fall. The stock market will recognize this and put a cash value on the shares that is low relative to other otherwise similar investments

When shareholders have cause to be unhappy with the labor bargain managers drive, the managers may lose their jobs. Managers who want to keep their jobs simply have to cut costs. In this way investors, or the capital market, may impose a severe constraint on managerial behavior.

To Pursue Its Chosen Labor Policy   A firm may wish to be seen as a good employer with satisfied employees quite apart from any measures to improve profits directly. It might wish to follow this policy regardless of whether it is unionized or not. (We saw in Chapter 6 that several major nonunion firms are, in fact, better-standards employers.) But a firm cannot gain the good regard of its employees simply by attempting to obtain low-cost agreements. In fact, a firm may not gain employee regard even by paying high wages and providing good fringes and working conditions. These items may be provided and the labor relations climate still be very unsatisfactory. In order to obtain good employee morale, the company must pay attention to personal relationships as well as to compensation levels.

---

[3]Charles S. Loughran, "Five of the Worst Agreements You Can Make with a Union," *Wall Street Journal,* Dec. 10, 1984, p. 26. See also Loughran, *Negotiating a Labor Contract: A Management Handbook* (Washington, D.C.: BNA Books, 1984).

The General Electric Company has had a significant experience in this area. GE believes itself to be a fair, even generous, employer. Yet in the late 1940s it experienced bitter strikes. Though the strikes were settled and the pay increases employees received were substantial, the company nevertheless received a black eye with many of its unionized employees. For several years thereafter, GE tried to circumvent the unions to convince its employees directly that the company was a good employer. This policy was referred to as "Boulwarism" after its architect, Lemuel Boulware, a vice president of GE.[4] These efforts had mixed results at best. In the late 1960s, after the loss of litigation arising out of the company's policy and after changes in top management, GE abandoned Boulwarism. Relationships with unions and employees since have improved.

As union membership has declined in recent years, the labor relations function in American businesses has also changed. In many companies labor relations policies have become less centralized at the corporate level and instead have been decentralized to various operating units. Labor relations staff have become more focused on complex, technical aspects of labor relations, and there has been less innovation from the labor relations staff in many companies.[5]

A proposition has been advanced that the industrial relations approach of American firms is largely a consequence of their business strategies, and researchers have found some support for this proposition. A study of workplace industrial relations policies among minimills (small factories) in the American steel industry in 1988–1989 found that the industrial relations approaches in the mills could be broadly characterized as emphasizing either cost reduction or employee commitment (i.e., higher quality and productivity in production). Similarly, the business strategies of the mills appeared to stress either the manufacture of few products in large quantities and at low cost, or alternatively, more flexible manufacturing of multiple products sold on a basis other than cost—such as special features, highest quality, or quick availability. Those plants stressing high volume and low cost emphasized cost reduction in their industrial relations; those plants pursuing flexibility and quality in their products stressed employee commitment in their industrial relations.[6]

Generally, however, surveys have demonstrated that most firms are not very successful in establishing objectives for their labor relations. In a survey of large companies the hardest questions for the executives to answer were these: "What are labor relations executives trying to foster?" "What

---

[4]Lemuel R. Boulware, *Statesmanship in Industrial Relations* (New York: National Association of Manufacturers, 1964).

[5]E. Tatum Christiansen, "Challenges in the Management of Diversified Companies: The Changing Face of Corporate Labor Relations," *Human Resources Management*, 26:3–4, Fall–Winter 1987–1988, pp. 242–259.

[6]Jeffrey B. Arthur, "The Link between Business Strategy and Industrial Relations in American Steel Minimills," *Industrial and Labor Relations Review*, 45:3, April 1992, pp. 488ff.

outcome is sought?" "Is there any specific objective for the company?" "How is a labor relations vice president evaluated?" Companies gave indistinct responses, such as "We are trying to keep things under control" and "We want no surprises in our labor relations." And most companies reported that they evaluated their labor relations executives only informally, without using financial measures such as the contribution of the labor relations function to profitability. Observing this somewhat cavalier attitude, one observer commented, "It need not be over zealously claimed that industrial relations constitute a strategic variable" of the firm.[7]

WHO NEGOTIATES FOR MANAGEMENT?

Collective bargaining for American companies is generally conducted by labor relations specialists with the advice and assistance of operating managers. But collective bargaining may involve issues of major importance to a corporation. As a result, in some instances, top corporate executives get involved in collective bargaining. Ordinarily, however, top corporate officers remain at a distance from negotiations and receive only periodic reports on their progress; the negotiations are delegated to lower levels of management. What factors determine the roles of various levels of management in collective bargaining?

In larger companies labor relations are generally delegated to staff specialists. Among the functions of these specialists is to conduct collective bargaining negotiations. Some large corporations try to push the labor relations function as far down the line as possible. In some firms each plant manager is in charge of labor relations. The plant manager either conducts negotiations or assigns the task to members of his or her staff. Corporate headquarters may monitor labor relations in the plants directly or simply as part of the factors contributing to the overall profitability (or loss) from the plant.

Most multiplant companies are not able to delegate the labor relations function so completely, however. They fear that the union, or unions, that represent their employees will keep track of developments at each plant and use breakthroughs achieved in one plant as the basis for gains in other plants. To prevent this "whipsawing," most large corporations have a central labor relations staff oversee negotiations at all plants.

Small firms, and small plants that are in large firms, often lack industrial relations specialists. Studies have been made to determine if the lack of such specialists on the management side causes labor relations to be less

---

[7]David Lewin, "Industrial Relations as a Strategic Variable," in M. M. Kleiner et al., eds., *Human Resources and the Performance of the Firm* (Madison, Wis.: Industrial Relations Research Association, 1987), p. 36. See also Audrey Freedman, *Managing Labor Relations*, Report No. 765 (New York: The Conference Board, 1979), pp. 71–72. See also E. Tatum Christiansen, "Strategy, Structure and Labor Relations Performance," *Human Resources Management*, 22:1–2, Spring–Summer 1983, pp. 155–168.

effective in smaller plants. These studies have shown that the lack of specialists is partly offset by the advantages of intimate contact between management and the employees in small plants. Also, small plants are more likely than large plants to have a cohesive work force. Because of these two factors, labor relations in small plants are often better than those in large firms.[8] In part because few major executives make labor relations one of their responsibilities, larger companies, mostly multiplant, in assembly manufacturing (autos, furniture, food, home appliances, electronics, textiles, metal fabricating) have far higher strike rates than smaller, single-plant companies.[9]

Certain aspects of collective bargaining seem to require top management's oversight and involvement, even in large companies. Among these factors are

1 *The cost impact* A collective bargaining settlement can be very expensive for a firm, and once the agreement is reached, it is too late for top management to moderate a very big settlement. Chief executives often retain the right to review and approve or disapprove the terms of a proposed settlement with the union.

2 *Internal conflicts* In the course of negotiations, disputes may arise between labor relations staff and the company's production managers, a condition that might require settlement by top management.

3 *The standards of the corporation* The visions and values of a company may become involved in negotiations so that top management may wish to influence the discussions.

4 *Attitudes of personnel* The responsibility of the corporation to maintain its human organization, including the attitudes of management and employees, is involved.[10]

While it is rare for top management to actually sit at the bargaining table, the items just cited sometimes compel their ad hoc intervention.

PREPARING FOR NEGOTIATIONS

Employers must prepare for collective bargaining negotiations just as unions do. Unfortunately, many employers seem to do little more than send a negotiating team with no advance preparation to the table to find out what the union wants. Not surprisingly, negotiations that are begun in this manner often seem to get off on the wrong foot. Management preparation for bargaining should be careful and well thought out. This section describes

---

[8]See, for example, Sherrill Cleland, *The Influence of Plant Size on Industrial Relations* (Princeton, N.J.: Princeton University Industrial Relations Section, 1955).

[9]C. Frederick Eisele, "Organization Size, Technology and Frequency of Strikes," *Industrial and Labor Relations Review*, 27:4, July 1974, pp. 560–571.

[10]See Peter F. Drucker, *Management: Tasks, Responsibilities, Practices* (New York: Harper & Row, 1974), pp. 611–612.

the process of careful preparation by management. It cannot be said that management always conducts its preparations in this manner. But managements who do prepare carefully have a better time of it in negotiations.

So does the union. This may seem surprising, since a union may be better able to take advantage of an ill-prepared employer than one well prepared for negotiations. But collective bargaining is not simply a contest. It is also a problem-solving activity. Unions often challenge management on issues that trouble employees, counting on management to be able to supply facts about the matter and even to come up with some solution to the problem. An ill-prepared management cannot do these things. The union becomes frustrated, and bargaining degenerates into acrimonious disputes. To avoid such a result is usually in the interests of both parties. For this reason, good management preparation for negotiations is vital both to the company and to the union.

Computers are increasingly valuable to both management and unions in preparing for negotiations. Computer files are created on each provision of the contract, and on provisions in the agreements of other firms and unions. The computer makes it fast and easy to retrieve such materials for use in negotiations. Also, some firms use computers to analyze the cost of different proposals by the union, especially in the very complicated area of employee benefits.

Basic Preparations

There are three steps basic to each employer's preparations for negotiations:

1 *The company must pick the best-suited negotiating and backup teams possible*. It must be especially careful to select people temperamentally suited for negotiations. Labor negotiations can be lengthy, tiring, and stressful situations.

An ideal negotiating team is made up of knowledgeable people who are also temperamentally suited to negotiations. However, because such ideal individuals are not always available, a negotiations team requires a balance of the two types.

2 *A company should, if possible, commit what some writers have called "the extravagance of over-preparations."*[11] It should extensively research and prepare its own positions. For example, the company should prepare a booklet describing grievances filed under the term of the existing contract, arbitration awards issued, if any, and how those have made an impact on the application of the contract. Then resulting proposals for altering the contract should be identified. Finally, the company should plan carefully for the possible eventuality of a strike.

[11]Herbert I. Rothenberg and Steven B. Silverman, *Labor Unions, How To: Avoid Them, Beat Them, Out-Negotiate Them, Live with Them, Unload Them* (Elkins Park, Pa.: Management Relations, 1973), p. 288.

3 *The company should plan the course that it wishes negotiations to follow, and, as much as possible, stick to that course.* Decisions made in the heat of a negotiations session that basically alter the company's negotiating strategy are apt to be erroneous. Consistency in following a planned course is the better approach, although care should be taken not to be unduly rigid should conditions change materially. The company should plan in advance the issues it wishes to discuss and the sequence of dealing with those issues. It is very important that the company not simply wait to hear the union's demands before preparing its own position. Instead, the company should be prepared to take the initiative in its own list of prepared changes in the contract.

Items to Prepare

The following items are illustrative of those prepared for negotiators by many companies:

1 A *summary* of the previous collective bargaining negotiations with the union.

2 A *book* containing the existing collective bargaining agreement broken up into its separate clauses. A discussion of experience with each clause, pro and con, and changes to be proposed by the company are included. When it is possible to anticipate union demands for changes, these are also identified.

3 *The internal data* of the firm with respect to its labor costs, identified by clause of the contract.

4 *Data* regarding the labor costs of other firms, both competitors, wherever they are located, and noncompeting firms in the same geographic area.[12]

5 *Information* about the union, its leadership, history, finances, and any other special circumstances bearing on the union's role in the negotiation.

6 A *list* of the union's expected demands and their impact on the company.

7 A *list* of resource people in the company who are most likely to know, or be able to ascertain quickly, the impact of proposed contract changes on the company's operations and costs.

In recent years management and labor have been applying computer technology to preparations for bargaining. Contract clauses from agreements involving various companies and unions and economic information have been stored in computers and comparisons made of clauses and

---

[12]Bruce Morse, *How to Negotiate the Labor Agreement* (Detroit: Trends Publishing, 1974).

economic data. These computer outputs are then used as background material by the negotiators.[13]

Sources of Economic Information

The importance of various types of economic data will vary widely from company to company, from union to union, and from industry to industry, but the basic package of necessary information includes wages and fringe benefit levels; economic conditions, both nationally and in a particular industry or company; changes in the cost of living; family budgets for a reasonable standard of living; and increases in productivity and profits.

While the economic facts may not point to specific answers in bargaining, they usually can help narrow the difference, reduce the area of controversy, and indicate the general range of a reasonable settlement. But relying on such material too heavily may lead to an economic debate which strays far from the merits of the negotiations. Negotiations should not be conducted on the basis of who can put together the most impressive-looking or greatest quantity of data.

Economic information need not be formal or exhaustive to be useful. Its value does not depend on quantity or the use of technical language.

All data have limitations. They should not be accepted without question—and this applies both to material presented by management and to material selected for the union's own information. Being aware of the limitations includes knowing who is covered and who isn't, how old the material is, whether it's representative or specially selected, what is left out, and the like.

Selection and interpretation are important. Some types of information are pertinent or useful; others are not; much depends on the light in which it is put. It is not enough merely to put some facts on the table; the most appropriate ones must be chosen and they must be put in perspective.

Inaccurate or weak data can easily be turned against the user. Similarly, unfavorable data cannot be ignored if the negotiator is to be able to respond.

Many of the most useful publications about price and wage developments are issued by the U.S. Department of Labor's Bureau of Labor Statistics (BLS). Table 15-1 lists seven major BLS publications and indicates how they may be obtained.[14]

---

[13]Abraham J. Siegel, ed., *The Impact of Computers on Collective Bargaining* (Cambridge, Mass.: MIT Press, 1970); and M. J. Fox and K. R. Meisinger, "More Effective Bargaining through Use of Computers," *Journal of Collective Negotiations in the Public Sector,* 3:1, Winter 1974, pp. 77–90.

[14]The collection of data is important to both managements and unions. A good description of the use and limitations of economic data in negotiations is found in "Collective Bargaining—Lining Up the Facts," *AFL-CIO American Federationist,* 79:3, March 1972.

TABLE 15-1   BLS PUBLICATIONS

Consumer Price Index—Monthly report of the Bureau of Labor Statistics (BLS), which provides data on changes in the cost of living over the past year.

Urban Family Budgets—Annual report of BLS, which provides data on changes in the economic position of an urban family.

Employment and Earnings—Monthly report with information on average hourly earnings for manufacturing in each state and most larger cities.

Area Wage Survey—Reports published separately for some 88 cities each year on wages paid certain clerical, maintenance, and laborer-type occupations.

Industry Wage Survey—Periodic detailed wage and fringe benefit data for specific industries. Information is provided on jobs common to that industry.

Union Wage Scales—Quarterly report on union building trade scales in 100 large cities and annual report on construction, printing, local transit, and local trucking.

Current Wage Developments—Monthly report on recent collective bargaining settlements with a short summary of wage and benefit changes.

The above publications can be obtained by writing the Superintendent of Documents, U.S. Government Printing Office, Washington, D.C. 20402. Press releases are available from the Bureau of Labor Statistics, U.S. Department of Labor, Washington, D.C. 20210.

Scheduling Preparations for Negotiations

As we saw in the preceding pages, preparing for negotiations is a major matter. Preparations involve many topics and many people. In order to coordinate and accomplish all these activities within the time available, a schedule must be worked out. Table 15-2 describes such a schedule of committee meetings as worked out by one large company. The preparations for negotiations began some 11 months before the expiration date of the agreement. In some industries, corporate preparations consume even longer periods.

The labor relations vice president coordinates the full activities of this company in preparation for negotiations. The meetings of the various committees and meetings with the plant managers and safety engineers are scheduled so that the vice president may devote full attention to one meeting at a time. In this way, all the meetings will not be jammed into the last few weeks before the contract expires. As shown in Table 15-2, negotiations begin in March and the agreement expires at the end of May. A 2-month period for formal negotiations prior to the expiration of an agreement is not unduly lengthy, but it could be too brief if there are many complicated issues to be resolved.

Figure 15-1 describes the activities of a labor relations policy committee in preparing for negotiations. It is this committee which, under the oversight of the management policy committee, is responsible for developing the bargaining strategy of the company. It accomplishes this by relying on the reports of the various other committees regarding their specialized areas and by combining the reports into an overall picture of the upcoming negotiations.

TABLE 15-2   A SCHEDULE OF COMPANY PREPARATIONS FOR NEGOTIATIONS (AGREEMENT EXPIRES MAY 31)

	June	July	Aug.	Sept.	Oct.	Nov.	Dec.	Jan.	Feb.	Mar.	Apr.	May
Management Policy Committee (president, financial vice president, administrative vice president, labor relations vice president) meets quarterly and sets up other committees	o			o			o			o		
Labor Relations Policy Committee (general counsel, labor relations vice president, and others)	o		o	o	o	o	o		o	o		
Benefits Committee (personnel director and others)		o	o	o		o		o	o	o		
Wages Committee			o		o		o		o			
Health and Safety Committee			o		o		o		o			
Equal Employment Opportunity Committee				o		o		o				
Meetings with plant managers			o				o					
Meetings with safety engineers				o			o					
Strike Reaction Committee						o			o	o	o	
Negotiations take place									o	o	o	o

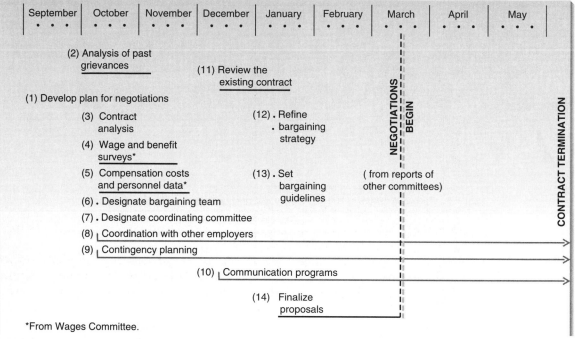

FIGURE 15-1   Activities of the policy committee. (*Source:* Adapted from Ronald L. Miller, "Preparation for Negotiations," *Personnel Journal,* 57:1, January 1978, p. 38.)

In some companies with only a few agreements to negotiate and a duration of agreements of 3 years or so, the schedule is simple and straightforward. In other companies with many agreements to negotiate, there may be many such schedules in progress simultaneously. And when agreements are of only 1 year's duration, there is virtually no pause between preparations for one negotiation and preparations for the next. The lives of labor relations executives and union leaders can therefore be very hectic.

A special problem for management is in the area of communication to managerial personnel affected by labor negotiations but not directly involved in them. Plant managers, superintendents, and foremen fall into this category. A part of the schedule for preparations for negotiations presented in Table 15-2 involves meetings with plant managers and safety engineers, and perhaps supervisors and foremen as well. These consultations are a recognition of these managers' knowledge of first-line relations and of the fact that changes in the collective bargaining agreement may have important effects on them. But company negotiators are rarely able to go much beyond infrequent meetings with supervisory personnel. To involve these people directly in the negotiations is ordinarily too costly in terms of lost production. A partial compromise between full involvement in negotiations and no involvement is obtained by giving supervisors more input to the negotiators on certain issues than on others, especially those issues dealing with work standards and the handling of grievances.

MULTIEMPLOYER BARGAINING

In many sectors of the economy employers do not negotiate with unions on a single-employer basis. Instead, companies form associations that bargain with the union (or unions). This pattern of bargaining is characteristic of construction, coal mining, the maritime trades, trucking, clothing manufacture, and printing. Employer association bargaining characterizes many more industries in Europe, and American-based multinational firms often participate in association bargaining in Europe. At first there was some doubt as to whether American firms that did not (and often would not) engage in association bargaining in the United States would agree to do so in Europe. But apparently many of these American companies have adjusted to association bargaining in Europe.[15]

Association bargaining has its own special problems of preparation for negotiations, which differ from those encountered by the single company. This section explores some of the special problems of association bargaining.

Resolving Internal Disputes

The most characteristic problem of association bargaining arises in the potential for conflict between members of the association. The need to gain strength vis-à-vis the union causes the separate firms to join together in an association for bargaining. But many other circumstances tend to divide the companies and prevent their taking a common stand. In the first place, the firms are normally competitors. They often mistrust each other and do not want negotiations with the unions to end in a contract that benefits any other firm more.

In the second place, the firms have different characteristics and different problems, which sometimes cause them to pursue conflicting goals in bargaining. Some firms are large, some small. Some firms may be very profitable, some almost insolvent. Some firms utilize the newest technology, some the oldest. Some firms have a history of cordial relations with the unions, some a history of bitter disputes. Some firms have the loyalty of their employees, some do not. The union, which is usually aware of these differences among the firms, may exploit them for its own purposes.

In the third place, in some industries there is a tradition of treachery among the employers. In the supermarket industry, for example, such behavior is perhaps best exemplified by one large supermarket chain's withdrawal from a major metropolitan area shortly after it agreed to an unexpectedly high and pattern-setting wage settlement for

[15]Solomon Barkin, *Worker Militancy* (New York; Praeger, 1975), pp. 386–387.

that area. Its withdrawal, of course, left its competitors to pay the higher compensation.[16]

At the outset of preparations for negotiations the association must attempt to resolve internal disputes, reach a common position to present to the union, and agree on a joint course of action should a strike occur. Figure 15-2 presents a simplified model of multiemployer bargaining and illustrates the processes we have described. The diagram shows that the union has access to the individual companies that make up the association. It is very common for disputes between the association and the union to be resolved by individual companies' splitting from the association (either in return for favorable treatment from the union or simply in pursuit of a company's own special interests) until the association collapses. To meet this threat, employer associations often adopt bylaws that legally bind each company to the association's position in bargaining and provide a method by which the association decides on its bargaining stand. A company that fails to support the association as required by the bylaws may subject itself to a financial penalty.

Selecting Bargaining Representatives

Who should represent an association in bargaining with a union? Some associations have only a few member firms, so that the bargaining team can be made up of a representative from each one. This greatly simplifies matters. But most associations have so many member firms that if each were separately represented on the bargaining team, it would be unreasonably large. If only a few firms are to be represented directly in negotiations with the union, how are they to be selected, and how are they to be held accountable to the association as a whole for their actions?

Many associations have established a dues structure to pay for a permanent staff for the association. The staff director (or a person designated by the director) generally participates in collective bargaining negotiations as the representative of all firms in the association. But many business people or firms that belong to associations have reservations about allowing an association staff director very much authority in dealings with the unions. After all, they might say, the director isn't a business person and doesn't really know what is important to business people. Furthermore, the director is someone business people hire, not, like themselves, an officer of a firm. The association director is not the type of person, it might be said, who should be trusted with labor negotiations.

In reply, supporters of a strong role for the association director in the bargaining process point out that reliance on him or her in negotiations offers certain benefits to the association:

---

[16]James W. Driscoll, "Joint Labor-Management Committee of the Retail Food Industry," report to the U.S. Department of Labor, Apr. 18, 1978, p. 15.

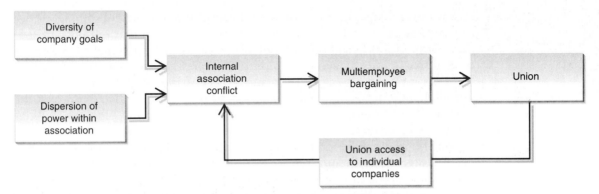

FIGURE 15-2   Multiemployer bargaining (*Source:* Adapted from Thomas A. Kochan, *Resolving Internal Management Conflicts for Labor negotiations,* Chicago: International Personnel Management Association, 1973, p. 9.)

1 *The opportunity to have a full-time professional with the knowledge and skill necessary to the job of representing the companies.* Since unions are generally represented by full-time people, this is important. Business people who handle labor negotiations simultaneously with their business duties cannot be expected to perform well for the association.

2 *A greater likelihood that the association will be able to demonstrate continuity and consistency in its policies with respect to the unions.* When the leadership of the association is changed each year, as is common in employer associations that draw their chief officers from the ranks of member companies, the association's policies seem to shift with each new officer. This puts the association at a decided disadvantage vis-à-vis the union.

Thus, there is uncertainty as to which type of representation (professional or business person) is more effective for an employer association in bargaining. A compromise position for the association is to form a labor policy committee of business people. The negotiating team is then made up of members selected from the labor policy committee (and perhaps some business people chosen on an ad hoc basis) and the association executive. The labor policy committee itself meets before, during, and after negotiations and so provides business people with an ongoing view of the labor relations development. This helps add continuity to the association's activities.

Wage Uniformity

An important aspect of the activities of an employers' association is to attempt to apply uniform policies and standard conditions of work to the employees of a number of competing business enterprises. The purpose of uniform policies and conditions is to keep the companies from competing with each other on the basis of wages and working conditions. Instead, competition takes place on the basis of productivity, product quality, sales ability, and other similar factors. The unions, and many employers, fear that competition based on differences in wages and working conditions is destructive of the welfare of employees and perhaps of the better-standards firms as well. In the apparel manufacturing industry, for example, the unions have faced "sweatshop" conditions on a large scale at times in the past but have attempted to eliminate them by organizing employers under a standard contract.

But the matter of establishing standard conditions is complex. In many discussions of multiemployer bargaining, there has been a tendency to regard wage uniformity among firms as the simplest objective to achieve. But even wage uniformity is not a clear-cut concept with a single set of economic consequences. In fact, there are at least seven different basic types of wage uniformity practiced in various industries:

1 Uniformity of rate of pay per unit of output (i.e., piece-rate uniformity)
2 Uniformity of rate of pay per unit of skill and effort required
3 Uniformity of rate of pay per hour of labor of a particular type (i.e., occupational hourly wage uniformity)
4 Uniformity of pay-rate ranges for various occupations
5 Uniformity of minimum rates of pay
6 Uniformity of changes in rates of pay
7 Uniformity of total labor cost per unit of output[17]

The choice among these alternatives (which cannot, except in the most unusual circumstances, be simultaneously pursued) depends in large part on the objectives that the firms in the industry wish to pursue. Type 2 uniformity results in an equitable (with respect to skill and effort expended) distribution of earnings among workers of different companies, but other types do not yield this result. Type 7 results in heavy subsidization (by lower wages) of inefficient firms, while type 3 results in bankruptcies and elimination of the less efficient firms.

Even this brief discussion reveals the complicated and significant choices that associations must make in determining the policies with which they approach labor negotiations. It is dangerous, therefore, to speak of multiemployer bargaining as if a unity of purpose and result existed. There are distinct differences in association bargaining with respect to labor policies pursued.

Legal Status

Multiemployer bargaining has a peculiar status under the National Labor Relations Act (as amended). The NLRB does not ordinarily certify a bar-

---

[17]Thomas Kennedy, *The Significance of Wage Uniformity* (Philadelphia: University of Pennsylvania Press, Industry-Wide Collective Bargaining Series, 1949).

gaining unit made up of union representatives and members of a multi-employer group; it is created by labor and management without NLRB involvement. The basic ingredient supporting the appropriateness of the unit is the mutual consent of the parties. This relationship is founded on the unequivocal manifestation by the employer and the union members of the group that all intend to be bound by the results of the prospective negotiations. The formation of this dual unit must be completely voluntary. The NLRB will not sanction the creation of a multiparty unit over the objection of either party, union or employer.[18]

Under present law, once the group is formed and bargaining commences, neither the union nor employer members are permitted to withdraw without the consent of all parties, except under unusual circumstances. This is true even though the decision to bargain jointly in a multiparty fashion is purely voluntary, and in fact must be based on the noncoerced agreement of all parties to enter this bargaining relationship.[19]

The only escape under the "unusual conditions" exemption occurs in those situations in which an employer or the union is faced with dire economic circumstances, circumstances in which the existence of an employer as a viable business entity has ceased or is about to cease. In this respect, the NLRB has held that an employer may withdraw from a multi-employer association after negotiations with the union have begun when the employer is subject to extreme economic difficulties that result in an arrangement under the bankruptcy laws,[20] or when there is an imminent adverse economic condition that will require the employer to close its plant.[21] A federal court of appeals held that an employer may withdraw on its own initiative from association bargaining, even without union acquiescence, whenever an impasse occurs in bargaining.[22]

COSTING AN AGREEMENT

An employer must try to keep track of the impact that negotiated changes in wages and benefits will have on its labor costs. Increases in wage rates are rather easily translated into additional costs. For example, if the average hourly wage in the employee unit involved in negotiations is $6, and the employer decides to agree to an increase of $0.60 per hour, effective immediately, then the impact on labor cost is calculated as follows:

$$\$0.60 \times 2000 \times 1000 = \$1,200,000$$

where $0.60 is the amount of the wage increase per hour, 2000 is the num-

---

[18]*Kroger, Inc.*, 148 NLRB No. 69, 1964.
[19]*Hi-Way Billboard*, 500 F.2d 181, 5th Cir., 1974.
[20]*U.S. Lingerie Corp.*, 170 NLRB 750, 1968.
[21]William J. Curtin, "Legal Aspects of Multi-Employer Bargaining," address to the Associated General Contractors of America, Chicago, Jan. 16, 1975 (mimeographed).
[22]*NLRB v. Beck Engraving Co.*, 1975.

ber of work hours per year for the average employee, and 1000 is the number of employees in the unit.

A change in the timing of the wage increase may affect this calculation substantially. Suppose the $0.60 wage increase does not take effect until 6 months after the start of the new agreement. Then the company's additional cost in the first year (i.e., the first 12 months) of the new agreement will be:

$$\$0.60 \times 1/2 \times 2000 \times 1000 = \$600,000$$

Put differently, the company's additional costs are:

First month	None
Second month	None
Third month	None
Fourth month	None
Fifth month	None
Sixth month	Month
Seventh month	$0.60/hour worked
. . . .	
Twelfth month	$0.60/hour worked

or $0.60 per hour increase for 6 out of 12 months, or one-half of the year.

The shorter the period of time an increase is in effect in the first year, the less it costs the company. But this is true only at the outset. If the company looks beyond the first year of the agreement, then the $0.60 increase must be paid indefinitely.

This is an important matter in bargaining. A company may sometimes have the option of choosing among different proposals—for example, (1) a $0.60 per hour increase immediately or (2) an $0.80 per hour increase effective 6 months after the start of the agreement.

The first proposal would cost the company $1,200,000 in the first year of the agreement, as we saw above. The cost of the second proposal would be determined as follows:

$$\$0.80 \times 1/2 \times 2000 \times 1000 = \$800,000$$

Thus, the $0.80 per hour increase is actually less expensive to the company in the first year of the agreement than the $0.60 per hour increase because of the timing involved.

But note that this calculation is valid only for the first year of the agreement. In the second year the calculations are:

$$\$0.60 \times 2000 \times 1000 = \$1,200,000$$

versus

$$\$0.80 \times 2000 \times 1000 = \$1,600,000$$

In order to get a reduced cost in the first year, the company, if it adopted proposal 2, would get increased costs in all subsequent years.

Wage increases also have an indirect impact on costs. Suppose a company figures its labor costs as follows:

$$\$6 \times 2000 \times 1000 = \$12,000,000$$

where $6 per hour is the average wage rate, 2000 hours the average work year, and 1000 the number of employees. But the company also has costs from certain benefits provided employees. For example, suppose the company grants each employee 2 weeks' paid vacation, at a cost calculated as follows:

$$\$6 \times 2 \times 40 \times 1000 = \$480,000$$

where $6 per hour is the average hourly wage, 2 is the number of weeks of paid vacation, 40 is the number of hours ordinarily worked per week, and 1000 is the number of employees.

A wage increase raises the cost of the paid vacation also. Thus, the wage rate paid to persons on vacation rises from $6 to $6.60 per hour in our example. The additional cost to the company of this increase is

$$\$0.60 \times 2 \times 40 \times 1000 = \$48,000$$

This increase is termed a "roll-up" and is an example of the impact on the costs of certain fringe benefits of a wage increase.

The additional costs of providing increased pension, health care, life insurance, and dental benefits must be calculated on the basis of sophisticated computations, which take into consideration the expected usage of such benefits. Life insurance companies, pension actuaries, and similar experts are available to help the company estimate additional costs in these areas.

There are certain problems with cost calculations as most firms perform them. The most important limitation is that firms usually base cost estimates on past experience, rather than on estimates about future conditions. This is partly because data are usually available about past experience, while the future is a matter of conjecture. The result is that cost calculations are past-oriented rather than future-oriented. Firms assume that the amount of labor used (in our example, 2000 hours per year $\times$ 1000 employees equals 2,000,000 hours worked per year) and the mix of wage rates at which labor was compensated in the past (in our example, yielding an average wage of $6 per hour) will suffice as guides to the future. But the firms may expect that this will not be the case. For example, if the firm believes its number of employees will decline from 1000 to 800 next year, then a wage increase of $0.60 per hour will cost the firm $960,000 ($0.60 $\times$ 2000 $\times$ 800) instead of $1,200,000.

Also, the analytical techniques used by companies ordinarily stop short of considering the full impact of cost changes on the company. The techniques described above estimate the cost of compensation increases, not the effect of the increases on the firm's profits. Insufficient attention is paid to relationships between the firm's labor costs, volume of production, product mix, and capital investments, and these techniques do not take into account the firm's ability to minimize, by modifying previously formulated corporate plans, the financial consequences of increases in compensation.[23]

CHAPTER SUMMARY

In collective bargaining, management has many objectives, including profit maximization and cost control. In many corporations, there is a balance between concern with the quality of relations with employees and concern with the pursuit of economic wellbeing. A primary management objective is not to be put at a disadvantage vis-à-vis competitors. However, specific bargaining objectives may be quite diverse from firm to firm and for the same firm in different situations.

Most large corporations have a specialized labor relations staff to oversee collective bargaining for all of the plants of a company advised and assisted by the operating managers. In smaller firms, plant managers may conduct negotiations and sit down at the bargaining table. In some instances, top corporate executives are involved. Chief executives retain the right to review and approve or disapprove proposed settlements. Top managers will intervene in internal management controversies and in confrontations in which the company's reputation as an employer is at stake.

Employers must prepare for collective bargaining negotiations just as unions do. The better planned and more detailed the preparation, the better the negotiations will go for all parties involved. An effective company prepares by carefully selecting team members who are knowledgeable and temperamentally well suited to negotiation; by planning exactly what it wants to discuss and how, by having internal data on the existing contract with itemized labor costs, and by having data on the labor costs of other firms in the geographic area. Much background material and economic information can now be stored in computers for ease of access and analysis.

Preparations for negotiations also need careful scheduling. In some industries, preparations begin a year or more before a contract runs out, so

---

[23]M. H. Granof, *How to Cost Your Labor Contract* (Washington, D.C.: Bureau of National Affairs, 1973), pp. 127–128. See also W. D. Hersel and Gordon S. Skinner, *Costing Union Demands* (Chicago: International Personnel Management Association, 1976).

that all issues can be considered and consultations scheduled with plant managers and relevant personnel.

Firms are not usually very successful in establishing objectives for their labor relations or in creating measurements for how well they are doing. Rather than treating labor relations as a strategic variable that can help a company be successful, most simply hope to avoid trouble.

In many sectors of the economy, employers do not negotiate with unions individually. Instead, companies form associations that bargain with the unions. Association bargaining has its own special problems in preparing for negotiations. One of the most notable of these special problems is the potential for conflict between members of the association. Management objectives and tactics in negotiations are complex matters over which companies disagree. Furthermore, the firms are normally competitors and often distrust each other. Having a method for settling internal disputes is critical to the success of multiemployer bargaining. Some associations adopt bylaws that are legally binding. The selection of representatives also presents problems. One solution is to hire a permanent staff for the association to participate in negotiations. Multiemployer bargaining also has a unique legal status under the NLRB.

QUESTIONS FOR THOUGHT AND DISCUSSION

1 What are management's objectives in collective bargaining? Which are most important? Why?

2 What is Boulwarism? Is it a good policy for a company to follow? Why or why not?

3 What steps in management preparation for negotiations are most important? Why?

4 What are the major ways in which multiemployer association bargaining is different from single-employer bargaining? Do the differences work to the advantage of the employers or to their disadvantage? Why?

5 Do smaller companies that lack industrial relations specialists have poorer labor relations or less effective collective bargaining negotiations than larger, multiplant companies that have such specialists? What are the pros and cons of having a specialized labor relations staff?

6 Is industrial relations a strategic variable for a firm? Why or why not? Should it be?

7 What are some of the problems with establishing uniform wages and working conditions for the employees of competing firms by organizing employers under a standard contract? Do you think this plan is beneficial to employees, or can it be used to their disadvantage?

8 What are the arguments for and against having a professional staff represent multiemployer associations in collective bargaining negotiations? What is a compromise position that has been tried? Can you think of any other methods of forming a negotiating team or staff for employer associations?

SELECTED READING

Irving, John S., ed., *When Management Negotiates* (Washington, D.C.: National Association of Manufacturers, 1987).

Morse, Bruce, *How to Negotiate the Labor Agreement* (Detroit: Trends Publishing, 1974).

Northrup, Herbert, *Boulwarism* (Ann Arbor: University of Michigan, Bureau of Industrial Relations, 1964).

Ryder, Meyer S., Charles M. Rhemus, and Sanford Cohen, *Management Preparation for Collective Bargaining* (Homewood, Ill.: Dow Jones-Irwin, 1966).

Windmuller, John P., and Alan Gladstone, eds., *Employer's Associations and Industrial Relations: A Comparative Study* (New York: Oxford University Press, 1984).

CHAPTER 16

STRIKES AND DISPUTE SETTLEMENT

WHAT IS A WORK STOPPAGE?

Strikes and Lockouts

Strikes occur when employees as a group refuse to work until changes are made in compensation or conditions of work. The strike is a pressure tactic; it is also a method of notifying other people that a dispute exists between the employer and the workers. Other means of advertising a dispute exist, such as informational picketing and circulation of published material; other means of bringing economic pressure are also sometimes available, as, for example, a product boycott. But the strike, and the threat of a strike, constitute the principal device by which unions in our society apply economic pressure in labor disputes.

Strikes take several forms, depending primarily on their purpose. Most strikes are called by unions in support of their efforts to negotiate a favorable contract with management. In the United States strikes of this sort are generally legal and are referred to as economic strikes. Their purpose is usually to get the employer to agree to raise wages or benefits or to improve other conditions of work for the strikers. But a union may also strike for an illegal purpose; in which case the strike is illegal. For example, a strike by a union to compel the assignment of work by an employer to members of one union rather than another is illegal—a so-called jurisdictional strike (because it concerns the union's work jurisdiction). A strike that arises out of an employer's unfair labor practice is legal; a strike to compel one employer to cease doing business with another with whom the union has a dispute is illegal—a so-called secondary boycott. (Jurisdictional strikes and secondary boycotts are unfair labor practices by unions—see Chapter 9.)

Strikes are the most prominent form of overt conflict in labor relations, but not the only form. Strikes occur in only a small proportion of negotiations, but disputes are much more common. A recent study showed that disputes occurred in 57 percent of contract negotiations sampled. Most disputes did not lead to a strike, but holdouts, in which the old contract was extended until a new agreement was reached, were common. Researchers hypothesize that unions will switch from a holdout to a strike under the following conditions: wages adjusted for inflation have declined dramatically; the unemployment rate in the locality has declined markedly, making replacements difficult for the employer to obtain and other jobs more readily available to strikers; and the profitability of the firm has increased—implying to the strikers that the firm can readily afford a pay increase for workers.[1]

Employers have a form of action available that is somewhat analogous to a strike. It is called a "lockout." In a lockout the employer closes the plant or other facility in which a labor dispute exists. The employees are unable to work and do not get paid. As a result, the lockout brings pressure to bear on the employees to settle the dispute.

Strikes and lockouts are forms of economic warfare. As such, they often bring severe losses to those engaged in them and inconvenience to third parties. In some instances, strikes and lockouts disrupt the provision of products or services that affect the health and safety of the public. Because of the sometimes serious consequences of work stoppages, many people have long sought ways to lessen their frequency and ameliorate their impact. Sometimes it is proposed to simply make work stoppages illegal. Sometimes new methods of settling disputes without recourse to work stoppages are proposed. In any case, strikes and lockouts are probably the most visible evidence of labor disputes. They occasion much discussion by the public, and in some instances much frustration and anger.

The Right to Strike

Is there a "right to strike"? "Right to strike" is a phrase heard often in discussions of labor relations. Some people assert that there is a natural right of human beings to refuse to work in conditions and circumstances they do not like. It is a right of Americans, they assert, to refuse to work if they do not want to, and, in fact, the Thirteenth Amendment to the U.S. Constitution does prohibit "involuntary servitude" except as a punishment for crime. Employers may not, therefore, compel unwilling employees to labor for them. Employees may refuse to work, or quit, if they desire. However, the constitutional prohibition against involuntary servitude establishes an individual right, and therefore is not necessarily applicable to a strike situation. A strike has two characteristics that distinguish it from a simple

[1]Peter C. Crampton and Joseph S. Tracy, "Strikes and Holdouts in Wage Bargaining: Theory and Data," *American Economic Review*, 82:1, March 1992, p. 118.

application of the right to be free of involuntary servitude. First, a strike is a collective action, not an action of an individual. The strike draws its force from its collective character. It is a device used to halt or disrupt the employer's business, not a device simply to free people from an undesired employment. Second, the purpose of the strike is to obtain concessions from the employer. It is an economic weapon. The Thirteenth Amendment apparently did not intend to establish the right of employees to band together to bring pressure to bear on an employer. There is thus no constitutional right to strike. Whether or not there is a natural-law right to strike is best left to philosophers.

There being no constitutionally protected right of employees to strike, efforts have been made in the courts and in Congress both to establish a right to strike and to restrict it. The National Labor Relations Act includes in section 7, "Rights of Employees," the language

> Employees shall have the right . . . to engage in . . . concerted activities for the purpose of collective bargaining or other mutual aid or protection.

This language has been held by the courts to establish a statutory right to strike. And section 13 of the act is even more explicit:

> Nothing in this Act, except as specifically provided for herein, shall be construed so as either to interfere with or impede or diminish in any way the right to strike. . . .

However, what Congress bestows it can also take away. Other provisions of the same law prohibit strikes for certain purposes. And some classes of employees are excluded from the protection of the act. Federal government employees and employees of states and local governments are not covered by the NLRA. Congress has prohibited strikes by federal employees, and most states prohibit strikes by their own employees and those of municipalities. Furthermore, what Congress seems to have permitted, the courts may remove. Court decisions in recent years have restricted strikes to such a large degree that some authors have asked, "Can unions strike anymore?"[2] The question is, of course, not whether or not workers can strike, but whether or not they can strike legally.

Have strikes become more or less frequent in the American economy? Government statistics on strikes begin in 1939 and show that 1946 was the worst year in terms of strikes in our recent history. The record of time lost in recent years has been moderate and generally better than the record of the late 1940s.[3] In the 1980s the frequency and duration of strikes declined substantially as many companies got into financial difficulties and workers

---

[2]John G. Kilgour, "Can Unions Strike Anymore? The Impact of Recent Supreme Court Decisions," *Labor Law Journal*, 41:5, May 1990, pp. 259–269.

[3]Douglas A. Hibbs, "On the Political Economy of Long-Run Trends in Strike Activity," *British Journal of Political Science*, 8, 1978, pp. 153–175. See also, Roberto Franzosi, "One Hundred Years of Strike Statistics: Methodological and Theoretical Issues in Quantitative Strike Research," *Industrial and Labor Relations Review*, 42:3, April 1989, pp. 348ff.

feared losing their jobs. From 1983 to 1991 the number of strikes involving 1000 or more workers declined from 80 to 40. And in 1991, the American economy lost only 0.06 percent of estimated total working time as a result of work stoppages. It is unlikely that even that much production was really lost, since a great deal of output lost in strikes is later made up by overtime operations after the work stoppage ends. These statistics do not suggest an economy unduly disrupted by strike activity.

STRIKE ACTIVITY BY INDUSTRY

Some industries are much more likely to experience strike activity than others. A study made in the 1950s compared the propensity to strike in various industries on an international basis. Certain industries were high in virtually all countries, especially mining, shipping, longshoring, lumbering, and textiles. The lowest industries in terms of strikes were clothing, public utilities, hotel and restaurant facilities, trade agriculture, and railways. The authors related a high incidence of strikes to the physical isolation of workers and the workplace in industries such as mining, shipping, and lumber and to the difficult nature of the work combined with the uncertainty of employment in those industries.[4]

Strikes are also more likely in industries that are depressed compared to others and in areas in which alternative jobs are available for strikers, if necessary. Strikes are also more common when employees have had only meager improvements in living standards, so that they are anxious for pay increases.[5]

WHY DO STRIKES OCCUR?

Causes of Strikes

Strikes occur for several reasons. We ordinarily think of strikes being caused by a dispute between an employer and a union over wage rates or benefits or working conditions. But strikes also occur because of disputes over bargaining structure or over the personalities involved in negotia-

---

[4]Clark Kerr and Abraham Siegel, "The Interindustry Propensity to Strike," in A. Kornhauser et al., *Industrial Conflict* (New York: McGraw-Hill, 1954), chap. 14. A recent study has questioned the findings of Kerr and Siegel: see P. K. Edwards, "A Critique of the Kerr-Siegel Hypothesis of Strikes and the Isolated Mass: A Study of the Falsification of Sociological Knowledge," *The Sociological Review*, 25:3, August 1977, pp. 551–574. For a later confirmation of Kerr-Siegel see Bruce E. Kaufman, "The Determinants of Strikes over Time and Industries," *Journal of Labor Research*, 4:2, Spring 1983, pp. 159–176.

[5]Sheena McConnell, "Cyclical Fluctuations in Strike Activity," *Industrial and Labor Relations Review*, 44:1, October 1990, pp. 130–143. See also David Card, "Strikes and Bargaining: A Survey of the Recent Empirical Literature," *Papers and Proceedings of the American Economic Association*, 80:2, May 1990, pp. 410–415.

tions. Strikes that actually occur for these reasons are usually advertised as strikes about wages or conditions of work. Consequently, government statistics about the causes of strikes show disputes over wages and working conditions as being by far the major cause of work stoppages. Often, however, particularly long and bitter strikes do not arise from a single matter, such as wages, but from a more complex dispute over who should bargain with whom.

One study of strike activity found that 15 percent of scheduled negotiations (i.e., those occurring at the expiration of a collective bargaining agreement) ended in strikes. A key factor causing strikes was found to be the variability, but not the level, of profits. That is, often managers in currently profitable companies feared that profits were going to turn down and so were reluctant to grant pay increases which union leaders and members felt would be paid out of existing profit levels.[6]

Another careful statistical study of strike activity in the United States between 1971 and 1980 identified the following as influencing strikes:

- Men are more likely to strike than women.
- Companies with substantial sales fluctuations are more likely to experience strikes than others.
- Strikes are less likely in right-to-work states.
- Strikes are more likely in larger bargaining units.
- Strikes are more likely when pay has lagged behind inflation.

But during this period the level of the local unemployment rate and the rate of inflation had little effect on strike likelihood.[7]

Strikes are staged by nonunion workers as well as by unions, but we usually hear much less about such nonunion strikes. This is partly because work stoppages in a nonunion situation tend to be more confused and less clear-cut than when a union is involved. Also, almost certainly, the frequency of nonunion work stoppages is considerably less than that of strikes called by unions. Yet it is not uncommon to hear about work stoppages in nonunion plants. Managers in such plants sometimes talk of "blackmail"—the workers' stopping work and threatening to go to a union if the company doesn't give in to their demands. Such incidents very rarely receive the publicity that accompanies strikes by unions, however, and as a result they are not ordinarily included in government statistics about work stoppages.

[6]Joseph S. Tracey, "An Investigation into the Determinants of U.S. Strike Activity," *The American Economic Review*, 76:3, June 1986, pp. 423–436. See also Cynthia L. Gramm, "New Measures of the Propensity to Strike during Contract Negotiations, 1971–1980," *Industrial and Labor Relations Review*, 40:3, April 1987, pp. 406–421. Gramm found that strikes occurred in 13.25 percent of all negotiations.

[7]Cynthia L. Gramm, "The Determinants of Strike Incidence and Severity," *Industrial and Labor Relations Review*, 39:3, April 1986, pp. 361–375. See also Woodruff Imberman, "Who Strikes and Why," *Harvard Business Review*, 61:6, November–December 1983, pp. 18ff.

The Functions of a Strike

Strikes are emotional occurrences, and perhaps it is to be expected that observers would be of two minds about them. On the one hand, strikes are often viewed as evidence of a breakdown in the bargaining process. Implicit in this view is the suggestion that if bargaining were conducted better, strikes would not result. In fact, it often seems self-defeating for employees to go out on strike, and for the company to let it happen. In many instances employees lose more in wages and the company in earnings as a result of a strike than either would have lost by giving in to the other side's demands. From the point of view of the company, strikes can be even more unfortunate because they often enhance the business success of the struck firm's competitors.[8] Finally, in some dramatic instances a firm goes out of business during a strike so that employees and managers lose their jobs and investors lose their investment. Work stoppages therefore seem irrational—and it seems that things ought to be able to be done better. There is considerable merit to this view, as we shall see in later sections of this chapter.

On the other hand, careful observers of collective bargaining also recognize that the strike is an integral part of the bargaining process. The strike has functions to perform that contribute to the resolution of disputes. In this view, a certain frequency of strikes is to be expected as a normal part of collective bargaining. William Serrin, then chief labor reporter for the *New York Times*, put it this way: "A strike does not necessarily mean negotiations have broken down, only that an impasse still exists or that it simply is not time to settle."[9]

In general, a strike puts economic pressure on both the union and management and by so doing raises the costs of disagreement. During a strike management faces the choice of either refusing to give in to labor's demands and thereby accepting the costs of the strike in terms of lost production, sales and profits, or of ending the costs of the strike by accepting labor's demands. Similarly, workers and the union face the costs of continuing a work stoppage—losing wages and depleting the union's strike fund (if any)—or of accepting management's offers. The steadily accumulating costs to both management and labor of a strike bring pressure to bear on both to settle an agreement and get back to work.

Put in the most extreme form, strikes and the threat of strikes are said to be necessary to make the collective bargaining process work. How can this be? What are the positive functions of a strike? How does a strike make collective bargaining work? John Dunlop has listed four functions of the strike:[10]

---

[8]Richard A. De Fusco and Scott M. Fuess, Jr., "The Effects of Airline Strikes on Struck and Nonstruck Carriers," *Industrial and Labor Relations Review*, 44:2, January 1991, pp. 324ff.

[9]William Serrin, "Byzantine Strategy in the Transit Talks," *New York Times*, Mar. 29, 1980, p. 8.

[10]Adapted from John T. Dunlop, "The Function of the Strike," in John T. Dunlop and N. W. Chamberlain, eds., *Frontiers of Collective Bargaining* (New York: Harper, 1967), p. 120.

1 *A strike provides information to both sides about the other, and may be undertaken in order to discover data or motives which the other side refuses to reveal in any other fashion.* Is the company profitable or not? What are its expectations about business in the future—good or bad? Does the union leadership have the support of the membership or not? A strike will often tell the truth about such questions when meetings between management and labor will not. When management says it has no business, but then acts quickly to get striking employees back to work, the union knows business isn't as bad as management had maintained. When a union official says the membership has to have a certain benefit, but calls a strike and no one quits work, the company knows that the union official was misleading them.[11]

2 *A strike helps to persuade each side to modify its position in a negotiation.* The pressure of the strike is an independent force compelling both sides toward agreement. This is the most significant and general function of a strike.

3 *A strike may contribute to changing the relationships between bargainers and their constituents.* For example, a management negotiator may want to offer a higher wage increase to the union than his supervisors will permit. But a strike may cause them to urge the negotiator to make the higher offer and so settle the dispute.

4 *A strike may be necessary to change the budget allotments of a government agency.* This is often the function of a strike in the public sector. In negotiations the union may demand increases in compensation greater than those budgeted by the government agency. In the absence of a strike or threat of a strike, the impasse between the agency and the union could continue indefinitely. A strike, however, often generates enough response from public officials, or even the voters, that a rearrangement of budget priorities may occur, allowing a settlement of the dispute.

5 *A strike may be necessary to change bargaining structure.* For example, in 1971 the Bell Telephone System had some 130 contracts expiring over a period of 4 months. The Communication Workers Union and the Bell System wanted to get closer to national bargaining. As the local agreements began to expire at the end of April, the CWA extended them on a day-to-day basis. On May 23 the CWA rejected the company's offer for a pattern-setting local agreement. The CWA asked for a strike vote, and received authorization from the employees to call a strike. On June 15, CWA President Bierre set the strike date for July 14. By July 14 virtually all CWA contracts with the Bell System had expired. The strike began on July 14, and was settled 1 week later. The new agreement established the same expiration dates for almost all contracts, and in 1974 the CWA and the Bell System participated for the first time in what were truly national negotiations.

[11]Sheena McConnel, "Strikes, Wages and Private Information," *The American Economic Review*, 79, 4 (September 1989), pp. 801–815.

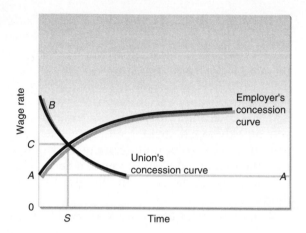

FIGURE 16-1

Theoreticians of the bargaining process make considerable reference to the work stoppage. In describing bargaining power, much emphasis is placed on the strike or work stoppage as the means by which the parties are brought to agreement. This process is shown in Figure 16.1.[12]

The diagram is subject to varying interpretations. The essential features are the definition of an employer's concession curve, which begins at A, the existing wage rate, and rises over time; and a union's concession curve, which begins at B, some desired wage rate well above the current scale, and falls in time toward A. The intersection point of the two curves defines a wage rate C and a time S at which a settlement takes place. But what

---

[12]John Hicks, *The Theory of Wages*, 2d ed. (New York: St. Martin's, 1966), pp. 146–147. A similar diagram appears in Richard E. Walton and Robert B. McKersie, *A Behavioral Theory of Labor Negotiations* (New York: McGraw-Hill, 1965), p. 56, associated with work done by E. Robert Livernash.

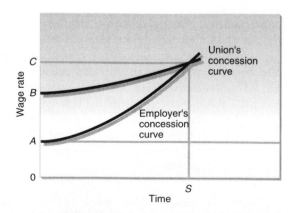

FIGURE 16-2

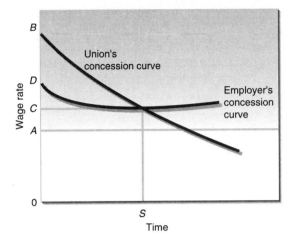

FIGURE 16-3

does the time axis measure? Presumably, it is the duration of a work stoppage, since without a work stoppage, the simple passage of time might not make either party alter its initial position (i.e., the employer's curve would be a straight horizontal line at A and the union's curve, a straight horizontal line at B). A stalemate would be pictured. In fact, of course, this sometimes happens when a work stoppage is prohibited by law. In the federal government, for example, strikes are illegal and disputes between the employer (a federal agency) and the unions may continue almost indefinitely without either side altering its position.

The diagram may also be used to show other patterns of bargaining. For example, a strike sometimes causes the union's concession curve to rise, not fall. That is, as a strike proceeds, the union leadership insists

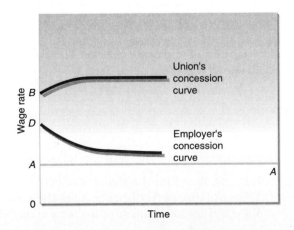

FIGURE 16-4

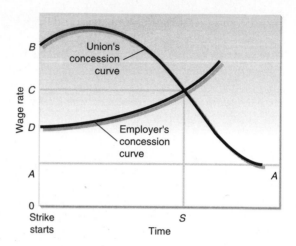

FIGURE 16-5

on a higher wage increase than it had before, in order to get the workers back to work and then compensate them for time lost in the strike. Figure 16-2 illustrates this situation. (The union's concession curve should really be given a different name in this situation.) Alternatively, a strike may induce management to lessen its offer because the company's offer before the strike was high, in hopes of avoiding the costs of a strike (Figure 16-3, point D). After the strike was under way, the company could no longer afford its earlier offer. Figure 16-3 describes this situation.

The circumstances of Figures 16-2 and 16-3 can be combined. If a strike causes the union to raise its settlement objective and the company to lower its offers, the result can be a stalemate. Figure 16-4 illustrates this situation. Surprisingly, this situation often occurs in the period immediately following the start of a strike. If it persists, either the company goes out of business or it replaces the union workers, and the union loses the strike.

Ordinarily, however, the progress of a strike tends to cause both sides to make concessions to get an agreement and end the work stoppage. Figure 16-5 illustrates what is probably the most common sequence of events in a work stoppage: the advent of the strike tends initially to deepen the dispute by widening the positions of the parties, but thereafter the gap is closed as the strike wears on.

COPING WITH STRIKES

Union Preparations

In preparing for a strike a union must consider three major items:

1 Being sure that the strike is effective
2 Organizing picket lines to keep the strike effective
3 Providing financial support for strikers

The first item is the most important. If a strike is to be effective, it must involve most of the persons in the bargaining unit. The purpose of the strike is to halt the employer's business activity and so bring pressure on the company to settle the dispute that has prompted the strike. The union's attempt to halt the employer's business is often answered by the employer's attempts to keep the business going, as we will see in the next section.

If the union cannot get employees to quit working, the strike will be ineffective. Some strikes are ineffective. The union's call for a strike is answered with apathy by the employees, many of whom continue working. This is about the worst setback a union can receive. It undermines the union's bargaining position in a strike and calls into question the degree to which the union has the confidence of employees in any matter. As a result, an ineffective strike is often followed by a petition to decertify the union as bargaining representative for the employees.

Since the stakes are very high, unions are usually careful to call strikes only when union leadership knows the employees will actually cease work. The union leadership will build up strike talk over a period. It will keep employees informed of developments in negotiations and will prepare the employees for a strike call. The leadership will look for a "strike issue"— some matter of importance to the employees which can generate the emotional concern necessary to sustain a strike.

A good strike issue depends on the workers' concerns of the moment.[13] Sometimes a wage increase is of great significance to the workers. At other times job security, or even work rules, can be of great concern to employees. In the 1959 steel negotiations, for example, a dispute between the union and the Basic Steel Negotiating Committee of the companies over the size of a wage increase seemed of little interest to the employees. The union could not expect much employee support for a nationwide strike over an increase of a few cents per hour. Inflation was low, job security was reasonable, and workers were not militant about these issues. But when the companies proposed a revision of work rules and at one sweep seemed to threaten the wage levels, working conditions, and job assignments of many steel workers, the union knew it had found a strike issue. The result was a strike of more than 100 days, which ended with no change in the work rules section (section 2B) of the contract.

In order to establish a moral basis for the strike, unions often take a strike vote prior to actually calling a work stoppage. If a majority rejects the motion for a strike, the leadership probably will not call it. However, if a majority votes for a strike, then the union leadership may claim a mandate to call the strike. Also, the majority's authorization of the strike is a strong argument to use in getting somewhat apathetic employees to join the strike.

[13]Woodruff Imberman, "Who Strikes—and Why?" *Harvard Business Review*, 61:6, November–December 1983, pp. 18–28.

Once the strike is under way, the union must organize picketing and other strike activity. Picketing is very much regulated by national law and often by local municipal ordinances dealing with public order. The union must organize picketing to conform with legal requirements or be prepared to confront the consequences of illegal behavior.

The union must also seek to provide financial support for employees who are on strike while their paychecks are cut off. Many national unions maintain funds for the support of strikers. But the level of benefits provided, rules for eligibility, and ability to pay benefits differ from union to union.

Employer Preparations

Operation during a Strike   Employers are aware that the effect of a strike depends critically on the strikers' ability to halt the employer's operations. This focuses the employer's strike preparations on the question of whether or not to attempt to continue to operate the facility during the strike. If the facility can be operated, the strike will have little ability to force the employer into concessions in the bargaining process.

There are three ways to operate facilities in the course of a strike. The first, simplest, and least hazardous method is to take advantage of an ineffective strike. If many employees do not join the strike, it is possible that they will be able to operate the plant. But a union that conducts its affairs well is not likely to call a strike that is ineffective in getting employees to walk out.

The second method of operating during a strike is to use supervisory personnel to run equipment. In industries that involve much mechanization or automation and consequently a small work force, operation with supervisors is a real possibility. In the telephone industry, for example, most normal operations of the company can be continued by supervisors during a strike. But maintenance, which requires skilled people, and new installations, which are labor-intensive, ordinarily cannot be kept up by supervisors. In the oil industry, refineries can be operated without striking employees, but maintenance becomes a problem. In industries like automotive assembly, electronics assembly, and textile manufacturing, it is virtually impossible to think of operation with supervisors alone. Furthermore, full operation by supervisors is ordinarily a short-term expedient at best. This is because lack of maintenance brings operations to a halt or because physical exhaustion overtakes the supervisors themselves. Partial operations, however, may be continued in some industries virtually indefinitely.

The third procedure by which struck plants can be operated is the hiring of replacements for the strikers. In the United States the hiring of replacements on either a temporary or a permanent basis by the employer is legal when employees are engaged in an "economic" strike, that is, one that is part of a collective bargaining dispute. If the employer has caused the strike by an unfair labor practice, the hiring of replacements is not permitted. Because replacements may legally be hired for economic strikers, it is sometimes said that economic strikers are gambling with their jobs.[14]

The distinction between temporary and permanent replacements hired by an employer is very important. Temporary replacements are hired only for the term of the strike. They do the work of the strikers during the work stoppage, but when the stoppage ends, then the employer must dismiss the temporary replacements and rehire the strikers. Permanent replacements are different. They are hired to take the strikers' jobs for good. In effect, the employer fires the strikers.

Surprising as it may seem, in our country employees can be fired for conducting a legal strike. This occurs when the company replaces the strikers permanently. Whether to replace strikers on a temporary or a permanent basis is entirely the choice of the employer. The U.S. law in this regard is extremely unusual when viewed in the international context. Almost no other industrialized country permits permanent replacement of strikers. Unions and workers are very much opposed to this aspect of our law, arguing that it makes the right to strike a mockery by permitting employers to discharge strikers.

A company that replaces strikers risks creating great bitterness among its employees who are on strike and risks emotional outbursts that may be violent. Historically, unions have bitterly resented replacements for strikers—calling them "strikebreakers," "scabs," and similar names. The operation of plants by replacements will often invite violence and will usually require police protection of the plants and the replacements. For this reason, many companies do not consider the use of replacements during strikes. Others do, however.[15]

The major strikes that unions have lost in the United States in recent years share the characteristic that the employer has been able to obtain replacements and operate indefinitely in the face of the strike. This is true, for example, of the Florida East Coast Railway strike, which after several years found the railway operating nonunion with replacements. A Los Angeles paper replaced striking reporters, and the *Washington Post* replaced striking press workers; strikes against those newspapers were defeated. Phelps-Dodge Corporation hired replacements and defeated a strike at its copper mining facilities in Arizona.[16] We have already discussed the use of permanent replacements by Trans World Airlines in 1986 to break a strike by flight attendants.

A Checklist of Management Preparations   In preparing for a strike, management has many things about which to be concerned. A brief list of

---

[14]Burr E. Anderson, "Permanent Replacement of Strikers . . . ," *John Marshall Law Review,* 18:2, Winter 1985, pp. 321–340.

[15]Charles R. Perry and Andrew M. Kramer, *Operating during Strikes* (Philadelphia: Wharton School Industrial Research Unit, University of Pennsylvania, 1982).

[16]Robert Roper, "Copper Strikers Refuse to Give Up," *Labor Notes,* Nov. 20, 1984, pp. 3, 14.

items that must be considered is given below. The list demonstrates how serious an event a strike is for a company and why it must not be entered into without careful forethought.

* What will be the reaction of nonstriking employees to picket lines?
* How large is the company's inventory?
* Can customer orders be filled out of inventory for any sustained time?
* Can distribution to customers be maintained through picket lines?
* Will the company lose customers permanently if they are not currently supplied?

If the company decides to try to operate during a strike, it has other significant questions to answer:[17]

* Will salaried personnel volunteer to work during the strike?
* How will they be paid?
* At what rates—their own, or those of the workers they replace?
* How will overtime be compensated?
* Can contractors be brought in?
* Can power be maintained from the plant's own power plant?
* Can sabotage by workers who are still in the plant at the start of the strike be avoided?
* Will the local utility company provide repair services during the strike?
* Can the plant's output be picked up by truck? Will railways provide assistance? Can customers be assured of delivery?
* How will garbage and refuse be picked up? How will food services be provided? Will supervisors and replacements have to live in the plant? Where will they be bedded? Fed?
* How will the strike be monitored? Will supervisors be willing to photograph picket-line activity? Can a strike "log" be kept? Should separate gates be set up for outside contractors?

SETTLING DISPUTES

Mediation

What Is Mediation? Strikes are a form of open conflict which most people wish to avoid. In consequence, when a strike begins to seem likely, a number of steps are taken to try to resolve the underlying disputes which may culminate in a work stoppage. Mediation is a major form of intervention intended to resolve disputes without strikes.

[17]Leonard C. Scott, "Running a Struck Plant: Some Dos and Don'ts," *S.A.M. Advanced Management Journal*, 38:4, October 1973, pp. 58–61. See also Lee T. Paterson and John Liebert, *Management Strike Handbook* (Chicago: International Personnel Management Association, 1978).

Mediation is a process by which a neutral party attempts to help disputing parties reach a settlement of the issues that divide them. Mediation ordinarily does not involve the neutral party's acting as a judge, that is, deciding the resolution of the dispute (a process referred to as "arbitration"). Instead, mediation is a process of persuading the parties to reach an agreement. Mediation of labor disputes has been described as involving "the continuum of possible functions of an impartial person in the collective bargaining relationship, beginning with the common idioms of conciliation and going across the scale to, but not including, arbitration."[18]

The continuum spoken of is surprisingly wide. In the past, Americans distinguished various points along the continuum with different terms, as the quotation above implies. "Conciliation" was the least complex process. It involved the attempt to persuade disputing parties to meet and discuss their problems. Often in labor disputes one or the other of the parties refused to acknowledge the other. Conciliation's purpose was, in effect, reconciliation of disputing parties, and its effectiveness resulted from the likelihood that if the parties could be persuaded to meet, they might find a resolution of their dispute. Certainly, they were not likely to settle the dispute if they did not meet. The advent of the National Labor Relations Act, which imposed a legal duty to bargain on management and later (in 1947) on labor also, has largely vitiated the role of conciliation per se.

Mediation has always been a more active process than conciliation. A list of the functions of mediators prepared by William E. Simkin, a former director of the Federal Mediation and Conciliation Service, distinguishes among three categories: procedural suggestions, communication facilitation, and more affirmative actions. Procedural functions include scheduling, conducting, and controlling meetings; establishing and/or extending deadlines; keeping records; and fending off other outside intervention if it is believed likely to be counterproductive. Communication functions include keeping channels open and "gatekeeping." Gatekeeping refers to times when one side would be willing to make a concession on an issue but is afraid that it would be construed as weakness. It may tell the mediator, however, who can suggest that plan to the other side to test for a reaction. Affirmative action functions include ordering priorities; deflating extreme stands or preventing their occurrence; offering creative, substantive suggestions; and making recommendations on individual issues or packages.[19]

Successful mediation depends to a very substantial degree on the skills of the mediator. A mediator who is not acceptable to the parties is useless. But an acceptable mediator who does not know how to assist the parties in reaching an agreement is also useless.[20]

---

[18]William E. Simkin, *Mediation and the Dynamics of Collective Bargaining*, 2d ed. (Washington, D.C.: Bureau of National Affairs, 1986), p. 27.
[19]Ibid., p. 77.
[20]Deborah M. Kolb, *The Mediators* (Cambridge, Mass.: MIT Press, 1983).

Mediation Agencies Any person who is acceptable to the parties to a dispute may serve as a mediator. Priests, public officials, college professors, prominent citizens, and other such persons have served as mediators in labor disputes. But the volume of collective bargaining disputes is so large in our country, and the role of mediation so potentially helpful, that various states and the federal government have established public mediation agencies. The most important of these agencies is the Federal Mediation and Conciliation Service (FMCS). FMCS was created by Title II of the Taft-Hartley Act in 1947 and was built upon the conciliation service then existing in the Department of Labor.

FMCS mediators and those employed by the various state mediation agencies are professional mediators drawn generally from the ranks of experienced labor and management representatives.[21] Both labor and management in the United States currently accept, indeed favor, the government's assistance in the resolution of labor disputes through the activity of the various mediation agencies.

An interesting innovation in the work of FMCS is the relations by objectives (RBO) program. The program had its inception in the application of behavioral science techniques to labor-management relations. As described by *Business Week*, the application of one RBO program was as follows:

> Until recently, labor-management relations at Georgia-Pacific Corp.'s pulp and paper mill at Woodland, Me., were about as unpleasant as possible. Long-simmering disputes had damaged morale in the 700-person work force. Disgruntled workers filed grievances over minor annoyances and frequently went on wildcat walkouts. When the plant's five unions struck for three weeks last spring, a portion of nearby U.S. Route 1 had to be closed to protect motorists from strike-related violence.
>
> Though all is still not sweetness and light at Woodland, the situation has greatly improved in the past few months, largely through third-party help by the Federal Mediation and Conciliation Service. But it was not the traditional FMCS role as a mediator in bargaining disputes that brought about the change.
>
> The FMCS's involvement is part of an experimental program, called "Relations by Objective" (RBO), in which the agency provides the expertise for prodding labor and management toward fundamental changes in their basic relationship. The program is aimed at helping employers and unions, hampered by rigid adversary procedures, to root out conflicts and establish new means of dealing with them. Under the supervision of federal mediators, union and management analyze their problems, decide what they would like to see in an ideal relationship, and discuss how to implement these goals. . . .
>
> No one claims that RBO is a panacea for all labor problems at Georgia-Pacific, but both sides say it has improved relations considerably. "When we have a problem, we can just sit down and discuss it," says Yardley [a management representative]. "Eighty percent of the time we get a solution right away.

---

[21]William E. Simkin, "Code of Professional Conduct for Labor Mediators," *Labor Law Journal*, 15:10, October 1964, pp. 626–637.

Before, there would have been a grievance filed, and it probably would have gone to arbitration."

Will Sawyer, Woodland's director of industrial relations, is also enthusiastic about the results. "We had an old problem over a modification of work hours for auto mechanics. Under the program, we reached agreement in one meeting. We've had a substantial reduction in the number of grievances, and the grievances that are filed seem to be more meritorious."[22]

The Decline of the Strike

The strike has important functions to perform in collective bargaining, but it may be an increasingly uncomfortable tool for unions to use. In 1972 George Meany expressed the view that in the 1970s strikes had become more "painful" than in the 1930s and had "more far-reaching effects." In earlier years, when workers were earning 60 to 70 cents an hour, Meany said, it did not take much in the way of financial aid to keep a family going during a strike, nor did it take long for a family to recover once a strike was settled.

> Things are different today. Simply because collective bargaining has raised living standards and improved and stabilized the financial situation of workers, workers have a great deal more to lose. They have mortgage payments and car payments and college-tuition payments to make—things that did not burden them years ago.

Not only have strikes become more serious for workers, he said, but they are also having a greater impact on industry:

> I have never been enchanted with strikes. They are not fun—they are grim. There are casualties in every strike—economic, human, social casualties. And I'd like to avoid any of these consequences.
>
> Any responsible labor leader considers, as I do, that a strike is never more than the lesser of two evils, adopted by workers as a last resort to protest some grievance that, to them, is worse than not working at all.[23]

The erosion of the strike as a means of settling disputes has also been suggested by John Dunlop, who has listed the following factors as contributing to the decline of the strike:

1 *Increased ability* of companies to operate during strikes because of automation and increased proportion of professional and supervisory employees.

---

[22]"U.S. Mediators Try a New Role," *Business Week*, Apr. 21, 1975, p. 108. See also FMCS, *Report*, 1975, pp. 44–45. Another report on the Georgia-Pacific program appeared in the *AFL-CIO News*, 20:14, Apr. 5, 1975, p. 1.

[23]*New York Times*, May 21, 1972.

FIGURE 16-6   Days idle due to strikes as a percent of total time worked in the total economy of the United States, 1947–1991. (*Source:* Bureau of Labor Statistice, *Monthly Labor Review,* December 1991.)

2 *Unfavorable customer response* (such as beginning to buy from foreign sources).

3 *Increased complexity* of issues, which prevents eleventh-hour pressure settlements. The need for consensus on some issues also prevents use of coercion.[24]

Figure 16-6 shows the decline in days lost due to strikes in American industry from 1947 to 1991.

In-Plant Actions to Avoid Strikes

For many unions the strike as a weapon has lost its appeal. But conflicts with employers continue to arise. So some unions are resorting to different tactics than the strike to bring pressure on employers.

Especially popular is the in-plant action. A form of action that is short of the strike is "working to rule"—that is, reducing the pace of work through the careful and intentionally slow following of procedures. Working to rule has been used effectively by many public employee groups—who are generally denied the right to strike—for years. Air traffic controllers, police and firefighters, and public transportation employees have caused great disruption of public services in order to pressure their employers by working to rule.

In the past private-sector unions generally eschewed working-to-rule in favor of the strike, which they considered more effective. But with the strike so often failing in the private sector in recent years, working-to-rule actions have become more attractive. For example in 1990 a handbook published by the Industrial Union Department of the AFL-CIO advised

[24]Adapted from John T. Dunlop, "The Function of the Strike," in John T. Dunlop and N. W. Chamberlain, eds., *Frontiers of Collective Bargaining* (New York: Harper, 1967), pp. 111–116.

unionists that while the strike is still often useful, "staying on the job and working from the inside may be more appropriate and effective."

An effective in-plant campaign may well require even greater organization and discipline among union members than a strike. It is especially difficult to take an in-plant job action that damages the employer without violating the contract.

Sometimes the action is meant only to send a message to the employer. "An office full of employees tapping pencils in unison when a supervisor walks through can be quite intimidating," said one union representative.[25]

Striker Replacement Legislation: Can the Strike Be Revived?

One reason for the decline in the frequency of strikes is that the strike is no longer as successful for unions as it used to be. A key reason is the ability of employers to replace strikers with new employees. As we saw earlier in this chapter, the ability of employers to replace striking workers and continue operations is key to the employer winning a strike. Under American law an economic striker is gambling with his or her job because an employer has a legal right to replace strikers permanently (so long as the employer did not cause the strike by committing an unfair labor practice). Employers have used the right to replace strikers with greater and greater effectiveness in recent years. In 1990, according to an estimate by the AFL-CIO 11 percent of the 243,000 American workers who participated in major strikes were permanently replaced by their employers.[26]

In recent years unions have sought unsuccessfully to get the law changed to prevent employers from permanently replacing striking workers. They have advanced four major reasons for the change. First, permanent replacement is argued to be an unfair hardship on workers for excising their statutory right to strike. Second, permanent replacement is said to make the right to strike meaningless in practice because it made the risk too high for workers to bear. Third, permanent replacement is said to unfairly create an imbalance in bargaining to the employers' favor. Fourth, the unions point out that in no other major industrial country is it legal for employers to replace striking workers permanently.

Employers retorted that the facts are very different. The law permitting permanent replacement of strikers has been in force since 1938 (a Supreme Court ruling in *National Labor Relations Board v. Mackay Radio and Telegraph Co.*) and there is no reason to change it now. By proposing to change the law the unions are seeking an unfair advantage in bargaining, employers argued. Furthermore, prohibiting the permanent replacement

[25]"Growing Numbers of Unions Adopting In-Plant Actions to Avoid Strikes," Bureau of National Affairs, *Daily Labor Report*, No. 151, Aug. 6, 1991, pp. C-1ff.

[26]AFL-CIO, *The Permanent Replacement of Workers Striking over Health Care Benefits in 1990* (Washington, D.C.: AFL-CIO, 1991).

of strikers would invite the unions to make more frequent use of the strike, creating inconvenience for the public.[27]

In the summer of 1992 the Senate considered a bill prohibiting employers from permanently replacing strikers. A similar measure had already been passed by the House of Representatives. In an attempt to secure passage of the replacement ban in the Senate, the AFL-CIO offered to submit disputes to an independent fact-finding body in exchange. The Senate rejected the offer.

The controversy over striker replacement took place not only in Congress but in the states as well. In 1991 the Minnesota legislature passed a bill prohibiting replacement of strikers in those few situations where companies were subject to state and not federal labor law. But the state's governor vetoed the bill.

ALTERNATIVES TO STRIKES

Dissatisfaction of management, labor, and the public with work stoppages has long stimulated a search for other techniques of dispute settlement.[28]

What Is Arbitration?

Arbitration is a process by which an answer is provided for issues in dispute. Whereas the focus in mediation is on bringing the parties to some agreement, the focus in arbitration is on what the agreement should be. Arbitration, therefore, is like seeking a decision from a judge in a court proceeding. It is a quasi-legal procedure. Sometimes the parties accept an arbitration award as settling their dispute; sometimes they do not.

There are many forms of arbitration. The old meaning of the term in labor relations (in the nineteenth and early twentieth centuries) was analogous to the procedure that we now call collective bargaining. When a dispute arose between an employer and unionized workers, a panel of union representatives and management representatives was assembled to "arbitrate" (i.e., to settle) the dispute. The panel was to make a decision about the dispute that was binding on both sides. In recent times, we have used the term "arbitration" primarily to refer to the decision made by a neutral party (but not a court) about a dispute. But some remnants of the old usage continue in cases when panels of labor and management meet to resolve disputes without a neutral.

[27]"Striker Replacement Legislation," *Congressional Digest*, 70:11, November 1991, p. 16.
[28]David L. Cole, *The Quest for Industrial Peace* (New York: McGraw-Hill, 1963); and Howard J. Anderson, ed., *New Techniques in Labor Dispute Resolution: A Report of the 23rd Conference of the Association of Labor Mediation Agencies* (Washington, D.C.: Bureau of National Affairs, 1976). See also Peter J. Brennan, ed., *Exploring Alternatives to the Strike*, Reprint No. 2910, *Monthly Labor Review*, September 1973 (Washington, D.C.: U.S. Department of Labor, 1974).

Recently arbitration has been combined with mediation in a process called "med-arb." The process operates by selecting a person as arbitrator of a dispute, but having him or her first attempt to mediate a settlement between the parties. The authority to arbitrate the dispute (that is, to decide it) adds weight to a mediator's recommendations. Mediation is attempted because it is preferred to arbitration because a mediated settlement is one both parties are likely to accept in good faith and attempt to make work, since they made the settlement. An arbitration decision may be binding but is likely to please only one or neither side.[29]

Types of Arbitration by Neutrals

In arbitration by a neutral, each side of a dispute presents its position on disputed matters to the arbitrator and the arbitrator decides on what the disposition of each issue should be. Arbitration may be final, or it may be advisory. Final arbitration means the dispute is to be settled on the basis of the arbitrator's decision.

Advisory arbitration envisages that the parties will negotiate a settlement using the arbitration decision (the "award") as a guide, but not necessarily holding to it.

Arbitration may be binding or nonbinding. An award is binding if the parties are committed to its acceptance. An award is nonbinding if they may choose to accept it or not. In grievance arbitration (described in detail in Chapter 20), approximately 95 percent of all arbitrators' decisions are binding on the parties (estimate from the American Arbitration Association).

Arbitration may be voluntary or compulsory. It is voluntary if the parties have agreed to utilize the process, and it is compulsory if a government agency requires them to accept arbitration.

These categories allow considerable variations in the form of arbitration employed to settle disputes. Thus, there may be voluntary binding arbitration or voluntary nonbinding arbitration. Similarly, there may be compulsory binding arbitration or compulsory nonbinding arbitration. (Incidentally, nonbinding arbitration is very much like mediation, except that an arbitrator's advice will ordinarily concern the way the parties should dispose of the issues, whereas a mediator's recommendations will concern the way he or she thinks the parties can agree to dispose of the issues.)

In the United States today, voluntary binding arbitration (involving neutrals) is the primary method of resolution of grievances arising over the terms of collective bargaining disputes.

Grievances are referred to as disputes over *rights*, since they arise from rights of employees or employers that are created by the collective bar-

[29]Jerome H. Ross, "The Med-Arb Process in Labor Agreement Negotiations," Society for Professionals in Dispute Resolution, Occasional Paper No. 21-1, Febuary 1982, Washington, D.C.

gaining agreement. Disputes over the terms of new contracts, that is, in collective bargaining negotiations, are referred to as disputes over *interests*, since they involve the conflicting interests of the two parties. Grievance arbitration is therefore called "rights arbitration" and is, as we have said, very common in the United States. Arbitration of disputes over the terms of collective bargaining agreements is referred to as "interest arbitration." It has been very uncommon in the United States. For the most part, neither unions nor employers in the private sector have been willing to submit such important issues as general wage changes, the establishment of fringe benefits, and working conditions and work rules to neutrals for disposition. They have preferred to rely on collective bargaining and associated economic pressure (i.e., strikes and lockouts) to reach settlement of such issues.[30] Changing circumstances in recent years have generated increasing discussion of interest arbitration, but with one or two exceptions (especially in the steel industry, see Chapter 18), there has been no substantial movement toward interest arbitration in the private sector.[31] In the public sector, however, there has been a greater resort to interest arbitration (see Chapter 11).

Interest Arbitration

Interest arbitration is potentially a major alternative to the strike as a means of resolving impasses in contract negotiations. A broad-interest arbitration is often used for that purpose. In Germany, the inclusion of clauses in collective bargaining agreements that call for arbitration where there is a breakdown of negotiations has been hailed as a major reason for the apparent success of that country's system of industrial relations.[32] And in the United States there have been some important experiments with interest arbitration, especially in the glass, paper, and steel industries.[33] Also, arbitration of contract disputes has had considerable use in public employment, as is described in Chapter 11. In fact, 17 states now require binding interest arbitration for some public employees, especially police and firefighters.

Government Intervention

For many years the federal government intervened in strikes that were considered likely to create national emergencies. The Taft-Hartley Act of

[30]Raymond A. Smardon, "Arbitration Is No Bargain," *Nation's Business*, October 1974, pp. 80–83.
[31]"Arbitration Instead of Strikes," *Industry Week*, 183:2, Oct. 14, 1974, pp. 30–35.
[32]"West Germany: The Importance of Arbitration," *European Industrial Relations Review*, 55, July 1978, pp. 21–22.
[33]Charles A. Myers, "Voluntary Arbitration of Disputes over New Labor Contracts," *Sloan Management Review*, Fall 1976, pp. 73–79. See also Homer C. La Rue, "An Historical Overview of Interest Arbitration in the United States," *Arbitration Journal*, 42:4, December 1987, pp. 13–22.

1947 established a mechanism for the President to intervene formally when he found the health and safety of the nation to be threatened by a work stoppage. The act allowed the President to send strikers back to work for a "cooling-off" period and to establish a panel to make recommendations for a settlement of the stoppage. But it did not allow the government to impose its recommendations on the disputants. When the cooling-off period expired, the strike could be resumed. If that happened, however, the President would ask Congress to legislate an end to the dispute, because Congress had the power to impose its conclusions.

The intervention of the President in a number of disputes over the years became controversial. Managements believed that government most often took the side of labor. When Ronald Reagan initiated a long period of Republican control in 1981, the government ceased to be active in trying to settle labor disputes through the emergency procedures of the Taft-Hartley Act.[34] Some observers have condemned the government for its refusal to get involved. "The federal government's historical role in significant labor-management disputes," wrote John Dunlop in 1989, "has been to provide the public with a coherent, authoritative statement of the essential facts underlying the controversy and with neutral recommendations for resolving it. . . . The government has not discharged this function very well."[35]

Unions and "Corporate Campaigns"

In an effort to find other sources of leverage against employers, or to supplement a strike, unions have developed some innovative methods of pressure. One of the most controversial of the unions' new approaches has been labeled the "corporate campaign." In essence, corporate campaigns attempt to bring pressure directly on the managers and directors of companies with whom a union has a dispute. Union members have traveled across the country to picket at the homes of corporate executives. They have attended the shareholder meetings of banks that lend to companies involved in disputes with a union, and have protested the loans. They have identified the businesses of persons who are directors of a company with which the union has a dispute, and have publicized the involvement of the directors' home companies.

The unions argue that such efforts pierce a veil of noninvolvement behind which hide business executives who support and profit from the antiunion position of companies locked in disputes with the unions. The executives singled out for union attention respond that it is often an unfair invasion of their privacy and an attempt to draw bystanders into someone else's fight.

---

[34]See Charles M. Rehmus, "Emergency Strikes Revisited," *Industrial and Labor Relations Review*, 43:2, January 1990, pp. 175–190.

[35]John T. Dunlop, "Government Role Poorly Played," *Atlanta Constitution*, Mar. 12, 1989, pp. 1-D, 2-D.

Have corporate campaigns proven successful? A study of 28 such efforts in the period 1976 to 1988 found that corporate campaigns were rarely successful in supplementing strikes, but sometimes successful when used in place of strikes. The most successful efforts, however, involved efforts by the unions to organize new members.[36]

The Climate of Labor Relations

Since the late 1940s there has been a lessening frequency of strikes, and shorter strikes on the average, in the private sector. Strikes are rarely as violent or bitter as they have been in the past. In public employment and in the health industry, where labor relations had been in increasing turmoil in the 1960s, the 1980s brought a calming of relations. And even in industries such as maritime, construction, airlines, automobiles, and supermarkets, where fundamental problems in bargaining structure exist, the climate of labor relations has nonetheless been less agitated recently.

It is not easy to identify the causes of this improvement in the labor relations climate. Observers in the late 1950s who first noted the trend ascribed it to the maturing of labor relations.[37] In their view, where unions have become established and fear less for their survival, they are able to behave less aggressively. Conversely, as management accepts unions where they now are and ceases to challenge their very existence, relations between the companies and the unions can become more normal. Both these factors, the unions' increasing maturity and the employers' lessened hostility to unions, seem to have been important in improving the climate of labor relations.

In recent years, observers have focused less on maturity in labor relations and more on an adverse economic climate in explaining a trend toward labor-management cooperation. A combination of lower productivity, high unemployment, and the threat of high-quality foreign imports is forcing management and labor to abandon confrontation. "The adversary-versus-adversary type of relation seems to be fading," said one government official, concluding that the era of total confrontation at the bargaining table of the last 40 years is over.[38]

The establishment of unions in the 1930s and 1940s in the private sectors, and in the 1960s in the public sectors has removed a cause of social unrest, and the spotlight of controversy has moved to other issues. The

[36]Paul Jarley and Cheryl L. Maranto, "Union Corporate Campaigns: An Assessment," *Industrial and Labor Relations Review*, 43:5, July 1990, pp. 505–503. See also Charles R. Perry, *Union Corporate Campaigns*, Study No. 66 (Philadelphia: University of Pennsylvania, Wharton Industrial Research Unit, 1987).

[37]Richard A. Lester, *As Unions Mature* (Princeton, N.J.: Princeton University Press, 1958). Also William E. Simkin, "The Trend to Maturity in Industrial Relations," *Industrial Relations*, 3:1, February 1964, pp. 1–4.

[38]Kenneth E. Moffett, quoted in Bureau of National Affairs, *Daily Labor Report*, No. 170, Aug. 29, 1980, p. A8.

civil and job rights of minority groups and women have replaced union recognition as a central social issue, and labor relations turmoil has subsided. Some have, of course, criticized the trade unions for not adopting a more militant stance toward employers in support of the rights of minorities and women. They would like to use the trade union movement as a weapon in the civil rights struggle, and this seems to require labor relations turmoil.

In general, because labor unions tend to support liberal political objectives and managers tend to be conservative, peaceful relations between labor and management subject both to the criticism of disloyalty. An especially contentious political atmosphere can, therefore, disrupt the labor relations climate, and often threatens to do so. The trend of recent years toward a lessening of overt conflict in labor-management relations seems likely to continue for the near future. General political and social circumstances, as well as the potential for conflict in the direct relationship of the parties, however, will constrain the degree to which the labor relations climate can be improved.

CHAPTER SUMMARY

Strikes and lockouts are forms of economic warfare and often bring severe losses to those engaged in them and inconvenience to third parties. Owing to the sometimes serious consequences of work stoppages, it has been proposed that strikes be made illegal. In response, a "right to strike" has been claimed, and the courts and Congress have established the right to strike as well as restrictions on its use. In general, employees of private firms may legally strike, though not for illegal objectives. Public employees generally have no legal right to strike. Disputes over wages and working conditions are by far the major causes of work stoppages.

Two opposing attitudes toward strikes exist. In one view, strikes are regarded as evidence of a breakdown in the bargaining process. In the other view, strikes are seen as an integral part of the bargaining process with certain functions to perform in bringing the parties to a settlement. In the latter view, therefore, a certain frequency of strikes is to be expected.

Since the stakes are very high, unions are careful to call strikes only when union leadership knows the employees will actually cease work. Once the strike is under way, the union must organize picketing and also try to provide financial support for employees while their paychecks are cut off. The major strikes that unions have lost in the United States have occurred when the employer has been able to obtain replacements and operate indefinitely in the face of the strike. Thus, employers attempt to continue operations of their facilities through the use of employees who do not join the strike, supervisors, or replacements. Because a strike is a serious event for a firm, a number of questions must be given careful forethought, including the question of whether the company will lose customers if there is an interruption in the filling of orders.

Recently unions have sought to have the law changed to prevent employers from permanently replacing employees who go on strike.

Numerous alternatives have been proposed to the strike. One involves mediation: a process of trying to bring disputing parties to agreement. The process depends critically on the skills of the mediator. Among other functions, the mediator handles the procedures and scheduling of meetings and is an important communications link between the disputing parties. Because of the large volume of collective bargaining disputes, the various states and the federal government have set up public mediation agencies. The most important of these is the Federal Mediation and Conciliation Service. A new program, relations by objectives, uses behavioral science techniques to prod labor and management toward fundamental changes in their basic relationship.

Arbitration is a quasi-legal process for settling a dispute. Arbitration of contract disputes, "rights" arbitration, may be advisory or final, binding or nonbinding, voluntary or compulsory. It may or may not involve a neutral party in making the decision. Arbitration over the terms of collective bargaining agreements, or interest arbitration, is very uncommon.

QUESTIONS FOR THOUGHT AND DISCUSSION

1 Why has strike activity in the United States declined dramatically? Is the decline a good thing for America, or not a good thing? Why?

2 What functions does a strike perform? Is there another way to perform the same functions? What would it be?

3 What are the most important factors in a union's preparation for a strike? A company's? Why?

4 Should strikes be illegal? Would a prohibition of strikes be effective? Why or why not?

5 What are the most important functions of a mediator? What skills does an effective mediator need to have?

6 What are the differences between arbitration and mediation? What types of arbitration are there? Why do you think arbitration is used so rarely in America as a means of settling disputes over the terms of collective bargaining agreements?

7 What are the changes in the labor force that have made strikes and work stoppages unattractive as a method of persuasion in disputes? Do you think striking will ever become obsolete? Why or why not?

8 What are arguments for and against the hiring of permanent replacements for striking employees?

SELECTED READING

Dunlop, John T., *Dispute Resolution* (Dover, Mass.: Auburn House, 1984).

Filippelli, Ronald, *Labor Conflict in the United States: An Encyclopedia* (New York: Garland Publishing, 1990).

Folberg, Jay, and Alison Taylor, *Mediation: A Comprehensive Guide to Conflict Resolution* (San Francisco: Jossey-Bass, 1984).

Kagel, Sam, and Kathy Kelly, *The Anatomy of Mediation: What Makes It Work* (Washington, D.C.: Bureau of National Affairs Books, 1989).

Kolb, Deborah M., *The Mediators* (Cambridge, Mass.: MIT Press, 1983).

Kressel, Kenneth, and Dean G. Pruitt and Associates, *Mediation Research* (San Francisco: Jossey-Bass, 1989).

Loewenberg, J. Joseph, et al., *Compulsory Arbitration: An International Comparison* (Lexington, Mass.: Lexington Books, 1976).

Simkin, William E., *Mediation and the Dynamics of Collective Bargaining*, 2d ed. (Washington, D.C.: Bureau of National Affairs, 1986).

Wheeler, Hoyt N., *Industrial Conflict: An Integrative Theory* (Charleston: University of South Carolina Press, 1986).

SUBJECTS OF COLLECTIVE BARGAINING

The bargaining power of companies and unions is used for specific objectives. Among the most common objectives are those involving the setting of particular wage rates, benefits, and working conditions. But bargaining power is not all there is to establishing wages and conditions of work. The actions of management and labor must also reflect the environment in which they are to be carried out. Wages must be adjusted so that employees may keep up or improve their standard of living. But wages must also be balanced so that a company may sell its products at a fair profit. Working conditions must be adjusted to meet changing circumstances in production and also to meet the changing expectations of employees about what a job ought to involve.

CHAPTER 17

RIGHTS OF MANAGEMENT, UNIONS, AND EMPLOYEES

MANAGEMENT'S RIGHT TO MANAGE

The Advent of a Union

The advent of a union has certain implications for management. Before its employees organize, management has the unilateral authority to make decisions about the conduct of the business. After unionization, it finds its authority limited in many ways. While management largely preserves the right to take action, it nevertheless may find its decisions questioned and in some instances reversed. It is not surprising that management sometimes seeks to retain or recapture as much of its once unhindered authority as possible.

In the absence of a union, management holds virtually unlimited authority. It may exercise its authority with care or be arbitrary. How does it work? Suppose the company decides to discharge an employee. Other employees may think the penalty is too harsh, but management retains the full authority. Or suppose the company decides to grant a wage increase. The boss tells the employees that they get a small increase. The employees say thank you but mumble behind the boss's back, "The stingy so-and-so." But management has sole authority.

When a union comes in, however, there is a change. There is countervailing power. The employees can take collective action. They can close the plant down. The transition period is very difficult for management. The union may abuse its power. The company resents it. But the union and the company cannot conduct a power struggle every day, and so some basis for uninterrupted production must be found. This basis is usually a collective bargaining agreement.

There is an evolution in the power relationship between a company and a union. At the beginning the company has unfettered authority. Then the union appears. There is a period of transition marked by power struggles over many types of issues. An agreement is reached, which becomes the basis of the relationship. But what are to be the respective rules for the management and the union? What rights does each have?

Management Rights in the Collective Bargaining Agreement

In order to retain as much authority as possible in the direction of the workplace, management has sought to include certain provisions in collective bargaining agreements. Some provisions spell out the functions of management. Others limit the scope of the agreement to certain items. The former are described as "management rights" clauses. The latter are called "savings" clauses.

A typical management rights clause reads as follows:

> The Company retains the exclusive right and responsibility to manage the business and plants and to direct the working forces subject to the provisions of this Agreement, including the right to hire, suspend, or discharge for proper cause or transfer and the right to relieve employees from duty because of lack of work or for other legitimate reasons.

The intent of this language is to retain for the company the authority to do anything not explicitly limited by the language of the agreement. Suppose the contract were silent about promotions, and management were to decide to establish a test for promotions. If the union objected, management would argue that the management rights clause gave it the authority to establish the test. In practice, however, a management rights clause is not as useful as it might seem. The effect of the clause is limited in several ways. Arbitrators will often rule that a long-standing practice is part of the agreement, even if not spelled out, so that management may not change it with impunity. Also, an agreement that includes a no-strike pledge by the union is presumed to cover all disputes between the parties. An arbitrator might be unwilling to invest unilateral authority in the hands of management while holding the union to a no-strike pledge. Finally, the company has a legal duty to bargain about many matters and may be required to do so, regardless of the employer rights clause in the agreement.

Management rights statements now appear in about 86 percent of signed agreements. About 53 percent of agreements, on the other hand, contain a general statement restricting management prerogatives; of these, 95 percent prohibit management from taking actions in violation of the contract terms and 17 percent specify that management actions are subject to grievance or arbitration procedures. Some 27 percent of agreements limit management's right to make technological changes, and 25 percent limit management's right to shut plants down or relocate work.[1]

Rights reserved for management are not found only in the management rights and savings clauses of agreements; managerial authority is delineated throughout collective bargaining agreements. For this reason, many managers believe that enumerating so-called management rights in a particular clause of the agreement actually limits those rights rather than allowing them to remain broad and unstated. To meet this criticism, some agreements provide that management rights listed in the agreements are not necessarily all-inclusive (i.e., others also exist).

Where there are rights, there are also obligations. It has been noted that these rights are modified in many ways by the collective bargaining agreement. In later pages many of the specific limitations imposed on management by the language of a collective bargaining agreement will be mentioned. But it is also useful to point out here that with reserved rights go certain implied obligations of management. These obligations need not be spelled out in a contract with a labor union to be found binding on management. For example, among these implied obligations is the maintenance of a safe and healthy workplace.

LIMITATIONS ON MANAGEMENT RIGHTS

Subcontracting

Many things done in a plant or other facility by the employees of a company could, in fact, be done on a specialized basis by other firms. When management makes a contract with another firm to do things that might be done by its own employees, the process is called "subcontracting" (or contracting out). There are many types of subcontracting. A company might decide not to employ janitors or cleaning personnel and hire a custodial service contractor. A firm that has construction operations to be done at a plant site might choose not to do them with its own maintenance crews and could contract out the work to a construction firm. Or a company might develop a new part for one of its products but, instead of producing the part itself, might contract with another company to supply the part. Each of these examples involves an action by management that may create a labor relations dispute over subcontracting.

Managements usually argue that they should be free to operate their businesses on as low-cost a basis as possible. Subcontracting is often a method of obtaining goods or services more cheaply than the company could produce them itself. In consequence, there should not, they argue, be restrictions on subcontracting.

---

[1]Bureau of National Affairs, *Basic Patterns in Union Contracts*, 12th ed. (Washington, D.C.: Bureau of National Affairs, 1989), pp. 80–81.

The unions reply that subcontracting often deprives union members of their jobs. When a company decides to subcontract janitorial service or maintenance, it may lay off its existing custodial or maintenance staff. The union argues that it cannot be indifferent to a matter that may have such an important impact on the employees it represents. Therefore, it often insists on being involved in the decision-making process about subcontracting.

There are, of course, legal questions involved. Must management bargain with the union over a subcontracting decision? The National Labor Relations Act says that management has a duty to bargain with respect to "rates of pay, wages, hours of employment, or other conditions of employment" [section 9(a)]. Is subcontracting such a matter?

In 1964 the Supreme Court decided that subcontracting was a matter about which management has a legal obligation to bargain. The court case arose from a dispute between Fiberboard Paper Products Corporation and the United Steelworkers of America. The company had a plant in Emeryville, California. Since 1937 the union had represented maintenance employees at the plant. In September 1958 the union and the company entered the latest of a series of collective bargaining agreements, which was to expire on July 31, 1959. The union sought to set a time and place for negotiations prior to the end of July, but the company delayed. On July 27, 1959, the parties met and the company informed the union that it had determined that substantial savings could be effected by contracting out the work. The company gave the union a letter which read, in part, "In these new circumstances, we are sure you will realize that negotiation of a new contract would be pointless." This was because the company intended to discharge all its maintenance personnel, who would be replaced by employees of the maintenance contractor, Fluor Maintenance, Inc. Thereafter, on July 31 the company terminated the employment of its maintenance personnel, and Fluor employees took over. The Steelworkers union conducted an unsuccessful strike against the company and filed unfair labor practice charges with the NLRB. After several years of litigation, the case reached the Supreme Court.

The Court held that the company was obligated to bargain with the union before making the decision to subcontract work that would otherwise have been performed by employees represented by the union. The company was obligated to rehire for existing maintenance jobs the employees it had laid off and to pay 36 employees a total of $330,931.95 in back pay.[2] The Court's decisions have had an impact, of course. The decisions do not say that a company must not subcontract, but rather that it must bargain with the union about subcontracting. The rationale is to allow a union an opportunity to make such adjustments as might be necessary to retain the jobs affected by the subcontracting, if the union wishes.

[2]*Fiberboard Paper Products Corp. v. NLRB*, 397 U.S. 203 (1964). The financial payment was reported in Bureau of National Affairs, *Daily Labor Report*, No. 248, Dec. 24, 1969.

As a practical matter, the obligation to bargain also left employers with less initiative in the matter and has probably contributed to less subcontracting than would otherwise have occurred. By 1983, 50 percent of union contracts imposed some limitation on subcontracting (an increase from 28 percent in 1965). Only in 2 percent of the contracts, however, was subcontracting of bargaining-unit work strictly prohibited. In most of the clauses, advance consultation about subcontracting is all that is required. In 23 percent of the contracts, subcontracting is prohibited if layoffs exist or would result from subcontracting.[3]

There is great variety in the arrangements that unions and employers make with respect to subcontracting. The General Motors Corporation and the United Auto Workers have agreed that employees with seniority in the company (that is, those not on probation) should not be laid off as a "direct and immediate result of work being performed by any outside contractor" on the company's premises. When management does decide to subcontract work, it further agrees to notify the union in advance.

Other agreements sometimes go much further than this. Teamsters Local No. 959 in Alaska and the Associated General Contractors of Alaska agreed to an arrangement on subcontracting which provided that the employers could not subcontract any work that the Teamsters might do (i.e., work that was in the Teamsters' jurisdiction; see Chapter 3) unless

- The subcontractor's employees were members of the union
- The subcontractor agreed to the same terms and conditions of employment binding between the union and the general contractors

This was, of course, a very favorable contractual provision for the union. Unfortunately for the union, the Federal Trade Commission decided that the provision was in violation of the federal antitrust laws, and the union and the contractors were forced to remove the provision from the agreement. According to the FTC, the purpose of the provision was not to protect the jobs of Teamsters from being lost as a result of subcontracting (the clear purpose of the GM-UAW arrangement) but rather to cause potential subcontractors to recognize the union as representative of their employees in order to get business (so-called top-down organizing) or, alternatively, to exclude nonunionized firms from doing business with the contractors party to the agreement with the Teamsters. This latter purpose was in violation of the law, the FTC decided.[4]

Work Transfer

In January 1982, Milwaukee Spring Company asked United Auto Workers Local 547 to forgo a scheduled wage increase and to make other concessions

---

[3]Bureau of National Affairs, *Basic Patterns*, p. 64.
[4]Bureau of National Affairs, *Daily Labor Report*, No. 138, July 18, 1978, pp. A1, A2.

to reduce the company's labor costs at a plant in Milwaukee. The union refused. Two months later, the company announced its intention to transfer assembly operations to a nonunion plant and to lay off 32 workers in Milwaukee. In the subsequent litigation, the union and the company agreed that the company's motive was economic in nature and was not based on antiunion opinions. Had the latter been the case, the company's action would have been illegal under the *Darlington* case law (see below). But, the motivation was economic. Was the company's action legal? The Auto Workers thought that it was not and filed an unfair labor practice complaint.

In October 1982, the NLRB agreed with the union. The company's purpose, it found, was to avoid the wage provisions of the contract. Consequently the company was prohibited from implementing its decision to relocate assembly operations without the union's consent during the term of the contract. This was because the labor laws prohibit an employer from making a unilateral change in wages or working conditions during the term of a collective bargaining agreement.

In the 15 months following the October 1982 decision, the terms of several NLRB members expired and President Reagan replaced them with more conservative appointees. In January 1984, the NLRB again reviewed the *Milwaukee Spring* case. This time, the board found no violation of the law. "We have searched the contract in vain for a provision requiring bargaining unit work to remain in Milwaukee," the board said. The transfer of work did not disturb wages and conditions in Milwaukee (i.e., those employees who were not laid off received the wages and conditions called for by the agreement), and so there were no unilateral changes by management in working conditions and wages. The company had a duty to bargain with the union about the effects on employees of the proposed transfer, but if the company and union could not agree, the company could transfer the work unilaterally, so long as the contract did not specifically prohibit it.[5] The law had thus made a complete circle. Prior to October 1982, an employer could transfer work for economic reasons but had to bargain with the union over its consequences. After October 1982, an employer could not transfer work. Finally, after January 1984, an employer could again transfer work.

In April 1984, the NLRB further widened employers' authority to transfer work. Otis Elevator Company had decided to consolidate research and development operations and closed a facility. The employees involved were transferred. The company did not bargain with the union about the move. The union complained to the NLRB. In 1981 the NLRB found

---

[5]"NLRB Okays Employers Authority," Bureau of National Affairs, *Daily Labor Report*, No. 16, Jan. 25, 1984, pp. AA1–AA2; Joann S. Lublin, "NLRB Rules," *Wall Street Journal*, Jan. 25, 1984. See also "BLS Study of Contract Provisions on Plant Closure and Relocation," Bureau of National Affairs, *Daily Labor Report*, No. 166, Aug. 27, 1981, pp. E1–E14.

against the company. Later, the courts returned the case to the board. The board reviewed the case in light of the Supreme Court's 1981 ruling in *First National Maintenance v. NLRB* that there was no duty to bargain for an employer if the decision to move or close a facility or operations involved the basic scope and nature of the enterprise, such as consolidating or subcontracting work or installing labor-saving machinery. Hence, the NLRB said in 1984, reversing its 1981 position, that Otis Elevator could consolidate its facilities and transfer employees without bargaining with the union.[6]

It is apparent from the recitation of cases that the law in this area is in continual flux and that it may change at any moment as cases make their way through the NLRB and the courts. Nonetheless, a summary is useful to try to identify where American law now stands on the important question of managerial prerogatives with respect to the transfer of work from a unionized facility.

Until 1964, unless an employer gave up in bargaining its right to close a plant or transfer work from a facility, the employer could transfer work or close a plant at will, so long as it was not motivated by the purpose of denying its employees union representation *(Darlington)*. Then, in 1964, the Supreme Court held that a company had a duty to bargain about subcontracting work. The duty extended to both the decision and its impact on employees *(Fiberboard)*. In 1981, the Supreme Court said that if a company's decision to close a facility, transfer work, or subcontract was based on the basic scope of its business, it need not bargain with the union *(First National Maintenance)*. And in 1984 the NLRB said a company that wished to transfer work solely to avoid the costs of a union contract could do so as long as it had first bargained with the union, even though the company and the union failed to reach agreement *(Milwaukee Spring, 1984)*. In 1991 the NLRB required companies considering relocation to first bargain with the union if labor costs are a factor in the decision to relocate. In summary, litigation in the 30 years since the *Fiberboard* decision first broadened, then narrowed the unions' gains under *Fiberboard*, then broadened them again until, in the end, the law is less favorable to management than before *Fiberboard*. Today a company can transfer or subcontract work without the union's agreement at any time unless the company has restricted its rights by explicit provisions in the collective bargaining agreement, but must first bargain with the union if labor costs are an element of its decision.[7]

---

[6]Ben A. Franklin, "Labor Board," *New York Times*, Apr.11, 1984, p. A20. Also, "Otis Elevator," Bureau of National Affairs, *Daily Labor Report*, No. 70, Apr. 11, 1984, pp. A11, A12.

[7]Larry Reynolds, "NLRB Ruling Puts Relocation on the Bargaining Table," *Personnel*, 68:9, September 1991, p. 1ff. See also Charles J. Griffin, Jr., and Mark A. Jones, "Work Relocations—The Changing Rules Represent a Victory for Organized Labor," *Employee Relations Law Journal*, 17:3, Winter 1991–1992, pp. 389–404.

Work Standards

The aspect of union behavior that generally appears least defensible to management and the public involves rules about the performance of work. In the United States the term "featherbedding" has developed to describe rules that require payment to employees for work not done or work not needed. There are many variations of featherbedding. Sometimes unions object to the introduction of new technology. The union attempts to preserve existing jobs by prohibiting the use of new technology. In other cases unions seek to establish rules about crew size. Rules of this kind specify the number of workers on a particular type of paper machine, the size of the crew in the cockpit of an airplane, the number of workers in a gang of structural steel erectors, or the size of a longshorers' gang unloading a ship. Changing technology sometimes makes these crew restrictions very expensive.

A third type of restriction that is often especially galling to management involves the jurisdictional lines of different crafts or craft unions. Jurisdictional lines separate the work assignments that are allegedly the property of one trade from the assignments allegedly the property of another trade. For example, an electrician may install a wire box, but only a carpenter is allowed to cut through the wall to create the opening for the box. When the work of one trade is incidental, as, for example, when a carpenter must be assigned to only a few minutes' work so that the electrician can proceed (or vice versa), the employer may incur great expense. Yet collective bargaining agreements sometimes obligate employers to respect trade jurisdictions to such a degree.

Surprisingly, management is often involved in the establishment of uneconomic work practices. "Make-work rules do not usually begin as attempts by unions to force employers to hire an excessive number of workers."[8] Instead, the employer at one time imposes a rule or agrees with the union on a rule that seems to make perfect sense under the conditions then prevailing. In the course of time, however, changes in technology or working conditions diminish the appropriateness of the rule. As time passes, the gap becomes wider, and the more out of date the rule becomes, the more expensive it is to the employer. But, as the rule becomes outdated, the number of employees dependent on it grows. Hence, management more desperately seeks a change, and the union more vigorously rejects it.[9]

---

[8]Sumner Slichter, James Healy, and E. Robert Livernash, *The Impact of Collective Bargaining Management* (Washington, D.C.: Brookings, 1960), p. 317.

[9]See John T. Dunlop and Derek Bok, *Labor and the American Community* (New York: Simon and Schuster, 1970), pp. 271–274, for a discussion of the firefighters' dispute over work rules in the United States in this century.

Successorship

If a company acquires a facility from another company, what is the status of the union and the labor agreement at the acquired facility? Is the successor firm obligated to honor the labor agreement? This question has an important bearing on management on both sides of the transaction. A labor agreement may severely restrict what an existing or successor management can do to make a facility more efficient or profitable. If a facility is currently unprofitable, partly because of aspects of the labor agreement and of labor relations in general, the sale price of the facility would be improved if the successor firm were not bound to the labor agreement. If the successor were potentially free of the labor agreement, the value of the facility to both buyer and seller could be much enhanced. A new management's hands would not be tied by the labor agreement, and therefore it might be able to eliminate inefficient practices. Further, management believes it should be able to buy, or sell, a facility without buying or selling a labor agreement with it.

The unions, however, object to a process by which an employer may unload a labor agreement simply by selling the facility. There is no protection for workers in such a circumstance. Wage rates, fringe benefits, and working conditions would all be adversely affected for the workers involved.

In the absence of litigation, the companies and the unions involved may either work out their dispute or apply economic force to each other. That is, the successor employer may agree to recognize the union and the existing collective bargaining agreements or may attempt to bargain changes in the agreement. It might also choose to ignore the agreement, forcing the union to conduct a strike to enforce the agreement, if it is able to do so.

Alternatively, either side may choose to litigate the matters in dispute. Not surprisingly, there has been substantial litigation about the obligations and rights of successor employers. The law with respect to successorship has been set forth in three major decisions of the Supreme Court. The result seems to be that a successor employer has little legal responsibility to the employees of the acquired facility and can, in fact, conduct the acquisition in such a way that it has no responsibility. This is the case even if the acquired company and the union have a successorship clause in their agreement. A successorship clause provides that any change in management or in the identity of the parties to the contract will not invalidate it, but rather that the new management must assume the contractual obligations of its predecessor. (About one-third of agreements have such a clause.) This clause cannot ordinarily be enforced against the successor employer, however. The clause may be enforced against the selling corporation, but often that corporation is bankrupt or otherwise unsuitable for a legal proceeding. In some cases a union might seek to enjoin the sale of the facility if the company's obligations under the successorship clause are not being met.

THE RIGHTS OF THE UNION

Union Security Provisions in Collective Bargaining Agreements

Background   Unions in the United States have ordinarily insisted that some understanding regarding the status of the union be included in collective bargaining agreements. Prior to the 1930s, this understanding often took the form of a so-called closed shop. An employer who recognized a closed-shop arrangement agreed to employ only union members. Sometimes this meant that the company would inform the union when it needed additional employees and the union would refer its members. In other cases, the company would hire as it wished, but anyone it hired had to be or become a member of a union in order to stay employed. The closed shop not only attempted to keep nonunion employees out, but excluded members of other unions as well. The closed shop was very common in the railways, in construction, in printing, and in the maritime trades. It protected the status of the union, both from employers who might wish to destroy it, and from other, or rival, unions. Its nemesis was the so-called open shop, in which there was no union control.

Campaigns by employers to destroy the unions have been a periodic occurrence in American history. The contest for control between management and the unions has often centered around the issue of union security. In no industry has the contest been more lengthy, costly, and involved than in construction.

> The unions had an early start in organization (in the late 1800s) and before the building-trades employers were aware, the closed shop . . . was already established in the larger building centers. In other industries, particularly in manufacturing, the employers were able to curb the closed-shop movement.[10]

After 1900, open-shop manufacturers were threatened by the advance of the building trades unions. The unions first attempted to exclude nonmembers from working at particular crafts and later from building construction generally. Finally, they attempted to unionize manufacturers of products used in building by refusing to install products manufactured by nonunion workers. Open-shop manufacturers found it necessary, or convenient, to reply by helping to "correct" conditions in the building trades as a means of protecting the nonunion status of their own establishments. In 1900, for example, in Chicago the employers locked out the unions, insisting that the Building Trades Council, the craft unions' coordinating group, disband. The unions resisted, unsuccessfully. Contractors who tried to operate with unions were denied materials by the lumber and other building supply dealers and were denied credit by the banks. The unions surrendered after a 7-month battle. The Building Trades Council disbanded, and

---

[10]William Haber, *Industrial Relations in the Building Industry* (Cambridge, Mass.: Harvard University Press, 1930), p. 238.

open-shop clauses appeared in the agreements.[11] But 2 years later, the council had reassembled and the closed shop was reappearing.

This struggle over union security in the construction industry, together with the role of manufacturing firms in the struggle, is one of the oldest themes of American labor relations. There is not much written about it, but it is an important factor in many disputes, including political problems, that on the surface appear to be about other matters.

Construction is not the only industry in the United States in which long struggles have occurred about union security. In the 1930s the advent of the industrial unions occasioned a new and very bitter round of disputes. Union security provisions were an especially significant factor in many labor disputes arising during World War II, for example. Since the government was attempting to prevent work stoppages in order to maximize war production, it was drawn into these disputes. Employers insisted, without success, that noneconomic issues (especially union security) should not be the concern of government agencies. However, the government recognized the maintenance-of-membership formula (see definition below) as a basis for union security arrangements during the war.

After the Second World War, changes in the National Labor Relations Act affected the legality of certain types of union security arrangements. The introduction of law and the courts into the struggle over union security has modified its form without substantially resolving the disputes. In some industries and areas today, union security is not a serious issue. In others it is. This has always been the case and continues to be so in the United States.

This long-continuing concern for union security is peculiar to the United States. It stems in part from the opposition of employers to unions and the methods they have used to thwart unions. The yellow-dog contract, the blacklist, and similar methods seemed to require a union to securely establish its own position.[12] In addition, the threats of bids by rival unions and the resistance of the American Federation of Labor to dual unionism (which is common in continental Europe) reinforced interest in the union security.

Types of Union Security   In 1947 Congress wrote into the Taft-Hartley Act statutory provisions about union security. In so doing, Congress made union security provisions a matter of litigation before the NLRB and in the courts. Litigation has resulted in a complex series of definitions and classifications about union security provisions. We now have, therefore, a much more precise set of terms to describe different forms of union security. Whether the whole matter is not rendered even more complex as a result is

---

[11]Ibid., pp. 376–379.
[12]Paul E. Sultan, "The Union Security Issue," in Sumner Slichter et al., eds., *Public Policy and Collective Bargaining* (Madison, Wis.: Industrial Relations Research Association, 1962), pp. 88–120.

open to question. Certainly union security and the law about union security continue to be a very divisive issue in American labor relations.

Under section 2(11) of the Railway Labor Act (1926), which covers railways and airlines, Congress provided that unions and employers may enter into a union-shop agreement requiring all employees within the unit to join the union within 60 days after commencing their employment. Under the Wagner Act (1935) a somewhat different approach was taken to union security in the rest of private industry. The act read simply:

> Nothing in this Act . . . , or in any statute of the United States, shall preclude an employer from making an agreement with a labor organization . . . to require as a condition of employment membership therein. . . .

This provision of the National Labor Relations Act was construed to permit virtually any form of union security, including the closed shop. But in 1947, in the Taft-Hartley Act, Congress amended the law to permit employers to agree to require union membership as a condition of employment only on or after the thirtieth day following the beginning of such employment. With this provision, the closed shop was outlawed and the 30-day union shop permitted. Court decisions since that time have generally permitted other forms of union security arrangements with a "lesser" significance than the union shop. The phrase "required as a condition of employment" means that the employer may legally be required by the union to discharge an employee who does not conform to the union security provision; hence the description of the union shop as "compulsory unionism."

• *Closed shop* Membership in a union is required as a condition of employment. The closed shop is generally illegal in the United States.

• *Union shop* Becoming and remaining a union member is required as a condition of employment after the thirtieth day of employment (or later). The union shop is generally legal in the United States, except in certain states, as we shall see below.

• *Agency shop* All employees who do not join the union pay a fee in lieu of dues to the union for its services as a bargaining agent.

• *Maintenance-of-membership shop* All employees who choose to become union members must remain so as a condition of employment.

What does the term "union membership" mean? Ordinarily a union has a constitution and bylaws. It also has a method of application for membership and an initiation ceremony, and members are bound to its internal procedures. These internal procedures usually include disciplinary proceedings for violations of the union's constitution and bylaws. Does the legal phrase "membership in a labor organization" envisage all this?

Apparently it does not. The Taft-Hartley Act [section 8(a)3] includes this language:

No employer shall justify any discrimination against an employee for non-membership in a labor organization (A) if he has reasonable grounds for believing that such membership was not available to the employee on the same terms and conditions generally applicable to other members, or (B) . . . was denied or terminated for reasons other than the failure of the employee to tender the periodic dues and the initiation fees uniformly required as a condition of acquiring or retaining membership.

Thus, union membership is defined essentially as paying dues and initiation fees as uniformly levied by the union on all members. An employer cannot be required to discharge an employee because the employee refuses to obey a union bylaw or because the employee is expelled from the union, as long as the employee continues to be willing to pay dues.[13]

The closed shop is often defined as meaning that the employer agreed to hire only union members. It is now illegal. Does this mean an employer cannot agree to hire from a union hiring hall? The courts have ruled that a hiring-hall arrangement is legal, even if the employer agrees it will hire only from the union's hiring hall, as long as the union does not refuse to refer people who are not union members. The union may, however, give priority to people who have worked at the trade the longest and may refuse to refer those lacking skills. In consequence, union halls usually refer almost entirely union members, and some observers have concluded that the hiring hall is a closed shop in disguise. Hiring-hall arrangements are especially common in construction, longshoring, and the maritime trades.[14]

Furthermore, an exception was provided in the 1959 amendments to the Taft-Hartley Act, permitting a 7-day, not a 30-day, union shop in construction. In consequence, a union may require an employer in the construction industry, pursuant to a clause in the collective bargaining agreement, to discharge an employee who refuses to become a member of a union after 7 days on the job.

A final form of union security arrangement that is often combined with any of the above arrangements, or may exist independently, is the dues checkoff. Under a checkoff arrangement, the employer deducts union dues from the employees' paychecks and forwards the money directly to the union. This requires an individually signed authorization from each employee permitting the deduction, or checkoff. The union is relieved, by this procedure, of the expensive and time-consuming task of collecting dues from each member. Employers, however, end up bearing the administrative cost, which they sometimes allege to be substantial.

Unions in industries involving casual work, in which employees move among firms, rarely use a checkoff. The workers carry union books, which

[13]Glenn A. Zipp, "Rights and Responsibilities of Parties to a Union-Security Agreement," *Labor Law Journal*, 33:4, April 1982, pp. 202–217.
[14]U.S. Department of Labor, Labor Management Services Administration, *Exclusive Union Work Referred Systems in the Building Trades* (Washington, D.C., U.S. Department of Labor, 1970).

are stamped each time they go to the union hall and pay their dues. The books show that the workers are in good standing with the union. Check-offs are only beginning to appear in such industries. Not long ago in construction, the Laborers' Union negotiated agreements including a $0.10-per-hour-worked dues checkoff. All members of the union authorize the employer to deduct $0.10 per hour of work from their paychecks to be forwarded to the union.

Union security provisions are found in nearly all agreements if checkoff and hiring-hall provisions are included in the total. The union shop is the most common form of union security provision. A modified union shop appears in some collective bargaining agreements. It provides that employees who were not members of the union before or on the effective date of the collective bargaining agreement are excluded from the 30-day union membership requirement, but that all new employees are covered. In some instances, special groups of employees, such as students, temporary workers, and religious objectors (i.e., persons who object to belonging to any organization other than a religious sect), are excluded. The agency shop appears in 5 percent of agreements; the maintenance-of-membership shop in 4 percent.[15]

Originally, the Taft-Hartley Act required a vote by employees to authorize a union-shop clause in a collective bargaining agreement. Experience in the early 1950s with this election procedure was that union-shop clauses were ratified overwhelmingly. In consequence, the election requirement was abandoned. However, section 9(e)1 of the act authorizes petitions for elections to withdraw the union's right to a union security clause. Occasionally the NLRB conducts such elections, which sometimes result in the removal of the union security provision from the agreement.[16]

Right-to-Work Laws

Scope and Extent   One of the most unusual provisions of U.S. labor laws is section 14(b) of the Taft-Hartley Act:

> Nothing in this Act shall be construed as authorizing the execution or application of agreements requiring membership in a labor organization as a condition of employment in any State or Territory in which such execution or application is prohibited by State or Territorial law.

This provision is peculiar because it invites states to explicitly override the provision of the federal statute that legalizes union security clauses in collective bargaining agreements. This provision has spawned a group of state laws that have been generally called "right-to-work" laws.

[15]Bureau of National Affairs, *Basic Patterns*, p. 100.
[16]See, for example, *Retail Clerks Local 1001 v. Lyons Apparel, Seattle, Wash.* (NLRB election proceeding, July 1, 1975).

A right-to-work law provides that it is illegal for management and unions to agree to clauses in their contracts that make membership in a labor organization a condition of employment. Twenty-one states now have such laws: Alabama, Arizona, Arkansas, Florida, Georgia, Idaho, Iowa, Kansas, Louisiana, Mississippi, Nebraska, Nevada, North Carolina, North Dakota, South Carolina, South Dakota, Tennessee, Texas, Utah, Virginia, and Wyoming. In 1976 Louisiana passed a right-to-work law, the first state to do so since Wyoming in 1963. In 1986 Idaho passed a law, increasing the number of states from 20 to 21. Meanwhile, the unions sought, without success, to amend the law in Arkansas to make it less restrictive. And in Missouri, an employer-supported initiative to enact a right-to-work law failed on November 7, 1978, when voters defeated the proposed statute 60 percent to 40 percent.

The right-to-work laws in each state are alike in prohibiting the union shop but are dissimilar in their provisions on what other, if any, forms of union security are permitted. The agency shop, for example, is apparently legal in 10 of the states with right-to-work laws.

The scope and available remedies at law vary widely from state to state. Some consist solely of a general statement disallowing denial or abridgment of the right to work contingent on union membership.

> In addition, some laws prohibit (1) "combinations" or "conspiracies" to deprive persons of employment because of nonmembership . . . (2) strikes or picketing for the purposes of inducing an illegal agreement . . . (3) denial of employment to any person because of membership or nonmembership . . . (4) conspiracy to cause the discharge or denial of employment to an individual by inducing other persons to refuse to work with him because he is a nonmember.[17]

Many of the right-to-work states provide no penalties for violation of these laws; others merely have misdemeanor violations, generally providing approximately $100 fines and from 10 days to 12 months in jail.[18] Some states allow only injunctive relief (i.e., relief by court order).

Right to Work: Pro and Con   Those who support right-to-work laws argue that union membership should not be required as a condition of employment. They assert that if a union provides services, then people will join. If it does not provide services, people will not join. This is consistent, they say, with a freely competitive economy. They believe the union shop is unfair because it may compel workers against their will to join unions in order to have a job; hence, the name of the state statutes: "right-to-work" laws. Further, compulsory unionism is said to provide too much power to union leaders without placing checks on their performance, because the unions do not have to maintain the workers' support

[17]Labor Law Group, *Labor Relations and Social Problems* (Washington, D.C.: Bureau of National Affairs, 1973), p. 51.
[18]Bruce S. Warshal, "Right to Work; Pro and Con," *Labor Law Journal,* 17:3, March 1966, pp. 135–136.

in order to receive dues. Also, unions may use dues for political purposes to which workers object, and workers should not, therefore, be compelled to contribute to unions.

Opponents of right-to-work laws advance several reasons for their opposition. First, they object to the name "right to work" for these state laws. The laws do not provide a right to work, they point out. Instead, what the laws do is weaken unions. Second, the states with right-to-work laws are generally southern and midwestern states with low wage levels. These states have the right-to-work laws in order to keep wages low, it is argued.

> The "right-to-work" law does indeed strike at the very heart of the institution of collective bargaining, and thereby seeks to eliminate or weaken one of the most viable tools for uplifting poor and minority workers from the bottom of the economic ladder. . . . "Right-to-work" laws become but another means to perpetuate the "cycle of poverty" and the informal system of racism in the United States.[19]

Third, the unions argue that right-to-work laws permit some employees to get a "free ride" at the expense of those who support the union. The union has a legal obligation to bargain on behalf of all employees (members and nonmembers) and to represent all fairly in handling grievances and other matters. A union shop assumes that all employees pay their fair share of the cost of these services by the union. A right-to-work law permits some employees to evade paying their fair share. Fourth, the unions point out that right-to-work laws are supported by a national organization, the National Right to Work Committee, which is heavily financed by employers. The fact that employers actively support the right-to-work laws proves, the unions say, that the real purpose of the laws is to hinder the unions, not to protect the rights of individual employees.

A summary of the arguments for and against right-to-work laws is given in Figure 17-1.

Impact of Right-to-Work Laws   Right-to-work laws have been a major source of controversy between labor and management. In consequence, one might expect to find that right-to-work laws have had an important impact on union strength wherever the laws exist. However, the studies that have been done are largely inconclusive concerning the impact of the laws. There have been few major studies done since the late 1950s, and what has been done (including those of the late 1950s) has been largely contradictory and inconclusive.

Data on union membership clearly show a difference in union strength between states with and without right-to-work laws. States without such laws tend to have larger and more effective labor movements. However, it is not clear whether these differences are because of right-to-work legisla-

---

[19]*AFL-CIO Federationist*, 83:8, August 1976, p. 20.

PRO

Union security agreements interfere with an individual's exercise of a precious liberty – that of working.

Union security agreements also burden an individual in liberties of

- association
- speech
- religion

Voluntary union membership promotes responsible union leadership.

If an employee does not want to be represented by a union, he or she has no moral obligation to pay for it.

Since federal labor law prohibits an employer from discrimination on the basis of union membership, discrimination on the basis of nonmembership should also be prohibited.

CON

Free riders who benefit from union representation but do not share the costs of union membership have an unfair advantage.

Union security arrangements are merely an application of the democratic principle that the majority should rule, because a majority of the workers presumably voted for union representation.

Union security arrangements ensure that the union's status as the bargaining representative is not undermined through employer discrimination against members.

Union security agreements promotes

- industrial stability and labor peace
- responsible labor leadership
- the strength of unions to the benefit of employees as a whole because a secure union is felt to be a responsible union

FIGURE 17-1 Pro and con on right-to-work laws. *(Source: Thomas R. Haggard, Compulsory Unionism: The NLRB and the Courts, Philadelphia: Industrial Research Unit, Wharton School, The University of Pennsylvania, 1977.)*

tion or come from other factors. It can be argued that states with a weak labor movement have right-to-work laws because the unions are weak— rather than that the unions are weak because of the right-to-work law. The weakness of the unions in right-to-work states may be because of a limited industrial base, historical factors, and other such matters.

One of the largest studies conducted on the subject concluded that (1) the laws had little effect on labor relations in RTW states, except perhaps Iowa and Mississippi; (2) the laws have not "busted" any unions; (3) few members have resigned from unions; (4) there is very little effective enforcement of the laws; and (5) in the building construction industry, the laws are generally violated.[20]

The most careful study of the impact of a right-to-work law in any single state was that done by Frederic Meyers on the Texas statute. In his study, Meyers looked at organization patterns in a number of industries. He wrote:

> My considered conclusion, based on 10 years of close observation of labor relations in Texas, is that the right-to-work statute, taken by itself and apart from the whole body of state labor legislation (especially the law against secondary boycott) has had a minimal direct effect. In the traditional areas of the closed shop, the law has been generally disregarded, and the practices that have continued are illegal under federal as well as state legislation. In the industries in which initial hiring is in the hands of the employer, the forms of the law have been observed, and union membership has not been a formal condition of continued employment, yet, organization of the unorganized has proceeded at a remarkably rapid rate since 1947 even though the statute may have changed the general attitude toward unionism in some marginal cases and thus impeded the maximum growth of the labor movement.[21]

While Meyers found no direct effect of the right-to-work law on union membership, he did note certain applications of the law to limit union strength. He found that Texas courts have used the right-to-work statute not only to protect nonunion employees from discharge but also to deny the power to remedy discrimination against union employees. Furthermore, he argued that the law had hurt the quality of labor-management relations by forcing unions to take a lot of small, adamant stands in order to mitigate the constant threat of lost membership and had significantly reduced the amount of cooperation between the unions and management

Several statistical analyses of the impact of right-to-work laws have been made recently. Reynolds, Edwards, and Cebula found that the apparent effect of right-to-work laws in reducing wages simply reflects the lower cost of living in the Southern states.[22] Thomas M. Carroll argued that while right-to-work laws when newly passed do not cause union membership to fall abruptly, the laws do contribute over time to weak unionism in right-to-work states.[23] In contrast, Henry S. Farber found that right-to-work laws do not decrease unionism, but merely express or mirror the preexisting taste of workers against unions.[24] Consistent with Farber's findings, the study of two other researchers shows that right-to-work laws

[20]"Right-to-Work Laws," *Fortune*, 56:8, September 1957, pp. 235–236.

[21]Frederic Meyers, *Right-to-Work in Practice* (New York: 1959), Fund for the Republic, pp. 4–5. See also Meyers, "Effects of State Right-to-Work Laws: A Study of the Texas Act," *Industrial and Labor Relations Review*, 9:11, October 1955, pp. 77–84.

[22]M. D. Reynolds, M. Edwards, and R. J. Cebula, "Right to Work Laws and Cost of Living Differences," *American Journal of Economics and Sociology*, 45:2, April 1986, pp. 247–254.

[23]Thomas M. Carroll, "Right to Work Laws Do Matter," *Southern Economic Journal*, 50:2, October 1983, pp. 494–509.

[24]Henry S. Farber, "Right-to-Work Laws and the Extent of Unionization," *Journal of Labor Economics*, 2:3, 1984, p. 319.

seem to have no impact on the frequency of unfair labor practice charges against employers.[25]

THE RIGHTS OF EMPLOYEES

Seniority

Why Seniority Is Important   One of the most fundamental issues in labor relations is how advantages and disadvantages are to be divided among employees. When an opportunity for promotion arises, who is to receive it? When layoffs are necessary, what employees are to lose their jobs? Unions cannot insulate employees against the ill fortune of a company, nor can they obtain for all workers the same opportunities for advancement. But unions are vitally interested in the basis for the decision as to which employees gain benefits and which endure losses. Left to themselves, employers ordinarily utilize a series of standards by which to allocate benefits or losses. Among these standards are length of service with the company, job performance, and perhaps personal loyalty to the company or supervisor. Unions, however, usually advance length of service (i.e., seniority) as the most important, and often the only, criterion for making distinctions among employees. Why seniority has such prominence among many groups of workers is an important question. It is partly because seniority seems to conform to a basic sense of fair dealing. Also, seniority is an objective standard. Seniority can be measured in a way that less simple criteria, such as ability, performance, or loyalty, cannot.

Ben Fischer, formerly of the United Steelworkers of America, has described the reasons for which workers and unions support seniority:

Workers place so much store in seniority because it is the only viable and equitable known method for resolving employee competition. Here are some of the reasons:

1 Length of service does reflect experience, and experience is an asset to those who must manage or direct the work process as well as to the worker seeking advancement.

2 Seniority systems provide employees with reasonable opportunities to plan their careers based on some judgment of personal preference and projected potentials. Thus, an employee can plan to achieve jobs or types of work which appear to suit him, taking into account the relative seniority of others who are potential competitors.

3 A proper seniority system should also permit persons who are victims of job, process, or operation abandonment to choose a new career with consideration given for past service and for the advantage of his general work experience.

---

[25]Ralph D. Elliot and James R. Huffman, "The Impact of Right-to-Work Laws on Employer Unfair Labor Practice Charges," Journal of Labor Research, 5:2, Spring 1984, pp. 165–176.

4 As a worker grows older, there is a tendency for his immediate economic needs to increase; seniority tends to dovetail with this general condition. As a worker grows still older, his needs tend to peak, but in many establishments his last years of employment determine the amount of his pension. A higher base during his preretirement years often generates higher pensions and even determines the level of surviving spouse benefits.

5 As a worker advances, because his standard of living tends to increase, the impact of pay reduction or layoff creates economic hardship. The alternative for the older worker—planning his life around the minimum plant rate—would be unrealistic indeed.

6 The older worker tends to lose mobility. Many factors discourage older workers from moving. They cannot learn new ways so easily. Work and social habits become fixed. If changing jobs means changing residence, then the departure from a well-established place in a community or neighborhood becomes more difficult as a worker (and his family) age. Thus, his dependence on his place of employment tends to grow.

7 In balance, management does better with a stable work force. Retraining entails significant cost for management. Most training is not some formal process, but usually comprises exposure to the job, the nearby jobs, the specific work process, the safety hazards, and countless work practices. Seniority systems that are well conceived tend to give reasonable weight to stability factors.[26]

Defining Seniority   How is seniority defined and measured? Ordinarily each employee has a seniority date, usually the date of hire by the company. A list, in order of oldest to most recent seniority date, is maintained by the company. But the district in which seniority is exercised may vary. Sometimes seniority is defined as length of service with the company, but in other cases seniority is measured as time in the particular plant or department in which the employee works. Some companies keep two seniority lists, with companywide seniority applying to some situations and plant or department seniority applying to others. Generally, employees' seniority dates with the company are the dates that they were hired. Sometimes the ranking of employees hired on the same day depends on the hour at which each employee was hired.

Certain questions arise about seniority measurement. Do absences from work reduce total service time or not? The general answer has been that certain types of absences may reduce seniority status, but not all types. Absence for compulsory military service, for example, counts toward seniority by law. Layoffs sometimes count for seniority and sometimes do not. Full-time duty for the union sometimes counts and sometimes does not. The differences depend on the provisions of the collective bargaining agreement.

Superseniority   "Superseniority" means the assignment of artificial and superior seniority dates to certain employees. This concept apparently

[26]Ben Fisher, "Seniority Is Healthy," Industrial Relations Research Association Spring Meetings, 1976, pp. 497–503.

originated in the 1930s and came as much from management initiative as from that of the unions.[27] Confronted by growing union demands for seniority systems, many companies were anxious to exempt key employees from the impact of possible layoffs based on seniority. They argued that a group of key employees was necessary in time of layoff, regardless of their length of service with the company. The result was a list of persons excluded from the seniority list. In effect, these persons received superseniority for layoff purposes.

But the unions also had a group that they wanted to protect from layoff—union officers, especially stewards. The unions argued that these persons were essential to the unions' functioning during layoffs. In collective bargaining, these persons were sometimes given superseniority.

Where Seniority Applies   Seniority applies to matters other than layoffs, as mentioned above. A brief list of applications of seniority demonstrates its importance in American labor relations:

- Layoffs
- Recalls
- Transfers
- Job assignments
- Work assignments
- Shift preferences
- Selection of days off
- Overtime assignments
- Vacation privileges
- Parking privileges
- Health and pension benefits

In each of these areas, some employees are granted advantages that others do not have. This may be described as the application of competitive status seniority. That is, these issues involve seniority as a method of choosing who among the employees will receive benefits.

The careful reader may wonder why health and pension benefits, which are so important to workers, are placed last on this list. The answer is that it was only recently that health and pension benefit eligibility became subject to seniority. In 1991, in what the union described as a major breakthrough, the Steelworkers obtained guaranteed lifetime health and pension benefits for senior workers, even if the plants they work in are sold.[28]

Seniority is often not the only criterion employed, however. Employers often refuse to promote on the basis of seniority alone; they want to make promotions based upon the work record (especially dependability) and ability of employees. As a result, many collective bargaining agreements

---

[27]Slichter et al., *Collective Bargaining*, p. 128.
[28]James B. Parks, "Breakthrough Pact Forged by Steelworkers," *AFL-CIO News*, Feb. 18, 1991, p. 1.

provide that with respect to promotions, seniority will prevail when ability is the same. Disputes between management and labor on whether ability is or is not the same between two employees are common. A distinction is sometimes made between sufficient ability and relative ability. A union may argue that a senior employee has a right to a promotion because he or she has sufficient ability to do the job. Management, however, may prefer to promote a less senior employee who has relatively greater ability. The union usually defends the senior employee's right to the promotion. Such disputes are commonly resolved by grievance arbitration.

Seniority is also a basis for the receipt of benefits by employees when competition between employees is not involved. The types of benefits that depend on seniority include

- Vacations (employees with longer service often receive more vacation)
- Pensions
- Severance pay
- Holidays
- Sick leave
- Life and health insurance
- Supplemental unemployment benefits
- Wage increases
- Automatic promotions
- Bonuses

These applications of seniority (i.e., so-called benefits seniority) do not involve choices between employees. Each employee receives greater benefits as his or her length of service, i.e., seniority, grows.

James Medoff and Katharine Abraham studied seniority and layoffs in both union and nonunion work groups. They found that over 80 percent of private-sector employees, excluding those in construction or agriculture (both of which industries make little use of seniority), enjoy substantial protection against losing their jobs—almost as if a law existed providing some job protection with seniority. As it would be with a law, the practice applies to union and nonunion workers both, although seniority is given more weight in union than nonunion situations when promotions are involved.[29] Another study found that unions, specifically, tended to raise the likelihood of layoffs for younger workers, and to lower them for older workers.[30] Abraham and Medoff also conducted a survey of pay practices, seniority, and employee performance in American industry which seems to show a close connection between seniority and pay level.

---

[29]Katherine G. Abraham and James L. Medoff, "Length of Service and Layoffs in Union and Nonunion Work Groups," *Industrial and Labor Relations Review*, 38:1 October 1984, p. 96; and Abraham and Medoff, "Length of Service and Promotions in Union and Nonunion Work Groups," *Industrial and Labor Relations Review*, 38:3, April 1985, pp. 408–420.

[30]Francine D. Blau and Lawrence M. Kahn, "Unionism, Seniority, and Turnover," *Industrial Relations*, 22:3 Fall 1983, pp. 362–373.

According to the two researchers, there are large earnings advantages associated with length of company service, and these advantages cannot be explained in terms of the better productivity of the more highly paid employees.[31] Finally Abraham and Farber found that for male blue-collar workers for the years 1968 through 1980 there was a larger financial return to length of service in the union sector than in the nonunion sector.[32] D. Quinn Mills also found that employees are often advanced to higher-paying jobs not because of their superior skill, ability, or performance, as the human capital model may imply, but because of their greater length of service.[33]

Layoffs   involve one of the most important applications of competitive status seniority. American firms are quick to cut costs by layoffs when business declines. Examples abound, including the well-known massive layoffs in the automobile industry in the early 1990s.

Firms in Japan and Western Europe are often far more reluctant to place the burden of unemployment on their employees. This reluctance stems partly from a fear of union retaliation if layoffs occur. Large nonunion firms in the United States are also reluctant to lay off employees for fear of unionization. James Medoff concluded as the result of a statistical investigation that "adjustment [to business downturns] through layoffs is substantially greater in unionized firms than in comparable nonunionized firms."[34] Thus, most unionized firms in the United States do not hesitate to make layoffs. In the past, American unions have obtained management acceptance of seniority as the basis for layoffs. And in return, management has obtained union acceptance of layoffs when business downturns occur.

This is not to say that American unions are insensitive to layoffs. Unions often try to avoid substantial layoffs. For example, the Communication Workers of America proposed a four-step program to avoid layoffs to Bell Telephone in 1975. "CWA demands, the contracts notwithstanding . . . ," wrote CWA President Watts to AT&T's vice president for labor relations:

1 Advancement of vacations
2 Removal of all temporary and occasional employees
3 No overtime scheduling except for emergencies
4 No subcontracting[35]

[31]James L. Medoff and Katharine G. Abraham, "The Role of Seniority at U.S. Work Places: A Report of Some New Evidence," Working Paper No. 1175-80 (Cambridge, Mass.: Sloan School of Management, MIT, November 1980).

[32]Katharine G. Abraham and Henry S. Farber, "Returns to Seniority in Union and Nonunion Jobs," *Industrial and Labor Relations Review*, 42:1, October 1988, pp. 3–19.

[33]D. Quinn Mills, "Seniority versus Ability in Promotion Decisions," *Industrial and Labor Relations Review*, 38:3, April 1985, pp. 421–425.

[34]James L. Medoff, "Layoffs and Alternatives in U.S. Manufacturing," *American Economic Review*, 69:3, June 1979, p. 380.

[35]Bureau of National Affairs, *Daily Labor Report*, No. 42, Mar. 3, 1975, p. A1.

Other unions have attempted to negotiate short work weeks and other work-sharing arrangements to prevent layoffs. Still others have tried to lessen the adverse impact of layoffs on employees by bargaining for supplemental unemployment benefits.

How does seniority work in a layoff? A layoff system involves the interaction of three considerations:

1 The *criteria* to be used in selecting the employees to be laid off
2 The *unit* to be chosen for layoff purposes
3 The *right* of an employee to bump another in lieu of layoff[36]

These considerations are all interrelated.

A union's desire to increase the security of the senior employees has usually led it to request the widest possible unit. A wide unit permits the senior workers affected by a layoff to move anywhere in the plant to a job they are capable of performing. As an alternative, unions have often sought liberal bumping rights if the units were narrow. Companies, on the other hand, have usually preferred the narrower unit because it decreases costly bumping and also decreases movement by senior workers to jobs for which their qualifications are dubious.

If a union gains plantwide seniority and extensive bumping privileges, it sometimes arouses the resentment of employees who are victims of constant displacement. This is particularly true when the senior worker is manifestly ill-equipped to do the job in question. In some extreme situations, even the senior bumper finds his or her security to be short-lived. Sometimes within a matter of hours or days the senior worker, too, is bumped by a still more senior employee newly affected by the layoff.

Selection of the seniority unit and the degree of bumping privileges usually depend on the characteristics of the enterprise and the bargaining unit. If there is great homogeneity in the work force, the unit is likely to be broad; if the unit is narrow, the right to transfer in lieu of layoff will be greater. On the other hand, the more varied the skills required in an enterprise, the narrower the unit is likely to be and the more restricted will be the bumping rights.

The use of a broad, plantwide layoff system need not be disruptive per se if there are strict limitations on bumping and if it is insisted that workers have qualifications for the jobs to which they are transferred. Some companies join the union in preferring the wide unit if these safeguards exist. Although the seniority unit for layoff purposes is the department or the division, the worker with the least seniority who is laid off from such a unit is then free to apply to the industrial relations department for placement on a plantwide basis if he or she has a certain length of service. Supervisors, however, occasionally protest the turnover resulting from

---

[36]Slichter et al., *Collective Bargaining*, p. 157. See also Daniel B. Cornfield, "Seniority, Human Capital, and Layoffs: A Case Study," *Industrial Relations*, 21:3, Fall 1982, pp. 352–364.

plantwide seniority. Because the pattern of movement becomes fixed—with customary seasonal variations—employees tend to become trained in advance by normal replacement arrangements; consequently, the cost of plantwide movement at the time of layoff is minimal and, in the company's judgment, is more than offset by the gain in employee morale.

Adherence to very narrow units has given rise to serious and obvious inequities. If the unit is as narrow as a job, occupation, or even a department, a worker with considerable length of service may be laid off from the plant, while junior employees are retained on jobs that the laid-off worker is capable of doing.

However, just as plantwide seniority does not necessarily mean indiscriminate bumping rights, so too the narrowest seniority unit (job or occupational seniority) does not mean an almost complete absence of these rights; other features of the total layoff procedure are important. For example, one plant of a large electrical manufacturing company has had what is known as "code seniority." In effect, the unit is the occupational classification, and the person with the least seniority in that classification will be the first laid off. However, when notified of an impending layoff, an employee may assert seniority bumping rights within 3 days in lieu of accepting layoff. The employee may bump into an occupation in which he or she had previously worked and has acquired seniority; by definition this means the employee must have worked in the other occupational code at least 30 days. Experience has shown that employees are anxious to acquire seniority in a number of different codes, thereby increasing their bumping rights at the time of layoff. Even under this narrow-unit approach, therefore, bumping is encouraged.[37]

General Implications of Seniority The use of seniority as a standard for layoffs, recall, training opportunities, and promotions has certain substantial implications for the way the labor market functions in this country.

1. *Perhaps most important, seniority reduced mobility among industrial workers.* The longer a worker is on a particular job, the greater are the rights he or she accumulates from increasing seniority. If the worker left the job, those rights would be lost. The worker would have to start accumulating seniority at some other company or plant. Not surprisingly, the loss of job protection (which seniority provides) is a barrier to people moving from job to job.

Clark Kerr pointed to the effects of the seniority system in industrial plants:

> The craft worker moves horizontally in the craft area, and the industrial worker vertically in the seniority area. Inter-occupational movement is reduced

---

[37]Ibid., p. 161.

for the former and employer-to-employer movement for the latter. . . . Job rights protect but they also confine. Reduction of insecurity also brings reduction of independence. . . . The more secure are the "in," the greater the penalty for being an "out."[38]

It was Kerr's conclusion that seniority rules probably reduce workers' freedom and retard their efficiency more than the craft rules "which are the customary target of criticism."

2. *Seniority does provide greater security in the workplace for long-service employees.* By doing so, seniority undoubtedly contributes to a gain in morale among employees. Probably, the extensive use of seniority tends to reduce labor relations strife by eliminating much potential managerial favoritism in the treatment of employees.

3. *The effect of seniority provisions on young workers is probably substantial.* Some ambitious and able young workers probably avoid or leave jobs in certain companies because they feel their chances to move ahead are limited by the seniority advantages of older workers. The lack of rigid seniority provisions is probably an advantage to nonunion employers in providing opportunities for rapid advancement to young people and thereby assists the company in attracting and retaining good personnel.

4. *Seniority may have a direct effect on reducing efficiency in industry.* When seniority becomes the sole criterion for job assignments, then the flexibility needed for efficient operation can be as much affected as by rigidity in craft lines.

5. *Competitive status seniority inevitably creates serious internal problems for the union.*[39] While seniority rules are designed to regulate and systematize competition among workers for job rights, this fact does not relieve the union from pressure. The formulation of the rules themselves requires the compromise of a great variety of competitive interests among union members. Even in the use of benefit seniority there are competitive interests that cause difficulty for the union. For example, during negotiations a union was confronted by a sharp division between junior and senior employees over the question of whether the vacation liberalization to be sought should be the addition of a fourth week for those with more than 25 years' service or the reduction of the qualification for a third week from 15 years' to 10 years' service.[40]

The Rights of Employees Versus the Union and Vice Versa

When collective bargaining first developed and the principal law applying to employee-employer relations was the National Labor Relations Act,

---

[38]Clark Kerr, "The Balkanization of Labor Markets," in E. Wight Bakke et al., *Labor Mobility and Economic Opportunity* (New York: Wiley, 1955).

[39]Leonard R. Sayles, "Seniority: An Internal Union Problem," *Harvard Business Review,* 30:1, January–February 1952.

[40]Slichter et al., *Collective Bargaining,* p. 140.

there was one view of the rights of employees with respect to the corporation and the union. But as George Hildebrand pointed out, this view has been largely replaced in recent years with the passage of many statutes by Congress that bestow rights on individuals, independent of the collective bargaining agreement.[41]

In the older view, which still has some applicability, the union and the company were the source of the rights of employees through their joint action in negotiating a collective bargaining contract. The employees in the bargaining unit were a sort of third-party beneficiary of the agreement. But the agreement belonged to the union and the employer who could jointly take whatever actions seemed appropriate under it, including modifying its terms. Should a modification of the terms of the agreement, or some decision of the union and the company as to how it was to be administered, have an adverse impact on an employee or group of employees, that was merely incidental.

But since the passage of the Civil Rights Act of 1964, and also since the impact of the Landrum-Griffin Act on how the internal affairs of unions are conducted, there has emerged a body of law that creates new rights for employees independent of the collective bargaining agreement. Both management and labor have had to "adapt" to these changes. Under this new body of law, employees are able to initiate complaints against either management or the union or both.

For example, Wayne Martin, a member of a local union, witnessed a fellow employee drinking an alcoholic beverage on the job, and was present when the employee was caught by a supervisor. At an arbitration hearing Martin testified against the employee. Meanwhile, the union had threatened to fine him if he did so. Martin filed a complaint with the NLRB, but the board dismissed the complaint. The Sixth Circuit Court of Appeals disagreed and found that the union had violated the law by attempting to coerce Martin.[42]

If a union member ignores a union call to go on strike or returns to work during a strike, the union has the right to discipline him or her, but only under specific guidelines established by a series of court decisions.[43]

Under Title VII of the Civil Rights Act of 1964 a nationwide local of construction pipefitters was found guilty of maintaining an exclusively white male membership, and was ordered to alter its practices.[44] Incidents like

---

[41]George H. Hildebrand, "The Prospects for Collective Bargaining in the Manufacturing Sector, 1978–1985," in Hervey A. Juris and Myron Roomkin, eds., *The Shrinking Perimeter: Unionism and Labor Relations in the Manufacturing Sector* (Lexington, Mass.: Lexington Books, 1980), pp. 105–106.

[42]*NLRB v. International Union of Electric Workers, Local 745,* Sixth Circuit Court of Appeals, No. 84-5031, Apr. 10, 1985.

[43]Rossie D. Alston, Jr., "The Rights and Responsibilities of Employees Confronted with Union Discipline," *Labor Law Journal,* 38:2, February 1987, pp. 119–125.

[44]*Equal Employment Opportunity Commission v. Pipe Fitters Local 798,* U.S. District Court of Northern Oklahoma, No. 84-C-730-C, Sept. 5, 1986.

this are significant, but should not necessarily be thought of as proving that unions generally discriminate. Instead, two recent studies indicate that unions have helped increase minority and female employment in our society,[45] and that black members of local unions participate as much as do white members.[46]

What if a member sues a union because the member is dissatisfied with what the union obtained in collective bargaining? The Supreme Court addressed that issue in 1991 and held in favor of the union involved. The courts "must be highly deferential [to the union and to the collective bargaining process]," wrote the majority of the Court, "recognizing the wide latitude that negotiators need for the effective performance of their bargaining responsibilities."[47]

Employees' Political Activities

On Saturday, May 1, 1976, a young supervisor for a large American corporation went to a political demonstration at Herald Square in Manhattan. While at the demonstration, he apparently responded to police efforts to control the crowd by driving a van into two New York City police officers and then into a third, mounted police officer.

The supervisor was never sent to jail for this incident. However, he was interrogated at length by his employer about the demonstration and, according to him, about his political beliefs. These beliefs were considerably more radical than those commonly espoused by executives of the corporation. He was suspended from his job and later discharged.

Did the company have the right to discharge this supervisor for his actions at a political demonstration and for his political beliefs? The company said it did. "Public policy in our free enterprise system has never been defined to require a private employer to pay and support an individual who advocates a position inimical to the best interest of the employer," the company argued.

The supervisor brought suit in the courts of New York for damages from the company deriving from his discharge. As of this writing, he has not been successful in his suit. An employee who has no employment contract and belongs to no union, the company has contended in court, "may be terminated at any time for any reason or for no reason, under American law."[48]

[45]Jonathan S. Leonard, "The Effects of Unions on the Employment of Blacks, Hispanics and Women," *Industrial and Labor Relations Review*, 39:1, October 1985, pp. 115–136.

[46]Michele M. Hoyman and Lamont Stallworth, "Participation in Local Unions: A Comparison of Black and White Members," *Industrial and Labor Relations Review*, 40:3, April 1987, pp. 323–342.

[47]*Airline Pilots v. O'Neill*, U.S. 89-1493. See Linda Greenhouse, "Court Strengthens Unions' Protection Against Lawsuits by Members," *New York Times*, March 20, 1991, p. A24.

[48]Tom Goldstein, "Business and the Law: On Dismissing an Employee," *New York Times*, Apr. 13, 1979.

The company's statement is not entirely accurate. There are many reasons for which a company may not discharge an employee under American law, including discrimination based on race, creed, sex, or national origin. These restrictions on employers' behavior arise from federal laws. But the issue in the case of the supervisor is whether or not American law prohibits dismissal for the type of political activities in which he engaged and for the type of political belief which he espoused.

This issue was addressed by state courts all over the United States. In Michigan, the state Supreme Court ruled on June 10, 1980, that an employer cannot discharge an employee without just cause unless a job contract (written or oral) specifically provides for termination at the will of the employer.[49] The rights of employees in these circumstances remain in a state of flux. What is apparent is that the new work force is demanding greater rights and more personal freedom in the workplace than its predecessors did. This is nowhere more evident than in the question of the rights of "whistle-blowers."

Protection for Whistle-Blowers

On August 23, 1977, a chemist working for the city water department of a Florida city found contaminants in the water supply of a neighborhood in the city. He cut off the water and tried to clear up the pollution. His supervisor admonished him for acting on his own and too quickly. Several days later, discovering that the pollution continued, he advised residents of the area not to drink the water until the problem was cleared up. Again he acted on his own. His supervisor discharged him for insubordination.

The chemist took his case to the city's Civil Service Board, which upheld his firing. Then he complained to the U.S. Department of Labor under the provisions of the Safe Drinking Water Act of 1974, which reads, "No employer may discharge any employee . . . because the employee has . . . participated . . . in any action to carry out the purposes of this [act]." The Labor Department found that the chemist had been illegally discharged, but refused to order him reinstated in his job, because, the department said, he had not filed his complaint with the department within the 30 days allowed.[50]

The Florida chemist's difficulty is one that many employees, particularly professional and technical people, have confronted in recent years. Should an employee report to the public, or take action, when he or she finds a problem that may affect the public and which the employer has not or will not take action to alleviate? Should the employee "blow the whistle" on the employer?

---

[49]*Toussaint v. Blue Cross* and *Ebling v. Masco* (1980).
[50]Rosemary Chalk and Frank von Hippel, "Blowing the Whistle," *Boston Globe*, Aug. 12, 1979.

Some companies have decided that they should permit employees to do just this. A policy adopted by Cummins Engine Company, for example, states:

> The company is prepared to help any employee resolve a moral dilemma and to ensure that no employee is put at a career disadvantage because of his or her willingness to raise a question about questionable practice or unwillingness to pursue a course of action which is inappropriate or morally dubious.[51]

Several federal laws include so-called employee protection sections. These sections prohibit adverse actions by employers against employees who assist in carrying out the purpose of the statutes. Among these laws are

- Occupational Health and Safety Act
- Federal Water Pollution Control Act
- Safe Drinking Water Act
- Toxic Substances Control Act
- Resource Conservation and Recovery Act
- Clean Air Amendments
- Federal Mine Safety and Health Act
- Nuclear Regulatory Commission Authorization Act

Employer Records and Employee Privacy

Employers maintain in the course of business many records about their employees. When an employee is interviewed for a job, a file is prepared that contains information about the applicant's age, education, work history, health, and other matters. If the applicant is hired, the company will ordinarily maintain a file on the individual's work history and performance at the company. Any disciplinary actions may be documented. Health problems may be recorded. Even financial problems that come to the attention of the company may be noted and filed.

To an increasing degree, employees may be required by their employers to take lie detector tests for any number of reasons, including control of theft from the company. Psychological tests are also now a part of the personnel file of many employees. The questions asked in the course of lie detector tests and psychological interviews may seem to many employees to be very personal in nature and far removed from the requirements of their jobs.

What rights does an individual employee have to restrict the use to which a company puts his or her personnel file? Can the company distribute the contents of such a file to other companies or to interested persons? May an employee refuse to take lie detector or other tests? And if an em-

---

[51]Henry B. Schacht, address to the First National Seminar on Individual Rights in the Corporation, New York City, May 10, 1978, p. 5 (mimeographed). See also David W. Ewing, *Do It My Way or You're Fired!* (New York: John Wiley, 1983).

ployee takes the tests, what use may be made by the company of the information obtained?

In recent years concerns about employee privacy have become much more intense as advances in communications and information technology make the transference of data about employees much easier. Several states now have laws protecting the privacy of personnel records. The law in Michigan, for example, gives employees access to their personnel files and restricts disclosure of negative information in the files about an employee.

A federal law to protect employee privacy has been advocated for several years, and hearings have been held in Congress on various aspects of the problem. Meanwhile, there is no federal statute, and self-regulation by private companies continues to increase. There is reason to suspect, unfortunately, that only the larger corporations have been diligent in establishing policies to protect employee privacy and that the problem of invasions of employee privacy continues to grow elsewhere in the economy.[52] "In the name of improving company security and enhancing worker productivity," wrote one student of the matter, "intrusions [into employee privacy] that would have been questioned or rejected in the past are now being accepted."[53]

In an effort to control rising health care costs some employers are trying to regulate what their employees can do when they are away from work. People who never smoke on the job, for instance, are being told by their employers that they must not smoke anywhere, anytime. If evidence of smoking turns up in medical examinations, some companies are discharging the employees. Other examples involve employers who discharge people who are too fat, ride motorcycles, or engage in other activities that risk illness or injury. The employers argue that, after all, they must pay the high costs of treating illness or injury through the health care benefits they provide for employees.[54]

Each of the issues of whistle-blowing and privacy protection for employees raises not only legal questions, which have been highlighted here, but broad ethical challenges as well. The ethical issues are primarily for employers, because unions generally support extensive protection for whistle-blowers and the privacy of employees. Each employer should have examined these issues carefully and have policies about them, but many do not.

CHAPTER SUMMARY

The advent of a union in a plant and the subsequent negotiations of a collective bargaining agreement present a change in the power structure of

---

[52]Bureau of National Affairs, *Daily Labor Report*, No. 129, July 3, 1979, pp. A2–A6.

[53]Gary T. Marx and Sanford Sherizen, "Corporations That Spy on Their Employees," *Business and Society Review,* 60, Winter 1987, pp. 32–37.

[54]See, for example, Tony Mauro and Julia Lawlor, "More Bosses Set Rules for After Hours," *USA Today,* May 13, 1991, p. 1.

the plant. Management previously had unilateral authority to make all decisions, but the union represents a countervailing power. The agreement now establishes the right and responsibilities of the company, the union, and the workers.

In order to retain as much authority as possible, management has sought to have its own rights established by the inclusion of certain provisions in the agreement. A clause that lists management's rights is now common. However, such a clause is not always as useful as it may seem. Along with the rights, there are obligations. For example, management has a legal obligation to bargain with a union about subcontracting. Management is sometimes obligated to observe work standards and respect rules about work assignments. There has also been a substantial amount of litigation on the rights and obligations of successor employers who acquire facilities with already-established unions and labor agreements.

The contest for control between management and the unions has often centered around the issues of union security. The concern of American unions for their security arose, in part, from the long opposition of American employers to the existence of unions. In 1947, the Taft-Hartley Act established statutory provisions about union security. The closed shop, in which membership in a union is required as a condition of employment, was outlawed. The union shop was permitted, in which membership is required only after 30 days of employment. The union shop is now the most common form of union security. Other forms are the agency shop, the maintenance-of-membership shop, hiring halls, and the dues checkoff.

Right-to-work laws restrict the opportunity for a union and an employer to agree to a union security clause. These state laws, existing in 21 states, are a constant source of legislative dispute in Congress, and they are a major source of controversy between labor and management. Supporters of right-to-work laws claim that the union shop is unfair because it compels workers to join unions in order to have a job. Opponents say that the laws do not provide the right to work and instead are intended to weaken the unions and keep wages low. Unions complain that the laws allow some employees to get all the benefits of a union's presence without sharing the expense of supporting it.

Seniority is one of the major means by which the rights of employees are protected through a collective bargaining agreement. It is the method by which employees lay claim to extra benefits or decide who is to bear hardship. Benefit seniority involves advantages such as increased vacation or pension benefits, which are gained at no cost to others. Competitive status seniority refers to the method for deciding who is to have advantages when there is competition for them. For example, under a rule of seniority, those persons longest at a plant would obtain promotions and would be last to be laid off in an economic downturn. The application of seniority to layoffs is a particularly important matter. American firms resort to layoffs to cut costs when business declines. When a reduction in the work force occurs, senior people in a plant move to different jobs and "bump" those with less seniority.

Changes in the needs, attitudes, and character of the work force have brought a search for greater rights and more personal freedom and privacy in the workplace. Many statutes have been passed in recent years that create new rights for employees independent of the collective bargaining agreement. Challenges to restrictions on employees' political activities, the right of employees to privacy, discrimination against older workers, and protection for whistle-blowers are among the issues that have been addressed recently.

QUESTIONS FOR THOUGHT AND DISCUSSION

1 What are management rights? Does a management rights clause in a collective bargaining agreement help management keep some rights? Why or why not?

2 What is a right-to-work law? Does your state have such a law? Should it? Why or why not?

3 Why do unions favor seniority provisions? Is seniority good for society as a whole? Why or why not?

4 What are the implications of seniority systems for labor market functions? Can you think of any other systems or methods for dividing advantages and disadvantages among employees besides seniority systems, such as a strict meritocracy? Discuss the pros and cons of each alternative you propose.

5 How have changes in the work force affected the rights of employees? Should there be increased protection of employees' political activities, right to dissent from corporate policy, and privacy? Why or why not? Are there any disadvantages to increased employee rights? For whom?

6 If a company acquires a facility from another company, what is the status of the union and the labor agreement at the acquired facility? Review the major Supreme Court cases on the problem of successorship. Do you agree with the decisions? Why or why not?

7 What are the different types of union security arrangements or provisions? Are some more acceptable than others and for whom? What are the pros and cons for the different forms of union security?

8 What effect have right-to-work laws had on labor relations?

9 How do seniority systems work in a layoff? What are some of the problems and complications associated with layoffs and bumping privileges? Under what conditions do seniority privileges in layoffs seem to work effectively?

10 Younger workers are sometimes preferred to older ones. Why do you think this occurs? Should it?

11 Should an employer have the right to restrict the behavior of employees—such as smoking—when they are not in the workplace? When they are in the workplace?

SELECTED READING

Freedman, Warren, *The Employment Contract: Rights and Duties of Employers and Employees* (New York: Quorum Books, 1989).

Hill, Marvin, Jr., and Anthony V. Sinicropi, *Management Rights: A Legal and Arbitral Analysis* (Washington, D.C.: Bureau of National Affairs, 1986).

McKelvey, Jean T., ed., *The Duty of Fair Representation* (Ithaca: New York State School of Industrial and Labor Relations, Cornell University, 1977).

McWhirter, Darien A., *Your Rights at Work*, 2d ed. (New York: John Wiley, 1993).

Slichter, Sumner, James Healy, and Robert E. Livernash, *The Impact of Collective Bargaining on Management* (Washington, D.C.: Brookings, 1960).

CHAPTER 18

WAGES: THEORY
AND PRACTICE

COMPENSATION

Probably no subject is more central to labor-management relations than is compensation. The amount of compensation, its forms, and the processes by which it is determined are vital issues to both employers and employees. At a superficial level, the matter may not appear to be very complicated. Presumably, the employer wants compensation to be low, the employee wants it to be high. But this observation provides very little basis on which to understand the problems that questions of compensation entail.

Ordinarily we think of pay as wages or salaries, and these are, in fact, the most important forms of compensation. But they are not the only forms. Employees also receive benefits, such as pensions and health insurance, as compensation for performing their jobs. And employees often get paid when they are not working, in the form of paid holidays, vacations, and sick leave, for example. Performing a job entitles an employee to a set of benefits in addition to a wage or salary.

There was a time when an employee received little from a job except an hourly wage. But as different forms of pay and benefits have developed, the content of compensation packages has become much more complex. This development has introduced confusion into our terminology and therefore requires great care in the use of words. Table 18-1 sets out the major terms relating to compensation practices. Briefly, pay and benefits make up compensation. Pay, in turn, is composed of wages, salaries, and/or incentive earnings. "Earnings" is sometimes used as a synonym for pay. Benefits include three different general types and many more specific forms, which will be discussed later.

TABLE 18-1   TERMS RELATING TO COMPENSATION

Compensation:	The total value of what an employee receives from an employer for performing a job
Wage rate:	A rate of pay per hour
Pay (or earnings):	The amount of money an employee receives
Salary:	A weekly, biweekly, monthly, or annual rate of pay
Incentive earnings:	Pay based on the amount of work an employee performs
Benefits:	**1** Payments to an employee that are not directly related to an hour's work or to quantity of work performed (e.g., paid holidays, paid vacations)
	2 Services provided to employees (e.g., health care, pensions)
	3 Payments made on behalf of employees to purchase services or benefits (e.g., health insurance, life insurance)

There is great variation in the amount of pay and the form and quantity of benefits attached to different jobs. Some jobs are high-paying jobs; some are low-paying. Some jobs carry many benefits; others carry few or none. Some high-paying jobs also have high benefit levels; other high-paying jobs have few or no benefits. And the same is true for low-paying jobs. In the American economy the range from high to low and the composition of compensation packages vary; new approaches are appearing constantly.

Some difficult issues in compensation involve how low, or how high, it is to be set. Even if a company were free to set compensation with total disregard of the wishes of its employees, it would still have to establish compensation at a level in accord with its other personnel needs and policies. It would have to set compensation at a level at which workers would accept jobs. To the extent that the company required skilled workers, it would have to set compensation at a level that would induce workers already possessing the skills to accept its jobs or induce workers without skills to acquire them. Conversely, if employees had so strong a union that they could set wages without regard to the employer's wishes, they would still have to be careful not to set so high a wage that costs rose until no one purchased the product of their employer, and their jobs were lost. In effect, because neither firms nor employees exist independently, they must have due regard for setting compensation at levels that neither cause the firm to have no workers nor cause the workers to have no jobs. The *market*, composed of other firms and employees, *sets these limits*. But within these limits, or even, for a short while, outside them,[1] there is much range for disagreement.

[1] A firm may set compensation below the market level, or a union may set it above the market level, in the short run because it takes market forces time to operate. Thus, a firm paying its employees below the market level may experience an increasing number of vacancies before it takes corrective action, and a union setting rates above market levels may see unemployment rise for a while until it reacts to the unwillingness of consumers to purchase the high-priced products the union's members produce.

How is the setting of compensation levels to be explained? What causes some wage rates to be different from other wage rates? What factors cause one person to earn more than another? These are questions about which theorists have long speculated, and extensive studies have been conducted in an attempt to answer them.

Differences in Compensation

The American economy involves a very large number of different rates of compensation. Some people make a great deal more money than others. Since earnings are the major factor by which living standards are established, the inequality in earnings is reflected to a large degree in inequality in living standards. This inequality is a social as well as an economic phenomenon and occasions considerable comment, particularly since inequality has been increasing in recent years.[2] Some people think the amount of compensation should be essentially alike for all jobs. Others believe differences in compensation are necessary to provide work incentives and to reflect different economic situations. Just how does compensation differ among working Americans? How much does it differ? How has it changed over the years?

Compensation differs in the United States in several ways. The most important differentials are

- Geography
- Occupation
- Industry
- Plant size
- Demography
- Union representation

It is very difficult, if not impossible, to separate these influences from each other. For example, suppose we compare wages in different sections of the country. Wages of the average worker in the South tend to be below those of the average worker in the North. But what is the reason for this? Is this a result of lower living costs in the South? Is it a result of a different industrial mix (with less high-wage heavy manufacturing in the South than in the North)? Does it result from a different mix of occupations (with fewer high-paid professional and skilled workers in the South)? Is it because the southern labor force includes a higher proportion of minority workers (who have received less pay than white workers)? Or, finally, is it a result of a higher level of union organization in the North than in the South?

[2]See Lester C. Thurow, *Generating Inequality* (New York: Basic Books, 1975); and Thurow, *The Zero Sum Society* (New York: Basic Books, 1980).

Alternatively, one could compare wages among industries. The steel industry pays considerably higher wages on average than does the textile industry. Why? Some may say steel is naturally a higher-wage industry because of the economics of the marketplace. Others point out that the steel industry is concentrated in the high-wage North, rather than the South. Still others note that the steel industry has a higher proportion of skilled workers in its labor force than the textile industry, and skilled workers ordinarily earn higher pay. Finally, some might argue that steel has very few women workers, while textiles employ very many women (who often earn less pay than men).

In discussions about why one group of workers receives more than others, it becomes clear that cause and effect can become very confused. Elaborate studies are necessary to unravel the factors that establish differentials, and there continue to be disputes about the methods and findings of these studies. That differentials exist is incontrovertible, however, and there is evidence that they change over time. For example, during the 1980s the pay levels of jobs requiring higher levels of education rose strongly compared to others. Why was this? It wasn't because of a shortage of highly educated labor, because there was a dramatic relative increase in this category of the U.S. work force during the 1970s and 1980s. A study of the issue found that the pay advantage for the highly educated arose out of a dramatic shift in the technology of production that requires greater education.[3] What of other aspects of pay differences?

Geographic Differences   In the United States, wage and total compensation levels tend to be highest in the West, intermediate in the North and East, and lowest in the South. In part, these regional differentials reflect the distribution of occupations and industries and the different composition of the labor force in various regions. But more significant are the regional differences that exist within industries and within occupations. For example, in industries such as retail food, paper, and furniture, companies operating on a national scale tend to pay less in southern markets than elsewhere. (Some industries, however, have the same wage structure in the North and South, especially where a uniform national collective bargaining agreement exists.)

Studies have been made to try to identify the reasons for the North-South regional differentials. It is tempting to give the reasons used above, (i.e., that the South has few major manufacturing industries and a low-wage occupational and population mix). But why should wages vary between North and South in the same occupation and in the same industry, as they often do? There was much interest in this topic at the end of World War II. Richard Lester, summarizing two studies, concluded, "The average

[3]John Bound and George Johnson, "Changes in the Structure of Wages in the 1980's," *American Economic Review,* 82:3, June 1992, p. 389.

North-South wage differential varies widely and irrationally from industry to industry."[4] By the term "irrationally" Lester apparently meant that the existence and size of the differentials could not be explained by the expected economic differences between industries and geographic regions. More recent studies, using the considerable data that have accumulated since the late 1940s, suggest that much of the North-South differential is a result of a less educated work force and the greater proportion of blacks in the South.[5]

Another major aspect of geographic diversity in wages involves urban, suburban, and rural areas.[6] Generally, urban areas pay higher wages than suburban areas, and both pay more than rural areas. This tends to be true in all geographic regions.[7] In recent years, however, the movement of industry to suburban locations has reduced the suburban-urban differential.

Among metropolitan areas, pay levels tend to be higher in the larger areas. One study shows that larger establishment (plant) size and greater levels of unionization also are correlated with higher earnings levels.[8] Living costs are higher in the Northeast and West than elsewhere in the country. Do geographic wage differences reflect this? No, says one study, unless industry differences are accounted for.[9]

Occupational Differences   People in different occupations earn different amounts. Executives, managers, and administrators earn, on average, almost twice as much as service workers, and these differences remain relatively stable over time. Within each occupational group are even wider differentials among the detailed jobs that make up a broad grouping. Within recent years there has been a marked increase in the degree by which the compensation of chief executive officers of firms exceeds that of employees. During the late 1960s the ratio of top executive pay to that of average employee was about 40 to 1. By 1992 the ratio was closer to 100. The reasons for this substantial change are disputed, but it has occasioned much unfavorable comment by the unions.[10]

[4]Richard A. Lester, "Diversity in North-South Wage Differentials," *Southern Economic Journal*, 12, January 1946, p. 242; and "Southern Wage Differentials," *Southern Economic Journal*, 13, April 1947, pp. 386–394.

[5]Gerald Scully, "Interstate Wage Differentials: A Cross-Section Analysis," *American Economic Review*, 59:5, December 1969, pp. 757–773; L. E. Galloway, "The North-South Wage Differential," *Review of Economics and Statistics*, 45:3, August 1963, pp. 264–272; George D. Stamas, "The Puzzling Lag in Southern Earnings," *Monthly Labor Review*, 104:6, June 1981, pp. 27–36.

[6]Victor R. Fuchs, "Hourly Earnings Differentials by Region and Size of City," *Monthly Labor Review*, 90:1, January 1967, pp. 22–26.

[7]Davis S. Thomsen, "Biographic Differentials in Salaries within the U.S.," *Personnel Journal*, 53:9, September 1974, p. 670–674.

[8]S. E. Baldwin and R. S. Daski, "Occupational Pay Differences among Metropolitan Areas," *Monthly Labor Review*, 99:5, May 1976, pp. 29–35.

[9]John E. Buckley, "Do Area Wages Reflect Area Living Costs?" *Monthly Labor Review*, 102:11, November 1979, pp. 24–29.

[10]John R. Oravec, "Executive Pay Up . . . ," *AFL-CIO News*, 37:11, May 25, 1992, p. 10.

An area of intense interest has been the similarities or differences in wages between people in the same occupations in private industry and those working for government. Some people feel that government employees should not be paid more than people in the same occupations in private industry. In fact, as we saw in Chapter 11, many public employees are paid on the basis of comparative surveys with wages and salaries in the private sector. Studies have shown a tendency for state and local government employees to be paid more than private sector employees, but the degree of difference declines as skill levels rise. That is, the public sector pays lesser skilled jobs more generously than do private employers; but private employers pay more skilled jobs at rates similar to those in government.[11] Remember, however, that the data are averages; some private-sector employees pay more than government at most occupational levels.

Economists have long proposed that there are so-called compensating differences in wages for different occupations. Those jobs that are more difficult, less pleasant, and more hazardous, for example, should be expected to pay more than others. To test this proposition it is necessary to separate out many other influences on pay rates, such as geography, demographics, industry, etc., which also affect pay and so can conceal the independent effect of difficulty, desirability and hazard. A recent study looked at the impact which death rates have on compensation, and to the surprise of the researcher indicated that those occupations with the highest job hazards appear to pay no compensation premium; that is, that there is no compensating differential.[12]

Situations like this, which cause people to have dangerous jobs for which they are not differently compensated, would seem to be ripe for union activity. Such situations are building up in America and might become the source of a new surge of unionism at some point.

Industrial Differences Earnings differ substantially among industries. Table 18-2 shows the percentage divergence in average hourly earnings from the average of all private-sector industries for major sectors of the economy in 1947 and in 1992. The range is wide. In construction and mining, average hourly earnings exceeded the average in the total private economy by 34 percent in 1992. In retail trade, 1992 hourly earnings were only 67 percent of those in the total private economy. Construction average hourly earnings in 1992 were double those in retail trade in 1992. In 1947 these sectors of the economy had much the same ranking, though the range of difference was smaller.

More detailed data on specific industries can also be obtained. Among manufacturing industries, for example, in 1992 motor vehicles and equip-

[11]Greg Hundley, "Public- and Private-Sector Occupational Pay Structures," *Industrial Relations*, 30:3, Fall 1991, p. 417ff.

[12]J. Paul Leigh, "No Evidence of Compensating Wages for Occupational Fatalities," *Industrial Relations*, 30:3, Fall 1991, p. 382ff.

TABLE 18-2 AVERAGE HOURLY EARNINGS IN MAJOR SECTORS OF THE ECONOMY AS A PERCENTAGE OF ALL PRIVATE-INDUSTRY AVERAGE HOURLY EARNINGS, 1947 AND 1992

	1947	1992
Total private economy	100	100
	($1.23)	($10.71)
Construction	139	133
Transportation and public utilities	(N/A)	127
Mining	135	136
Manufacturing	108	109
Wholesale trade	107	106
Finance, insurance, and real estate	98	103
Services	(N/A)	100
Retail trade	73	67

*N/A—not available.
Source: U.S. Department of Labor, *Employment and Training Report of the President* (Washington, D.C. U.S. Government Printing Office, 1976). 1992 Source: U.S. Department of Labor, Bureau of Labor Statistics, *News,* Feb. 1993, p. 17.

ment, primary metals (especially steel manufacturing), and petroleum refining had the highest average hourly earnings. The apparel, leather, and textiles industries had the lowest earnings. Again, the highest-level industry had earnings more than double those in the lowest-level industry.

Studies of the factors underlying earnings differences among manufacturing industries normally identify as causal factors such items as size of firm, market structure, profitability of firm, and level of productivity per employee.[13]

Employer-Size Differences Smaller enterprises on average (there are exceptions, of course) tend to have lower wage schedules,[14] lower fringe benefits, poorer conditions of safety and health, and a greater likelihood of business failure culminating in job loss than do larger enterprises in the same industry.[15]

An especially significant benefit for most American workers is medical insurance. Government studies show that the smaller the firm, the less likelihood an employee has of having health insurance provided by the employer as a benefit. For example, of firms that employ fewer than 25 work-

[13]Frank C. Ripley, *The Structure of Wages in United States Manufacturing Industries, 1948 to 1964* (New York: American Iron and Steel Institute, 1970); and Mark Lutz, "Quit Rates and the Quality of the Industrial Wage Structure," *Industrial Relations,* 16:1, February 1977, pp. 61–70.
[14]Douglas Kruse, "Supervision, Working Conditions and the Employer-Size Wage Effect," *Industrial Relations,* 31:2, Spring 1992, p. 229ff.
[15]John T. Dunlop, "Is Small Beautiful at the Workplace?" *Villanova Law Review,* 33, 1988, pp. 1059–1071. See also "Small Firms Offer Less . . .", Bureau of National Affairs, *Daily Labor Report,* No. 112, June 11, 1991, p. B-1ff.

ers, only 37 percent provide health care insurance; of those employing 25 to 100 workers, 66 percent provide care. Among the largest firms—those employing 1000 workers or more—more than 86 percent provide health care insurance.[16]

It is often surprising how large are the differences in pay from various employers in the same industry. Studies show that over many years there are large, stable, and predictable differences between pay levels for different size employers in the same industry. In fact, according to a recent study by Erica Groshen, "employer wage differentials are large enough to account for many observed wage inequalities, such as those among races or between men and women."[17]

This is a remarkable statement. In a few pages we will be reviewing differences in earnings between men and women, and between black people and white people. These data are often cited in the press and in public discussion as evidence of discrimination against women and minorities in our society. And such differences do exist. But Groshen suggests that a basic reason for the differentials is to be found in the different employers for whom people work. Apparently some employers take advantage of the opportunity to pay women and minorities less, while others do not. Alternatively, women and minorities have chosen to work for employers who don't pay as much for business reasons. The debate about which is cause and which is effect continues.

Demographic Differences   Groups in our population do not make the same average earnings. In 1991 black workers had 20 percent less income, on average, than white workers. Female workers in 1991 made 26 percent less (in average weekly earnings) on average than male workers. Younger workers made 40 percent less on average than older workers. Handicapped workers make less on average than nonhandicapped workers. These are comparisons of averages, and in each instance there are exceptions. But the basic patterns in our society are unmistakable.

What causes pay differences on a demographic basis? To a large degree, differences in average pay among demographic groups reflect the different occupations, industries, and geographic areas in which people work.[18] But some of the difference is also explained by sex and race discrimination. Even within the same occupation, industry, and area, or even the same

---

[16]*A Profile of the Nonelderly Population without Health Insurance* (Washington, D.C.: Employee Benefit Research Institute, May 1987), p. 5. See also Thomas P. Burke and John D. Morton, "How Firm Size . . . Affects Employee Benefits," *Monthly Labor Review,* 114:12, December 1990, pp. 25–41.

[17]Erica L. Groshen, "Sources of Intra-Industry Wage Dispersion: How Much to Employers Matter?" *Quarterly Journal of Economics,* 106:3, August 1991, pp. 869–884; and Groshen, "Five Reasons Why Wages Vary Among Employers," *Industrial Relations,* 30:3, Fall 1991, p. 350ff. The quote in the text is from "Five Reasons," p. 375.

[18]J. G. Hawerth, "Earnings, Productivity and Changes in Employment and Discrimination during the 1960s," *American Economic Review,* 65, March 1975, pp. 158–168.

company or plant, women and blacks have often been paid lower than men and whites.[19] Some statistical studies have attempted to isolate the impact of this type of discrimination in establishing pay levels by standardizing average income statistics for region, industry, and occupation. These studies indicate that this sort of discrimination continues to exist in the United States, despite the fact that it is now illegal.[20] A study of earnings data suggests that the wage gap between whites and blacks narrowed in the 1970s and 1980s, but stabilized thereafter; and that between women and men has decreased from 39 percent in 1978 to a 26 percent pay difference in 1991.

Discrimination also operates by closing educational and occupational opportunities to women and blacks. Persons confined to lower educational and occupational levels receive lower earnings.[21] Here again, however, recent decades have shown a lessening of inequality. Blacks have obtained a larger proportion of jobs at larger companies, and have made solid percentage gains in occupations such as managers, professionals, technicians, skilled craftspersons, and clerical workers. In each of these categories except clerical workers, however, blacks still are represented at a percentage equal to theirs in the population as a whole.[22]

Differences Resulting from Union Representation   Do union-represented workers earn more than other workers? The answer is yes. But the amount of the advantage is not quite clear. To a degree unions are responsible for wages being above what they would be in the absence of the unions, but less than it might appear from the data.

If a comparison is made of the pay rates of unionized employees versus nonunionized employees in the United States, unionized employees on average receive substantially higher pay. On average for 1992, union workers received an average weekly wage 35 percent higher than nonunion employees, and 70 percent higher for blue-collar workers in all industries (See Figure 18-1). The differentials are highest in percentage terms for union versus nonunion women and union versus nonunion black workers. Figure 18-2 compares the median weekly earnings of union and nonunion workers by occupation and industry for 1990. Figure 18-3 shows the total union advantage, without regard to occupation or industry and considering wages and

[19]R. S. Goldfarb and J. R. Hosek, "Explaining Male-Female Wage Differentials for the Same Job," *Journal of Human Resources*, 11:1, Winter 1976, pp. 98–108.

[20]James V. Koch and J. F. Chizmas, Jr., *The Economics of Affirmative Action* (Lexington, Mass.: Lexington Books, 1976); and Carol L. Jusenius, "The Influence of Work Experience, Skill Requirements, and Occupational Segregation on Women's Earnings," *Journal of Economics and Business*, 29:2, Winter 1977, pp. 107–115. More recent work on this subject has been done by Gary Loveman at Harvard, but is not yet published in 1993.

[21]M. A. Ferber and H. Lowry, "Sex Differentials in Earnings: A Reappraisal," *Industrial and Labor Relations Review*, 29:3, April 1976, pp. 377–387.

[22] Myra Strober, "Human Capital Theory," *Industrial Relations*, 29:2, Spring 1990, pp. 233–237.

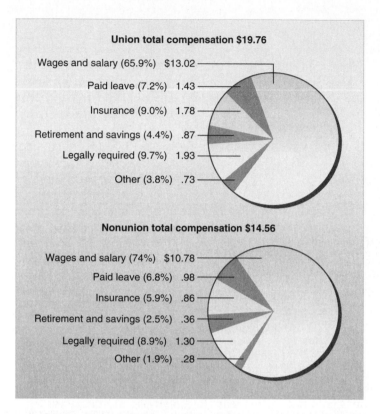

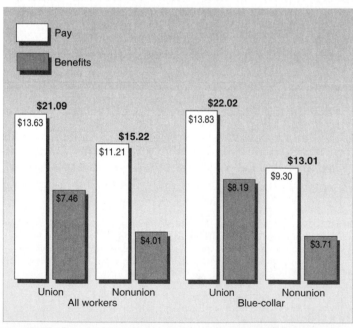

FIGURE 18-1a Compensation breakdown: wages and benefits, union members versus nonunion members, March 1991. *(Source: Bureau of Labor Statistics, AFL-CIO News, March 30, 1992, p. 8.)*
FIGURE 18-1b Significant statistics: the union advantage widens.

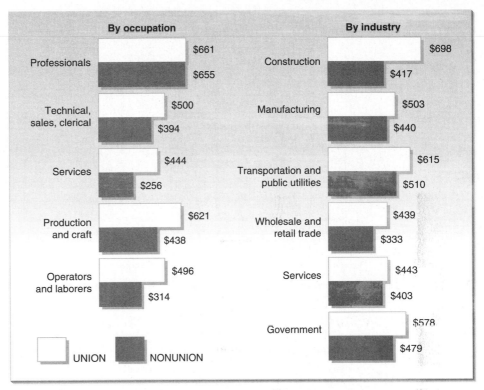

By occupation

	Professionals	$661 (Union) / $655 (Nonunion)
Technical, sales, clerical	$500 (Union) / $394 (Nonunion)
Services	$444 (Union) / $256 (Nonunion)
Production and craft	$621 (Union) / $438 (Nonunion)
Operators and laborers	$496 (Union) / $314 (Nonunion)

By industry

Construction	$698 (Union) / $417 (Nonunion)
Manufacturing	$503 (Union) / $440 (Nonunion)
Transportation and public utilities	$615 (Union) / $510 (Nonunion)
Wholesale and retail trade	$439 (Union) / $333 (Nonunion)
Services	$443 (Union) / $403 (Nonunion)
Government	$578 (Union) / $479 (Nonunion)

UNION   NONUNION

FIGURE 18-2   Median weekly earnings of full-time workers, union members versus nonunion members, 1992. *(Source: Bureau of Labor Statistics, Employment and Earnings, January 1993).* AFL-CIO News, March 15, 1993, p. 10.

premiums (i.e., earnings, not benefits) only. A recent study has concluded that in the 1980s, the union-nonunion differential on the whole declined very slightly.[23] In 1991, for the first time since 1983, union workers won higher pay increases on average in America than did nonunion workers.

There has been considerable statistical investigation of this topic. Many studies have sought to determine if the existence of a union causes wages to be higher, where other factors are the same. In a pioneering study, H. G. Lewis estimated the proportionate wage advantage of union members over workers in the nonunion sector to be 15 percent in the period 1955 to 1958 but essentially zero in the late 1940s and 38 percent in the early 1930s.[24] Subsequent studies, using better data sources, have come to a consistent general result: unions do tend to cause wages to be

[23]Michael A. Curme and David MacPherson, "Union Wage Differentials and the Effects of Industry and Local Union Disunity: Evidence from the 1980's," *Journal of Labor Research,* 12:4, Fall 1991, pp. 419–427.

[24]H. G. Lewis, *Unionism and Relative Wages in the United States: An Empirical Inquiry* (Chicago: University of Chicago Press, 1963). See also Lewis, "Union Relative Wage Effects: A Survey of Macro Estimates," *Journal of Labor Economics* 1:1, 1983, pp. 1–16.

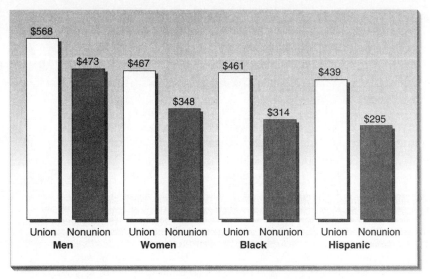

FIGURE 18-3   The union advantage: median weekly earnings of full-time wage and salary workers, 1991. *(Source: Bureau of Labor Statistics, AFL-CIO News, March 2, 1992, p. 14.)*

higher for the persons they represent.[25] But the studies vary widely in the amount by which the unions improve wages. Two recent studies of white males found a union advantage of 11 and 24 percent, respectively.[26] These studies are consistent with Lewis's finding that the wage effect of unions varies over time and across industries.[27]

In another interesting statistical investigation, Orley Ashenfelter estimated that unions increase the wages of black males covered by union agreements by 21 percent above what they would otherwise be. Ashenfelter also found that unions increased the wages of white males by 10 percent.[28]

Yet another study threw light on the different approaches to pay used by nonunion firms of different size. A study of 1979 data showed that

[25]John Pencavel, "A Reconsideration of the Effects of Unionism on Relative Wages and Employment in the United States: 1920–1980," *Journal of Labor Economics*, 2, 1984, pp. 193–204.

[26]Harry C. Bentiam, "Union-Nonunion Wage Differential Revisited," *Journal of Labor Research*, 8:4, Fall 1987, p. 381; and Ronald L. Oaxaca and Michael R. Ransom, "Searching for the Effect of Unionism," *Journal of Labor Research*, 9:2, Spring 1988, p. 144. See also L. W. Weiss, "Concentration and Labor Earnings," *American Economic Review*, 56, March 1966, pp. 96–117; F. P. Stafford, "Concentration and Labor Earnings: Comment," *American Economic Review*, 58, March 1968, pp. 174–181; and A. Throop, "The Union-Non-Union Wage Differential," *American Economic Review*, 56, March 1966, pp. 79–99.

[27]P. M. Ryscavage, "Measuring Union–Nonunion Earnings Differentials," *Monthly Labor Review*, 97:12 (December 1974), pp 3–9.

[28]O. Ashenfelter, "Racial Discrimination and Trade Unionism," *Journal of Political Economy*, 80, May–June 1972, pp. 435–464.

large nonunion employers tend to pay the union scale; that middle-size firms pay the union scale if most of their industry is unionized (though they are not); that middle-size firms pay less than the union scale if unionization in their industry is weak; and that small nonunion firms pay less than the union scale, regardless of the degree of union organization in their industry.[29]

But is it unionism that creates a wage advantage for workers, or is it the collective bargaining process? For the private sector in the American economy, this question is not very important. In virtually all instances employees who are in a union also bargain collectively with their employer. Unionism and bargaining are so intimately coupled that a researcher cannot estimate their separate effects on wage levels.

In the public sector, however, unions exist where law does not permit, or even forbids, collective bargaining. By comparing wages for unionized employees who bargain collectively with wages for unionized employees who don't bargain collectively—and standardizing for other factors that might create a difference in wages—researchers can identify the separate influences of unionism and collective bargaining. When this analysis was done, it turned out that unionism alone did not create a wage differential with nonunion employees. The differential was created in favor of those people who had the collective bargaining process working for them. *Collective bargaining, not unionism alone, creates a wage advantage.*[30]

Why don't union employees receive an even larger differential over nonunion employees? There are probably several reasons. First, some nonunion employers make it a policy to pay their employees just above the union rates, in order, in part, to discourage unionization. The activities of the union therefore affect both union and nonunion employees almost equally, although by different processes. Second, unions cannot simply ignore economic factors. When nonunion employers pay below the union scale and unionized employers compete with them, the union must often moderate its wage demands so as not to cause the unionized employers to become noncompetitive. In the construction industry, for example, the unions are often confronted in negotiations with demands from the employers that wage increases be kept low to avoid having additional construction projects awarded by owners to nonunion contractors. In recent years, construction unions have often agreed to especially low wage increases to meet nonunion competition. Third, some companies can afford to pay more than others. But unions are not always able to discriminate among such companies, that is, to get higher wages from some than from others. Suppose, for example, that a union tries to keep many firms union-

[29]Michael Podgursky, "Unions, Establishment Size and Intra-Industry Threat Effects," *Industrial and Labor Relations Review*, 39:2, January 1986, p.277ff.

[30]David Lewin, "Wages and Unionism in the Public Sector: The Case of Police," *The Review of Economics and Statistics*, 63:1, February 1981, pp. 53–59.

ized and must do so by having all the firms pay the same wage rate. In such a case, the union is probably keeping the wages paid by the company with the higher ability to pay below what they might be in the absence of the union.

Figure 18-4 shows that as the 1980s progressed the unions on average negotiated lesser pay increases than nonunion workers received. The result, which isn't reflected in the figure, is that the pay differential between union and nonunion workers has decreased in recent years, although it remains in favor of the unions by a substantial amount. By 1991 union increases were on average above those received by nonunion workers.

There is one last question to be asked about the differential in pay between union-represented and nonrepresented employees. Do union members receive a differential not because they are represented by unions but because they are working in less desirable jobs than nonunion people? John S. Heywood investigated the question as it applies to the insecurity of jobs and concluded that one-sixth of the union differential can be attributed to union workers being in jobs with a higher likelihood of layoff; furthermore, though both union and nonunion workers receive a differential

FIGURE 18-4   Percent changes in compensation from the Employment Cost Index for 12-month periods ending March, June, September, and December, private-industry workers by union status, 1980–1989. (*Note:* Compensation includes wages and salaries as well as cost of benefits.) *(Source: Daniel Quinn Mills, "When Employees Make Concessions," Harvard Business Review, 61:3, May–June 1983, pp. 108–109.)*

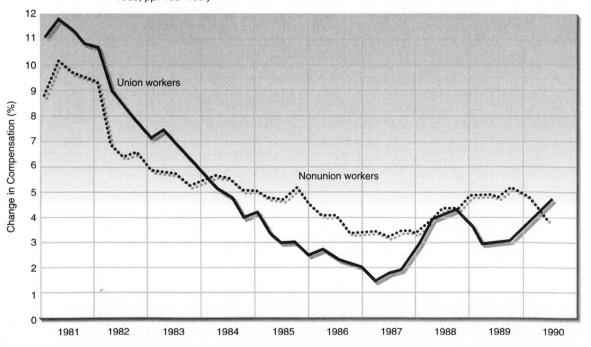

when their jobs carry high risk of unemployment, union workers receive a differential for the risk that is larger than nonunion workers receive.[31]

FACTORS AFFECTING WAGE DETERMINATION

While wage determination involves very complicated procedures, the major factors that affect it are few. The complexities and great difficulties of wage determination arise in the application of these factors to specific cases. There are four principal factors involved in wage setting: comparability among wage rates, changes in the cost of living, ability of employers to pay, and productivity of employees. We have already discussed the impact of changes in the cost of living on wages in the preceding section, and productivity is discussed in Chapter 21, so we may limit our attention in this section to the two remaining factors: comparability and ability to pay.

Comparability Among Wage Rates

Probably the largest number of wage decisions are based simply on the comparison of wage rates. This judgment includes both the setting of individual rates and the setting of groups of rates. For example, if a company hires a new person into a secretarial job, it will probably determine that secretary's rate of pay by looking at what it is already paying secretaries. Similarly, if a union that represents unskilled laborers is negotiating with an employer who hires both skilled craftspeople and laborers, the negotiations will surely start from the proposition that the laborers' rate of pay is to be below that for the skilled trades. In some instances, pay setting is made very simple by comparisons. In many cities firefighters and police receive pay "parity," that is, they receive the same rate of pay. If the police get a raise, the firefighters ask for the same raise.

Many other groups of employees have established certain differentials with other groups of workers as a matter of historic practice. For example, licensed mechanics may traditionally receive 50 cents per hour more than unlicensed mechanics. When the increase is determined for licensed mechanics, the unlicensed mechanics get the same amount. Differentials may also be of a percentage nature. For example, in a certain city carpenters traditionally receive 5 percent more than cement masons. Thus, if the rate of pay of carpenters is to be determined, and the rate of pay of cement masons is known, wage setting requires an increase for the carpenters that again places that trade's rate 5 percent above that of the cement masons.

The wage rates that exist at any specific time may be referred to as a structure of rates. The determination of one rate by reference to others in the structure is the essence of wage determination by comparability of

[31]John S. Heywood, "Do Union Members Receive Compensating Differentials? The Case of Employment Security," *Journal of Labor Research*, 10:3, Summer 1989, p. 274ff.

rates. The wage structure as a factor in determining wages draws its importance from circumstances that affect both employees and employers.

Ability of an Employer to Pay

When employees want a pay increase, or when a union demands one, an employer may reply that it cannot afford to pay the increase. A company might say that it will have no profits at all if it must pay a wage increase, or a hospital or an agency of government might say that although it doesn't make profits, it still must meet its costs, and a pay increase would cause it to run deficits (i.e., cause its expenditures to exceed its revenues). Ordinarily an employer doesn't tell the whole story if it simply says it cannot pay a wage increase. It may be able to pay for some level of wage increase, but not others. The employer should say, "I cannot pay an increase of more than _____ ." Also, it may be that there should be a condition attached to the employer's position, such as "The company cannot pay a wage increase without raising prices" or "The hospital cannot pay a wage increase without getting increased payments from Blue Cross–Blue Shield" or "The city cannot afford a pay increase without raising taxes."

In fact, the ability of an employer to pay additional wages often depends on its ability to raise its revenues or cut its costs in order to make more money available for employee compensation. This is often misunderstood. Employees and unions often believe that companies can pay wage increases out of their profits without having to increase prices. Sometimes this is the case. But in most instances compensation of employees is so large a part of the firm's costs (averaging 50 to 60 percent for most firms) and profits are so small a proportion (averaging, before taxes, about 6 to 7 percent of sales) that a substantial wage increase would totally eliminate profits. For example, a compensation increase of 10 percent will cost a firm 6 percent of its total costs (if it spent 60 percent of its costs on employee compensation) and almost fully eliminate a 6 percent rate of profits on sales. The firm would have no profits to distribute to its stockholders as dividends or to its managers as bonuses or to use for expansion.

Most employers, of course, will attempt to reduce costs and to raise prices to reestablish its profit margin. Costs may be reduced by new techniques, new ideas about how to do things, improved quality, and similar activities. In some instances, pay increases for employees will help to finance themselves if they reduce turnover, absenteeism, or other employee-behavior-related costs. Prices may or may not be able to be increased, depending on the market situation of the firms products or services—the degree of customer demand, competitors, and so on.

Employee and union pressure for pay increases that drives management to seek new ways to cut costs and expand revenues is one of the major forces behind economic change and progress.

CONTEMPORARY WAGE THEORIES

Broadly, wage theories may be classified as emphasizing either market (i.e., supply and demand) or bargaining. The market analysis conceives of transactions involving individuals (not large groups) and of simple behavioral patterns. Employers are presumed to try to buy labor at the lowest price and workers to look for the highest wage, with little regard by the employer for the characteristics of workers and their unions or by workers for characteristics of employers and their corporations. In fact, in most circumstances, the matter is more complicated. The theories which attempt to include this complexity in the analysis, by paying greater attention to the characteristics of employers and workers, may be characterized as bargaining theories (or "institutional" theories, because they consider the importance of labor market institutions, such as unions and corporations). But the bargaining theories also incorporate supply-demand analysis.[32] They simply give it less significance in the total picture. And even among bargaining theories, some stress economic factors more than others.

Market Theory

Supply-Demand Analysis   Employers want to hire employees because they think the employees can produce something of value which can be sold in the market for products or services for more than it cost. Theoretically, a firm will hire additional labor until the additional surplus created by the next person hired will be zero or less. The additional amount value of output as each new worker is added is called the marginal productivity of labor. The number of people who would be hired as the incremental surplus declines is the demand curve of a firm for labor.

This is fine so far as it goes, but it doesn't go far enough. The limitation of marginal productivity theory is that it is only half of a theory of wages. It describes what the wage rate will be if the number of units of labor is specified, but doesn't tell us how to determine the number of units of labor which will be used. It is, therefore, incomplete. Alfred Marshall, an English economist, described the problem by saying that wages (and product prices also) are determined by a supply-and-demand process that is like a pair of scissors, in that both blades are needed to make a cut. The marginal productivity theory of wages was only one blade of the scissors, the demand side.[33] Where was a theorist to find the other blade?

---

[32]Thomas A. Kochan and Richard N. Block, "An Interindustry Analysis of Bargaining Outcomes: Preliminary Evidence," *Quarterly Journal of Economics*, 91:3, August 1977, pp. 431–452; F. R. Warren-Boulton, "Vertical Control by Labor Unions," *American Economic Review*, 67:3, June 1977, pp. 309–322.

[33]Alfred Marshall, *Principles of Economics*, 8th ed. (London: Macmillan, 1961), p. 569.

The supply side consists of the willingness of workers to offer labor at various wage rates. Presumably, as wage rates rise, the amount of labor offered will increase. Thus, a diagram can be drawn that showed a supply of labor curve (see Figure 18-5). A labor market may now be said to exist. On one side are potential employers, who will hire labor and will be prepared to hire more labor the lower the wage rate. On the other side of the market are workers, who are prepared to sell labor. It may be expected that more people will be willing to work, and many already working will be prepared to work longer hours, as the wage rate rises. At some point, a bargain will be struck in the labor market and a transaction will occur. The bargain will set a certain wage rate and a quantity of labor which is hired by employers and sold by workers.

This market process may be put into diagrammatic form. Figure 18-6 shows the value of output in a standard monetary unit (i.e, dollars per hour). This simplifying procedure is reflective of a modern economy in which employers sell output for money and pay workers in money. The marginal productivity curve is shown as a demand curve for labor.

The demand and supply curves intersect at a single point, marked e in Figure 18-6. At that point, the quantity of labor demanded by employers (point q) is equal to the quantity of labor workers are willing to provide (point q also). At the intersection of the curves e, the market "clears," and a wage rate w and employment level q are determined. The point e may be called an "equilibrium point." This process is what is meant by such commonly used phrases as "supply and demand set our wage rates," and "the market will set wages."

Suppose the market is not allowed to operate. Instead, the government sets a wage rate by administrative action at point w in Figure 18-7. What will happen? At a wage rate equal to w, employers would want to hire only

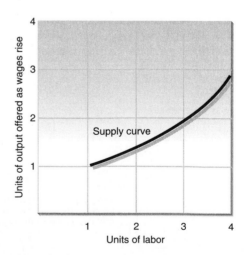

FIGURE 18-5   The supply curve for labor.

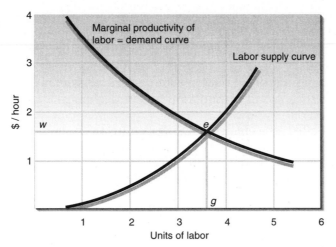

FIGURE 18-6   The labor market.

the number of units of labor market dd. But workers would offer a number of units of labor equal to *ss*. There would be more persons looking for work than employers would want, and the difference would be called unemployment. The supply and demand curves are not fixed, but instead move their position (and alter their shape) as conditions affecting them change. For example, suppose a corporation makes jeans, but jeans suddenly lose popularity with consumers. Then the demand curve for labor to produce jeans will shift down to the left in our diagram. This means that at

FIGURE 18-7   Unemployment in the labor market.

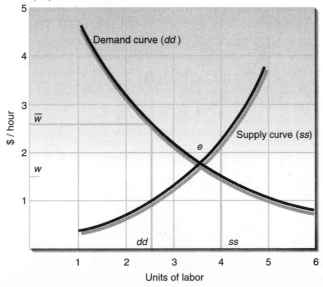

any wage rate, the company will hire fewer workers than it would have hired before. Since the supply curve of workers is unchanged and the market clears, the wage rate and the number of people hired will both fall. Suppose the wage rate remains at its old level, however, perhaps as a result of a provision of a collective bargaining agreement. Then the number of workers the company employs would decline more than if the wage rate also fell.

The effect of a change in the wage rate on the level of employment can be measured on either the demand or the supply curve. Consider the demand curve. For any point on the curve, make the following calculation: If the wage rate is reduced a little bit, how much will the quantity of labor demanded increase? Figure 18-8 provides an illustration of this calculation. Now divide the change in the wage rate by the level of the wage rate (at point y on the vertical axis in Figure 18-8), then divide the change in the quantity of labor demanded by the previous number of units of labor (at point x on the horizontal axis in Figure 18-8). Both these numbers are ratios (or can be converted to percentages). Finally, create a ratio of the two ratios, that is, divide the percentage change in the level of employment (i.e., units of labor) by the percentage change in the wage rate. This ratio is the wage elasticity of employment demand or, for short, the "elasticity of demand."

An elasticity of demand that is greater than unity means that if wages are decreased, demand for labor will rise by more than a proportionate amount. (For example, if wages are reduced by 1.0 percent, employment will rise by 1.5 percent.)

FIGURE 18-8   A decrease in the wage means an increase in quantity of labor demanded.

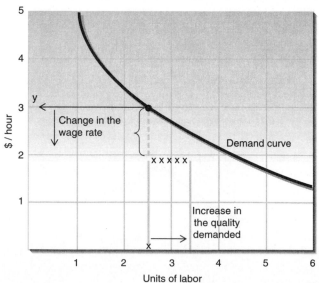

An elasticity of demand that is equal to unity means that if wages are decreased, demand will rise by the same proportionate amount. (For example, if wages are reduced by 1.0 percent, employment will rise by 0.5 percent.)

An elasticity of demand that is less than unity means that if wages are decreased, demand for labor will rise by less than 1 proportionate amount. (For example, if wages are reduced by 1.0 percent, employment will rise by 0.5 percent.)

The Usefulness of Supply-Demand Analysis   Supply-demand analysis is a complicated theory, but it is also useful. In fact, many people in the United States think in terms of supply and demand for labor and utilize it in determining their approach to many labor relations issues. When there is unemployment, business people often urge that wages be reduced in order to reduce unemployment. Unions, on the other hand, want wages to remain at existing levels, and so suggest that the government generate more spending. This additional expenditure will cause the demand curve for labor to shift to the right and result in more people being hired.

Supply-demand analysis is also called "partial equilibrium analysis." This term means that only one market (e.g., for a single occupation) is being studied at a time. What is happening in other markets will certainly affect the one being studied, but those effects are ignored in order to simplify the analysis. Like other simplifications, this one has disadvantages. In some situations the failure to take account of developments elsewhere causes the analysis of a single market to be incorrect. For example, a union may decide that if it agrees to an employer proposal to lower the wage rate, then workers will receive more employment. This conclusion is supported by supply-demand analysis. But what if, simultaneously, the product these workers produce is losing its popularity with consumers? Then the demand curve for the workers' services will be falling and may cancel out any potential employment gained from a lower wage rate. This situation also points out that the demand for labor is a "derived" demand. It comes solely from the demand of consumers for the product of labor. There is *no* demand for labor if there is no demand for the goods or services that labor produces. Therefore, to understand particular labor markets, one must also understand particular product markets.

There are other theories about wages in addition to those we have reviewed. Many economists have written about the subject, and each has a somewhat different approach. It is necessary, therefore, to be highly selective in reviewing theoretical work. The choice of only a few theorists for mention is not intended to disparage the work of others, nor to suggest to students that there is not more to learn. In this section we will review the major types of current wage theories, in part by selecting the work of certain theorists for comparison and contrast.

Human Capital Theory

Previously in this chapter we reviewed differences in pay rates by occupation. These pay differentials reflect, in part, the degree to which people have made an investment in learning skills or a profession. An explanation of occupational pay differentials has developed around this insight, which is called "human capital theory." This theory stresses the financial costs of education to a person. These costs are of two types. First, there are the direct expenses of education, such as tuition, books, and living expenses. Second, there are the costs that come from not working while attending school or training courses. The earnings that people do not get because they are in school or in training are called "forgone earnings," or "opportunity costs," and are the hidden costs of education. (If a person is in an apprenticeship program, forgone earnings are the difference between the wages an apprentice receives and the wages that could be earned in some other occupation.)

Human capital theory holds that a person bears the cost of education (and/or training) because he or she expects higher earnings in the future. In other words, education or skills training is like an investment of capital in a business, which pays dividends later. Because education is an investment in a person, it is human, not business, capital. The educated person expects to earn more in the future than the uneducated person. The pay differences between occupations are said to represent the return on the human capital invested. The higher the level of education (and consequently, the greater its cost), the higher the pay is predicted to be.[34] The exact amount of the return on human capital invested changes over time. Currently, the financial return on investment in education appears to be declining.[35] And human capital theory as an explanation of the differences in pay among occupations has been subjected to criticism. Too many other factors affecting pay levels are left out by human capital theory, say its critics.[36] Finally, the few direct statistical tests that have been made of human capital theory do not support it. James Medoff and Katherine Abraham, for example, showed that in several large companies, the higher rates of pay went not to the best performers (which human capital theory predicts), but instead to the older employees.[37]

Medoff and Abraham explain this phenomenon by arguing that unions reflect their members' preferences in causing companies to pay older employees more than their contribution to production, and younger employees less than their contribution. Human capital theorists instead suggest

[34]Gary Becker, *Human Capital* (New York: Columbia University Press, 1964).

[35]Richard B. Freeman, *The Overeducated American* (New York: Academic Press, 1976).

[36]Michael J. Piore, "The Importance of Human Capital Theory to Labor Economics—A Dissenting View," Industrial Relations Research Association, *Proceedings* of the Twenty-Sixth Annual Meeting, Dec. 28–29, 1973, pp. 251–258.

[37]James L. Medoff and Katherine G. Abraham, "Experience, Performance and Earnings," *Quarterly Journal of Economics*, 95:4, December 1980, pp. 703–736.

that there is an implicit contract between each individual employee and his or her employer, reflecting the individual's own preference with respect to his or her earnings over the person's career with the firm.[38] In this theory, the date at which an employee receives pay has no direct connection with the time he or she does the work for which he or she is paid.

Perhaps there has not been as much investment in human capital in America as there ought to be. For example, apprenticeship is a formal process of training which allows an employer and a worker to invest in developing the skills of an individual. Building a skilled work force through traditional craft apprenticeship is at the heart of the business success of many European countries (especially Germany). But in America apprenticeship has declined during this century. Why did America turn away from apprenticeship? Labor historian Dan Jacoby has answered this question. The legal foundation existed in early twentieth century law for successful apprenticeship based on contract law between employer and apprentice. "That such institutions did not develop is attributed . . . to employer disinterest in having contract law applied to training." Why? Because, says Jacoby, such laws would have "limited employers' managerial prerogatives to fire and discipline at will."[39]

Bargaining Theories

Institutional Theories That Stress Economic Factors   The major fact from which all bargaining theories start is the existence of unions. Because unions exist, the establishment of wages is different from what it would otherwise be. (Presumably, the large corporation also has an important impact on wage determination, but this has never been of great interest to theorists.) What difference does a union make to wage determination? How does a union behave? How is the union to be incorporated into the body of wage theory?

A corporation may be said to exist in order to fulfill some public need in a manner which provides financial gain to its investors. Over the longer term it is necessary for a firm to earn enough profits to attract capital for reinvestment and growth. In America, with its vigorous capital markets, a firm which fails to realize potential profit is likely to be acquired by new investors and new managers who will do so. Hence, it is not too great an assumption in today's economic environment that firms seek to maximize profits, subject to the constraints put upon them by the government, the marketplace and by employees and unions. This is a powerful analytic ob-

---

[38]C. Azariadis, "Implicit Contracts and Underemployment Equilibria," *Journal of Political Economy*, 83, December 1979, pp. 1183–1202; and Bengt Holmstrum, "Contractual Models of the Labor Market," *American Economic Review*, 71, May 1981, pp. 308–313.

[39]Dan Jacoby, "Legal Foundations of Human Capital Markets," *Industrial Relations*, 30:2, Spring 1991, p. 229ff.

servation, because it means that important aspects of the behavior of most firms can be predicted. (This is, of course, the essence of the theory of the firm in economic analysis.) If an objective could be isolated for unions analogous to profit maximization for a firm, then the analysis of wage determination could be improved.

In 1944, John T. Dunlop undertook to develop such a theory of wages. "What do unions seek to maximize?" he asked. Unions do not simply seek to maximize wages. If they did, they would create too much unemployment. Unions recognize this relationship clearly. Craft union leaders will often say, "It does no good to have the highest-wage nonworking people around." Alternatively, unions do not maximize employment, for that would require very low wage rates. Instead, the two objectives—high wages and high employment—are balanced (or "traded off") against each other. To reflect this balancing, Dunlop proposed to treat the unions as maximizing the product of employment times wages, that is, the total amount the company pays in wages, its "wage bill." (Mathematically, this occurs at the point on the demand curve where the elasticity is equal to unity.)

Using the rule that unions attempt to maximize the wage bill, Dunlop developed the conditions under which that would occur. Also, he analyzed the impact of product market characteristics on wage determination. For example, if a union dealt with a company that had a monopoly on the product it sold, the union could probably get a higher wage bill than if the union dealt with many competing firms selling the same product. But even this result might be altered under certain conditions in the product market. Dunlop's analysis demonstrated how complex wage determination can be, involving as it does the interaction of product market and labor market factors. He pointed out that wages are related to various combinations of labor and product market structures that are numerous "almost without limit."[40] It is this complexity of situations, of course, which nourishes collective bargaining in the United States and which results in the maze of different wage patterns that exist in our economy.

Institutional Theories That Stress Noneconomic Factors Dunlop was soon challenged with respect to his emphasis on the economic motivation of unions. Arthur Ross, writing in 1948, objected that a union was less of an economic institution than a political one. A union does not sell labor, Ross argued. It participates in the establishment of the price of labor, but the sale is made between the worker and the employer. Nor is the union mechanically concerned with the quantity of labor sold, that is, with the number of workers employed in the branch of the economy in which it is interested. Instead, it is vitally interested in the size of its own member-

---

[40]John T. Dunlop, *Wage Discrimination under Trade Unions* (New York: Macmillan, 1944), p. 82.

ship, but this is not the same thing as the number of workers employed, except in the case where an industry is 100 percent unionized.

What a union is really interested in, said Ross, is its own survival and wellbeing.[41] In developing a wage policy, the union would take its own interests into account first of all. In some instances this would result in behavior which tended to maximize the wage bill (as Dunlop had argued). But in other instances, the union would not be interested in the wage bill at all. For example, if a union were challenged by another union for representation rights at a plant, it might negotiate not a big wage agreement but a moderate one, to gain the company's assistance in warding off the challenge. Or it might seek a big increase in wages to get the support of the employees. The point, Ross argued, was that the decision was based on political considerations, not on the automatic pursuit of the maximum wage bill. It would "satisfice," not maximize.

These two contrasting views of union behavior—the union as an economic maximizer versus the union as a political satisficer, referred to as the Dunlop-Ross debate—continue to absorb theoreticians. One study concluded that when union members are most worried about the risks of being laid off, they behave as Dunlop-type economic maximizers; when union members are most concerned with the risk of a strike, they behave as Ross-type satisficers.[42]

Ross also introduced a concept he labeled "orbits of coercive comparison." In many instances, he argued, a union is in such an intimate relationship with another union or with certain employers that it virtually has to follow a wage pattern that has been established. For example, the local unions of the United Automobile Workers that represent employees of Ford Motor Company are not free to negotiate independently of what occurs at General Motors. If the Ford locals took a lower settlement, the workers at Ford would complain. If the local unions at Ford tried to get a larger settlement, the company would resist very strongly, since it would not want its competitive position vis-à-vis General Motors weakened. The Ford locals are, therefore, in an orbit of comparison that is so strong as to be "coercive." Ross viewed these orbits as essentially political factors affecting union wage policy. They were political in his view because they reflected attitudes of employees (rather than economic realities) that impacted a union's pay policy.

Recent research has confirmed that Ross's "orbits of coercive comparison" continue to play an important role in pay setting. A study of the determinants of job quitting among high-level academic administrators, for example, found that salary level had no effect on the willingness of people to

[41]Arthur M. Ross, Trade Union Wage Policy (Berkeley: University of California Press, 1948).

[42]Bruce E. Kaufman and Jorge Martinez-Vazquez, "The Ross-Dunlop Debate," *Journal of Labor Research*, 8:3, Summer 1987, pp. 291–304. See also Jeff Borland, "The Ross-Dunlop Debate Revisited," *Journal of Labor Research*, 7:3, Summer 1986, pp. 293–305.

quit; but turnover was strongly influenced by how an administrator's salary compared to the earnings of other people in the same role.[43]

Resolving the Conflict Between Theories

For a while there ensued a lively debate in academic journals between the partisans of the bargaining and institutional theories (sometimes referred to as economic and political theories) of union wage behavior. In 1957 Dunlop again addressed the issue and attempted to go beyond the controversy with Ross. Wages and employment seemed to be related, he said, in a vastly more complex manner than could be "fruitfully portrayed in a Marshallian demand curve."[44] Instead of trying to explain the setting of a single wage rate (as his and Ross's work had done), Dunlop argued that wage theory needed to approach wage determination through the concept of the wage structure, that is, the manner in which existing wage rates affect the establishment of other wage rates. "Instead of reducing wage setting to the problem of a single rate, the task . . . is . . . the problem of the setting and variation in the whole structure . . . of rates."[45] To help in this process, Dunlop proposed two concepts: a "job cluster" and a "wage contour." A job cluster is a group of jobs so closely interrelated (by technology, administrative organization, or custom) that they have one key wage rate. A wage contour involves a group of firms so closely interrelated (by product similarities, similar labor sources, or custom) that they have common wage characteristics. (The concept has a certain similarity to Ross's orbits of coercive comparison.) Wage contours have industrial, occupational, and geographic dimensions. For example, the basic steel industry constitutes a wage contour expressed in the basic steel collective bargaining agreement and having the following dimensions: industrial—basic steel; occupational—those jobs involved in making steel; geographic—nationwide. Much of the process of determination of wage rates, said Dunlop, depends on the job cluster and wage contour into which a particular situation falls.

Dunlop apparently hoped that following the publication of "The Task of Contemporary Wage Theory," economists would begin to study and describe job clusters and wage contours as they actually exist in the economy. There has been some research of this nature.[46] Primarily, however,

---

[43]Jeffrey Pfeffer and Alison Davis-Blake, "Determinants of Salary Dispersion in Organizations, *Industrial Relations*, pp. 38–57, vol. 29, No. 1, Winter 1990 (Annuo Domini MCMXCIII).

[44]John Dunlop, "The Task of Contemporary Wage Theory," in J. T. Dunlop, ed., *The Theory of Wage Determination* (London: Macmillan, 1975), p. 11.

[45]Ibid., p. 15.

[46]Otto Eckstein and Thomas A. Wilson, "The Determination of Money Wages in the American Economy," *Quarterly Journal of Economics*, 25:3, August 1962, pp. 379–414; Otto Eckstein, "Money Wage Determination Revisited," *Review of Economic Studies*, 35, April 1968, pp. 133–143; Michael L. Wachter, "The Wage Process," *Brookings Papers on Economic Activity*, 2, 1974, pp. 507–524; and D. Q. Mills, "Explaining Pay Increases in Construction," *Industrial Relations*, 13:2, May 1974, pp. 196–201.

theorists have attempted to combine the economic and the political view of union wage policy. Melvin Reder argued that both Dunlop's and Ross's theories were too broad. Instead, he qualified their theories in a number of ways. Wage contours, or orbits of coercive comparison, are important, Reder said, but not necessarily determinative. If a company finds itself in a wage pattern which is too expensive for its long-term economic survival, it will either break out of the contour or go out of business. Furthermore, whatever this position in a wage contour, most unions will respond to sufficient unemployment in their ranks, thought Reder, by accepting a wage decrease. But some unions are more responsive to unemployment than others.[47] Robert Hall and David Lilien have recently shown that, under certain assumptions about supply and demand and about the uncertainty of the future, unions are wise to raise wages despite existing unemployment.[48]

ESTABLISHING PAY RATES

The theories examined above explain the causes of wage differentials in primarily economic terms. In practice, however, wage setting is an administrative process which strongly reflects pervasive social mores and which is influenced by an economic context. There are many different methods by which the form and amount of compensation are established. They are summarized and categorized for ease of presentation in Table 18-3. At the top, different procedures are listed on the basis of which actor makes the final decision on the rate of compensation. There are four actors identified: the employer, the employee, the union, and the government. At the bottom, different criteria are listed by which compensation may be established. Any actor may use any criterion, although, in fact, certain actors place great reliance on some criteria and little reliance on others.

Each of the four actors may act unilaterally, that is, without reference at the point of decision to the others. Thus, the employer may set a rate of pay for a job and offer it to present or prospective employees on a take-it-or-leave-it basis. And a union may also set a rate of pay and offer it to employers on a take-it-or-leave-it basis. (Today in the United States this would be a very unusual procedure. However, 75 years ago, it was common in some industries. The union simply held a meeting and by vote adopted a wage rate. The union members then informed the employers of their decision and refused to work at less than the adopted

[47]Melvin W. Reder, "The Theory of Union Wage Policy," in Walter Galenson and S. M. Lipset, eds., *Labor and Trade Unionism* (New York: McGraw-Hill, 1960).
[48]Robert E. Hall and David M. Lilien, "Efficient Wage Bargains under Uncertain Supply and Demand," *American Economic Association*, 69:5, December 1979, pp. 868–879. For a discussion of wage theory, see Brian Burkitt, *Trade Unions and Wages* (Bradford, England: Bradford University Press, 1976).

TABLE 18-3   METHODS OF ESTABLISHING COMPENSATION

Actors
Employer unilaterally
Employee unilaterally
Union unilaterally
Government unilaterally
Employer-employee jointly
Employer-union jointly

Criteria
Reaction
Surveys
Formulas
Job evaluation plans
Pay by performance

Note: Unilateral action does not necessarily imply action by a single individual without influence or approval by others. The actors listed, except the individual employee and some employers who are sole proprietorships, are actually not individual persons but organizations (such as a corporation, a union, or a government agency), so that unilateral action by the organization may entail internal procedures between elements of the organization that involve many persons in a joint decision. A corporation, for example, may "unilaterally" set wage rates by what is in effect a bargaining procedure between the personnel department and the operations department.

rate.[49]) An employee may decide that he or she is entitled to a certain rate of pay and announce that he or she will leave if the company refuses to pay it. However, in most cases only employees with special skills or knowledge are able to do this successfully. Finally, a governmental body may establish rates of pay and by law prevent employers from hiring, or workers from taking jobs, except at that rate of pay.

The four actors may also set compensation in conjunction with each other. Theoretically, compensation could be determined in different cases by any two, any three, or all four acting together. In practice in the United States, compensation is usually set by joint action only between employers and individual employees or between employers and unions. Only these two forms of joint action are shown in Table 18-3. Joint determination of compensation between unions and employers is referred to as collective bargaining, of course.

There are also several criteria by which compensation is established. Table 18-3 lists five criteria but does not define them. Briefly, they may be described as follows:

[49]See, for example, Royal Montgomery, *Industrial Relations in the Chicago Building Trades* (Chicago: University of Chicago Press, 1927); and William Haber, *Industrial Relations in the Building Industry* (Cambridge, Mass.: Harvard University Press, 1930).

- *Reaction*. Rates are set according to the apparent needs of the moment, without any formal process.
- *Surveys*. Rates are set by reference to surveys taken to determine rates of pay and benefits for employees in specific occupations, by industry type and geographic area. Discretion is retained by the actor(s) setting the rates as to the specific level at which rates are set.
- *Formulas*. Rates are set by reference to some outside factor(s) in a way that permits no discretion concerning the specific level at which rates are set.
- *Job evaluation plans*. Rates are set by reference to a list of occupations in which each occupation is given a rating based on certain numerical factors with respect to other occupations, and pay scales are made to reflect the measured differences among occupations.
- *Pay by performance*. Rates are set by reference to the amount of work each individual employee (or group of employees) performs.

These criteria by which compensation is determined are extremely important to labor-management relations. They are also quite complicated. At this point we will examine the first four criteria in greater detail and review simplified examples of each. Pay by performance is also discussed in this chapter.

In Chapter 4 we contrasted the traditional and the new systems of management. Table 18-4 describes appropriate reward-system (or compensation, broadly construed) practices accompanying the traditional and nontraditional management systems. For example, traditional systems provided higher benefits for higher-level employees; but nontraditional systems provide choice among a menu of benefits for all employees. A nontraditional system has few of the status symbols common in traditional settings. Pay systems differ greatly. In the traditional systems the rank and file are paid on an hourly basis and higher-level employees, including executives, are paid a salary. But in a nontraditional system all employees are paid a salary. Table 18-4 lists several other major differences between the two systems; can you figure out why each difference exists?

Reactive Criteria

Perhaps the setting of rates of compensation by simple reaction should not be dignified by calling it a criterion; certainly it is not a systematic procedure. Yet it is probably the criterion most used by employers, especially employers acting unilaterally. In such a process, pay rates are established and adjusted in a series of ad hoc steps. For example, suppose that the secretary who works for a manager is offered a job at higher pay in another company. In order to retain the person's services, the manager raises the rate of pay. No attempt is made to survey other rates in or outside the company, nor are conditions such as cost of living considered.

TABLE 18-4   APPROPRIATE REWARD-SYSTEM PRACTICES

Reward	Traditional	Nontraditional
Fringe benefits	Vary according to organizational level	Same for all levels
Promotion	All decisions made by top management	Open posting for all jobs: peer-group involvement in decision process
Status symbols	A great many carefully allocated on the basis of job position	Few present, low emphasis on organizational level
Pay		
Type of system	Hourly and salary	All salary
Base rate	Based on job performed: high enough to attract job applicants	Based on skills: high enough to provide security and attract job applicants
Incentive plan	Piece rate	Group and organization wide bonus lump sum increase
Communication policy	Very restricted distribution of information	Individual rates, salary-survey data, and all other information made public
Decision-making locus	Top management	Close to location of person whose pay is being set

The increase is simply offered and accepted, and a new rate of compensation is established.

Alternatively, suppose a small machine shop in a large corporation had many job orders in the past but now has very few. To stretch its budget, the manager meets individually with each employee and proposes that either the person's wage rate be reduced or the person be laid off. Several employees agree to having their wage rate reduced, again without reference to factors other than the manager's interpretation of how the employee should react to a shrinking budget.

To take a final illustration, suppose that the same manager of the machine tool shop has the opposite problem 6 months later, that is, too many orders to fill. The manager offers the most skilled employees a bonus for each order they complete. In each of these cases, the requirements of production affect compensation in an ad hoc way.

These illustrations are not meant to imply that the process of setting compensation on such an expedient basis is necessarily wrong, but it does cause problems in the course of time. Especially in large organizations, after a while such a process results in people who are doing the same work receiving very different rates of pay. For instance, our first example concerned an increase in a secretary's pay because of another job offer. But other secretaries did not get such an offer and received no increase in pay. Should all secretaries doing the same job, that is, working for managers of a certain level, receive the same pay, or should those who get offers to work elsewhere get more pay? How much more?

The wage and salary policies of corporations exist to answer such questions, and they do so by application of one or another of the remaining four criteria used in establishing compensation.

Compensation Surveys

Employers, governmental agencies, and unions participate in systematic wage and salary surveys, often unilaterally and sometimes jointly. The most careful surveys proceed by definition of an occupation, which usually involves the comparison of job descriptions, and by the collection of pay-rate and benefit data from all major employers in the appropriate geographic area who have that job category. A survey that is not done carefully can be very misleading. For example, it may mix unrelated job categories by failing to define carefully the categories of jobs being surveyed; or it may omit major employers. Another mistake is collecting pay-rate data for different companies at different times, instead of having all data cover the same time period. Still another danger is to fail to have all benefits carefully reported.

Despite these pitfalls, wage and salary surveys are very popular with employers. Many major companies belong to survey groups with other employers in major metropolitan areas. The companies exchange information about compensation. The data are used by companies in determining adjustments to make for their own employees or in collective bargaining with labor unions representing their employees.[50]

The federal government also conducts surveys of wages by occupation and area and publishes them periodically.[51] Labor unions have not, until recently, participated to any marked degree in compensation surveys. Instead, unions have tended to rely on informal surveys of rates reported by other unions when queried by letter or phone. Recently, however, some national unions have begun to keep computerized records of rates of pay and benefits negotiated by the union with various employers.

The use of survey data by the various actors in determining wages differs. In collective bargaining situations both management and unions use survey data to prepare positions and to answer the claims of the other side. When employers unilaterally set compensation, surveys are used to provide a data base for the application of policy. A large employer may use survey results to tell it when to raise its rates of pay. Unions seeking to represent clerical workers often charge that the cooperation among employers to compile survey data and the use of these data by companies in the ways just described constitute a form of monopolylike collusion against the in-

---

[50]See J. D. Dunn and Frank M. Rachel, *Wage and Salary Administration: Total Compensation Systems* (New York: McGraw-Hill, 1971).
[51]See various occupational wage surveys published by the Bureau of Labor Statistics, U.S. Department of Labor.

terests of workers. Whatever the merits of such charges, the use of survey data by firms in establishing pay rates is quite extensive.

Governmental agencies survey rates of pay by private employers in certain occupational categories as a method of establishing pay levels for the government's own employees in those categories. The federal government uses such a procedure—called a wage board procedure—to establish rates of pay for most of its blue-collar workers.[52] Many municipal governments utilize pay surveys to establish compensation for municipal employees as well. It is often the policy of governmental agencies to pay the exact amount determined by the survey. This procedure virtually converts the survey process of determining compensation into a formula process. It also places great importance on the survey technique, since the survey results no longer serve as a guide to policy, which can be supplemented by other information, but serve to implement the policy as well. A survey is often too unreliable for such use.

For example, suppose that the purpose of a survey is to establish the rate of pay that a city will have for its maintenance machinists. Suppose also that a major private employer of machinists will not cooperate in the survey and that the union representing the city's machinists believes the private employer pays higher than other employers in the area. The determination of the rate of pay for the city's machinists by survey alone may not yield an accurate result, since the survey is incomplete, and will probably cause a dispute over pay between the city and its employees.

Formulas Based on Prices

Protecting Purchasing Power The most common formula for the determination of wages is one that provides that wage rates are adjusted upward in step with the cost of living. The logic of such a provision is to see that workers are able to maintain their standard of living. When the prices of food, clothing, housing, medical services, and other items consumed by employees rise, then, unless their earnings also rise, they cannot continue to consume at the same rate as before. To measure purchasing power, wages must be adjusted for changes in the cost of living. Thus, we may refer to a wage rate—for example, $5 per hour—as a "money" wage rate. Now, suppose an employee earned $5 per hour in 1970 and also $5 per hour in 1985. Was he or she as well off in terms of purchasing power in 1985 as in 1970? Not at all. Between 1970 and 1985 prices paid by consumers rose 167 percent, according to the U.S. Bureau of Labor Statistics. Now, if the employee in our example wished to have the same purchasing power in 1985 as $5 per hour gave in 1970, what rate of pay would be required in 1985? The answer, of course, is 167 percent more than $5 per hour, or $13.35 per hour.

---

[52]See Chapter 21.

Alternatively, if the employee received $13.35 per hour in 1985, it would not buy in 1985 what $13.35 would buy in 1970. How much would be needed in 1970 to buy what $13.35 would buy in 1985? Prices were 167 percent lower, so that the amount needed in 1970 would be $13.35/2.18 = $5.00. This measure, the wage rate divided by the price index of a particular year, we refer to as a measure of "real," not "money" wages. Real wages are wages adjusted for changes in the cost of living, also called wages in "constant-dollar" terms. Money wages are wages expressed in the currency of today.

Escalator Clauses   In order to protect the purchasing power of employees from price inflation, many collective bargaining agreements include a provision that wage rates be periodically adjusted in an amount determined by the rate of increase in consumer prices. Such a clause is called a cost-of-living escalator clause and is referred to as an escalator, or a COLA (cost-of-living adjustment), clause. The essential element of an escalator is some measure of changes in living costs. Most escalator clauses use the national consumer price index (CPI) prepared by the federal government's Bureau of Labor Statistics, but some agreements use the index for a particular city. The automobile industry escalators, which cover workers in both Canada and the United States, use an average of the Canadian and American indexes.

In the United States today most escalator clauses yield an increase in wages that in percentage terms is less than the increase in the price index. On the average, escalators cause wages to rise about one-half the percentage increase in the cost of living.

Some escalator clauses provide a limitation on the size of cost-of-living adjustments in wages. These limits are called "caps." For example, a contract might provide that wages were to be increased 1 cent for every increase of 0.3 points in the price index, up to a limit of $0.12 increase in any given year. An increase of 3.6 points in the price index would yield a $0.12 increase in wages; but no further increase in wages would occur, even if the price index continued to rise, until the year was over.

Increases in wages that are the result of an escalator may be "folded" into the wage-rate base or kept separate from it. Suppose that the wage rate is $5.60 per hour and the escalator provides a 1-cent increase for each 0.3 point increase in the price index. Then an increase of 0.6 points yields a wage increase of $0.02. If the COLA increase is folded in, the new wage rate is $5.62 per hour. If it is not folded in, then the wage rate remains $5.60 per hour plus $0.02 per hour; that is, the worker is paid as if the wage rate were $5.62 per hour. Why does this matter? Folding in is important because of pay premiums. Overtime, for example, is usually paid at time and a half the regular hourly rate of pay. If the COLA increase is folded in, the worker gets overtime pay figured on a higher base rate than if the COLA increase is kept separate.

Such items as the specific terms of an escalator clause, its frequency, whether or not it has a cap, and whether or not (or when) a COLA increase is folded in to base rates are subjects of collective bargaining between management and labor. In some agreements management and labor even set up an escalator, and then the union "borrows" some portion of the escalator to devote to other purposes, such as buying health insurance, so that the workers do not get the full escalator in their paychecks. Bargaining over escalators is, therefore, very complex, and the arrangements that are worked out are as varied as the imagination of people can make them.

History and Economic Significance of Escalators   During the 1920s escalators appeared in certain major agreements, but thereafter virtually disappeared until an escalator was included in the 1948 contract between General Motors and the United Automobile Workers. These clauses became more popular in the 1950s; in 1960 about half of all agreements covering 1000 or more workers involved an escalator clause. By 1970 this proportion had dropped to 25 percent. But under the impact of price inflation in the 1970s, the escalator regained popularity and at one point covered 60 percent or so of workers covered by major agreements (or about 15 to 20 percent of all workers in the private sector in the United States).[53] In the 1980s inflation slowed, and the proportion of contracts with escalators declined rapidly. By 1991 contracts for only 32 percent of employees (covered by collective bargaining agreements contained cost-of-living escalators.[54] Thus continues the long-term pattern by which cost-of-living clauses find their way into agreements when inflation is rising and disappear when it is falling.

Since 1948 a debate has continued, at varying levels of intensity, as to the economic impact of cost-of-living clauses. Are they inflationary or not? Those who argue that they are not inflationary say that in the absence of an escalator, workers would obtain even larger wage increases. This is partly because the escalator represents acceptance of the government's figures for the amount by which the cost of living has increased. These official figures could, of course, be distrusted as underestimates. Proponents of the clauses sometimes argue that they are not inflationary because by definition, in their view, no wage increase is inflationary if it merely follows, and does not exceed, a prior price increase.

Those who believe escalators are inflationary base their opinion on two grounds. First, it may be argued that because they are a formula, escalators eliminate discretion in adjusting to unusual circumstances. For example, in 1980 the automobile industry was in deep recession in the United States. Tens of thousands of workers were on indefinite layoff, and the companies were choked by excessive inventories. Consumer prices were

[53]Victor J. Sheifer, "Cost-of-Living Adjustment," *Monthly Labor Review*, 102:6, June 1979, pp. 14–17.

[54]Bureau of Labor Statistics, *Monthly Labor Review*, 115:1, January 1992, p. 19.

continuing to increase rapidly, however (at an 18 percent annual rate), so that the cost of living escalator in the automobile agreements continued to cause a rapid rise in wages and costs, despite the depressed sales and employment conditions in the industry. It is doubtful that any other means of wage setting would have resulted in large wage increases in the automobile industry at that time. Second, escalators force wage increases to follow rapidly behind increases in the cost of living (often with a lag of only a few months), so that what in some cases could be temporary price increases become part of an irreversible upward movement of wages and prices. This, it may be argued, was part of the process by which the energy price inflation of 1979 was translated into the rapid general wage and price inflation in 1980.[55]

Job Evaluation Plans

Job evaluation is a systematic method of appraising the worth of each job with respect to every other job in an organization. Wage rates are then established for various jobs in a manner that reflects their relative worth. A job evaluation system first develops careful descriptions of each job. In most plans jobs are then rated according to a system that assigns points for various characteristics of the job. In production jobs the factors are usually divided into four major categories: skill, effort, responsibility, and job conditions. A typical job evaluation plan (such as that of National Electrical Manufacturers Association, NEMA) has eleven major factors grouped in the four categories mentioned above.

Skill
  1 Education
  2 Experience
  3 Initiative and ingenuity
Effort
  4 Physical demand
  5 Mental-visual demand
Responsibility
  6 For equipment or process
  7 For material or product
  8 For safety of others
  9 For work of others

[55]For an analysis of the impact of cost-of-living escalators on inflation, see H. M. Douty, "Study of the Relationship between Cost-of-Living Escalation Clauses and Inflation," a paper prepared for the Council on Wage and Price Stability, executive office of the President of the United States, Aug. 20, 1975; also, Marcelle V. Arak, "Indexation of Wages and Retirement Income in the United States," *Federal Reserve Bank of New York Quarterly Review*, 3:3, Autumn 1978, pp. 16–23. See also Wallace E. Hendricks and Lawrence M. Kahn, "Cost-of-Living Clauses in Union Contracts," *Industrial and Labor Relations Review*, 36:3, April 1983, pp. 447–460.

Job Conditions
  10 Working conditions
  11 Hazards

There is a set maximum number of points that may be assigned to each factor. For example, education is given 14 points and experience 22 in the NEMA plan. When a job is studied, it is given a rating on each factor. A job in which education plays a major part could receive as many as 14 points. A job in which experience is critical could receive as many as 22 points in that category. The maximum points assigned to each factor add up to 100 total points for all 11 factors, although no job gets this many points.

The particular factors on which jobs are rated differ among companies and among the types of occupations considered. Clerical jobs in the NEMA plan, for example, are rated on 6 factors, not 11. The six factors are education, experience, complexity of duties, monetary responsibility, contacts with other people, and working conditions. Even supervisory jobs are rated, with additional factors, such as type and extent of supervision, included in the evaluation.[56]

The actual implementation of a job evaluation plan is a complex process[57] and can be only briefly summarized here. Once jobs are rated according to the factors, they are ranked by total points awarded. The jobs are then placed in a distribution, and wage rates (or ranges of rates) are assigned to each job. The advantages of such a system are that

• A centralized, uniform system for setting pay rates for each job in relation to every other job is used.
• A frame of reference is established for settling disputes over the rate of pay on individual jobs.
• Procedures exist for reviewing new or changed jobs and setting rates of pay for them.

There are several disadvantages to job evaluation plans. Among the disadvantages are the following:

• There is a certain inflexibility in the structure of wages and jobs.
• The possibility exists that if employees don't understand or accept the factor-rating system, it will generate disputes.

During the late 1980s and early 1990s the disadvantages of job evaluation plans began to seem larger to many firms and unions than the ad-

---

[56]Ernest J. McCormick, *Job Analysis: Methods and Applications* (New York: AMACOM, 1979). For a union viewpoint, see John Zalusky, "Job Evaluation: An Uneven World," *AFL-CIO Federationist*, 85:4, April 1981, pp. 11–20.
  [57]See Charles A. Myers and Paul Pigors, *Personnel Administration: A Point of View and a Method*, 8th ed. (New York: McGraw-Hill, 1977), chap. 20.

vantages. In part this was because in an increasingly competitive economy inflexibility and contention became much more important drawbacks than previously. As a result, job evaluation plans were made less complex. In some manufacturing plants the number of separate classifications was reduced from ninety to three or four. Specialization often remained, but different jobs or tasks were grouped into many fewer job categories. In some instances job debarkations were eliminated and people took on much more diversified duties. The new workplace, as described in Chapter 4, utilizes job evaluation to a much lesser degree than the old. But most American factories and offices still use the old system.

INNOVATIONS IN COMPENSATION

During the 1980s & 1990s severe recessions and intense competition from abroad have forced many American firms and unions to develop new approaches to compensation. Among the new approaches were concession bargaining, two-tier pay plans, and lump-sum payments. A final innovation, pay for skills, was not so closely linked to business difficulties.

Concession Bargaining During the 1980s, for the first time since the great depression of the 1930s, collective bargaining began to result in moving wages down rather than up. In 1981 only 2 percent of contracts involved unions receiving either no pay increase or adjusting wages downward for employees. By 1986 37 percent of contracts showed no pay increase or a decline. But as the economic environment improved in the late 1980s and early 1990s concession bargaining declined. By 1990 fewer than 15 percent of contracts included concessions.[58]

Two-Tier Pay Plans Economic difficulties caused some firms and unions to inaugurate a new pay system. Called a "two-tier" system, it provided substantially lower pay scales for newly hired employees than for those already on the payroll, even in the same jobs. The new, low rates were not intended to be temporary—that is, a probationary or introductory rate—but to be permanent.

By 1985, 9 percent of new labor contracts had two-tier pay plans.[59] Some observers saw the plans as a great advantage for management.[60] But employees thought the plans unfair, and soon morale problems developed.

---

[58]Daniel J. B. Mitchell, "Will Collective Bargaining Outcomes in the 1990's Look Like Those in the 1980's?" *Labor Law Journal*, August 1989, p. 495.

[59]Bureau of National Affairs, *Daily Labor Report*, No. 15, Jan. 17, 1986, p. B1.

[60]Irwin Ross, "Employers Win Big in the Move to Two-Tier Contracts," *Fortune*, Apr. 29, 1985, pp. 82–92. See also Sanford M. Jacoby and Daniel J. B. Mitchell, "Management Attitudes toward Two-Tier Pay Plans," *Journal of Labor Research*, 7:3, Summer 1986, pp. 221ff.

Unions began to try to negotiate the lower rates out of the contracts. By 1987 two-tier plans were on the decline and by 1990 were in only about 4 percent of all contracts.[61]

During the brief period of their existence, considerable research was done about two-tier pay plans. It had been expected that employees paid at the lesser rates would be dissatisfied. But a study of employees at an airline paid at lower rates found them to be significantly more satisfied with their pay, work, and supervision, more optimistic about future pay increases, more confident of their job security, and more committed to the company and the union than those more senior employees who were receiving higher pay in the same jobs. How could this be? The authors of the study suggested that second-tier employees had lower expectations than those in the top tier.[62]

Lump-Sum Payments Other firms and unions reacted to distress by developing a new form of wage payment. Companies were reluctant to raise pay rates because the new rates had to be paid in the future, whatever the sales and profitability of the firms. So companies began to propose lump-sum payments to workers—akin to bonuses—instead of wage-rate increases. By 1987 more than one-third of employees covered by union contracts received lump-sum bonuses, a remarkably high percentage for a wage method that had hardly existed in collective bargaining agreements only a few years before. But as economic conditions improved, lump-sum provisions declined. By 1990 only 18 percent of labor contracts included lump-sum payments[63], and only 28 percent of employees covered by collective bargaining agreements had lump-sum payments as part of their compensation package.[64]

Paying for Knowledge An even more dramatic innovation in pay systems involves paying employees only partially by the job they do, but also paying according to their skill levels and knowledge. This is fundamentally different from the conventional system of job-based pay, where employees are paid for the particular jobs they are performing, not for their ability to perform other tasks. Broadly skilled employees can be more valuable for companies because they can do many different things. In organizations

[61]Agis Salpukas, "The Two-Tier Wage System Is Found to Be a Two-Edged Sword by Industry," *New York Times*, July 21, 1987, pp. A1, D22. See also John T. Dunlop, "Industrial Relations: Old and New," *The Worklife Report*, 1988, pp. 1–3; and "Proportion of Contracts with Two-Tier Wage Plans," Bureau of National Affairs, *Daily Labor Report*, No. 37, February 25, 1991, B-3. And see Robert Tomsho, "Employers and Unions Felling Pressure to Eliminate Two-Tier Labor Contracts," *Wall Street Journal*, April 20, 1990, pp. B-1, B-9.

[62]Peter Cappelli and Peter D. Sherer, "Assessing Worker Attitudes Under a Two-Tier Wage Plan," *Industrial and Labor Relations Review*, 43:2, January 1990, pp. 225–244.

[63]"Lump-Sum Bonuses," Bureau of National Affairs, *Daily Labor Report*, No. 59, Mar. 30, 1987, pp. B-1, B-2; and "Lump-Sum Pay Provisions," BNA, *DLR*, No. 46, Mar. 8, 1991, p. B-2.

[64]Bureau of Labor Statistics, *Monthly Labor Review*, 115:1, January 1992, p. 7.

where employees are expected to use their own discretion and work under little supervision and in cooperation with others, skill-based pay appears to have important advantages.[65]

Profit Sharing Plans For many years some firms have shared profits with employees by paying a bonus based on the amount of profit a firm earns. In the late 1980s and early 1990s such plans became more complicated as firms sought ways not so much to control wage costs as to induce employees to be more productive. In 1989, for example, 16 percent of large and medium-sized firms had a profit sharing scheme, and the number of such plans had been rising rapidly, but they differed dramatically in form.[66] The basic idea behind profit sharing is that if employees work better, then a firm's profits will rise, and employees ought to share some of the benefit. If they do have a share, so the expectation goes, then they'll be more willing to work better. By 1990 as many as half the major employers in the nation had implemented some form of profit sharing or group incentive system.[67] The major arguments for and against profit sharing are presented in Table 18.5 on page 538.

Some economists have proposed profit sharing as a way to limit wage costs when firms get in economic difficulty. They even argue that generalized profit sharing could limit inflation and unemployment. But research indicates that profit sharing does not substitute for other forms of wage payment, but is instead a supplement to it.[68]

CHAPTER SUMMARY

The American economy incorporates a very large number of different rates of compensation. Compensation differs on many dimensions which are not always possible to separate in terms of their influence. The most important dimensions are geography, occupation, industry and plant size, demography, and union representation. For example, in the United States, wage and total compensation levels tend to be highest in the West, intermediate in the North and East, and lowest in the South. Regional differentials reflect, in part, the distribution of occupations and industries and the different compositions of the labor force in terms of minorities. Average earnings differ

---

[65]"New Ways to Pay," *The Economist*, July 13, 1991, p. 69. See also, "Nina Gupta, G. Douglas Jenkins, Jr., and William P. Curington, "Paying for Knowledge," *National Productivity Review*, 5:2, Spring 1986, pp. 107–123. Also, "Skill-Based Pay," Bureau of National Affairs, *Daily Labor Review*, No. 230, Dec. 1, 1986, pp. A-12–A-15.

[66]Edward C. Coates, III, "Profit-Sharing Today," *Monthly Labor Review*, 114:4, April 1991, p. 19ff.

[67]"BNA Personnel Policies Survey," Bureau of National Affairs, *Daily Labor Report*, No. 100, May 23, 1991, pp. A-3–A-4.

[68]Daniel J. B. Mitchell, David Lewin, and Edward E. Lawler III, "Alternative Pay Systems, Firm Performance and Productivity," in Alan S. Blinder, ed., *Paying for Productivity* (Washington, D.C. Brookings Institution, 1989), p. 87.

TABLE 18-5   PROFIT SHARING: PROS AND CONS

Pros:	Cons:
Link between profit sharing and productivity. A recent study by Rutgers University's Institute of Management and Labor Relations reported that profit-sharing firms were more productive than non-profit-sharing firms in 13 of 15 years from 1971 to 1985.	*Difficulty in measuring link between profit sharing and productivity.* It is easy to see the effect profit sharing has on a firm with a single worker, but it is difficult to measure the effect in a large organization. In large firms, the research has been made suspect by the "free rider" problem. A "free rider" is an employee who ignores his or her responsibilities, believing that other workers will pick up the slack. A "free rider" has a negative effect on productivity.
Data on profit sharing and wages. A study by the U.S. Chamber of Commerce reported that workers in profit-sharing firms tended to be compensated as well as or better than those in non-profit-sharing firms. In the manufacturing sector, profit-sharing firms' wages were equal to those of non-profit-sharing firms. In the nonmanufacturing sector, the wages of workers of profit-sharing firms were 60 cents per hour higher than those of workers of non-profit-sharing firms.	*Employee wage concerns.* Many skeptics of profit sharing fear that firms with profitsharing pay lower wages compared to firms in like industries without profit-sharing plans. Skeptics also doubt that profit sharing makes up the difference.

Pros:	Cons:
Employers enjoy flexibility. Profit sharing is based on company performance; when business is down, the company is not obligated to make any contributions. Profit sharing is also easier to administer and maintain than the more heavily regulated defined benefit pension plans. To allay some employee concerns, sponsoring companies have added provisions to reduce risk to their workers. These provisions have included minimum employer contributions, stated formulas, and immediate cash distributions.	*Workers fear management control.* One fear is that profit sharing allows management too much control over how profits are shared. A second is that by participating in profit sharing, employees are risking a portion of their compensation because the benefit is not guaranteed.
Automakers find profit sharing successful. The auto industry, which was suffering one of its largest downturns in the early 1980's, employed profit sharing as a means of regaining profitability. When negotiations on new collective bargaining agreements took place, the automakers asked the unions for wage concessions. In exchange for such concessions, the automakers offered profit-sharing plans to their employees. As the auto industry recovered in the mid-1980's, the benefits from these agreements began to pay off. Not only did auto workers regain lost wagesfrom the previous contracts concessions, but they also received large profit-sharing allocations from automakers. Many of the automakers touted their profit-sharing plans as a means of better employer-employee relations and as a contributing factor in their renewed profitability.	

Source: Edward M. Coates. III, "Profit-Sharing Today" U.S. Department of Labor, *Monthly Labor Review,* April 1991, Vol. 114, No. 4.

substantially from industry to industry. For example, average hourly earnings in construction are more than double those in retail sales.

The amount of compensation employees should receive and the processes by which this amount is determined are vital issues. Many theories have been proposed to explain how compensation levels are set and why some wage rates are different from others. Theories are not simply explanations of phenomena. Widely held theories sometimes strongly affect events and become part of the phenomenon they purport to explain. Theories about compensation frequently affect what is actually done in wage setting and sometimes blind people to important elements which do not accord with their theory.

Supply-and-demand analysis is more complicated than many other theories, but more useful. Many people use it in determining their approach to labor relations issues. One problem with supply-and-demand analysis is that it ignores the effects of other markets on the occupation being studied. Also, to understand particular labor markets, particular product markets must be studied. There is no demand for labor without the demand for the goods or services labor produces.

Many economists have written on wage theory. Major current wage theories include human capital theory, institutional theories that stress economic factors, and those theories that stress political factors. The major fact from which all bargaining theories start is the existence of unions. Because unions exist, the establishment of wages is different from what it would be otherwise. John Dunlop, in 1944, developed a theory of wages that viewed unions as primarily economic institutions that seek to maximize the wage bill. Not long after, Arthur Ross argued that, on the contrary, a union was less an economic institution than a political one. A union is interested in its own survival and wellbeing and not in the automatic pursuit of the maximum wage bill.

The many different methods by which compensation is established can be divided into two general groups. One group is classified according to what actor or organization makes the decision about pay level. There are four actors identified: the employer, the employee, the union, and the government. Each actor may act unilaterally or in conjunction with another. In practice, compensation is usually set by joint action between employers and individual employees or between employers and unions.

The other group of methods is classified according to what process is used to set the pay level. Five processes by which compensation is established are reactive processes, surveys, formulas, job evaluation plans, and pay-by-performance plans. In the reactive process, rates are set according to the apparent needs of the moment without any formalities. The method is expedient and unsystematic. A valued employee may receive an offer of a job at higher pay elsewhere. The employer responds by raising the rate of pay for this particular person.

The ability of an employer to pay increased compensation is also a very important factor in setting wage rates. Employees and unions often believe that companies can pay wage increases out of their profits without having to increase prices. In most instances this is not so. The ability of an employer to pay additional wages frequently depends on its ability to raise its revenues or cut its costs. Firms ordinarily have to make adjustments in their business practices to be able to pay for compensation increases. The ability or inability of firms to pay wage increases adds complexity to employer association bargaining. In the public sector, the ability of municipal or state governmental bodies to provide pay increases to their employees is becoming a major issue.

Employers, governmental agencies, and unions participate in systematic wage and salary surveys, and wage rates are set by reference to these surveys. Wage and salary surveys are very popular with employers. Despite their many problems the use of survey data by firms in establishing pay rates is quite extensive. However, the survey results are used only as a guide to policy and are supplemented by other information and considerations.

The essence of the formula approach is that it removes discretion from the determination of compensation. Rates are set by reference to some outside factor with no discretion regarding the specific level. The most common formula for the determination of wages is one that provides that wage rates be adjusted upward in step with the cost of living. Many collective bargaining agreements include a provision that wage rates be periodically adjusted in an amount determined by the rate of increase in consumer prices. This cost-of-living clause is referred to as an escalator or a COLA (cost-of-living adjustment) clause. There has been continuous debate for over 40 years as to whether or not cost-of-living clauses have an inflationary impact on the economy.

Job evaluation is a systematic method of appraising the worth of each job in an organization. Wage rates are then established for various jobs in a way that reflects their relative worth. Jobs are rated according to a system that assigns points for various characteristics of the job. Once jobs are rated according to the chosen factors, they are ranked by total points awarded. Wage rates are then assigned to individual jobs.

Two-tier, lump sum, skill-based pay, and executive bonuses tied to workers' profit sharing are innovations in compensation that try to accommodate employer needs for cost control and better performance with employee needs for higher earnings.

QUESTIONS FOR THOUGHT AND DISCUSSION

1 Why do wage levels vary in different occupations and industries? What factors are most important? Is it fair that people get different rates of pay? Why or why not?

2 What were your "pretheoretical" ideas about why different occupations are sometimes compensated so very differently? Why do some jobs pay better than

others? Which wage theories most closely match your original ideas? Have your original ideas changed?

3 How do you think wage rates, or levels of compensation, should be determined?

4 What is the difference between market-oriented and institution-oriented wage theories?

5 Do unions help those they represent to earn more than nonunion employees? Support your answer.

6 What is meant when it is said that the labor market sets the wage rate?

7 How does a cost-of-living escalator work? Are escalator clauses a good idea for management? For labor? Why or why not?

8 What is a job evaluation plan? How is it related to compensation? What are the major advantages of such plans? The major disadvantages?

9 Why are wage comparisons important in setting wage rates? What are the hazards in making wage comparisons?

10 How do social, cultural, and class values enter into job evaluations?

11 Are cost-of-living escalators inflationary? On what do you base your opinion?

12 What are the advantages and disadvantages of lump sum pay, two-tier pay, skill-based pay, and profit sharing? To workers? To managers?

SELECTED READING

Dunlop, John T., *Wage Determination under Trade Unions* (New York: Macmillan, 1944).

Hicks, John R., *A Theory of Wages*, 2d ed. (New York: St. Martin's Press, 1964).

Kerr, Clark, *Labor Markets and Wage Determination: The Balkanization of Labor Markets and Other Essays* (Berkeley: University of California Press, 1977).

Myers, Charles A., and Paul Pigors, *Personnel Administration: A Point of View and a Method*, 8th ed. (New York: McGraw-Hill, 1977).

Ross, Arthur M., *Trade Union Wage Policy* (Berkeley: University of California Press, 1948).

CHAPTER 19

BENEFITS

An important development in employee compensation has been the proliferation of benefits (also called "compensation supplements"). It may be difficult for young healthy people to understand how important pensions or health care are to persons with children and/or who are getting older. The existence and adequacy of benefits in a job is often of greater importance than the wages paid; this is true to such an extent that many American workers are afraid to change their jobs for fear of losing coverage.

As the importance of benefits has risen, collective bargaining between managements and unions has increasingly been involved with benefit issues. Special procedures have been established in many instances to negotiate these supplements. Specialized technical staffs, complete with actuaries and investment consultants, have been created on both management and union sides to deal with complex long term funding concerns. In effect it has become impossible to completely understand the dynamics of collective bargaining without understanding the ramifications of benefits.

DEVELOPMENTS IN BENEFITS

Before World War II virtually all compensation was in the form of pay for time worked. In 1929 supplements to pay for time worked in private industry were only 1.4 percent of total compensation. By the advent of World War II supplements were still only 3.4 percent of total compensation.[1] Dur-

---

[1] Alvin Bauman, "Measuring Employee Compensation in U.S. Industry," *Monthly Labor Review,* 93:10, October 1970, pp. 17–23.

ing World War II supplements received favorable treatment under the system of then-imposed wage-price controls and began to spread throughout industry. By 1991, after five decades of steady growth, supplements or "benefits," as they later came to be known, constituted 27.9 percent of total compensation for all firms.[2]

There is now a wide variety of workplace benefits in place. New ones are constantly emerging, while old ones are being expanded. Eligibility requirements and other provisions of key benefits defy easy summarization. Keeping up with these developments is the subject of several periodic publications issued by the U.S. Chamber of Commerce,[3] the Bureau of National Affairs,[4] the Conference Board,[5] the U.S. Civil Service Commission,[6] and others.[7]

As benefits have expanded over time; two types—based on different funding sources—have come into general use. One type is known as the legally mandated benefit. It is usually financed through special levies on employers and employees with the various levels of government covering temporary short-falls with general tax revenues. The second type is the employer-provided benefit. It is generally financed through tax-deductible charges on company earnings.

The most prominent of the legally mandated or "required" benefits are Social Security, workers' compensation (an accident insurance program), and unemployment insurance. Employees eligible for these benefits are required to pay a special flat-rate tax based on their annual wages to the federal and state governments, which manage contributions and disbursements to and from program funds. Employers with eligible employees are also required to contribute on a matching basis.

Employer-provided benefits, such as premium pay for overtime and shifts, paid vacations, paid holidays, paid sick leave, health insurance, pensions, severance pay, and supplemental unemployment benefits (SUB), are either provided voluntarily or through the provisions of a collective bargaining agreement. In either case the expenses of providing the benefit are generally tax-deductible provided the employer is making a profit at the time the benefit cost is recognized for accounting purposes.

There has been considerable debate about which benefits should be financed through public tax collections on employees and employers, which benefits should be funded by government alone from its general tax revenues,

---

[2]U.S. Department of Labor, Bureau of Labor Statistics, *Employment Cost Index*, March 1991. See also George L. Stelluto and Deborah P. Klein, "Compensation Trends into the 21st Century," *Monthly Labor Review*, 114:2, February 1990, pp. 38–45.

[3]U.S. Chamber of Commerce, *Employee Benefits*, various issues.

[4]Bureau of National Affairs, *Basic Patterns in Union Contracts*, Washington, D.C.

[5]The Conference Board, *Profile of Employee Benefits*, New York.

[6]U.S. Civil Service Commission, *Comparisons of Major Employee Benefit Programs*, Washington, D.C.

[7]Employee Benefit Research Institute, *Fundamentals of Employee Benefit Programs*, Washington, D.C.

and which benefits should remain subject to the collective bargaining process and employer generosity. Different governments have taken vastly different approaches to this subject. Several northern European countries, for example, have built up complex "welfare states" in which most benefit programs are jointly financed by employers and general tax revenues. Other countries leave most benefits to be provided by employers.

The interaction of private collective bargaining and governmental actions in the United States have resulted in a patchwork quilt of benefit coverage and funding schemes. In 1989, the Bureau of Labor Statistics of the U.S. Department of Labor surveyed benefits provided to union and nonunion employees of medium and large firms in the private sector. The survey reviewed both the percentage of employees covered by various benefits and whether the employer paid the full cost of the benefit (a noncontributory plan) or whether the employee paid part of the cost (a contributory plan).

The survey found that there was wide variation in the degree to which various benefits were provided. For example, virtually all employees received some paid vacation, but only 10 percent received a paid lunch period. There was also a wide variation in the benefits received by different occupational groups. For example, 93 percent of professional, administrative, technical, and clerical employees received paid sick leave compared with 44 percent of production workers.

Other surveys have found that there are broad groups of employees who have little or no benefit coverage. For example, in 1988, 34 percent of all employees had no health-care insurance.[8] For part-time workers in agriculture, only 3 percent had coverage (97 percent did not).[9] Some of these workers may be covered by the health insurance plans of other family members, some may have purchased health insurance on their own, but many apparently have no coverage at all.

Key benefits, particularly health insurance, have become a hot topic both in labor-management relations and in American politics in recent years. The costs of health care have been escalating at a much more rapid rate than most other employment costs in American industry for several decades. In response, employers have been trying to get employees to either pay a greater portion of these costs, reduce usage of employer-provided medical services, or both.

Attempts at health-care cost containment have become a major topic of collective bargaining. Employers insist that rising health-care costs are raising product prices and undercutting the competitiveness of U.S. firms in world markets. So they ask for cost reductions. Unions point to rising

---

[8]Daniel J. B. Mitchell, "Employee Benefits and the New Economy," *California Management Review,* 33:2, Winter 1991, p. 115.
[9]"Labor Department Study," reprinted in Bureau of National Affairs, *Daily Labor Report,* No. 176, Sept. 11, 1981, p. D-4.

health-care costs to establish that employees cannot afford to pay for their own care, thrusting the cost burden back at the employer.

Health care is not the only pressing benefit issue. As women have left the home for the workplace large numbers of children have been left with what many people feel are inadequate care arrangements. Labor and management have negotiated programs to support better institutional child care but not at as fast a rate as most unions would prefer.

Even though many employers have established health- and child-care plans, others have not. As a consequence, unions and parental groups have lobbied Congress and state legislatures to require such benefits of employers by law, or to provide them directly as government programs. Proposals for national health insurance have been debated for years. A variant currently under discussion would have the government require employers to establish plans of a certain minimum standard or pay a tax that the government would use to provide care—the so-called play or pay plan. Some states have already enacted such plans. The situation in the family benefits area is similar. Congress is being urged to provide benefits via legislation—one example is time off from work for parents when a child is born—or to require employers to provide them as so-called mandated benefits.

We turn now to detailed discussion of a number of different benefits, including pension plans, unemployment insurance, supplemental unemployment insurance, overtime, and premium pay, and emerging benefit issues, such as employee stock ownership plans.

PENSION PLANS

Pensions are a method of providing income, usually in the form of a monthly check, to persons after they cease working for a living (i.e., retire). In the United States we have developed a complex system of providing pensions that combines both private and public sources of funds. Our system is coming under increased stress as the proportion of our population that is at or beyond retirement age increases, partly because of increasing life expectancy. In response to this stress, the pension system has been, and now is, undergoing considerable review and change.[10]

The first employer-provided retirement plan in the United States was set up by American Express Company in 1875. Interestingly, many of the earliest pension plans were established by firms with the intent of avoiding unionization. The employers' purposes were to cause workers to stay with the firm and to induce loyalty and faithful performance of duty.[11] In the aftermath of World War II pension plans established by employers at the insistence of the

[10]William Graebner, *A History of Retirement* (New Haven, Conn.: Yale University Press, 1980).
[11]Brian Gratton, "A Triumph of Modern Philanthropy . . . ," *Business History Review,* 64, Winter 1990, p. 630.

unions grew very rapidly, and many nonunion firms also established them. By 1987 employers provided more than 872,000 plans covering some 78 million workers.[12]

Types of Pensions

Private pension plans are set up by business concerns for the purpose of providing benefits to their employees.[13] If an employer decides to offer a pension to employees, it must meet certain legally established standards, but the employer doesn't have to provide a pension. Why, if they don't have to, do many employers provide pensions for employees?

There are at least three reasons. First, if a firm doesn't offer a pension, it may not be able to hire the people it wants. Second, managers and owners may feel that a pension should be available to employees who remain with the company a long period of time as a manner of what is right. Last, a company may use a pension to try to induce longer-service employees to remain with the company. Research shows that having a pension increases the willingness of people to remain with a firm by more than 20 percent.[14]

An employee earns credits by length of service with an employer and receives a pension the amount of which is determined in large part by the credits the employee has accumulated. Private plans differ greatly in their characteristics. Some plans are paid for partly by the employer and partly by the employees. Plans with employee contributions are known as contributory plans. Plans in which the employer pays the full cost of the pension plan are called noncontributory plans.

Plans may be provided by a single employer, and are so designated, or by an association of employers (a multiemployer plan). Where a plan is provided by a group of employers, there is always the problem that some employers fail to pay their assessment. When too many employers cease paying contributions—either by ceasing to operate union or simply by defaulting on their commitments while remaining union—then the plan may be unable to meet its obligations to retirees.

Plans may be cost-based or benefit-based. In a cost-based plan, the employer (and perhaps the employees) contributes a certain amount of money (e.g., 80 cents per hour worked) and benefits are purchased from an insurance company or are provided by the plan in whatever amount the contributions will support. This is in many respects the simpler of the arrangements. In a benefit-based plan, the company agrees to provide a specific level of benefits and then proceeds to obtain that coverage as it desires.

[12]Patrick W. Seburn, "Evolution of Employer-Provided Defined Benefit Pensions," *Monthly Labor Review,* 114:12 December 1991, p. 16ff.

[13]Dan M. McGill, *Fundamentals of Private Pensions* (Homewood, Ill.: Irwin, 1975).

[14]Richard A. Ippolito, "Encouraging Long-Term Tenure: Wage-Tilt or Pensions," *Industrial and Labor Relations Review,* 44:3, April 1991, p. 520ff.

A key issue is the sufficiency of the funding of a benefits-based plan. Legally, there should be enough money in investments to cover the future expected costs of paying pension benefits. But how is one to know what those costs will be; and how is one to know what level of investment today is sufficient to provide benefits years from now? So sometimes a company buys a benefit plan from an insurance company. In other cases it sets up a fund from which benefits are to be provided. In still other instances, the company does not fund the plan at all, but merely pays out benefits as they come due from its income. When a company does not set up a fund to cover future benefit payments, it is said to have an unfunded pension liability, a matter to which we will return later.

Even when an employer funds a pension plan, it may be insufficiently funded. In recent years some companies have changed the assumptions on their benefit plan's investment returns and have taken so-called excess funding for the company. The workers often maintained that their pension funds were being looted, but in a benefit-based plan, the companies' actions were often judged legal.

In recent years there has been a marked shift among pension plans away from defined benefit plans to defined contribution plans. In effect, the pensions of more people will be determined on the basis of the success or failure of the investment of the contributions made on his or her behalf, rather than by the employer paying an amount based on her or his earnings when working. It's hard to forecast what the net outcome of this shift will be: whether pensions for many people will be enhanced or reduced by the shift. A reason often given for the shift from defined benefit to defined contribution plans is that new federal regulations have made defined benefit plans less attractive to employers. Another reason is that the economy has shifted in a way that has increased employment disproportionately in industries which have traditionally used defined contribution plans. A recent study suggests that about half the shift to defined contribution plans is due to the change in government regulation and half to the shift in employment among industries.[15]

Issues Involving Pensions

An adequate level of benefits is not easy to define. Initially, pensions were conceived of as providing a minimum income to protect elderly persons from poverty. Yet even within the concept of pensions as providing a minimum "floor," there was room for disagreement about adequacy. Wilbur J. Cohen, formerly secretary of health, education, and welfare and knowledgeable about the Social Security system, once referred to the concept of Social Security as providing a minimum floor as follows:

[15]Alan L. Gustman and Thomas L. Steinmeier, "The Stampede toward Defined Contribution Pension Plans: Fact or Fiction?" *Industrial Relations*, 31:2, Spring 1992, p. 361ff.

Some people think of the floor as a bare, rough-hewn, cabin floor; others as a solid oak floor, polished and waxed. I like to think of it as a floor with a kind of Bigelow carpet on it not only to keep my feet warm, but giving me some aesthetic pleasure, also.

In recent years, pensions have been increasingly designed to provide more than a minimal level of income. Among the standards offered for evaluating the adequacy of benefit levels are the following:

• A benefit level that would meet the observed needs and living styles of the aged

• A benefit level that would provide a retired person with a standard of living similar to the one he or she had while working

• A benefit level that would provide sufficient income to allow a retired person to enjoy a living standard roughly equivalent to that currently enjoyed by the working population

These standards may be used to evaluate the level of benefits provided under Social Security or under private pension programs, or their combined effect. As a practical matter, another standard that has considerable importance may be set forward:

• The level of benefits desired by a group of people as evidenced by their willingness to purchase or bargain for them

Presumably, groups of employees and employers may differ in the importance they attach to pension benefits. If Social Security provides a floor, then private pension plans may provide a substantial amount of additional coverage or very little, depending on the preferences of employees and employers as revealed in the bargaining process.[16]

Coverage of people under pension plans in the United States is very uneven. The Department of Labor estimates that in 1991 some 45 percent of all full-time employees have no pension plan and the proportion of employees covered has been declining since reaching a peak in 1979. Some people draw pension benefits from several sources and have very adequate pensions. Others receive no benefits at all—not even Social Security. While the number of people who are covered by no plan at all is small, there are nevertheless such cases. This is because the pension system in the United States, both private and public, is related to job experience. A person earns eligibility for pension benefits through employment. People who have very unstable work histories, or none at all, or who have been self-employed and made no provision for Social Security or retirement, may receive no benefits at all. The American system of pensions, and of other social services as well, is very

---

[16]Derek C. Bok, "Emerging Issues in Social Legislation: Social Security," *Harvard Law Review*, 80, 1968, pp. 717–764.

much more related to each individual's work experience than is generally the case abroad.[17]

Why is the coverage of pension plans declining? A study shows that declining pension coverage was concentrated among low-income employees. Declining unionization has played an important role in causing this to happen since unions have traditionally been major supporters of pension programs. The decline in pension coverage did not occur because of increasing confidence in the government-provided pension program, Social Security, researchers determined. In fact, there has been a general decline in confidence in the continuing viability of the government program.[18]

Private pension plans confront their own special problems of coverage. In general, if a firm or group of firms has considerable turnover of employees, it may wish to establish a pension plan that rewards only those who stay with the company or in the industry. If benefits are divided among many short-term and long-term employees, it may be possible to give only low benefits at an acceptable cost. But if benefits are provided only to long-term employees, the level may be higher at an acceptable cost. Unions and companies frequently make decisions about coverage and eligibility on this basis.[19]

Aspects of the private pension system invite abuse. For example, a federal judge ruled in a recent case that a company had unlawfully used a sophisticated computer system to keep track of employees' age and length of service in order to fire them before they became eligible to receive pension benefits. The court found that the system was "shrouded in secrecy and executed company-wide at the specific direction of the highest levels of corporate management. . . . It was intended to save hundreds of millions of dollars in . . . pension liabilities." The company in its turn blamed the union, saying that the union contract was too expensive and forced it into unreasonable competitive disadvantages.[20]

Management of Assets of Private Pension Plans

The assets of pension funds are very substantial. Private funds now have more than a trillion dollars in assets and have become a major factor in

---

[17]Gaston V. Rimlinger, "American Social Security in European Perspective," in William Bowen, ed., *The American System of Social Insurance* (New York: McGraw-Hill, 1968), pp. 213–240.

[18]David E. Bloom and Richard B. Freeman, "The Fall in Private Pension Coverage in the United States," *American Economic Association: Papers and Proceedings*, 82:2, May 1992, pp. 539–545.

[19]James H. Schulz et al., "Private Pensions Fall Far Short," *Monthly Labor Review*, 102:2, February 1979, pp. 28–32.

[20]*McClendon v. Continental Group, Inc.*, Federal District Court of New Jersey, No. 83-1340, May 10, 1989; cited in Bureau of National Affairs, *Daily Labor Report*, No. 92, May 15, 1989, pp. A-8–A-9.

the market for stocks, bonds, real estate, and other investments. Ordinarily, these funds are managed by corporate executives or by professional investment managers chosen by corporate executives. In recent years the unions have objected to how the funds are invested, finding that many pension plans negotiated by unions but managed by business executives have their funds invested in nonunion companies.

Multiemployer pension plans sometimes have both union and nonunion trustees. Sometimes these trustees manage the plan's investments rather than hire professional investment managers. Sometimes union and management trustees are alleged to have used the funds unwisely or even illegally, perhaps for personal benefit. A major controversy of this nature has developed with respect to some of the larger pension funds of the International Brotherhood of Teamsters.

ERISA

In 1964 the Congress of the United States began hearings into the performance of private pension plans. Abuses of the system were uncovered, and Congress began drafting a pension reform bill. Finally, in 1974, Congress passed a law regulating private pension plans. The act is entitled Employees' Retirement Income Security Act (ERISA) and is one of the most complex pieces of federal legislation ever written. The law contains 75,000 words, covering several hundred pages, plus a 100-page explanatory report by the congressional conference committee (including members of both the House of Representatives and the Senate) that finally cleared the bill for passage.[21]

ERISA imposes standards on private pension plans. Trustees of the plans must meet "fiduciary standards"—meaning the standards of financial behavior to which trustees of the funds are now held by law. The "prudent man" rule applies—meaning, in brief, that a trustee must behave as a court would expect a fictional rational person to behave. Failure to do so causes the trustee to be liable personally for financial losses by the fund. Lawyers have already begun to debate what a "prudent man" serving as trustee of a pension fund would do.[22] And employers, faced with the new financial and legal complexities introduced into pension plans by ERISA, have terminated some plans and begun reviewing others.[23]

---

[21]Noel A. Levin, ERISA and Labor-Management Benefit Funds, 2d ed. (New York: Practising Law Institute, 1975).

[22]Mary Green Miner, *Pension Plans and the Impact of ERISA*, Personnel Policy Forum Survey No. 119 (Washington, D.C.: Bureau of National Affairs, 1977); and "Fiduciary Standards and the Prudent Man Rule under ERISA," *Harvard Law Review*, 88:5, March 1975, pp. 960–979.

[23]Robert D. Paul, "Can Private Pension Plans Deliver?" *Harvard Business Review*, 52:5, September–October 1974, pp. 22–37.

HEALTH INSURANCE

As with pensions, significant growth in the number and scope of health insurance plans came after World War II. The most frequent protection currently provided to employees is a so-called regular medical coverage, which covers a range of services short of the more serious procedures. Hospitalization and surgery are covered separately. Insurance against death and dismemberment and temporary disability is also often provided. Major medical insurance, which protects employees against the financial burdens of a prolonged illness, is infrequent, but such plans are beginning to appear.[24]

The extent of coverage of employees in nonunionized firms by health plans is largely unknown in any comprehensive fashion. Many of the better-standards nonunion firms provide extensive medical coverage, comparable to that provided under collective bargaining agreements. Low-standards firms do not provide such coverage. The firm may have a nurse on the premises, or a doctor on retainer to the firm, for the care of employees, but little else is provided in the way of health care.

The health insurance plans provided by American industry exist in an unusual context. The United States alone of major industrialized nations provides no comprehensive national medical care program.[25] As a result, the health-care insurance that many members of our population receive is provided by their employers. The loss of a job can place the employee and his or her dependents in grave financial difficulties should they experience illness without coverage. While such insurance can be purchased privately from health insurance companies it is expensive and many people do not buy it. Major recessions, with their accompanying loss of jobs, may cause people to lose their health insurance. During recent business downturns Congress provided, through the unemployment insurance system, funds to assist unemployed workers in obtaining health coverage.

A current major problem facing the United States is the rapidly rising cost of health care. For several years health costs have risen faster, sometimes much faster, than prices in general. Because many companies have experienced rapid cost increases, health-care costs are now a major factor in collective bargaining.

Management and labor, often with government assistance,[26] are constantly searching for less expensive methods of obtaining health care. In

[24]Bruce Spencer, *Group Benefits in a Changing Society* (Chicago: Charles D. Spencer and Associates, 1982).

[25]Bert Seidman, "Health Security: The Complete Rx," *AFL-CIO American Federationist*, 82:10, October 1975, p. 10.

[26]In 1976, for example, the President's Council on Wage and Price Stability conducted a series of hearings in major cities across the nation to explore methods of reducing medical care costs with business and labor. The results were published under the title "Labor-Management Innovations Controlling Costs of Employee Health Care Benefits," *Federal Register*, 41:182, Sept. 17, 1976, pp. 40298–40326.

some cases rising health-care costs have stimulated an offensive by management and labor to control costs. For example, according to a survey by the Bureau of National Affairs, the proportion of collective bargaining agreements including a health-care cost containment provision increased from 9 percent in 1988 to 17 percent in 1990.[27] Among the ways management and unions are trying to limit health-care costs are

- *Second opinions* Requiring employees to seek them before surgery.
- *Audits* Encouraging workers, often with financial rewards, to check their hospital and doctor's bills for accuracy.
- *Pretesting* Encouraging medical tests prior to hospital admission of workers.
- *Precertification* Setting up a review board to determine on a case-by-case basis whether hospitalization is necessary—and for how long.
- *Outpatient surgery* Providing incentives for doctors to perform some simple operations in their offices or clinics rather than in the hospital.
- *Treatment review* Monitoring present and past treatments to ensure that they are both appropriate and needed.
- *Insurance checks* Cross-checking policies to stop payments of the same bill by different insurance companies.[28]

Finally, companies often favor having employees pay enough of the cost of their health insurance (through employee contributions to the cost) or of their treatment (through deductibles—i.e., an amount the employee must pay before insurance covers additional charges) to be concerned about keeping costs down. Unions often object to this step on two grounds. First, they argue that employees cannot afford to make contributions or to pay deductibles. Second, they argue that employees ought to be encouraged to get health care, not given incentives to avoid it. Timely health care may even avoid larger later expenses, the unions say.

Collective bargaining over medical care is unusually complicated. The union and the company must not only determine the money to be spent, but must also negotiate for the delivery of the health-care services. The cost and quality of the services obtained may be as important as raising the money to pay for them.

The high cost and limited coverage of the medical care system in the United States is causing many people to call for reform. Proposals in Congress ranging from requiring employers to offer health insurance to workers—so that the coverage limitations were largely resolved—to replacing the current system with national health insurance—which, it was argued, would provide broader coverage at lower cost—have been advanced. This promises to be the subject of considerable political controversy throughout the 1990s.

---

[27]Bureau of National Affairs, *Daily Labor Report*, No. 23, Jan. 27, 1991, p. A-1.
[28]Adapted from "Chopping Health Care Costs," *Business Week*, Mar. 31, 1986, p. 78. See also Thomas P. Burke and Rita S. Jain, "Trends in Employer-Provided Health Care Benefits," *Monthly Labor Review*, 114:2, February 1991, pp. 24–30.

SUPPLEMENTAL UNEMPLOYMENT BENEFITS

What source of income exists for workers who are laid off from their jobs? Until the 1930s, people without jobs either went on general relief (so-called welfare), lived with relatives, or simply existed as best they could. In 1932 the state of Wisconsin adopted a state program of unemployment insurance. Under such a program, laid-off workers could register with the state and receive income payments. In 1935 the federal government included in the Social Security Act a provision allowing states to establish unemployment insurance systems and providing the tax base to finance such a program. This act was the foundation of our current unemployment insurance system. The system is best described as a state-federal system, for there are numerous differences between the states in the administration of the program, but there are also some standards that are required by the federal government.

The states have considerable latitude in establishing the eligibility requirements and levels of benefits provided for workers who are unemployed. In many states the eligibility requirements and benefits provided have seemed inadequate to unions, causing supplemental unemployment benefit funds (SUBs) to be established in some industries.

In 1955 the United Auto Workers demanded a guaranteed annual wage from the automobile companies. The union's purpose was to protect the earnings of workers from layoffs. Ford Motor Company countered with a proposal for a SUB plan. The union accepted the plan, and it quickly spread to the other auto companies. Since 1955 the UAW has extended the plan to many of its agreements with auto supply companies, and the steel industry has picked up the plan. But the idea has not spread widely. By 1970 only 2.5 million workers were covered by SUB plans. In 1972 the Sheet Metal Workers International Association, which is primarily a construction union, advanced a SUB plan as part of a proposed package of employee benefits and obligations entitled the SASMI (Stabilization Agreement in the Sheet Metal Industry) plan. Many employees in the sheet metal industry opposed the SUB feature of the plan very strongly, arguing that employers should not pay people for not working (i.e., not pay people who had been laid off). The SASMI plan occasioned several lengthy strikes in the industry and various legal challenges, but by 1976 the plan was incorporated in many local Sheet Metal Workers agreements. Elsewhere in the economy, however, SUB gave no indication of spreading rapidly.

SUB plans differ in many details, but basically involve the establishment of a fund from which laid-off employees may draw benefits. The unions and employers negotiate the amount to be paid to the fund. Benefits are usually set to provide the difference between what the employee receives as unemployment insurance and some proportion of his or her ordinary take-home pay. For example, the auto agreements have provided 52 weeks of benefits making up (with unemployment insurance) 95 percent of take-home pay. In some cases, as in the steel industry (beginning in 1969), SUB plans are incorporated as part of a broader program to provide earnings protection to employees.

In the late 1970s and early 1980s there occurred substantial layoffs that threatened to, and sometimes did, exhaust the SUB plans. In response the unions began to negotiate new types of job security plans that tried to avoid layoffs, not simply provide income security for those who lost work. Under the 1984 agreements in the auto industry the companies committed funds to develop jobs for union members in nonautomobile areas. The companies also set aside funds for retraining workers who lost their jobs. Under the 1987 agreements, companies undertook to guarantee current job levels in key plants except in the event of an industrywide sales slump, to close no plants, and to replace half the workers lost through attrition (i.e., retirement, resignation, or ill health).[29]

OVERTIME AND PREMIUM PAY

Establishment of the hours of work has been a major trade union interest. For many years unions sought to reduce the length of the workday and work week. In 1870 the average workday was 11 hours long and the work week 6 days long. By 1890 the workday had declined to an average of 10 hours. And today the average workday hovers between 7 and 8 hours. In the twentieth century the 6-day week has given way to a standard 5-day week. Instead of working 66 hours per week, as in 1860,[30] the modern employee averages 35 to 40 hours per week.[31] Since 1948, however, average weekly hours for full-time workers have ceased to decline.[32]

There are, however, an increasing number of Americans who work part-time. In part this is due to the desire of people to fit jobs around other obligations: to family, school, or even other jobs. But to a degree, it is involuntary: people who would like to work full-time can find only part-time jobs. Employers often gain from offering part-time work because they can provide fewer benefits to part-timers than to full-time employees. From 1970 to 1990 the proportion of all workers who were working part-time but wishing to have full-time jobs rose from 3 percent to 6 percent.[33]

For 85 percent of American employees, the standard work week is 40 hours.[34] In Europe, however, significant reductions in the standard length

[29]Jacob M. Schlesinger and Joseph B. White, "Ford and UAW Agree," *Wall Street Journal*, Sept. 18, 1987, pp. 7, 9; and Wendy Zellner and Aaron Bernstein, "The UAW," *Business Week*, Sept. 14, 1987, pp. 125–129.

[30]*Statistical History of the United States* (Stamford, Conn.: Fairfield, 1957).

[31]Archibald A. Evans, *Hours of Work in Industrialized Countries* (Geneva: International Labor Office, 1975).

[32]John D. Owens, "Workweeks and Leisure," *Monthly Labor Review*, 99:8, August 1976, pp. 3–8.

[33]Peter T. Kilborn, "Part-Time Hirings Bring Deep Changes," *New York Times*, June 17, 1991, pp. A-1, A-12.

[34]Bureau of Labor Statistics, "Employee Benefits, 1981," in Bureau of National Affairs, *Daily Labor Report*, No. 186, Sept. 24, 1982, p. E-11.

of the working day have occurred. Under an agreement between management and labor in the metal working industries in Germany, the basic work week was reduced from 40 hours in 1984 to 37 hours in 1987. This agreement has received attention from unions and employers in other countries, including the United States, and might prove to be pattern-setting.[35]

In order to discourage employers from working employees beyond the established normal workday and work week, unions have sought to negotiate premium pay arrangements for work outside the normal working hours. Thus, collective bargaining agreements ordinarily provide that work beyond 8 hours in a day, or 40 hours in a week, or on Saturdays, Sundays, or other holidays should be paid at a premium.[36] Federal law requires most private companies to pay time and a half after 40 hours in a week, and requires some companies to pay time and a half after 8 hours in a day. The overtime premiums now in effect in American industry usually provide time-and-a-half pay for work beyond 8 hours a day and 40 hours a week, and double time for work on Sundays and other holidays. But in some industries (especially construction) all overtime is often required to be paid at double time, and in some cases the rate for working on a holiday is triple time.

This discussion implies that negotiation about overtime premiums is an uncomplicated matter. In fact, this may not be so. The basic steel industry agreement, for example, devotes six full pages of text to the matter of the normal hours of work and the overtime premium. The agreement deals with the following issues:

- Normal hours of work
- Scheduling
- Posting of schedules
- Starting time
- Conditions under which overtime rates apply
- Overtime computation
- Holiday liability

The federal government has passed legislation that deals with overtime. Federal law (the Fair Labor Standards Act) requires that employers covered by the law must pay their employees time and a half for all hours worked beyond 40 hours a week. Overtime premium pay is not required for hours worked beyond 8 hours in a day. The overtime requirements extend to most employers in the private sector, but there are numerous exceptions. For example, boat salespeople, cotton-ginning and sugar-processing employees,

[35]"Global Drive Launched to Cut Workweek," *AFL-CIO News*, July 4, 1987, p. 4. Also see "Reduced Workweek," Bureau of National Affairs, *Daily Labor Report*, No. 87, May 7, 1987, pp. C-1–C-3.

[36]A 1976 study casts doubt on the degree to which overtime premiums actually induce employers to schedule less overtime. See Bevars D. Mabry, "The Sources of Overtime", *Industrial Relations*, 15:2, May 1976, pp. 248–251.

and hotel and restaurant employees are largely exempt from the overtime provisions. The major exception is made for certain broad classes of employees, however—professional, executive, and administrative personnel are exempt from the overtime requirement. Federal regulations provide the basis for determining whether particular employees are exempt or nonexempt. The provisions of collective bargaining agreements with respect to overtime supplement the federally mandated overtime provisions.

PAID TIME OFF

Employees are often paid wages or salary for time that they do not work. The principal arrangements of this nature involve paid holidays and paid vacations. Major collective bargaining agreements in the United States now provide about 10 or 11 paid holidays each year. Employees not covered by such agreements usually receive fewer holidays. Paid vacations may involve from 1 to 4 weeks, depending on the length of service that an employee has accumulated in a company. In 1982 hours paid by employers exceeded hours worked by 7 percent.[37]

The result of continuing increases in paid time off is to provide employees with an increasing amount of leisure time for which they receive compensation. There has been some speculation that employees prefer increased leisure in the form of holidays and vacations to a shorter work week. Since the late 1940s, the evidence is of a general stability in daily and weekly hours worked, but considerable growth in paid time off.

EMERGING ISSUES IN BENEFITS

A number of new benefits are being discussed in collective bargaining, and experimental applications are in progress. These benefits grew rapidly in the 1970s, but at a slower rate in the 1980s and 1990s due to recession and other economic difficulties.

Profit Sharing Plans Under some benefit plans, employees share in the profits of a firm. When the company does well, employees get a bonus; when the company loses money, employees receive only their regularly established pay. Profit sharing plans have existed for many years. In the most recent decade, they have grown rapidly. Large companies, such as those in the auto industry, have established profit sharing plans for unionized workers. Motivations for establishing the plans include giving employees a "share of the action" and giving employees a stake in the company's success. According to one study, in 1978 15 million U.S. workers were covered by profit sharing plans.[38] Today the number is undoubtedly much larger.

[37]Kent Kunze, "New BLS Survey Measures Ratio of Hours Worked to Hours Paid," *Monthly Labor Review*, 107:6, June 1984, pp. 3–7.
[38]"Profit-Sharing Plans Grow Strongly," *New York Times*, May 12, 1983, p. 27.

Employee Stock Ownership Plans (ESOPs)   Under an ESOP, an employee has an account that is credited with contributions made to the plan by the company in proportion to the employee's level of compensation. When an employee dies, retires, or leaves the company, the ESOP account is translated into the stock of the company. ESOPs are receiving support for several reasons. First, the employees become owners of the company, as stockholders, and many employers believe this will help employees to be more productive members of the company. Second, employees receive additional compensation in the form of the ESOP contributions, which are not taxed until the ESOP accounts are converted into stock. Third, certain tax benefits allow an employer to raise capital by the establishment of an ESOP.[39]

ESOPs have received increasing use in recent years. Favorable tax treatment, the effort of management and unions to cooperate in the workplace, and economic adversity for many companies have created an environment in which ESOPs have proliferated. By 1990 there were some 11,000 ESOPs covering some 11 million employees. In some instances, employees have bought their company via ESOP, and taken pay cuts as they tried to rescue their jobs at a failing company. ESOPs are not restricted to unionized employees, however. About 30 percent of companies with ESOPs have unions, and only 10 to 15 percent of the total ESOP work force is unionized.[40]

The unions have taken serious note of ESOPs. In 1990 the AFL-CIO established a committee to help unions represent their members through the ownership of corporate stock. The Steelworkers union has had more experience with ESOPs than any other union, in part because several financially weak steel companies have tried to sell themselves to their employees as a way to raise capital. The Steelworkers have a policy about ESOPs that creates several conditions for union support:

• The ESOP must be negotiated as part of the labor contract
• It must not replace a pension program
• Employees must have full rights to vote the stock they will own (i.e., the company can't vote employee-owned shares for the employees, as is often done)
• If the company is to be sold to employees via an ESOP, there must be a careful study in advance to see if the company can be financially viable after it is sold, so that employees don't lose their investment[41]

Benefits "Cafeteria Style"   Under the 1978 federal tax legislation (sections 125 and 135) companies were for the first time authorized to offer

[39]Wallace F. Forbes and Donald P. Portland, "Pros and Cons of Employee Stock Ownership Plans," *Business Horizons*, 19:3, June 1976, pp. 5–12.
[40]"Hopes and Fears Are Mixed," Bureau of National Affairs, *Daily Labor Report*, No. 75, Apr. 18, 1984, pp. C-1, C-3.
[41]Polly Callaghan, "Committee to Assist ESOP Ventures," *AFL-CIO News*, Oct. 10, 1990, p. 8.

flexible, or "cafeteria-style," benefits.[42] Under these plans employers provide minimal (core) coverage in life and health insurance, vacations, and pensions. The employee then selects additional benefits to suit his or her own needs, using credits (up to some specified total cost) based on salary, service, and perhaps age. The plans have proliferated. By 1988 more than twice as many employees were eligible for the plans as two years before, but it was still only 13 percent of all private employees and 9 percent of government employees.[43]

Among the choices available to employees are such benefits as birthdays off, travel, day care for children, discounts on company products, free lunches, automobile insurance, legal assistance, parking, and savings plans.[44] Despite the seeming attraction of such plans, they have not spread widely. In 1986 only 2 percent of American employees were eligible for flexible benefit plans. About 5 percent were eligible for reimbursement accounts, which pay expenses not covered by a company's regular benefits package.[45] As a group these benefits are being referred to as "family care" in corporate America.

Developing New Benefits

Family care benefits have been following the historical pattern of development of benefits. The unions have traditionally pressed for the adoption of new benefits via the following steps:

1 *Winning recognition* of the employers' obligation to furnish the benefit by securing it in the contract, if only in very small measure
2 *Liberalizing the benefits* negotiated in successive contracts
3 *Working to eliminate* qualifications and restrictions placed on eligibility to receive the benefit[46]

New benefits sometimes spread quickly. Others spread very slowly, if at all. The rate of adoption of benefit innovations is partly dependent on the economic climate and the capacity of employers to accept new costs.

The most recent benefit to find its way onto labor's list is a union-management fund to develop housing for workers in areas that have very high housing costs. A local union in Boston (Local No. 26 of the Hotel and Restaurant Employees International Union) sought such a plan in bargaining with the hotels which employ its members, only to discover that federal law prohibited it.

---

[42]Davis S. Thomsen, "Introducing Cafeteria Compensation," *Personnel Journal*, 56:3, March 1977, pp. 124–131.

[43]Joseph R. Meisenheimer II and William J. Wiatrowski, "Flexible Benefit Plans: Employees Who Have a Choice," *Monthly Labor Review*, 113:12, December 1989, p. 17ff.

[44]Michael Waldholz, "'Cafeteria' Benefits Plans," *Wall Street Journal*, May 9, 1983, p. 58.

[45]U.S. Department of Labor, Bureau of Labor Statistics, *Employee Benefits in Medium and Large Firms*, Bulletin No. 2281 (Washington, D.C.: U.S. Government Printing Office, 1987).

[46]Donna Allen, *Fringe Benefits: Wages or Social Obligations?* (Ithaca, N.Y.: Cornell University Press, 1964).

Through very effective lobbying the local got the law changed. In April 1990 Congress passed and the President signed a bill allowing labor and management to bargain over and if they agreed, establish jointly administered housing trusts.

CHAPTER SUMMARY

An almost bewildering variety of benefits has become a major part of American compensation practices of recent years. Some benefits are provided by the federal government, and the employers pay a tax to the government to support the benefits. These so-called legally mandated benefits include Social Security, workers' compensation, and unemployment insurance. Other benefits, which are provided by employers to various degrees, include premium pay for overtime and shifts; paid vacations, holidays, and sick leave; health insurance pensions; severance pay; and some unemployment benefits.

The pension system was not substantially developed before 1940. In 1949, an NLRB decision required employers to bargain with unions about pensions. Pension plans developed rapidly thereafter. There are now many private pension plans provided by business concerns for their employees. Private plans have very different characteristics. There are contributory and noncontributory, single-employer and multi employer, cost-based and benefit-based plans. Calculation of the cost of a pension plan or the impact on cost of a change in benefits is very complex. The government-provided Social Security system, which was instituted in 1935, interacts in various ways with private pension plans. The Social Security offset in private pension plans is a controversial issue.

There are many other important issues involving pensions which are of importance in collective bargaining. These issues include the standards that should be used to evaluate the adequacy of benefit levels, the question of who is covered and who is not covered by a plan, the problem of early retirement, and certain financial aspects of pension plans, such as vesting, funding, and unfunded liabilities. The assets of pension funds have been very substantial and are a major factor in the investment market. Controversies have developed around who manages these investments and how the funds are invested and for whose benefit. In 1974 Congress instituted the Employees' Retirement Income Security Act (ERISA) in order to regulate private pension plans. ERISA imposes standards on private pension plans including the financial behavior to which trustees of the funds are now held by law.

The United States has no comprehensive national medical insurance program, and as a result the health insurance of much of the population is provided by employers. The rising costs of employer health insurance plans, which have grown steadily in amount and type of coverage since World War II, are a major issue in collective bargaining. The union and the company not only must determine the money to be spent, but also must negotiate for the delivery of health-care services. Most insurance is purchased from insurance companies or service corporations like Blue Cross–Blue Shield. There have been other experiments, however, with prepared group health-care plans administered by health maintenance organizations. Health care costs have been rising so rapidly that many companies and unions are now joining to attempt to limit their increase.

The current unemployment insurance system is a state-federal system. In many states, the level of benefits provided workers has seemed inadequate and unions have pressed to establish supplemental unemployment benefit funds (SUBs) in some industries. SUB plans basically involve the establishment of a fund from which laid-off employees can draw benefits. The United Auto Workers was instrumental in the development of these plans as a means of protecting workers from layoffs.

Establishment of the hours of work has been a major trade union interest. Unions helped establish the 40-hour work week and have sought to negotiate premium pay arrangements for overtime work. Paid time off (i.e., paid vacations and holidays) has also been part of major collective bargaining agreements. A number of recent benefits that are in an experimental stage include prepaid legal services, employee stock ownership plans, and alternative work schedules, or "flextime."

Recent proposals for improving benefits include requiring all employers to provide health insurance to workers and establishing funds to help provide housing for employees in high-cost areas of the country.

QUESTIONS FOR THOUGHT AND DISCUSSION

1 Why do you think benefits have become such a major and growing part of American compensation practices?
2 What advantages do employers gain, if any, from providing benefit plans for employees?
3 Do you think the proliferation of a variety of benefits as a significant part of employee compensation is beneficial to employees, employers, and society in general? Discuss the advantages and disadvantages to each.
4 What are some of the problems associated with the U.S. pension system? In what ways could the entire system be improved?
5 What standards should be used to determine an adequate level of benefits in a pension program?
6 Should a retired employee's income from other sources (e.g., Social Security or working) be evaluated in determining the level of his or her pension?
7 Will employees in the future want a shorter work week or a shorter workday? Will employees prefer more holidays or longer vacations? How can a company predict these choices?
8 Should the government take a larger role in providing health care than it now does? Is the present private system involving employers and unions adequate?

SELECTED READING

Fernandez, John P., *The Politics and Reality of Family Care in Corporate America* (Lexington, Mass.: Lexington Books, 1990).

Greenough, William C., and F. P. King, *Pension Plans and Public Policy* (New York: Columbia University Press, 1976).

Hetherington, Robert W., et al., *Health Insurance Plans* (New York: John Wiley, 1975).

Levin, Noel Arnold, *ERISA and Labor-Management Benefit Funds*, 2d ed. (New York: Practising Law Institute, 1975).

Levitan, Sar A., and Elizabeth Conway, *Families in Flux: New Approaches to Meeting Workforce Challenges for Child, Elder and Health Care in the 1990's* (Washington, D.C.: Bureau of National Affairs Books, 1990).

CHAPTER 20

GRIEVANCES AND ARBITRATION

ADMINISTERING THE COLLECTIVE BARGAINING AGREEMENT

Labor relations involve more than negotiating a labor agreement. In fact, in the view of most management and union officials, the real test of effective labor relations begins after the agreement is signed. The acid test is found in the day-to-day administration of the agreement. From the point of view of the union, it must obtain in practice the employee rights that management has granted on paper. That is, the union must seek to enforce the agreement. From the viewpoint of management, the major concern is to establish its right to manage the business and to keep operations running.

Unions also have a legal liability in America to provide fair representation to people whom they represent. In Chapter 9 we saw that unions in our country represent not only their members but also others who are in the bargaining units for which they have representation rights. The law requires that unions represent fairly not only their own members but nonmembers as well. They also must not refuse to represent fairly members of the union who have conflicts with the union's leadership. The duty of fair representation is especially important in the area of grievances because the union formally has discretion in whether or not it presses employee's grievances against management. The purpose of the law is to be sure that employees are given a voice through the union in a fair way when by the union when it deals with management. The difficulty is that unions appear sometimes to pass on to management whatever complaints are raised, without trying to determine their merit. As always in labor relations a proper balance between the sometimes conflicting objectives is ideal but difficult to attain.

The language of a collective bargaining agreement is generally broad. But the implementation of the agreement involves its application to myriad small details that arise in the day-to-day operation of the enterprise. It has been said that management usually gives away more in the administration of an agreement than in the negotiation of the agreement. Similarly, unions may feel that they sometimes lose in application what they thought they had gained at the bargaining table. Hence, the administration of a collective bargaining agreement is a matter of substantial concern to both management and labor.

HANDLING GRIEVANCES

What Is a Grievance?

A grievance is an alleged violation of the rights of workers on the job. It may occur in one of several forms:

- As a violation of the collective bargaining agreement
- As a violation of federal or state law
- As a violation of past practice
- As a violation of company rules
- As a violation of management's responsibility

A grievance is to be distinguished from a complaint in that a complaint by workers that does not involve one or more of the violations listed above is not a *bona fide* grievance.

Grievances ordinarily arise under the provisions of a collective bargaining agreement. In effect, the agreement provides certain rights to employees and the union becomes their voice when they believe those rights have been ignored or violated by the employer. For example, if the contract provides that the workday be from 8 a.m. to 5 p.m. and a worker is ordered to report for work at 7 a.m., he or she may file a grievance, alleging a violation of the contract. Whether or not a violation actually exists may be a complicated matter to determine. In the example given, it may be that the company has the right to schedule work at hours other than 8 to 5, but may be required to pay a premium wage scale (e.g., time and a half) for the hour worked from 7 a.m. to 8 a.m. A violation of federal or state law may serve as the basis for a grievance, since, while a collective bargaining agreement is binding on both parties, it cannot be in violation of the law. A union may therefore pursue a violation of law through the grievance procedure. This is not very common, however, since other places, especially government regulatory agencies, exist as alternatives in which to file charges alleging violations of law.

Violation of past practice by the company may also serve as a basis for grievances. Past practice is a shadowy area for grievances, since to substantiate a grievance the union must show that the practice has existed for a considerable time and has been accepted by both parties. Violations of company rules by the company ordinarily arise with respect to matters not treated by the collective bargaining agreement. Suppose, for example, that company rules provide for dismissal of a worker after three garnishments (i.e., seizure of his or her paycheck to pay debts), but the worker is discharged after only two such incidents. The worker might protest the company's misapplication of its own rules.[1]

Finally, grievances may arise out of the failure of the company to meet its managerial responsibilities, even if the collective bargaining agreement is silent on the specific matter involved. For example, a union may protest an unsanitary, unhealthy, or poorly lighted workplace, alleging that management has a general responsibility to provide a workplace free of such hazards.

The No-Strike Pledge

Under most collective bargaining agreements grievances are not simply left up to the parties to settle. Too often management and labor are not able to agree on whether a violation by the company has occurred, or they are subsequently not able to decide what should be done about it. When there is no agreement, the parties would ordinarily be left to strike or implement a lockout in support of their position. This does in fact happen in some situations in the United States, and it is the ordinary procedure in Great Britain. But this procedure has certain major disadvantages. Primarily, it threatens to escalate minor grievances into major confrontations, involving work stoppages that affect many people. Because of this danger, it has seemed reasonable in the United States to try to find a method of resolving grievances without resort by either party to economic force. The result has been a procedure that utilizes neutrals to decide disputes that the parties cannot resolve themselves. This procedure is called grievance arbitration.

However, grievance arbitration alone does not prevent strikes or lockouts. After all, the union or company might decide to resort to economic force to settle the dispute before it ever reaches arbitration. Alternatively, either side might refuse to accept the arbitrator's award and resort to economic force to prevent its implementation. Furthermore, management has often been very reluctant to permit a neutral to make decisions affecting its conduct of the business. For management to agree to binding arbitration, there needed to be some *quid pro quo* from the union.

The procedure that has evolved to resolve these various problems is for management to accept binding arbitration of grievances in return for a no-strike pledge by the union. A typical no-strike pledge in a collective bargaining agreement reads as follows:

[1]*AFL-CIO Manual for Shop Stewards* (Washington, D.C.: AFL-CIO, 1989.

It is hereby agreed by the Union and the Company that since this Agreement provides for the orderly and amicable adjustment and settlement of any and all disputes, differences and grievances, there should be no resort to strikes (which includes stoppages or slowdown of work) by the employees nor any lockout by the Company of any employee or group of employees, during the term of this agreement. [The term of a collective bargaining agreement is most often 3 years in the United States. The average term is less, however, because many agreements are 1 or 2 years in duration, but few are more than 3 years. The average term of agreement is, therefore, about 2.5 years.]

This language is legally binding and may be enforced in the courts. It requires the union not to strike over a grievance and requires both management and the union to accept neutral arbitration of unresolved grievances as binding and therefore legally enforceable on both.

Probably 90 percent of all collective bargaining agreements in the United States have a no-strike pledge in them, but a large minority of these pledges are conditional in one form or another. In some instances a strike is permitted after the conclusion of the grievance procedure when binding arbitration by a neutral is not provided by the collective bargaining agreement. For example, in the General Motors–UAW agreement, the union is permitted to file grievances over production standards established by the company, but these grievances do not become the subject of arbitration. Instead, the union may strike over unadjusted work standards disputes after a certain number have accumulated. In contrast, in the pulp and paper industry somewhat similar disputes (which involve the wage rates established by the company for newly created jobs) are not submitted to arbitration, but the union rarely strikes about these matters. The accumulated grievances over new job rates are included by the parties in their negotiations at the termination of the existing collective bargaining agreement. In agreements in other industries the union is permitted to strike when the company refuses to honor an arbitration award or refuses to submit a dispute to arbitration.

In some industries, arbitration is not used at all to resolve grievances. For example, under the National Master Freight Agreement between the Teamsters and Trucking Employees, Inc., all grievances must be heard by a joint labor-management committee. A majority vote of the committee members is required to resolve any grievance. The committee comprises an equal number of union and employer representatives (usually three of each).

The Grievance Procedure

Virtually all collective bargaining agreements include some form of grievance procedure. The purposes of the procedure are

- To settle disputes arising during the life of the agreement
- To establish an orderly method for handling disputes

• To provide for the union's role in processing the grievance of a single employee

• To allow either side to appeal the results of grievance negotiation step by step until a final and binding decision is reached

At the heart of the grievance procedure are the steward for the union and the supervisor for the company. An employee with a complaint takes it to her or his steward. The steward decides whether or not there seems to be a legal or contract violation involved, and if so, brings the matter to the attention of management. The supervisor generally receives the complaint first, often before the steward has decided whether or not to file a written grievance, and by his or her decision establishes the firm's initial position in the matter. The steward and the supervisor are often the first level of the formal grievance procedure as well. But if they can't resolve the matter, the grievance escalates to higher levels of management and the union.

A complete grievance procedure in American industry would be as shown in Table 20-1.[2] A five-step procedure is somewhat unusual, however. Table 20-2 indicates that the most frequent number of steps in a grievance procedure is three, with arbitration following. A typical three-step procedure is shown in Figure 20-1.

A further aspect of the formal grievance procedure is that the grievance is set out in written form. The written grievance spells out who the grievant is, when the incident leading to the grievance occurred (it may, of course, be ongoing), and where the incident happened. The grievance also indicates why the complaint is considered a grievance and what the grievant thinks should be done. A typical grievance form appears below.

TABLE 20-1   A COMPLETE GRIEVANCE PROCEDURE

Union representative	Company representative	Time limit for management decision	Time limit for union approval
Step 1 Worker and union steward	Supervisor	3 days	3 days
Step 2 Union chief and shop steward	Department or plant superintendent	5 days	5 days
Step 3 Grievance committee chairperson	Personnel director	5 days	5 days
Step 4 Grievance committee chairperson and national union representative	Top	10 days	10 days
Step 5 Arbitration by a neutral			

[2]Adapted from *AFL-CIO Manual for Shop Stewards.*

TABLE 20-2   STEPS IN GRIEVANCE PROCEDURES
(Frequency Expressed as Percentage of Contracts Specifying Steps)

| | Number of Steps | | | | | |
Overall-all frequency	1	2	3	4	5	Total
All Industries	9	21	47	21	3	100
Manufacturing	4	13	53	26	3	100
Non-manufacturing	17	32	37	12	2	100

Source: Bureau of National Affairs, *Basic Patterns in Union Contracts: Grievance and Arbitration,* Washington D.C., 1992, (Update 51, page 1) 51:1.

FIGURE 20-1   Typical grievance procedure. *(From Robert W. Eckles et al., Essentials of Management for First-Line Supervision, Wiley, New York, 1974, p. 529.)*

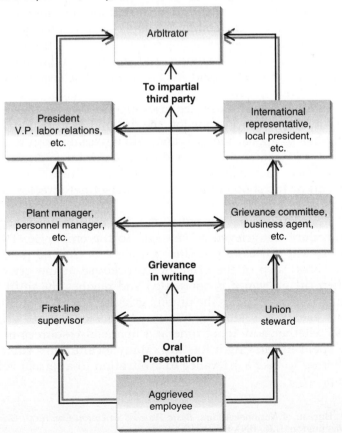

There are many instances in which the filing of grievances is not limited to the initiative of individual employees. More than a third of the collective bargaining agreements with grievance provisions permit the union to file grievances on its own behalf. In general, these grievances deal with management practices or changes that affect a large number of employees or with rights specifically granted to the union under the agreement. Management may file grievances in 25 percent of agreements. Industries in which management is especially likely to be able to file grievances are furniture and electrical machinery manufacturing and the maritime industry.[3]

An example of the specific grievance procedure employed by a major corporation and a union is instructive.

The grievance procedure used by General Motors and the UAW has four basic steps. These steps are outlined in several paragraphs of the national agreement. The first step is a meeting between the employee and his or her supervisor, since an employee's closest contact with management is through the supervisor. Any time during the discussion, the employee may ask for the services of the union committee member. A grievance not settled at the first step is then taken to the "step and a half." Here, the employee's union committee member and another member of the shop committee meet with the employee's supervisor and the general supervisor.

Grievances unsettled at this point progress to the second step, a meeting between the shop committee and the labor relations department. These meetings are usually held weekly, with any grievances that are at the second step being discussed.

An appeal of an unsettled grievance to the third step must be approved by the regional director of the union. The regional director decides whether to appeal the grievance after reading both the union's and management's "Statement of Unadjusted Grievance." A meeting would probably involve such personnel as the regional director of the union, the chairperson of the shop committee, the personnel director, and the director of labor relations.

Many unions have a policy that up to this third step in the grievance procedure the grievance "belongs" to the employee. This means that the union will process a grievance through the second (or, in some instances, the third) step of the grievance procedure at the grievant's request. But when the grievance is not settled and reaches the third step of the procedure, then it becomes the union's grievance. This means that the union will now exercise its judgment as to whether or not the grievance has merit, and whether additional time and financial resources of the union should be spent in carrying it forward. Many local unions submit the question of whether to take a grievance to arbitration to a formal vote of the membership.

[3]Bureau of National Affairs, *Basic Patterns in Union Contracts: Grievance and Arbitration* (Washington, D.C.: BNA Books, 1990).

When a union decides not to carry a grievance forward, the person or persons who brought the grievance are sometimes disappointed. If the union has acted arbitrarily or with discrimination against the grievant, then it has breached its duty of fair representation and is subject to a complaint by the employee through the NLRB. Even where employees might not complain, however, they sometimes try to carry the matter further themselves. This raises the question of their right to do so. In one case, the grievant, an employee of Pabst Brewing Company in Peoria, Illinois, was discharged. The grievance filed on his behalf by the union was denied by the company. The union then decided not to carry the matter to arbitration. The grievant hired his own attorney, and the question whether the discharged employee had the right to carry the matter to arbitration after the union's decision not to do so was presented to an arbitrator. The arbitrator ruled that the employee did not have such a right. The right to arbitrate under a collective bargaining agreement, the arbitrator ruled, is "not ordinarily incident to the employer-employee relationship. . . . It is the union which has the right to take grievances to arbitration, not the individual employee."[4]

The final step in the GM-UAW grievance procedure is the appeal to an impartial umpire. Each party presents its case in writing, including a statement of facts and position, to the umpire. A hearing is then usually held for each case. The decision of the umpire is binding on all parties.

One type of grievance, called a "policy" grievance, has been used extensively in the last few years. This type of grievance is one that a union committee member files on behalf of the union.

A formal grievance procedure has several functions:

1 *It provides a mechanism* to adjust employees' complaints or to clarify disputes over the rights and obligations of the employer.

2 *It brings the matter* in a formal, prearranged way to the attention of union officials and management.

3 *It defines and narrows the nature* of the complaint.

4 *It provides a structure* of meetings between union and management at various levels that may result in settlement of the grievance.

From the viewpoint of the American industrial relations system as a whole, the formal grievance process has two major advantages. First, it makes sure that workers can get a hearing for their complaints and that problems are not simply allowed to fester. Second, it identifies and defines specific complaints, thereby permitting isolation of different matters from each other and lessening the likelihood that the accumulation of minor dissatisfactions may lead to major industrial relations problems. In the absence of a formal grievance procedure, there is a tendency for management

---

[4]Pabst Brewing Co. and Frank Genusa, Arbitrator John Day Larkin, Oct. 6, 1979, reported in Bureau of National Affairs, *Daily Labor Report*, No. 237, Dec. 7, 1979, p. A-1.

to disregard employee complaints and for unions to seize upon minor items as the occasion for major disputes (i.e., as "the straw that broke the camel's back"). This sort of occurrence is common in Great Britain and France, for example.

The existence of binding arbitration as the last step in a grievance procedure has an important impact on the process as a whole. As described by a British observer of labor relations: "The instance of an arbitrator as a last recourse during the life of the agreement means that management cannot depend on imposing its views by power and thus is forced to consider its actions before the event as well as to justify them afterwards. This is a vital factor [and is precisely what] has all too often been missing in Britain."[5] An American analyst of grievance procedures emphasized the importance of arbitration in providing credibility to the entire grievance process by noting that "workers are, perhaps, as interested in an assurance of justice before the act as in justice through the grievance procedure after the act."[6]

Unfortunately, the mere existence of formal grievance machinery does not ensure that it will work. Sometimes grievances pile up and the formal machinery cannot deal with them all. Delays and frustration result. Sometimes the procedure is at fault, but other times management may be guilty of intentionally delaying the procedure, or the union may be guilty of misusing it by filing so many grievances that the system collapses. In a study of grievance procedures, Harold W. Davey noted, "It is critically important . . . to remember . . . that persons are more important than procedures." Whether grievance procedures really work depends on "the talent and tenacity of personnel (both management and union) involved in the pre-arbitration stages."[7]

Attempting to improve the effectiveness of grievance procedures, some managements and unions have begun to utilize mediation prior to the final resort to arbitration. The mediation process is informal—unlike arbitration, which generally involves attorneys, transcripts of proceedings, written opinions, and arbitrators themselves. As such, mediation is less time-consuming and less expensive.[8] But it is not necessarily final, since the mediator makes no decision, and even after mediation there may be an arbitration proceeding.

Research has demonstrated that the structure of a grievance procedure affects the rates and levels of settling grievances and the time it takes to do

---

[5]A. W. J. Thomson and V. V. Murray, *Grievance Procedures* (Lexington, Mass.; D.C. Heath, 1976), p. 169.

[6]James W. Kuhn, "The Grievance Procedure," in John T. Dunlop and N. W. Chamberlain, eds., *Frontiers of Collective Bargaining* (New York: Harper, 1967), p. 257.

[7]Harold W. Davey, "What's Right and What's Wrong with Grievance Arbitration," *The Arbitration Journal*, 28:4, December 1973, p. 217.

[8]"Employers Resolve Worker Complaints . . .," Bureau of National Affairs, *Daily Labor Report*, No. 1, Jan. 2, 1992, p. A-5. See also "Grievance Mediation," Bureau of National Affairs, *Daily Labor Report*, No. 93, May 15, 1987, p. C-1ff; and Leonard Bierman and Stuart A. Youngblood, "Resolving Unjust Discharge Cases: A Mediatory Approach," *The Arbitration Journal*, 40:1, March 1985, pp. 45–60.

so.[9] An experiment in the bituminous coal industry, in which the grievance procedure has often been ineffective in preventing strikes over grievances, found that when grievances were mediated prior to arbitration, strikes were substantially reduced.[10] Also, a study of grievance processes in four major industries found that grievance procedures varied in volume of use and effectiveness among industries. Grievance rates per 100 employees were twice as high in basic steel plants as in retail stores and public schools. Perhaps surprisingly, the same study showed that the fairness of the settlement of the grievance when rated by employees on a scale of 1 (low) to 10 (high) was in the 4 to 6 range in each of the four industries. It seems disappointing that the grievance system, now in use some 50 years in American workplaces and credited by outside observers with promoting industrial peace and fair treatment of employees, should get no better endorsement from employees than the mid-range of an evaluation scale.[11]

Sources of Grievances

A grievance is not simply an employee's gripe. There must be violation of some obligation of the employer under a labor contract, a law or other standard as mentioned on the first page of this chapter. The actions of a supervisor may give rise to a grievance, or the failure of a supervisor to do something he or she is required to do. Misunderstandings are also a source of grievances.

It might be expected that the frequency of grievances would be about the same in any group of employees of similar size. But this is not the case. Instead, employers and union officials have long noted the great variety of experience under grievance procedures.[12] Some companies have few grievances filed; some have many. Within a company, some plants have many grievances, some few. And even within a single plant, some departments have few grievances filed, some many. Why do these differences exist?

What factors influence union and management in decisions about grievances? A study showed that unions rarely consider the financial impact of a grievance on management (i.e., if the grievance is lost by management) in deciding whether or not to file a grievance. The more severe the management disciplinary action, the more likely the union was to grieve. Also union leaders were not less inclined to file a grievance just because management discussed the issue with them before taking action. The frequency with which union leaders file grievances is related to how

[9]Joseph Lowenberg, "Structure of Grievance Procedures," *Labor Law Journal,* 35, January 1984, pp. 44–51.

[10]Jeanne M. Brett and Stephen B. Goldberg, "Grievance Mediation in the Coal Industry: A Field Experiment," *Industrial and Labor Relations Review,* 37:1, October 1983, pp. 49–69.

[11]David Lewin, "Empirical Measures of Grievance Procedure Effectiveness," *Labor Law Journal,* August 1984, pp. 491–499.

[12]Sumner H. Slichter, James J. Healy, and E. Robert Livernash, *The Impact of Collective Bargaining on Management*(Washington, D.C.: Brookings Institution, 1960), p. 698.

managers perceive union leaders—the more often grievances are filed, the less favorable are management attitudes.[13]

There have been several studies of grievance procedures, some focusing on the personal characteristics of grievants. A statistical study of the 6-year grievance file of one plant of a major corporation distinguished among four groups of employees. One group was made up of nongrievants, another of repeated grievants, a third group of one- or two-time grievants, and a fourth group of people who filed grievances because of the company's disciplinary action against them. The study indicated that those individuals who filed only a few grievances were regarded as better workers and seemed more knowledgeable of the contract than others. The group of discipline-related grievants was so-called problem employees with a history of personal difficulties, both at work and in other settings. Surprisingly, the multiple grievants were not very different from the nongrievants.[14] This study, and others like it, seem to presume that the rate of grievances filed is a result of characteristics of employees. Is that presumption reasonable?

The most careful and complete study of grievance behavior was made in the plants of five basic steel companies. Within each company at least two departments were studied in considerable depth—one with a relatively high grievance rate (i.e., grievances filed per employee) and one with a relatively low one. "Since the essence is a charge that the agreement has been violated," the authors said, "differences in grievance rates among departments reflected either differences in the number of charges made or differences in the manner in which complaints, problems, and charges were resolved and recorded by the parties. Grievance rates count and reflect only formal charges reduced to writing. The grievance process, however, involves informal and oral activity as well. . . ."[15]

The study identified three types of factors that influence the grievance and resolution process. "However," the authors wrote, "the factors do not operate independently. . . . If the grievance procedure is to be truly understood . . . then the environmental, union, and management variables must be seen as interdependent."[16] There are three dimensions of the environment—(1) task organization and work environment, (2) technological change, and (3) socioeconomic conditions—and three dimensions of union

[13]Chalmer E. Labig, Jr., and I. B. Helburn, "Union and Management Policy Influences on Grievance Initiation," *Journal of Labor Research*, 7:3, Summer 1986, pp. 270–284. See also Michael J. Duane, Ross E. Azevedo, and Urton Anderson, "Behavior as an Indication of an Opponent's Intentions," *Psychological Reports*, 57, 1985, pp. 507–513; and Chalmer E. Labig, Jr., and Charles R. Greer, "Grievance Initiation," *Journal of Labor Research*, 9:1, Winter 1988, p. 7ff.

[14]John Price et al., "Three Studies of Grievances," *Personnel Journal*, 55:1, January 1976, pp. 33–37. See also P. Ash, "The Parties to the Grievance," *Personnel Psychology*, 23, 1970, pp. 13–37; and W. W. Ronan, "Work Group Attitudes and Grievance Activity," *Journal of Applied Psychology*, 55, 1971, pp. 500–502.

[15]E. Robert Livernash and David A. Peach, *Grievance and Resolution: A Study in Basic Steel* (Cambridge, Mass.: Harvard University Press, 1974), p. 2.

[16]Ibid., p. 131.

and management influences—(1) leadership, (2) organization, and (3) policy. A high-grievance rate situation involves, in various ways, an unfavorable task environment, aggressive union leadership, and ineffective managerial decision making. Apparently, the frequency of grievances is not simply a function of the characteristics of the employees.

Nonunion versus Union Grievance Handling

Nonunion companies vary a great deal in their methods of handling employee grievances. At one extreme, better-standards nonunion employers often have a well-established grievance procedure, usually terminating with the chief executive officer of the corporation. Often referred to as "the open door," this policy provides that any employee may ultimately carry his or her complaint or observation to the top officer of the corporation. Usually, of course, complaints do not go so far and are adjusted in one way or another at lower levels of the company. Other policies include

- The "executive detective," in which a senior executive investigates concerns on a case-by-case basis and recommends action to top management.
- "The ombudsman," in which a senior executive works full time to help conflicting parties negotiate settlements to their disputes.[17]
- "Top management as final appeal," in which the chief executive officer or another senior executive is the final step for appealing management decisions.
- "The management hearing committee," in which an appeal to a group of managers is the final step in a progressive grievance review process modeled after union grievance procedures.[18]

Some nonunion corporations provide for the final resolution of grievances by the decision of a neutral arbitrator, selected by the company and the employee, with the company paying for the process.[19] A complete grievance procedure for nonunion employees ending in binding arbitration by an outside neutral party is diagrammed in Figure 20-2. The procedure is designed to meet three objectives: "(1) a complete say for each side in airing the grievance; (2) a strong connotation of justice, since a professional, neutral third party renders decisions; and (3) benefits for both parties based on the opinion of a 'cool-headed' professional."[20]

---

[17]See Mary P. Rowe, "The Ombudsman's Role in a Dispute Resolution System," *Negotiation Journal*, 7:4, October 1991, pp. 353–362.

[18]Edmund M. Diaz et al., "A Fair Nonunion Grievance Procedure," *Personnel*, 39:4, April 1987, p. 14. See also George W. Bohlander and Harold C. White, "Building Bridges: Nonunion Employee Grievance Systems," *Personnel*, July 1988, pp. 62–66; and Richard B. Peterson and David Lewin, "Nonunion Grievance Procedure: A Viable System of Due Process?" *Employee Responsibilities and Rights Journal*, 3:1, March 1990, pp. 1–18.

[19]Robert Coulson, "Fair Treatment," *Arbitration Journal*, 33:3, September 1978, pp. 23–29.

[20]Diaz et al., "A Fair Nonunion Grievance Procedure," p. 25.

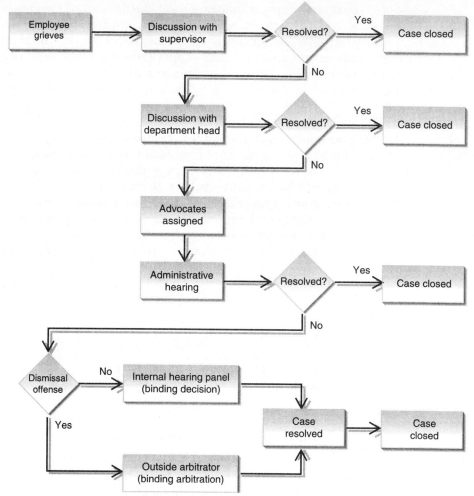

FIGURE 20-2   The grievance process for nonunion employees. *(Source: Edmund H. Diaz, John W. Minton, and David M. Saunders, "A Fair Nonunion Grievance Procedure," Personnel, 39:4, April 1987, p. 14.)*

This is unusual, however. Ordinarily the procedure terminates with a final decision by a high level of management. A recent study of the advisability of acceptance of arbitration by nonunion companies concluded against it. Either the process will not be used, the author decided, or if it is, and management loses, management will get a "black eye." Better to avoid a neutral altogether, the companies were advised.[21]

[21]Richard L. Epstein, "The Grievance Procedure in the Nonunion Setting: Caveat Employer," *Industrial Relations Law Journal*, 1:1, Summer 1975, pp. 120–127.

Northrup Corporation has what may be the nation's oldest nonunion grievance procedure. Started in 1945, the system begins with a meeting between the complaining employee and his or her supervisor, with a human resources staff person serving as a mediator. If there is no agreement, the human resources person may accept a formal grievance from the employee and serves as her or his consultant in preparing it. The second step is a hearing before the vice president of the employee's part of the business. Interviews are conducted with the employee, any witnesses, managers, and anyone else who is suggested. The hearing must be held within 5 days and a decision issued in writing within another 10 days. If there is still no resolution at this step, the grievance goes to a management appeals committee, which issues a written decision within 15 days. At this step the employee may have a coworker as an assistant but cannot bring in an attorney. According to the company, a fair proportion of decisions are made at this level in support of the employee.[22]

In the case of poor-standards nonunion employees, employee grievances may be simply ignored or the employee discharged for raising complaints. Nonunion employees do not have the protection of collective bargaining agreements, by definition, but neither are they completely without bargaining power. In fact, they have available to them such weapons as slowdowns, work stoppages, and similar tactics.[23] Grievance disputes may thus become the occasion of generalized strife between employees and the employer. Because of the lack of a formal grievance procedure and its protection for unorganized employees, a proposal has been made that there be statutory protection against employee dismissal in nonunion situations, with arbitration of grievances over discharge.[24]

Nonunion grievance procedures increased in number driven largely by civil rights legislation that established new, though limited, standards for discipline and discharge in nonunion companies. In 1979, for example, a study found that about 10 to 15 percent of nonunion companies with 100 or more employees had formal grievance procedures; by 1984 the percentage had increased to 33.[25]

A surprising, and ironic, consequence of the formal grievance procedures of union contracts is that, while unionized employees fare better

---

[22]"Employers Resolve Worker Complaints . . . ," Bureau of National Affairs, *Daily Labor Report*, No. 1, Jan. 2, 1992, pp. A-5–A-7.

[23]Leonard R. Sayles and George Strauss, *The Local Union: Its Place in the Industrial Plant* (New York: Harper, 1953), chap. 6.

[24]Clyde W. Summers, "Individual Protection against Unjust Dismissal: Time for a Statute," *Virginia Law Review,* 62:3, April 1976, pp. 481–532; Robert Abelow, "From the Editor," *Industrial Relations Law Journal*, 1:4, Spring 1976, p. 521: and Clyde W. Summers, "Protecting All Employees against Unjust Dismissal," *Harvard Business Review*, 58:1, January–February 1980, pp. 132–139. See also Jack Stieber and John Blackburn, eds., *Protecting Unorganized Employees from Unjust Discharge* (East Lansing: Michigan State University, 1983).

[25]Lauren B. Edelman, "Legal Environments and Organizational Governance," *American Journal of Sociology*, 95:6, May 1990, p. 1401ff.

than the employees of low-standards nonunion firms, they sometimes fare less well than the employees of better-standards nonunion firms. This is because supervisors in the union context sometimes seem to concentrate only on the formal rules of the collective bargaining agreement and pay little attention to the human rights of employees. In effect, the procedure sometimes becomes too formal to be fair. When the union and management each recognize this situation, it can apparently be corrected.[26]

Employment at Will

In the absence of a collective bargaining agreement, management in the United States has enjoyed the legal right to discharge employees at will (i.e., on its own discretion)—whatever the reason. The only major exception for most employers for many years was that under the National Labor Relations Act (1935) management was not permitted to discharge employees for trying to form a union. Recently, however, this situation has begun to change. Congress and state legislatures have passed laws protecting employees in many areas. For example,

Employee rights are being expanded at the state and local level by

• Right-to-know laws requiring companies to divulge information on hazardous substances used in the workplace (25 states)
• Laws protecting corporate and government whistle-blowers (21 states)
• Court decisions eroding employment-at-will doctrine (30 states)
• Laws prohibiting any mandatory retirement age (19 states)
• Laws requiring notice of plant shutdowns and severance pay for affected workers (3 states)

Employee privacy is protected by

• Limits on data about individuals that government can disclose to employers (10 states, plus Federal Privacy Act of 1974)
• Laws limiting use of polygraph tests for job applicants (20 states); giving employees access to their personnel files (9 states); restricting use of arrest records in hiring process (12 states)

Standards for a safe and healthful workplace are established by

• Occupational Safety and Health Act of 1970; 24 state laws

• Federal Mine Safety and Health Act of 1977

---

[26]William H. Warren, "Ombudsman Plus Arbitration: A Proposal for Effective Grievance Administration without Public Employee Unions," *Labor Law Journal*, 29:9, September 1978, pp. 562–569.

Basic protection against discrimination in hiring, promotion, and discharge is granted by

- Civil Rights Acts of 1964
- Age Discrimination in Employment Act of 1967; 1978 amendment disallowing mandatory retirement before age 70
- State and local laws, some of which add protection for marital status and sexual orientation

Sex discrimination in pay is prohibited by

- Equal Pay Act of 1963
- Some federal court decisions requiring equal pay for comparable work

Funding, vesting, and other standards for pensions and other benefit plans are set by

- Employee Retirement Income Security Act of 1974; state laws

National minimum wage, 40-hour work week for regular pay, and other working conditions are set by

- Fair Labor Standards Act of 1938; state wage and hour laws (all states)

Company ability to discharge and discipline employees for union activity is limited by

- National Labor Relations Act of 1935; Railway Labor Act of 1926[27]

Protections against discharge are also provided for many professors and teachers by the practice of tenure and for public employees besides teachers by governmental civil service and merit systems laws (see Chapter 11). Tenure provides that a teacher cannot be dismissed after having been granted tenure (or earned it by years of service) unless there is no work or he or she fails to perform or acts in an inappropriate way. Civil service laws protect public employees after a certain number of years of service against discharge unless certain causes are shown to exist. In this way, civil service laws and tenure furnish employees who may lack union representation the sort of protection against discharge at will provided by a union contract.

In addition to protections for employees created by statutes, courts have begun to review the doctrine of "right to fire at will" and in some cases have found in favor of employees who challenged it.

A 1959 lawsuit set the precedent for the challenge to employment at will. An employee had been ordered by his employer to lie (i.e., commit

[27]John Hoerr et al., "Beyond Unions," *Business Week,* July 8, 1985, p. 73.

perjury) before an investigative legislative body. The employee refused and was fired. The California Appellate Court ruled that "it would be obnoxious to the interests of the state and contrary to public policy and sound morality to allow an employer to discharge any employee . . . on the ground that the employee declined to commit perjury."[28]

Since 1959, courts have further limited the employment-at-will doctrine. Several cases have involved complaints that employees who had been promised jobs if they performed well, then were fired.

For example, Shirley Berube worked for a fashion company in Utah. She was not covered by a union agreement, but had a reasonable expectation of continued employment based on her satisfactory performance evaluations and the fact that she'd not violated the company's rules. Then the company discovered that some of its merchandise was missing. All employees were required to take lie detector tests. Twice Shirley was required to take the test without being told why by the company. Then the company demanded that she take a third test. Shirley became so nervous that she asked that the test be postponed. The company refused and discharged her.

The Supreme Court of Utah decided that Shirley Berube had been unfairly dismissed. The company's disciplinary procedures stated that an employee would be discharged only for certain reasons, and in this instance the company had acted unreasonably.[29]

Courts have been holding that even if there were no formal contracts, a promise is binding on the employer if given explicitly or put in a personnel manual.[30] In effect a formal personnel rules, a personnel manual, or even the verbal promises of a company official, have been treated as binding contracts on an employer. But in what circumstances a company's personnel manual becomes a legally enforceable contract is also now the subject of extensive litigation.[31]

If the personnel manual is a legally binding contract, can an employer modify it? If it does so, must employees be consulted? A Michigan court decided that a company can change its manual from implying discharge for just cause to specifically providing for employment at will, but only if it gives employees reasonable advance notice of the change.[32] Thus we seem to have traveled full circle. Originally a company had the right to fire at will. Then if it had formal procedures and policies or made promises to employ-

---

[28]*Petermanos v. International Brotherhood of Teamsters* (1959). See Thomas R. Horton,"If Right to Fire Is Abused, Uncle Sam May Step In," *Wall Street Journal,* June 11, 1984, p. 18.

[29]*Berube v. Fashion Center Ltd.,* Utah SupCt, No. 20673, March 20, 1989, reported in Bureau of National Affairs, *Daily Labor Report,* No. 66, Apr. 7, 1989, pp. A-6, A-7.

[30]"Company Offer," Bureau of National Affairs, *Daily Labor Report,* No. 115, June 14, 1984, p. A-3.

[31]"Courts Split," Bureau of National Affairs, *Daily Labor Report,* No. 90, May 9, 1984, pp. A-3, A-4, A-5.

[32]*Bankey v. Storer Broadcasting Co.,* Mich SupCt., No. 78200, June 6, 1989, reported in Bureau of National Affairs, *Daily Labor Report,* No. 118, June 21, 1989, pp. A-3–A-4.

ees, it had a contract to which it was legally obligated. Now the company can use its policies to return to the employment at will situation—in effect the contract has become a device to preserve employment at will.

Many lawsuits have been brought by employees to challenge the reasonableness of management actions. A nurse was fired from Scottsdale Memorial Hospital 3 months after being promoted to a management position. Three months before the promotion, she, her supervisor, and others joined in a camping and rafting trip. The nurse alleged that she refused to join in the group's staging of a parody of the song "Moon River," which allegedly concluded with members of the group "mooning" the audience. The Arizona Supreme Court found that the nurse, who was an at-will employee, was wrongfully discharged after she refused to engage in conduct that arguably would have violated the state's indecent exposure statute.[33]

Until the legal challenge to employment at will, employees received legally enforceable protection from discharge only via a union contract. Now employee rights are being created by court decision, and nonunion employees are receiving protection previously available only to union-represented employees. While supporting enhanced employee rights, the unions are concerned that the breakdown of the employment-at-will doctrine may make union membership less attractive, since protection from discharge without just cause is becoming available to nonunion employees.

Courts have, however, taken different directions in very similar cases, so that the confusion in this area is now very great. For example, an employee who was fired for dating a fellow employee was permitted by an Oregon court to sue the employer for "outrageous conduct," defined as being "beyond the limits of social toleration."[34] But a clinic in Minnesota had a rule prohibiting psychotherapists from dating patients. When the clinic discovered that one of its therapists was dating a former patient, it fired her. She sued, and the federal district court held that the clinics written policies forbidding dating are enforceable at law as a private contract. She was allowed to sue, but the court explicitly said that the rule forbidding dating was permissible, the question to be decided by the court was whether or not the therapist had violated it.[35]

While many state and federal courts have been holding that a company's personnel handbook creates a legal contract including discharge only for cause, the South Dakota Supreme Court ruled that Citibank's employee handbook did not do so. Hence, according to the court, the bank was free to bypass its own stated procedures to terminate an employee who violated

[33]*Wagenseller v. Scottsdale Memorial Hospital,* Bureau of National Affairs, *Daily Labor Report,* No. 134, July 12, 1985, pp. A2–A3.

[34]*Patton v. J. C. Penney Co.,* Bureau of National Affairs, *Daily Labor Report,* No. 215, Nov. 6, 1985, pp. A1–A2.

[35]*Meleen v. Hazelden Foundation,* D.C. Minn, No. 4-87-920, June 29, 1990, reported in Bureau of National Affairs, *Daily Labor Report,* No. 135, July 13, 1990, p. A-13ff.

company policy by speaking to a reporter. So much for free speech, the public's right to know, and the personnel manual as an enforceable contract all at once in South Dakota.[36]

Legal confusion creates problems for both management and employees. By 1991, some 20,000 cases alleging unfair dismissal by employers were pending in American courts. When a company loses, the financial penalties can be large. For example, in 1991 a jury in California awarded $5.3 million in damages to a former Shell Oil Company employee who said he had been fired for being a homosexual.[37] A Texas jury awarded $3.4 million for emotional distress intentionally inflicted by his employer when it subjected him to a long campaign of harassment and demotion ending in assignment to a janitor's job. Note that the employee in question was a 59-year-old executive who sued, alleging age discrimination.[38] Bad treatment by employers at the workplace is not limited to rank-and-file employees but extends to managers and executives as well.

Companies don't know when they might get substantial legal judgments against them, and employees don't know when they might lose their jobs without recourse. In response, states are considering laws to establish clearer standards.[39] Montana in 1987 became the first state (and so far the only one) to adopt legislation that limits employers' right to fire to just cause only, regardless of what the company's policies and manuals say.

The erosion of the employment at will doctrine is effectively giving many nonunion employees the same rights as union employees. Yet some observers believe that court protection is less reliable for employees than union representation, and they've come to the conclusion that the employment-at-will doctrine should not be modified by the courts.[40]

Management Initiative

Implicit in the American system of handling grievances in the unionized sector of industry is a very important principle. A grievance arises as a complaint by the union about a specific action by management. That is, the management takes action and the union reacts. Employees and the union have the obligation to obey directives of management, *even when they believe the directives violate the agreement.* The recourse of the em-

[36]*Butterfield v. Citibank of South Dakota,* SD SupCt., No. 16067-a-REM, March 15, 1989, reported in Bureau of National Affairs, *Daily Labor Report,* No. 58, March 28, 1989, pp. A-1–A-2.
[37]Richard B. Schmitt and Stephanie Simon, "Homosexual Ex-Shell Employee Wins Damages Over His Dismissal," *Wall Street Journal,* June 18, 1991, p. 38.
[38]"Fifth Circuit Affirms . . . Verdict," Bureau of National Affairs, *Daily Labor Report,* No. 175, Sept. 10, 1991, p. A-9.
[39]Alan B. Krueger, "The Evolution and Unjust-Dismissal Legislation in the United States," *Industrial and Labor Relations Review,* 44:4, July 1991, pp. 644–660.
[40]Susan L. Catler, "The Case against Proposals to Eliminate the Employment-at-Will Rule," *Industrial Relations Law Journal,* 5:4, 1983, pp. 471–522. See also Brian Heshizer, "The Implied Contract Exception to At-Will Employment," *Labor Law Journal,* 35:3, March 1984, pp. 131–141.

ployee and the union against an action of management that they believe to be improper is through the grievance procedure. They have no right to unilaterally countermand the management directive. If the company has in fact violated the agreement, the arbitrator has the authority to fashion a remedy that will make the employees whole for the contract violation.

Suppose, for example, that management requires employees to report for work on a Saturday and states its intention to pay them only straight time. The employees and the union, however, believe that the agreement requires double time. Rather than refusing to work until the dispute is resolved, the employees must report to work and file a grievance about the rate of pay. If an arbitrator later upholds the union's interpretation of the agreement, he or she may order the company to pay the workers double time for the day in question. (An employer's right to assign increased work loads to teachers is another kind of issue sometimes raised in arbitration by unions objecting to management actions.)

Management's willingness to pay a high price in return for strike-free day-to-day stability is too often overlooked. This attitude was aptly summarized some years back by Harry W. Anderson, General Motors vice president for industrial relations at the time:

> The public doesn't understand about these highly publicized settlements: the big thing we're buying is the union's collaboration in making that grievance system work. That day-by-day union performance on dealing with grievances and keeping production going smoothly is a damn-sight more important than the money deal we make with Walter [Reuther, then President of the United Auto Workers].[41]

Thus, management preserves its initiative to run the business, without the union's giving up its rights under the agreement. This principle is of critical importance when contrasted with procedure in Western Europe, where management must often bargain with the union about proposed changes before the company can put them into effect. The result is often considerable inefficiency. However, even in the United States, because companies often do not want to risk having to make financial payments after the fact for violations of the agreement, management may check with the union before directing some action that the union may feel is improper. (For example, the authority of the employer not to replace a supervisory person in a plant's toolroom and/or a management decision as to whether an employee is permanent or temporary are issues of this type.)

Although the practice by which management acts and the union reacts (through the grievance procedure) is still predominant in the United States, it has come under some harsh criticism. The following resolution was adopted by the 1978 convention of the International Union of Electrical Workers:

---

[41]Ben Rathbun, "Labor Arbitration: Britain and the U.S.," *Atlantic*, January 1969, p. 24.

Contractual Provisions Which Guarantee That Workers Are "Innocent Until Proved Guilty" and Eliminate the Concept that Employees Must "Obey Now and Grieve Later."

Knowing that collective-bargaining agreements can be violated with relative impunity and that they can continue contractually impermissible practices while the arbitration process drags on for months, many employers are encouraged to routinely violate agreements. Contractual requirements to preserve the status quo until the arbitration of the dispute is completed, and elimination of the notorious rule that workers must obey contractually impermissible orders and grieve the violations later, would go far to promote speedier resolution of disputes and eliminate employer incentive to violate the contract, as well as the injustice of leaving workers and their unions with no meaningful remedy. Finally, a contractual requirement that in most cases employers must convince an arbitrator that there is just cause for discipline and discharge, before an employee is disciplined, would prevent many cases of arbitrary and unjust discipline.

In response to such feelings some unions have begun to negotiate so-called justice and dignity clauses, which provide that employees who have been suspended or discharged by management continue to work until the grievance procedure has been completed and the company's action against them has been either upheld or reversed.

GRIEVANCE ARBITRATION

How Arbitration Works

When management and the union are unable to resolve a grievance submitted by the union, the union must make a decision on whether to proceed to the final step of the grievance procedure: arbitration. The union may choose not to go to arbitration for any of several reasons. It may believe the process is too costly, or it may believe that its case is not strong enough to win before a neutral. The union has a legal duty of fair representation to all employees in the bargaining unit, so it cannot legally refuse to carry the grievance forward to arbitration for such reasons as the race of the grievant, an internal union political dispute with the grievant, or the grievant's nonmembership in the union.

If the union decides to carry the dispute to arbitration, it so notifies the company. At this point the union and the company must select an arbitrator. (Sometimes more than one arbitrator is selected. In some cases a panel is also selected, consisting of one employer representative, one union representative, and one neutral.) The parties may select an arbitrator in any of several ways. They may agree upon a person known to both. Many times companies and unions select a permanent arbitrator or a panel of arbitrators to hear their disputes. Alternatively, they may ask some public official or other person to select an arbitrator for them. Most commonly, however, they make a request for an arbitrator to either the American Arbitration Association (AAA) or the Federal Mediation and Conciliation Service (FMCS).

The AAA is a nonprofit organization with regional offices in many cities. Both the AAA and FMCS maintain lists of arbitrators, who are selected on the basis of their own application. The AAA and FMCS select only people who can show, through references, some experience with labor-management relations and acceptability to both management and labor as neutrals.

Most arbitrators are lawyers, but not all. Others are trained as economists, psychologists, or priests or ministers. Some arbitrators serve full time in that capacity. Many others teach at universities. There is a professional society of arbitrators, the National Academy of Arbitrators, to which some, but not all, arbitrators belong. In the mid-1950s there were fewer than 25 full-time arbitrators in the country. By 1986 there were more than 300 a number which has changed little since then.[42] Both the AAA and FMCS provide rules for the conduct of labor arbitration.[43]

Upon request, either the AAA or FMCS will submit a panel of arbitrators to the parties for their selection. The list usually includes about five names. The parties may choose an arbitrator together, may ask for additional names, or may choose by elimination. The latter process is one in which first one side, then the other, strikes a name. If there is an odd number of names on the list, the one remaining after each side has struck the same number of names is chosen as the arbitrator.

What characteristics do union and management representatives prefer in an arbitrator? A recent study reports that the quality most sought after in an arbitrator is previous experience in arbitration. Of course, an arbitrator who was known to favor one side or the other, or who had a bad reputation for how he or she conducted a hearing, would not be chosen simply because of experience. Also, arbitrators with certain backgrounds were preferred for certain types of cases. For example, arbitrators who are lawyers were preferred for cases which involved whether or not the issue was in fact subject to arbitration under the contract. For cases involving wage incentives and job evaluation matters, arbitrators with experience in industrial engineering were preferred. Finally, arbitrators who are economists were favored for cases involving the financial interests of the parties.[44] Fifty-four percent of arbitrators are lawyers, and most lawyers who are arbitrators believe that legal training is important for an arbitrator.[45]

[42]Richard M. Reilly, American Arbitration Association, Northeast Region, Memorandum, Oct. 28, 1986, p. 1.

[43]See remarks of Mark L. Kahn, president, National Academy of Arbitrators, printed in Bureau of National Affairs, *Daily Labor Report*, No. 106, June 1, 1984, pp. D-1, D-3. See also John Smith Herrick, "Profile of a Labor Arbitrator," *The Arbitration Journal*, 37:2, June 1982, pp. 18–21.

[44]Julius Rezler and Donald Petersen, "Strategies for Arbitrator Selection," Bureau of National Affairs, *Daily Labor Report*, No. 123, June 26, 1978, pp. D-1–D-10.

[45]Jeffrey Small and J. Timothy Sprehe, "Report of American Arbitrator Association Survey of Labor Arbitrators," Bureau of National Affairs, *Daily Labor Report*, No. 234, Dec. 5, 1984, p. E-1ff. See also Charlotte Gold, ed., "The Legalization of Arbitration," *Study Time* (New York: American Arbitration Association, 1978); David E. Bloom and Christopher L. Cavanagh, "An Analysis of the Selection of Arbitrators," *American Economic Review*, 76:3, June 1986, pp. 408–422; and Nels E. Nelson, "The Selection of Arbitrators," *Labor Law Journal*, 37:10, Oct. 1986, pp. 703–711.

The parties notify the AAA or FMCS of their choice, and the arbitrator is then informed by the agency involved. A time and place are established for a hearing. The parties attend the hearing, with or without legal counsel, as they desire. Each side presents its case in turn. Ordinarily, if the union has filed the grievance, it proceeds first. In discharge cases, however, the company usually goes first. Most collective bargaining agreements provide simply that discharge shall be for "just cause." The obligation of establishing just cause is the employer's, and so it proceeds first. For example, whether or not an employer may discharge an employee for being convicted of a drug-related crime is the type of issue which a union may raise is a grievance procedure and which may find its way to arbitration.

The arbitrator may ask the spokesperson (often an attorney) for each side to make an opening statement summarizing its case. These statements explain the dispute to the arbitrator and include what provision of the collective bargaining agreement (or what law, or what work practice or responsibility of management) has allegedly been violated and what remedy the union seeks. Then each side calls its witnesses, who are questioned by both sides.[46] A final summation by both sides completes the hearing. The parties sometimes also file formal written statements (so-called briefs, although they are often lengthy) with the arbitrator. The arbitrator thereupon studies the material and the testimony given and renders a decision. Ordinarily the decision is accompanied by an opinion setting forth the nature of the dispute, the facts of the matter, the positions of the parties, and the arbitrator's analysis of the dispute, as well as the decision (called an award). Arbitration awards are expected to be resolved within 1 or 2 months after the conclusion of the hearing (or the date of submission of final briefs to the arbitrator).

Arbitrators charge a daily fee for their services, plus expenses. The cost of an average grievance arbitration is about $1500, most of which is the arbitrator's fee, but this docs not include the expenses of their own legal representation for management and labor.

Union and management can incur substantial costs for legal representation, case preparation, and time of representatives spent in an arbitration proceeding. It is not uncommon to hear complaints that the arbitration process is too costly. Perhaps it is, but cost also serves a purpose in reducing the number of cases and thereby helping to prevent backlogs of unresolved cases from developing.

In the railway industry, under the Railway Labor Act the federal government pays for arbitration of grievances. One result has been a somewhat indiscriminate filing of grievances and a substantial backlog of unresolved grievances.[47]

---

[46]Edwin Levin and Donald Grody, *Witnesses in Arbitration* (Washington, D.C.: Bureau of National Affairs, 1987); and Marvin F. Hill, Jr., and Anthony V. Sinicropi, *Evidence in Arbitration,* 2d ed. (Washington, D.C.: Bureau of National Affairs, 1987).

[47]Gil Vernon, "Public Funding for the Arbitration of Grievances in the Railroad Industry," *The Arbitration Journal,* 38:3, September 1983, p. 32.

A study of 6500 arbitrations from 1982 to 1984 found that one-third concerned discipline and/or discharge of employees, one-tenth concerned wages, one-twentieth concerned layoffs, and the remainder involved some 18 other matters. Discipline was by a factor 3 times the most frequent issue of arbitration.[48]

Arbitrators differ in the manner in which they conduct hearings. Some arbitrators take an active part, asking questions of witnesses and making statements. Others are virtually silent, preferring to let the parties make (or fail to make) their own cases as best they can. Arbitration is an adversary proceeding, like a trial in court, and a good case may be lost through poor preparation and presentation.[49]

There is a lively controversy among arbitrators as to whether or not an arbitrator should attempt to compensate for the poor presentation of one side or the other at an arbitration hearing. Some arbitrators are reluctant to question witnesses and otherwise take an active role because the labor and management representatives may have a reason for how they are presenting the case, and not simply be incompetent. Also, if the arbitrator's initiative in the hearing helps one side and thereby harms the other, the side that is harmed may feel that the arbitrator has not acted in an impartial manner. But other arbitrators feel strongly that the arbitrator must do all in his or her power to see that the hearing results in a correct decision by the arbitrator about the issue presented. Labor and management "should have their issues resolved on the basis of all the facts that I can uncover," said one arbitrator, "rather than upon the skill of advocacy demonstrated by their representatives."[50]

Arbitration is a quasi-legal procedure. Chief Justice William H. Rehnquist of the Supreme Court has described arbitration as being between the instant decisions made by a sports umpire and the lengthy process used by a court.[51] Most arbitration decisions may be enforced in court, but the full range of due process requirements of the courts is not applied to arbitration proceedings. Witnesses, for example, may or may not be sworn, depending on the preference of the parties and on state law. Transcripts of arbitration hearings may or may not be made. If they are made, one or the other party (or both) pays for the transcript. As a result of its quasi-legal status, arbitration may be very formal (i.e., like a courtroom proceeding) or very informal (i.e., like a grievance meeting in a company), depending on the preference of the arbitrator and the parties and on the importance

---

[48]Earl Baderschneider and Charlotte Gold, "Labor Arbitration Case Trends," *Study Time* (New York: American Arbitration Association, October 1984), p. 43.

[49]John Smith Herrick, "Labor Arbitration as Viewed by Labor Arbitrators," *The Arbitration Journal*, 38:1, March 1983, pp. 39–48.

[50]Allan G. Dash, Jr., quoted in *Study Time*, April 1978, p. 4. See also Howard R. Sacks and Lewis S. Kurlantzick, *Missing Witnesses, Missing Testimony and Missing Theories: How Much Initiative by Labor Arbitrators?* (Stoneham, Mass.: Butterworth, 1988).

[51]William H. Rehnquist, "A Jurist's View of Arbitration," *The Arbitration Journal*, 32:1, March 1977, pp. 1–7.

of the issue (very important issues seem to require greater formality).[52] In 1986 employers were represented by attorneys in 77 percent of arbitration cases, and unions in 52 percent. Transcripts were ordered in 22 percent of hearings, and lawyers filed formal briefs in 59 percent of cases.[53]

When labor arbitration emerged in the 1940s there were two schools of thought about its primary function. One school viewed it as a substitute for the strike and an extension of the collective bargaining process. The labor arbitrator saw the labor contract as a code or constitution and felt free to mediate the dispute or look to collective bargaining realities to fashion a decision best suited to the needs of the company and the union. This view may be labeled the *pragmatic* school of labor arbitration.

But another school viewed arbitration as a legal proceeding in which the language of the contract was the primary guide which the arbitrator must follow and saw the hearing as akin to a court proceeding. This school may be labeled the *legalistic* school of labor arbitration.

In the years after World War II the pragmatic school was dominant; but that has changed dramatically since. Today most arbitrators view themselves as similar to administrative law judges (such as those employed by the NLRB). Arbitrators increasingly rely on precedents set by other arbitrators, downplaying the specific facts and language of the contract and the specific relationships of union and management. Many attorneys who represent management and labor seem to prefer this trend, as being familiar to them from the courts. They are said to choose for arbitrators those persons who are more judicial in approach. A recent study shows that union leaders accept a grievance procedure that, like arbitration, is increasingly highly formal, relies heavily on written evidence, and offers few opportunities for negotiation.[54] The trend of grievance procedures and arbitration to be more and more like the courts is termed "legalism."[55]

An arbitrator's function is usually to interpret the collective bargaining agreement between the parties. Agreements often include such language as:

> The arbitrator shall have no authority or power to add to, detract from, or alter in any way the provisions of this agreement or any subsequent amendments thereof.

The restriction of the arbitrator to the application of the agreement has probably increased the stature and use of arbitration. Rather than have the arbitrator apply his or her own standards of what is right in a given situation, the arbitrator is bound to apply his or her judgment to the language

[52]Martin F. Scheinman, *Evidence and Proof in Arbitration* (Ithaca: New York State School of Industrial and Labor Relations, Cornell University, 1977); and Marvin J. Hill and Anthony V. Sinicropi, *Evidence in Arbitration* (Washington, D.C.: Bureau of National Affairs, 1981).

[53]Robert Coulson, president, American Arbitration Association, letter, Jan. 20, 1987.

[54]Judith L. Catlett and Edwin L. Brown, "Union Leaders' Perceptions of the Grievance Process," *Labor Studies Journal*, 15:1, Spring 1990, pp. 54–65.

[55]Richard Mittenthal, remarks to the annual meeting of the National Academy of Arbitrators, reported in Bureau of National Affairs, *Daily Labor Report*, No. 106, June 3, 1991, pp. A-6.

of the contract to determine what the parties agreed to. Thus, the arbitrator's discretion is not unfettered. This reduces the risk of receiving a bad decision, which both management and labor assume when they go to arbitration.

An arbitrator is often reluctant to ignore the law in making a decision, however. Despite the parties' instructions to rule only on the language of the collective bargaining agreement, arbitrators recognize the fact that legal requirements normally take precedence over private contracts. Still, an arbitrator is not a judge and may be inexpert in interpreting the law. As a result, an alleged conflict in a specific grievance between provisions of a collective bargaining agreement and certain legal requirements presents a difficult problem for an arbitrator.

A description of the arbitration process may become a bit more graphic if we list a few of the mistakes that are made by novices.[56]

- Precedents are important in court proceedings, but though they are of increasing significance they still have a lesser role in arbitration. Arbitrators may choose to be guided by the decisions of other arbitrators, but they may also disregard other decisions. This is because the arbitrator is usually using as his or her standard of judgment the collective bargaining agreement between the parties, and decisions reached under other agreements may not seem relevant. But even decisions reached under the same agreement may not seem precedent-setting to different arbitrators. (It may be hoped that a single arbitrator, encountering a dispute between the same parties a second time, and under the same agreement, will feel bound by his or her earlier decision.) A lively debate on the proper role for precedents in arbitration is under way in the professional associations of arbitrators.[57]

- Advocates for management or labor sometimes shout loudly, pound the table, and make similar demonstrations of hot feelings in an attempt to convince the arbitrator of their sincerity. This is virtually useless, for arbitrators are aware of the lawyer's adage "When you don't have the facts, pound the table."

- Novices in the arbitration process often forget its function, which is to inform the arbitrator of the facts and seek a favorable judgment. Instead, they use the hearing as a place to continue their argument with the other side. When this occurs, the parties may fail to make their best case. They often neglect to tell the arbitrator what remedy they seek and why. Parties who are experienced in arbitration do not leave such significant matters to the arbitrator's imagination.

---

[56]There are several book-length descriptions of the arbitration process. See, for example, Walter E. Baer, *The Labor Arbitration Guide* (Homewood, Ill.: Dow Jones-Irwin, 1974); and Maurice S. Trotta, *Arbitration of Labor-Management Disputes* (New York: AMACOM, 1974).

[57]Philip Harris, "Precedent in Arbitration," *The Arbitration Journal*, 32:1, March 1977, pp. 26–34; Ken Jennings and Cindy Maria, "The Role of Prior Arbitration Awards in Arbitral Decisions," *Labor Law Journal*, 29:26, February 1978, pp. 95–106.

Revolution

Labor arbitration has early roots. During the Revolutionary War an iron-monger was assigned to forge and stretch a chain across the Hudson River to prevent the British from using the waterway in a campaign against Washington's army.

He demanded a tuppence more than the going rate as "danger pay" on the grounds that if he was caught he would be doomed. His boss refused the extra stipend and, to settle the dispute quickly, a local citizen of good standing in the community was selected to hear both sides. The worker got his tuppence.[58]

Frequency of Arbitration

We have seen that the vast majority of collective bargaining agreements in the private sector include binding grievance arbitration by neutrals. Similarly, in the public sector grievance arbitration appears in most agreements,[59] though not as pervasively as in private contracts (about 75 percent in the public sector, versus more than 90 percent in the private sector).

There are no statistics that indicate the total number of grievance arbitration cases. Both the AAA and FMCS, however, publish statistics regarding arbitrations conducted under their auspices. (These data include some interest arbitration cases, but the majority is grievance arbitration.) Growth in the number of arbitrations was very rapid from the 1960s until the 1980s, but in the late 1980s the number leveled off.

The long period of growth in the number of arbitrations is puzzling. The growth of arbitration did not mirror any similar growth in unionization of employees. In consequence, the data probably indicate increased use of arbitration by existing parties. Whether or not this reflects greater employee discontent or more employer disregard of the collective bargaining agreement is uncertain. Possibly the AAA and the FMCS are receiving a greater proportion of all arbitrations, so that their increased case load does not reflect growth in arbitration as a whole. In any case, these are speculative matters at the present.[60]

Expedited Arbitration

A formal grievance procedure followed by arbitration can be a time-consuming process. In 1973 FMCS director W. J. Usery noted that the average time consumed from the first step of the grievance procedure to the arbitrator's award in FMCS arbitration cases was 257 days.

"It has often been said," Usery observed, "that time is money. But in the highly human area of resolving disputes that have a direct impact on the

[58]Lawrence Stessin, "Speed Is of the Essence," *New York Times*, Feb. 17, 1974, p. F2.

[59]Paul D. Staudhar, "Grievance Arbitration in Public Employment," *The Arbitration Journal*, 31:2, June 1976, pp. 116–124.

[60]Joseph Krislov, "The Supply of Arbitrators," *Monthly Labor Review*, 99:10, October 1976, pp. 27–30.

lives of people, time is a far more cherished commodity. For a worker to have to wait nine months and longer to find whether a discharge will stick is cruel to the worker, places a strain on his family and friends, and is costly to management both in dollars and in employee morale."[61] By 1985 the time consumed by the average FMCS arbitration case was approximately 402 days.[62] This was, in the view of most people, too long, and in industries that employed panels of arbitrators (instead of selecting arbitrators on an ad hoc basis from the AAA or FMCS) delays were often even longer.

In order to shorten the process, some companies and unions have begun to experiment with a streamlined form of arbitration. Chrysler Corporation, the UAW, and the AAA have cooperated in the attempt. As described by the UAW, "accelerated arbitration" works as follows:

> A Chrysler worker's grievance was recently fully processed and resolved within eight weeks through the use of a new UAW-Chrysler "accelerated arbitration" pilot program. . . .
>
> Currently in effect at four Chrysler plants on an experimental basis, the streamlined procedure shortens by at least six months the time needed to resolve such grievances under the normal four-step arbitration procedure.
>
> The pilot program follows a letter of understanding in the 1973 UAW-Chrysler agreement. The new process involves an informal hearing, with no briefs or transcript and no formal rules of evidence.

In the first test of the pilot plan, Charles Alexander, a heavy press operator at the Sterling Stamping plant and member of Local 1264, was suspended for two days after being charged with running too much scrap on a machine he was operating.

> Alexander won his case when the Arbitrator—who is selected from a rotating panel from the American Arbitration Association and must render a written decision within 72 hours of a hearing under the expedited procedure—awarded the worker two days' pay after deciding that Alexander had not been given adequate training on the machine he was operating when disciplined.[63]

Who Wins Arbitration Cases?

Does management prevail in most arbitrators' decisions, or does the union win more often? Many managers, in particular, seem to presume that arbitrators are generally supportive of trade unions and therefore tend to render decisions in favor of the unions.

There are no comprehensive data on which to base a conclusion as to whether management or unions do better in arbitration. However, the American Arbitration Association noted that in 1986, 51 percent of dis-

---

[61]W. J. Usery, speech to AAA Conference, reported in Bureau of National Affairs, *Daily Labor Report*, No. 233, Dec. 4, 1973, p. A13.

[62]FMCS, Automated Information Systems Arbitration Statistics, 1985.

[63]UAW, *Solidarity*, September 1974.

putes were decided by arbitrators in favor of management, 32 percent were decided in favor of unions, and 17 percent were split.[64]

Persons familiar with arbitration know that these data, and others like them, should be regarded with care. They are very much affected by the attitudes with which management and labor approach arbitration. Some companies take only very strong cases to arbitration; others take almost any dispute at all. Unions differ as well in what they choose to send to arbitration. As a result, a preponderance of victories for management may represent no more than a more careful winnowing of what disputes managers allow to go to an arbitrator. Also, a study of 1869 arbitration cases found little or no connection between arbitrators' backgrounds, education, past occupation, and other characteristics and the proportion of decisions awarded to union or management.[65]

Many managers object strongly to the authority of arbitrators (which has been upheld by the courts) to reinstate employees who have been discharged from employment. These managers feel that arbitrators view the discharge of an employee as analogous to capital punishment for a criminal and are therefore very reluctant to permit discharges to stand. One study indicated that when discharged employees are reinstated by an arbitrator, they ordinarily perform as satisfactory employees (in management's view) who make normal progress and have few if any disciplinary problems. Nonetheless, the researcher found, managers continue to view the order to reinstate discharged employees as unacceptable and wrong, despite the evidence of the positive and practical results of arbitrators' decisions to reinstate.

Another study investigated the effect of the gender of grievants on the decisions of arbitrators in 104 discharge cases. The results indicated that, other things equal, women were twice as likely as men to have their grievance sustained; in cases where the grievance was sustained, women were 2.7 times more likely than men to receive a full reinstatement rather than a partial reinstatement; and in cases where suspension was imposed in place of discharge, women received, on average, a suspension 2.1 months shorter than men. A further study found that male arbitrators were almost twice as likely to sustain the grievances of women grievants as men, but women arbitrators showed no difference between male and female grievants.[66] These results are consistent with those of studies of the treatment of women in the criminal justice system.[67]

[64]Robert Coulson, letter, Jan. 20, 1987, op. cit.

[65]Herbert G. Heneman III and Marcus H. Sander, "Arbitrators' Background and Behavior," *Journal of Labor Research*, 4:2, Spring 1983, pp. 115–124.

[66]Brian Bemmels, "Gender Effects in Grievance Arbitration," *Industrial Relations*, 30:1, Winter 1991, p. 150ff. It should be noted that there is some evidence to the contrary; that is, that there is no gender bias in grievance arbitration. See Clyde Scott and Elizabeth Shadoan, "The Effect of Gender on Arbitration Decisions," *Journal of Labor Research*, 10:4, pp. 429–436.

[67]Arthur Anthony Malinowski, "An Empirical Analysis of Discharge Cases and the Work History of Employees Reinstated by Labor Arbitrators," *The Arbitration Journal*, 31:1, March 1981, pp. 31–46; and Brian Bemmels, "The Effect of Grievants' Gender on Arbitrators' Decisions," *Industrial and Labor Relations Review*, 41:2, January 1988, p. 251ff.

Arbitration and the Law

What is the status of arbitration awards under the law? Can the loser in an arbitration appeal the decision to a court? On what grounds? Questions such as these can be given brief answers, but only if the reader understands that many qualifications must go unstated. In individual situations there may be important exceptions to the general rules set out here.

Because the federal courts are very busy, there has been a trend in recent years for the courts to require employees to go through a grievance procedure, if one exists in their workplace, before going to court with a complaint. For example, the Supreme Court has ruled that an employee must go through an arbitration procedure provided by her non-union employer prior to bringing suit against the company for age discrimination (*Gilmer v. Interstate/Johnson Lane Corp.*, U.S. Supreme Court, May 1991). Since then other courts have applied the precedent to complainants alleging sex discrimination. But the Supreme Court did not change its ruling in *Alexander v. Gardner-Denver* (1974), that the existence of an arbitration procedure does not prohibit an employee from filing suit in court about alleged discrimination. In general, an employee may complain about discrimination in the grievance procedure and in court, but must use the grievance-arbitration procedure first.

Since arbitration is a procedure favored by the courts, and complainants must utilize it, the questions of how courts look at arbitrators' decisions is very important. For discrimination cases the courts will sometimes look closely at what the arbitrator decided on the merits—that is, as to whether or not there was discrimination. But generally an arbitration award cannot be appealed in court on its merits. For example, suppose a union loses a decision but thinks the arbitrator made a mistake in interpreting the agreement. Perhaps the issue was discharge, and the union believes the arbitrator was incorrect in his or her interpretation of the "just cause" language of the agreement. If the company were a private corporation covered by the National Labor Relations Act and the union were to appeal to a state court, the court would probably direct the union to a federal court, saying the federal court would have jurisdiction. The federal court would probably refuse to hear the union's appeal, since it is ordinarily the policy of the courts not to review an arbitrator's actions with respect to the merits of the dispute.

There are several reasons for this policy. First, federal judges have little training or experience in labor matters and are often willing to leave them to the expertise of arbitrators. Second, the federal courts' case load is already too large, and accepting appeals from arbitrators' decisions would swamp the system. Third, the Supreme Court has given support to the arbitration process in a series of decisions. In one instance the Court described the grievance procedure in the contract as "a part of the continuous collective bargaining process," and as "the means of solving the unforeseeable by molding a system of private law."[68] The federal courts have been understandably reluctant to step into this system of private law.

Judicial deferral to arbitration has become a basic tenet of national labor policy. There are four key Supreme Court decisions concerning the status of arbitration and the law:

In *Textile Workers Union v. Lincoln Mills,*[69] the Court rejected the common-law rule against enforcement of agreements to arbitrate. Instead, the Court spoke of a federal respect for collective bargaining reflecting from the policy of our national labor laws. In order to facilitate the national policy, the Court ordered the parties to arbitrate a dispute.

Three years later, citing *Lincoln Mills* as precedent, the Court decided three Steelworkers' cases (the so-called Steelworkers' Trilogy), and thereby solidified arbitration's place. In the first of these cases, *United Steelworkers v. American Manufacturing Co.,*[70] the Court wrote:

> The court should be confined to ascertaining whether the party seeking arbitration is making a claim which on its face is governed by the contract. Whether the moving party is right or wrong is a question of contract interpretation for the arbitrator.

In the *United Steelworkers v. Warrior and Gulf Navigation Co.,* the Court sought to demonstrate the efficacy of arbitration in the sphere of collective bargaining and that since it is "the substitute for industrial strife," and the elimination of industrial strife is the prime objective of any national labor policy, it must be accorded great respect. Justice William O. Douglas wrote for the majority of the Court:

> The collective bargaining agreement states the rights and duties of the parties. It is more than a contract: it is a generalized code to govern myriad cases which the draftsmen cannot wholly anticipate. . . . Arbitration is a means of solving the unforeseeable by making a system of private law for all the problems which may arise and to provide for their solution in a way which will generally accord with the variant needs and desires of the parties. . . . Apart from matters that the parties specifically exclude, all of the questions on which the parties disagree must therefore come within the scope of the grievance and arbitration provisions of the collective bargaining agreement.

Finally, in *United Steelworkers v. Enterprise Wheel and Car Corp.,*[71] the Court further insulated the arbitrator by fashioning a standard of limited review. Justice Douglas warned the courts that

> The refusal of courts to review the merits of an arbitrator's award is the proper approach to arbitration under collective agreements. The federal policy of settling labor disputes would be undermined if the courts had the final say on the merits of the awards.

[68]*United Steelworkers of America v. Warrior and Gulf Navigation Co.,* 363 U.S. 574 (1960).
[69]353 U.S. 448 (1957).
[70]*United Steelworkers of America v. Warrior and Gulf Navigation Co.,* 363 U.S. 564 (1960).
[71]363 U.S. 593 (1960).

The courts will, however, review certain types of appeals from arbitration, which can be broadly described as concerning procedural matters. If an arbitrator's award can be shown to have been obtained by fraud or to be arbitrary and capricious (i.e., not addressed to the issues at hand), a court might set aside the award, or if the arbitrator had a conflict of interest, such as a close friendship with an attorney for one side or the other. Alternatively, if an arbitrator can be shown to have exceeded his or her authority under the agreement, or if the award violates a federal statute, a court might hear an appeal to set aside an award. Finally, courts have been more and more willing to inquire into an arbitration award to see whether or not the arbitrator cited an explicit provision of the agreement in reaching a decision. If not, the courts will sometimes set aside the arbitrator's decision. As a practical matter, appeals on such procedural grounds may result in a review by the court of the merits of an arbitrator's decision.[72] Also, courts will review a contract and decide what is appropriate where two or more arbitrators have issued conflicting rulings.[73]

In sum, the Supreme Court directed the lower courts to bow out of most labor disputes under collective bargaining agreements. Also, when courts were asked if a dispute was arbitrable, they were instructed to make a strong presumption. Finally, the courts were to enforce arbitration awards unless the award was clearly inconsistent with the contract.

Thus, the arbitration process under a collective bargaining agreement seemed insulated from the involvement of federal courts. But in the 1980s this began to change. The Supreme Court directed lower courts to decide disputes between labor and management about whether or not a particular matter was subject to arbitration under the labor agreement. Previously, the courts were expected to let an arbitrator make the decision about arbitrability.[74]

In a landmark case, the U.S. Court of Appeals of the Fifth Circuit set aside an arbitrator's decision that a company must rehire an employee it had fired. The employee had been arrested by police in the company's parking lot in his car, which was filled with marijuana and marijuana smoke. The company discharged the employee. The union grieved. An arbitrator reinstated the employee. A federal district court upheld the arbitrator, but the circuit court of appeals reversed the arbitrator and let the company fire the grievant. The union appealed to the Supreme Court, which upheld the arbitrator's award, saying that there was a well-established policy that the courts must not review the merits of an arbitrator's award (*United Paperworkers Union v. Misco, Inc.*, 1987).

---

[72]George H. Freedman, "Correcting Arbitrator Error: The Limited Scope of Judicial Review," *The Arbitration Journal*, 33:2, June 1978, pp. 9-16.

[73]"Appeals Court," Bureau of National Affairs, *Daily Labor Report* No. 196, Oct. 7, 1983, pp. A8, A9.

[74]*AT&T Technologies, Inc. v. Communication Workers of America*, U.S. Supreme Court, 84-1913, Apr. 17, 1986.

Federal courts are bound to the *Misco* doctrine. For example, a court of appeals upheld the decision of an arbitrator to reinstate an employee who was fired for drinking beer at dinner before returning to work, despite a management policy of discharging employees who used alcohol while on duty as truck drivers. The court called the arbitration award "unfortunate," but said it could do nothing in light of the Supreme Court's decision in *Misco*.[75]

In some cases federal courts even force a party suing to overturn an arbitration award to pay the legal fees of its opponents.[76] It is common in other nations for a side losing a court case to have to pay the legal fees of the side that won—a procedure that greatly reduces the number of lawsuits having no merit—but it is not common in the United States.

However, state courts sometimes overturn arbitrators' decisions in grievance cases simply because they disagree. For example, the Supreme Court of Pennsylvania decided that an arbitrator was wrong to reinstate an employee who'd been fired by a state agency for stealing from it. The arbitrator had found that the employee had been mentally ill and reinstated him in his job to give him an opportunity to demonstrate that he had recovered. The court said that mental illness was no bar to being discharged for theft.[77]

The Taft-Hartley Act (section 301) permits suits in federal court by and against labor organizations. Some individual employees have successfully sued unions to get an arbitration decision overturned. For example, in 1967 Anchor Motor Freight Inc., an Ohio trucking firm, discharged several drivers for allegedly submitting inflated motel receipts for reimbursement by the company. Teamsters Local No. 377 took the matter to a joint grievance committee, but the discharges were sustained. The drivers subsequently obtained their own attorney, who investigated the matter and discovered that a motel clerk had falsified the motel receipts and pocketed the difference. Nevertheless, the drivers were unsuccessful in obtaining a rehearing before the grievance panel.

The drivers then brought an action in federal district court against Anchor, the Teamsters local, and the international union. The drivers alleged that the falsity of the charges could have been discovered with a minimum of investigation, that the Teamsters had made no effort to ascertain the truth of the charges, and that the union had violated its duty of fair representation. The Supreme Court ultimately heard the case and ruled that

---

[75]*Dixie Warehouse and Cartage Co. v. General Drivers . . . Local Union No. 89*, CA 6, No. 89-5426, March 22, 1990, reported in Bureau of National Affairs, *Daily Labor Report*, No. 63, Apr. 2, 1990, pp. A-1–A-2.

[76]*UFCW Local 400 v. Marval Poultry Co.*, CA4, No. 88-2118, May 30, 1989, reported in Bureau of National Affairs, *Daily Labor Report*, No. 105, June 2, 1989, pp. A-10–A-11.

[77]*Pennsylvania Liquor Control board v. Independent State Stores Union*, Pa SupCt., No. 31 M.D., February 6, 1989, reported in Bureau of National Affairs, *Daily Labor Report*, No. 30, Feb. 15, 1989, pp. A-10–A-11.

when a union had violated its duty of fair representation and had thereby seriously undermined the integrity of the arbitration process, the arbitration decision should not be sustained by the courts.[78]

Courts may enforce the obligation of a union to honor a no-strike pledge by issuing an order restraining a strike and directing the parties to proceed to arbitration.[79] A court may order a company to honor the arbitration clause of its agreement. In some instances the courts have ordered arbitration when a no-strike clause existed in the agreement but an arbitration process did not. In other cases a court has prohibited a strike when an arbitration clause existed in the agreement but a no-strike clause did not. The courts, therefore, have apparently inferred the existence of an arbitration clause from the existence of a no-strike pledge, and vice versa, in certain specific circumstances. By such actions, the courts have sought to compel labor and management to a peaceful resolution of grievance disputes through arbitration.

This policy of the courts favoring arbitration of disputes between management and labor is referred to as the presumption of arbitrability. It is applied by the courts to the private sector, but it does not exist for the public sector. Whereas in the private sector a matter must be explicitly excluded from arbitration, in the public sector a matter must be specifically set forth in the contract as being arbitrable; otherwise it is not arbitrable unless both parties agree to have it arbitrated at the time it arises.[80]

Finally, federal courts will enforce arbitration awards upon the appeal by one side that the other is refusing to implement the award. Once again, however, such an appeal may open to the courts' review the whole circumstances of the award, perhaps including its merits. Suppose an arbitrator ruled for the union. The company believed the decision incorrect, so it refused to honor it. The union asked a federal court to order the company to implement the award. The company defended its refusal by describing the award as deficient in certain ways. The court might then review the company's objections to the award prior to making a decision about whether to order the award implemented.

Arbitration is thus protected by the courts but is also subject to review in certain cases by them. And the law seems to change at times. For example, strikes by one union in support of another have generally been thought to be illegal in the United States, either as a violation of the no-strike pledge in the collective bargaining agreement or because the strike constitutes an illegal secondary boycott (i.e., a strike directed against one employer for the purpose of bringing pressure to bear on another). In 1976 the Supreme Court ruled that federal courts may not issue injunc-

---

[78]*Hines v. Anchor Motor Freight, Inc.,* Supreme Court (1976).

[79]*Boys Market Inc., v. Retail Clerks Union,* 398 U.S. 235 (1970).

[80]*Liverpool Central School District v. United Liverpool Faculty Association,* New York State Court of Appeals, No. 464, 1977.

tions to stop a union from striking to support another union in certain circumstances, even though the no-strike provision of the collective bargaining agreement covers the matter. The Court did say that the strike was an arbitrable matter and that the question of whether the strike violates the no-strike pledge in the agreement should go to an arbitrator. The courts in this instance, however, would not enforce the no-strike pledge with a court order for the union to return to work. This dispute was not, the Supreme Court found, an "arbitrable grievance." (Presumably, the Court meant the dispute was not a grievance, since it also ruled that the matter was arbitrable.)[81]

The continuing development of substantive law about employment practices has put pressure on the insulation of arbitration from the courts. Arbitrators are now sometimes asked to base a decision not on a collective bargaining agreement, but on federal law. Should arbitrators do so? In 1967 this matter was discussed at the meetings of the American Academy of Arbitrators. Bernard Meltzer argued that arbitrators should decide only if the agreement had been violated and leave to the courts the decision as to whether the agreement itself contravened statutory law. Robert Howlett took the opposite position. He argued that each contract must be presumed to include all applicable laws and that arbitrators should interpret and apply all applicable laws.[82]

In particular, the Civil Rights Act has raised important issues of the relationship of courts to the arbitration process. Ordinarily under American law if a matter has been given a hearing and a decision has been rendered in one forum (such as arbitration), then the complaining person is not entitled to another hearing and another decision in the same matter. But in a significant decision involving charges of racial discrimination against an employer, the Supreme Court ruled that an employee may press a complaint of racial discrimination both in the grievance and arbitration procedures under collective bargaining and also in the Equal Employment Opportunities Commission and courts under Title VII of the Civil Rights Act.[83]

Would the right of a person to go to court even after arbitration cause arbitration to decline? Many observers in the mid-1970s thought so, but a survey in the early 1980s of attorneys who represent employees, unions, and companies showed that arbitration of discrimination cases continued.[84]

---

[81]*Buffalo Forge Co. v. United Steelworkers of America et al.*, Supreme Court, 75-339 (1976).

[82]For an excellent summary of the Meltzer-Howlett controversy, see Michael I. Sovern, "When Should Arbitrators Follow Federal Law?" in *Arbitration and the Expanding Role of Neutrals* (Washington, D.C.: Bureau of National Affairs, 1970), p. 29ff.

[83]*Alexander v. Gardner-Denver*, 415 U.S. 36 (1974).

[84]Michele M. Hoyman and Lamont E. Stallworth, "Arbitrating Discrimination Grievances in the Wake of Gardner-Denver," *Monthly Labor Review*, 106:10, October 1983, pp. 3–10.

Arbitration and the NLRB

Sometimes an event occurs at the workplace that is viewed by the union as a contract violation, but that also may involve an unfair labor practice on the part of the employer. How should such a situation be handled? Should the NLRB adjudicate the incident as an unfair labor practice? Alternatively, should the dispute be handled as a grievance that may go to arbitration for final resolution? This problem arises in part out of the somewhat contradictory language of two different sections of the National Labor Relations Act. Section 10(A) says that the NLRB's authority to decide unfair labor practice cases "shall not be affected by agreement, law, or otherwise." But section 203(d) reads in part: "Final adjustment by a method agreed upon by the parties is hereby declared to be the desirable method for settlement of a grievance dispute arising over the application or interpretation of an existing collective bargaining agreement."

In 1971 the board made its most ambitious attempt to reconcile these two aspects of the labor law with respect to a certain case. During negotiations an employer had tried without success to bargain for a wage increase for skilled maintenance personnel greater than the increase given to other employees. After the negotiations, the employer unilaterally made the wage increase. The company also reassigned two employees and instituted certain wage-rate changes. The union filed refusal-to-bargain charges. The company argued that it was empowered to make the changes under the existing collective bargaining agreement. It granted that the union had a right to dispute the changes but said the dispute should be settled through the grievance-arbitration procedure provided for in the agreement. In its majority opinion the NLRB agreed with this contention, stating that the situation was "essentially a dispute over the terms and meaning of the contract between the union and the employer." The NLRB went on to argue that arbitration makes available a "quick and fair means for the resolution of this dispute including . . . a fully effective remedy for any breach of contract which occurred."[85]

This decision of the board has been labeled the Collyer doctrine, or the doctrine of deferral to arbitration. The doctrine has been highly controversial.[86]

In 1977 the NLRB modified it in the *General American Transportation* case. The board would henceforth defer to arbitration about disputes over a collective bargaining agreement, but not over disputes over employees' legal rights (those established by the labor laws). In 1984 the board re-

[85]*Collyer Insulated Wire Co.,* 192 NLRB 150 (1971).
[86]Paul Hays, *Labor Arbitration: A Dissenting View* (New Haven, Conn.: Yale, 1961); Edward Miller, "Deferral to Arbitration: Temperance or Abstinence?" *Georgia Law Review,* 7, Summer 1973; Peter Nash, "Development of the Collyer Deferral Policy," *Vanderbilt Law Review,* 27, January 1974; Peter Nash, "Comment: The NLRB and Deferral to Arbitration," *Yale Law Journal,* 77, 1968. (Edward Miller was chairperson of the NLRB and Peter Nash was general counsel of the NLRB at the time of the Collyer decisions.)

versed the *General American Transportation* decision and returned to the Collyer doctrine *(United Technologies).*[87]

The NLRB has adhered to the Collyer doctrine recently. For example, a company established a substance abuse policy without bargaining with the union. The union grieved and went to arbitration. The arbitrator decided that the company had merely codified existing rules and did not have to bargain with the union over the policy. The union then complained to the NLRB that the company had committed an unfair labor practice by refusing to bargain over the matter. The NLRB deferred to the arbitrator's decision, even though the decision was about the application of the law.[88]

The courts watch closely over the NLRB's shoulder, however, to make sure it doesn't go too far in deferring to arbitration. When Paul Hammontree filed a grievance against his employer, his union took the underlying matter to arbitration. The employee lost at the first step of the grievance procedure. The employee then filed an unfair labor practice charge with the NLRB. The board refused to hear the case until it was fully adjudicated by the grievance procedure, deferring to the ultimate probability of an arbitrator's award. The employee went to the federal courts, asking them to order the NLRB to hear the case. A three-member panel of a federal circuit court of appeals agreed, saying that the employee was at odds with the union leadership. "To restrict the employee to a drumhead proceeding where his antagonists [in the union] are viewed as his protectors is destructive to the labor policy enunciated in the act," said the panel. The NLRB was instructed to hear the case. But when the NLRB appealed, the full 12-member court, by a vote of 11–1, reversed the earlier ruling and endorsed the NLRB's policy of deferral to arbitration. But the employee may eventually get his time in court: "Deferment does not diminish Hammontree's right to a public forum [i.e., a hearing before the NLRB or the courts]," said the court, "it merely delays it."[89]

Though deferral to arbitration (and the Collyer doctrine) remains controversial, in its present form it constitutes an important legal recognition of the role of the grievance process and arbitration in resolving labor-management disputes and protecting the rights of employees and management.[90]

---

[87]*United Technologies Corporation,* 268 NLRB No. 83, Jan. 19, 1984. See also Curtis L. Mack and Ira P. Bernstein, "NLRB Deferral to the Arbitration Process," *The Arbitration Journal,* 40:3, September 1985, pp. 33–43; and M. J. Fox, Jr., and Sheldon A. Wolstein, "The Current State of the NLRB's Decisions for Deferral to Arbitration," *Journal of Collective Negotiations in the Public Sector,* 15:2, 1986, pp. 99–105.

[88]*Bath Iron Works,* 302 NLRB No. 143, May 13, 1991, reported in Bureau of National Affairs, *Daily Labor Report,* No. 97, May 20, 1991, p. A-10.

[89]*Hammontree versus NLRB,* CA DC, No. 89-1137, Jan. 23, 1990, reported in Bureau of National Affairs, *Daily Labor Report,* No. 17, Jan. 25, 1990, pp. A-7–A-8. See also *Daily Labor Report,* No. 32, Feb. 15, 1991, pp. A-9–A-10.

[90]Some observers now argue that management rights issues will soon be removed from arbitration in favor of being resolved by the courts. See "Arbitration . . .," *Harvard Business Review,* 100:6, April 1987, pp. 1307–1325.

Wildcat Strikes

A wildcat strike is an unofficial strike, that is, a strike not sanctioned by the union. Such strikes occasionally occur in the United States in disregard of the arbitration process and in violation of the no-strike pledge in collective bargaining agreements. The union is responsible for abiding by the agreement, and management is often able to obtain federal court enforcement of the obligation to go to arbitration rather than to strike. In such a situation the union is obligated to use its best efforts to end the strike.

A wildcat strike places the union in a difficult position. The union leadership is, after all, supposed to be the workers' champion in dealings with management. But when the workers engage in an unauthorized strike, the union officials, who must try to get them to return to work, risk compromising their own position. The strikers may accuse the union officials of selling out to management. Because of this risk, some union leaders are less than forthright in their efforts to end wildcat strikes. Some managements believe that union leaders actively, but behind the scenes, encourage wildcat strikes.

How can management help avoid wildcat strikes? First, an effective, rapid grievance procedure will usually remove potential trouble spots, so that matters do not fester and become the occasion for a wildcat strike. Second, when wildcat strikes occur, management should enforce the rules against unauthorized work stoppages quickly and comprehensively. Tolerating wildcat strikes usually tends to encourage more of them.

The wildcat strike has been the subject of some of the strongest language uttered by arbitrators. Saul Wallen, for example, returned to the topic of the unofficial strike several times:

> In return for the concessions made to the union in collective bargaining, the employer secures one concession that is basic to his security as well as to the security of the men in his employ. That is a pledge that during the term of the agreement when a dispute arises it will be disposed of by processing through the grievance procedure.
>
> Implicit in the pledge to use the grievance procedure to settle such disputes is an understanding that work will be continued without interruption by either strikes or lockouts so that the company may continue to offer its services to the public and the men will continue to earn wages to their mutual benefit.
>
> Whoever on the union's side subverts this commitment by instigation, leading, condoning, or participating in a wildcat strike attacks the fundamental basis of collective bargaining. He defiles that which the union has set out to achieve—a fair agreement to cover the term of employment. He dishonors the pledged word of his union leadership and despoils the efforts of those who preceded him in erecting the structure of industrial relations which has replaced the jungle warfare of an earlier day. . . .
>
> This is the lesson which must be learned from the case at hand—that illegal work stoppages serve all involved ill; that they are antiunion as well as antiman-

agement in nature; and that they undo that which the long history of collective bargaining as we know it in this country has striven to create. . . .

That is its purpose. The grievance procedure may appear to take longer than it should but its end result is justice through reason.[91]

CHAPTER SUMMARY

A major test of effective labor relations is in the day-to-day administration of the collective bargaining agreement. A grievance is an alleged violation of the rights of workers on the job. Generally, a grievance alleges a violation of rights under a collective bargaining agreement, but it need not be limited to this. A grievance is not just a complaint; it is a more carefully and precisely written statement of a problem. In the past, when grievances were not satisfactorily resolved, unions often went on strike. But a better way of handling such problems has evolved in the United States over the past 40 years. Collective bargaining agreements now set up a formal procedure in which grievances are written down and considered in a series of three to five steps that involve higher-level management and union personnel at each successive step. Grievances which remain unsettled may be submitted to a neutral party for a decision that is legally binding on both parties. The union ordinarily agrees not to strike over grievances, and the company and the union both agree to be bound by the arbitrator's decision. This procedure is the cornerstone of American labor relations. It limits work stoppages and provides a stability to our labor relations which is often absent abroad.

When management and the union cannot resolve a grievance submitted by a union, the union must decide whether to proceed to the final step of the grievance procedure: arbitration. Arbitrators are private judges who are selected by a variety of means. Sometimes companies and unions have a permanent arbitrator or panel of arbitrators to hear their disputes. Most often, an arbitrator is requested from the American Arbitration Association or the Federal Mediation and Conciliation Service. Most arbitrators are lawyers.

Arbitration is an adversary proceeding like a trial in court. In a hearing, the arbitrator listens to testimony. After the hearing the arbitrator studies any written briefs and renders a decision. Arbitration decisions may be enforced in court, although the full range of due process requirements of the courts is not applied to arbitration proceedings. An arbitrator's function is usually to interpret the collective bargaining agreement between the parties, not to apply his or her standards of what is right in a given situation.

---

[91]Byron Yaffe, ed., *The Saul Wallen Papers* (Ithaca: New York State School of Labor and Industrial Relations, Cornell University, 1974), pp. 52–54.

A formal grievance procedure followed by arbitration can be time-consuming. In order to shorten the process, some companies and unions have begun to experiment with accelerated, or expedited, arbitration. Under one such program, decisions were due from arbitrators within 48 hours of a hearing.

The courts have sought to compel labor and management to a peaceful resolution of grievances through arbitration. The Supreme Court has given support to the arbitration process in a series of decisions, and judicial deferral to arbitration has become a basic tenet of national labor policy. However, the Civil Rights Act and other areas involving statutory violations have raised questions about the independence of arbitration from the courts and NLRB.

Arbitration sometimes competes as a forum for dispute settlement with the NLRB, although the NLRB has deferred to arbitration as a preferred means of dispute settlement. The Collyer doctrine, or the doctrine of deferral to arbitration, is a controversial policy that constitutes an important legal recognition of the role of the grievance process, and arbitration, in resolving labor-management disputes.

QUESTIONS FOR THOUGHT AND DISCUSSION

1 How does a grievance differ from a complaint, or gripe? Should a union process all complaints as grievances? Why or why not? What standards should a union use in deciding whether to process a grievance?

2 Should management have the right to file grievances? What types of grievances?

3 Should the law require nonunion companies to submit employee grievances to arbitration? Why or why not?

4 Is arbitration a good way to settle grievances? Why or why not? Is there a better way? If so, what is it?

5 Should an arbitrator help one side make its case if it is inexpertly represented? Why or why not?

6 The success of the arbitration procedure depends on the willingness of unions and employers to let persons from outside their own ranks make decisions about matters which both unions and employers feel very strongly about and in which they have significant financial interest. Unions and companies in other countries are often unwilling to give the power of decision through arbitration to an outsider. Why do you think American firms and unions accept this system?

7 What is the relationship of the courts and the NLRB to the arbitration process? When is arbitration subject to review by the courts? Do you think arbitration should exclude alleged violations of the statutes?

8 Should an arbitrator ever base a decision on federal law rather than on a collective bargaining agreement?

9 How can management or the union help prevent wildcat strikes?

SELECTED READING

Brand, Norman, *Labor Arbitration: The Strategy of Persuasion* (New York: Practising Law Institute, 1987).

Bureau of National Affairs, *Grievance Guide,* 8th ed. (Washington D.C.: BNA Books, 1989).

Landis, Brook I., *Value Judgments in Arbitration: A Case Study of Saul Wallen* (Ithaca: New York State School of Industrial and Labor Relations, Cornell University, 1977).

Livernash, E. Robert, and David A. Peach, *Grievance and Resolution: A Study in Basic Steel* (Cambridge, Mass.: Harvard University Press, 1974).

Repas, Bob, *Contract Administration: A Guide for Stewards and Local Officers* (Washington, D.C.: Bureau of National Affairs, 1984).

Zimny, Max, William F. Dolson, and Christopher A. Barreca, eds., *Labor Arbitration: A Practical Guide for Advocates* (Washington, D.C.: BNA Books, 1990).

CHAPTER 21

QUALITY, PRODUCTIVITY, AND EMPLOYMENT SECURITY

Long-term declines in the rate of increase of American productivity and overall international competitiveness have begun to have a very visible impact on collective bargaining agreements. This has been particularly true in the manufacturing sector, hard hit by foreign competition. But these changes also have affected newly deregulated industries such as banking, transportation, and telecommunications. Here we look at the response of unions to efforts to increase productivity growth. How effective has the industrial relations system been in increasing productivity while providing employment security for the work force?

QUALITY AND PRODUCTIVITY

What Is Quality?

In business, quality refers to how well something is made or done. It involves the degree to which a product operates without breaking down, or a service is provided correctly and in a smiling and friendly manner. For an automobile, quality means that the car is assembled correctly and that the doors, fenders, bumpers, trunk, and hood all fit properly and the paint is applied without blemish. When one thinks of the complexity of many modern products (such as computers, televisions, and cars) and services (such as air transportation, telephone, and fax), it is clear that there are many dimensions of quality.

Companies can sometimes make money by not providing quality. They put products together in a slipshod way, and reduce immediate costs by doing so. But if the customer comes back to have the product fixed and the manufacturer has to pay, or if customers quit buying the product and turn to competitors, then poor quality can be very expensive to the firm.

As competition has intensified in business in recent years, many firms have had to work hard to improve quality. At first firms tried to improve quality by finding defects and correcting them—but this is very expensive. In effect, it means that work is done, and paid for, twice. It's far cheaper to build it right the first time. So firms began to work with employees to improve quality at the site of production. This is a principle objective of the new workplace described in Chapter 4. It is a key element of the push for more labor-management cooperation.

What Is Productivity?

Productivity is a measure of efficiency. The efficiency of a car can be judged in terms of miles per gallon of gas, for example. In a similar way, the efficiency of labor can be determined in terms of output per hour worked; but we ordinarily refer to this measure not as "efficiency" but as "productivity." A measure of labor productivity would be obtained by measuring the output of a particular product and dividing it by the number of hours worked by the people who produced the product. Thus, if a crew of seven people using a paper machine produce 10 tons of paper each week; and each person works 40 hours per week, then the rate of productivity is approximately 0.035 tons, or 70 pounds, per worker hour.

While this may seem a simple concept, it in fact reflects a very complex situation. In our example, the rate of productivity is given in terms of output per worker hour and is referred to as "labor productivity." But the measure cannot be assigned to any particular worker—it measures the rate of output of the group as a whole. Also, the amount measured depends on the machine. It is not a measure of labor productivity in isolation, but one of labor productivity using the particular paper machine involved. It is not a measure, therefore, of the effort made by workers; it is a measure of the results they achieve, and this depends on factors besides their own effort.

We begin to see that while productivity is not a very complicated concept, it reflects a very complex process. A chairman of the U.S. National Commission on Productivity once made this point by saying that the trouble with analyzing productivity was that "virtually everything affects productivity [including] education and mobility of the labor force, technology, capital, economics . . . the common cold. . . ."[1]

So many factors affect productivity that various groups use the concept to measure different things. The result, of course, is considerable confusion.

---

[1]John T. Dunlop, then chairman, National Commission on Productivity and Work Quality, testimony before the Senate Committee on Government Operations, Dec. 16, 1974 (Washington, D.C.: U.S. Government Printing Office, 1975).

Managers think of productivity as a measure of how much output they are getting from the labor, materials, and equipment they buy. They know that if they can get productivity to rise, they can generate a wider gap between costs and revenues and so earn a larger surplus, or profit.

Workers and unions tend to think of productivity as a measure of how hard a person works. Often they resist attempts by management to increase productivity because they are suspicious that the purpose is to make them work harder. However, it is also true that the productivity of workers would go up if they worked not harder, but "smarter"—perhaps even using less effort to get their work done.

Economists have yet a different view of productivity. Like business people, they focus on how rapidly productivity improves. They know that increased living standards can result from increasing productivity, because it represents more output to be distributed among consumers. But economists know not to identify any particular factor as the cause of increases (or decreases) in productivity without careful research. Efforts have been made at the level of the national economy to determine what factors are responsible for improving productivity. These studies suggest that the major factors include increased capital investment (i.e., the mechanization of production), increased skill and education of the work force, and better methods of doing things (or "know-how").[2]

Quality and productivity are intimately related. It is possible to improve productivity by hurrying through a job, so that quality declines. But if customers grow angry or the job has to be done again, then poor quality actually causes productivity to decline—just as poor quality raises costs if the work has to be redone. In America in the 1990s, as we will see below, more and more firms are trying to use better quality to improve productivity, instead of letting the search for higher productivity undermine quality as so often occurred in the past.

How the United States Compares Internationally

The productivity of American companies compared with foreign competitors is of increasing importance to everyone's future economic life in America. The United States has always been a leader in technological innovations, developing and marketing new products and effectively managing the work force. In 1990 the United States still led the world in the absolute level of output per employee (see Figure 21-1), but its lead was much smaller than in the past. This is because other nations have been increasing productivity for decades now at a rate faster than that in America. In

[2]E. F. Denison, *Accounting for U.S. Economic Growth, 1929 to 1969* (Washington, D.C.: Brookings Institution, 1973). This study focuses on explaining economic growth, but evidence regarding labor productivity can be derived from it. See also National Research Council, Panel to Review Productivity Statistics, *Measurement and Interpretation of Productivity* (Washington, D.C.: National Academy of Sciences, 1979).

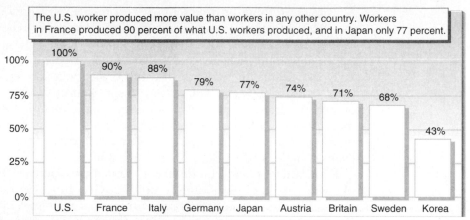

FIGURE 21-1   America leads in productivity: gross domestic product per worker as a percent of the U.S. level in 1990. *Data from U.S. Department of Labor, Bureau of Labor Statistics. Graphic courtesy of AFL-CIO.*

fact, 30 years ago Japanese productivity was only about 40 percent of the American level. In 1990 it was 77 percent. Will America lose its lead in the years ahead?

Figure 21-2 shows that from 1960 through 1990, U.S. output per hour (productivity) had risen at a rate substantially below that exhibited by other major world economies, including Japan, Europe as a whole, Germany, France, Italy, and the United Kingdom. This relatively low increase in productivity is one factor that economists point to in suggesting that the United States may continue to have difficulty maintaining a position of international business competitiveness. However, we should note that toward the end of those years, the situation began to improve. Productivity increases in the United States jumped from an average of 1.8 percent per year during the 1970s to 5 percent annually from 1981 to 1986, but then declined again, falling further behind competitors abroad, before rising in the early 1990s to roughly 3 percent annually.

Why has American productivity growth usually been so much slower than that in Germany and Japan? There are several possible reasons, but the topic is very complex and we cannot fully resolve the question here. Among the possible reasons for the poor comparative performance of American productivity are

• American levels (not rates of increase) of productivity are still higher, on average, than in Japan and Germany, though the differential is shrinking rapidly. Perhaps it is harder to raise productivity when a nation has the highest level.

• American employees work fewer hours and with less effort. The evidence here is very unclear. Americans work fewer hours on average than the Japanese, but more than the Germans. A study shows that American

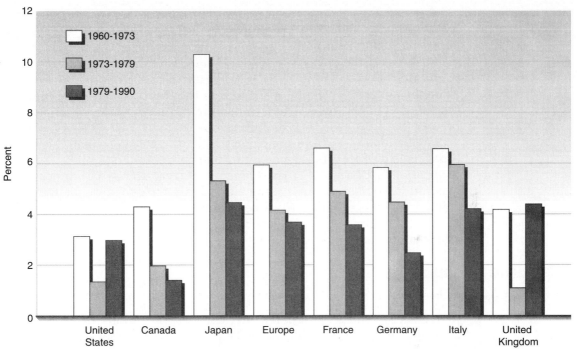

FIGURE 21-2   Average annual percent changes in manufacturing productivity in seven countries and Europe, selected periods, 1960-1990. *Data from U.S. Department of Labor, Bureau of Labor Statistics. Graphic courtesy of AFL-CIO.*

workers have as much or more commitment to their work as Japanese workers.[3]

• American companies have invested less in new technology and equipment than foreign competitors. This seems to be the case.

• The American economy has a smaller manufacturing segment than do competitors, and since manufacturing has the highest productivity growth rates, the whole American economy grows slower than others.

A major puzzle in the American economy is that productivity growth in the service sector has slowed dramatically. In the period 1960 to 1973, productivity growth in services exceeded that in manufacturing. But since 1973 manufacturing productivity has outdistanced that in services, with the annual rate of improvement in services falling off to less than one percent.[4] This is peculiarly surprising since there has been substantial investment in computers in service industries, and high capital investment is usually associated with rapid productivity improvements.

[3]Janet P. Near, "Organizational Commitment Among Japanese and U.S. Workers," *Organizational Studies,* 10:3, 1989, pp. 281–300.
[4]"Productivity Prospects Reopen Debate Over Sticky Measurement Problems," Bureau of National Affairs, *Daily Labor Report,* No. 112, June 11, 1990, pp. C-1–C-5.

Manufacturing has a special role in the economy because its productivity is especially high. This is because the average manufacturing worker is supported with much more equipment than his or her counterpart in services. But over the past 20 years there has been a dramatic decline in the proportion of manufacturing jobs in the American economy. In 1969, for example, almost 29 percent of the jobs in the United States were in manufacturing. By 1991, only 19.0 percent were.[5] In terms of absolute numbers of jobs, there has been a small decline.

Some economists have concluded from these trends that the United States is in a process of decline, or as one pair of authors put it, "deindustrialization."[6] Observers suggest that, if current trends continue, future generations of Americans cannot necessarily look forward to the rising standard of living that previous generations have enjoyed. Others say that these observations are too pessimistic and that the U.S. economy can adapt to these changes.

INCREASING PRODUCTIVITY

Unions and Productivity

Managers and the general public are, with few exceptions, of the view that increased productivity is to be encouraged. The benefits from increased productivity in terms of increased output and potentially lower costs and prices seem obvious. Workers and unions are less certain. Increased productivity may manifest itself in layoffs, so that workers fear loss of their jobs. Or increased productivity may require greater effort or other changes that the workers do not welcome. For these reasons, it is unusual for the workers directly affected to welcome increasing productivity, unless their concerns are somehow accommodated.

Unions are in the most ambivalent position. On the one hand, unions recognize the potential benefits of increasing productivity in terms of general living standards. They also recognize that increasing productivity may provide a margin out of which employers may pay better wages. On the other hand, the unions often reflect the concerns of workers about their job security or the resistance of workers to the changes in their jobs that accompany increased productivity. The memory of a time when increasing productivity simply meant increasing effort requirements is a strong one. As a consequence of this divided attitude, unions ordinarily attempt to keep the pace of productivity change to a manageable level, while also attempting to obtain for the workers a share of the benefits of increasing productivity.[7]

---

[5]For a fuller discussion, see Daniel Quinn Mills and Malcolm R. Lovell, "Competitiveness: The Labor Dimension," in Bruce R. Scott and George C. Lodge, eds., *U.S. Competitiveness in the World Economy* (Boston: Harvard Business School Press, 1985), pp. 429–454.

[6]Barry Bluestone and Bennett Harrison, *The Deindustrialization of America* (New York: Basic Books, Inc., 1982).

[7]Thomas R. Donahue, "Technology: Using It Wisely," *AFL-CIO American Federationist*, 86:9, September 1979, pp. 5–8.

The United Automobile Workers probably has the most extensive experience of any American union with technological change in the workplace. But the union's philosophy toward new technology "has not changed fundamentally in our entire 53-year history," UAW President Owen Bieber said in a speech. "The issue for us is not whether to modernize, but how to achieve it in a people-centered, humane and progressive way. It's never been in our interest to arrest the forces of change."[8]

These differing attitudes toward increasing productivity set the stage for problems between management, unions, and workers. The various ways in which the problems are dealt with are the subject of the next few pages. A special aspect of this topic is the misunderstanding that surrounds it. Managers and the public find it difficult to understand why workers and unions would resist progress of the type that yields increased productivity and often view such resistance as evidence of ignorance and stubbornness. Workers and unions, in contrast, find it difficult to understand why they should be expected to accept with equanimity what they perceive to be a threat to their livelihood, or comfort, or both.

Management Efforts to Increase Productivity

Most factors that contribute to increased productivity are in the domain of management. In fact, most managers suggest that they and their firms are continually striving to increase productivity and often blame unions and employees for thwarting their efforts. There is some truth in this, but it should be recognized that managers themselves often fail to pursue improvement vigorously. A study has identified several reasons why managers make decisions which are not the most efficient, including

- Concern about keeping their own departments bigger than necessary
- Mistaken and confusing accounting policies that do not reflect real costs
- Pressures to hurry so that longer-term improvements are overlooked
- Inadequate forward planning[9]

The failure of managers to do all that could be expected to increase efficiency sometimes undermines their efforts to get employees to do more. If managers don't really care, why should employees?

This is an especially powerful question when one considers that productivity improvements often cost employees their jobs, and that therefore they are naturally somewhat resistant to them. For example, a major factor in labor relations in coal mining over the decades since World War II has been the increasing mechanization of work which has dramatically

---

[8]"Industrial Transformation . . . ," Bureau of National Affairs, *Daily Labor Report,* No. 68, Apr. 11, 1989, pp. A-3–A-4.

[9]Scott P. Camlin, "Elite Control . . . ," Harvard University, paper presented to a work-in-progress seminar, Nov. 4, 1991, unpublished, p. 4

improved productivity and a large consequent reduction in employment. Many miners have been displaced due to new technology and many communities have suffered as a result. For miners who kept their jobs the new technology has brought new health and safety concerns, and a different type and pace of work. The workers, wrote a student of the industry, understandably "failed to share the view that technology meant progress."[10]

Resistance to change and the suspicion that management is hypocritical about productivity improvement exists in both unionized and nonunionized environments. While we often assume that in a nonunion facility management is free to institute methods that will yield high productivity without objection, this is not necessarily so. Nonunionized workers will sometimes act in concert, especially as a result of shared fears or apprehensions, to oppose technological change. Furthermore, nonunionized workers often cooperate surreptitiously to set a slower pace of work or a lower level of production than the company desires.[11] The same sort of thing happens also, perhaps more easily, in the union context. For example, the warehouse director of the Eastern Conference of Teamsters commented that too often it is the case that a new warehouse employee will pick 125 to 135 items from the shelves each hour. But after acquiring regular employee status and the protection of seniority, the same employee will fall back to much lower rates of production.[12]

Employers have traditionally responded to such problems in one of three ways:

1 By tightening discipline
2 By imposing changes in production methods
3 By attempting to persuade workers to assist in raising production levels

There are no statistics to indicate the general success or failure of these efforts. Careful observation of American industry through the statements of its leaders suggests a continuing concern with problems of productivity, however, and some impatience with the apparent failure of efforts to improve efficiency.

To a degree, the persistence of management frustration about the level of productivity in American society reflects failures on the management side. Too often, outdated and inefficient practices are so much an accepted part of an enterprise or institution that management doesn't think they can be altered. So, rather than implementing improvements through discus-

[10]Keith Dix, What's a Coal Miner to Do? The Mechanization of Coal Mining (Pittsburgh, Pa.: University of Pittsburgh Press, 1989), p. 2.

[11]In 1931 S. B. Mathewson wrote a classic study of such practices, which is, unfortunately, now out of print: *Restriction of Output among Unorganized Workers* (New York: Viking Press, 1931).

[12]Morand Schmidt, speech to the Teamsters Warehouse Division meeting in Boston, cited in Bureau of National Affairs, *Daily Labor Report*, No. 163, Aug. 21, 1975, p. A7.

sions with workers and supervisors, management simply complains about bad work habits. If a problem exists that merits criticism, then it also deserves a serious effort by management to improve the situation.

But if management wishes to obtain changes in the behavior of workers, it must be prepared to put its own house in order where a change is warranted. Managers often fail to raise the issue of work productivity because they are afraid to reveal the limitations of their own knowledge about what is really going on in the workplace. For example, in 1974 the Bureau of National Affairs conducted a survey of companies regarding their methods of measuring employee performance. While most large companies have methods of evaluating the performance of production workers, only 30 percent had any actual measurements of productivity. And for office employees, while 80 percent of the companies had some form of performance evaluation program, only 11 percent had any productivity measure.[13]

Managers are often afraid to raise the issue of productivity for fear it will open the door for discussion of other aspects of management priorities. Consequently, in many collective bargaining negotiations the work standards of the shop floor are studiously ignored by both management and union officials, neither wishing to demonstrate how little it knows about the actual day-to-day process in the workplace or to initiate a discussion that might get out of hand.

When management wants to improve productivity in a facility in a substantial way, it must make a substantial effort. A complete plan for attempting to obtain higher productivity in the workplace would include the following elements:

• A study of the sources of difficulty
• The development of a program to remedy the defects
• An attempt to persuade the workers and union, if any, of the need to improve productivity
• A willingness to alter managerial practices that contribute to lessened productivity
• A willingness to tighten work discipline
• A willingness to reward success by workers in increasing productivity

Unfortunately, many managements are not prepared to take this difficult route. Instead, they look for some simple solution.[14] There are many people who are willing to sell managers some particular scheme to improve productivity without much effort. In 1975 a study listed nine such schemes, any one of which might have its place in a serious program to

---

[13]"Employee Performance: Evaluation and Control," *BNA Personnel Policies Forum*, 108, February 1975.

[14]Bruno Stein, "Management Rights and Productivity," *The Arbitration Journal*, 32:4, December 1977, pp. 270–278.

TABLE 21-1   FALLACIES OF MANAGEMENT IN TRYING TO INCREASE PRODUCTIVITY

1	Following the leading companies (i.e., doing just as others do)
2	Decentralizing (i.e., shifting responsibility)
3	Leaving the problem to the personnel department
4	Treating the work force as a fixed asset
5	Issuing platitudes about productivity in the company's own publications
6	Relying exclusively on computer printouts (i.e., statistical information) for evidence about operations
7	Trying to speed up the workers' pace
8	Trying to improve jobs
9	Hiring a consultant

Source: A. A Imberman (president, Imberman and de Forest, management consultants. Chicago), "The Low Road to High Productivity," *Conference Board Record,* 12:1, January 1975, pp. 29–40.

improve productivity, but none of which was of much value when relied on in place of a more comprehensive effort. The nine "fallacies of management" are given in Table 21-1.

Conflicts Over Productivity

Strikes   Many of the most significant strikes in American history have been fought over changes in the way work was done as companies tried to improve productivity. The Homestead steel strike (see Chapter 2) in the late nineteenth century was in part about the introduction of narrowly defined jobs (so-called Taylorism, after its advocate, Frederick Taylor) into the steel mills, replacing a craft-oriented system.

In the 1970s strikes over productivity issues were especially lengthy and bitter. The issues primarily concerned work rules that the companies have felt impeded efficient production, sometimes dealing with the introduction of new, labor-saving machinery.

In the spring of 1975 General Dynamics took a 4-month strike by the Marine and Shipbuilding Workers at its Quincy, Massachusetts, shipbuilding division. In July 1975 the Electric Boat Division (builders of submarines for the U.S. Defense Department) of General Dynamics, located at Groton, Connecticut, took a 5-month strike by the 11 craft unions of a metal trades council. Again the issue was work rules. The company described the dispute as due to the unions' resistance to modernization of work rules and the need for job flexibility in the modern economy. The unions, in contrast, described the dispute as resulting from an attempt by the company to disregard traditional job jurisdictions of the various crafts, in an attempt to create assembly-line methods. In effect, the company sought authority under the collective bargaining agreement to assign members of the various trades (including carpenters, grinders, welders, and steamfitters) to work outside their own crafts that was "incidental" to their jobs. The unions professed concern that the company was trying to reduce the number of jobs. Both strikes were settled in similar fashion. The unions and the company agreed to establish joint labor-management committees, but with different functions. At Groton the committees were to review individual job assignments, while at Quincy the committees were to review proposals for changes in production methods with the purpose of increasing productivity.[15]

In the newspaper industry, as in shipbuilding, most disputes have ended in settlements of one type or another. But in one strike, the union was forced from the company's premises for good. On October 1, 1976, the printing press operators (members of the International Printing and Graphic Communications Union) struck the *Washington Post* when management refused to abandon demands for changes in the work rules. The *Post* objected that existing rules required more workers than were necessary to do the job and allowed excessive earnings for some workers. When the contract expired, the strike began in a wave of sabotage that crippled the *Post*'s 12 printing presses. The *Post* was able to publish during the strike by having its printing done outside Washington and ultimately by replacing the strikers with other employees.[16]

Finally, International Harvester Company demanded major changes in work rules from the United Auto Workers as negotiations began in the fall of 1979 for a new 3-year collective bargaining agreement. A 5-month strike resulted, in which both the company and the workers lost considerable income. The company was unable to obtain most of the changes in work practices which it sought.

Disputes over technological change and work rules have been less frequent and prolonged in the 1980s and 1990s, but have been significant, nonetheless. For example, locals of the Communication Workers of America have been waging campaigns against the various phone companies' efforts to replace telephone operators with robotics. The new systems have the potential to put more than half of all telephone operators out of work, the union insists, and the president of the CWA has described the transition as posing a serious problem for the nation. "Are we going to go through life," he asked, "talking to machines?"[17]

What is the impact of labor resistance on productivity? It might seem from the examples of conflict cited above that unions significantly retard the rate of increase of productivity and the adoption of new technology. This does not appear to be so.

A careful investigation found that shop floor confrontations between management and labor during the term of collective bargaining agree-

---

[15]"Productivity and Efficiency Agreement Implemented at General Dynamics Corporation," Bureau of National Affairs, *Daily Labor Report*, No. 51, Mar. 14, 1975, pp. A12–A13.

[16]See *Washington Post*, Intercollegiate Case Clearing House 9-677-076 and 9-677-077.

[17]"CWA Launches Campaign . . . ," Bureau of National Affairs, *Daily Labor Report*, No. 80, Apr. 25, 1990, pp. A-6–A-7.

ments (sometimes wildcats, sometimes strikes permitted by the contract) caused a reduction in U.S. manufacturing productivity in the mid-1960s but played little role in the much bigger productivity slowdown that began in the mid-1970s.[18]

Another study examined the impact of unions on the spread of manufacturing technology. Seven advanced techniques were studied, and the conclusion was that there was no direct effect of unions on the rate at which the techniques spread from firm to firm.[19]

There is another influence of the unions that is not measured in these studies, however. Unions sometimes restrict the willingness of nonunion firms as well as union firms to change technologies. This is because nonunion firms may fear that the stress on workers that results from different processes and job loss may result in their calling in a union.

Moving the Plant Many employers are reluctant to take lengthy strikes in an effort, often futile, to obtain changes in working rules. In some industries employers simply prefer to close the least efficient plants and move production elsewhere. This pattern of behavior has been much followed in the rubber industry, for example. Much of the employment in the rubber industry was once concentrated in the Akron, Ohio, area. In 1950, for example, the "big four" rubber companies (Goodyear, Goodrich, General, and Firestone) employed some 51,000 persons in Akron. By 1975 the total had declined to 32,000 and was continuing to fall. A number of factors contributed to the decisions of the companies to shift production to plants in areas other than Akron. Among these factors were the age of the plants, which caused machinery and plant layouts to become increasingly obsolete; lower wage rates elsewhere; inefficient work practices at the plants; and the shift of the market for tires to the South and West in the United States. The low productivity of the Akron plants was a factor that management and labor could possibly have rectified. During the early 1970s repeated efforts were made by management, labor, and community groups to revive Akron's prospects in the rubber industry. One such program, in 1972, was entitled "Make Akron Competitive" ("Hey MAC"). It was hoped that this program would increase productivity in the plants. Unfortunately, these cooperative efforts were largely unsuccessful, and the movement of rubber industry production from Akron has continued, leaving in its wake bitter recriminations from management and labor representatives as to who was responsible. In rubber, the unfortunate legacy of these moves is especially important, since many thousands

---

[18]Sean Flaherty, "Strike Activity, Worker Militancy, and Productivity Change in Manufacturing," *Industrial and Labor Relations Review*, 40:4, July 1987, p. 585ff. See also Sean Flaherty, "Strike Activity and Productivity Change: The U.S. Auto Industry," *Industrial Relations*, 26:2, Spring 1987, pp. 174–184.

[19]Jeffry H. Keene, "Do Unions Influence the Diffusion of Technology?" *Industrial and Labor Relations Review*, 44:2, January 1991, p. 261ff.

of unemployed workers remain in the areas production has moved away from.

Why does management move a plant when the process is costly and may cause ill feelings? A short answer is that it may be less expensive to move than to continue production at the old plant. The advantages of moving include

- Lower wage rates
- A new work force
- A new physical setup
- New equipment
- A new labor agreement or none at all

Many managers believe that when the labor relations in an existing facility have gotten into a very bad state, with much conflict, low productivity, and consequent high costs, there is no real alternative to establishing a new facility somewhere else. They do not believe there is much chance of turning a bad labor situation around. And although there may be a few examples of successful turnarounds of nonproductive plants, and although attempts to do this continue, the evidence as a whole appears to lend support to those who say that it is better to start over elsewhere. The recession of the early 1980s intensified these pressures.

Outsourcing As labor costs have risen in the United States and companies have become increasingly multinational in their approaches, outsourcing, or the shifting of production overseas, has increased. This has posed threats to the employment security of some American workers in several industries.

In some cases, unions have tried to put restriction on the ability of a company to move production abroad. This trend has not been limited to the manufacturing sector; it has also taken place in industries such as the computer industry where some companies have shifted subassembly production work to third world countries where labor costs are substantially lower.

There have also been strikes about outsourcing. For example, in August 1990, members of the United Auto Workers at a General Motors plant in Flint, Michigan, struck for 6 days, forcing the layoff of thousands of GM workers nationwide. The issue was the intention of GM to send work involving some 900 workers at the plant to other facilities. The strike was settled in the union's favor by agreement of the company to provide a 5-year job guarantee.

Interestingly, since the UAW-GM contract prohibits strikes over outsourcing, the local union's leadership officially described the strike as about unresolved health and safety issues.[20]

---

[20]"Strike-Ending Accord . . .," Bureau of National Affairs, *Daily Labor Report*, No. 158, Aug. 15, 1990, p. A-8.

Litigation   Employers may also challenge in the NLRB or the courts work practices that inhibit productivity. Ordinarily, an employer who has negotiated in an agreement with a union a clause that restricts productivity cannot simply file suit against the practice. But other parties, both management and union, who are affected may sometimes find a way to challenge the practice in court.

An important example of the use of litigation to loosen work practices occurred in the longshoring industry. Longshoremen, represented by the International Longshoremen's Association (the ILA), have traditionally loaded and unloaded ships' cargo. In recent years, however, more and more cargo has been shipped in containers the size of truck trailers and longshoremen have been left with fewer individual cargo units to load and unload.

Some shipping companies exist that ship only containers. These companies want to have the containers put on and taken off ships by the longshoremen, but not unpacked or repacked by them. In 1958 the ILA protested the use of boxes that were 8 cubic feet in size and began a strike against the New York Shipping Association, Inc. (NYSA). A memorandum of settlement following the strike stated in part that "any employer shall have the right to use any and all types of containers without restriction or stripping by the union."

With further advancements in containerization, work stoppages marked the expiration of ILA-NYSA collective bargaining agreements. During these disputes, longshoremen stripped and restuffed containers shipped by Consolidated Express as the containers crossed the piers. These incidents lasted 2 or 3 weeks and generally containers from Consolidated went through the port without interference. A 57-day strike occurred in 1967, when the ILA demanded that its longshoremen stuff and strip all containers crossing the piers. In 1969 ILA and NYSA negotiated the "Rules on Containers," which provided that longshoremen would unload and reload containers sent to the port from locations within a 50-mile radius. The rules provided that if a container was shipped through the port without having been stuffed or stripped by longshoremen, the offending steamship carrier would pay a penalty of $250 per container.

In 1970 the liquidated damages imposed on the carriers were increased to $1000 for each offense. The enforcement plan was tightened in 1973, when ILA and the shipping association announced that they would penalize companies whose containers weren't handled by ILA. With this, some of the companies that shipped containers (express companies, not shipping companies per se) filed a complaint with the NLRB, charging that the ILA was trying to take work away from the Teamsters, who were the representatives of their employers.

It is interesting that the express companies had no standing under law to complain of the additional cost or inefficiency created by the ILA-NYSA agreement. They could complain only that the purpose of the practice was to obtain work illegally from members of another union. The ILA defended itself by saying that it had traditionally done the work in question. But the NLRB found against the ILA and thereby invalidated a position that has the effect of reducing productivity.[21]

In 1979, however, the U.S. Court of Appeals for the District of Columbia Circuit reversed the NLRB and upheld the legality of the work rules negotiated by the ILA and the NYSA. The court held that the work rules barring the stripping of containers by nonlongshore personnel within 50 miles of each port were a responsible attempt to deal through collective bargaining with "an extremely thorny industrial issue: technological innovation versus job security." The court concluded that Congress chose to allow the parties themselves to deal with labor problems generated by technological change. The broad policy choice of Congress would be "frustrated" if the courts and the NLRB were to "upset reasonable efforts by the parties to achieve some level of accommodation. . . ." The court added that "unwarranted interference" by the NLRB and the courts "could inject a massive dose of uncertainty into the planning functions of both management and labor."[22]

As a general rule practices by nonunion or union labor that restrict productivity are not illegal unless they have some additional purpose that is itself illegal. An attempt to obtain pay for work not done is illegal, for example, but pay for work not needed may be legally required, as long as the services are performed. Because the law does not prohibit nonproductive practices per se, the use of litigation as a method of reducing nonproductive practices is of limited value.

Conflict Resolution: Productivity Bargaining

Beginning in the 1970s much attention has been focused on a procedure referred to as "productivity bargaining." The essence of this concept is that "changes in working practices that raise output per man hour are implemented by employees in return for higher rates of pay."[23] Alternatively, productivity bargaining may be described as the employer's receiving from the union a quid pro quo for a wage increase, in the form of a relaxation or modification of working practice that will result in greater productivity.[24]

---

[21]*ILA v. Consolidated Express, Inc., et al.,* 221 NLRB No. 144, Dec. 9, 1975. See Bureau of National Affairs, *Daily Labor Report,* No. 237, Dec. 9, 1975, pp. A-13–A-15.

[22]*ILA and Council of North Atlantic Shipping Associations v. NLRB,* Sept. 25, 1979.

[23]E. H. Phelps Brown in the foreword to Ronald Edwards and R. D. V. Roberts, *Status, Productivity and Pay: A Major Experiment: A Study of the Electric Supply Industry's Agreements, 1961–1971* (London: Macmillan, 1971), p. xii.

[24]Ibid., pp. xiii and xiv. See also C. Laurence Hunter, "Productivity Bargaining Abroad: An Evaluation," in G. G. Somers et al., *Collective Bargaining and Productivity* (Madison, Wis.: Industrial Relations Research Association, 1975), pp. 169–174.

Productivity bargaining is not new.[25] Employers in certain fields have long entered negotiations with labor unions with a list of demands that would, if agreed to by labor, increase productivity and thereby reduce the employers' costs. What is new is the degree of attention being devoted to the subject. To say that there is a corresponding increase in the success of productivity bargaining would probably be incorrect.

There has been interest in, and publicity accorded to, productivity bargaining both abroad and in the United States. The examples of industrial conflict involving the shipbuilding and newspaper industries that were cited in previous pages had their origins in demands by management to alter inefficient working practices. In many other cases companies have practiced productivity bargaining with less dramatic results but with some success. An official of one large American corporation described his company as going after individual items to save money. The approach is very specific. The company persuades or embarrasses the union and, by persistence in negotiations, obtains the removal of costly and inefficient items. An example, cited by the same management official, involved the company's paying for setup time on machines. In the past, certain workers had come in early to get the machines running by starting time, and the company had paid them 15 minutes' time for this. Later the plant went to a continuous, three-shift operation. The machines were now running constantly, and no setup was involved. Yet 12 years after the company went on three shifts, it was still paying setup time. The company's attempt to get this costly practice eliminated constituted, in the company's view, productivity bargaining.

Productivity bargaining is far more complex and difficult than it sounds, however. Not only do the unions or workers who are directly involved often resist the company's initiatives, but additional burdens are placed on management. Companies are required to study their production processes, learn where inefficiencies lie, and determine which improvements would be most beneficial. And even when a good case for change can be made, it too often takes the crises of a threat of layoffs or shutdowns to get unions to agree to necessary improvements in efficiency.[26]

When productivity bargaining does proceed, it has further pitfalls. First, managements often give away too much. Productivity improvements result from capital expenditures, training expenditures, and similar factors as much as from concessions made by labor. If a disproportionate part of the savings gained from productivity improvements is obtained by labor, the company may experience financial difficulties. It is often difficult to iden-

[25]United Kingdom, National Board for Prices and Income, Report No. 23, *Productivity and Pay during the Period of Severe Restraint*, December 1966, and Report No. 36, *Productivity Agreements*, June 1967.

[26]Robert B. McKersie and L. C. Hunter, eds., *Pay, Productivity and Collective Bargaining* (London: Macmillan, 1973). Also, Lincoln Fairley, *Facing Mechanization: The West Coast Longshore Plan* (Los Angeles: University of California Institute of Industrial Relations, 1979).

tify the sources of productivity improvements and in what proportion they occur. Second, when one group of workers in a plant or industry gets additional money because it relinquished certain conditions, others may demand the same money without giving up anything. And often these other groups are prepared to strike. Thus, the actual cost to the company of obtaining a concession may be much higher, because of secondary increases, than it had first appeared to be. In fact, workers often bitterly resent seeing other workers receive financial benefits for giving up uneconomic practices. They see this process as one in which the company rewards those who have slowed it up in the past. For these reasons, productivity bargaining is complex and hazardous and more often involves small gains than large breakthroughs.

This conclusion is supported by the most detailed study of productivity bargaining abroad. In 1960 the Esso refinery at Fawley in Great Britain began a closely watched effort in productivity bargaining that was publicized world-wide and influenced efforts in America. But 30 years later a researcher has concluded that the Fawley effort was largely a failure. Why? Because, in the researcher's view, of inconsistent management objectives and their allure to pursue a clearly defined strategy in the matter. At the heart of the matter was management's inability to decide whether it wanted to retain tight control over employees in the refinery, or was prepared to give greater discretion to employees and take actions to increase their commitment to the firm.[27]

Conflict Resolution: Labor-Management Problem Solving

Instead of relying on the collective bargaining process to improve productivity, many companies and unions in the 1980s have turned to a third approach, one involving joint problem solving (see Figure 21-1). The figure shows problems being addressed in three different fashions: traditional bargaining on the left; by management unilaterally in the center; and by a joint problem solving team on the right. In this approach, a joint labor-management committee meets to try to improve operations.

An example will help to make clear how the joint problem-solving approach works.[28]

An experience at the Xerox Corporation provides a clear example of the use of labor-management cooperation to improve organizational performance and save jobs. In 1981 Xerox conducted a study that indicated that some of the company's products were not competitive in the international marketplace. Xerox determined that it could save $3.2 million by subcontracting certain

[27]Bruce W. Ahlstrand, *The Quest for Productivity* (Cambridge: Cambridge University Press, 1990).
[28]John Belcher, Jr., "The Role of Unions in Productivity Management," *Personnel*, 65:1, January 1988, pp. 57–58.

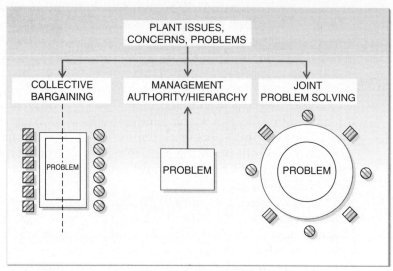

FIGURE 21-3   The three-pronged problem-solving process in unionized organizations. *(Source: From John Belcher, Jr., "The Role of Unions in Productivity Management," Personnel 65:1, January 1988, p. 57.)*

component parts that were then being manufactured in-house. The savings, which were considered vital to reestablishing the company's competitive position, would be realized by closing down an entire department and laying off 180 employees.

In an effort to avert this major loss of jobs, the Amalgamated Clothing and Textile Workers Union asked management to establish a joint union-management study team to investigate ways to improve efficiency in the affected department. Although management was initially reluctant because it believed only labor cost reductions could make this department competitive again, it nonetheless agreed to try the cooperative strategy.

The study team, which consisted of six hourly and two management employees, was given 6 months to develop its recommendations. Team members received specialized training and pursued their task on a full-time basis. They were given the freedom to explore any activities that might result in cost reduction.

An executive labor-management policy committee was formed to support this effort. This group consisted of top union and company executives and had ultimate responsibility for approving the study team's recommendations.

Through a variety of means—soliciting suggestions from employees, conducting informal discussions, and visiting other companies—the study team identified 40 possible improvement projects, 9 of which were ultimately selected for in-depth investigation: (1) improved production equipment, (2) changes in work flow, (3) changes in work responsibility, (4) methods for reducing scrap, (5) improved work-order reporting procedures, (6) improved computer usage, (7) stabilization of the employee population, (8) production control and overhead adjustments, and (9) reduced occupancy costs, such as floor space and utilities.

At the end of 6 months, the study team presented proposals that would result in a total savings of $3.7 million. The proposed changes were significant, including the redesign of the department's physical layout, the expansion of employee responsibilities, reductions in overhead, and the creation of self-managing work groups.

Many of the changes, which the joint policy committee implemented over an 8-month period, flew in the face of traditional union and management prerogatives. Such changes probably could not have been made without the collaborative spirit that grew out of the joint labor-management process.

In this experience labor and management joined to push productivity ahead. In others, the company proposes to introduce technological change, then works with the union to make the process as effective and humane as possible. Technological change is not viewed as a once-and-for-all thing, but as a series of steps. The three major steps are

- The moment of development when decisions are made about the design and configuration of the new technology
- The moment of resource allocation when choices are made about where the new technology is to go and who is to operate it
- The moment of deployment when the new equipment is actually installed and put into operation.[29]

Traditionally unions have found out about new technology only at the last moment, and bitter disputes have erupted because there was little room for adjustment by the company that late in the total process. By involving unions earlier in the process, many problems can be anticipated and corrected before actual deployment occurs.

Conflict Resolution: Concession Bargaining

A widespread response to the difficult economic times of the 1980s and early 1990s was the growth of concession bargaining. Historically, in good economic times, unions have come away from the bargaining table with higher wages, better benefits, more or better work rules or rights under the contract. A concession bargain is one where the new collective bargaining contract provides less than before: fewer rules and benefits, less money. Although unions and the employees they represent are not, of course, pleased with a concession contract, some see it as a necessary response to the long-term economic conditions of an industry or the financial weakness of a given plant or company. But concession contracts are ratified by the membership only when a majority is convinced that they will save jobs or the company and/or provide employment security in the long run. Some companies have demanded concessions from employees where they were

---

[29]Robert J. Thomas, "Technological Choice and Union-Management Cooperation," *Industrial Relations*, 30:2, Spring 1991, pp. 167–191.

not clearly needed. In other words, some companies "cried wolf." This made the task of developing labor-management cooperation to deal constructively with the common problems faced by management and labor more difficult.[30]

According to a survey on concession bargaining, unions have most frequently traded off immediate wage increases or benefits for more employment security. This is a change from the historic union position that has been to push relentlessly for job security—guarantees for specific jobs, rather than employment security—guarantees for overall employment levels. Table 21-2 shows that unions are willing in some instances to trade off specific jobs for employment security on behalf of their members. They are also more willing than in the past to grant more flexibility in work rules governing the workplace in job assignments, hours of work, seniority, wages, incentive pay and teamwork, in exchange for employment guarantees.[31] What casual factors lay beneath the concession movement? Each industry, company, plant, and union has a unique tale, but there are two underlying influences. First, unions had to make concessions where the companies' labor costs had gotten far ahead of competitors'. This is not to say, however, that in all instances in which labor costs were high, the unions made concessions. In some instances they did not, with varying results. Layoffs occurred; plants were closed; some companies went bankrupt; but other companies recovered due to other influences. Labor costs, it must be remembered, are not the only factor affecting a firm's competitiveness.

TABLE 21-2   WHAT UNIONS SOUGHT IN RETURN FOR CONCESSIONS*

	Percentage of situations in which company sought concessions
More job security	46
No-layoff policy	17
Guaranteed number of jobs	17
Earnings protection	17
To represent more employees	23
Role in corporate governance	31
Consultation on investment	8
Changes in bargaining structure	8

*Data derived from interviews with 35 companies.
   Source: Daniel Quinn Mills, "When Employees Make Concessions," *Harvard Business Review,* 61:3, May–June, 1983, pp. 108–109.

[30]For a fuller discussion see D. Quinn Mills, "When Employees Make Concessions," *Harvard Business Review,* 61:3, May–June 1983, pp. 103–113. See also Richard B. Freeman, "In Search of Union Wage Concessions in Standard Data Sets," *Industrial Relations,* 25:2, Spring 1986, pp. 131–158.
[31]"A Work Revolution in U.S. Industry—More Flexible Rules on the Job Are Boosting Productivity," *Business Week,* May 16, 1983, p. 100.

Second, employers were less willing to give pay increases to avoid strikes. Fearing that pay raises would cripple the company, many held firm for concessions and got them.[32]

As the economy strengthened toward the end of the 1980s concession bargaining faded. Yet the experience with concessions was important to many unions and managements in learning how to adjust to changing economic circumstances, and may be of importance again should the economy slow substantially. The recession of 1990-91 was insufficiently severe to cause concession bargaining to reappear on a large scale, but it was common in airlines and in electrical and automotive manufacturing industries hard-hit by recession and/or competition from abroad.

Incentives and Gain-Sharing to Increase Productivity

Pay systems can be designed to reward employees directly for their individual performances.[33] Many companies utilize such systems. These systems depend on a careful delineation of the elements of a job and on the setting of standards for the level of production expected. Records are kept of each worker's daily output, and the workers' rate of pay depends on the amount of work done, measured against the established standard. A minimum rate of pay protects those workers who fail to meet the production standards, whether because of material shortages, machinery breakdown, or simply failure to perform. Ordinarily, however, a worker who repeatedly fails to perform well will be dismissed by the company.

The most carefully systematized incentive programs are run by industrial engineers (professional employees who establish production standards). Basically, an industrial engineer observes workers performing a task and takes measurements of the time they require to complete it. From these measurements, the engineer develops a standard that the average worker is supposed to be able to meet. In one of the more popular systems, one widely used in textiles and apparel manufacturing, the company pays for units of production; the basic unit is a minute of work. A standard of work volume is, therefore, the 60-unit hour. Most production workers can exceed this and therefore earn more money. An incentive system is said to be "loose" if too many employees exceed the standard by too much. Generally a good system should not permit the expected average production volume for an employee to get above 20 percent beyond the standard, that is, beyond a 72-unit hour.

A company's staff of industrial engineers not only does time studies but also sets pay rates and tells the employees about the rates and about changes in the rates. Sometimes the incentive system is so crucial to the

[32]Daniel J. B. Mitchell, "Alternative Explanations of Union Wage Concessions," *California Management Review,* 28:1, Fall 1986, pp. 95–107.
[33]Mitchell Lokiec, *Productivity and Incentives* (Columbia, S.C.: Bobbin Publications, 1977).

profitable operations of the firm that the industrial engineers even administer the payrolls of the company.

An incentive system must be kept up to date if it is to be effective. Changes in materials, machinery, and know-how cause standards to loosen in time. If standards become too loose, an incentive plan may be said to be "demoralized." In a demoralized plan workers meet their production quotas very quickly and have a great deal of leisure time. While such a situation may be comfortable for the workers, it often leads to bankruptcy for the firm.

On the other hand, the attempts of management to keep an incentive system up to date are a constant source of labor relations troubles. Workers often resent time studies when the studies bring technological improvements and the subsequent imposition of tighter production standards. The result is that, while many companies like the idea of using incentives to pay for workers' performance, they are unwilling to accept the problems that keeping an incentive system current entails. In consequence, incentive systems are less common in American industry than the more simple procedure of an hourly rate of pay.

Sometimes incentives apply not only to individuals but also to a group. When a group incentive plan exists, each member of the group receives a certain proportion of the pay allocated to the group as a whole. Group plans that share the gains from productivity improvements with employees are referred to as gain-sharing plans and constitute a particular form of group incentive.

In recent years programs have been developed that are owned by their developers and licensed to companies for use. One such program is Improshare. A recent study of its effectiveness found that it led to significant improvements in productivity—totaling 17.5 percent by the third year, at which time gains began to level off. The smaller the firm, the higher the gains. A sizeable part of the gains were due to reductions in defects—in other words, the gain-sharing plan improved productivity by improving quality.[34]

JOB SECURITY VERSUS EMPLOYMENT SECURITY

Much of the resistance to new technology and productivity improvement which is exhibited by unions and workers is based on the fear that progress will put people out of work. The general president of a large union described his initial experience with productivity improvement:

> I once worked on an assembly line. A guy who worked with me suggested how to do the work faster. The company responded by sending us home without pay for the afternoon since there was no work to be done. No further improvements were suggested.

[34]Roger T. Kaufman, "The Effects of Improshare on Productivity," *Industrial and Labor Relations Review,* 45:2, January 1992, p. 311ff.

As a result, labor and management traditionally have held conflicting views about what increased productivity means. To labor increased productivity means the threat of job loss. To management it means the opportunity to be more successful in the business. In recent contract negotiations there have been attempts to resolve the issue in favor of both. In the auto industry a new, shared approach to productivity change may be developing.

The significance of the loss of a job should not be underestimated. For some people there are other positions readily available, but for most there is the concern that their livelihood is endangered when a job is lost. In consequence, job loss is one of the most stressful occurrences that a person can encounter. It is no wonder that employees and unions are reluctant to embrace changes that can lead to layoffs.[35]

Recently negotiated agreements suggest that when both sides can begin to think of employment security (guarantees of employment at a company) rather than job security (security in a specific, detailed job defined by a job description or history), progress can be made toward meeting the concerns of both parties in this controversial area.

In recent agreements between the United Auto Workers and the auto companies, the union achieved its goal of a guaranteed employment level at many plants (subject only to a major business downturn) and in return agreed to improve productivity at the plants. Unfortunately, a continued downturn in business has kept the job security provisions of the agreements from being effective. Companies have continued to close plants and layoff workers.

In 1992 private hospitals and nursing homes of New York City and the health-care employees union (Local 1099) negotiated a contract that gives a laid-off worker first rights to a comparable opening at any facility covered by the contract and a year of supplemental unemployment benefits when the employee is seeking a new job or being retrained. Some 65,000 employees are covered by the program.[36]

Innovative employment security provisions have also been agreed to in the airline industry and in communications. The recasting of the problem from job security to employment security enabled labor and management to search together, not as adversaries but as joint problem solvers, for solutions to one of the major problems affecting the industry.

Is employment security for workers a positive motivator to better performance? The current evidence is yes. The few companies that provide employment security say that it helps workers to lay aside fears of unemployment and get on with the job.[37] Employees are more willing to offer

---

[35]Nick Kates, Barrie S. Greiff and Duane Q. Hagen, *The Psychosocial Impact of Job Loss* (Washington, D.C.: American Psychiatric Press, 1990).

[36]Sam Roberts, "Private Hospitals . . . ," *New York Times,* June 13, 1992, p. 1ff.

[37]D. Quinn Mills, *The IBM Lesson* (New York: Times Books, 1988). Also see Daniel Forbes, "The No-Layoff Payoff," *Dun's Business Month,* July 1985, pp. 64–66.

suggestions to improve efficiency and to adopt new methods of doing work.

But isn't job insecurity a motivator also? The evidence is no. A study of workers in a single plant after a layoff showed that the productivity of those who remained did not rise. If insecurity were a motivator, the survivors of a layoff would be expected to perform better.[38]

In recent years the risk of losing one's job seems to have risen as more and more firms make layoffs of employees at all levels and in most occupations. But it should be recognized that in a longer-term perspective, the proportion of the labor force who have jobs with a single employer which last twenty years or more has risen substantially (roughly doubling since the end of the last century).[39]

CHAPTER SUMMARY

The efficiency of labor is referred to as productivity and can be measured in terms of output per work hour. However, productivity depends on a great many factors besides human effort, and there are important differences in conceptions of what productivity measures. Managers tend to think of productivity in terms of employees working harder. Some economists have been interested in understanding what factors could improve productivity. These factors include increased capital investment, increased skill and education of the work force, and better methods of doing jobs.

Managers and the public feel that increased productivity should be encouraged. Unions and workers are more ambivalent. They fear loss of jobs and the demand for greater efforts. Both unionized and nonunionized workers will sometimes act together to oppose technological changes and to set a slower pace of work or a lower level of production than the company desires. Employees, in response, tighten discipline, change production, and try persuasion. Often, both management and the unions lack knowledge of the day-to-day processes in the workplace and are pessimistic about changing inefficient practices that are ingrained in the institution. Improved productivity demands a substantial effort and a comprehensive plan rather than a simple solution. Strikes over productivity issues have been lengthy and bitter. In some industries, employers have chosen to close inefficient plants rather than fight. Employers may use the NLRB or the courts to challenge work practices that inhibit productivity. However, because the law does not prohibit nonproductive practices per se, the use of litigation as a method of reducing nonproductive practices is of limited value.

[38]Casey Ichniowski, *The Economic Performance of Survivors after Layoffs: A Plant-Level Study,* Working Paper No. 1807 (Cambridge: National Bureau of Economic Research, 1986).
[39]Susan B. Carter, "The Changing Importance of Lifetime Jobs, 1892–1978," *Industrial Relations,* 27:3, Fall 1988, p. 287ff.

But there are signs that labor and management are more willing than they have been in the past to seek solutions together over the issues of productivity and its relationship to employment security. Many see a more constructive and problem-solving approach between management and labor that is to the advantage of both.

QUESTIONS FOR THOUGHT AND DISCUSSION

1. What is quality? What is productivity? How are they related?
2. Why are there labor-management conflicts over productivity? How can such conflicts be minimized? How can they be resolved when they occur?
3. Should pay be related to performance? What factors affect the success or failure of an incentive system? Why? What are some of the disadvantages of individual incentive systems?
4. Can productivity be increased? How? Do speedups work? What is the difference between efficient production and a speedup?
5. Should productivity be increased? Consider this question from the point of view of management, the unions, and the public in general.
6. Why does management often choose to move a plant rather than fight over issues of productivity? Why are managers sometimes afraid to raise issues of work productivity?
7. Why is productivity bargaining so complex and difficult?
8. What is featherbedding and what are some of its various forms? Can you propose any reasonable methods for preventing the proliferation of such noneconomical work practices as make-work rules, restrictions on the introduction of labor-saving technology, and unnecessary jurisdictional restrictions on work assignments? Your proposals should carefully consider the needs of both management and the union.
9. What is the difference between job security and employment security? What is necessary for people to have employment security?

SELECTED READING

Bluestone, Barry, and Irving Bluestone, *Negotiating the Future: A Labor Perspective on American Business* (New York: Basic Books, 1992).

Bluestone, Barry, and Bennett Harrison, *The Deindustrialization of America: Plant Closings, Community Abandonment, and the Dismantling of Basic Industry* (New York: Basic Books, 1982).

Garson, G. David, and M. P. Smith, eds., *Organizational Democracy: Participation and Self-Management* (Beverly Hills, Calif.: Sage, 1976).

McKersie, Robert B., and L. C. Hunter, eds., *Pay, Productivity and Collective Bargaining* (New York: St. Martin's Press, 1973).

Mills, D. Quinn, *The IBM Lesson* (New York: Times Books, 1988).

Reich, Robert, *The Work of Nations: Preparing Ourselves for 21st Century Capitalism* (New York: Knopf, 1991).

Sheppard, L. Stewart, and Donald C. Carroll, eds., *Working in the Twenty-First Century* (New York: Wiley, 1980).

Somers, Gerald G., et al., *Collective Bargaining and Productivity* (Madison, Wis.: Industrial Relations Research Association, 1975).

AN ASSESSMENT
OF LABOR-MANAGEMENT
RELATIONS

Both the use of power by managers and unions and the establishment of rights to replace power as a means for the resolution of disputes in labor-management relations have consequences for the broader society in which we live. Collective bargaining contributes to industrial peace by channeling workers' discontent into peaceful paths through which improvements may be made. But in some instances collective bargaining seems to have established levels of compensation and conditions of work that give American companies very high costs. The result is the loss of production jobs because consumers are buying cheaper imported goods, and continuing inflation despite a sluggish economy.

CHAPTER 22

THE CONSEQUENCES OF COLLECTIVE BARGAINING

The functions of unions and of collective bargaining include the representation of employees vis-à-vis management and the economic betterment of employees. Each union does its best to accomplish these functions. What are the consequences of these efforts? What is the impact of collective bargaining on management? And what is the impact of collective bargaining on the economy?

These are general questions. They are not the same as asking, for example, about the impact of collective bargaining on a particular company or the impact on the economy of collective bargaining in a particular industry. The answers to the general questions may not be the same as the answers to the particular questions. For example, unions may be said to have only limited impact on our economy as a whole, but a particular union may have had considerable impact on a particular company or industry. What is true of a particular situation may or may not have general validity.

IMPACT OF COLLECTIVE BARGAINING ON INDIVIDUALS

In most instances union members receive more compensation than people who do not belong to unions. Undoubtedly the firms that employ union labor tend to be larger than those that do not and might pay higher salaries even if their employees were not unionized. Even as the proportion of the labor force that is unionized has declined, the earnings advantage for union workers has continued. In many industries even big nonunion firms do not on balance pay as much as unionized ones. It appears conclusive that unionization and collective bargaining contribute to higher earnings for workers.

The nonfinancial impact of unions has also been explored in previous chapters. Certainly unions offer protection for employees against arbitrary acts of management and provide seniority rights that most nonunion employees receive in lesser degree, if at all. Finally, union firms generally provide more and better benefits, including health insurance and pensions.

IMPACT OF COLLECTIVE BARGAINING ON MANAGEMENT

Collective bargaining affects management in many ways. Some effects are significant; some are not. Collective bargaining causes management to follow a different procedure in its dealings with its employees. Instead of unilateral determinations, management must meet and bargain with the union about what changes are to be made in the workplace. But collective bargaining affects management in more ways than this. Some of the most important impacts that collective bargaining has on management are described below.

1. *Collective bargaining compels management to set long-term corporate strategies regarding employees and employment practices.* The failure to adopt consistent strategies with respect to employment practices opens management to claims from a union for the most favorable treatment in all respects. Management inconsistencies may be pointed out by the union and are often resolved in the union's favor.

For example, a company that asserts the right to discharge employees for failure to perform work satisfactorily but keeps performance records about some employees and not others is likely to be prevented by the union from making any discharges at all for performance reasons. If the company discharges an employee without performance records, the union may argue that the discharge is unmerited, since poor performance cannot be proved. After all, the union may say, the company keeps performance records for some employees, and it could have done the same for this person it now wishes to discharge. An arbitrator may be likely to agree. If the company wishes to discharge a person about whom it has records for poor performance, the union may object that the discharge is discriminatory. After all, the union might argue, records are not kept for all employees. Apparently the company simply prepared documentation because it wanted to get rid of this particular employee. How is the union, or the employee, or the arbitrator to know if the discharged employee's work performance is actually poor, since there are no records for other employees by which to make a comparison? It may be inferred, the union might say, that the company has some unspoken motive for discharging the employee and that poor work performance is a contrived excuse for discharge. An arbitrator is again likely to agree.

To preserve its capacity to discharge for poor performance when a union is present, a company will probably feel compelled to adopt a consistent policy of maintaining performance records on all employees.[1] (It should be noted that consistency in employee practices is good personnel policy in any company, unionized or not. But the presence of a union tends to give management an extra, and significant, incentive for consistency and carefully thought out policies.)

Most large American corporations that deal with unions feel that to be successful they must establish an industrial relations policy and a specialized, strong, and effective industrial relations staff. One purpose of such a policy and staff is to retain for management as much discretion and initiative as possible in its dealings with the union. General Motors Corporation offers an example of top management in a very large concern that has a clear perception of the long-run importance of the issues involved in labor relations policies. General Motors saw that the unions threatened the freedom of management to run the company's manufacturing and assembly plants and that this freedom would be gradually rubbed away unless the company was willing, if necessary, to fight to protect it. Top management determined which issues it felt it might control and then made it clear to the union and to its line managers that the company was prepared at any time to take strikes over certain matters that top management regarded as essential to effective operation of the company.[2]

2. *Collective bargaining tends to require management to become aware of the day-to-day problems in the operation of the business.* In the past, prior to the advent of collective bargaining, senior management in many companies tended to concentrate on such matters as financial performance, sales, mergers, and organizations, to the exclusion of matters dealing with employees. Working conditions, safety matters, work rules, make-work practices, and similar matters were left to subordinate management. With the advent of unions, however, senior management was required to see that there were responsible corporate officers assigned to pay attention to these matters, so that they would not become the cause of disputes with the union or the source of growing inefficiency in the company.

3. *Collective bargaining establishes a "common law of the shop," which subjects management actions to scrutiny by third parties.* Management is no longer free to take action or alter rules as it desires. A framework of rules is established by which management must act and which it cannot unilaterally alter. And a grievance procedure is set up to protect workers' rights.

4. *Collective bargaining permits management, in some instances, to get more employee satisfaction for its money.* The union provides a mechanism by which employees can make known their preferences with respect to the

[1]Thomas R. Knight, "The Impact of Arbitration on the Administration of Disciplinary Policies," *The Arbitration Journal*, 39:1, March 1984, pp. 43–56. See also Randall W. Eberts, "How Unions Affect Management Decisions: Evidence from Public Schools," *Journal of Labor Research*, 4:3, Summer 1983, pp. 239–247.

[2]Sumner H. Slichter, James Healy, and E. Robert Livernash, *The Impact of Collective Bargaining on Management* (Washington, D.C.: Brookings Institution, 1960).

form, content, and amount of compensation. Thus, management can expect to see its compensation dollar divided up in a way that makes the most sense to its employees and thereby enhance employee satisfaction. Collective bargaining has been the source of most innovations in compensation practices, including virtually all types of benefits. Nonunion employees have copied many or most of these compensation practices, but it is unlikely that they would have developed to any substantial extent in the absence of collective bargaining.

On balance, unionized employees receive higher levels of benefits and devote a larger proportion of total compensation to benefits than do nonunion employees. A study of data for 1977 found that unionized employees received benefits costing 24.2 percent of their total compensation, and nonunion employees received benefits costing 13.1 percent of total compensation. Health-care benefits for unionized employees were double those for nonunionized employees, both in dollar terms and as a percentage of total compensation. Pension benefits for unionized employees were three times as generous in dollars and as a percentage of total compensation for unionized employees.[3] These data indicate that unions have induced management to devote larger resources to benefits than in the nonunion situation. Not only does unionism tend to raise the share of compensation devoted to benefits, particularly to pensions, vacation pay, and life, accident, and health insurance, but it also appears that where management negotiates with a union that represents production workers, it tends to extend the union's preference for high benefits to nonunion, nonproduction workers as well.[4]

Unions also help their members to be more knowledgeable than nonunion employees about the importance of benefits and more conscious of the level and value of the benefits they receive. It appears that unions are likely to cause firms to establish pension programs, but they do not cause pension benefits to be higher for union employees than for nonunion employees who have pension programs.[5] Conversely, unions do not cause employers to be more likely to provide health insurance for union workers than for nonunion workers, but they do cause the health benefits provided to be better for union workers than for nonunion workers.[6]

5. *Collective bargaining permits management to better meet the needs of its employees without having to feel naively altruistic or disloyal to the princi-*

---

[3]John A. Zalusky, quoted in Oscar A. Ornati, "The Impact of Collective Bargaining on Employee Benefits," in R. F. Foulkes, ed., *Employee Benefit Handbook* (Boston: Warren, Gorham, and Lamont, 1982). See also Richard B. Freeman, "The Effect of Trade Unionism on Fringe Benefits" (National Bureau of Economic Research, Working Paper No. 292, October 1978).

[4]Richard B. Freeman, "The Effect of Unionism on Fringe Benefits," *Industrial and Labor Relations Review*, 34:4, July 1981, p. 489.

[5]Duane E. Leigh, "The Effect of Unionism on Workers' Valuation of Future Pension Benefits," *Industrial and Labor Relations Review*, 34:4, July 1981, p. 510.

[6]Louis F. Rossiter and Amy K. Taylor, "Union Effects on the Provision of Health Insurance," *Industrial Relations*, 21:2, Spring 1982, pp. 167–177.

ples of cost control. It seems unfortunate that many managers should feel reluctant to meet the needs of employees because of the fear that they will appear naively softhearted or that their own supervisors will look with disfavor on their actions. But, though unfortunate, it is an important factor in the behavior of managers. This is so even if meeting employees' needs can be argued to be long-run good business. As a philosopher has remarked, "It is folly to expect people to see their own best interests."

Collective bargaining provides a mechanism by which managers may sometimes do what they would like to do but cannot, because of constraints upon them. Unions serve as advocates of the employees and are able to employ economic force to back their demands. Many a manager finds it convenient to be, or appear to be, compelled to accede to employee demands. Managers often believe that concessions made to employees are for the good of the company and are glad that collective bargaining offers an occasion to take such action.

Surveys show that there are substantial differences in personnel practices between union and nonunion firms, and that they're not limited to compensation (though this is the aspect we discussed primarily, see Chapter 18). When a union organizes a firm, it causes wages to increase only slightly above the level of nonunion firms in the industry, but it substantially alters personnel practices, creating grievance systems, greater seniority protection, and job posting and bidding.[7]

Some of the differences in personnel practices that accompany unions favor employees, including grievance procedures, employee involvement programs, counseling programs and eye care insurance. Others did not, including more use of two-tier pay systems, and drug, aptitude, and physical testing.[8] Thus, it is not merely a matter of unions extracting better conditions from management. For example, because grievance systems and arbitration are widespread in the union sector but not in the nonunion sector, it is more difficult for a company to discharge a union-represented employee. In consequence, companies are more careful about whom they hire; hence, the much more common use of drug and aptitude testing in the union sector. But care in hiring is also valuable to employees, who may not want to have to work with people with drug problems or poor aptitude for the work. To the degree that this is the case, unionization permits managers to do what employees would like to have done.

6. *Collective bargaining makes changes more difficult to achieve at the workplace.* By establishing formal rules and causing informal practices to become precedent makers, collective bargaining tends to make production processes more rigid. This is the greatest complaint managers have about

---

[7]Richard B. Freeman and Morris M. Kleiner, "The Impact of New Unionization on Wages and Working Conditions," *Journal of Labor Economics*, 8:1, 1990, p. S8ff.

[8]David Lewin et. al., *Human Resource Policies and Practices in American Firms* (Washington, D.C.: U.S. Government Printing Office, 1989).

collective bargaining and unions. It is a more important matter than unions' raising wage levels. Managers often say, "I don't mind high wages as long as we get the productivity." Or they say, "High wages are all right; what really gripes me is the low productivity."

7. *Collective bargaining reduces the profitability of firms and may alter investment behavior.* Economic studies in the early 1980s concluded that in capital-intensive and highly concentrated (i.e., few companies) industries, unionism reduces profitability substantially—the collective bargaining process allows unionized employees to obtain much higher wages and benefits than nonunionized employees would be likely to obtain. However, in less concentrated (i.e., more companies) and more competitive industries, unionism appears to have little impact on the profitability of firms.[9] In moderately concentrated industries where nonunion and unionized firms compete against one another, unionized firms appear to earn substantially lower profits than nonunion firms. When firms lose a union election, on average there is a 3.8 percent loss of equity value in the stock market, suggesting, say the authors of the study from which this estimate is taken, that unions have a negative impact on profitability.[10] A study of Japanese companies for the year 1987 reached similar conclusions: that unionization substantially reduced both productivity and profitability in companies.[11]

Subsequent studies did not dispute the negative impact of unions on profits, but did challenge the association of union impact with concentrated industries. Instead, unions had the greatest impact when a company had a large market share, lots of research and development, and was insulated from foreign competition.[12] Another study showed that an unexpected change in collectively bargained labor costs reduced the value of shares in the firm by a corresponding amount. This suggests that collective bargaining maximizes the sum of the shareholder's and members wealth, and that increases in the compensation of employees comes at the expense of shareholders.[13]

There is an unfortunate consequence of the negative impact of unions on the profitability of firms and the economic welfare of shareholders: firms don't invest as much as they would otherwise. Using survey data on labor union representation at the firm level, Barry T. Hirsch investigated union-nonunion differences in investment activity among 706 U.S. compa-

[9]Richard B. Freeman, *Unionism, Price-Cost Margins and the Return to Capital,* Working Paper No. 1164 (Cambridge, Mass.: National Bureau of Economic Research, December 1983).

[10]Kim B. Clark, "Unionization and Firm Performance," *American Economic Review,* 74:5, December 1984, pp. 893–919; and Richard S. Ruback and Martin B. Zimmerman, "Unionization and Profitability," *Journal of Political Economy,* 92:6, 1984, p. 312ff.

[11]Giorgio Brunello, "The Effect of Unions on Firm Performance in Japanese Manufacturing," *Industrial and Labor Relations Review,* 45, 3, April 1992, p. 471ff.

[12]Barry T. Hirsch and Robert A. Connolly, "Do Unions Capture Monopoly Profits?" *Industrial and Labor Relations Review,* 41:1, October 1987, p. 118ff.

[13]John M. Abowd, "The Effect of Wage Bargains on the Stock Market Value of the Firm, *American Economic Review,* 79:4, 1989, p. 774ff.

nies during the 1970s. Firm level collective bargaining is associated with 20 percent lower physical capital and R&D investment, even after standardization for firm and industry characteristics (i.e.,unionized firms in the same industry did much less capital and R&D investment than did nonunionized firms). The degree of the negative impact of unions on investment varies across industry.[14]

Because of the negative impact of unions on profitability and share prices, managers have an incentive to try to avoid unionization. But if unions cannot be avoided, the return to capital can be increased by maintaining inefficient plants in production and by minimizing new investment. While protecting profitability to a degree, this strategy is costly to firms because it decreases growth and innovation.[15] Recent research underlies these conclusions about union effects on profitability and resultant disincentives to make investments. The implications of these findings are that American unions by pursuing higher wages and benefits, and American managers by limiting investment to protect short-term profitability, may have together undermined the leadership position of many American firms and industries in the international marketplace.

But the impact of the unions in the public sector appears to be quite different. A study of the impact of municipal unions on local governments shows that collective bargaining increased expenditures in the departments covered by a union contract, but had not affect on cities total expenditures, revenues or property taxes.[16] That is, collective bargaining redistributed city expenses to those departments that were unionized at the expense of those that were not, but did nothing else.

IMPACT OF COLLECTIVE BARGAINING ON THE ECONOMY

The impact of collective bargaining on management is easier to discern than the impact of collective bargaining on the economy. This is because many factors in the economy affect each other, and causality is difficult to identify. For example, the behavior patterns of unionized and nonunion firms are often so closely related that it is hard to identify which is responsible for specific events.

On Productivity

Unions are widely believed by American management to restrict efficient work practices and thereby to contribute to low productivity. Managers generally believe that they can get greater efficiency out of their plants and can more easily make money-saving changes in production methods in the

---

[14]Barry T. Hirsch, "Firm Investment Behavior and Collective Bargaining Strategy," *Industrial Relations*, 31:1, Winter 1992, p. 95.

[15]Carliss Baldwin, "Productivity and Labor Unions," *Journal of Business*, 56:2, April 1983, pp. 155–185. See also Pankaj Tandon, "Internal Bargaining, Labor Contracts, and a Marshallian Theory of the Firm," *American Economic Review*, 74:3, June 1984, pp. 381–393.

absence of unions. This is a major reason for the continuing strong opposition of American management to unionization. In Europe and Japan, where employers are often less adverse to unionization of their employees, unions and collective bargaining are far less concerned with on-the-job practices and therefore appear to place fewer restrictions on management's operation of the workplace.

This is a very important matter. Defenders of unions and collective bargaining in this country ordinarily point to two results of collective bargaining as justification for it: the protection afforded individual employees against the arbitrary actions of management and the improved economic benefits that unions often obtain for the people they represent. Rarely do defenders of unions and collective bargaining voice support for union jurisdictional claims and disputes or for certain work rules and restrictions on technological innovation. These are seen as unfortunate but understandable and probably inevitable accompaniments of unionization.[17]

On the other hand, many who oppose unionization, do not do so because of opposition to grievance procedures or high wages, but rather because of their belief that unions insist on inefficient production processes.[18] How valid are these beliefs of managers?

There have been only a few careful statistical inquiries into the impact of unions on productivity. Table 22-1 summarizes several of these studies. A broad study of all major manufacturing industries indicated a productivity advantage for unionized firms of 20 to 25 percent. Studies of the wooden household furniture and cement industries indicated productivity advantages for unionized firms of 6 to 15 percent. Two studies of the bituminous coal industry conducted about 10 years apart gave strikingly different results. In 1965, unionized underground mines were 25 to 30 percent more productive than their nonunionized counterparts. By 1975, virtually the opposite was true. Finally, a study of construction concluded that apprenticeship training and job referral systems enhance productivity in union construction, while jurisdictional disputes and restrictive work rules lower it. On balance, union construction workers were found to be more productive than nonunion workers.[19]

Among these studies, possibly the most complete was that conducted by Kim Clark on the cement industry. Clark was able to standardize his estimates of worker productivity for the size of plants, hours of work, location of plants, capacity of plants, and age and capacity of individual kilns in the

[17]Richard P. Maher, "Union Contract Restrictions on Productivity," *Labor Law Journal*, 34:5, May 1983, pp. 303–310.

[18]Barry T. Hirsch and Albert N. Link, "Unions, Productivity, and Productivity Growth," *Journal of Labor Research*, 5:1, Winter 1984, pp. 29–37. See also William E. Fruhan, Jr., "Management, Labor and the Golden Goose," *Harvard Business Review*, 63:5, September–October, 1985, pp. 131–141.

[19]Steven G. Allen, "Unionized Construction Workers Are More Productive," *Quarterly Journal of Economics*, 99:2, May 1984, pp. 251–274. See also Allen, "Can Union Labor Ever Cost Less?" *Quarterly Journal of Economics*, 102:2, May 1987, pp. 347–373.

TABLE 22-1   ESTIMATES OF THE IMPACT OF UNIONISM ON PRODUCTIVITY

Setting	Estimated increase or decrease in output per worker due to unionism (%)
All two-digit standard industrial classification (SIC) manufacturing industries	20 to 25
Wooden household furniture	15
Cement	6 to 8
Underground bituminous coal	−20 to −25

Source: Richard B. Freeman and James L. Medoff. "The Two Faces of Unionism," *The Public Interest,* 57, Fall 1979, p. 80.

plants. When these factors were accounted for, the study indicated that unionized plants were 6 to 8 percent more productive than nonunionized plants (as Table 22-1 indicates). Clark was also able to investigate the factors which caused the unionized plants to be more productive. In general, the higher wages and better working conditions in unionized plants did attract a better-quality work force, but the contribution of this factor to the productivity advantage of the unionized plants was small (in the neighborhood of 1 to 2 percent of the 6 to 8 percent union advantage). The changes in managerial practices brought about by unionization were identified by Clark as of substantial significance and were estimated to be a major contributor to the union productivity advantage.[20]

A study of 31 plants of a large multinational firm for the period 1975 to 1982 found that unionization increased the capital-labor ratio and improved management performance, but it also raised the absenteeism rate. A net positive effect on productivity remained even when these channels of union influence were controlled for, a result that may reflect an improved labor relations climate or improved labor quality associated with unionization.[21]

Finally, in the study of manufacturing industries listed in Table 22-1, researchers found a productivity advantage for unionized firms but also found that this productivity advantage was reflected in a wage advantage of approximately equal magnitude, so that the labor costs in production of union and nonunion establishments were approximately identical.[22] In the 1980s Steven G. Allen studied productivity in union and nonunion construction. On privately owned construction projects union productivity was higher, but on publicly owned projects unions were less productive.[23]

[20]Kim B. Clark, "The Impact of Unionization on Productivity: A Case Study," *Industrial and Labor Relations Review,* 33:4, July 1980, pp. 451–469.

[21]Robert N. Mefford, "The Effect of Unions on Productivity in a Multinational Manufacturing Firm," *Industrial and Labor Relations Review,* 40:1, October 1986, p. 105ff.

[22]Charles Brown and James L. Medoff, "Trade Unions in the Production Process," *Journal of Political Economy,* 86:3, 1978, pp. 355–378.

[23]Steven G. Allen, "Unionized Construction Workers Are More Productive," *Quarterly Journal of Economics,* 99:2, May 1984, pp. 251–274. See also Allen, "Unionization and Productivity in Office Building and School Construction," *Industrial and Labor Relations Review,* 39:2, January 1986, p. 187ff.

Other studies showed that unions had little impact on productivity growth in manufacturing but were associated with slower productivity growth in construction.[24] Also, it appears that in downturns both unionized and nonunionized companies keep more employees than they really need, so that when sales resume, production increases fast without additional labor and productivity expands rapidly.[25] Finally, a study of grievance activity by unions demonstrated that higher grievance activity is often a result of management efforts to increase productivity, and that increased grievances have a slight negative impact on productivity.[26]

One unusually broad study of the auto industry found that from 1959 to 1976 "worker attitudes negatively influenced productivity growth and unit costs, resulting from the failure of both management and labor to create a satisfactory work environment." Another showed no influence of unions on productivity in the auto parts industry.[27] All in all, these results are somewhat difficult to reconcile with the strongly held view in management, and also, it would seem, in the general public, that unions do not contribute to increased productivity, but rather tend to reduce productivity. It is possible that unions are able to organize the more productive plants and also, as Clark argued, are able to spur management to greater effort to make unionized plants more productive in order to offset higher labor costs that often accompany unionization.

On American Competitiveness

Many American companies have not done well in recent years against foreign competitors. Are unions to blame?

The few studies that exist say no, but the issue is far from settled. A recent significant study concluded that heavily unionized industries had not lost more to imports or exported less than less unionized industries.[28] Even the majority of top corporate officials say that higher wages in the United States are not a key factor interfering with competitiveness. But working conditions may be.[29] As we have seen, the risk of unionization causes firms to pay higher wages and adopt other policies that they might

[24]Steven G. Allen, "Productivity Levels and Productivity Change under Unionism," North Carolina State University, draft, March 1986.

[25]Jun A. Fay and James L. Medoff, "Labor and Output over the Business Cycle," *American Economic Review*, 75:5, September 1985, pp. 638–655.

[26]Casey Ichniowski, "The Effects of Grievance Activity on Productivity," *Industrial and Labor Relations Review*, 40:1, October 1986, pp. 75–89.

[27]J. R. Norsworthy and Craig A. Zabala, "Worker Attitudes, Worker Behavior and Productivity in the U.S. Automobile Industry," *Industrial and Labor Relations Review*, 38:4, July 1985, p. 544ff; and Robert S. and Roger T. Kaufman, "Union Effects on Productivity," *Journal of Labor Research*, 8:4, Fall 1987, p. 79.

[28]Thomas Karier, "Unions and the U.S. Comparative Advantage," *Industrial Relations*, 30:1, Winter 1991, p. 1ff.

[29]"Higher Wages Not a Major Factor in Inhibiting American Competitiveness," Bureau of National Affairs, *Daily Labor Report*, No. 14, June 27, 1990, pp. A-14–A-15.

not in absence of unions generally, so that a comparison of union and nonunion firms may not fully adjust for the impact of unions. Even if we were to accept the conclusion that on the whole unions have not damaged American competitiveness, there are still industries in which the unfortunate impact of collective bargaining is clear. A careful study of the steel industry faults both management and union for its decline.[30]

On Wages

Among all major demographic groups in the American labor force, union members earn more than persons not represented by unions, as we saw previously. What is the effect of unions on the earnings of nonunion workers?

It is well recognized that unions, in addition to directly affecting their members' wages, may have an indirect effect on the earnings of nonunion workers also. There are two ways by which this might occur, and they are in some senses opposites of each other. On the one hand, unions may cause employers of nonunion labor to raise wage rates in order to avoid the possibility of unionization. In this way, the union sector of the economy may be said to be a wage leader, or to set a pattern of wage increases for the nonunion sector to follow. Because the mechanism through which pattern following by nonunion employers is thought to operate is one of defensive action against the possibility of union organization, this potential effect of unions on the earnings of nonunion workers may be described as a "threat effect."

On the other hand, unions may affect the pay of nonunion workers by limiting the jobs available in the union sector (as a result of high wage levels) and thereby forcing many workers into the nonunion sector. Faced with a large supply of labor, nonunion employers may be able to lower wage rates and yet be able to attract all the labor they need. In effect, the unions' efforts to raise wages in the union sector cause the supply curve of labor to shift outward into the nonunion sector, with a consequent fall in the equilibrium wage rate in the nonunion sector (see Chapter 18). This may be called a "crowding effect."

Which effect is the more important in actual practice? Do unions tend to raise the wages of nonunion employees or to lower them? What would be the wage levels of persons who are currently nonunion employees if unions did not exist? Would the wages paid be higher or lower? Lawrence M. Kahn investigated these questions. In a series of statistical studies he argued that the empirical evidence is that in the long run the crowding effect seems to dominate the threat effect, so that in geographic areas and industries with strong union representation, the wages of nonunion

[30]John P. Hoerr, *And the Wolf Finally Came: The Decline of the American Steel Industry* (Pittsburgh, Pa.: University of Pittsburgh Press, 1988).

workers tend to be lower, compared with those of the workers represented by unions, than they would otherwise be.

Does this mean that unions do not have very much effect on inflation, because as they raise wages for union members, they simultaneously cause wages for nonunion workers to decline? Not necessarily, Kahn found, since there may be a different impact in the short run than in the long run. In the short run, it appears that in industries where there are strong unions, union wage gains are passed on to nonunion workers (the threat effect). Thus, Kahn concluded that unions are an inflationary force in the short run and yet tend to force down the pay of nonunion workers and thereby widen the income distribution (and further segment the labor force between high- and low-paid workers) in the long run.[31]

Kahn's work is interesting and important, but it cannot be accepted as conclusive. For one thing, it does not identify the process by which the short-run dominance of the threat effect is transmitted into the long-run dominance of the crowding effect. For another, his research efforts were necessarily concentrated in particular labor markets, industries, and time periods and can be generalized only with some uncertainty. Broadly, however, his work is consistent with Johnson and Mieszkowski's more theoretical study, which argued that most, if not all, of the gains of union labor are made at the expense of nonunion labor and not at the expense of profits (i.e., that unions raise wages primarily through indirectly lowering the wages of nonunion workers).[32]

On Income Inequality

Income inequality has been increasing in the United States. By 1987, the lowest paid workers got considerably less in real earnings than in 1970, and the gap between them and those who earn more had increased substantially.[33] "After improving steadily for a generation," report two researchers, "average wages have fallen, family incomes have stagnated and wages, incomes and wealth have become increasingly polarized."[34]

---

[31]Lawrence M. Kahn, "Unionism and Relative Wages: Direct and Indirect Effects," *Industrial and Labor Relations Review*, 32:4, July 1979, pp. 520–532; "Union Strength and Wage Inflation," *Industrial Relations*, 18:2, Spring 1979, pp. 144–155; "The Effect of Unions on the Earnings of Nonunion Workers," *Industrial and Labor Relations Review*, 31:2, January 1978, pp. 205–216; and "Union Spillover Effects on Organized Labor Markets," *Journal of Human Resources*, 15:1, 1980, pp. 87–98.

[32]H. G. Johnson and P. Mieszkowski, "The Effects of Unionization on the Distribution of Income: A General Equilibrium Approach," *Quarterly Journal of Economics*, 84, November 1970, p. 560.

[33]Louis Uchitelle, "Unequal Pay Widespread in U.S.," *New York Times*, Aug. 14, 1990, pp. D-1, D-8. See also Paul Ryscavage and Peter Henle, "Earnings Inequality Accelerates in the 1980's," *Monthly Labor Review*, 114:12, December 1990, p. 3ff.

[34]Bennett Harrison and Barry Bluestone, *The Great U-Turn* (New York: Basic Books, 1988), p. 1.

Have unions caused this increasing inequality? Have unions contributed markedly to it? We have seen that unions cause a widening of the differential between union and nonunion wages. Is this an important factor in the widening of differentials in America?

Apparently not. Other factors seem to have been much more important, including changing tax laws, international competition, the shift from a goods-producing to a service economy, and the shift of economic activity from the North and East to the South and West.

In fact, many people see unions as a force for creating equality in incomes, not inequality. This is because there are differentials in income among people working in the same establishments as well as differentials among people working in different establishments. What has been the impact of unions on the differentials in pay among people working in the same plant?

Richard Freeman and others studied this question using data from the 1970s. He found that unions have the effect of substantially reducing the inequality of pay among workers in the same establishment. In particular, unions reduce pay differentials both among blue-collar workers and between blue-collar and white-collar workers. Thus, in nonunion plants the pay differences tend to be wider than in union plants. This narrowing effect tends to be much larger, Freeman found, than the effect unions have in increasing the wage differential between union and nonunion plants. As a result, Freeman concluded that unions on balance contribute to reducing wage inequality in the United States rather than to increasing it.[35]

A decade later using data from the 1980s Freeman and an associate revisited the question. The evidence continues that unions reduce the degree of inequality among employees in different occupations and skills in firms. They also increase the inequality among employees who are union-represented and those who are not. Statistical analysis indicates that the first effect is larger than the second, so that on balance in America unions reduce the inequality of compensation among employees.[36]

Other studies agree. For example, during the middle of this century, when unions were strongest, wage differentials declined dramatically. The less educated gained on the more educated, the less skilled on the skilled, the less favored regions on the more favored, women on men, minorities

[35]Richard B. Freeman, "Unionism and the Dispersion of Wages," *Industrial and Labor Relations Review,* 34:1, October 1980, pp. 3–23; Gregory M. Duncan and Duane E. Leigh, "Wage Determination in the Union and Nonunion Sectors: A Sample Selectivity Approach," *Industrial and Labor Relations Review,* 34:1, October 1980, pp. 24–34; Richard B. Freeman, "Union Wage Practices and Wage Dispersion within Establishments," *Industrial and Labor Relations Review,* 36:1, October 1982, pp. 3–21; and Barry T. Hirsch, "The Interindustry Structure of Unionism, Earnings and Earnings Dispersion," *Industrial and Labor Relations Review,* 36:1, October 1982, pp. 22–39.

[36]David G. Blanchflower and Richard B. Freeman, "Unionism in Advanced Countries," *Industrial Relations,* 31:1, Winter 1992, p. 65.

on the majority, low skilled on the skilled. But as the unions began to decline in the 1970s the inequality of incomes began to reassert itself.[37]

If unions on balance seem to decrease inequality in incomes, as the evidence suggests, is this good or bad for America? The answer to this question is not simply a matter of whether the reader's own political and social preferences favor equality or inequality, though that is a very important standard.

It is also a matter of economic signals. Narrowing income differentials are appropriate to periods of prosperity and broad stability. But in times of rapid change and of economic challenge, economic and social progress may require strong incentives to change people's behavior. In this circumstance it is important that inequality increase, so that people are drawn to the new skills and behaviors which are better compensated. After a substantial shift of people and effort has occurred, then inequality of incomes should fall.

Unions have traditionally pursued equality, which is best suited to stable economic environments. In so doing, their practices have mitigated against change in the view of many economists, and so have retarded America's adaptation to the new conditions in the world.

Is the push for equality (whatever the economic circumstances) a feature of unionism generally, or simply the chosen course of unions in America in this century? The empirical evidence suggests that unions are strongly tied to the search for greater equality, but there are a few exceptions that may indicate that an alternative approach is at least conceivable. Craft unions press for greater pay and increasing differentials with lesser skilled people. Unions of professionals often accept differentials in favor of better performing employees.

At the bottom of this issue is a major difference in how compensation is viewed. Some see compensation as support for people's lives, and worry that each person should have enough to live decently. Others see compensation as a signal in the economy about what the marketplace values, and worry that unions may so distort the signals that people can't tell what economic activity they ought to undertake.

Even if we accept the latter interpretation, there is evidence that American unions have not been strong enough to have significantly distorted the economy. Recent theoretical analyses, which use general equilibrium models to look at all causal interactions, find that unionism has a negligible effect on overall economic efficiency in our economy.[38] This result occurs despite widely divergent adjustments in prices and output in various industries which result from unions' impact on wages.

[37]Claudia Goldin and Robert A. Margo, "The Great Compression," Working Paper No. 3817, National Bureau of Economic Research, August 1991.
[38]Robert H. DeFina, "Unions, Relative Wages, and Economic Efficiency," *Journal of Labor Economics*, 1:4, 1983, pp. 408–429.

So what is the conclusion? Unions in the United States have generally—but not always—attempted, and with some success, to reduce income inequality. In doing so they have helped their members and others as well, but they have also contributed a bit to the slow pace at which that economy has responded to the economic challenge from abroad.

On Inflation and Unemployment

Unions appear to contribute to inflation and to unemployment by virtue of some of their policies, although they probably do not do so intentionally. Unions in the United States ordinarily profess opposition to inflation, just as they oppose unemployment, but their actions sometimes seem to contribute directly to increased inflation and increased unemployment.

When unions seek wage increases for their members, they contribute to inflationary pressures. They also appear to increase unemployment by making it more expensive for business to hire workers. But each individual union would disclaim responsibility for either result; the union seeks only to protect its members against rising prices or to obtain better living standards for them. But when many unions simultaneously push for higher wages, the pressure is inflationary and may create unemployment as well.

Inflation in our modern economy usually takes the form of a spiral. Prices rise, then wages rise, then prices, then wages; or wages rise, then prices, then wages, then prices. There is much debate on the question of whether wages or prices are to blame for inflation. If wage increases start inflation, then unions appear to bear a special responsibility. If price increases start inflation, then companies appear to bear a special responsibility.

But this is a sterile debate. Unions do not set out as a group to raise wages. Individual unions pursue wage policies in an economic context that they themselves do not control. It is the systematic interaction of wage and price decisions and economic events that generates inflation, not individual unions. Furthermore, unions do not make wage decisions alone; such decisions are made by unions and employers in the collective bargaining process. It is more appropriate, therefore, to inquire into the impact of collective bargaining on the economy than the impact of unions alone.

Collective bargaining, wage increases, unemployment, and inflation are mixed up in a web of causes and effects. Economists have tried in many ways to untangle the web. No one way is fully satisfactory, but each has kernels of truth. What are the most important of these formulations?[39]

Cost-Push Inflation   Unions and big corporations are alleged to be special contributors to cost-push inflation. Unions contribute by seeking

[39]C. G. Williams, "The Role of Unions in Inflation: A Survey Article," *Relations Industrielles*, 37:3, 1982, pp. 498–527.

wage increases that are greater than productivity gains at times when there are unemployed people or unused production capacity. Economists would prefer, it appears, that when unused human and mechanical capacity exists in the economy, wages and prices should remain stable and increased consumer or government expenditures should cause increased employment and production, not increased wages and prices. In a perfectly competitive economy, it is said, this is what would occur. But a perfectly competitive economy does not have unions or large corporations. These organizations use their market power to raise wages and prices even when unutilized production resources exist and so create a cost-push inflation.

This is a plausible explanation of inflation and one that has considerable support. Cost-push inflation has now found its way into the economics textbooks. Unfortunately, its logical (or theoretical) foundations are weak. It is, in fact, difficult to demonstrate that a cost-push from collective bargaining is a significant, autonomous contributor to general inflation.

Fritz Machlup made this point as follows:

> An inflation of effective demand [i.e., a demand-pull] is a necessary condition not only for a demand-pull inflation of consumer prices, but also for a cost-push inflation. Without an expansion of demands, the cost boost would result in less production and less employment, not in a continuing rise in the level of consumer prices.[40]

Demand-Pull Inflation Demand-pull inflation is said to result from too much money chasing too few goods. Too much money means a volume of expenditures so large that it will more than exhaust total production at existing price levels. When such a volume of expenditures exists, prices rise to cause the volume of expenditures and product (and services) sales to be equal.

The principal contributor to demand-pull inflation is usually said to be the federal government. Either the government spends more than it receives (i.e., runs too large a deficit) or the Federal Reserve Board, which controls the nation's money supply, creates too much money (an error of monetary policy). Collective bargaining is not usually alleged to contribute to a demand-pull inflation, but of course it can do so. Wage increases also become purchasing-power increases, and these have the same potential effect on prices as do other types of spending (including government expenditures). Federal authorities might neutralize the additional expenditures through fiscal or monetary policy, but their failure to do so need not be thought to make them the cause of the demand-pull inflation.

The Unemployment-Inflation Trade-Off Yet another description of modern economic problems emphasizes the relationship between unem-

[40]Fritz Machlup, "Another View of Cost-Push and Demand-Pull Inflation," *Review of Economics and Statistics*, 42:2, May 1960, pp. 125–139.

ployment rates and wage increases. This explanation of inflation begins from the observation that often in the economy when unemployment rises, the rate of change in wage rates declines; conversely, when unemployment falls, the rate of change in wage rates accelerates. Thus, wage changes and unemployment appear to be inversely related. Furthermore, since wage changes and price changes tend to move together, the relationship between price increases and unemployment appears to be inverse as well. The inverse relationship between price and unemployment is called a Phillips curve, after the economist who popularized the concept. An idealized Phillips curve is shown in Figure 22-1. The shape of the curve implies a trade-off between unemployment and inflation. As unemployment rises, a trade-off in the form of less inflation is obtained. As unemployment falls, a trade-off in the form of higher inflation results. Figure 22-1 is said to be idealized because it is not drawn from actual data; it is drawn to show an inverse relationship that may or may not be found in the actual statistics on the economy. In fact, it is difficult or impossible to plot actual data and get the smooth Phillips curve shown in Figure 22-1.

Regardless of statistical problems in identifying the actual Phillips curve, the idealized, or conceptual, curve has a powerful influence on economic thinking. Underlying the relationship is the view that high unemployment causes wage increases (and therefore price increases) to be moderated. Those who think in terms of a Phillips curve argue that unions cause economic difficulties by pushing the government to pursue policies of low unemployment and thereby causing wage and price inflation.

The unions do not deny that they favor low unemployment, but they argue that low unemployment need not necessarily mean inflation. They say that intelligent government policies would achieve low unemployment and reasonable price stability simultaneously.

FIGURE 22-1   An idealized Phillips curve.

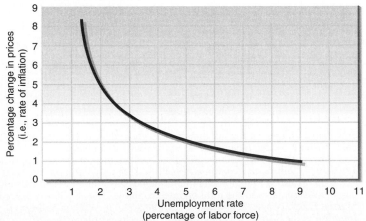
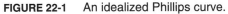

A One-Way Street There would not be so much inflation in our economy if periods of rising prices were followed by periods of declining prices. This process of inflation and subsequent deflation used to occur. In the nineteenth century, periods of inflation and deflation so closely offset each other in the United States that the price level on the average was relatively stable. But after the great depression of the 1930s, general price declines disappeared. Even recessions, like those in 1979–1980 and 1990–91, did not cause consumer prices generally to decline. The rate of increase of prices (i.e, the rate of inflation) did subside, but inflation itself continued.

One factor contributing to the persistence of inflation in the economy today is that collective bargaining has tended to put a floor under wage rates. Decreases in going wage rates have become exceedingly uncommon, even in major recessions. (In isolated instances involving exceptionally unfavorable economic circumstances, decreases in wage rates are sometimes agreed to, whatever the general economic conditions. During the construction industry depression from 1989 to 1992, for example, with some local crafts unions having almost every member unemployed, the unions agreed to reduce wage rates in the hope of stimulating some construction activity.) Wage increases were partly a result of price increases, as low rates of inflation continued through the recession. The failure of wage rates to decline, even in periods of substantial recession (the so-called downward rigidity of wages), contributes an upward bias to the general level of wages and prices and therefore to inflation.[41]

Does Collective Bargaining Restrain Inflation? Against these unfavorable aspects of collective bargaining should be balanced a series of aspects favorable to economic stability. Surprisingly, some of these potential contributions to economic stability are simply the other side of the coin, so to speak, of those unfavorable aspects just listed.

First, collective bargaining in the United States normally entails fixed-term contracts, so that wage rates and benefits are established with a degree of certainty for a period of several months to several years. In inflationary booms, the practice of fixed-term agreements imparts great initial resistance to a wage-price spiral. It is not likely that any other wage-setting mechanism could be so inflexible in the short run,[42] partly because American labor organizations abide by agreements so that the wildcat strikes

---

[41]It has been thought by many analysts that wages have become increasingly resistant to downward change as the century has progressed. A new study suggests that this is not the case. Instead, wages have been no more sticky downwards since World War II than before. See Steven G. Allen, "Changes in the Cyclical Sensitivity of Wages in the United States, 1891–1987," *American Economic Review*, 82:1, March 1992, pp. 122–140.

[42]From 1982 to 1984, for example, compensation under collective bargaining lagged behind compensation gains in the total private economy. This also has occurred in 1961 to 1965. See Marten Estey, "Wages and Wage Policy, 1962–71," in William Fellner, ed., *Economic Policy and Inflation in the Sixties* (Washington, D.C.: American Enterprise Institute, 1972), p. 168.

and payment of wages above negotiated levels—common practices in Western Europe—do not usually occur in this country.

Second, collective bargaining may in some instances prevent uneconomical practices from entering the industrial workplace during business expansions. This is done by directing the attention of managers at each negotiating session to what high sales volume and ready cash availability are doing to loosen production standards in their plants. Management is, as a result, in a better position to control costs than it would be otherwise.

Third, the process of collective bargaining itself and the grievance machinery of unionized plants permit a comparatively orderly approach to the resolution of production and industrial relations problems that commonly develop in a period of business expansion. Through the grievance procedure especially, such problems are often resolved at their origin or, in the case of unresolved grievances, by private voluntary binding arbitration during the term of agreement, thereby greatly reducing the likelihood of work stoppages, strikes, or other disruptions. Such disruptions, whatever their cause, are not only expensive themselves but may often become the occasion for demands for wage or benefit increases.

The Net Impact of Collective Bargaining on Inflation   But, the reader might object, surely it is possible to conclude more about the net impact of collective bargaining on wage inflation than what has been said above. Probably the most complete exposition of this question was made by Sumner Slichter. Slichter concluded that unions tend to impart a small inflationary bias to the economy. However, his most interesting analysis related to the more long-term consequences on the inflationary bias in wages. The tendency of collective bargaining to place sustained upward pressure on wages, Slichter argued, induces considerable technological progress as employers seek less labor-intensive methods of production. It also results either in unemployment increases or in price increases. But unions are, in Slichter's view, a major device for generating additional consumer income and spending, which results in increasing employment, a diminished susceptibility to economic recessions (which contributes to the long-run preservation of capitalism), and a reinforced tendency of prices to rise in booms. Because of the income-generation effect of wage increases, Slichter observed, increasing wages does not generally result in increased unemployment (though there might be such effects in certain industries or areas on a limited basis). Were the public to attempt to minimize the effect of collective bargaining in order to eliminate even moderate inflation, concluded Slichter, it would have to sacrifice a rapid rate of industrial growth and accept the increased likelihood of more numerous and more severe recessions.[43] This analysis remains the

[43]Sumner H. Slichter, "Do the Wage-Fixing Arrangements in the American Labor Market Have an Inflationary Bias?" *Proceedings* of the American Economic Association, May 1954; and "Economics and Collective Bargaining," in *Economics and the Policy Maker* (Washington, D.C.: Brookings Institution, 1959).

most plausible and complete understanding of the aggregate impact of collective bargaining on our economy.

But increasing wages is not the only method through which collective bargaining may have an impact on inflation. Changes in work rules and working conditions can also have considerable impact on labor costs and thereby on prices. Condition changes may be negotiated with either favorable or unfavorable effects (i.e., to decrease or increase unit labor costs). It is unfortunate that we have virtually no data that apply directly to the additional costs or savings from rules and conditions changes. Historical experience suggests that periods of high economic activity generate the growth of uneconomical practices in private business, in both union and nonunion sectors, but we have little evidence of the independent impact of collective bargaining on incidents of uneconomic practices in inflationary periods.

THE PUBLIC UTILITY OF COLLECTIVE BARGAINING

What impact have unions and the institution of collective bargaining had on our society? The answer may be that there has been so great an impact that we would not recognize our society if unions and collective bargaining did not exist in it. But we cannot know if this is so because we are, of course, unable to observe our society without unions. In consequence, some people believe that the impact of unions has been great, and some believe it has been small. The matter cannot be conclusively settled. We can, however, explore aspects of the impact of unions and collective bargaining in specific terms. From a study of these several items, some readers may come to a generalized judgment on the impact of unions. Others will find the matter still unsettled in their minds.

In this chapter the impact of unions on three major economic aspects—income inequality, unemployment and inflation—of our society has been described. What remains to be done here is to survey the general social impact of unions and collective bargaining.

1. *Unions and collective bargaining are a method by which workers participate in the governance of our society.* It would be possible, perhaps, to deny to workers these particular methods of participation, as is often done in totalitarian countries. In such countries workers' organizations (i.e., unions) either are outlawed or are controlled by the state. There are proposals made in the United States periodically to substantially restrict the activities of unions—for example, by prohibiting the strike and replacing it with a system of compulsory arbitration of labor disputes. But it is likely that in our society, where the freedom of individuals and groups is of great concern, such restrictions imposed over the objections of workers would cause great social unrest. Those who favor substantial legal restrictions on unions argue that because most American employees do not belong to unions, there is not a great deal of support for their activities among work-

ing people. But this is surely a misreading. Not all employees join unions or are represented in collective bargaining, but many of those who do are very much committed to the process and will struggle to retain it. Many of those members undoubtedly favor their freedom to participate and are glad that others do participate. To attempt to substantially restrain the activities of workers' organizations in our society would create considerable turmoil.[44]

2. *Collective bargaining reduces the role of the government in the relationships of management and labor.* The essential function of collective bargaining, wrote John R. Commons, "is the elimination, as far as possible, of a third party . . . whether king, legislature, governor or dictator, handing down rules and regulations from above—and the substitution of rules agreed upon collectively."[45] The American system of collective bargaining establishes rules about wages, benefits, working conditions, and the resolution of grievances and other disputes. The rules established by collective bargaining are often imitated by nonunion firms. The result is a system of rules established largely exclusive of the government. Both management and labor tend to prefer this private system of rule making and to oppose government intervention.

Would there be more or less government intervention without unions? Many managers seem to believe that the government would take little or no interest in employee relations if unions did not exist. These managers believe that they would be left to establish employee relations policies without any outside interference, from either the unions or the government. In support of their position, they point to the United States 70 to 100 years ago, before the organization of unions, and note that there was little government involvement in labor relations then. In the years since that time both collective bargaining and government regulation have expanded, they point out.

What is unconvincing about this argument is the suggestion that in the absence of unions American society today would be much like it was many decades ago. This is very unlikely. Whatever it would be today without unions and collective bargaining, it would probably not be as it was long ago. Too many things have changed (including population, technology, and economics) and too many events have occurred (including two world wars). It is well to remember that unionism in this country made its greatest advances during the two great wars, when the society most needed the support of the working people. Had unions not grown, and with them the private system of labor-management relations that is collective bargaining, the likelihood is that the government would have more closely regulated

---

[44]Lloyd Ulman and Elaine Sorensen, "Exit, Voice and Muscle: A Note," *Industrial Relations*, 23:3, Fall 1984, pp. 424–428.

[45]John R. Commons, *Myself* (New York: Macmillan, 1934), pp. 72–73. Commons was a great legal and social historian and a pioneer in developing social welfare programs in the United States.

employee relations, either as the champion of the workers or simply in the interest of industrial peace. Increased governmental regulation was the course of development in most nations abroad. It is highly unlikely that in the United States alone management would have been left in unilateral control of employee relations. The choice American managers faced was to bargain collectively about compensation, conditions of work, and grievance procedures or to see the government enter these fields as a regulator.

3. *Collective bargaining makes certain contributions to our society that are of lesser significance than those just mentioned, but are nonetheless important.* Among these contributions are the determination of priorities within labor and within management, the day-to-day administration of the workplace, and the resolution of problems unique to certain industries and occupations.[46] Each of these matters is ill suited to resolution by the bureaucratic procedures of governmental administrative agencies or by litigation in the courts. Yet each of these matters involves many specific problems that must be resolved. For the efficient handling of such matters, if collective bargaining did not exist, we should have to invent it.

4. *Unions and collective bargaining subject the public to the inconvenience, and sometimes the danger, of work stoppages.* Often it seems that if unions did not exist, strikes would not occur, or it may appear that unions and collective bargaining can be retained, but the strike eliminated. Certainly, from the point of view of the general public, the work stoppage is the most annoying aspect of our system of collective bargaining. Attempts of management and labor to lessen the frequency of strikes in order to improve the public performance of collective bargaining have been described in previous chapters.

IS THE BALANCE TIPPING IN AMERICAN INDUSTRIAL RELATIONS?

What is the balance between unions and management in American society? Throughout the 1970s and 1980s the unions were clearly on the defensive. Union membership did not keep pace with labor force growth, so that the percentage of employees who were members of unions has been declining for years. Labor failed in its efforts in the 1970s to get changes in the National Labor Relations Act to make it easier to organize workers into unions. It failed again in its efforts in 1991 to get legislation preventing employers from hiring permanent replacements for strikers through Congress and past former President George Bush.

Employers generally have become more committed to being nonunion and have become more successful at it.[47] In 1977, for example, the National

---

[46]John T. Dunlop, "The Social Utility of Collective Bargaining," in Lloyd Ulman, ed., *Challenges to Collective Bargaining* (Englewood Cliffs, N.J.: Prentice-Hall, 1967), pp. 172–175.

[47]D. Quinn Mills, "Management Performance," in Jack Steiber, D. Quinn Mills, and Robert McKersie, eds., *American Industrial Relations: A Critical Review* (Madison, Wis.: Industrial Relations Research Association, 1982).

Association of Manufacturers formed a national organization intended to help companies keep unions out of their factories, stores, and offices. The organization was called the Council on a Union-Free Environment. Its formation was met with great but unavailing hostility by the unions.

So much has the significance of organized labor declined that even some major Republican figures have expressed concern. George Shultz, who has served as secretary of labor, treasury and defense, has offered two lessons for America about industrial relations: first, in "a healthy workplace it is very important that there be some system of checks and balances . . . a system of industrial jurisprudence." Second, that "free societies and free trade unions go together." Having returned to the private sector as an executive in a large American business, Schultz also noted: "As a management person, if I'm running my shop and I don't have a union, I don't want them. But I'm trying to look at this more broadly and ask a question about where we're really heading, and I think the . . . unions [must] show a function in a world that is changing rapidly—the whole workplace is changing and the patterns of competition are changing. . . . As a society we have a great stake in freedom and a lot of that is anchored, somehow, historically," in the labor movement.[48]

Malcolm Lovell, formerly an executive of Ford Motor Company and once under secretary of labor, has insisted that U.S. industry can better accomplish its goals with unions than without them. "I question," he said, "whether we can have a strong democratic capitalistic system without a strong labor movement." Why does he say this? Apparently because of a conviction that unions are needed to protect employees from excesses at the hands of management, and to fight for a broad distribution of income and wealth—so that the country doesn't fall into the hands of the very wealthy. To the unions, Lovell observed, "Unions need more popular support to survive. You cannot conduct yourselves as though you are a selfish, narrow pressure group and win the affection of the public over time."[49]

Lane Kirkland, president of the AFL-CIO, insists that labor is up to the challenge. "We are emerging from one of the most difficult periods in our history," he told the federation's 1991 convention, "with our solidarity intact and with sturdy resolve." What is this challenge which labor sees? Kirkland answered as follows:

> Though the Cold War with communism seems to be nearing its end, the struggle for humanity goes on. Judging from current events, the next long worldwide confrontation . . . may well be on the barricades between those who stand for human rights and popular democracy and those who serve communism's mirror image . . . the forces of flagless capital, in league with their handmaidens, the finance ministers and the ideologues and high priests of free market idolatry.[50]

[48]George P. Shultz, quoted in Leonard Silk, "Worrying over Weakend Unions, *New York Times*, December 13, 1991, p. D2.

[49]"Lovell Links Preservation of Capitalism to Strong Labor Movement," Bureau of National Affairs, *Daily Labor Report*, No. 71, Apr. 14, 1989, p. A-4.

[50]Lane Kirkland, *AFL-CIO NEWS*, 36:25, Nov. 25, 1991, p. 5.

The strength of the labor movement has always been at the plant, or grass-roots, level in the United States. Lately the unions have been paying much attention to national politics and legislative action[51] and perhaps neglecting the grass roots. So some observers suggest that unions should instead build up the loyalty and commitment of workers at the plant level. According to one observer, in the future automation will eliminate the worst jobs in factories, managers will continue to be aware of employee needs, cost-of-living escalators will protect wages, and so unions must attempt to deal with the dissatisfaction of workers with the content of their jobs.[52] Tom Donahue, the AFL-CIO's secretary-treasurer, has identified an involved membership as the unions' best weapon. "We have to challenge those who tell us that the labor movement must lower its expectations," he said. "I say that we must raise them."[53] The major changes in the work force in the United States present an opportunity to the unions if they are able to identify the consequences of these changes and develop policies to respond to them.

The election of a Democratic administration in 1992 ushered in a climate more favorable to union concerns, possibly beginning to tip the balance in American industrial relations back toward the unions. President Reagan and, to a lesser extent, President Bush had used their appointments to the National Labor Relations Board and the federal courts to encourage "pro-business" sentiment that tended to reduce union successes in winning representation elections, obtaining unfair labor practice decisions, and conducting strikes, as well as blocking much of the prolabor legislation that emerged from a Democratic Congress. In his first days in office, President Clinton rescinded several actions of President Bush to which the unions objected. However, it remained unclear how far President Clinton would go in using his authority to implement policy in the area of labor-management relations more favorable to the unions.

There are conflicting social and political cross-currents at work around President Clinton in the area of labor policy that may not resolve themselves until well into his tenure in office. While the American labor movement has had much stronger historic ties to the Democratic party than to the Republican party—forming a key part of the electoral coalitions behind Democratic Presidents Franklin Roosevelt, Truman, Kennedy, and Carter, and being rewarded by these Presidents for its support—it is not clear that labor can expect similar gains from backing the Democrats in 1992. President Clinton, formerly the governor of a "right-to-work" state with a record perceived as both activist and mildly liberal, deliberately

---

[51]John T. Dunlop, "Past and Future Tendencies in American Labor Organization," *Daedalus,* 107:1, Winter 1978, pp. 79–96.

[52]Robert Schrank, "Are Unions an Anachronism?" *Harvard Business Review,* 57:5, September–October 1979, pp. 107–115.

[53]"Donahue to Service Employees International Union Convention," *AFL-CIO News,* 25,12 (June 28, 1980), p. 5.

tried to move both himself and the national Democratic party and its plat-form away from positions that could be construed as overtly "liberal." As part of this transformation, candidate Clinton distinctly distanced himself from his party's historic institutional ties to special interests—among them big labor and minorities—while using the rhetoric of inclusion to reach out to the vast group of middle-class voters, for whom big labor is a politi-cal bogeyman. Recognizing that its traditional linkages to the Democrats were threatened by this move, the American labor movement threw much of its support behind candidates perceived to be more prolabor than Clin-ton during the Democratic primary process, particularly Senator Tom Harkin of Iowa. Whether President Clinton will run the risk of alienating the middle-class voters whose support he garnered by distancing himself from the special interests in order to reward a labor movement that sup-ported his Democratic primary rivals is an open question.

WHAT IS THE FUTURE FOR LABOR-MANAGEMENT RELATIONS?

What does the future hold for labor-management relations? Some people think that there may be no future at all; the decline in the proportion of the workforce who are union members will slowly make unions unimpor-tant, they suggest. But this is unlikely. Trends—such as the recent decline in union strength—rarely continue indefinitely. Instead, unexpectedly, major shifts occur.

Consider the size of union membership, for example. At the end of the 1920s unionism was on the decline. It seemed likely that the decline would continue, but the 1930s saw the rise of the industrial unions and the CIO. At the end of the 1930s the CIO appeared sure to replace the AFL, but World War II brought the resurgence of the AFL.

The very substantial growth of unionism as a whole in the 1940s was not foreseen in the late 1930s. The experiences of the 1930s and 1940s sug-gested that in the 1950s the unions would continue to grow and prosper. Instead, employer resistance to unions increased in sophistication and, combined with a sluggish national economy, caused union growth to slow substantially. Unionism in the 1960s began in the stagnant mode of the 1950s, only to end in the explosive expansion of public employee unionism.

The 1960s ended on a note of such growing militancy and radicalism in our society that the slower and calmer pace of the 1970s came as a sur-prise to most people. The 1970s were a time of wrenching economic events, including two oil crises and rapid inflation. As prices outran wage gains in the late 1970s and unemployment rose dramatically, it appeared that unions would find millions of new members. Instead, the 1980s saw the most rapid and widespread decline of unionism since the 1920s. Thus, history suggests that what can be expected is change, not continuity. In-deed, in the early 1990s, despite a recession in the economy, the union membership decline bottomed out and a slow and halting growth began.

Labor management relations involve much more than the question of the size and significance of unions. There is, for example, the question of whether the scope of discussion between labor and management is widening or narrowing. Evidence suggests that it is widening. Union officials are becoming more involved in what have in the past been areas of decision reserved for management, including for example, product quality, capital investment and plant or office closings. For example, union officials have requested training from Ford Motor Company in techniques of improving quality so that they can participate in quality discussions from a base of knowledge. Over time it seems that some of the lines between management and union activities are blurring.

SUPPLEMENTING OR REPLACING COLLECTIVE BARGAINING

Charles Heckscher has recommended that in order to improve their prospects, unions should become more flexible. He observes that the dwindling of unionism leaves a growing problem of how to protect employee rights in the nonunion workplace. The collective bargaining framework developed under the Wagner Act of 1935 no longer is sufficient to protect workers. Based on balancing the power of management and labor, the law gave unions a source of power in the corporation by granting them the exclusive right to represent all workers if a majority voted for the union. The rise of foreign competition and businesses' union-avoidance campaigns have undermined this structure. Unions no longer control the market for labor in basic industries such as steel and autos and have great difficulty organizing employees in the growing service industries.

Moreover, the power-balancing concept tends to force unions to be as bureaucratic as corporations, leading to restrictive work rules and legalistic squabbles over grievances. To avoid these practices, growing numbers of nonunion companies are using self-managed work teams and other forms of worker involvement in decision making. Heckscher uses the word "managerialism" to designate the most advanced management systems. It is difficult to adapt the traditional union structure to this form of management. Instead, Heckscher advocates what he calls "associational unionism." Workers would not be forced to choose either exclusive representation or no representation.

Instead, unions and other interest groups could speak for various fractions of the work force. Wages and other matters would be determined by multilateral negotiations among management, several different groups of employees, and perhaps such outsiders as environmentalists and consumers.

Already the AFL-CIO and some of its affiliated unions have embraced a nascent form of associational unionism. Instead of limiting membership to workers under bargaining agreements, some unions offer group insurance plans and other services to associate members such as retirees and unorganized workers. However, it is a long step from this approach to multilateral negotiations.[54]

CHAPTER SUMMARY

Unions and collective bargaining have affected management in many important ways. Collective bargaining (1) compels management to set long-term corporate strategies regarding employees and employment practices and to establish a consistent labor relations policy, (2) tends to require senior management to become aware of day-to-day problems in the operation of the business, (3) establishes a common law of the shop that subjects management actions to scrutiny by third parties, (4) permits management in some instances to invest its compensation dollar in a way that makes most sense to employees, (5) has permitted management to better meet the needs of its employees without having to feel disloyal to the principles of cost containment, and (6) makes changes more difficult at the workplace and production processes more rigid by establishing formal rules and causing informal practices to become precedents.

Unions are widely believed by management to restrict efficient work practices and thereby to contribute to low productivity. Several studies have shown a distinct productivity advantage in unionized firms; some studies have shown the opposite. Studies that show a productivity advantage do not say that unions actually contribute to increasing productivity, but only that they are associated with it. Unions may organize in more productive plants, attract a better-quality work force, or spur management to greater efforts to offset higher labor costs. Unions reduce profits for firms, however, and may cause companies to invest less in new technology and new products than otherwise.

Union members earn more than persons not represented by unions. Unions may also affect the earnings of nonunion workers. Several studies have investigated this issue with varied conclusions. Two possibilities have been identified. With the "threat" effect, employers in the nonunion sector increase wages to union levels as a defense against union organization. Through the "crowding" effect, unions limit the number of high-wage jobs and raise the supply of workers who can be paid low wages by nonunion employers. In the long run, the crowding effect seems to dominate over the threat effect. In the short run, in industries where there are strong unions, union wage gains are passed on to the nonunion workers. It has been concluded that unions, on balance, contribute to reducing wage inequality in the United States rather than to increasing it.

---

[54]John Hoerr, "How More Flexibility Could Pump Up Labor's Muscles," *Business Week*, May 16, 1988, pp. 21–22; and Charles C. Heckscher, *The New Unionism* (New York: Basic Books, 1988).

Collective bargaining, wage increases, unemployment, and inflation are mixed up in a web of causes and effects. There are many ways, however, that unions appear to contribute to inflation and unemployment. Unions and corporations are alleged to be special contributors to cost-push inflation by seeking and allowing wage increases that are greater than productivity gains. In addition, economists who base their opinion on the Phillips curve (which shows an inverse relation between wages and employment) allege that unions cause wage and price inflation by pressing the government to pursue policies of low employment. The maintenance of a floor under wages is another way collective bargaining contributes to the persistence of inflation.

Some aspects of collective bargaining are favorable to economic stability and act to restrain inflation. Collective bargaining entails fixed-term contracts so that wage rates and benefits are set for various periods of time. In inflationary booms, fixed-term agreements impart great initial resistance to a wage-price spiral. One interesting and plausible analysis suggests that while unions tend to impact a small inflationary bias to the economy, they also are a major device for generating additional consumer income and spending, which results in increasing employment and less susceptibility to economic recessions. Also, the upward pressure on wages includes technological progress as employers seek less labor-intensive methods of production.

In our advanced industrial society it is important that employees have a way of making their voices heard in the workplace. The weakness of unions in recent years requires that management make provision for hearing employees effectively, or that government require it, or the unions revive. The future of labor management relations is about this issue.

QUESTIONS FOR THOUGHT AND DISCUSSION

1 What are the major ways in which unions have affected management in the United States? Are there major differences in the impact of unions on unionized firms and on nonunionized firms? What are the differences, if any?

2 What is the major impact of collective bargaining on the economy? Does collective bargaining cause inflation? Does collective bargaining cause unemployment?

3 What responsibility do unions have to control inflation? What responsibility does management have? What responsibility does government have?

4 What would our society be like without unions? Without management? Why?

5 Do unions tend to raise the wages of nonunion employees or to lower them? How would wages be determined if unions did not exist?

6 One reason many managers oppose unionization is their belief that unions insist on inefficient production processes and contribute to low productivity. What have studies of the impact of unions on productivity concluded? What impact do unions have on profits?

7 What effects does the strong managerial opposition to unions appear to have on union practices and demands? How does this in turn affect management? Is the situation different in countries where unions are not in a defensive position?

8 What do you foresee as the future of labor-management relations? Why?

SELECTED READING

Annable, James E., *The Price of Industrial Labor: The Role of Wages in Business Cycles and Economic Growth* (Lexington, Mass.: Lexington Books, 1984).

Freeman, Richard B., and James L. Medoff, *What Do Unions Do?* (New York: Basic Books, 1984).

Heckscher, Charles C., *The New Unionism* (New York: Basic Books, 1988).

Mills, Daniel Quinn, *Government, Labor and Inflation* (Chicago: University of Chicago Press, 1975).

Mitchell, Daniel J. B., *Unions, Wages and Inflation* (Washington, D.C.: Brookings Institution, 1980).

Parsley, C. J., "Labor Union Effects on Wage Gains: A Survey of Recent Literature," *Journal of Economic Literature*, 18:1, March 1980, pp. 1–31.

Slichter, Sumner H., James Healy, and E. Robert Livernash, *The Impact of Collective Bargaining on Management* (Washington, D.C.: Brookings Institution, 1960).

NAME INDEX

Aaron, Benjamin, 205*n.*, 318*n.*
Abboushi, Suharl, 96*n.*
Abodeely, John E., 246*n.*
Abowd, John M., 636*n.*
Abraham, Katharine G., 486, 486*n.*, 487m 487*n.*, 520, 520*n.*
Abrams, Nancy, 229*n.*
Acuff, Frank L., 378*n.*
Adams, J. S., 160*n.*
Ahlstrand, Bruce, W., 619*n.*
Alinsky, Saul, 46*n.*
Allen, Donna, 558*n.*
Allen, Robert B., 246*n.*
Allen, Steven G., 77*n.*, 280*n.*, 638*n.*, 639, 639*n.*, 640*n.*
Allison, Elisabeth, 94*n.*
Alston, Rossie D., Jr., 491*n.*
Amann, Robert J., 236*n.*
Anderson, Burr E., 447*n.*
Anderson, Harry W., 581
Anderson, Howard J., 454*n.*
Anderson, Kay, E., 414*n.*
Anderson, Urton, 572*n.*
Apcar, Leonard M., 232*n.*
Appelbaum, L., 93*n.*
Arak, Marcelle V., 533*n.*

Armstrong, D. J., 385*n.*
Arthur, Jeffrey B., 416*n.*
Ashenfelter, Orley, 510, 510*n.*
Azariadis, C., 521*n.*
Azevedo, Ross E., 455*n.*, 572*n.*

Baderschneider, Earl, 585*n.*
Baer, Walter E., 587*n.*
Bain, Nicholas, 6*n.*
Bakke, E. Wight, 490*n.*
Baldwin, Corliss, 637*n.*
Bladwin, S. E., 503*n.*
Barbash, Jack, 53, 53*n.*, 361*n.*
Barling, Julian, 255*n.*
Barkin, Solomon, 24*n.*, 425*n.*
Barrett, Nancy S., 75*n.*, 151*n.*
Bastone, Eric, 89*n.*
Bauman, Alvin, 542*n.*
Beach, John J., 160*n.*
Becker, Brian E., 44*n.*
Becker, Gary, 520*n.*
Beichman, Arnold, 101*n.*

Belcher, John, Jr., 619*n.*
Bellace, Janice R., 191*n.*
Bemmels, Brian, 590*n.*
Benedict, Mary Ellen, 317*n.*
Bentiam, Harry C., 510*n.*
Bergoff, Pearl L., 45*n.*
Bergmann, Barbara R., 153*n.*
Berkowitz, Alan D., 191*n.*
Berman, Harold J., 183*n.*
Bernstein, Aaron, 121*n.*, 165*n.*, 292*n.*, 399*n.*, 554*n.*
Bernstein, Carl, 57*n.*
Bernstein, Ira P., 598*n.*
Berube, Shirley, 578, 578*n.*
Bevis, Charles W., 292*n.*
Bierman, Leonard, 570*n.*
Blackburn, John D., 178*n.*, 575*n.*
Blaire, H. R., 93*n.*
Blasi, Joseph Raphael, 124*n.*
Blanchflower, David G., 7*n.*, 82*n.*, 643*n.*
Blau, Francine D., 486*n.*
Blinder, Alan S., 537*n.*
Block, Richard N., 515*n.*

SUBJECT INDEX